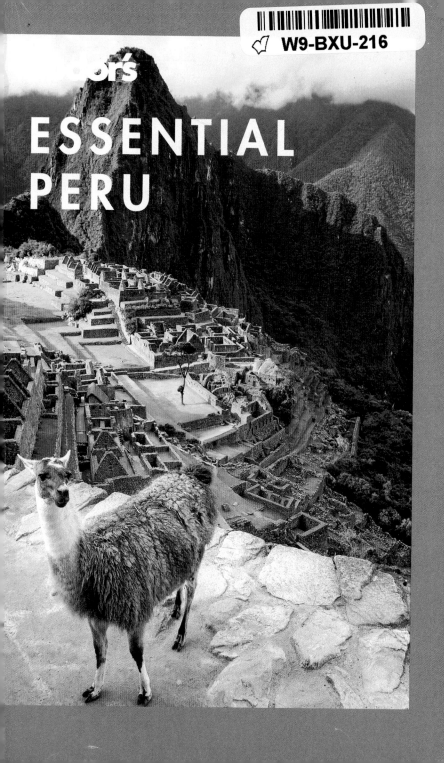

ESSENTIAL PERU

Fodor's

WELCOME TO PERU

Peru inspires wonder, from the majestic ruins of Machu Picchu and the mysterious Nazca Lines to the Cordillera Blanca's soaring peaks and Lake Titicaca's floating islands. Stroll Cusco's cobblestone streets and take in stunning Inca and colonial architecture, or visit an Andean community where daily life remains rooted in tradition. Savor intriguing flavors: the country of pisco sours and cebiche is now a hotbed for fusion food. Surfing, trekking, and bird-watching satisfy a thirst for outdoor adventure, and world-class hotels offer creature comforts.

TOP REASONS TO GO

★ **Machu Picchu:** The famous Inca city is simply awe-inspiring—it lives up to the hype.

★ **Local Culture:** Festivals, open-air markets, and homestays reveal the real Peru.

★ **Inca Trails:** Ancient paths blazed by the Inca entice with ruins and fantastic views.

★ **Food:** In Lima and beyond, buzz-worthy chefs innovate with spectacular produce.

★ **Shopping:** Colorful hand-woven textiles, baby alpaca sweaters, and ceramics.

★ **Museums:** Past civilizations come alive through displays of gold, mummies, and more.

Fodor's ESSENTIAL PERU

Editorial: Douglas Stallings, *Editorial Director*; Salwa Jabado and Margaret Kelly, *Senior Editors*; Alexis Kelly, Jacinta O'Halloran, and Amanda Sadlowski, *Editors*; Teddy Minford, *Associate Editor*; Rachael Roth, *Content Manager*

Design: Tina Malaney, *Art Director*

Photography: Jennifer Arnow, *Senior Photo Editor*

Maps: Rebecca Baer, *Senior Map Editor*; Mark Stroud (Moon Street Cartography), David Lindroth, *Cartographers*

Production: Jennifer DePrima, *Editorial Production Manager*; Carrie Parker, *Senior Production Editor*; Elyse Rozelle, *Production Editor*; David Satz, *Director of Content Production*

Business & Operations: Chuck Hoover, *Chief Marketing Officer*; Joy Lai, *Vice President and General Manager*; Stephen Horowitz, *Head of Business Development and Partnerships*

Public Relations: Joe Ewaskiw, *Manager*

Writers: David Dudenhoefer, Michael Gasparovic, Maureen Santucci

Editors: Salwa Jabado (lead editor), Jacinta O'Halloran, Rachael Roth, Denise Leto

Production Editor: Carrie Parker

Production Design: Liliana Guia

1st Edition

ISBN 978-0-14-754698-2

ISSN 2476–0978

All details in this book are based on information supplied to us at press time. Always confirm information when it matters, especially if you're making a detour to visit a specific place. Fodor's expressly disclaims any liability, loss, or risk, personal or otherwise, that is incurred as a consequence of the use of any of the contents of this book.

PRINTED IN THE UNITED STATES OF AMERICA

10 9 8 7 6 5 4 3 2 1

CONTENTS

Fodor's Features

MAPS

ABOUT THIS GUIDE

Fodor's Ratings

Everything in this guide is worth doing—we don't cover what isn't—but exceptional sights, hotels, and restaurants are recognized with additional accolades. Fodor's Choice★ indicates our top recommendations. Care to nominate a new place? Visit Fodors.com/contact-us.

Trip Costs

We list prices wherever possible to help you budget well. Hotel and restaurant price categories from $ to $$$$ are noted alongside each recommendation. For hotels, we include the lowest cost of a standard double room in high season. For restaurants, we cite the average price of a main course at dinner or, if dinner isn't served, at lunch. For attractions, we always list adult admission fees; discounts are usually available for children, students, and senior citizens.

Hotels

Our local writers vet every hotel to recommend the best overnights in each price category, from budget to expensive. Unless otherwise specified, you can expect private bath, phone, and TV in your room. For expanded hotel reviews, facilities, and deals visit Fodors.com.

Top Picks	Hotels & Restaurants
★ Fodor's Choice	🏨 Hotel
Listings	➷ Number of rooms
✉ Address	🍴 Meal plans
✉ Branch address	✕ Restaurant
☎ Telephone	☜ Reservations
🖶 Fax	👔 Dress code
⊕ Website	▭ No credit cards
✎ E-mail	$ Price
🎫 Admission fee	**Other**
⊘ Open/closed times	⇨ See also
Ⓜ Subway	☞ Take note
⊹ Directions or Map coordinates	🏌 Golf facilities

Restaurants

Unless we state otherwise, restaurants are open for lunch and dinner daily. We mention dress code only when there's a specific requirement and reservations only when they're essential or not accepted. To make restaurant reservations, visit Fodors.com.

Credit Cards

The hotels and restaurants in this guide typically accept credit cards. If not, we'll say so.

EUGENE FODOR

Hungarian-born Eugene Fodor (1905–91) began his travel career as an interpreter on a French cruise ship. The experience inspired him to write *On the Continent* (1936), the first guidebook to receive annual updates and discuss a country's way of life as well as its sights. Fodor later joined the U.S. Army and worked for the OSS in World War II. After the war, he kept up his intelligence work while expanding his guidebook series. During the Cold War, many guides were written by fellow agents who understood the value of insider information. Today's guides continue Fodor's legacy by providing travelers with timely coverage, insider tips, and cultural context.

EXPERIENCE
PERU

WHAT'S WHERE

1 Lima. In Peru's cultural and political center, experience some of the best dining in the Americas, vibrant nightlife, and great museums and churches. See the Catedral and the catacombs at the Convento de San Francisco, and stroll about Miraflores and Barranco.

2 The Southern Coast. Head south for wines and piscos around Ica, dune boarding in Huacachina, the mysterious Nazca Lines, and the marine life of the Paracas National Reserve. The inland area, particularly Pisco, was devastated by an earthquake in 2007 but is rebuilding.

3 The Southern Andes and Lake Titicaca. Colca and Cotahuasi Canyons are the world's two deepest canyons. Peru's "second city," Arequipa, may also be its most attractive. Lake Titicaca is the world's highest navigable lake and home to the floating Uros Islands.

4 Cusco and the Sacred Valley. Cusco (11,500 feet above sea level) is a necessary stop on your journey to Machu Picchu. The former Inca capital is gorgeous, and packed with fine restaurants, hotels, churches, and museums. Visit the nearby Inca ruins of Sacsayhuamán, take a day trip to the Pisac Market and Ollantaytambo, and spend a night in the Sacred Valley.

5 Machu Picchu. The great Machu Picchu, crowded or not crowded, misty rains or clear skies, never ceases to enthrall, and the Inca Trail is still the great hiking pilgrimage. Stay in Aguas Calientes for the best access.

6 Amazon Basin. Peru's vast tract of the Amazon may contain the world's greatest biodiversity. Fly into Iquitos or Puerto Maldonado for the wildlife preserves, jungle lodges, rain-forest hikes, and boat excursions.

7 The Central Highlands. Festivals and market towns dominate Huancayo and the Mantaro Valley, while the passionate Semana Santa celebrations are the rage in Ayacucho. From Lima to Huancayo, the world's second highest railroad tops out at 15,685 feet.

8 The North Coast and the Northern Highlands. Go up the coast for beach life and inland to the Cordillera Blanca for some of the world's highest mountains. Many of Peru's greatest archaeological discoveries were made in the north. Sites are still being uncovered near Chiclayo, Trujillo, and Chachapoyas.

NEED TO KNOW

PERU

Lima ☆

Atlantic Ocean

AT A GLANCE

Capital: Lima

Population: 31,380,000

Currency: *Nuevo sol*

Money: ATMs in bigger cities; U.S. dollars often not accepted.

Language: Spanish, Quechua, Aymara

Country Code: 51

Emergencies: 105

Driving: On the right

Electricity: 220v/60 cycles; plugs are U.S. standard or European standard. Power converter needed.

Time: Same time as New York except during daylight savings

Documents: Up to 90 days with valid passport

Mobile Phones: GSM (850 and 1900 bands)

Major Mobile Companies: Movistar, Claro, Nextel, Entel

WEBSITES

Trade: ⊕ www.peru.travel/en-us

Visit Peru: ⊕ www.visit-peru.com

Andean Travel Web: ⊕ www.andeantravelweb.com

GETTING AROUND

✈ **Air Travel:** International point of entry is Lima's Aeropuerto Internacional Jorge Chávez; other airports include Arequipa, Cusco, Iquitos, and Trujillo.

🚌 **Bus Travel:** The intercity bus system is extensive, and fares are quite reasonable but getting around mountain ranges and poor safety records make flying a better option.

🚗 **Car Travel:** In general, it's not a great idea to have a car in Peru; hire a driver instead.

🚆 **Train Travel:** Trains run along four different routes, including Cusco to Machu Picchu and Cusco to Lake Titicaca.

PLAN YOUR BUDGET

	HOTEL ROOM	MEAL	ATTRACTIONS
Low Budget	S/280	S/24	Museum of Pre-Colombian Art, S/20
Mid Budget	S/650	S/40	O/W standard train to Machu Picchu, S/350
High Budget	S/1,200	S/70	O/W luxury train to Machu Picchu, S/1,652

WAYS TO SAVE

Load up on lunch. Most smaller restaurants offer a lunchtime menu, a prix-fixe meal (US$3–US$6) that consists of an appetizer, a main dish, dessert, and a beverage.

Stay in a local B&B. B&Bs are popular all over Peru, but especially in Cusco, Arequipa, and Puno. Many are in charming older buildings, including colonial-era homes built around flower-filled courtyards.

Negotiate taxi fare in advance. Taxis are often not metered. Agree on a fare when you get in. Taxi drivers have a reputation for overcharging tourists.

Book with a local company. Though you may be reluctant to buy a package directly from a Peruvian company, keep in mind that you may get the same tour you would buy from a U.S. company for considerably less money.

PLAN YOUR TIME

Hassle Factor	Medium. Flights to Lima are frequent and domestic flights easily connect Lima to Peru's far reaches.
3 days	Make a beeline for Cusco. Enjoy this magical city and, of course, visit Machu Picchu. It is all that it is cracked up to be.
1 week	Spend more time enjoying the Cusco/Sacred Valley/Machu Picchu combination. You really need five days to see the region in full. Then head back up to Lima and experience the city's foodie revolution, or head to the coastal city of Paracas and visit the Nazca Lines.
2 weeks	Combine Machu Picchu and Cusco with the rain forest of nearby Madre de Dios. Then head toward the southern attractions such as Lake Titicaca, Arequipa, and the Colca Canyon, or head to Iquitos instead of Madre de Dios for a cruise on the Amazon River.

WHEN TO GO

High Season: Most people visit Peru between June and September, which is the dry season. During this winter in the Southern Andes, it often freezes at night, but the days are sunny. Nevertheless, the coastal areas are rainy, and Lima is enveloped in a chilly fog.

Low Season: December through April is considered low season because it is the rainy season in the Andes and Amazon. But the weather is lovely in Lima and such coastal sites as the Nazca Lines, Paracas, and the pre-Incan ruins near Trujillo and Chiclayo.

Value Season: If you prefer to avoid the crowds or the cold, consider doing your Cusco–Machu Picchu trip in late April, May, October, or November. You are likely to get some great weather and interact with fewer tourists.

BIG EVENTS

February: During the Festival of the Virgin de la Candelaria in Puno, you'll enjoy street parties and choreography displays from more than 140 traditional dances.

February–March: Peru's largest grape harvest festival, Festival de la Uva, or La Vendimia Wine Festival, is held in Ica, close to the town's pisco vineyards.

June: Hundreds of thousands make the pilgrimage to Cusco for the Festival of the Sun, or Inti Raymi, paying homage to the Inca sun god.

October: Of Peru's myriad Catholic celebrations, El Señor de los Milagros in Lima is the largest.

READ THIS

■ **Turn Right at Machu Picchu,** Mark Adams. Retracing the steps of explorer Hiram Bingham.

■ **The Green House,** Mario Vargas Llosa. Peruvian Nobel laureate's second novel.

■ **The Last Days of the Incas,** Kim MacQuarrie. A chronicle of the Spanish conquest of Peru.

WATCH THIS

■ **Secret of the Incas.** 1954 romantic adventure film shot in Cusco and Machu Picchu.

■ **The Motorcycle Diaries.** Biopic about Che Guevara.

■ **Sigo Siendo.** Documentary on Peruvian folk music.

EAT THIS

■ **Cebiche:** raw fish marinated in lemon juice

■ **Chupes:** soups made of shrimp and fish with potatoes and more

■ **Paiche:** huge fish found in jungle lakes

■ **Cuy:** guinea pig

■ **Pisco sour:** Peru's national drink made with pale grape brandy, lemon juice, sugar, bitters, and egg white.

■ **Chicha de jora:** low-alcohol corn beer

PERU MADE EASY

How Much Can I See in One Week, or Two Weeks?

The minimum amount of time to experience Peru is one week, but you really should consider setting aside two weeks if you can, because that would allow you to move more slowly and catch a few more of the country's amazing sights. One week is enough time to get a taste of Lima and complete the Cusco–Sacred Valley–Machu Picchu circuit, either with an Inca Trail trek, or a more leisurely train itinerary. If you don't mind a quick pace, you could do that circuit in four days, then fly to Puerto Maldonado for a couple of nights in the Amazon rain forest at one of the nearby nature lodges.

A two-week trip allows you to visit more of the sites along the Cusco–Sacred Valley–Machu Picchu route and head deeper into the Amazon rain forest, or do the Lake Titicaca–Arequipa–Colca Canyon circuit. The Nazca–Paracas trip can easily be added to the above in a two-week trip. Alternatives to the chilly Titicaca–Arequipa circuit is to return to Lima after Machu Picchu and fly to either Trujillo or Chiclayo: coastal cities that lie near important pre-Incan sites, to Huaraz for high-altitude adventure, or to Jaen to visit Chachapoyas and the Incan fortress of Kuelap. If outdoor adventure is your passion, you could extend your stay in the highlands for a white-water rafting trip or trekking in either the Cusco region or the Cordillera Blanca.

How Difficult Is Peru to Get Around?

A growing selection of domestic flights means it is much easier to move about within Peru. Almost every worthwhile destination is within a two-hour flight from Lima. Train travel is limited, but fun and easy. Traveling by car is trickier—roads are improving, but signage is spotty. Buses go everywhere, and the most expensive seats are comfortable, but bus accidents are a frequent occurrence in Peru, so only travel with reputable companies. In cities, cabs are abundant and cheap, but stick to the big companies such as Easy Taxi, Taxi Seguro, or Remisse. Many destinations in the Amazon Basin can only be reached by river.

Is It Hard to Get to Machu Picchu?

Travel to Machu Picchu is almost too easy. Many people do the trip in a day out of Cusco, but it is worth two or three days, with overnights in Aguas Calientes and the Sacred Valley. The most common method is to hop on a train from Ollantaytambo to Aguas Calientes, which is a 20-minute bus trip from the ruins. Or you can do as the Incas did and walk the trail, which is a two- to four-day hike and a highlight for those who do it. Keep in mind that you need to book an Inca Trail trek six months ahead of time.

What Languages Do People Speak?

The official language is Spanish and nearly everyone speaks it. But in the highlands the language the Incas spoke, Quechua, is still widely used. Older people in indigenous communities often don't know Spanish, but younger generations do. Aymara, a pre-Incan language, is spoken in the towns around Lake Titicaca, and dozens of native tongues are spoken in the Amazon Basin. And a growing number of Peruvians speak English.

Will I Have Trouble If I Don't Speak Spanish?

Although it's helpful to know some Spanish, it's not a necessity, especially on an organized tour or in tourist areas. There's a strong push for tourism professionals to learn English, but cab drivers or store clerks aren't likely to know a lick. We suggest learning a few simple phrases. *Cuánto cuesta?* (How much?) is a good one to start with.

Is the Water Safe to Drink?

Nope. But bottled water is cheap and sold nearly everywhere. Drink as much as you can, it'll help you beat altitude sickness.

Will I Get Sick?

Stomach bugs are a frequent problem for visitors, but if you avoid salads, ice, and only eat fruits that you peel, you'll reduce your likelihood of suffering from one. Cebiche and other "raw" seafood dishes popular in Lima carry a risk, but are so tasty that it would be a shame to avoid them. Stirring your cebiche a bit and waiting 10 minutes before eating it should allow the citric acid to kill any bacteria. Bring antidiarrhea medicines and play it by ear. If you are pregnant or plan to become pregnant and are headed to areas of Peru below 6,500 feet, you should talk to your doctor about Zika virus.

What Are the Safety Concerns?

Petty crime is the primary concern. You'll probably have a camera, iPod, watch, jewelry, credit cards, cash—everything a thief wants. Pickpocketing and bag slashing are the most common methods. Thieves are fast and sneaky, so be alert, especially in crowded markets and bus stations. Distraction is a common technique, so if a stranger touches you—a wobbly drunk, or somebody who wants to clean off a cream that has inexplicably gotten on your coat—be aware that their accomplice may try to rob you. Never walk on a deserted street at night. There have been cases of several robbers mugging travelers on side streets, but if you stick to the busy streets in Lima's Centro and Barranco, you should be fine. Taxi

kidnappings, in which people are forced to withdraw money from ATMs at gunpoint, are also a problem, albeit rare. Use only taxis from the big companies.

Should I Worry About Altitude Sickness?

If you have health issues, you should check with your doctor before heading to high altitudes. You can also consider getting a prescription for altitude sickness medication from your doctor. Don't worry too much because nearly everyone experiences a little altitude sickness. The lucky ones may have a headache for the first 24 hours, while others may endure several days of fatigue, nausea, and headaches. When up high, lay off the booze, limit physical activity, hydrate, drink lots of coca tea, suck coca hard candy, or chew coca leaves. If the headache persists, take an ibuprofen, hydrate some more, and sleep it off. Some hotels have oxygen, so don't hesitate to ask for it.

Do I Have to Pay Any Fees to Get into the Country?

No. But you pay to get out. The departure tax system (which nearly every South American country embraces) is alive and well in Peru, but the US$31 fee for international departures from Lima is included in the cost of your ticket.

Are There Cultural Sensitivities I Should Be Aware Of?

You'll notice that men and women kiss each other on the cheek when saying hello, and the same goes for women to women. It's nonsexual and a sign of friendliness. People talk, walk, and sit close in general. Peruvians, like many South American countries, are also on "Latin time," meaning they often arrive late for social engagements, though tours and transportation tend to run on time.

WHAT'S NEW IN PERU

Lima's Dining Scene Is Red Hot

Peruvian cuisine has been gaining international fame for years, but the restaurant scene in Lima has never been hotter. The 2017 edition of the "World's 50 Best Restaurants" included three Lima eateries, while the list of the "50 Best Restaurants in Latin America" compiled by the same organization—Walter Reed Business Media Ltd.—included nine, and rated Lima's Central and Maido as the region's best and second-best restaurants, respectively. If you want to eat at either of them, you should make your reservation two or three months ahead of time, but you should be able to get a table at any of the other seven on the list by calling a day or two ahead. And the truth is, there are at least 50 restaurants in Lima—and quite a few in other cities—that are just as good, or nearly as good as the ones on that list; so you'll have no shortage of places to savor the country's culinary delights during your time there.

Barranco Is Lima's Modern Art Mecca

Long considered Lima's most bohemian neighborhood, Barranco has recently established itself as the epicenter of the country's art scene. The attractive southern neighborhood is home to the city's modern art museum—El Museo de Arte Contemporáneo de Lima (MAC Lima) —and several galleries. Barranco also boasts two boutique hotels that have more impressive collections of modern art than any of the city's galleries—Hotel B and Second Home Peru—though most of it isn't for sale. Barranco also has a fair amount of street art, and is home to a growing number of boutiques that sell eclectic selections of colorful creations by local artists and artisans.

Barranco's vibrant art scene peaks during four days in late April, when the city's two most important art fairs take place simultaneously. Art Lima, held in the stately Escuela Superior de Guerra—just south of Barranco in the neighborhood of Chorrillos—and Peru Arte Contemporáneo (PARC), which is held in the MAC Lima. Together, those two art fairs exhibit an impressive array of works from some of Latin America's best contemporary artists, represented by galleries from across the region. As might be expected, Barranco's bars and restaurants are especially busy during that long weekend.

Northern Highlands Now More Accessible

The Amazonas Region, in Peru's northern highlands, holds one of the country's best archaeological sites and some impressive natural attractions, yet few travelers visited this area in the past because it took so long to get there. The trip from Lima to the colonial city of Chachapoyas—from where travelers can visit the pre-Incan city of Kuelap and Gochta Waterfall on day trips—used to be a long day's journey that began with a 90-minute flight to the coastal city of Chiclayo followed by a 9- to 10-hour bus trip. Because Chachapoyas is located in a narrow valley that is often foggy, it's airport was closed to commercial flights years ago, but in 2015–16, the government renovated the city of Jaen's airport, in a wider, lower-altitude valley. In late 2016, LATAM Airlines inaugurated a daily, 90-minute flight between Lima and Jaen, which is less than four hours by road from Chachapoyas, making the trip there less of an expedition. As demand grows, other airlines will likely begin flying to Jaen as well.

Visiting Kuelap has also gotten much easier, thanks to improvements to the road between Chachapoyas and Nuevo Tingo—the closest town—and the 2016 inauguration of Telecabinas Kuelap: a gondola lift that carries passengers up the mountain from a station outside Nuevo Tingo to a station a mere 20-minute walk from the archaeological site. Before the gondola lift was built, getting from Nuevo Tingo to Kuelap entailed several arduous hours of hiking, so the site was only accessible to people in good physical condition. Now that impressive walled city can be reached via a 20-minute gondola ride that costs a very reasonable S/20.

National Trademark

As part of its efforts to promote the country's exports and tourism, the government of Peru held a contest for the design of a national trademark. You're bound to notice the winning design—the word Perú written in cursive with a spiral beneath the P—on everything from brochures to T-shirts. The curlicue in the P was inspired by the tail of the monkey in the Nazca line figures, so Peru's 21st-century marketing campaign celebrates the country's pre-Columbian heritage.

2017 Floods

Though Peru is responsible for only a tiny fraction of the world's greenhouse gas emissions, scientists consider it to be one of the countries most vulnerable to climate change. This was affirmed during the first months of 2017, when record high surface water temperatures in the Eastern Pacific Ocean—linked to El Niño—triggered weeks of torrential rains along Peru's Northern Coast and Amazon Basin that produced unprecedented flooding. Floods and mudslides destroyed or damaged roads, bridges, farms, and more than 140,000 homes, killing approximately 120 people and injuring hundreds more. Travelers who visit Peru's northern coastal cities or beach towns can expect to encounter structures that were damaged by this national disaster, but the government prioritized repairing routes to tourist destinations, so the damage shouldn't affect overland travel significantly.

Aviation Evolution

The options for flying to and within Peru continue to evolve. The Chilean company LAN Airlines merged with the Brazilian carrier TAM to form LATAM Airlines in 2016, creating one of the world's largest airlines. LATAM has direct flights to Lima from five U.S. cities, several European capitals, and cities across Latin America. It is also the biggest airline in Peru, with flights to more than a dozen domestic airports and hourly flights between Lima and Cusco. Peru's domestic airline lineup expanded from five to six carriers in 2017 with the inauguration of the discount airline Viva Air Peru. The U.S. discount airline Jet Blue also has daily flights to Lima from Ft. Lauderdale. What it all means for travelers is that there is more competition, which should keep prices down, and there are more flights to more destinations in Peru than ever before.

PERU TODAY

Traditional and Chic

With its ancient ruins, snowcapped Andes, and vast Amazon wilderness, Peru has long captured the imagination of people in distant lands. But for much of the 1980s and '90s, few dared to visit the country, which was wracked by a violent conflict between the Shining Path guerrilla movement and Peru's armed forces. Even after the violence subsided in the '90s, the country's tourism infrastructure was quite limited, catering primarily to backpackers and other budget travelers.

Thanks to two decades of economic growth and its growing popularity as a tourist destination, Peru now has more options for experiencing its cultural and natural heritage than ever before. A growing number of the country's tourism businesses are becoming environmentally and socially responsible, and the industry is helping countless Peruvian's to work their way out of poverty, which remains the country's biggest problem.

Government

Peru is a constitutional democracy in which the president and congress are elected for five-year terms, and presidents are prohibited from running for reelection while in office, though they can run for the subsequent term, President Pedro Pablo Kuczynski took office in July 2016 and will serve till July 28, 2021, which is the bicentennial of Peru's independence from Spain. A former investment banker and World Bank official with degrees from Oxford and Princeton, Kuczynski was elected on promises to revive the country's lagging economic growth and improve life for the approximately seven million Peruvians who live in poverty. He is building upon the democratic reforms and economic growth of the three democratic administrations that preceded his, which marks an important continuity after decades on a political roller coaster.

Economy

For much of the past decade and a half, Peru has experienced some of the highest economic growth in Latin America, averaging 3%–6% annually. From 2004 to 2014, economic growth was driven by high mineral prices, largely due to demand from China, but since 2014, mineral prices have been weak, and exports of agricultural products such as asparagus, coffee, cocoa, seafood, textiles, and tourism have kept the economy afloat. Per capita income has more than doubled since 2003, and though much of that increase has gone to the upper echelons, the percentage of Peruvians living in poverty has dropped from more than 50% to less than 22% over the past 20 years. Tax revenues have likewise grown, which is reflected in the refurbished government buildings, new infrastructure, and a bigger police force. For travelers, this means safer, cleaner neighborhoods, but also higher prices than in years past.

Social Unrest

Marches and road barricades are part of Peruvian political life as communities, unions, and other groups periodically take to the streets to protest projects or policies they don't like, or to demand government help. The protests usually end peacefully, but there have been too many occasions where police fire has resulted in deaths. Cusco residents stage occasional protests and strikes, sometimes stranding travelers for a day. Unfortunately, many of that region's residents perceive little benefit from tourism and don't hesitate to disrupt transportation to pressure the government. Nevertheless, the likelihood that a protest will interfere with your travel plans is small.

Religion

As a result of centuries of Spanish rule, Peru remains predominantly Roman Catholic, with more than 80% of the population identifying themselves as such. Catholicism influences the daily lives of most Peruvians, as well as state affairs. The newly elected president's inauguration ceremony begins with a mass in Lima's Cathedral, for example, and the country's archbishop is frequently in the news. Despite this overwhelming presence, many Peruvians have moved toward Protestantism and Evangelicalism, which currently represent about 12% of the population. Indigenous Peruvians fused Catholicism with their preconquest religion, with Pachamama (an Earth spirit) representing the Virgin Mary, so in the highlands, people observe both Catholic and pre-Columbian holy dates, with rituals that meld traditions from both cultures. If you're lucky, you'll witness a religious procession, celebration, or other display of faith during your travels.

Sports

As with most of South America, *fútbol* (soccer) is Peru's second religion. The country's best teams are Universitario de Deportes and Alianza Lima, and a game between Universitario and Alianza is considered a "clasico." Peru's national team hasn't managed to qualify for the World Cup in more than two decades, which causes much frustration and debate. On the other hand, female athletes such as boxer Kina Malpartida and surfer Sofía Mulanovich have both been world champions.

Literature

Peru's most famous writer is the Nobel laureate Mario Vargas Llosa, who has written several books set in Peru, which makes him a good author to read before or during a trip there. *The Story Teller* and *The Green House* are especially Peruvian novels, though *The Time of the Hero, Conversation in the Cathedral, The Dream of the Celt*, and comic novels *Aunt Julia and the Script Writer* and *Captain Pantoya and the Special Service* are also set in the country.

Other important 20th-century writers are José María Arguedas, Ciro Alegría, and Manuel Scorza, all of whom wrote about the country's indigenous culture. Daniel Alarcón, who was born in Peru but raised in the United States, sets his fiction in the country. Peru's most famous poet is César Vallejo, who only produced three books of poetry, but is considered one of the most innovative poets of the 20th century.

Music

Peruvian music can be split by regions: the sounds of the Andes and the sounds of the coast. *Huayno*, the music of the Andes, is traditionally played on acoustic guitars, a small stringed instrument called the *charango*, and a panpipe called the *zampoña*, but its more popular form now relies on synthesizers and electric guitars. Coastal *música criolla* has Spanish, Gypsy, and African roots and is played on acoustic guitars and a percussion instrument called the *cajón*—a large wooden box. Popular singers in this genre include Susana Baca, Tania Libertad, and Eva Allyón. Peru's most popular music is probably cumbia, which is originally from Colombia but is popular across Latin America.

PERU
TOP ATTRACTIONS

Machu Picchu and the Inca Trail

(A) This "Lost City of the Incas" is the main reason people come to Peru. The citadel of Machu Picchu was built around the 1450s, only to be abandoned a hundred years later. Spanish conquistadors never found it, and for centuries it stayed hidden. It was rediscovered by an American historian in 1911. If you're adventurous, and in good shape, the four-day Inca Trail is the classic route to Machu Picchu. You'll need to reserve a tour six months in advance.

Colca Canyon

(B) Twice as deep as Arizona's Grand Canyon, Colca Canyon is typically a side trip from Arequipa, which is a three-hour drive away. Adventure enthusiasts head for the Canyon's Colca River for white-water rafting, while those less inclined toward danger hike along the canyon for gorgeous vistas. The highlight is the Cruz del Condor, a mirador where lucky visitors might spot the Andean condor in flight.

Chan Chan

(C) A UNESCO World Heritage site, this archaeological site was home to the second largest pre-Columbian society in South America: the Chimú. The estimated 30,000 Chimú residents built the mud city between 850 and 1470. You can roam the ruins—which contain 10 walled citadels that house burial chambers, ceremonial rooms, and temples—on a half-day trip from the nearby northern city of Trujillo, or the beach town of Huanchaco.

Lake Titicaca

(D) At 3,812 meters (12,500 feet), Lake Titicaca is the highest navigable lake in the world. More than 25 rivers empty into it, and according to Inca legend, it was the birthplace of the Sun god who founded the Inca dynasty. On Isla Taquile and other islands here Quechua-speaking people preserve the traditions of their ancestors.

Tambopata National Reserve

(E) This vast protected area near Puerto Maldonado, a short flight east of Cusco, is an excellent place to experience the myriad flora and fauna of the Amazon Basin. A dozen nature lodges scattered along the Tambopata and Madre de Dios Rivers provide comfortable bases for hikes and boat trips into the surrounding wilderness to see several types of monkeys, dinosaurian caimans, giant rodents called capybaras, and some of the reserve's hundreds of bird species.

The Nazca Lines

(F) Between 900 BC and AD 600 the Nazca and Paracas cultures constructed the Nazca Lines: geometric figures drawn into the Pampa Colorado (Red Plain) near Nazca, a city south of Lima. Three hundred geoglyphs and 800 straight lines make up these mysterious figures. No one knows why these massive drawings—which include representations of a lizard, monkey, condor, and spider—were created. The only way to get a good view is to take a flight.

Sacsayhuamán

(G) Machu Picchu isn't the only must-see Inca ruin to visit from Cusco. Used as a fortress during Pizarro's conquest, the military site of Sacsayhuamán is made of huge stone blocks; the largest is 8.5 meters (28 feet) high and weighs more than 300 tons (600,000 pounds). It's believed that some 20,000 men built it.

Cordillera Blanca

(H) The highest part of the Peruvian Andes, the Cordillera Blanca (White Range) has more than 50 peaks that reach 5,500 meters (18,000 feet) or higher, and stretches 20 km (12.5 miles) wide and 180 km (112 miles) long. Mountain climbers and hikers of all skill levels can enjoy this majestic range.

IF YOU LIKE

Sun, Surf, and Seafood

During the summer months (December–April), beach lovers around Peru head west to enjoy a day of surfing the Pacific Ocean waves, sunbathing, and devouring the country's freshest seafood.

Huanchaco. This beach town west of Trujillo has a long left-hand surf break that is complemented by an ample dining and lodging selection. Surfers of all skill levels can find suitable waves year-round, and take lessons, if needed, but the biggest swells roll in between March and August.

Lima. While the ocean views from Miraflores and Barranco are impressive, the capital's greatest marine asset is the food. Lima has restaurants that specialize in everything, but *cebicherías* (restaurants dedicated to seafood) are the place to head for lunch. Check out Punta Sal, Segundo Muelle, Amoramar, Pescados Capitales and chef Gastón Acurio's upscale La Mar.

Máncora. This fishing town on Peru's northern coast is the country's worst-kept secret. Ask any Peruvian which is the best beach in Peru and they will all mention this stretch of pale-gray sand lined with coconut palms and hotels. Máncora is sunny year-round and visited by beach lovers from Lima and abroad.

South of Lima. Urbanites from Lima flock southward from December to April to beach towns such as Punta Hermosa and San Bartolo, an hour from the capital. Cerro Azul, a small beach town in Cañete, 90 minutes south of Lima, is a tranquil alternative to the beaches closer to town. In contrast, Asia, also in Cañete, is where the wealthiest Limeños summer.

Ancient Archaeological Sites

The main reason most travelers visit Peru is to see the ancient ruins left by the Inca and pre-Incan civilizations. Machu Picchu is the biggie, but don't stop there. Here are a few archaeological sites that are worth the trip.

Caral. Four hours north of Lima, the archaeological ruins of Caral in the Supe Valley shocked the world when their origins were discovered to date back to 2627 BC—1,500 years earlier than what was believed to be the age of South America's oldest civilization. Growing numbers of visitors make the day trip to Peru's most recently discovered ancient wonder.

Chan Chan. This capital of the pre-Incan Chimú Empire was the largest pre-Columbian city in the Americas and is the largest adobe city in the world. A 5-km (3-mile) trip from the northern city of Trujillo, Chan Chan is a UNESCO World Heritage site. Unfortunately, it is threatened by erosion because of its close proximity to the coast, which experiences seasonal rains.

Choquequirau. The Inca ruins of Choquequirau, in Cusco province, is the ideal destination for hikers who want to stray from the beaten trail. Five-day trekking tours are available to this remote site, which has been called "Machu Picchu's sacred sister" because of the similarities in architecture.

Ollantaytambo. Sixty kilometers (37 miles) northwest of Cusco, the extensive Inca fortress of Ollantaytambo is one of the few locations where the Incas managed to defeat Spanish conquistadors. The fort held a temple, with a ceremonial center greeting those who manage to get to the top.

Natural Beauty

With more than 50 conservation areas—in the form of national parks, reserves, sanctuaries, and protected forests, Peru is a great place to experience nature.

Colca Canyon and Cotahuasi Canyon. The two deepest canyons in the world are in Peru's dry, southern Andes. Dipping down 10,600 feet and 11,000 feet, respectively, they are skirted by hiking trails, whereas the rivers that flow through them offer intense kayaking and rafting. Near this exceptional geology are villages offering glimpses into the indigenous culture.

The Cordillera Blanca. Towering over the town of Huaraz, the "White Mountain Range" holds Peru's highest peaks, as well as countless glacier lakes and highland valleys. Much of it is protected within Huascarán National Park, which was established to protect the mountain range's priceless flora and fauna and landscapes. A UNESCO World Heritage site, the park is home to such rare species as the spectacled bear and the Andean condor.

Manu Biosphere Reserve. This remote protected area extends from the cloud forest to the rain forest, and is home to an array of rare species that includes the cock of the rock, giant river otter, and jaguar. Its mountains, rivers, oxbow lakes, and forests are also stunningly beautiful.

Tambopata National Reserve. This vast rain-forest reserve covers an area where relatively few people live, so it suffers less hunting than other areas of the Amazon Basin, and is consequently one of the best places to see wildlife. This, together with its proximity to the Puerto Maldonado airport, make Tambopata one of the country's most popular natural destinations.

Museums

It could be argued that Peru is one big open-air museum. Nevertheless, a little background information before you head to the ruins is always helpful. Museums in Peru do an excellent job of documenting the history and culture of a country overflowing with both.

Museo de Arte de Lima (MALI). The permanent exhibition on the second floor of Lima's biggest art museum includes an extensive collection of pre-Columbian pottery, textiles and other artifacts, as well as colonial and 19th-century art.

Museo Larco. Lima's best archaeology museum was constructed on the site of a pre-Columbian pyramid. It's most famous for its titillating collection of erotic ceramics, but it has more than 40,000 other ceramic pieces, textiles, and gold work on display.

Museo Nacional Sicán. Twenty kilometers (12.5 miles) north of Chiclayo, this modern museum focuses on the ancient Sicán civilization, which originated in AD 750. Learn about the life and death of one of their leaders, the Lord of Sicán, who represented the "natural world" in their culture.

Museo Santuarios Andinos. Home to the famed "Juanita, the Inca Ice Maiden" mummy, the Museo de Arqueología de la Universidad Católica de Santa María, as it's formally known, is an obligatory stop for anyone visiting the city of Arequipa. Juanita was discovered in southern Peru and is now kept in a cold glass box to preserve her body so that future visitors can learn about her sacrificial death.

TOP EXPERIENCES

Join a Celebration

Clanging bells, chanting, and wafting incense rouse you before dawn. You peer out your window: scores of people draped in bright, colorful costumes walk down the street carrying a saint's figure. Catholic observances and indigenous traditions pack the calendar with *fiestas* (festivals)—from Lima's birthday in January to the *Semana Santa* (Holy Week) in spring, to the Incan ritual Inti Raymi, held near Cusco on June 24.

Puno is best known for its traditional Carnaval, but each November citizens reenact the birth of the first Incan emperor, Manco Capac, who, legend has it, rose out of Lake Titicaca. Among the crosses, saints, and colorful costumes, townspeople try their luck at bingo, beauty queens compete for the crown, Huayno music blasts from speakers, and the beer flows freely.

Explore a Market

Wandering through a market provides a wonderful window into the lives of local people. All of Peru's cities have central markets, some of the more interesting of which include Cusco's Mercado Central, the Mercado San Camillo in Arequipa, and the market in the neighborhood of Belén, in Iquitos. Certain highland towns are known for their market days, when vendors set up shop on central streets, one of the most popular of which is Pisac, in the Sacred Valley. Vendors pack their stalls with everything from dried potato chunks to medicinal herbs to love potions. They'll likely invite you to step inside for a look, and if you see something you like, don't forget to bargain.

Visit the Wild Things

Squirrel monkeys leap between branches, fish break the muddy water's surface, parrots squawk in the treetops. The colors and sounds of the Amazon Basin's wildlife are unforgettable, and each of those creatures has a story, because they all play specific roles in the complex web of jungle life. Peru is one of the easiest countries in which to experience the beauty and diversity of the Amazon, whether on the river that region was named for or one of its many tributaries. There are dozens of nature lodges where naturalist guides can take you deep into the wilderness, and show you some of the thousands of species that live there, most of which are found nowhere else on Earth.

Enjoy the Dances

Peruvian folkloric dances vary dramatically between the coast and mountains. The coastal *marinera* is performed to the music of a brass band by a courting couple who execute elegant, complex movements, but never touch. Afro-Peruvian dance, which is also coastal, is more sensual, performed to the music of guitars and the rhythm of a *cajón,* a sonorous wooden box on which the percussionist sits. Andean dances are more varied and spectacular, with many more dancers in colorful costumes. The most impressive one is the *danza de tijeras* (scissors dance), which involves gymnastic leaps with scissors in hand. Folk dancing plays a central role in the country's festivals, but any of the above can be enjoyed at the varied *peñas* and dinner shows in Lima and other cities.

PACKING AND PREPARATIONS

What you pack depends on where and when you travel. If you're heading to several regions, you'll need a good variety of clothing. If you visit the Amazon Basin or Andes between November and May, pack rain gear and plastic bags to protect cameras and other items. Good walking shoes or boots are essential everywhere, as are sunblock and insect repellent.

Weather-Appropriate Clothing

Peru's varied geography means a diversity of climates, with the major climate regions being the *Costa* (coast), *Sierra* (mountains), and *Selva* (Amazon rain forest). Add to this the fact that southern Peru experiences distinct summer and winter, which are the opposite of the northern hemisphere's seasons, whereas northern Peru has less seasonal climate variation. When it's torrid in Manhattan, Lima is chilly and gray, but when New Yorkers are bundling up, Lima is hot and sunny. It can get quite cool in the mountains at night, with frequent freezes between June and September, but it is warm and sunny during the day then. The coast is a desert, but it rains most afternoons in the mountains from October to May and pretty much year-round in the Amazon Basin, though more between October and May. If you visit then, you'll need rain gear. Nevertelss, the mountains don't get as cold at night during the rainy months, so you may not need that down jacket.

The best policy is to bring a good mix of clothes that go well together so that you can layer, because a mountain day begins brisk, but quickly warms. Once the clouds roll in, or the sun gets low, you'll need a raincoat or a jacket. Rather than packing a sweater, hat, and gloves, you may want to buy them in Lima or Cusco, where the shops and markets hold a kaleidoscopic selection of sheep and alpaca wool clothing.

You'll want light clothing, a hat, and rain gear for the Amazon Basin, where it is usually scorching. Long pants and sleeves will help you avoid insect bites and sunburn. Keep in mind that the Madre de Dios region gets little rain from May to September, when it gets hit by occasional cold fronts that can make you break out your mountain clothes.

Toiletries

Sunblock is essential everywhere, and can be purchased at any Peruvian pharmacy. Insect repellent, preferably with DEET, is essential in the Amazon Basin and eastern Andes (Machu Picchu), but the local brands aren't as good as what you can buy at home. Pack an antidiarrhea medicine, such as Imodium, just in case, and always carry a small packet of tissues, since rural bathrooms may not have toilet paper. You'll want a skin moisturizer if you spend much time in the mountains between May and October. If your camera or other electronic goods use unusual-size disposable batteries, pack extras.

Vaccines

The Centers for Disease Control and Prevention recommend that travelers to Peru be up-to-date on routine shots and consult their doctor about getting vaccinated against hepatitis A and B and typhoid. Travelers heading to the Amazon Basin should get a yellow fever vaccine and consider taking an antimalarial drug other than chloroquine. Diligent use of insect repellent, long pants, and long-sleeve shirts is the best policy in the jungle, because they can protect you against various insect-borne diseases.

GREAT ITINERARIES

If this will be your first trip to Peru, Cusco and Machu Picchu are practically obligatory. The question is "What else?" And the answer depends on how much time you have and what your interests are. You can combine Machu Picchu with a number of other Andean attractions, the Amazon rain forest, or pre-Incan archaeological sites on the coast. If this is not your first trip to Peru, the last itineraries in this section offer you something a little different.

ESSENTIAL PERU

The former Incan capital of Cusco and citadel of Machu Picchu are two of the most impressive places in South America and the reasons that most people visit Peru. If you only have a week, this is where you head, but it is easy and highly recommended to combine a Machu Picchu pilgrimage with a visit to the rain forest in the nearby Madre de Dios province.

Day 1: Lima

Lima has more to see than you could possibly pack into a day. You should definitely take a tour of Lima's historic Centro, or give yourself a few hours to explore it on your own, visiting **San Francisco** church and monastery and the **Museo de Arte de Lima (MALI)**. In the afternoon, head to Pueblo Libre to visit the **Museo Nacional de Antropología y Arqueología** and the **Museo Rafael Larco Herrera,** or explore Miraflores and visit the **Parque de Amor**. In the evening, stroll around historic Barranco and have dinner there or at the **Huaca Pucllana**, in Miraflores, where you can explore a pre-Inca site before you eat.

Day 2: Cusco

From Lima, take an early-morning flight to the ancient Inca capital of **Cusco**. Try to get seats on the left side of the plane for an amazing view of snow-draped peaks toward the end of the flight. You'll want to take it easy upon arriving in Cusco, which is perched at almost 11,000 feet above sea level. Take a half-day tour, or visit a couple of sights such as the **Cathedral, Qorikancha,** the **Museo de Arte Precolombino,** or the **Museo Hilario Mendivil** on your own. Be sure to stop by the **Plaza de Armas** at night, before dining at one of the city's many excellent restaurants.

Day 3: Sacred Valley

Dedicate this day to the sights of the surrounding highlands, starting with **Sacsayhuamán**, the Inca ruins above town. You could do a day trip to the **Sacred Valley,** or spend this night at one of the many hotels located there. The valley holds an array of interesting sites, such as the market town of **Pisac, Chinchero,** and the massive Inca fortress at **Ollantaytambo**. It is also lower, and thus warmer, than Cusco, and lies on the route to Machu Picchu, which means you can sleep a little later if you stay there.

Days 4 and 5: Machu Picchu

Enjoy a local site in the morning, then take a Machu Picchu train, which winds its way past Incan ruins and luxuriant forest, to the town of **Aguas Calientes**. Check into your hotel, then stroll down the road along the Urubamba River. On Day 5, get up early and take the bus to **Machu Picchu**, the majestic citadel of the Incas. Head up the steep trail on the left shortly after entering the park and climb to the upper part of the ruins for a panoramic view before you start exploring. If you're up for a tough hike up a steep,

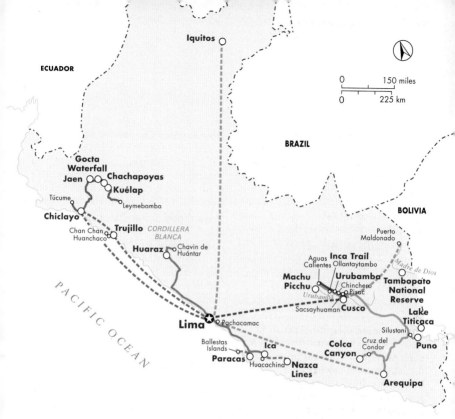

slightly treacherous trail, climb **Huayna Picchu,** the backdrop mountain, for vertiginous views of the ruins and surrounding jungle. ■TIP→ Admission tickets to hike Huayna Picchu must be purchased months in advance for visits during the May–September high season. You may instead opt for the longer hike through the forest to the **Temple of the Moon.** After all the hiking, you should be ready for a late lunch in Aguas Calientes before taking the train and bus back to Cusco.

Day 6: Cusco to Lima
Take advantage of the morning to visit a site you missed on your first day in Cusco, or to visit a few of the city's countless shops and markets. Fly to **Lima** (one hour) early enough to have lunch at one of the city's cebicherías. Use the afternoon to visit a museum or another attraction you missed on your first day there.

MADRE DE DIOS EXTENSION

The Essential Peru tour can easily be combined with a visit to the Amazon Basin by taking a short flight from Cusco to the adjacent Madre de Dios region on Day 6.

Days 6–8: Tambopata National Reserve
Take an early-morning flight from Cusco to **Puerto Maldonado,** where someone from your nature lodge will meet you and take you to your lodging by boat. Your next three days will be filled with constant exposure to tropical nature on rain-forest hikes, boat trips on oxbow lakes.

Days 9–10: Lima
On Day 9, travel by boat to Puerto Maldonado and fly to Lima. You should arrive in time for a late lunch and some sightseeing. On Day 10, visit Lima attractions that you missed on Day 1.

AMAZON RIVER EXTENSION

An alternative to the nature lodges of Madre de Dios is to visit the Amazon River proper, with a three-night river cruise or a stay at one of the nature lodges near Iquitos.

Day 6: Cusco to Iquitos

Fly to Lima in time for a connection to **Iquitos,** so that you can spend the night in that Amazon port city.

Days 7–9: Amazon Cruise or Lodge

Board a riverboat for a three-day cruise up the **Amazon River,** or head to one of the area's nature lodges. You'll explore Amazon tributaries and lakes in small boats on daily excursions, and perhaps visit an indigenous village.

Day 10: Iquitos to Lima

Disembark in Iquitos and fly directly back to Lima.

CLASSIC ANDEAN JOURNEY

Day 1: Lima

Follow Day 1 of the Essential Peru itinerary.

Day 2: Arequipa

From Lima, take an early-morning flight to **Arequipa,** a lovely colonial city with a backdrop of snowcapped volcanoes. Explore the city's historic center with its rambling **Monasterio de Santa Catalina** and the **Museo Santuarios Andinos,** home of a pre-Columbian mummy known as "Juanita." Be sure to enjoy some traditional arequipeña cooking, such as *rocoto relleno* (a hot pepper stuffed with beef), or *chupe de camarones* (river prawn chowder).

Day 3: Colca Canyon

Rise early for the drive to **Colca Canyon,** the deepest canyon in the world and one of the best places in Peru to spot an Andean condor. After lunch, take a hike, go horseback riding, or relax.

Days 4 and 5: Puno and Lake Titicaca

Rise early and head to **Cruz del Condor,** the best place to spot those massive birds. Spend the rest of the day traveling overland through a series of Andean landscapes to **Puno,** on Lake Titicaca, the highest navigable lake in the world. Puno's 3,830-meter (12,500-feet) altitude can take your breath away, so have a light dinner and rest for the day ahead.

Rise early on Day 5 and take a boat tour of **Lake Titicaca,** stopping at one of the **Uros Islands. Isla Taquile,** an island whose indigenous inhabitants are famous for their weaving skills, is also worth a visit. In the afternoon, visit the pre-Inca burial ground and stone *chullpas* at **Sillustani.**

Day 6: Puno to Cusco

Rise early for a full-day train or bus trip across more Andean landscapes to the ancient Inca capital of **Cusco,** a 330-meter (1,083-foot) drop in altitude. See Day 2 of the Essential Peru itinerary.

Day 7: Cusco

Follow Day 3 of the Essential Peru itinerary.

Days 8 and 9: Machu Picchu

Follow Days 4 and 5 of the Essential Peru itinerary.

Day 10: Cusco to Lima

Follow Day 6 of the Essential Peru itinerary.

CUSCO, INCA TRAIL, AND MACHU PICCHU

Travelers in good physical condition can combine Peru's top cultural attractions with an unforgettable hike through phenomenal scenery.

Day 1: Lima
Follow Day 1 of the Essential Peru itinerary.

Day 2: Cusco
Follow Day 2 of the Essential Peru itinerary.

Days 3–6: Inca Trail and Machu Picchu
Rise early this morning and catch the train to Machu Picchu, but get off at Km 82, where the four-day trek on the **Inca Trail** begins. You'll start by following the Urubamba River to the ruins of **Llactapata**, from which you climb slowly to the first campsite, at 9,691 feet. The next day is the toughest; you'll hike over **Warmiwanusca** pass (13,776 feet) and camp at 11,833 feet. On Day 3 of the trek, you hike over two passes and visit several small Inca ruins. The last day is short, mostly downhill. You'll want to rise very early to reach Machu Picchu's **Inti Punku** (Sun Gate) by sunrise. Spend the morning exploring **Machu Picchu**, then bus down to Aguas Calientes and check into your hotel.

Day 7: Sacred Valley
On Day 7, sleep in, have a leisurely breakfast, and take an afternoon train to Ollantaytambo. If you spend the night there, explore the fortress above town in the late afternoon, when the crowd thins. But you may opt for spending this night at one of the lodges near Urubamba.

Day 8: Cusco to Lima
Bus to Cusco and follow Day 6 of the Essential Peru itinerary.

NORTH COAST AND MACHU PICCHU

This trip lets you trace the development of Lima's indigenous cultures by combining the pre-Inca archaeological sites of northern Peru with the classic Inca sites of southern Peru.

Day 1: Lima
Follow Day 1 of the Essential Peru itinerary.

Days 2 and 3: Chiclayo
Catch an early flight to the northern city of **Chiclayo**, which lies near some of the country's most important pre-Inca sites. A small, pleasant city near several excellent museums, Chiclayo is noticeably warmer than Lima. Spend two days visiting the nearby pyramids at **Túcume**, the **Museo Nacional Sicán, Museo Nacional Tumbas Reales de Sipán**, and the **Museo Arqueológico Nacional Brüning**.

Days 4 and 5: Trujillo
Catch an early flight (40 minutes) to **Trujillo**, an attractive colonial city near the ancient structures of two other pre-Incan cultures. After checking into your hotel, explore the old city, which holds some well-preserved colonial and 19th-century architecture. In the afternoon, head to the rambling ruins of **Chan Chan**. On Day 5, visit the archaeological sites of **Huaca de La Luna** and **Huaca del Sol**, and the beach and fishing port of **Huanchaco**, where fishermen still use the tiny, pre-Columbian reed boats called *caballitos de totora*.

Day 6: Lima
Take a quick flight back to Lima and visit some of the sights you didn't have time for on Day 1. Be sure to hit Barranco, a lovely area for an evening stroll and dinner.

Day 7: Cusco
Follow Day 2 of the Essential Peru itinerary.

Day 8: Sacred Valley
Follow Day 3 of the Essential Peru itinerary.

Days 9 and 10: Machu Picchu
Follow Days 4 and 5 of the Essential Peru itinerary.

Day 11: Cusco to Lima
Follow Day 6 of the Essential Peru itinerary.

SOUTHERN COAST AND CORDILLERA BLANCA

This tour combines cultural and natural wonders and takes you through an array of landscapes—from the desert to offshore islands to snowcapped mountains.

Day 1: Lima
Follow Day 1 of the Essential Peru itinerary.

Days 2 and 3: Ica
Head south on the Pan-American Highway for four hours to **Ica**. After checking into your hotel, head for the **Huacachina** oasis for a dune buggy ride or sandboarding, or arrange a tour of one of the nearby wineries. *The Southern Coast, Chapter 3.*

Day 4: Nazca and Paracas
In the morning, do the flight over the enigmatic **Nazca Lines**. Then transfer to **Paracas**, on the coast. In the afternoon, take a boat tour to the **Ballestas Islands**, where you'll see thousands of sea lions, birds, and tiny Humboldt penguins, as well as the massive candelabra etched on a hillside. *The Southern Coast, Chapter 3.*

Day 5: Lima
The next day, return to **Lima**. If possible, stop at the pre-Inca site of **Pachacamac** on the way. Sightsee and shop in the afternoon, then enjoy a memorable meal at one of the city's great restaurants. *Lima, Chapter 2.*

Days 6–10: Huaraz
Travel overland to **Huaraz**, in the country's central Andes, where you'll want to take it easy while you acclimatize. If you're up for it, spend the next four days trekking on the Santa Cruz circuit, a gorgeous route into the heart of the **Cordillera Blanca**. If you aren't up for the trek, spend a couple of days doing less strenuous hikes to one of the Cordilleras turquoise lakes and visit the ruins of **Chavín de Huantar**. *The North Coast and Northern Highlands, Chapter 9.*

Day 11: Huaraz to Lima
Travel overland back to Lima. Follow Day 6 of the Essential Peru itinerary once you arrive.

NORTHERN ANDES AND CULTURES

The Northern Andes have some of Peru's most spectacular landscapes and the second most impressive Incan site after Machu Picchu: Kuélap. If you want to stray from the beaten path, explore this remote and fascinating region.

Day 1: Lima
Follow Day 1 of the Essential Peru itinerary.

Day 2: Jaen and Chachapoyas
Catch the 90-minute flight to the northern city of **Jaen** and take ground transportation (four hours) to **Chachapoyas**. Spend the afternoon exploring that attractive highland town.

Day 3: Chachapoyas and Gocta

Rise early and take a tour to **Gocta**, one of the world's highest waterfalls, which involves several hours of hiking. If you're not up for the hike, take a tour to see the burial monuments of the pre-Inca, Chachapoyas culture.

Day 4: Kuélap

Rise early for the four-hour drive up the Uctubamba Valley to the massive pre-Inca fortress of **Kuélap.** Spend several hours exploring that impressive site, which contains more than 400 structures, before returning to Chachapoas.

Day 5: Chachapoyas to Lima

Rise early for the four-hour drive to Jaen and the flight to Lima. Spend the afternoon visiting sights you missed on Day 1. A longer, archaeology-intensive alternative is to continue by land to Chiclayo, and spend Days 6–9 following the itinerary for Days 2–5 of the North Coast and Machu Picchu tour.

Day 6 or 10: Lima

Fly to Lima and follow Day 6 of the Essential Peru itinerary.

TOUR OPERATORS

WHY GO WITH AN OPERATOR?

There are plenty of good reasons to entrust the details of your Peru travels to a tour company, and convenience and security are high among them. Do you prefer to have your itinerary planned to the minutest details? If so, you can save time that you might otherwise spend researching and booking your trip by letting travel professionals take care of it. And once your trip has begun, you can see more in less time on a tour. You'll also get more out of your trip if you have a Peruvian guide who can point out and explain things that you might otherwise miss. You can rest assured that if something goes wrong, someone will straighten things out for you, and in the unlikely event that you have an accident, they'll take care of you.

On the other hand, if you prefer flexibility and spontaneity, you'll probably want to do things on your own, or hire a guide for day trips. There are areas, or activities, for which you can't avoid joining a tour. For many outdoor adventures, such as trekking or a trip into the Amazon rain forest, you simply have to travel with an outfitter. In the case of the Amazon, this might simply be the eco-lodge you visit. There will also be moments when you'll want things explained, or want to do a specific excursion or event if you're traveling independently. You can always book a day tour, or a short itinerary, from a local operator. You also have the option of simply showing up and hiring a guide in places such as Machu Picchu, Pachacamac, or other archaeological sites, where authorized freelance guides are available for hire at the entrance.

Whether you take a packaged tour for your entire Peru trip or prefer to book shorter itineraries with local outfitters, the decision of which tour operator or operators to use will likely be the most important one you make for your vacation. We've consequently compiled a list of some of the best tour companies operating in Peru, from the big international outfitters to the best local companies, to provide a good range of specializations and budget options.

WHO'S WHO

There is no shortage of companies selling tours to Peru, but not all of them have the same level of experience and reputation. Most U.S., Canadian, and British tour companies offering trips to Peru merely sell tours that are designed and run by Peruvian operators. However, there are also international companies that run their own tours in Peru. Others send a trip leader to accompany each group, who will often team up with a Peruvian guide, while the tour is operated by one or more Peruvian companies.

If you've traveled with a company to other destinations and had good experiences, you have good reason to use them in Peru. Though you may be reluctant to buy a package directly from a Peruvian company, keep in mind that you may get the same tour you would buy from a U.S. company for considerably less money. If you want to stray from the beaten path, you may have no choice but to book directly with a Peruvian company. Rest assured that the local operators included in this section have decades of experience and good reputations.

WHERE TO GO

While every company offers trips to Machu Picchu—Peru's must-see attraction—the country has much more to offer, including the Amazon wilderness, vibrant indigenous cultures, colonial cities, and jaw-dropping mountain landscapes. The great thing is that many of those attractions are easy to combine with Machu Picchu.

Nearly all first-time visitors do some sort of a Cusco/Sacred Valley/Machu Picchu combination, a tour that every company offers. Whether you hike there on a four-day Inca Trail trek or roll in luxuriously on the classic *Hiram Bingham* train, Machu Picchu is all that it is cracked up to be. There is enough to see between that ancient citadel, the Sacred Valley, and Cusco to fill a week, though many people cover the area in a few days. Some tours combine Machu Picchu and Cusco with the rain forest of nearby Madre de Dios, whereas others combine it with southern attractions such as Lake Titicaca, Arequipa, and the Colca Canyon or a cruise on the Amazon River. A longer extension or second trip is needed to include the ancient sites and impressive landscapes of northern Peru.

WHAT TO DO

Peru's combination of culture, history, scenery, and biodiversity make it a great place to visit, and you get exposure to all of the above on the classic Cusco–Machu Picchu trip. It is also a world-class destination for people who want to concentrate their vacations on one thing, be it bird-watching (Peru is the number-two country for avian diversity), surfing (the swells are sometimes as big as Hawaii's), or trekking (there are countless highland trails). Travelers with that kind of focus will want to book their tour with an outfitter that specializes in their passion, and we've included experts in each of those activities here.

The following outfitters are some of the best international and local tour outfitters offering trips in Peru, ranging from companies that accommodate thousands of tourists per month to smaller operations that specialize in custom tours. While nearly all of them offer Cusco–Machu Picchu tours, some have expertise, or hotels in certain regions, while others focus on specific activities. Sample prices of popular itineraries included here are per person, double occupancy.

TOUR OPERATORS

Top Companies

Abercrombie & Kent. Established as a safari outfitter in Kenya in 1962, this luxury travel company now has offices in the United Kingdom, United States, and Australia, and organizes trips on seven continents. The company offers a good selection of Peru itineraries that includes such emblematic attractions as Machu Picchu and the Amazon River as well as less-visited sites such as the Colca Canyon. Abercrombie & Kent also has tours that combine Peru with other South American destinations such as Bolivia and Ecuador's Galapagos Islands, as well as signature trips specifically for couples or families. Itineraries last anywhere from 8 to 19 days.

Destinations serviced: Lima, Cusco, Machu Picchu, Sacred Valley, Amazon River, Colca Canyon, Nazca, and Paracas.

Most popular package: Peru: Machu Picchu & the Sacred Valley, nine days, from $6,495. Combines time in Cusco, the Sacred Valley, and Machu Picchu.

Customized trips: Yes.

What they do best: Provide quality local guides, luxury accommodations, and private visits to spots few travelers get to.

Corporate responsibility: Support an organization in the Sacred Valley that provides meals, medical care, and education for children from poor families. ☏ *800/554–7016 in U.S., 01/421–7625 in Peru* ⊕ *www.abercrombiekent.com.*

Belmond. This venerable company offers a small selection of luxury itineraries in Peru using its own trains and hotels, which are some of the best in the country: the Miraflores Park, in Lima, the Palacio Nazarenas, and Hotel Monasterio in Cusco, the Hotel Rio Sagrado, in the Sacred Valley, and the Machu Picchu Sanctuary Lodge and Las Casitas, near Colca Canyon.

Destinations serviced: Lima, Cusco, Sacred Valley, Machu Picchu, Colca Canyon.

Most popular package: Essential Peru, five days, starting at $4,550; combines Lima, the Sacred Valley, Cusco, Machu Picchu, and a trip on the luxurious Hiram Bingham train.

Customized trips: Yes

What they do best: Luxury tours to Peru's top sites, with first class train and accommodations.

Corporate responsibility: The company has provided support for various schools, an orphanage, and an organic gardening center. ☏ *800/524–2420 toll-free in U.S., 0845/077–2222 toll-free in U.K., 01/610–8300 in Peru* ⊕ *www.belmond.com.*

Kensington Tours. One of the world's top-rated tour operators, Kensington Tours offers a dozen Peru itineraries with small groups and overnights in some of the country's best hotels. The company specializes in custom tours based on itineraries that range from a five-day Cusco and Machu Picchu trip to a two-week expedition that combines those highland treasures with a cruise on the Amazon River. Kensington also offers extra activities, such as a culinary tour, and have set itineraries that combine Lima, Cusco and Machu Picchu with Easter Island, Chile, or Galapagos, Ecuador.

Destinations serviced: Lima, Cusco, Sacred Valley, Machu Picchu, Puerto Maldonado area, Amazon River, Arequipa, Colca Canyon, Puno, Lake Titicaca.

Most popular package: Machu Picchu and Amazon Signature, 12 days, from $5,112; combines the classic Cusco-Sacred Valley-Machu Picchu trip with three nights on the Madre de Dios River.

Customized trips: Yes

What they do best: Organize custom luxury travel with top-rate local guides.

Corporate responsibility: The company's nonprofit, Kensington Cares, supports schools, clinics, and orphanages in East Africa. ☏ *888/903–2001 in U.S.* ⊕ *www. kensingtontours.com.*

Kuoda Travel. Cusco-based Kuoda Travel specializes in personalized, custom itineraries, primarily for families and couples. The Peruvian owner, Mery Calderon, manages the business, which has a series of suggested itineraries, but can work with clients to design custom trips. They also offer tours in Bolivia and Ecuador's Galapagos Islands.

Destinations serviced: Lima, Cusco, Sacred Valley, Machu Picchu, Tambopata, Arequipa, Colca Canyon, Puno, Lake Titicaca, Amazon River, Nazca.

Most popular package: The Jungle, Machu Picchu, and Lake Titicaca, 12 days, from $4,050; starts with three nights at the Reserva Amazonica, in Madre de Dios, followed by Cusco, the Sacred Valley, and Machu Picchu and ending with a couple days at Lake Titicaca.

Customized trips: Yes.

What they do best: Plan and run trips that cater to the interests and needs of each client.

Corporate responsibility: The company has a small foundation that runs development projects and after-school, computer literacy programs in half a dozen highland communities. ☎ *800/986–4150 toll-free in U.S. and Canada, 084/222–741 in Peru ⊕ www.kuodatravel.com.*

Overseas Adventure Travel. This U.S. company offers midrange tours with small groups (usually 10–16 travelers) led by knowledgeable guides that give travelers opportunities to meet local people. Their most popular Peru tour combines Cusco and Machu Picchu with the Galápagos, with possible extensions on the Amazon River or Lake Titicaca and La Paz, Bolivia.

Destinations serviced: Lima, Cusco, Sacred Valley, Machu Picchu, Amazon, Lake Titicaca.

Most popular package: Machu Picchu and the Galápagos, 16 days, from $5,795; combines Cusco, the Sacred Valley, and Machu Picchu with the Galápagos and Quito, Ecuador.

Customized trips: No.

What they do best: Provide quality guided tours to top sights at competitive prices.

Corporate responsibility: The company funds the Grand Circle Foundation, which provides school supplies and other support to six schools in poor Peruvian communities in the Sacred Valley and Amazon Basin. ☎ *800/955–1925 in U.S. ⊕ www.oattravel.com.*

Recommended Companies

Adventure Life. The South and Central America specialist Adventure Life has plenty of options for active travelers, including treks on the Inca Trail and less-hiked routes such as Ausangate Glacier and the Cordillera Blanca, white-water rafting, and trips into the rain forest of Manu and Tambopata. They also offer less strenuous options, ranging from the classic Cusco-Machu Picchu tour to a Peru cuisine tour or an Amazon cruise. For travelers who want more contact with local people, they offer homestays and extensions to volunteer with a community that the company has helped.

Destinations serviced: Lima, Cusco, Sacred Valley, Machu Picchu, Inca Trail, Ausengate, Lake Titicaca, Manu, Tambopata, Amazon River, Paracas, Trujillo, Chiclayo, Huaraz, Chachapoyas.

Most popular packages: Machu Picchu by train, seven days, $1,675; combines Cusco, the Sacred Valley and Machu Picchu. Manco Multisport with Machu Picchu, 10 days, $3,225; includes mountain biking, hiking, rafting, and two days in Machu Picchu.

Customized trips: Yes.

What they do best: Take travelers off the beaten track to experience Peru's amazing scenery, nature, and culture up close.

Corporate responsibility: Treat porters and other local staff well; work with rural community on route to Machu Picchu to improve livelihoods; support a shelter for single mothers in Cusco. ☎ *406/541–2677 in U.S.* ⊕ *www.adventure-life.com.*

Andean Treks. A pioneer in outfitting Inca Trail treks, Andean Treks was one of the first companies to organize treks to less-visited areas such as Choquequirao and Ausangate. From its humble beginnings outfitting hikes in 1980, Andean Treks grew to include an array of nonhiking trips in the highlands and the Amazon Basin, and eventually expanded to cover Argentina, Bolivia, Chile, and Ecuador as well. Their trips range from strenuous treks with overnights in tents or rustic lodges to Amazon cruises or tours of Lake Titicaca.

Destinations serviced: Cusco, Sacred Valley, Inca Trail, Machu Picchu, Choquequirao, Ausangate, Salcantay, Cordillera Blanca, Lake Titicaca, Arequipa, Colca Canyon, Tambopata, Amazon River, Nazca, Trujillo, Chiclayo.

Most popular packages: Inca Trail to Machu Picchu, five days, from $990; the classic trek, should be booked six months in advance. Moonstone to Machu Picchu trek, five days, from $953 (minimum four people) is an alternative route to Machu Picchu.

Customized trips: Yes

What they do best: Outfit quality treks through several cordilleras with experienced guides and arrange custom trips for an array of travelers.

Corporate responsibility: Pay decent wages, donate school supplies, and support economic alternatives in rural communities while working to reinforce traditional values. ☎ *800/683–8148 toll-free in U.S., 617/924–1974* ⊕ *www.andeantreks.com.*

Earthwatch. A nonprofit organization that provides volunteers and uses trip revenues to support scientific research, Earthwatch allows travelers to work on studies, enriching their understanding of the natural world while contributing to conservation. In Peru, Earthwatch runs expeditions up the Amazon Basin that let travelers participate in wildlife surveys in Pacaya-Samiria National Reserve. Some of those expeditions cater to teenagers. Fees for participating in Earthwatch expeditions are tax deductible.

Destinations serviced: Amazon River.

Most popular package: Amazon Riverboat Exploration, eight days, from $2,675; participants contribute to long-term survey of wildlife populations.

Customized trips: No.

What they do best: Allow travelers to contribute to the understanding and conservation of nature.

Corporate responsibility: All Earthwatch profits support scientific research and conservation. ☎ *800/776–0188 in U.S., 44/1865–318–838 in U.K.* ⊕ *earthwatch.org.*

Field Guides. The international birdwatching specialist Field Guides runs half a dozen tours to different regions of Peru led by expert birding guides, who help their clients spot as many of the country's more than 1,800 bird species as possible.

Destinations serviced: Cusco, Sacred Valley, Machu Picchu, Manu, Tambopata, Amazon River, northwest Peru.

Most popular package: Machu Picchu and Abra Malaga, 10 days, starting at $4,295; travels from the highlands to the cloud forest to the Amazon Basin.

Customized trips: No.

What they do best: Getting bird-watchers to areas where they can see the greatest variety of species possible.

Corporate responsibility: Field guides make regular contributions to conservation organizations. ☎ 800/728–4953 in U.S. ⊕ www.fieldguides.com.

InkaNatura Travel. One of the country's oldest ecotourism companies, InkaNatura Travel offers trips to its own nature lodges deep in the wilderness of the Manu Biosphere Reserve and Tambopata National Reserve, in the Amazon Basin. These can be combined with visits to Cusco and Machu Picchu, and the company also has a selection of itineraries to the archaeological sites of northern Peru. They cater to bird-watchers, nature lovers, archaeology buffs, and travelers who want to experience a bit of everything.

Destinations serviced: Manu, Tambopata, Cusco, Sacred Valley, Inca Trail, Machu Picchu, Trujillo, Chiclayo, Chachapoyas, Kuelap, Cajamarca, Mancora, Punta Sal.

Most popular packages: Sandoval Lake Lodge and Macaw Clay Lick, six days, from $1,493; this excellent tour offers the most affordable access to Amazon wildlife at an ox-bow lake, macaw clay lick, and in the rainforest with overnights in the Sandoval Lake and Heath River Lodges.

Customized trips: Yes.

What they do best: Help travelers experience Peru's diversity of flora and fauna.

Corporate responsibility: Company practices sustainable tourism and donates a portion of profits to Peru Verde, a small environmental organization. ☎ 888/870–7378 in U.S. and Canada, 0800/234–8659 in U.K., 01/203–5000 in Peru ⊕ www.inkanatura.com.

Inkaterra. This Peruvian company arranges customized luxury trips that combine access to the rain forest of Madre de Dios with the classic Cusco–Sacred Valley–Machu Picchu route with overnights Inkaterra hotels, which are among the country's best.

Destinations serviced: Cusco, Sacred Valley, Machu Picchu, Madre de Dios, Arequipa, Colca Canyon, Lake Titicaca.

Most popular package: Inkaterra's most popular package running seven days, and starting at $3,850; combines the Amazon Rain Forest, Cusco, and Machu Picchu, with nights at Inkaterra properties.

Customized trips: Yes.

What they do best: Provide high-quality service and accommodations and exposure to some of the country's greatest attractions.

Corporate responsibility: The company conserves 42,000 acres of rain forest in Madre de Dios, supports scientific research, and has adopted sustainable tourism. Its tours are carbon neutral. ☎ 800/442–5042 in U.S. and Canada, 800/458–7506 in U.K., 01/610–0400 in Peru ⊕ www.inkaterra.com.

International Expeditions. An ecotourism pioneer, International Expeditions specializes in taking travelers deep into tropical nature and helping them experience local wildlife and culture while mitigating tourism's negative impacts. The company has been running Peru trips for more than three decades and it offers longer itineraries to its most popular and off-the-beaten-path attractions. Its tours feature small groups led by knowledgeable local guides and competitive prices.

Destinations serviced: Lima, Cusco, Sacred Valley, Inca Trail. Machu Picchu, Amazon River, Puno, Lake Titicaca, Colca Valley, Arequipa, Trujillo, Chiclayo, Chaparri Nature Reserve, Gochta Waterfall, Kuelap, Madre de Dios.

Most popular packages: Amazon Voyage, 10 days, from $5,398; after sightseeing in Lima, travelers fly to Iquitos to start an eight-day cruise up the Amazon and Ucayali Rivers on the *Zafiro*.

Customized trips: Yes.

What they do best: Allow travelers to experience Peru's varied natural and cultural attractions safely and in comfort.

Corporate responsibility: The company promotes conservation on the Amazon River while improving life in local communities by donating water treatment plants, donating school supplies to 120 rural schools, and sponsoring an urban garden project in Iquitos. ☎ *844/795–8367* ⊕ *www.ietravel.com.*

Journeyou. A relatively new Peruvian company established by a team with decades of experience operating tours in Peru, Journeyou offers competitively priced package tours and customized trips. In addition to tours to the most popular destination, the company can arrange specialty travel, adventure activities, and trips to areas that few tourists visit.

Destinations serviced: All of Peru's destinations and highlights of other South American nations

Most popular package: Adventure in the Peruvian Andes, 11 days, from $1,750; visits Lima, Arequipa, Colca Canyon, Lake Titicaca, Cusco, the Sacred Valley, and Machu Picchu.

Customized trips: Yes.

What they do best: Customize suggested itineraries to the interests and budgets of individual travelers.

Corporate responsibility: The company has worked with Rainforest Alliance's sustainable tourism program. ☎ *855/888–2234 in U.S., 808/134–9965 in U.K.* ⊕ *www.journeyou.com.*

PERUVIAN HISTORY

by Paul Steele

About 15,000 years ago, the first people to inhabit what is now Peru filtered down from North and Central America. They were confronted by diverse and extreme environments at varying altitudes. An ocean rich in fish contrasts with sterile coastal valleys that are only habitable where rivers cut through the desert. To the east the valleys and high plateau of the Andes mountains slope down to the Amazon rainforest, home to exotic foods, animals, and medicinal plants.

Modern Peru incorporates all of these environmental zones. Long before the centralized state of the Inca empire, people recognized the need to secure access to varied resources and products. Images of animals and plants from coast and jungle are found on pottery and stone monuments in highland Chavin culture, c. 400 BC.

Around AD 500 the Nazca Lines etched out in the desert also featured exotic jungle animals.

In the 15th century the Incas achieved unprecedented control over people, food crops, plants, and domesticated animals that incorporated coast, highlands, and the semitropical valleys. Attempts to control coca leaf production in the warmer valleys may explain Machu Picchu, which guards an important trading route.

When the Spaniards arrived in the 16th century, the search for El Dorado, the fabled city of gold, extended the Viceroyalty of Peru into the Amazon lowlands. Since independence in 1821, disputes, wars, and treaties over Amazon territory have been fueled increasingly by the knowledge of mineral oil and natural gas under the forest floor.

(far left) Moche ceramic, portrait of a priest; (above) Cerro Sechin ca. 1000 BC on Peru coast; (left) Mummified corpse skull.

BIG OLD BUILDINGS

2600–1000 BC

Peru's first monumental structures were also the earliest throughout the Americas. Coastal sites like Aspero and Caral have platform mounds, circular sunken courtyards, and large plazas that allowed public civic-ceremonial participation. At Garagay and Cerro Sechin mud and adobe relief sculptures show images connected to death, human disfigurement, and human to animal transformation. A developing art style characterized by pronounced facial features like fanged teeth and pendant-iris eyes reached its height later in Chavin culture.

■ Visit:
Kotosh, Sechín

CHAVIN CULTURE

900–200 BC

Chavin de Huantar, a site not far from Huaraz, was famous for its shamans or religious leaders who predicted the future. A distinctive and complex imagery on carved stone monuments like the Lanzón and Tello Obelisk featured animals and plants from the coast, highlands, and especially the jungle. The decline of Chavin de Huantar coincided with the emergence of other oracle temples such as Pachacamac, south of modern Lima. The distinctive Chavin art style, however, continued to influence later cultures throughout Peru, including Paracas on the south coast.

■ Visit:
Chavin de Huantar

ALL WRAPPED UP IN ICA

600–50 BC

On the Paracas Peninsula, the desert holds the remains of an ancient burial practice. Corpses were wrapped in layers of textiles, placed in baskets, and buried in the sand. Many elaborately woven and embroidered garments that could be tens of meters long were only used to bury the dead and never worn in life. The mummy bundles of high status individuals were often accompanied by offerings of gold objects, exotic shells, and animal skins and feathers.

■ Visit:
Museo Histórico Regional

(above) Chavin de Huantar;
(top right) Huaca de la
Luna deity; (bottom right)
Nazca ground picture
of whale.

THE NASCANS

50 BC–AD 700

On Peru's south coast followed the Nasca, who are famous for the geoglyph desert markings known as the Nazca Lines. Thousands of long straight lines were constructed over many centuries, while around fifty animal outlines date to a more concise period of AD 400–600. An extensive system of underground aqueducts channeled water from distant mountains. In such a barren environment the Nazca Lines were probably linked closely to a cult primarily devoted to the mountain water source.

■ Visit:
Cahuachi, Nazca Lines

MOCHE KINGDOM

AD 100–800

On Peru's north coast the Moche or Mochica controlled a number of coastal river valleys. Large scale irrigation projects extended cultivable land. The Temples of the Sun and Moon close to the modern city of Trujillo were constructed from millions of adobe or mud bricks and were some of the largest buildings anywhere in the ancient Americas. The high quality of Moche burial goods for individuals like the Lord of Sipan indicated a wide social gulf not previously seen in Peru. Full-time artisans produced metalwork and ceramics for Moche lords. The pottery in particular is famous for the realistic portrayal of individuals and for the naturalistic scenes of combat, capture, and sacrifice that could have been narrative stories from Moche mythology and history. Some themes like the sacrificing of war captives in the presence of the Lord of Sipan and the Owl Priest were probably reenacted in real life. A number of severe droughts and devastating el niño rains precipitated the decline of the Moche.

■ Visit:
Pañamarca, Huaca de la Luna, Huaca del Sol

(above) Wari face neck jar; (top right) Chan Chan, (bottom right) Kuélap.

WELCOME TO THE WARI EMPIRE

550–950

A new dominant highland group, the Wari, or Huari, originated close to the modern city of Ayacucho. Wari administrative centers, storage facilities, and an extensive road network were forerunners to the organizational systems of the Inca empire. The Wari were influenced by the iconographic tradition of a rival site, Tiahuanaco, in what is now Bolivia, which exerted control over the extreme south of Peru. After Wari control collapsed, regional kingdoms and localized warfare continued until the expansion of the Inca empire.

■ Visit:
Pikillacta, Huari

CHIMÚ KINGDOM

900–1470

On the north coast the Chimú or Chimor succeeded the Moche controlling the coastal river valleys as far south as Lima. The capital Chan Chan was a bustling urban sprawl that surrounded at least 13 high-walled citadels of the Chimú lords. The city was built close to the ocean shore and continual coastal uplift meant that access to fresh water from deep wells was a constant problem. An extensive canal network to channel water from rivers never worked properly.

■ Visit:
Chan Chan, Huaca Esmeralda

THE FIGHTIN' CHACHAPOYAS

800–1480

In the cloud forests of the eastern Andean slopes the Chachapoyas kingdom put up fierce resistance against the Incas. The Chachapoyas are famous for their mummified dead placed in cliff-top niches and for high quality circular stone buildings at sites like Kuélap, one of the largest citadels in the world. Kuélap may have been designed as a fortification against the Wari. Later the Incas imposed harsh penalties on the Chachapoyas who subsequently sided with the Spaniards.

■ Visit:
Kuélap (Cuelap)

(left) Mama Occlo, wife and sister of Manco Capac, founder of the Inca dynasty, carrying the Moon; (above) Machu Picchu.

INCA ORIGINS

C. 1400

The Inca empire spanned a relatively short period in Peruvian history. The mythical origins of the first Inca Manco Capac, who emerged from a cave, is typical of Peruvian ancestor tradition. Spanish chroniclers recorded at least 10 subsequent Inca rulers although in reality the earlier kings were probably not real people. The famous Inca, Pachacuti, is credited with expansion from the capital Cusco. Inca iconographic tradition that followed geometric and abstract designs left no representational images of its rulers.

■ Visit:
Isla del Sol

INCA EMPIRE

1450–1527

Within three generations the Incas had expanded far beyond the boundaries of modern Peru to central Chile in the south and past the equator to the north. The Amazon basin was an environment they did not successfully penetrate. Although the Incas fought battles, it was a two-way process of negotiation with *curacas*, the local chiefs that brought many ethnic groups under control. The empire was divided into four *suyu* or parts, centered on Cusco. At a lower level communities were organized into decimal units ranging from 10 households up to a province of 40,000 households. Individual work for the state was known as *mit'a*. Com-

munities forcibly resettled to foreign lands were called *mitimaes*. The Incas kept a regular population census and record of all the sacred idols and shrines. The Incas spread the language Quechua that is still spoken throughout most of Peru and in neighboring countries.

■ Visit:
Ollantaytambo, Machu Picchu, Pisac Ruins

EXTENSIVE DEPOPULATION THROUGHOUT PERU

| 1600 | 1650 | 1700 |

(above) The execution of Tupa Amaru; (left) Francisco Pizarro, Diego de Almagro, and Fernando de Luque planning the conquest of Peru.

ARRIVAL OF THE CONQUISTADORS

1527–1542

The Spanish conquistadors arrived on the coast of Ecuador and northern Peru bringing European diseases like smallpox that ravaged the indigenous population and killed the Inca king. They also introduced the name Peru. In 1532 a small band of conquistadors led by Francisco Pizarro first encountered the Inca ruler Atahualpa in Cajamarca. This famous confrontation of Old and New World cultures culminated with the capture of Atahualpa, who was later strangled. The Spaniards arrived in Cusco in 1533 and immediately took the city residences and country estates of the Inca elite for themselves. The resistance of Manco Inca could not drive the Spaniards out of Cusco, and by the end of the 1530s the Inca loyal supporters had retreated to Ollantaytambo, and then to the forested region of Vilcabamba that became the focus of Inca resistance for the next 30 years. In 1542 the Viceroyalty of Peru was created and a new capital city, Lima, became the political and economic center of Spain's possessions in South America.

■ Visit:
Cajamarca, Ollantaytambo, Sacsayhuamán

END OF THE INCAS

1542–1572

A relatively small number of Spaniards overthrew the Incas because of support from many groups disaffected under Inca rule. Native Peruvians quickly realized, however, that these new lighter-skinned people were intent on dismantling their whole way of life. The 1560s nativist movement Taqui Onqoy, meaning dancing sickness, called on native gods to expel the Spaniards and their religion. In 1572 the Inca Tupa Amaru, mistakenly called Tupac Amaru, was captured and executed in public in Cusco.

■ Visit:
Cusco

1

IN FOCUS PERUVIAN HISTORY

(above) Battle of Ayacucho, Bolivar's forces establish Peruvian independence from Spain 1824; (left) Simon Bolivar, aka "The Liberator."

SPANISH COLONIAL RULE

1572–1770

The Spanish crown increasingly sought more direct control over its American empire. A new viceroy, Toledo, stepped up the policy of *reducciones* in which formerly dispersed native communities were resettled into more easily controlled towns. This made it easier to baptize the native population into the Catholic church. The indigenous population was forced to work in mines such as Potosí, which became the biggest urban center in the Americas. Huge quantities of gold and silver were shipped to the Caribbean and then to Europe, and helped fund Spain's wars in Europe. Spanish hacienda estates introduced new food crops such as wheat, and new livestock like pigs and cows. The scale of native depopulation—more acute on the coast—is today reflected by the number of abandoned hillside terraces. The Inca elite and local chiefs started to adopt European dress; some found ways to prosper under new colonial regulations (like avoiding Spanish taxes if demonstrating Inca ancestry).

■ Visit:
Colonial architecture of Arequipa, Ayacucho, Cusco, Lima, Trujillo

END OF COLONIAL RULE

1770–1824

The execution of the last Inca ruler in 1572 did not stop continued rebellions against Spanish colonial rule. In the eighteenth century an uprising led by the local chief José Gabriel Condorcanqui, who called himself Tupa Amaru II, foreshadowed the wars of independence that ended colonial rule in Peru and elsewhere in the Americas. Peru declared its independence in 1821 and again in 1824, when Símon Bólivar arrived from Colombia to defeat the remaining royalist forces at the battle of Ayacucho.

■ Visit:
Pampas de Quinua

TIMELINE
| Slavery abolished
Quechua language officially recognized |
└ *POPULATION MIGRATION TO BIG CITIES* ┘
Earthquake devastates
South Peru
| 1900 | 1950 | 2000 | PRESENT |

(above) Ollanta Humala; (right) Lima, Peru.

REPUBLICAN ERA

1824–1900

Despite an initial 20 years of chaos, when every year seemed to bring a new regime, the young republic was attractive to foreign business interests. Particularly lucrative for Peru were the export of cotton and guano—nitrate-rich bird droppings used for fertilizer. Peru benefited from foreign investment such as railroad building, but an increasing national foreign debt was unsustainable without significant industrial development. Disputes with neighboring countries, especially the War of the Pacific against Chile in which Lima was sacked, land to the south ceded, and the country bankrupted, deeply affected the nation.

20TH-CENTURY PERU

1900–2000

The twentieth century saw Peru's democracy repeatedly interrupted by military coups. The left-wing government of General Juan Velasco (1968–75) instituted agrarian reform and nationalized businesses. Democratically elected President Alan Garcia (1985–90) tried socialist policies that resulted in hyperinflation and capital flight. Economic insecurity combined with growing violence by the Shining Path guerrilla caused many Peruvians to emigrate and millions to move from the highlands to Lima. President Alberto Fujimori (1990–2000) reestablished economic stability and largely defeated the Shining Path, but authoritarianism and widespread corruption led to his downfall.

RECENTLY . . .

2000–PRESENT

This century has brought Peru's longest stretch of democracy and economic growth, resulting in a reduction in the number of Peruvians living in poverty from more than 50% in 2000 to less than 22% in 2017. Fujimori was convicted and imprisoned for human rights abuses and corruption, but has significant support among Peruvians, and his daughter Keiko has nearly been elected president twice. Former investment banker Pedro Pablo Kuczynski, who defeated Fujimori in 2016, will govern until 2021. He aims to catalyze economic growth in order to create opportunity, while using government programs to improve life for the poor.

LIMA

WELCOME TO LIMA

TOP REASONS TO GO

★ **Amazing Food:** From *cebiche* (raw fish marinated in lemon juice) to Peruvian fusion, Lima's dining scene is all the rage and offers some of the best bites on the continent.

★ **Lima Baroque:** In El Centro, churches such as the Iglesia de San Francisco have elaborate facades and interiors in the "Lima baroque" style of architecture.

★ **Cool Digs:** More than 30 archaeological sites are scattered across Lima's neighborhoods, such as the pre-Inca temple Huaca Pucllana in Miraflores and the Huaca Huallamarca temple in San Isidro.

★ **Handicrafts:** Calle La Paz and Avenida Petit Thouars in Miraflores have stores selling everything from hand-carved wooden masks to silver-filigree jewelry.

★ **Park Life:** On weekends families and couples fill Lima's parks, especially the ones that line Miraflores' ocean-view *malecónes* (piers) such as the colorful Parque del Amor.

1 **El Centro.** The Plaza Mayor (the city's main square) and nearby Plaza San Martín are two of the most spectacular public spaces in South America. Nearly every block has something to catch your eye, whether it's the elaborate facade of a church or the enclosed wooden balconies on centuries-old houses, but unfortunately, much of the neighborhood is dilapidated.

2 **San Isidro.** The city's nicest residential neighborhood surrounds Parque El Olivar, a grove of olive trees, where half-timbered homes are set among the gnarled trunks. Nearby are a pre-Columbian pyramid and the city's oldest golf course, but the main attraction for travelers is its selection of restaurants and hotels.

3 **Miraflores.** A mix of modern and early 20th century, Miraflores has the city's best selection of hotels, restaurants, bars, and boutiques, which are a draw for locals, so the neighborhood is always bustling. Visit Parque del Amor and the string of other parks along the malecón, which runs along the coastal cliffs—the view is unforgettable.

4 **Barranco.** The city's most bohemian and also most charming neighborhood,

Barranco combines historic architecture, nightlife, a vibrant art scene, and ocean views. Bars and eateries surround the Parque Municipal and nearby Bajada Los Baños, a cobblestone path leading down to the beach. In the evening, this area fills with young people in search of a good time.

5 **Pueblo Libre.** Home to Lima's best museum, the Museo Arqueológico Rafael Larco Herrera, this neighborhood retains its village feel, from before it was swallowed by the greater metropolitan area.

RÍMAC

Cerro San Cristóbal

García Rivero
Av. Caquetá
Pizarro
Río Rímac
Vía de Evitamiento

Av. 9 de Octubre

Cotonial
Zorritos

Plaza Mayor
Av. Tacna
Iglesia San Francisco
Av. Ancash

EL CENTRO 1

Av. Arica
Plaza San Martín
Jirón de la Vega
G. de Vega
Av. Grau

EL AGUSTINO

Av. Brasil
Av. Tingo María
Av. Ugarte

BREÑA

Marco Capac
Av. 28 de Julio

Unanue

Isabela Católica

Paseo de la República
Vía Expresa
Av. Arequipa

JESÚS MARÍA

Av. Salaverry

LA VICTORIA

Av. México

SAN LUIS

Av. N. Arriola

Parque Zonal Tupac Amaru
Av. Cañada

Av. Sánchez
Carrión

LINCE

Av. N. Arriola

Av. Javier Prado

SAN BORJA

Av. Javier Prado

Huaca Huallamarca

Campo de Golf

SAN ISIDRO

Parque El Olivar 2

Aramburú

Av. Guardia Civil

Av. Aviación

Av. Galvez B.

Av. Santa Cruz

Huaca Pucllana

SURQUILLO

Paseo de la República

Av. Angamos

Av. Tomás Marsano

Av. José Pardo

Playa Makah
MIRAFLORES

Parque del Amor 3

Playa Costa Verde

Av. M. Benavides

Av. Panamá

PACIFIC OCEAN

Playa la Estrella

Río Surco

BARRANCO 4

Av. Grau

SANTIAGO DE SURCO

Av. Santiago de Surco

Bajada Los Baños
Parque Municipal

Playa Barranco

0   2 mile
0   2 km

GETTING ORIENTED

Most of Lima's colonial-era churches and mansions are in **El Centro,** along the streets surrounding the Plaza de Armas. From there a speedy expressway called Paseo de la República (aka Via Espress) or a traffic-clogged thoroughfare called Avenida Arequipa takes you south to **San Isidro** and **Miraflores,** two fairly upscale neighborhoods where you'll find the bulk of the city's dining and lodging options. Southeast of Miraflores is **Barranco,** where colonial architecture is complemented by art galleries, ocean views, and a bohemian atmosphere.

Updated by David Dudenhoefer

When people discuss great South American cities, Lima is often overlooked. But Peru's capital can hold its own against its neighbors with its oceanfront setting, colonial-era splendor, sophisticated dining, and nonstop nightlife.

It's true that the city—choked with traffic and fumes—doesn't make a great first impression, especially since the airport is in an industrial neighborhood. But wander around the regal edifices surrounding the Plaza de Armas, among the gnarled olive trees of San Isidro's Parque El Olivar, or along the winding lanes in the coastal community of Barranco, and you'll find yourself charmed.

In 1535 Francisco Pizarro found the perfect place for the capital of Spain's colonial empire. On a natural port, the so-called Ciudad de los Reyes (City of Kings) allowed Spain to ship home all the gold the conquistador plundered from the Inca. Lima served as the capital of Spain's South American empire for 300 years, and it's safe to say that no other colonial city enjoyed such power and prestige during this period.

When Peru declared its independence from Spain in 1821, the declaration was read in the square that Pizarro had so carefully designed. Many colonial-era buildings still stand near the Plaza de Armas. Walk a few blocks in any direction and you'll find churches and elegant houses that reveal just how wealthy this city once was. But the poor state of most buildings reminds that the country's wealthy families moved to neighborhoods to the south decades ago.

The walls that surrounded the city were demolished in 1870, making way for unprecedented growth. A former hacienda became the graceful residential neighborhood of San Isidro. In the early 1920s, the construction of tree-lined Avenida Arequipa heralded the development of neighborhoods such as bustling Miraflores and bohemian Barranco.

Almost a third of the country's population of more than 30 million lives in the metropolitan area, most of them in the more impoverished *conos* (newer neighborhoods on the outskirts of the city). Most residents of those neighborhoods moved there from mountain villages during the political violence and poverty that marked the 1980s and

'90s, when crime increased dramatically. During the past decade and a half, the country has enjoyed peace and steady economic growth, which have been accompanied by many improvements and refurbishment in the city. Residents who used to steer clear of the historic center now stroll along its streets; many travelers who once would have avoided the city altogether now plan to spend a day here, and end up staying for two or three.

PLANNING

WHEN TO GO

The weather in Lima is a relative opposite of North America's. Summer, from December to May, is largely sunny, with temperatures regularly rising above 80°F, while the nights and mornings are cool. From June to November it is mostly cloudy and cool, sometimes dipping below 60°F, though there are occasional sunny days. The coastal region gets little precipitation so you'll rarely find your plans ruined by rain, but there are winter days when you'll have to endure a miserable foggy drizzle.

GETTING HERE AND AROUND

AIR TRAVEL

If you're flying to Peru, you'll touch down at Aeropuerto Internacional Jorge Chávez, in the northern neighborhood of El Callao. Once you're in the main terminal, hundreds of people will be waiting. Do yourself a favor and arrange for a transfer through your hotel. You can also hire a cab from one of the companies stationed in the corridor outside of customs, or take an Airport Express Lima bus, which drops passengers off at seven major hotels in the city.

Contacts Airport Express Lima. ⊠ *Av. Faucett s/n, Callao* ☏ *01/446–5539* ⊕ *www.airportexpresslima.com.* **CMV Taxi.** ☏ *01/517–1891.* **Taxi Green.** ☏ *01/484–4001* ⊕ *www.taxigreen.com.pe.*

Various airlines handle domestic flights, so getting to and from major tourist destinations is easy. LATAM is the carrier with the most national flights, with a dozen per day to Cusco, and several daily departures to Arequipa, Cajamarca, Chiclayo, Iquitos, Juliaca (Puno), Piura, Puerto Maldonado, Trujillo, and Tumbes. Avianca is a close second, with daily flights to Arequipa, Cusco, Piura, Puerto Maldonado, and Trujillo. These are the most convenient airlines, but also the most expensive, charging foreigners twice as much as locals. Peruvian Airlines offers the best deals for travelers, with daily flights to Arequipa, Cusco, Iquitos, Piura, and Tacna, on the border with Chile. Star Peru is relatively inexpensive and flies to Ayacucho, Cusco, Huanuco, Iquitos, Juliaca, Puerto Maldonado, and Trujillo. Viva Air is an even more affordable discount airline, and flies to Arequipa, Chiclayo, Cusco, Iquitos, Piura, Tacna, Trujillo, and Tarapoto. The smaller LCPeru also has competitive rates, and flies to Ayacucho, Cajamarca, Cusco, Huanuco, and Huaraz.

Airport Information Aeropuerto Internacional Jorge Chávez. ⊠ *Av. Faucett s/n, Callao* ☏ *01/517–3100* ⊕ *www.lima-airport.com.*

Carriers Avianca. ✉ *Av. José Pardo 811, Miraflores* ☎ *01/511–8222* ⊕ *www. avianca.com.* **LATAM.** ✉ *Av. José Pardo 513, Miraflores* ☎ *01/213–8200* ⊕ *www.latam.com.* **LC Peru.** ✉ *Av. Jose Pardo 269, Miraflores* ☎ *01/204–1313* ⊕ *www.lcperu.pe.* **Peruvian Airlines.** ✉ *Av José Pardo 495, Miraflores* ☎ *01/716–6000* ⊕ *www.peruvian.pe.* **Star Peru.** ✉ *Av José Pardo 265, Miraflores* ☎ *01/705–9000* ⊕ *www.starperu.com.* **Viva Air.** ✉ *Av. Faucett s/n, Callao* ☎ *01/705–0107* ⊕ *www.vivaair.com.*

BUS TRAVEL

A mix of buses patrol the streets of Lima. Fares are cheap, usually S/1–S/2 for a ride, but don't expect a lot of comfort. Watch your belongings, as pickpockets and bag-slashers can be a problem. A quicker way to travel between Barranco, Miraflores, and El Centro is El Metropolitano, a modern bus that runs down the middle of the Paseo de la Republica to the underground Estación Central, in front of the Sheraton Lima Hotel. El Metropolitano runs from 6 am to 10 pm and each trip costs S/2.50, but it gets quite crowded during rush hour. The system uses recharge-able electronic cards that you can buy from a vending machine for S/5. Stations on Avenida Bolognesi in Barranco and Avenida Benavides in Miraflores are walking distance from hotels, but the route is far from San Isidro lodgings.

Contacts Metropolitano. ☎ *01/203–9000* ⊕ *www.metropolitano.com.pe.*

CAR TRAVEL

Lima can be a difficult and confusing city to drive in, but most rental agencies also offer the services of a driver. In addition to offices down-town, Avis, Budget, and Hertz have branches at Jorge Chávez Interna-tional Airport that are open 24 hours.

Contacts Avis. ✉ *Av. 28 de Julio 587, Miraflores* ☎ *01/207–6000* ⊕ *www.avis. com.pe.* **Budget.** ✉ *Av. José Larco 998, Miraflores* ☎ *01/444–4546* ⊕ *www. budgetperu.com.* **Hertz.** ✉ *Pasaje Tello 215, Miraflores* ☎ *01/447–2129* ⊕ *www.hertzperu.com.* **National.** ✉ *Av. Faucett s/n, Callao* ☎ *01/578–7878* ⊕ *www.nationalcar.com.pe.*

TAXI TRAVEL

Taxis are the best way to get around Lima. The safest options are to use one of the black taxis that service the tourist hotels or to have somebody call a taxi for you. There are plenty of more affordable taxis cruising the main streets, but be sure to look for those with a company logo and the driver's license prominently displayed. Negotiate the fare before getting in the car. A journey between two adjacent neighborhoods should cost between S/8 and S/12; longer trips run between S/20 and S/30.

Contacts Taxi Peru Remisse. ☎ *01/480–0500* ⊕ *www.taxiperuremisse.com.* **Taxi Seguro.** ☎ *01/200–2000* ⊕ *www.taxiseguro.com.pe.*

HEALTH AND SAFETY

Drink only bottled water, and avoid lettuce and other raw vegetables. As for cebiche and *tiradito* (thinly sliced, marinated fish), both made with raw seafood, the citric acid in the lime-juice marinade is as efficient at killing bacteria as cooking, but because they are often prepared to order, it's best to let yours stew in the lime juice for a bit before eating to be safe.

El Centro is safe during the day, but the neighborhood grows dicey at night, when you should stick to the two main plazas and Jirón de la Union (the pedestrian mall that connects them). Residential neighborhoods such as Miraflores, San Isidro, and Barranco have far less street crime, but you should be on guard when away from the main streets. Always be alert for pickpockets in crowded markets and on public transportation.

In case of trouble, contact the Tourist Police. The department is divided into the **northern zone** (*01/423–3500*), which includes El Centro, and the **southern zone** (*01/445–7943*), which includes Barranco, Miraflores, and San Isidro. English-speaking officers will help you report a crime. For emergencies, call the **police** (*105*) or **fire department** (*116*) emergency numbers.

EMERGENCIES

Several clinics have English-speaking staff, including the Clinica Anglo-Americana in San Isidro. There is a pharmacy on every other (or every third) block of Lima's main streets.

Hospitals Clinica Anglo-Americana. ⊠ *Av. Alfredo Salazar 350, San Isidro* ☎ *01/616–8900* ⊕ *www.angloamericana.com.pe.*

Pharmacies Mifarma. ⊠ *Av. José Larco 518, Miraflores* ☎ *01/612–5000* ⊕ *www.mifarma.com.pe.* **Mifarma.** ⊠ *Av. José Larco 401, Miraflores* ☎ *01/612-5000* ⊕ *www.mifarma.com.pe.*

TOURS

Bike Tours of Lima. If you prefer to pedal, this company offers half-day bike tours of Miraflores and San Isidro or Barranco, as well as a full-day tour that includes the historic El Centro. ⊠ *Calle Bolivar 150, Miraflores* ☎ *01/445–3172* ⊕ *biketoursoflima.com* 🖾 *From $30.*

Ecocruceros. Wildlife enthusiasts will enjoy the half-day boat tour to the Islas Palomino, off the coast of El Callao and home to more than 4,000 sea lions and abundant bird life. This is a very chilly trip from June to December, but you can swim with the sea lions from January to May. ☎ *01/226–8530* ⊕ *www.islaspalomino.com* 🖾 *From $48.*

Lima Vision. Lima Vision offers the best selection of city tours, by day or night, including a full-day excursion that combines a city tour with a visit to the ruins of Pachacamac. They also offer a Peruvian Paso horse show, a gastronomic tour, and a full-day tour to the ruins of Caral—the oldest urban center in the Americas. ☎ *01/447–7710* ⊕ *www.limavision.com* 🖾 *From $26.*

Mirabus. This company offers a variety of tours on open-top double-decker buses, from the classic city tour to a selection of night tours, including one that visits the city's oldest cemetery, Cementerio Presbítero Maestro. Mirabus also runs tours to the pre-Columbian ruins of Pachacamac or Caral. Most tours depart from Avenida Diagnol across the street from Miraflores' Parque Kennedy (next to Starbucks), however 20-minute tours of Lima's historic center depart regularly from the Plaza de Armas in El Centro from 3 pm to 7 pm. ⊠ *Av. Diagonal cuadra 3, Parque Kennedy, Miraflores* ☎ *01/242–6699* ⊕ *www.mirabusperu.com* 🖾 *From $3.*

Turibus. Turibus offers three- and four-hour city tours on double-decker city buses as well as a 45-minute tour of Barranco and Miraflores. The company also has night tours, including one to Lima's oldest cemetery, and a tour of the Real Felipe Spanish fortress in El Callao. Tours depart from Malecón de la Reserva across from the Casino Miraflores, by the Larcomar shopping center, but the ticket booth is in the lower level of Larcomar, across from La Bombonniere restaurant. ⊠ *Larcomar, Malecón de la Reserva, Miraflores* ☎ *01/234–0249* ⊕ *www.turibusperu. com* ⛴ *From $7.*

VISITOR INFORMATION

Travelers can find information about Lima and the rest of Peru at iPerú, which has English- and Spanish-language materials. The city runs the Oficina de Información Touristica, or Tourist Information Office, in the rear of the Municipalidad de Lima.

Information iPerú. ⊠ *Jorge Basadre 610, San Isidro* ☎ *01/421–1627, 01/574–8000 24 hrs* ⊕ *www.peru.travel* ⊠ *Larcomar, Malecón de la Reserva and Av. José Larco, Level 2, Stand 211, Miraflores* ☎ *01/234–0340* ⊕ *www.peru. travel.* **Oficina de Información Turística.** ⊠ *Pasaje Nicolás de Ribera El Viejo 145, El Centro* ☎ *01/632–1542* ⊕ *www.visitalima.pe.*

EXPLORING LIMA

Once a compact city surrounded by small towns, Lima is now a vast metropolitan area that is home to nearly 9 million people. Most of it has little to offer travelers, so you'll want to limit your exploration to the *distritos*, or neighborhoods, listed here. Most of the city's best hotels and restaurants are in three adjacent neighborhoods—Barranco, Miraflores, and San Isidro—to the south of the historic center, El Centro, but the bulk of its attractions are clustered in El Centro and nearby Pueblo Libre. You'll consequently need to take taxis between neighborhoods, though an express bus called the Metropolitano provides a quick connection between El Centro and the neighborhoods of Miraflores and Barranco. The airport is in a separate city called El Callao, about half an hour to the west of El Centro and an hour from most hotels. Trips between Barranco and Miraflores or San Isidro should take 10 to 20 minutes, whereas travel time between any of them and El Centro is 20 to 30 minutes. During rush hour (7:30 to 9 am and 5:30 to 7:30 pm) travel times double.

EL CENTRO

In the colonial era, Lima was the seat of power for the Viceroyalty of Peru. It held sway over a swath of land that extended from Panama to Chile. With power came money, as is evident by the grand scale on which everything was built. The finely carved doorways of some mansions stand two stories high. At least half a dozen churches would be called cathedrals in any other city. And the Plaza de Armas, the sprawling main square, is spectacular.

HISTORICAL WALK

Almost all of Lima's most interesting historical sites are within walking distance of the **Plaza de Armas**. The fountain in the center can be used as a slightly off-center compass. The bronze angel's trumpet points due north, where you'll see the **Palacio de Gobierno**. To the west is the neocolonial **Municipalidad de Lima**, and to the east are the **Catedral** and the adjoining **Palacio Episcopal**. Peek inside the cathedral, one of the most striking in South America. Head north on Jirón Carabaya, the street running along the east side of the Palacio de Gobierno, until you reach the butter-yellow **Estación de Desamparados**, the former train station. Follow the street as it curves to the east, and in a block you'll reach the **Convento de San Francisco**, which has one of the city's most spectacular colonial-era churches, complete with eerie catacombs.

But history has not always been kind to the neighborhood known as El Centro. Earthquakes struck in 1687 and 1746, leveling many of the buildings surrounding the Plaza de Armas. Landmarks, such as the Iglesia de San Augustín, were nearly destroyed by artillery fire in skirmishes that have plagued the capital. But most buildings are simply the victims of neglect. It's heartbreaking to see the wall on a colonial-era building buckling or an intricately carved balcony beyond repair. But the city government has made an effort to restore its historic center. After years of decline, things are steadily improving.

An unhurried visit to the historic district's main attractions takes a full day, with at least an hour devoted to the Museo de Arte Nacional, though a half day will suffice if you're in a rush. ■TIP→ Make sure to take the guided tour of the Convento de San Francisco, and don't miss Plaza San Martín.

GETTING AROUND

Chances are you're staying in Miraflores, Barranco or San Isidro, which are all a quick taxi ride from El Centro. As taxis usually take the expressway, you'll get to downtown in 20–30 minutes. For a slower but more interesting route with views of gorgeous architecture, ask your driver to take Avenida Arequipa and do a loop on Paseo Colón (roughly a 40-minute drive, longer during rush hour). A Metropolitano bus takes 20–30 minutes to get to El Centro. The best way to get around El Centro once you're there is on foot; the historic area is rather compact.

TOP ATTRACTIONS

Casa Riva-Agüero. A pair of balconies with *celosías*—intricate wood screens through which ladies could watch passersby unobserved—grace the facade of this rambling mansion from 1760. Step inside and the downtown traffic fades away as you stroll across the stone courtyard and admire the ancient balconies and woodwork. The Catholic University, which administers the landmark, uses it for changing exhibitions, but the real reason to come is for a glimpse into a colonial-era home. ✉ *Jr. Camaná 459, El Centro* ☎ *01/626–6600* 💲 *S/2* ☉ *Weekends.*

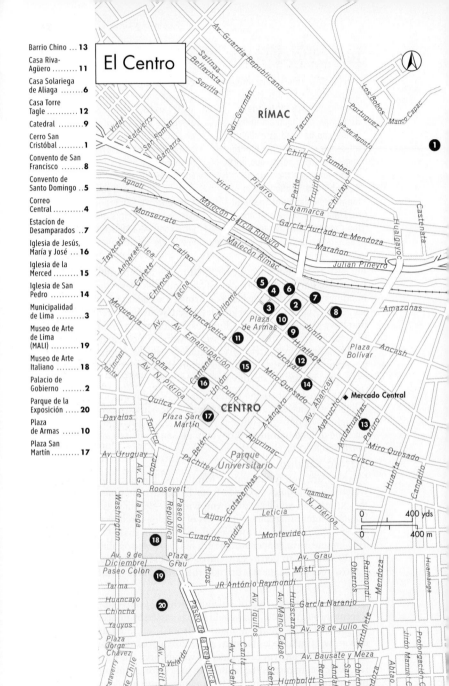

El Centro

RÍMAC

RÍMAC

Plaza
de Armas

Plaza
Bolívar

Mercado Central

CENTRO

Plaza San
Martín

Parque
Universitario

Plaza
Grau

Paseo Colon

Plaza
Jorge
Chávez

Estadio
Nacional

Estadio
Alianza
Lima

0   400 yds
0   400 m

Catedral. The first church on the site was completed in 1625. The layout for this immense structure was dictated by Francisco Pizarro, and his basic vision has survived complete rebuilding after earthquakes in 1746 and 1940. Inside are impressive baroque appointments, especially the intricately carved choir stalls.

Because of changing tastes, the main altar was replaced around 1800 with one in a neoclassical style. At about the same time the towers that flank the entrance were added. Admission includes a recorded 40-minute tour. Visit the chapel where Pizarro is entombed and the small museum of religious art and artifacts. ⊠ *Jr. Carabaya s/n, El Centro* ✛ *East side of Plaza de Armas* ☎ *01/427–9647* ◻ *S/10* ⊘ *Closed Sat. after 1, Sun. before 1.*

Fodor's Choice   **Convento de San Francisco.** With its ornate facade and bell towers, ancient
★   library, and catacombs full of human skulls and other bones, the Convento de San Francisco is one of Lima's most impressive sites. The catacombs hold the remains of some 75,000 people, some of whose bones have been arranged in eerie geometric patterns (the dusty narrow tunnels here aren't for the claustrophobic, though). The convent's massive church, the Iglesia de San Francisco, is the best example of Lima baroque architecture. Its handsome carved portal would later influence those on other churches, including the Iglesia de la Merced. The central nave is known for its beautiful ceilings painted in a style called *mudéjar* (a blend of Moorish and Spanish designs). The 50-minute tour includes the church, the monastery's library packed with antique texts, ample colonial art, and the catacombs. ⊠ *Jr. Ancash 471, El Centro* ☎ *01/427–1381* ⊕ *www.museocatacumbas.com* ◻ *S/10.*

Correo Central. Inaugurated in 1924, this regal structure looks more like a palace than a post office. You can buy a postcard or send a package, but most people come to admire the exuberance of an era when no one thought twice about placing bronze angels atop a civic building. At one time locals deposited letters in the mouth of the bronze lion by the front doors. About half of the building is given over to the Casa de la Gastronomía Peruana, dedicated to the country's culinary traditions, which charges admission. The museum entrance is on Jirón Conde Superunda, whereas the post office entrance is on Jirón Camana. ⊠ *Jr. Camana 157, El Centro* ☎ *01/427–9370* ◻ *S/3.*

Iglesia de la Merced. Nothing about this colonial-era church could be called restrained. Take the unusual baroque facade: instead of stately columns, the powers-that-be decided they should be wrapped with carefully carved grapevines. Inside are a series of retablos that gradually change from baroque to neoclassical styles. The intricately carved choir stalls, dating from the 18th century, have images of cherubic singers. The first house of worship to be built in Lima, Our Lady of Mercy was commissioned by Hernando Pizarro, brother of the city's founder. He chose the site because it was here that services were first held in the city. ⊠ *Jr. de la Unión at Jr. Miro Quesada, El Centro* ☎ *01/427–8199* ◻ *Free* ⊘ *Closed 1–3:30.*

DID YOU KNOW?

For more than 400 years, Lima's cathedral has undergone numerous reconstructions and face-lifts thanks to earthquakes.

Iglesia de San Pedro. The Jesuits built three churches in rapid succession on this corner, the current one dating from 1638. It remains one of the finest examples of early-colonial religious architecture in Peru. The facade is remarkably restrained, but the interior shows all the extravagance of the era, including a series of baroque retablos thought to be the best in the city. Many have works by Italians like Bernardo Bitti, who arrived on these shores in 1575. His style influenced an entire generation of painters. In the sacristy is *The Coronation of the Virgin*, one of his most famous works. ■TIP→ Don't miss the side aisle, where gilded arches lead to chapels decorated with beautiful hand-painted tiles. ⊠ *Jr. Azángaro 451 at Jr. Ucayali, El Centro* ☎ *01/428–3010* ⊕ *www. sanpedrodelima.org* ⊠ *Free* ⊗ *Closed daily 1–5 pm.*

Fodor's Choice ★ **Museo de Arte de Lima (MALI).** Built in 1871 as the Palacio de la Exposición, this mammoth neoclassical structure was designed by the Italian architect Antonio Leonardi, with metal columns from the workshop of Gustav Eiffel (who later built the famous Parisian tower). The ground floor holds temporary exhibitions by both national and international artists, and the second floor houses a permanent exhibition that spans Peru's past, with everything from pre-Columbian artifacts to colonial-era art to republican-era paintings and drawings that provide a glimpse into Peruvian life in the 19th and early-20th centuries. One of the museum's treasures is the collection of *quipus*, or "talking knots": collars of strings tied with an array of knots, each with a distinct meaning (the closest thing the Incas had to writing). ■TIP→ Leave time to sip an espresso in the café near the entrance. ⊠ *Paseo Colón 125, El Centro* ☎ *01/204–0000* ⊕ *www.mali.pe* ⊠ *S/30* ⊗ *Closed Mon.*

Palacio de Gobierno. The neobaroque palace north of the Plaza de Armas is the official residence of the president. It was built on the site where Francisco Pizarro was murdered in 1541 and has undergone several reconstructions, the most recent of which was completed in 1938. The best time to visit is at noon, when you can watch soldiers in red-and-blue uniforms conduct an elaborate changing of the guard. It's not quite Buckingham Palace, but it is impressive. Tours are offered on Saturday 9–10:30 am, but reservations must be made at least a few days ahead of time. ⊠ *Conde de Superunda 1501, El Centro* ☎ *01/311–3908.*

Fodor's Choice ★ **Plaza de Armas.** This massive square has been the center of the city since 1535. Over the years it has served many functions, from an open-air theater for melodramas to an impromptu ring for bullfights. Huge fires once burned in the center for people sentenced to death by the Spanish Inquisition. Much has changed over the years, but one thing remaining is the bronze fountain unveiled in 1651. It was here that José de San Martín declared the country's independence from Spain in 1821. ⊠ *Jr. Junín and Jr. Carabaya, El Centro.*

Fodor's Choice ★ **Plaza San Martín.** This spectacular plaza is unlike any other in the city. It is surrounded on three sides by neocolonial buildings dating from the 1920s, the pale facades of which are lit at night, when the plaza is most impressive. Presiding over the western edge is the Gran Hotel Bolívar, a pleasant spot for a pisco sour. Even if you're not thirsty, you should step inside for a look at its elegant lobby. At the plaza's center is a massive statue of José de San Martín, the Argentine general who led the independence of Argentina, Chile, and Peru from Spain. ⊠ *Between Jr. de la Unión and Jr. Carabaya, El Centro.*

WORTH NOTING

Barrio Chino. A ceremonial arch at the corner of Ucayali and Andahuaylas marks the entrance to Lima's tiny Chinatown. It consists of little more than a block-long pedestrian mall where the benches and kiosks are topped with traditional Chinese roofs and the street is decorated with tile representations of the Chinese zodiac. The best restaurants are around the corner on Paruro. ⊠ *Jr. Ucayali between Andahuaylas and Paruro, El Centro.*

Casa Solariega de Aliaga. Lima's oldest house, commonly known as Casa Aliaga, is a beautiful example of Spanish-colonial architecture a block from the Plaza de Armas. It was built by Jeronimo de Aliaga, one of Pizarro's officers, in 1536. His descendents lived in it for centuries, restoring it following an earthquake in 1746. Rooms are furnished with antiques, and walls decorated with historic paintings and colonial religious art. You must make a reservation and hire a guide to visit the house, so the best way to see it is as part of a city tour. ⊠ *Jr. de la Unión 224, El Centro* ☎ *01/427–7736* ⊕ *www.casadealiaga.com* 🖂 *S/30.*

Casa Torre Tagle. This mansion sums up the graceful style of the early 18th century. Flanked by a pair of elegant balconies, the stone entrance is as expertly carved as that of any of the city's churches. Casa Torre Tagle currently holds offices of the Foreign Ministry and is open to the public only on weekends, when you can check out the tiled ceilings and carved columns of the ground floor and see a 16th-century carriage. Across the street is **Casa Goyeneche**, which was built some 40 years later in 1771, and was clearly influenced by the rococo movement. ⊠ *Jr. Ucayali 363, El Centro* ☎ *01/204–2400* 🖂 *Free* ☉ *Closed weekdays.*

Cerro San Cristóbal. Rising over the northeastern edge of the city is this massive hill, Cerro San Cristóbal, recognizable from the cross at its peak—a replica of the one once placed there by Pizarro. On a clear day, more common during the southern summer, you can see most of the city below. ■TIP→ **The neighborhood at the base of the hill is sketchy, so hire a taxi or take a tour to the summit and back.** ⊠ *Calle San Cristóbal, El Centro.*

Convento de Santo Domingo. The 16th-century Convent of Saint Dominic offers a glimpse of life in a cloister. This sprawling structure shows the different styles popular during the colonial era in Lima. The bell tower, for instance, has a baroque base built in 1632, but the upper parts rebuilt after an earthquake in 1746 are more rococo in style. The convent's two cloisters are decorated with hand-painted tiles imported from Spain in the early 17th century. The stately library holds 25,000 antiquarian books. If you visit between 11 and 4, you can ascend the bell tower for a view of the old city. The church is quite popular as it holds the tombs of the first two Peruvian saints, Santa Rosa de Lima and San Martín de Porres. Independent guides who wait by the entrance offer short tours for a negotiable fee. Night visits are possible on the last Friday of every month from 7 pm to 9 pm. ⊠ *Conde de Superunda and Camaná, El Centro* ☎ *01/426–5521* ⊕ *www.museosantodomingo.com* 🖂 *S/10.*

2

RETABLOS EXPLAINED

You can tell a lot about colonial-era churches by their *retablos* (retables), the altarpieces that are almost always massive in scale and over-the-top in ornamentation. Most are made of elaborately carved wood and coated with layer upon layer of gold leaf. Indigenous peoples often did the carving, so look for some atypical elements such as symbols of the sun and moon that figure prominently in the local religion. You may be surprised that Jesus is a minor player on many retablos and on others doesn't appear at all. That's because these retablos often depict the life of the saint for which the church is named. Many churches retain their original baroque retablos, but others saw theirs replaced by the much simpler neoclassical ones with simple columns and spare design. If you wander around the church, you're likely to find the original relegated to one of the side chapels.

Estación de Desamparados. Inaugurated in 1912, Desamparados Station was the centerpiece for the continent's first railway, which stretches from the port of Callao to the Andean city of Huancayo. The station was named for a Jesuit church and monastery that stood next door at the time of its construction but has since been demolished. It now holds the Casa de la Literature Peruana (House of Peruvian Literature), which hosts literary exhibitions. It's well worth stepping inside to admire the building's elegant art nouveau interior, especially the stained-glass sky-light. ⊠ *Jr. Ancash 207, El Centro* ☎ *01/426–2573* ⊕ *www.casadelaliteratura.gob.pe* ⊠ *Free* ☉ *Closed Mon.*

Iglesia de Jesús, María y José. The 1659 Church of Jesus, Mary, and Joseph may be smaller than some of El Centro's other churches, but inside is a feast for the eyes. Baroque retablos representing various saints rise from the main altar and line both walls. ⊠ *Jr. Camaná and Jr. Moquegua, El Centro* ☎ *01/427–6809* ⊠ *Free* ☉ *Closed noon–3 daily and all day Sun.*

Municipalidad de Lima. Although it resembles the colonial-era buildings that abound in the area, City Hall was constructed in 1944. Step into the foyer to see the stained-glass windows above the marble staircase. To the south of the building is a popular pedestrian walkway called the Paseo Los Escribanos, or Passage of the Scribes, lined with restaurants. On the right, you'll find the entrance to a small gallery run by City Hall that hosts exhibitions by Peruvian artists. ⊠ *Jr. de la Union 300, El Centro* ☎ *01/315–1542.*

Museo de Arte Italiano. Italian art in Peru? This small museum is one of the city's most delightful. Most of the art is about a century old, so it captures the exact moment when impressionism was melting into modernism, and the building itself is a work of art. Don't overlook the magnificent iron door by Alessandro Mazzucotelli. ⊠ *Paseo de la República 250, El Centro* ☎ *01/321–5622* ⊠ *S/6* ☉ *Closed Mon.*

Parque de la Exposición. Eager to prove that it was a world-class capital, Lima hosted an international exposition in 1872. Several of the buildings constructed for the event still stand, including the neoclassical Palacio de la Exposición, which now serves as the Museo de Arte de

Lima. Stroll through the grounds and you'll find the eye-popping Pabellón Morisco, or Moorish Pavillion. Painstakingly restored, this Gothic-style structure has spiral staircases leading to a stained-glass salon on the second floor. The nearby Pabellón Bizantino, or Byzantine Pavilion, most closely resembles a turret from a Victorian-era mansion. ⊠ *Paseo Colón and Av. Wilson, El Centro* 🏛 ⌑ *Free.*

SAN ISIDRO

While strolling through the ancient olive grove of Parque El Olívar, you might be surprised by the light traffic and pastoral atmosphere. But just a few blocks away, you'll find the busy boulevards such as Camino Real, Conquistadores or Avenida Arequipa, and the sleek towers of the Centro Empresarial, which serve as reminders that San Isidro also holds the offices of the country's largest companies and banks, as well as most foreign embassies. It also has some of the city's best hotels and restaurants, so you are bound to spend some time here. Nevertheless, San Isidro's only real tourist attraction is the Huaca Huallamarca, where you can clamor atop the ruins of a pre-Columbian temple.

Like nearby Miraflores, San Isidro is big on shopping, though most of its boutiques sell designer goods and international brands. Its restaurants dish out amazing cuisine and it has a few nice bars, but San Isidro has a more subdued atmosphere than you'll find in the other neighborhoods.

GETTING AROUND

The easiest way to travel between the widely dispersed attractions in San Isidro (Lima's safest neighborhood) is by taxi, but you could also explore the neighborhood on foot in two or three hours.

TOP ATTRACTIONS

FAMILY **Huaca Huallamarca.** This mud brick pyramid, thought to be a place of worship, predates the Incas. Painstakingly restored on the front side, it seems out of place among the neighborhood's upscale homes and apartment buildings. Here you'll find a small museum with displays of objects found at the site, including several mummies. From the upper platform you can take in views of the San Isidro. ⊠ *Av. Nicolás de Rivera and Av. El Rosario, San Isidro* 🏛 *01/222–4124* ⌑ *S/5* ⊙ *Closed Mon.*

WORTH NOTING

Country Club Lima Hotel. Two royal palms stand guard, and a red carpet leads up the stairs to the entrance of this stately hotel built in 1926. Widely regarded as the city's most elegant hotel, its lobby and halls are decorated with colonial art on loan from the Museo Pedro de Osma. Even if you stay elsewhere, it's worth dropping by for a drink on the terrace or in the pub. If you feel like a light meal in the early evening, consider the English-style high tea. ⊠ *Calle Los Eucaliptos 590, San Isidro* 🏛 *01/611–9000* ⊕ *www.hotelcountry.com.*

FAMILY **Parque El Olívar.** For years this rambling olive grove was slowly disappearing as homes for wealthy citizens were built on its perimeter and within it. The process was halted in the 1960s, in time to save more than 1,500 gnarled olive trees. Some of the trees are centuries old and still bear fruit. A network of sidewalks, flower beds, fountains, and playgrounds make

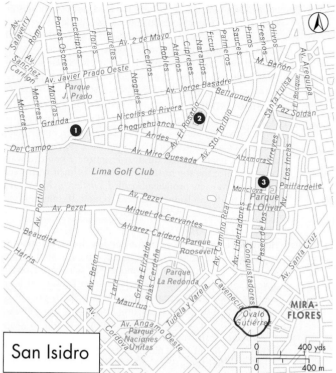

this 50-acre park a popular spot on weekend afternoons. ⊠ *Av. Los Incas, between Choquehuanca and República, San Isidro* ⊕ *msi.gob.pe/portal/ nuestro-distrito/turismo-distrital/bosque-el-olivar.*

MIRAFLORES

With flower-filled parks and wide swaths of green overlooking the ocean, it's no wonder travelers flock to this seaside suburb. Miraflores has Lima's best selection of hotels and restaurants, and is also a bustling cultural hub. There are plenty of boutiques and cafés, bars and dance clubs here. Some people who find themselves in Lima for a short time never leave this little haven.

At its center is Parque Miraflores, sitting like a slice of pie between Avenida José Larco and Avenida Diagonal. On the eastern side is the Iglesia de la Virgen Milagrosa, the neighborhood's largest church. The colonial-style building next door is the Palacio Municipal de Miraflores, where most governmental business takes place. The park is surrounded by shops, bars and restaurants, including several sidewalk cafés.

If you're interested in ancient cultures, head to Huaca Pucllana, the massive temple complex, which is especially attractive at night. The tiny Museo Amano, six blocks to the west, contains a small but impressive collection of ancient weavings. If you want to shop, head for Avenida Petit Thouars just a block northeast of the park, where a series of handicraft markets hold dozens of shops that offer some of the best deals in town. For some fresh air and an ocean view, head to Parque del Amor and adjacent parks, or nearby Larcomar, for splendid views of the coast and sea below. These areas attract young lovers, joggers, paragliding enthusiasts, and just about everyone else on a sunny afternoon.

GETTING AROUND

A popular walk is the 20-minute stroll south from Parque Miraflores, down busy Avenida José Larco to Larcomar, an open-air mall built into the side of a cliff. Its gorgeous views and ocean breezes complement the shops, bars, and restaurants. From there you can walk either east or west, since the top of the coastal cliff is lined with a series of parks and an ocean-view promenade called a *malecón*. Miraflores is about 10 minutes from San Isidro or Barranco, and 30 minutes from El Centro by taxi or the Metropolitano bus.

TOP ATTRACTIONS

FAMILY
Fodor'sChoice
★

Huaca Pucllana. Rising out of a nondescript residential neighborhood is this massive, mud-brick temple complex. You'll be amazed at the scale—this pre-Inca *huaca* (pronounced "wha kah"), or temple, covers several city blocks. The site, which dates back to at least the fourth century, has ongoing excavations, and new discoveries are occasionally announced. A tiny museum highlights a few of those finds. Knowledgeable, English-speaking guides will lead you through reconstructed sections and over the ruins to an area that is being excavated. ■ TIP→ This site is most beautiful at night, when parts of it are illuminated. Thirty-minute partial tours are available during this time. ⊠ *Calle General Borgoño cuadra 8 s/n, Miraflores* 🕾 *01/617-7148* ⊕ *huacapucllanamiraflores.pe* 🖾 *S/12 in day, S/15 at night* ☉ *Closed 5–7 pm daily; closed at night Mon. and Tues.*

FAMILY
Fodor'sChoice
★

Parque del Amor. You could imagine you're in Barcelona when you stroll through this lovely park designed by Peruvian artist Victor Delfin. Like Antoni Gaudí's Park Güell, the park that provided the inspiration for this one, the benches are decorated with broken pieces of tile. In keeping with the romantic theme—the name translates as "Park of Love"—the mosaic includes sayings such as *Amor es como luz* ("Love is like light"). The centerpiece is a massive statue of two lovers locked in a passionate embrace. The park affords a sweeping view of the Pacific, and on windy days, paragliders take off from an adjacent green. ⊠ *Malecón Cisneros, Miraflores.*

FAMILY

Parque Miraflores. What locals call Parque Miraflores is actually two parks. A smaller section, near the roundabout, is Parque 7 de Junio, whereas the rest of it is Parque Kennedy. To the east of Parque Kennedy stands Miraflores's stately Iglesia de la Virgen Milagrosa (Church of the Miraculous Virgin), built in the 1930s on the site of a colonial church. The equally young colonial-style building behind it is the Palacio Municipal de Miraflores (town hall). Two open-air cafés along Parque Kennedy's eastern edge serve decent food and drink. At night, a round cement structure in front of those cafés called La Rotonda fills up

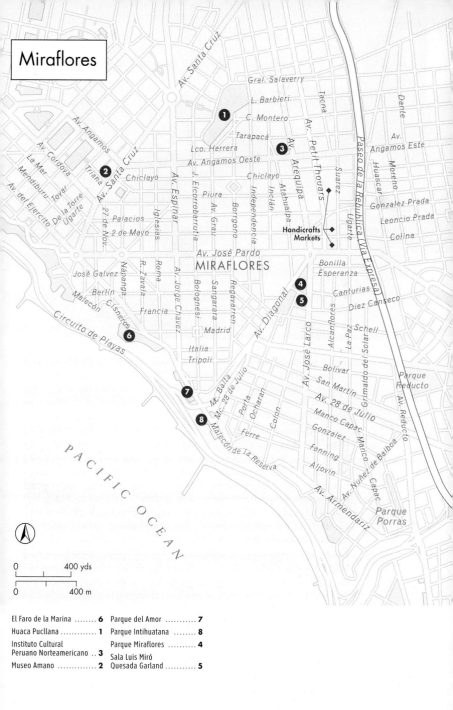

Miraflores

The tile mosaics of Parque del Amor in Miraflores take their inspiration from Barcelona's Park Güell.

with handicraft vendors, and the park becomes especially lively. Street vendors sell popcorn and traditional Peruvian desserts such as *picarones* (fried donuts bathed in molasses), *mazamora* (a pudding made with blue corn juice and fruit) and *arroz con leche* (rice pudding). ✉ *Between Av. José Larco and Av. Diagonal, Miraflores.*

WORTH NOTING

FAMILY **El Faro de la Marina.** Constructed in 1900, this little lighthouse at the north end of Parque Antonio Raimundi, a short walk north from the Parque del Amor, has guided ships for more than a century. On sunny weekends, the large park that surrounds it is one of the most popular spots in Miraflores, with paragliders floating overhead and bicyclists and skate boarders rolling along the ocean-view *malecón* (promenade). Children of all ages play on the lawns and playground. ✉ *Malecón Cisneros at Calle Madrid, Miraflores.*

Instituto Cultural Peruano Norteamericano. The large gallery in the lower floor of the Instituto Cultural Peruano Norteamericano primarily exhibits the work of contemporary Peruvian artists, with a new show every month. Each year in July or August, however, it exhibits a collection of traditional Andean folk art, which is well worth seeing. ✉ *Av. Angamos Oeste at Av. Arequipa, Miraflores* ☎ *01/706–7000* ⊕ *www.cultural.icpna.edu.pe* ☺ *Closed Mon.*

Museo Amano. Although relatively small, this private museum of pre-Columbian artifacts holds some of the city's best weavings, as well as well-preserved ceramics and other handiwork. The museum was founded by Japanese businessman and collector Yoshitaro Amano in 1962 and was expanded and remodeled by his offspring in 2015. The chronological exhibition charts Peru's artistic development from

800 BC to the 15th century across four halls packed with well-preserved artifacts from pre-Inca cultures such as the Paracas, Nasca, Moche, and Chanchay, as well as Incan handicrafts. The impressive collection of weavings contains some that are almost 2,000 years old, yet they've retained their vivid colors and intricate (and sometimes comic) imagery. Displays are in English and Spanish, but you can call ahead to reserve an English-speaking guide. ⊠ *Calle Retiro 160, Miraflores* ☎ *01/441–2909* ⊕ *www.museoamano.org* 🖭 *S/30* 🕙 *Closed Mon.*

WHERE TO PARAGLIDE

PerúFly. If you visit any of the parks in Miraflores with ocean views on a windy day, you'll likely see brilliantly colored paragliders in the sky above the cliffs. PerúFly offers 10-minute tandem flights that take off from a spot just north of Parque del Amor and cost S/260, which includes a video. Call ahead to make sure there is enough wind to fly. ⊠ *Malecón Cisneros at Venecia, Miraflores* ☎ *994–567–802* ⊕ *www.perufly.com.*

Parque Intihuatana. A massive cement sculpture called *Intihuatana*, designed by Peruvian artist Fernando de Szyszlo, dominates this plaza across the bridge from Parque del Amor. *Intihuatana* is the Quecha term for sundial, and the artist was no doubt inspired by *intihuatanas* in Machu Picchu and other Incan sites. It's a great spot to grab a snack or beverage and watch the surfers ride the waves below. It marks the beginning of the Malecón de la Reserva, which winds its way southward along the adjacent Parque Champagnat to the Larcomar shopping center and Parque Domodossola. ⊠ *Malecón de la Reserva s/n, Miraflores.*

Sala Luis Miró Quesada Garland. On the southern end of the Palacio Municipal de Miraflores (town hall), around the corner from Parque Miraflores, is the Sala Luis Miró Quesada Garland: one of the district's most popular galleries. It exhibits the work of Peruvian painters, sculptors, and photographers, with a new artist exhibiting each month. ⊠ *Palacio Municipal de Miraflores, Av. José Larco 450, Miraflores* ☎ *01/617–7264* 🖭 *Free* 🕙 *Closed Mon.*

BARRANCO

Barranco is a mix of bohemian, historic, and run down, but the area along the coast is the most charming of Lima's neighborhoods, thanks to its architectural treasures and ocean views. Travelers and locals alike come for art exhibitions, concerts or folk dancing performances, and high-quality handicrafts. It also has Lima's best boutique hotels.

On weekend nights, Barranco is a magnet for young people who come to carouse in its bars. Sleepy during the day, the neighborhood comes to life around sunset, when its central square and nearby streets begin filling up.

Founded toward the end of the 19th century, Barranco was where wealthy *limeños* built their summer residences. The streetcar line that once connected it to El Centro brought crowds of beachgoers on weekends and holidays. The view proved so irresistible that some built huge mansions on the cliffs above the sea. Many of these have fallen into disrepair, but little by little they are being renovated.

GETTING AROUND

To get your bearings, head to Parque Municipal, one of the nicest of the city's plazas. To the south, the brick-red building with the tower is the Biblioteca Municipal, or Municipal Library. To the north is the parish church called La Santisima Cruz. To the west, steps lead down to Lima's own Bridge of Sighs, the Puente de los Suspiros. Directly below, in the shade of ancient trees, is the Bajada de Baños, lined with wonderful old houses and colorful bougainvillea. Head down this cobblestone street to the waves of Playa Barranquito by day or to various bars and restaurants by night.

TOP ATTRACTIONS

Bajada de Baños. The cobbled road that leads down to the "Baths"—the beaches—is shaded by massive trees and lined with historic architecture. Once the route that local fishermen used to reach their boats, it is now a popular promenade at night, since many of the former homes that line it hold restaurants and bars. At the bottom of the hill a covered wooden bridge spans a busy road, called Cirquito de Playas, to a coastal sidewalk that leads to several beaches and restaurants. A short walk to the north is Playa Barranquito, and Playa Agua Dulce is half a mile south. ⊠ *1 blk. west of Parque Municipal, Barranco.*

2

El Mirador. Walk down the path to the left of La Ermita church and you will find El Mirador, a scenic lookout with a view of the sea and coastline. It's especially attractive at night, when a cross and a Christ statue on the ridge to the south of the city are illuminated. The path is lined with bars that also have nice views. ⊠ *End of Ermita path, Barranco.*

Galleria Lucia de la Puente. Lucia de la Puente represents some of the best artists in Peru, as well as other South American nations, at Lima's premier gallery, inside a historic house on Barranco's most charming street. Some of de la Puente's private collection is on display next door, in the public areas of Hotel B, which art enthusiasts should definitely stop by and see. ⊠ *Paseo Sáenz Peña 206, Barranco* ☎ *01/477–9740* ⊕ *www.gluciadelapuente.com* ☾ *Closed Sun.*

Museo de Arte Contemporáneo—Lima (MAC). Lima's newest art museum, inaugurated in 2013, the MAC Lima was built and is run by a privately funded institute on land donated by the Municipality of Barranco. Its minimalistic, rectangular exhibition halls house a permanent collection of work by Latin American and European artists, dating from the past 60 years, as well as temporary shows that change every few months. The main hall overlooks a metal sculpture by Veronica Wiesse perched over a reflection pond, beyond which lies a small park, sometimes used for fairs and other events. ⊠ *Av. Grau 1511, Barranco* ☎ *01/514–6800* ⊕ *www.maclima.pe* ☞ *S/10* ☾ *Closed Mon.*

Museo Mario Testino (MATE). Occupying a refurbished, turn-of-the-century house near the Museo Pedro de Osma, this small museum exhibits photos by renowned fashion photographer Mario Testino, who is Peruvian. It has rooms dedicated to the likes of Kate Moss, Gisele Bündchen, and Madonna as well as a few photos of indigenous Peruvians in traditional Andean dress. A separate building holds a sampling from the last photo shoot of Princess Diana before her untimely death. The gift shop has some great postcards, and the museum's café is a pleasant spot for a light meal or drink. ⊠ *Av. Pedro de Osma 409, Barranco* ☎ *01/200–5400* ⊕ *www.mate.pe* ☞ *S/10* ☾ *Closed Mon.*

Fodor'sChoice ★ **Museo Pedro de Osma.** Even if there were no art inside this museum, it would still be worth the trip to see the century-old mansion that houses it. The mansard-roofed structure—with inlaid wood floors, delicately painted ceilings, and breathtaking stained-glass windows in every room—was the home of a wealthy collector of religious art. The best of his collection is permanently on display. The finest of the paintings, the 18th-century *Virgen de Pomato* represents the Earth, with her mountain-shape cloak covered with garlands of corn. A more modern wing contains fine pieces of silver, including a lamb-shape incense holder with shining ruby eyes. Make sure to visit the manicured grounds. ⊠ *Av. Pedro de Osma 423, Barranco* ☎ *01/467–0063* ⊕ *www.museopedrodeosma.org* ☞ *S/20* ☾ *Closed Mon.*

Parque Municipal. Elegant royal palms, swirls of colorful bougainvillea, and the surrounding colonial architecture make this park stand out from others in Lima. The southern end is lined with historic buildings, the most prominent of which is the library with its yellow clock tower. To the north of the park stands Barranco's bright red Iglesia de la Santísima Cruz (Church of the Holy Cross), which opens for mass every evening and on Sunday mornings. To the west of the park is a staircase that leads down to the Puente de los Suspiros and the Bajada a los Baños. ⊠ *Between Av. Pedro de Osma and Av. Grau, Barranco.*

Puente de los Suspiros. The romantically named Bridge of Sighs is a wooden walkway over the tree-shaded Bajada de los Baños. Though the bridge itself is nothing special, the view of the surrounding historic buildings is priceless. It is also the most direct route between the Parque Municipal and La Ermita, a little yellow chapel dating from 1882. ⊠ *Bajada de Baños, Barranco.*

WORTH NOTING

Yvonne Sanguineti Galería de Arte. Housed in an ornate, turn-of-the-century home near the corner of Avenida Miguel Grau and Avenida Sáenz Peña, this small gallery exhibits the work of Peruvian artists, primarily painters. It also has a shop that sells smaller paintings and sculptures that are easier to pack. ⊠ *Av. Miguel Grau 810, Barranco* ☏ *01/247-2999* ⊕ *yvonnesanguinetigaleria.com* ☉ *Closed Sun.*

NEED A BREAK

✕ **Bisetti.** The best coffee in Lima and a tempting selection of desserts are served in this cozy, refurbished early 20th-century home across the street from the Parque Municipal. ⊠ *Av. Pedro de Osma 116, Barranco* ☏ *01/247-4399* ⊕ *www.cafebisetti.com.*

PUEBLO LIBRE

Instead of hurrying past, residents of Pueblo Libre often pause to chat with friends. Despite forming part of a metropolis, it retains the feel of a small town. Plaza Bolívar, the park at the heart of Pueblo Libre, is surrounded by colonial-era buildings, many of which are home to shops and restaurants. On the south side, in the Municipalidad de Pueblo Libre, are governmental offices. A small gallery on the ground floor sometimes hosts painting and photography exhibitions.

Despite the pleasant surroundings, there would be little reason to venture this far if it weren't for the Museo Nacional de Antropología, Arqueología e Historia del Perú, and the Museo Larco, both must-visit museums.

GETTING AROUND

The most convenient way to reach Pueblo Libre is a taxi ride, which takes 20–30 minutes.

TOP ATTRACTIONS

Fodor'sChoice
★

Museo Larco. Fuchsia bougainvillea tumbles over the white walls surrounding the colonial bishops mansion built atop a pre-Columbian temple. It houses the city's most impressive collection of ancient art, with works from all the country's major pre-Colombian cultures spanning several thousand years. Most intriguing are the thousands of ceramic "portrait heads" crafted more than a millennium ago. Some owners commissioned more than one, allowing you to see how they changed over the course of their lives. The *sala erótica* reveals that these ancient artisans were surprisingly uninhibited, creating everyday objects adorned with explicit sexual images. This gallery is across the garden from the rest of the museum. Guides are a good idea, and are just S/35 per group. The café overlooking the museum's garden is an excellent option for lunch or dinner. ⊠ *Av. Bolívar 1515, Pueblo Libre* ☎ *01/461–1312* ⊕ *www.museolarco.org* ✆ *S/30.*

WORTH NOTING

FAMILY **Museo Nacional de Antropología, Arqueología e Historia del Perú.** The country's most extensive collection of pre-Columbian artifacts can be found at this sprawling museum. Beginning with 8,000-year-old stone tools, Peru's history is revealed through the sleek granite obelisks of the Chavín culture, the intricate weavings of Paraca peoples, and the colorful ceramics of the Moche, Chimú, and Inca civilizations. A fascinating pair of mummies from the Nazca region is thought to be more than 2,500 years old. They are so well preserved that you can still see the grim expressions on their faces. The exhibits occupy two colonial houses, in one of which Venezuelan general Simón Bolívar, who led South America's war of independence from Spain, lived for awhile following independence. ■TIP→ Not all the exhibits are labeled in English, but you can hire a guide for S/15. ⊠ *Plaza Bolívar, Pueblo Libre* ☎ *01/321–5630* ⊕ *mnaahp.cultura.pe* ✆ *S/10* ⊗ *Closed Mon.*

NEED A DRINK? ╳ **Antigua Taberna Queirolo.** Be sure to stop by the Antigua Taberna Queirolo, a charming little bar on the west side of Pueblo Libre's central plaza, where locals lean against the marble-top tables and historic photos hang on the walls. The place serves good ham sandwiches smothered in pickled onions and pisco bottled in the factory next door. ⊠ *Jr. San Martín 1090, Pueblo Libre* ☎ *01/460–0441* ⊕ *antiguatabernaqueirolo.com.*

ELSEWHERE AROUND LIMA

A few of Lima's most interesting museums are in outlying neighborhoods such as Monterrico and San Borja. The most convenient way to reach them is a quick taxi ride.

TOP ATTRACTIONS

Museo "Oro del Perú". When you see examples of how Peru's pre-Columbian societies manipulated gold—from a mantle made of postage-stamp-size pieces worn by a Lambayeque priest, to an intricately designed sheet that once decorated an entire wall of the Chimú capital of Chan Chan—you begin to imagine the opulence of the cities that the Spanish conquistadors plundered. The Gold Museum contains items like a child's poncho made of yellow feathers, a skull with a full set of pink-quartz teeth, and several mummies. The main floor holds a less-flashy museum of military uniforms and weapons, which most visitors skip. None of the displays are particularly well marked, so you may want to rent a recorded tour or visit the museum as part of a city tour. ⊠ *Alonso de Molina 1100, Monterrico* ☎ *01/345–1271* ⊕ *www.museoroperu.com.pe* ✆ *S/33.*

WORTH NOTING

Pachacamac. Dating back to the first century, this complex of plazas, palaces, and other structures was for centuries a stronghold of the Huari people. Here they worshipped Pachacamac, creator of the world. It was a pilgrimage site, and people from all over the region came to worship.

In the 15th century the city was captured by the Incas, who added structures such as the *Acllahuasi*, the Palace of the Chosen Women. When the Spanish heard of the city, they dispatched troops to plunder its riches. In 1533, two years before the founding of Lima, they marched triumphantly into the city, only to find a few remaining objects in gold. The extensive ruins are spread across a desert ridge with views of the verdant Lurin River valley, the Pacific Ocean, and Pachacamac Island. The site has both pre-Incan temples and several that were built by the Incas, such as the Templo del Inti (Temple of the Sun), with its grand staircase leading up to colonnaded walkways. A large museum holds an extensive collection of ceramics, textiles, and other artifacts. The easiest way to visit Pachacamac, located 31 km (19 miles) south of Lima, is on a half-day guided tour offered by several Lima agencies. If you prefer to hire a taxi, there are knowledgeable guides available at the entrance (S/25). ⊠ *Km 31.5, Panamericana Sur* ☎ *01/321–5606* ⊕ *pachacamac. cultura.pe* 🗃 *S/15* ☾ *Closed Mon.*

OFF THE BEATEN PATH

Caral. Few people realize it, but the oldest urban site in the western hemisphere is just 220 km (120 miles) north of Lima. Caral was first settled around 5,000 BC, long before the rise of ancient Egypt, though Caral's squat Pirámide Mayor is slightly younger than Egypt's Great Pyramid of Giza. It may not be as spectacular as other Peruvian sites, but Caral has some interesting structures that evoke a well-developed people, who archaeologists have dubbed the Caral-Supe culture. It takes nearly four hours to drive to Caral and it is not easy to find, so the best way to visit it is on an organized tour. ⊠ *Panamericana Norte, Caral* ☎ *01/205–2500* ⊕ *www.zonacaral.gob.pe* 🗃 *S/11.*

WHERE TO EAT

Lima has long been a popular destination among foodies, but its dining scene is now hotter than ever. Three of the city's eateries were listed in the World's 50 Best Restaurants in 2017; nine were included in the list of 50 Best Restaurants in Latin America; and the World Travel Awards has named Peru the World's Leading Culinary Destination for five years in a row. When Peru's celebrity chefs Gastón Acurio and Astrid Gutsche moved their flagship Astrid & Gastón to a refurbished colonial mansion called Casa Moreyra, they inaugurated it with a week of activities attended by some of the world's top chefs and restaurant critics, and the reservation book was already filled for the next four months. Luckily, there are other world-class dining options in Lima, and the midranged restaurants are pretty impressive, too.

WHAT IT COSTS IN NUEVO SOLES			
$	$$	$$$	$$$$
Restaurants	under S/35	S/35–S/50	S/51–S/65	over S/65

Restaurant prices are the average cost of a main course at dinner or, if dinner is not served, at lunch.

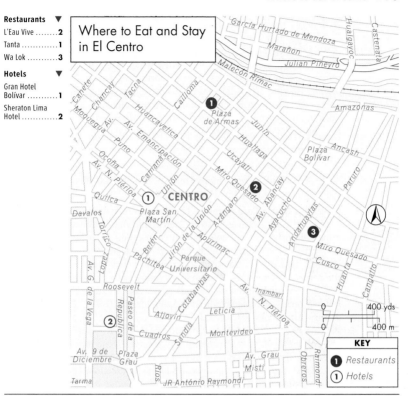

Where to Eat and Stay in El Centro

KEY

❶ Restaurants

① Hotels

EL CENTRO

El Centro has both high-quality cuisine and cheap, filling food. A highlight is the Barrio Chino, packed with dozens of Chinese-Peruvian restaurants called *chifas,* but the run-down neighborhood that surrounds it makes it inadvisable to head there for dinner. Restaurants on the main plazas are better dinner options.

$

FRENCH FUSION

✕ **L'Eau Vive.** Run by nuns who serve satisfying (though not extraordinary) French food, and sing "Ave Maria" nightly at 9, L'Eau Vive sits in a restored mansion across the street from Palacio Torre Tagle. Trout baked in cognac and duck in orange sauce are two dishes that bring the locals back time and again. **Known for:** singing nuns; inexpensive three-course lunches; delicious trout baked in cognac. $ *Average main: S/32* ⊠ *Ucayali 370, El Centro* ☎ *01/427–5612* ⊘ *Closed 3:30–7:30 and Sun.*

$$

PERUVIAN

✕ **Tanta.** Overlooking a quiet plaza behind the Municipalidad, this chic Peruvian-Italian fusion restaurant is a pleasant spot for a break from sightseeing. The menu, which is the work of chef Gastón Acurio, offers an excellent mix of light fare such as a plate of *causushis* (cold mashed-potato appetizers with varied fillings), and more hearty dishes such as fettuccine in a *huancaina* (yellow pepper–cheese) sauce with a sirloin scaloppine topped with mushrooms. **Known for:** inventive empanadas (meat pastries); thirst-quenching mixed-fruit juices; amazing desserts.

$ *Average main: S/49* ⊠ *Pasaje Nicolás de Rivera 142, El Centro* ☎ *01/428–3115* ⊕ *www.tantaperu.com* ⊘ *Closed Sun. dinner.*

$$ ✕ **Wa Lok.** The best *chifa* in Chinatown, Wa Lok is known for such
CHINESE memorable dishes as *calamares rellenos* (shrimp-stuffed squid tempura), *taipá* (wok-fried chicken, pork, shrimp, and vegetables) and *pato pekines* (Peking duck). It's best to go with a group and share, or ask for half orders. **Known for:** traditional Chinese cuisine; excellent Peking duck; many vegetarian options. $ *Average main: S/44* ⊠ *Jr. Paruro 878, El Centro* ☎ *01/427–2750* ⊕ *www.walok.com.pe.*

SAN ISIDRO

Most of San Isidro's restaurants are on or near Avenida Conquistadores, the neighborhood's main shopping street.

$$$$ ✕ **Astrid & Gastón Casa Moreyra.** The flagship restaurant of Peru's most
PERUVIAN celebrated chefs, spouses Gastón Acurio and Astrid Gutsche, occupies
Fodor's Choice a meticulously restored colonial mansion called Casa Moreyra. They
★ serve a fixed tasting menu, with nine separate dishes at dinner and seven at lunch, taking you on a journey through Peru's culinary traditions over the course of two hours. **Known for:** exquisite tasting menu; both meat and seafood dishes; reserve at least two weeks in advance. $ *Average main: S/669* ⊠ *Av. Paz Soldán 290, San Isidro* ☎ *01/442–2774* ⊕ *www. astridygaston.com* ⊘ *Closed 3–7 and dinner Sun.*

$ ✕ **Como Agua Para Chocolate.** One of Lima's few Mexican restaurants,
MEXICAN this colorful spot near Parque El Olivar serves some innovative dishes as well as the usual Tex-Mex fare. The house specialties are *barbacoa de cordero* (lamb grilled in avocado leaves), *pescado a la veracruzana* (fish in a slightly spicy tomato sauce), and *albóndagas al chipotle* (spicy meatballs served with yellow rice), but you can also get tacos, burritos, and enchiladas. **Known for:** great margaritas; traditional Mexican fare; house specialty is barbacoa de cordero. $ *Average main: S/34* ⊠ *Pancho Fierro 108, San Isidro* ☎ *01/222–0174* ⊘ *Closed Sun.*

$$$ ✕ **Lima 27.** This dark gray mansion with a bright red foyer looks like
PERUVIAN Dracula's love shack at night, but inside you'll find a chic lounge and two elegant dining rooms. Local epicureans gather here to savor a creative fusion of Peruvian and Continental cuisine, from *cabrito loche* (roast kid with squash ravioli) to *atún costra* (tuna in a sesame-pepper crust), to *gnocchis crocantes* (crispy gnocchi smothered in a mushroom and artichoke heart ragout). **Known for:** inventive Peruvian and Continental fusion dishes; popular terrace bar on weekends; local favorite. $ *Average main: S/63* ⊠ *Calle Santa Luisa 295, San Isidro* ☎ *01/421– 9084* ⊕ *www.lima27.com* ⊘ *No dinner Sun.*

$$$$ ✕ **Malabar.** Foodies flock to Malabar for one-of-a-kind dishes. Chef-
PERUVIAN owner Pedro Miguel Schiaffino travels the Peruvian Andes and Amazon in search of weird and unfamiliar ingredients that most chefs—and locals—overlook, and then incorporates them into the menu at Malabar. **Known for:** true foodie experience; organic ingredients; five- and nine-course set menus. $ *Average main: S/66* ⊠ *Camino Real 101, San Isidro* ☎ *01/440–5200* ⊕ *malabar.com.pe* ⊘ *Closed Sun.*

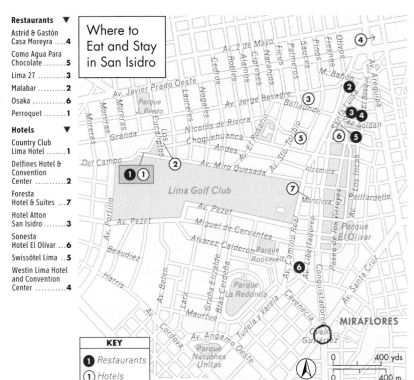

Restaurants ▼

Astrid & Gastón
Casa Moreyra **4**

Como Agua Para
Chocolate **5**

Lima 27 ....**3**

Malabar **2**

Osaka **6**

Perroquet **1**

Hotels ▼

Country Club
Lima Hotel **1**

Delfines Hotel &
Convention
Center **2**

Foresta
Hotel & Suites ...**7**

Hotel Atton
San Isidro **3**

Sonesta
Hotel El Olívar ...**6**

Swissôtel Lima ..**5**

Westin Lima Hotel
and Convention
Center **4**

Where to Eat and Stay in San Isidro

KEY

1 *Restaurants*

1 *Hotels*

$$$ ✕**Osaka.** Osaka has a sushi bar and also serves Peruvian standards
ECLECTIC such as cebiches and tiraditos, plus Chinese dishes like broiled scallops
braised in a spicy sauce. Settle into one of the low tables and sink your
teeth into *quinua maguro* (seared tuna medallions served with mashed
lucuma fruit and crunchy quinua), or grilled sirloin and sautéed mush-
rooms atop miso mashed potatoes. **Known for:** Peruvian-Asian fusion;
excellent seafood; great service. $ *Average main: S/58* ⊠ *Av. Pardo y
Aliaga 660, Miraflores* ☎ *01/222–0405* ⊕ *www.osaka.com.pe* ⊘ *No
dinner Sun.*

$$$$ ✕**Perroquet.** There's not a more elegant dining room in the city than Per-
PERUVIAN roquet, tucked away in the Country Club Lima Hotel, and the inventive
selection of Peruvian and Continental cuisine is on par with the set-
ting. The main room features upholstered chairs, polished crystal, and
china, and on the terrace are brass chandeliers. **Known for:** exquisite
food and setting; Sunday lunch buffet; delicious lamb shank roasted in
red wine. $ *Average main: S/70* ⊠ *Country Club Hotel, Los Eucalip-
tos 50, San Isidro* ☎ *01/611–9007* ⊕ *www.hotelcountry.com/dining/
perroquet-restaurant.*

MIRAFLORES

Miraflores has some of Lima's best restaurants. Although a few of them are clustered around Parque Miraflores, many are scattered farther afield and are best reached by taxi.

$$$ PERUVIAN 🍴 **ámaZ.** Chef Pedro Miguel Schiaffino (of Malabar fame) spent years exploring the Peruvian Amazon and experimenting with its ingredients and traditional recipes before opening ámaZ, where you can experience the flavors of the rain forest in the urban jungle. His versions of traditional Amazonian dishes such as *pataraschca* (catfish filet cooked in a *bijau* leaf), or *tacacho* (fried plantain-and-smoked-pork balls) are excellent, but so are inventions like chunks of *paiche* (Amazon fish) stewed in coconut milk. **Known for:** traditional Amazonian dishes; nine-dish "abruta fiesta" menu; upscale, eclectic environment. [$] *Average main: S/62* ✉ *Av. La Paz 1079, Miraflores* ☎ *01/221–9393* 🌐 *amaz.com.pe* 🕓 *No dinner Sun.*

$$$ PERUVIAN 🍴 **Brujas de Cachiche.** Though its name evokes folklore, "Witches of Cachiche" is an elegant, modern spot that offers variations on traditional Peruvian cuisine. The results include such delicacies as *corvina en salsa de camarones* (sea bass in a roasted crayfish sauce) or *cabrito a la norteña* (stewed kid) . **Known for:** elegant atmosphere; extensive wine list; cozy bar in back open early for appetizers. [$] *Average main: S/64* ✉ *Calle Bolognesi 472, Miraflores* ☎ *01/447–1133* 🌐 *www.brujasdecachiche.com.pe* 🕓 *Closed Sun. night.*

$$$$ PERUVIAN Fodor's Choice ★ 🍴 **Central Restaurante.** After years working in some of the best kitchens of Europe and Asia, Virgilio Martínez returned to Lima to convert his childhood home into this chic, airy venue for his culinary talents, and quickly established a reputation as one of Latin America's best chefs. Martínez and his wife, chef María Pía Leon, change their menu every six months, but each one celebrates the country's edible biodiversity with fresh and often organic ingredients. **Known for:** reserve months in advance; 11- and 18-course menus; coastal, Andean, and Amazonian cuisine. [$] *Average main: S/400* ✉ *Calle Santa Isabel 376, Miraflores* ☎ *01/242–8515* 🌐 *www.centralrestaurante.com.pe* 🕓 *Closed Sun. No lunch Sat.*

$$$ PERUVIAN 🍴 **El Señorío de Sulco.** Owner Isabel Alvarez has authored several cookbooks of traditional Peruvian cuisine, which is the specialty here. Start with one of various cebiches or *chupe de camarones* (a creamy river prawn soup) if in season, then move on to *arroz con pato* (rice and duck with a splash of dark beer), or *huatia sulcana* (a traditional beef stew). **Known for:** cebiche; traditional food; good service. [$] *Average main: S/54* ✉ *Malecón Cisneros 1470, Miraflores* ☎ *01/441–0389* 🌐 *www.senoriodesulco.com* 🕓 *No dinner Sun.*

$$$ PERUVIAN Fodor's Choice ★ 🍴 **Huaca Pucllana.** The view of the 1,500-year-old pre-Inca ruins is reason enough to dine at Huaca Pucllana, but the sumptuous Peruvian and international cuisine is a close second. The best tables are outside, with a view of the *huaca* (ruins), which are spectacularly lighted at night. The Peruvian fusion menu includes treats such as grilled alpaca in a mustard sauce with corn soufflé and paiche (an Amazon fish) fillet with Brazil-nut flakes and a *cocona* (jungle fruit) and *aji* chili sauce. **Known for:** priceless view of pre-Inca ruins; quality Peruvian cuisine; reservations essential. [$] *Average main: S/56* ✉ *Huaca Pucllana, Calle General Borgoño at Calle Ayacucho, Miraflores* ☎ *01/445–4042* 🌐 *www.resthuacapucllana.com* 🕓 *Closed 4–7 pm.*

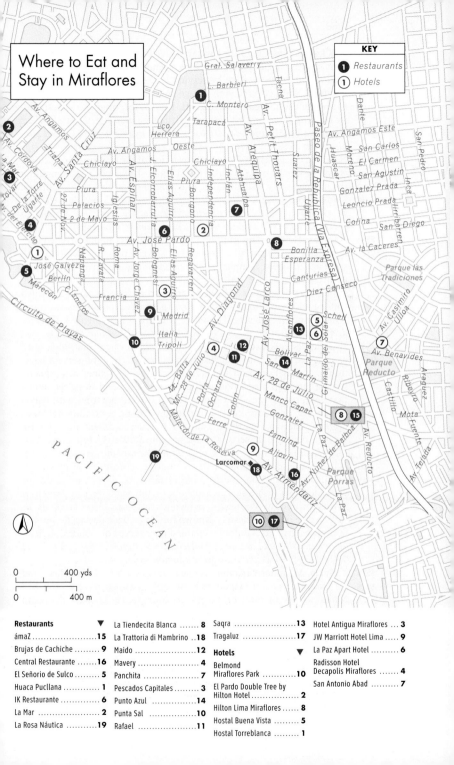

Where to Eat and Stay in Miraflores

KEY

1 Restaurants
1 Hotels

PACIFIC OCEAN

Larcomar

0   400 yds
0   400 m

$$$$ PERUVIAN 🍴 **IK Restaurante.** Chef Ivan Kisic was killed in a tragic automobile accident shortly before IK Restaurante opened, but his family keeps his dream and memory alive by serving his recipes in the restaurant he designed. Walls covered with foliage and wood reflect the commitment to serving fresh, organic ingredients. **Known for:** original recipes; family run; top-notch grilled octopus. [$] *Average main: S/70* ✉ *Calle Elias Aguirre 179, Miraflores* ☎ *01/652–1692* 🌐 *ivankisic.pe* 🕒 *Closed Sun. No lunch Mon.*

$$$ SEAFOOD Fodor's Choice ★ 🍴 **La Mar.** Chef Gastón Acurio's reinvention of the traditional cebichería is one of Lima's most popular lunch spots. The decor is minimal, but the menu offers a kaleidoscopic selection of delectable seafood dishes. **Known for:** amazing seafood; busiest from 1 to 3 pm; large shareable portions. [$] *Average main: S/56* ✉ *Av. La Mar 770, Miraflores* ☎ *01/421–3365* 🌐 *www.lamarcebicheria.com* 🕒 *No dinner.*

$$$$ SEAFOOD 🍴 **La Rosa Náutica.** This rambling Victorian-style complex perched over the Pacific at the end of a breakwater serves up quality seafood with spectacular views, complete with surfers riding the waves by day. Signature dishes include scallops sautéed with hot peppers, a mixed fish, scallops, and octopus *cebiche* (marinated in lime juice), and grilled corvina with a leek fondue sauce. **Known for:** great ocean views; various cebiche options; sunsets. [$] *Average main: S/72* ✉ *Espigón 4, Circuito de Playas, Miraflores* ☎ *01/445–0149* 🌐 *www.larosanautica.com.*

$$$ SWISS 🍴 **La Tiendecita Blanca.** This old-fashioned Swiss eatery first flung open its doors in 1937, and little has changed since. They still serve a selection of quality European and Peruvian cuisine in a refined atmosphere, with ornately painted wooden detail on the doors and along the ceiling that conjures up the Old Country. *Rösti* (grated potatoes with bacon and cheese) and three kinds of fondue are among the traditional Swiss options. **Known for:** three kinds of fondue; excellent three-course lunches; decadent desserts. [$] *Average main: S/60* ✉ *Av. José Larco 111, Miraflores* ☎ *01/445–9797* 🌐 *www.latiendecitablanca.com.pe.*

$$ ITALIAN 🍴 **La Trattoria di Mambrino.** After a quarter century in business, this remains one of Lima's best Italian restaurants. The proof is on the plate: delicious dishes such as artichoke ravioli and fettuccine magnifico (with a prosciutto, Parmesan, and white truffle sauce) are favorites; be sure to save room for dessert. **Known for:** homemade pastas; desserts by famous pastry chef Sandra Plevisani; dinner served on Sunday. [$] *Average main: S/49* ✉ *Larcomar, Malecón de la Reserva, 610, Miraflores* ☎ *01/447–5941* 🌐 *www.latrattoriadimambrino.com.*

$$$$ PERUVIAN Fodor's Choice ★ 🍴 **Maido.** Mitsuharu Tsumura is one of Lima's most creative chefs, and his exquisite *nikkei* (Japanese-Peruvian) creations have established Maido as one of the world's best restaurants. He changes the menu frequently, but it always includes cebiches, *nigiris* (sushi with Peruvian flavors), and dishes such as *asado de tira mitsuke* (braised short ribs with pickled ginger and fried rice), cod *misayaki* (marinated in miso with sweet potato and Brazil nuts), and *sanguichitas* (a plate of unique sandwiches). **Known for:** nikkei cuisine; 13-course tasting menu; reserve one month in advance. [$] *Average main: S/75* ✉ *Calle San Martín 399, at Calle Colón, Miraflores* ☎ *01/447–9333* 🌐 *www.maido.pe* 🕒 *No dinner Sun.*

Continued on page 84

FOOD IN PERU

by Mark Sullivan

When Peruvians talk about *comida criolla*, or typical food, they aren't talking about just one thing. This is a vast country, and dishes on the table in coastal Trujillo might be nowhere in mountainous Cusco. And all bets are off once you reach places like Iquitos, where the surrounding jungle yields exotic flavors.

REGIONAL CUISINE

THE CAPITAL
Lima cooks up the widest variety of Peruvian and international foods. One of the most influential immigrant communities is the Chinese, who serve traditional dishes in restaurants called *chifas*. One favorite, *lomo saltado*, strips of beef sautéed with onions, tomatoes, and friend potatoes, is now considered a local dish.

THE COAST
When you talk about the cuisine of the country's vast coastal region, you are talking about seafood. Peruvians are very particular about their fish, insisting that it should be pulled from the sea that morning. The most common dish is *cebiche,* raw fish "cooked" in lime juice. It comes in endless variations—all delicious.

THE ALTIPLANO
Hearty fare awaits in the altiplano. Because it keeps so well over the winter, the potato is the staple of many dishes, including the ubiquitous *cau cau*, or tripe simmered with potatoes and peppers. A special treat is *pachamanca*, a Peruvian-style barbecue where meat and potatoes are cooked in a hole in the ground lined with hot rocks. In Huancayo, the local specialty is *papa a la huancaina*, boiled potato covered in yellow chili-cheese sauce.

THE AMAZON
Fish is a staple in the Amazon, and you'll know why once you taste paiche and other species unknown outside this area. One of the best ways to try local fish is *patarashca*, or fish wrapped in bijao leaves and cooked over an open fire. Restaurants here are very simple, often just a few tables around an outdoor grill.

A woman preparing *anticuchos.*

Cebiche

IT'S ALL ABOUT THE FISH

Peru's high-altitude lakes, including Lake Titicaca, and rivers spawn some very tastey *trucha* (trout).

In Peru, restaurants known as *cebicherías* serve more than the marinated fish called cebiche. The menu may intimidate those who can't tell *lenguado* (sole) from *langosta* (lobster). Don't worry—just order a series of dishes to share. Local families pass around huge platters of *pescado* until they are picked clean, then gesture to the server for the next course.

The fragrant *parihuela* is soup overflowing with fish, shrimp, and *chorros* (mussels) still in their shells. *Tiradito* is similar to cebiche but leaves off the onions and adds a spicy yellow-pepper sauce. A platter of *chicharrones de calamar*, little ringlets of deep-fried squid, should be given a squeeze of lime. For a nice filet or whole fish, many restaurants suggest a dozen or more preparations.

ON THE SIDE

CHOCLO
A pile of large-kernel corn.

Camote
Boiled sweet potatoes. The sweetness is a wonderful contrast to the citrus marinade.

Cancha
A basket full of fried corn that's usually roasted on the premises. Highly addictive.

Chifles
A northern coast specialty of thin slices of fried banana.

Zarandajas
A bean dish served in the northern coast.

Papas
Potatoes, boiled, fritas (fried), or *puré* (mashed).

SPUD COUNTRY

POTATO ON THE PLATE

The potato, or its cousin the yucca, is rarely absent from a Peruvian table. Any restaurant offering *comida criolla*, or traditional cuisine, will doubtless serve *cau cau* (tripe simmered with potatoes and peppers), *papa a la huancaina* (potatoes in a spicy cheese sauce), or *ocopa* (boiled potatoes in peanut sauce). Just about everywhere you can find a version of *lomo saltado*, made from strips of beef sautéed with tomatoes, onions, and fried potatoes. Some 600,000 Peruvian farmers, most with small lots in the highlands, grow more than 3,250,000 tons of potatoes a year.

GET YOUR PURPLE POTATOES HERE!

Peru's potatoes appear in all colors of the spectrum, including purple, red, pink, and blue. They also come in many strange shapes.

SCIENCE POTATO

The International Potato Center (Centro Internacional de la Papa), outside of Lima, conducts spud research to help farmers and open markets, particularly for the great variety of Andean potatoes. Its genebank preserves seeds and *in vitro* plantlets of more than 10,500 potato varieties and 8,500 sweet potato varieties, in order to conserve that diversity and share it with crop breeding programs around the world.

POTATO HISTORY

The potato comes from the Andes of Peru and Chile (not Idaho or Ireland), where it has been grown on the mountain terraces for thousands of years. There are endless varieties of this durable tuber: more than 7,000 of them, some of which are hardy enough to be cultivated at 15,000 feet. The Spanish introduced potatoes to Europe in the late 1500s.

(above) Preparing *pachamanca;* (left) Discovering the potato.

OTHER STAPLES

CORN: Almost as important as potatoes is corn. You might be surprised to find that the kernels are more than twice as large as their North American friends. Most corn dishes are very simple, such as the tamale-like *humitas*, but some are more complex, like the stew called *pepián de choclo*. A favorite in the humid lowlands is *inchi capi*, a chicken dish served with peanuts and toasted corn. A sweet purple corn is the basis for *chicha morada*, a thick beverage, and *mazamorra*, an even thicker jelly used in desserts. Even ancient Peruvians loved popcorn, kernels were found in tombs 1000 years old in eastern Peru. Also discovered were ceramic popcorn poppers from 3000 AD.

PEPPERS: Few Peruvian dishes don't include *ají*, the potent hot peppers grown all over the country. You'll find several everywhere—*amarillo* (yellow pepper), *rocoto* (a reddish variety), and *panca* (a lovely chocolate brown variety), but there are hundreds of regional favorites. Some, like ají *norteño*, are named for the region of origin, others, like the cherry-sized ají *cereza*, are named for what they resemble. Such is the case with the ají *pinguita de mono*, which, roughly translated, means "small monkey penis." It is one of the hottest that you'll find.

Hot pepper tip: Never rub your eyes after handling a hot pepper, and avoid contact with your skin.

FOR ADVENTUROUS EATERS

CUY: What was served at the Last Supper? According to a baroque painting hanging in the Iglesia de San Francisco in Lima, it was guinea pig. The painting shows a platter in the middle of the table with a whole roasted guinea pig, including the head and feet.

This dish, called *cuy chactado* or simply *cuy*, has long been a staple of the altiplano. Cuy is a bit hard to swallow, mostly because it is served whole. The flavor is like pork, and can be sweet and tender if carefully cooked.

ANTICUCHOS: When a street vendor fires up his grill, the savory scent of *anticuchos* will catch your attention. Beef hearts in the Andes are a delicacy. Marinated in herbs and spices, these strips of meat are incredibly tender. They have become popular in urban areas, and you're likely to run across restaurants called *anticucherías* in Lima and other cities.

ALPACA: Nearly every visitor to Cusco and the surrounding region will be offered a steak made of alpaca. It's not an especially tasty piece of meat, which may be why locals don't eat it very often. But go ahead—you can impress the folks back home.

(Top, right) *humita*; (bottom) Peruvian eating guinea pig.

$ ✕ **Mavery.** This rustic-looking restaurant, with log walls and tables made
PIZZA from sliced tree trunks, specializes in pizza and deep-fried *empanadas*
(meat pastries), with nine fillings, ranging from the traditional *carne*
(ground beef) to *cangrejo y queso* (crabmeat and cheese). They also
have good pasta dishes, and the typical Peruvian *pastel de choclo* (corn
casserole with beef, raisins, and olives). **Known for:** popular nighttime
hangout; delicious pizzas; deep-fried empanadas. ⓢ *Average main: S/25*
✉ *Av. Del Ejercito 182, Miraflores* ☎ *01/441–3134* ⊕ *www.pastasmav-
ery.com* ⊙ *Closed Mon.*

$$$ ✕ **Panchita.** Lima's premier steak house features much more than just
STEAKHOUSE prime beef cuts: also on offer are Peruvian specialties, such as a sam-
pling of six traditional dishes called the *jarana criolla*, the best salad
bar in the city, plus a few seafood options. Beef lovers can choose
between U.S. **Known for:** excellent beef; best salad bar in the city; six-
dish sampler. ⓢ *Average main: S/59* ✉ *Av. Dos de Mayo 298, Miraflores*
☎ *01/242–5957* ⊕ *panchita.pe* ⊙ *No dinner Sun.*

$$$ ✕ **Pescados Capitales.** This vast, whitewashed restaurant with a laid-back
SEAFOOD vibe is popular with limeños, who flock here for its inventive recipes
and fresh seafood. The name is a play on the Spanish term for the seven
deadly sins, and *gula* (gluttony)—fettuccine with a mix of scallops,
shrimp, and squid in a spicy cream sauce—is one of many sins worth
committing here. **Known for:** inventive seafood dishes; busy lunches;
fresh fish. ⓢ *Average main: S/53* ✉ *Av. Mariscal La Mar 1337, Miraflores* ☎ *01/421–8808* ⊕ *www.pescadoscapitales.com* ⊙ *No dinner Sun.*

$$ ✕ **Punto Azul.** Healthy portions of quality seafood at reasonable prices is
SEAFOOD the reason there's usually a wait here. Classic Peruvian dishes such as cebi-
che, rice with seafood, and *parihuela* (a seafood soup) keep the locals com-
ing back. **Known for:** traditional seafood dishes; affordable; local favorite.
ⓢ *Average main: S/38* ✉ *Ca. San Martín 595, Miraflores* ☎ *01/445–8078*
⊕ *puntoazulrestaurante.com* ⊙ *No dinner Sun., no lunch Mon.*

$$ ✕ **Punta Sal.** On a sunny afternoon, the view of the malecón and the grace-
SEAFOOD ful paragliders from the upper floors of this restaurant is as good as the
food—which is quite good. Dishes include classic *cebichería* fare such as
tiradito criollo (thin slices of marinated fish covered in a yellow pepper
sauce), *conchitas a la parmesana* (scallops on the half shell smothered
in garlic and toasted cheese), or *pescado a la Chorrillana* (fish fillet in
a tomato, onion, and chili sauce). *Piqueos,* platters with various dishes,
are fun to share. **Known for:** classic limeño seafood; great view; packed
on weekends. ⓢ *Average main: S/42* ✉ *Malecón Cisneros at Av. Tripoli,
Miraflores* ☎ *01/242–4524* ⊕ *www.puntasal.com* ⊙ *No dinner.*

$$$ ✕ **Rafael.** This small corner house seems inconspicuous, but at mealtimes
PERUVIAN it is invariably packed with gourmands feasting on Rafael Osterling's
Fodor's Choice culinary creations. One of Lima's best chefs, Osterling mixes Peruvian,
★ Mediterranean, and Asian influences in a menu brimming with innova-
tion. **Known for:** pastas such as gnocchi with seafood; Peruvian and
Mediterranean flavors; need to reserve. ⓢ *Average main: S/64* ✉ *Ca.
San Martín 300, Miraflores* ☎ *01/242–4149* ⊕ *www.rafaelosterling.pe.*

$$ ✕ **Saqra.** The name of this attractive eatery is a Quechua word for
PERUVIAN "mischievous child," which refers to its playful variations on Peruvian
cuisine, such as gnocchi served in a *huancaina* sauce, or panko-crusted

prawns with a passion fruit ginger-pisco sauce. Start with quinua tabouleh on a tomato pesto with goat cheese, then sink your teeth into *Adobo arepiqueño* (pork loin stewed in a chili sauce), octopus on an olive risotto, or wok-fired chicken, tomatoes, and mushrooms on spaghetti. **Known for:** creative recipes; colonial-style building; pleasant terrace. $ *Average main: S/40* ⊠ *Pasaje El Suche, Av. La Paz 646, Miraflores* ☎ *01/650–8884* ⊕ *www.saqra.pe* ☽ *Closed Sun.*

$$$ ✕ **Tragaluz.** The patio tables at Tragaluz (part of the Belmond Miraflores
PERUVIAN   Park Hotel), which overlook lush Parque Domodossola, rank among Lima's most pleasant spots to enjoy a meal. The food runs a close second, with a Peruvian-international fusion menu that ranges from grilled calamari with quinua tabouleh to Thai tuna curry linguini with sautéed vegetables. **Known for:** delectable seafood dishes; verdant view; murals by Lima artist Mateo Liébana. $ *Average main: S/64* ⊠ *Belmond Miraflores Park Hotel, Los Carolinos at Malecón de la Reserva, Miraflores* ☎ *01/610–4018* ☽ *Closed 3–7 pm.*

BARRANCO

In keeping with its reputation as a bohemian neighborhood, Barranco has a slew of bars and cozy cafés, but it also has some excellent restaurants, most of which are a short walk from the neighborhood's best hotels.

$$$ ✕ **Amoramar.** Amoramar doesn't look like much from the street, but step
PERUVIAN   through the door and you'll discover an oasis of poinciana trees in a
Fodor'sChoice   restored adobe house. Seafood dominates the menu, with a selection
★   ranging from the traditional *pulpo parrilla* (grilled octopus) to creative recipes such as *atun saltado* (tuna strips sautéed with onions and aji peppers), *chaufa de quinua* (vegetarian stir-fry with quinua), and *canilla de cordero* (roast lamb in a mild chili sauce). **Known for:** excellent seafood; eclectic dining setting; best to take a taxi to and from here at night. $ *Average main: S/58* ⊠ *Jiron Garcia y Garcia 175, Barranco* ✛ *Near corner of Miraflores and Bolognesi* ☎ *01/619–9595* ⊕ *www. amoramar.com* ☽ *Closed 4–8 pm. No dinner Sun.*

$$ ✕ **Antica Pizzeria.** This Italian eatery is the place to head on a cool night,
ITALIAN   offering a rustic but warm ambience and great food. The extensive menu includes a wide array of salads and fresh pastas served with your choice of a dozen sauces, but Antica is best known for its pizza: more than 50 different kinds baked in a wood-fired oven. **Known for:** more than 50 kinds of super-thin-crust pizza; rustic ambience; great place to warm up on a cool night. $ *Average main: S/40* ⊠ *Av. Prolongación San Martín at Jr. Alfonso Ugarte, Barranco* ☎ *01/247–3443* ⊕ *www. anticapizzeria.com.pe.*

$$$ ✕ **Cala.** One of the city's few waterfront dining options, Cala has an
SEAFOOD   impressive selection of dishes to complement the ocean view. The Peruvian fusion cuisine ranges from crab ravioli in seafood soup, to quinua-crusted salmon, to tenderloin with mushrooms, quinua, and spinach. **Known for:** great seafood and sushi bar; ocean view; popular bar. $ *Average main: S/52* ⊠ *Playa Barranquita, Circuito de las Playas, Barranco* ☎ *01/477–2020* ⊕ *www.calarestaurante.com* ☽ *No dinner Sun.*

Where to Eat and Stay in Barranco

KEY

① Restaurants
① Hotels

$$$ ✕ **Isolina Taberna Peruana.** Meat lovers wait in line here for a chance to
PERUVIAN   savor chef José del Castillo's slow-cooked osso buco, *seco de asado de
tira* (short rib stew), or *costillar de cerdo a la chorrillana* (crispy pork
ribs with tomatoes and onions). It's the kind of food Peruvians have
eaten for centuries, impeccably prepared and served in a tavern set-
ting. **Known for:** traditional meat dishes; big portions; worth the wait.
$ *Average main: S/51 ⊠ Av. San Martín 101, Barranco* ☎ *01/247–5075*
⊕ *isolina.pe.*

$ ✕ **Las Mesitas.** It's easy to miss this tiny historic café half a block north
PERUVIAN   of Barranco's Parque Municipal, but it is known for serving inexpen-
sive, traditional dishes such as *carapulcra* (stewed beef and potatoes),
and *pescado a la chorrillana* (fish fillet in a tomato, onion, and aji chili
broth). Traditional limeño puddings such as *manjar de lucuma* (made
from a native fruit) or the vanilla-and-cinnamon *suspiro a la limeña*
are the best reasons to stop by. **Known for:** inexpensive set lunches;
traditional limeño desserts. $ *Average main: S/22 ⊠ Av. Grau 341, Bar-
ranco* ☎ *01/477–4199.*

$$ ✕ **Segundo Muelle.** This airy restaurant on the waterfront offers a good
SEAFOOD   introduction to traditional Peruvian seafood dishes, complete with
photos on the menu. The selection includes 10 types of cebiche, and
classics such as *pescado a lo macho* (fish fillet in a creamy seafood
sauce) *chupe de langostinos* (creamy shrimp chowder) and *jalea del*

pescador (deep-fried fish and seafood). **Known for:** traditional Peruvian seafood; ocean view; Mediterranean and Asian fare. $ *Average main: S/42* ⊠ *Circuito de playas, Blvd. Bordemar, Barranco* ☎ 01/713–0066 ⊕ *www.segundomuelle.com* ☾ *No dinner Sun. and Mon.*

$ ✕ **Songoro Cosongo.** This family-run restaurant serves the kind of tradi-
PERUVIAN tional dishes that limeños have eaten for generations, such as *anticuchos* (cow's-heart brochettes served with corn on the cob) and *sudado* (fish fillet in a spicy broth). Owner Hernan Vega doesn't strive for gourmet; he focuses on authentic cuisine. **Known for:** home-style Peruvian cooking; excellent pisco sours; owner performs music here at night. $ *Average main: S/34* ⊠ *Ayacucho 281, Barranco* ☎ 01/247–4730 ⊕ *www. songorocosongo.com.*

PUEBLO LIBRE

$$ ✕ **Café del Museo.** Sequestered inside the walls of the colonial palace
PERUVIAN that houses the Museo Larco, this is one of the most charming places in Lima to enjoy a meal. The Peruvian fusion menu offers everything from empanadas to ravioli stuffed with squash, and *seco de cordero* (stewed lamb) served with rice and beans. **Known for:** gorgeous setting; Peruvian fusion cuisine. $ *Average main: S/45* ⊠ *Museo Larco, Av. Bolivar 1515, Pueblo Libre* ☎ 01/462–4757 ⊕ *www.museolarco. org/cafedelmuseo.*

WHERE TO STAY

There's no shortage of lodging in Lima. Across the city, flags wave above the doorways to hotels, indicating that international travelers are welcome. If you have some money to spend, the capital has some astonishing accommodations. For something special, bypass the towers of glass and steel and opt instead for such charmers as the Country Club Lima Hotel, Hotel B, or Second Home Peru. *Hotel reviews have been shortened. For full information, visit Fodors.com.*

WHAT IT COSTS IN NUEVO SOLES			
$	$$	$$$	$$$$
Hotels	under S/250	S/250–S/500	S/501–S/800	over S/800

Hotel prices are the lowest cost of a standard double room in high season.

AIRPORT

$$$ 🏨 **Costa del Sol Wyndham Lima Airport.** Lima's only airport hotel makes up
HOTEL for the lack of a view with a soothing, minimalist interior, decent restaurant and a spa. **Pros:** next to the airport; comfortable rooms; spa. **Cons:** overpriced; far from Lima attractions. $ *Rooms from: S/730* ⊠ *Aeropuerto Internacional Jorge Chávez, Av. Elmer Faucett s/n* ☎ 01/711–2000 ⊕ *www.costadelsolperu.com* ⇥ *130 rooms* ⦿ *Breakfast.*

EL CENTRO

$$ ⊞ **Gran Hotel Bolívar.** Although this grande dame retains the grandeur
HOTEL of the days when guests included Ernest Hemingway, it lacks some of
the comforts and conveniences offered by newer hotels. **Pros:** historic
atmosphere; convenient location; good value. **Cons:** rooms are a bit
worn; spotty Wi-Fi coverage; no a/c or heat. *$ Rooms from: S/280*
⊠ Plaza San Martín, Jr. de la Unión 958, El Centro ☎ 01/619-7171
⊕ www.granhotelbolivar.com.pe ⤵ 99 rooms ⏇ Breakfast.

$$$ ⊞ **Sheraton Lima Hotel.** This massive hotel is removed from the city's best
HOTEL dining and nightlife options but close to the historic district and a short
drive from the airport, San Isidro, Miraflores, or Barranco. **Pros:** plenty
of amenities; close to many attractions and airport; on-site Brazilian
buffet restaurants. **Cons:** massive; far from most restaurants; lacks personality. *$ Rooms from: S/615 ⊠ Paseo de la República 170, El Centro*
☎ 01/315-5000 ⊕ www.sheratonlima.com ⤵ 430 rooms ⏇ Breakfast.

SAN ISIDRO

$$$ ⊞ **Country Club Lima Hotel.** Historic paintings from the Museo Pedro de
HOTEL Osma hang in the lobby and in each stately room of this colonial-style
Fodor's Choice hotel, which is itself a work of art. **Pros:** architectural gem; doting service;
★ excellent restaurant. **Cons:** a bit removed from the action; new wing
less charming. *$ Rooms from: S/780 ⊠ Los Eucaliptos 590, San Isidro*
☎ 01/611-9000 ⊕ www.hotelcountry.com ⤵ 82 rooms ⏇ Breakfast.

$$$ ⊞ **Delfines Hotel & Convention Center.** Once one of Lima's best, this hotel's
HOTEL star has faded slightly, but it's still a pleasant spot with good views.
Pros: quiet location; golf course views; competitive rates. **Cons:** decor
a bit dated; removed from most restaurants and bars. *$ Rooms from:*
S/565 ⊠ Los Eucaliptos 555, San Isidro ☎ 01/215-7000 ⊕ www.los-
delfineshotel.com ⤵ 205 rooms ⏇ Breakfast.

$$ ⊞ **Foresta Hotel & Suites.** With a selection of shops and restaurants within
HOTEL walking distance, this hotel offers a convenient location along with
most of the amenities—except a pool—of the city's top hotels at a much
cheaper rate. **Pros:** central location; offers discounted rates. **Cons:** chain-
hotel feel. *$ Rooms from: S/460 ⊠ Av. Libertadores 490, San Isidro*
☎ 01/630-0000 ⊕ forestahotellima.com ⤵ 60 rooms ⏇ Breakfast.

$$$ ⊞ **Hotel Atton San Isidro.** This plain cement building with square windows
HOTEL doesn't look like much from the street, but step into its sleek lobby, or
browse the menu at its chic Peruvian fusion restaurant Chabuca, and
you'll begin to see why this is one of Lima's more popular hotels. **Pros:**
friendly staff; convenient location; heated lap pool. **Cons:** nothing Peruvian about the decor. *$ Rooms from: S/520 ⊠ Av. Jorge Bassadre 595,*
San Isidro ☎ 01/208-1220 ⊕ www.atton.com ⤵ 252 rooms ⏇ Breakfast.

$$ ⊞ **Sonesta Hotel El Olívar.** Standing at the edge of an old olive grove, this
HOTEL dark-green hotel has one of the most relaxing settings in San Isidro,
especially when you experience it from the sundeck and pool on the top
floor. **Pros:** convenient location; view of the park at on-site restaurant
El Olívar; relaxing setting. **Cons:** small standard rooms; interior rooms
are dimly lit. *$ Rooms from: S/490 ⊠ Pancho Fierro 194, San Isidro*
☎ 01/712-6000 ⊕ www.sonesta.com/lima ⤵ 144 rooms ⏇ Breakfast.

WHERE SHOULD I STAY?

	Neighborhood Vibe	Pros	Cons
EL CENTRO	Colonial-era splendor	Walking distance to the city's best-known sights	Clogged with traffic by day, deserted at night
SAN ISIDRO	Mostly residential area with a few commercial strips	Peace and quiet, especially around Parque El Olivar	No major sights, a bit far from the action
MIRAFLORES	Bustling neighborhood filled with shops, restaurants, and hotels	Hundreds of dining options, nightlife, ocean views, scenic parks	Traffic noise even on side streets
BARRANCO	Bohemian, historic atmosphere, nightlife hot spot	Plenty of bars, restaurants, galleries, eye-catching architecture, ocean views	Area to the east of Metropolitano is sketchy, traffic noise

$$$$ HOTEL **Swissôtel Lima.** A popular hotel with business travelers, the Swissôtel has well-appointed rooms, excellent in-house dining, and a convenient location in an office complex a few blocks from many shops and restaurants. **Pros:** plush rooms; first-rate service; four excellent on-site dining options. **Cons:** slightly isolated location; expensive. [$] *Rooms from: S/860* ✉ *Centro Empresarial Real, Av. Santo Toribio 173, San Isidro* ☎ *01/421–4400* 🌐 *www.swissotellima.com.pe* 🛏 *345 rooms* 🍴 *No meals.*

$$$$ HOTEL **The Westin Lima Hotel and Convention Center.** This 30-story glass tower is impressive from the moment you step into the airy lobby, with its soaring walls of aluminum and glass, geometric patterns, and abundant art. **Pros:** marble baths with tubs and showers; incredible views from room; great indoor lap pool. **Cons:** far from most restaurants and sights; pricey; busy during conferences. [$] *Rooms from: S/936* ✉ *Calle Las Begonias 450, at Av. Javier Prado, San Isidro* ☎ *01/201–5000* 🌐 *www.westinlima.com* 🛏 *301 rooms* 🍴 *Breakfast.*

MIRAFLORES

$$$$ HOTEL Fodor's Choice ★ **Belmond Miraflores Park.** The spacious ocean-view rooms here overlook a verdant park, the city's coastline, and the sea beyond, a panorama that is complemented by a rooftop pool, spa, and first-class restaurant. **Pros:** ocean-view rooms worth the splurge; executive lounge access means free food and drinks; luxurious bedding. **Cons:** pricey; city-view rooms disappointing. [$] *Rooms from: S/2200* ✉ *Malecón de la Reserva 1035, Miraflores* ☎ *01/610–4000* 🌐 *www.belmond.com* 🛏 *81 rooms* 🍴 *Breakfast.*

$$ HOTEL **El Pardo Double Tree by Hilton Hotel.** The comfortable rooms, central location, rooftop pool, and large health club make this hotel a good option for travelers. **Pros:** well-stocked business center; 12 conference rooms; walking distance from Miraflores sights. **Cons:** impersonal feel. [$] *Rooms from: S/485* ✉ *Jr. Independencia 141, Miraflores* ☎ *01/617–1000* 🌐 *doubletreel3.hilton.com* 🛏 *241 rooms* 🍴 *Breakfast.*

$$$
HOTEL
⌸ **Hilton Lima Miraflores.** Located on a quiet residential street a short walk from both Larcomar and Parque Miraflores, this sleek hotel offers chic rooms with urban views and the service and amenities you'd expected from a Hilton. **Pros:** attractive rooms with spacious baths; rooftop deck with pool and Jacuzzis; charming on-site restaurant. **Cons:** mediocre views. $ *Rooms from: S/780* ⌧ *Av. La Paz 1099, Miraflores* ☎ *01/200–8000* ⊕ *www3.hilton.com* ↩ *207 rooms* ⍾ *No meals.*

$
B&B/INN
⌸ **Hostal Buena Vista.** This affordable colonial-style house furnished with antiques and hemmed by an exuberant garden is one of Lima's loveliest B&Bs. **Pros:** charming house; near restaurants and bars; complimentary breakfast. **Cons:** street noise, especially rooms 13 and 14; quality of rooms varies; lacking in service. $ *Rooms from: S/195* ⌧ *Grimaldo del Solar 202, Miraflores* ☎ *01/447–3178* ⊕ *www.hostalbuenavista.com* ↩ *19 rooms* ⍾ *Breakfast.*

$$
HOTEL
⌸ **Hostal Torreblanca.** Although this eclectic older building is a little far from the center of Miraflores, it's just a block from a park overlooking the ocean and a good option for travelers with a limited budget. **Pros:** has character; near oceanfront park. **Cons:** smallish rooms; on a busy traffic circle; far from most bars and restaurants. $ *Rooms from: S/290* ⌧ *Av. José Pardo 1453, Miraflores* ☎ *01/242–1876* ⊕ *www.torreblan-caperu.com* ↩ *24 rooms* ⍾ *Breakfast.*

$$
B&B/INN
Fodor's Choice
★
⌸ **Hotel Antigua Miraflores.** Black-and-white marble floors and crystal chandeliers greet you as you stroll through the antique-filled lobby of this salmon-color mansion, where boutique-hotel-style accommodations are surprisingly affordable. **Pros:** courtyard gardens and soothing fountains; spacious rooms; friendly and attentive staff. **Cons:** additional charge for certain breakfast items. $ *Rooms from: S/360* ⌧ *Av. Grau 350, Miraflores* ☎ *01/201–2060* ⊕ *www.antiguamiraflores.com* ↩ *81 rooms* ⍾ *Breakfast.*

$$$$
HOTEL
Fodor's Choice
★
⌸ **JW Marriott Hotel Lima.** In addition to being in the heart of the action, across the street from the Larcomar shopping mall, rooms in this gleaming glass tower have impressive ocean views. **Pros:** stunning ocean views; attractive, airy lobby lounge; indoor pool. **Cons:** corner deluxe rooms lack ocean view; Wi-Fi costs extra. $ *Rooms from: S/845* ⌧ *Malecón de la Reserva at Av. José Larco, Miraflores* ☎ *01/217–7000* ⊕ *www.marriotthotels.com* ↩ *300 rooms* ⍾ *No meals.*

$$
HOTEL
⌸ **La Paz Apart Hotel.** Most rooms here are small apartments with a dining/living room, making it popular for lengthier stays. **Pros:** close to shops and restaurants; big rooms; large windows. **Cons:** lots of street noise. $ *Rooms from: S/325* ⌧ *Av. La Paz 679, Miraflores* ☎ *01/242–9350* ⊕ *www.lapazaparthotel.com* ↩ *27 rooms* ⍾ *Breakfast.*

$$$
HOTEL
⌸ **Radisson Hotel Decapolis Miraflores.** Bright, comfortable rooms, a convenient location, and competitive rates make this hotel a good option for travelers who like high-end amenities but don't want to pay a fortune for them. **Pros:** some rooms come with ocean views; competitive rates; great on-site Peruvian fusion restaurant, Miso. **Cons:** not quite up to luxury hotel standards. $ *Rooms from: S/526* ⌧ *Av. 28 de Julio 151, Miraflores* ☎ *01/625–1200* ⊕ *www.radisson.com* ↩ *105 rooms* ⍾ *Breakfast.*

Changing of the guard, Peru-style, in front of the Palacio de Gobierno (Government Palace) in El Centro.

$

B&B/INN

San Antonio Abad. This mansion in a residential neighborhood offers atmosphere, tranquillity, and very reasonable rates; the rambling old building has common areas with colonial-style furnishings overlooking a small courtyard. **Pros:** short walk to parks, shops, and restaurants; cozy furnishings; good breakfast. **Cons:** some dated furnishings. *$ Rooms from: S/225 ⊠ Ramón Ribeyro 301, Miraflores ☎ 01/447–6766 ⊕ www.hotelsanantonioabad.com ⇆ 26 rooms |⊙| Breakfast.*

BARRANCO

$$$$

B&B/INN

Fodor'sChoice

★

Hotel B. Also known as Arts Boutique Hotel B, this boutique hotel-cum–art gallery in a refurbished, turn-of-the-century mansion in the heart of artsy Barranco is a feast for the senses with its impressive collection of works by up-and-coming Latin American artists, 1920s charm, rooftop deck, and impeccable service. **Pros:** contemporary art collection; excellent service; complimentary breakfast and afternoon tea. **Cons:** pricey; noisy. *$ Rooms from: S/1334 ⊠ San Martín 301, at Av. Sáenz Peña, Barranco ☎ 01/206–0800 ⊕ hotelb.pe ⇆ 17 rooms |⊙| Breakfast.*

$$

B&B/INN

Fodor'sChoice

★

Second Home Peru. This 100-year-old Tudor-style house on a cliff overlooking the sea and surrounded by a sculpture garden is one of Lima's loveliest lodging options. **Pros:** gorgeous setting; home of sculptor Victor Delfín; oceanfront rooms with jaw-dropping views. **Cons:** limited guest services. *$ Rooms from: S/400 ⊠ Ca. Domeyer 366, Barranco ☎ 01/247–5522 ⊕ www.secondhomeperu.com ⇆ 8 rooms |⊙| Breakfast.*

$$

B&B/INN

3B Barranco's Bed & Breakfast. Budget-watching travelers appreciate this modern B&B's sleek rooms, convenient location, and reasonable rates. **Pros:** quiet rooms; reasonable rates. **Cons:** short on personality.

$ *Rooms from: S/285* ⊠ *Jr. Centenario 130, Barranco* ☎ *01/247–6915* ⊕ *www.3bhostal.com* ⇨ *16 rooms* ◎| *Breakfast.*

$$$
B&B/INN
Fodor's Choice
★

🛏 **Villa Barranco.** Staying in this meticulously restored 1920s mansion on a quiet street near Barranco's malecón is a bit like staying with friends thanks to the laid-back atmosphere and helpful staff. **Pros:** gorgeous historic home; ocean views; friendly, helpful staff. **Cons:** some rooms have small bathrooms. $ *Rooms from: S/700* ⊠ *Ca. Carlos Zegarra 274, Barranco* ☎ *01/396–5418* ⊕ *www.ananay-hotels.com/villa-barranco* ⇨ *9 rooms* ◎| *Breakfast.*

NIGHTLIFE AND PERFORMING ARTS

Lima may not be the city that never sleeps, but it certainly can't be getting enough rest. Limeños love to go out, as you'll notice on any Friday or Saturday night. Early in the evening they gather outside movie theaters and concert halls, and late at night they're piling into taxis headed to the bars and clubs of Miraflores and Barranco.

NIGHTLIFE

EL CENTRO

BARS

El Bolivarcito. Legend has it that the pisco sour was invented by a bartender at the Gran Hotel Bolivar, and it remains a popular spot to imbibe that tangy cocktail. You can have one in El Bolivarcito, the popular bar to the right of the hotel's entrance, overlooking Plaza San Martín, or step inside and veer to the left to the main bar and restaurant, which also has tables on an elevated terrace with a street view. ⊠ *Gran Hotel Bolivar, Jr. de la Unión 958, El Centro* ☎ *01/619–7171.*

SAN ISIDRO

BARS

Chocolate Bar. Above the restaurant Como Agua Para Chocolate, Chocolate Bar has the best selection of tequila in Lima and serves a great margarita. ⊠ *Pancho Fierro 108, San Isidro* ☎ *01/222–0174.*

Lima 27. This popular restaurant also features a low-lighted lounge in front, and a lively back patio. ⊠ *Calle Santa Luisa 295, San Isidro* ☎ *01/422–8915* ⊕ *www.lima27.com.*

MIRAFLORES

BARS

Huaringas. Occupying several floors of a lovely old house next to the restaurant Brujas de Cachiche, Huaringas is a pleasant place for a drink, though it can get packed on weekends. ⊠ *Ovalo Bolognesi 460, Miraflores* ☎ *01/243–8151* ⊕ *huaringas.com/.*

La Cuina de Bonilla. One of a dozen bars on Calle Manuel Bonilla, La Cuina is known for its ample selection of tapas—from mushrooms sautéed with garlic to *tortilla española* (Spanish omelet)—and selection of microbrewery beers, but the tables out front are a nice spot for a drink. ⊠ *Ca. Manuel Bonilla 124, Miraflores* ☎ *01/241–2189* ⊕ *www.lacuina.pe.*

Peña Party

A great way to experience Peruvian folk music and dance is to visit a *peña:* a bar and restaurant that offers *música criolla,* rhythmic ballads performed with guitars and *cajones* (wooden boxes used for percussion), *huaynos* (Andean folk music), and folk dances from the country's coastal and Andean regions.

La Candelaria. Drawing a mix of locals and foreigners, La Candelaria is located in an attractive art deco building a couple blocks east of Barranco's Parque Municipal. The restaurant opens at 9 pm and shows combining the folklore of the coast, mountains, and jungle start at 10:30 on Friday and Saturday night, and end around 2 am. There's a cover charge for the show, and food and drink are à la carte. ⊠ *Av. Bolognesi 292, Barranco* ☎ *01/247–1314* ⊕ *www.lacandelariaperu.com.*

La Dama Juana. The most tourist-friendly peña, La Dama Juana offers 90-minute shows in an atmospheric Spanish colonial-style building in Barranco. Performances start at 8:30 pm, and a traditional Peruvian buffet is served from 7:30 to 10 pm. They also have a Sunday afternoon show that starts at 2:30; the buffet opens at 12:20. ⊠ *Av. República de Panama 230, Barranco* ☎ *01/248-7547* ⊕ *ladamajuana.com.pe.*

Marcelino Restaurante Peña Show. Though this restaurant and bar on Miraflores's *Calle de las Pizzas* has little to offer during the week, later on Friday and Saturday nights it becomes a *peña,* attracting an almost exclusively Peruvian crowd that comes for the traditional musica criolla and Afro-Peruvian sounds. The show starts at 11:30 pm and ends at 2:00 am. ⊠ *Calle de las Pizzas, Pasaje San Ramón 260, Miraflores* ☎ *934–098–157.*

Sachún. With more than three decades in business, Sachún's mix of Andean folk dancing and musica criolla draws a predominantly older crowd. ⊠ *Av. del Ejército 657, Miraflores* ☎ *01/441–4465.*

Nuevo Mundo Draft Bar. This second-floor pub in the heart of Miraflores sells draft and bottled beers from several microbreweries. Window tables and a small balcony afford nice views of Parque Miraflores. ⊠ *Av. Larco 421, Miraflores* ☎ *01/249–5268.*

Sukha. The giant Buddha statue that presides over this vast, airy club and Asian appetizers may seem a bit out of place, but this place is quite popular, in part because they don't charge a cover. There's often a good DJ, and even though there's no dance floor, people dance wherever there's room as the night progresses. ⊠ *Ca. Dos de Mayo 694, Miraflores* ☎ *01/223–1542* ⊕ *www.sukha.pe.*

DANCE CLUBS

Gotica. Down several flights of stairs from the lower level of the Larcomar Shopping Center is this cavernous dance club, one of Lima's top spots for electronic music. The club and the shopping center are built into a cliff, so if you need a dance break, step out back and you'll enjoy a sweeping view of the Lima coast. It's open Thursday to Saturday from 11 pm to 5 am, and the cover charge is S/100. ⊠ *Larcomar, Malecón de la Reserva 610, next to Pardos, Miraflores* ☎ *01/256–2320* ⊕ *www.gotica.com.pe.*

Son de Cuba. There are plenty of places to dance in Miraflores, but this Cuban-owned bar on the Calle de las Pizzas is among the most entertaining. On weekends, it offers salsa classes from 7 to 9, and a live band plays Cuban beats from 11:30 pm to 2:30 am. A DJ spins Latin dance music the rest of the time. ⊠ *Calle San Ramon 277, Miraflores* ☎ *941–494–941.*

GAY AND LESBIAN CLUBS

Downtown Vale Todo. After midnight, head to one of Lima's most popular dance clubs, Downtown Vale Todo, which draws a young, largely LGBT crowd. A balcony filled with comfy couches overlooks the cavernous dance floor, where revelers move and mingle. Not only do they open early (9 pm), but they close late, with drag queens performing around 3 am on weekends. ⊠ *Pasaje Los Pinos 160, Miraflores* ☎ *01/446–8222* ⊕ *www.mundovaletodo.com.*

Legendaris. With its big dance floor and convenient location a few blocks west of Parque Miraflores's southern end, Legendaris is a popular weekend spot, drawing a young, mostly gay and lesbian crowd. Open Thursday through Sunday. ⊠ *Calle Berlin 351, Miraflores* ☎ *01/446–3435.*

LIVE MUSIC

Cocodrilo Verde. Two blocks west of Parque Kennedy, Cocodrilo Verde features some of Peru's best musicians and visiting acts that play everything from jazz to salsa to bossa nova. Shows start anytime between 9 pm to 11 pm, depending on the night. ⊠ *Francisco de Paula Camino 226, Miraflores* ☎ *01/242–7583* ⊕ *www.cocodriloverde.com.*

El Tayta. On the second floor of an old building across from Parque Kennedy, El Tayta has live guitar from duos or trios that play mostly Latin pop. ⊠ *Av. José Larco 437, Miraflores* ☎ *01/444–3317* ⊕ *www. eltayta.com.*

Jazz Zone. It's easy to miss the Jazz Zone, hidden in a colonial-style shopping complex called El Suche. Head up a bright red stairway to the dimly lit second-story lounge for performances of everything from Latin jazz to blues to flamenco, with salsa or other dance music on weekends. Shows start at 10:30. ⊠ *Av. La Paz 656, Miraflores* ☎ *01/241–8139* ⊕ *www.jazzzoneperu.com.*

BARRANCO

BARS

Ayahuasca. The refurbished 19th-century mansion that houses Ayahuasca would be worth visiting even if it wasn't Barranco's chicest bar. The wild decor—it is named for the hallucinogen used by Amazonian tribes—and light menu only adds to the allure. ⊠ *Av. Prolongación San Martín 130, Barranco* ☎ *981–044–745* ⊕ *www.ayahuascarestobar.com.*

Barranco Beer Company. Bored with Peru's beer selection? This microbrewery a block north of Barranco's Parque Municipal not only offers several house brews, but also has sandwiches on home-baked bread, empanadas, and blue-corn pizza. ⊠ *Av. Grau 308, Barranco* ☎ *01/247–6211* ⊕ *barrancobeer.com.*

Juanito. Facing Barranco's main square is Juanito, one of the neighborhood's most venerable establishments, though it is rather bare-bones and bohemian. Built by Italian immigrants in 1905, the former pharmacy is packed nightly with limeños drawn by the cheap drinks, historic setting, and ham sandwiches. ⊠ *Grau 274, Barranco.*

La Posada del Mirador. When you're in Barranco, a pleasant place to start off the evening is La Posada del Mirador, at the end of the path behind La Ermita. The bar has a second-story balcony that looks out to sea, making this a great place to watch the sunset or enjoy a nightcap. ⊠ *Ca. Ermita 104, Barranco* ☎ *01/256–1796.*

Picas. In a remodeled old building next to the Puente de los Suspiros, Picas is the hippest bar on the Bajada de Baños. There are usually DJs on weekends, when it gets so crowded that it feels like dancing in an elevator. It also has a decent kitchen, perfect for a late-night snack. ⊠ *Bajada de Baños 340, Barranco* ☎ *01/252–8095* ⊕ *www.picas.com.pe.*

Piselli. This lovely little bar in an adobe building one block south of Barranco's main square is a memorable spot for a drink, with its high beamed ceilings and glass cabinets filled with liquor bottles. Nights draw a substantial crowd. ⊠ *Av. 28 de Julio, Barranco* ☎ *01/252–6750.*

Santos Café & Espirituosos. Popular with a young crowd, Santos occupies one floor of a historic building up the steps from the Puente de los Suspiros. Its long balcony overlooking the Bajada de los Baños affords one of the best views in Barranco. ⊠ *Jr. Zepita 203, Barranco.*

DANCE CLUBS

Rustica. In the back of this restaurant on the Parque Municipal is an airy bar with a big dance floor that gets packed on weekend nights, when DJs spin Latin and international hits. ⊠ *Parque Municipal 105–107, Barranco* ☎ *998/191–720.*

Victoria Bar. With outdoor seating on the porch and terrace of this restored mansion built in 1905, and a cozy indoor cellar bar, Victoria Bar offers both intimate and lively options, along with its Old Barranco setting, trendy crowds, and excellent cocktails. DJs spin dance music on weekend nights. ⊠ *Av. Pedro de Osma 135, Barranco* ☎ *01/247–2180.*

LIVE MUSIC

La Noche. La Noche is in a funky old house at the far end of the pedestrian street lined with bars known as El Boulevard de Barranco. The building includes a theater with a separate entrance (and admission fee) where local rock, Latin pop, and jazz bands perform. It's a great place for a drink even if you don't see the show. ⊠ *Sanchez Carrion 307, at Bolognesi, Barranco* ☎ *01/247–1012* ⊕ *www.lanoche.com.pe.*

Posada del Ángel. Posada del Ángel is decorated with a wild collection of antiques and art, including statues of angels. It's one of the few bars in Barranco suited to conversation, and guitarists perform Latin American classics from 10 pm to 2 am. The bar has two more locations just down the street at Prolongación San Martín 157 and Avenida Pedro de Osma 222. ⊠ *Av. Pedro de Osma 164, Barranco* ☎ *01/247–0341.*

PERFORMING ARTS

MUSIC

Auditorio Los Incas. Peru's Orquestra Sinfónica Nacional (Naional Symphony), and Conjunto Nacional de Folklore (Folk Dancing Company) perform in the Auditorio Los Incas, in the Ministerio de Cultura building. ⊠ *Museo de la Nación, Av. Javier Prado Este 2465, San Borja* ☎ *01/618–9393.*

Centro Cultural Juan Parra del Riego. This small cultural center in a historic building in the heart of Barranco sponsors exhibitions by local artists and other activities. ⊠ *Av. Pedro de Osma 135, Barranco* ☎ *01/247–8643.*

Centro Cultural Ricardo Palma. There is always something going on at the Centro Cultural Ricardo Palma, a municipal cultural center three blocks south of La Municipalidad de Miraflores. It hosts nightly concerts, dance performances or plays at very affordable prices. ⊠ *Av. José Larco 770, Miraflores* ☎ *01/617–7266.*

Instituto Cultural Peruano Norteamericano. The Instituto Cultural Peruano Norteamericano offers frequent concerts ranging from jazz to classical, as well as dance and theater. ⊠ *Av. Angamos Oeste and Av. Arequipa, Miraflores* ☎ *01/706–7000* ⊕ *cultural.icpna.edu.pe.*

SHOPPING

Hundreds of stores around Lima offer traditional crafts of varying quality. The same goes for silver and gold jewelry. Wander down Avenida La Paz in Miraflores and you'll be astounded at the number of shops selling silverware and jewelry; the street also has several antiques dealers. Miraflores is also full of crafts shops, many of them along Avenida Petit Thouars. For upscale merchandise, many people now turn to the boutiques of San Isidro. For original works of art and the highest quality of handicrafts, Barranco has excellent small galleries.

EL CENTRO

MARKETS

Mercado Central. The official name is Mercado Municipal Gran Mariscal Ramón Castilla, but limeños simply call this massive market the Mercado Central. Its hundreds of vendors display the ingredients of the city's varied cuisine, including hooks hung with slabs of meat and poultry and trays piled high with seafood. Wheels of cheese are stacked above tubs of olives, open sacks hold everything from dried potato chunks to ají peppers, and bundles of spices lie next to natural remedies. ⊠ *Jr. Ucayali 640, at Jr. Ayacucho, El Centro* ☎ *01/427–5182.*

The courtyard of the mansion-museum Casa Riva-Agüero in El Centro

SAN ISIDRO

CLOTHING

Kuna. Kuna offers an array of quality alpaca wool clothing, from ponchos to coats, with bright colors and some of the nicest designs in the country. ⊠ *Av. Jorge Bassadre Grohmann 380, San Isidro* ☎ *01/440–2320* ⊕ *kuna.com.pe.*

HANDICRAFTS

Indigo. On a quiet street in San Isidro, Indigo invites you to wander through at least half a dozen different rooms filled with unique items. There's a selection of whimsical ceramics inspired by traditional designs, as well as modern pieces. In the center of it all is an open-air café. ⊠ *Av. El Bosque 260, San Isidro* ☎ *01/440-3099* ⊕ *www.galeriaindigo.com.pe.*

JEWELRY

Ilaria. If you're looking for silver jewelry, gifts, or household items, you can't do better than the chic designs of Ilaria, which also has small shops at Calle Los Eucaliptos 578, next to the Country Club Lima Hotel, in the lobby of The Westin, and at the airport. ⊠ *Av. Dos de Mayo 308, San Isidro* ☎ *01/512-3530* ⊕ *www.ilariainternational.com.*

MIRAFLORES

ANTIQUES

Avenida La Paz is the best street for rare antique finds in Miraflores.

El Frailero. Brooding saints dominate the walls of this small shop on Avenida La Paz, which also has some interesting ceramic and silver figures. Open only for a few hours in the afternoon and evening, the owners live nearby and are happy to open the store at other times if you give them a call. ⊠ *Av. La Paz 551, Miraflores* ☎ *999–691–029.*

El Nazareno. One of several small antiques shops in the Pasaje El Suche (a small, colonial-style complex), El Nazareno has an eclectic selection of antique statues and religious art, as well as handicrafts such as woven rugs. ⊠ *Av. La Paz 646, No. 5, Miraflores* ☎ *01/447–8344.*

La Linea del Tiempo. This store offers a mix of old and new in two small shops in the Pasaje El Suche complex; the main store sells antique paintings, ceramics, and other collectables, whereas a smaller shop on Av. La Paz has new jewelry, paintings, and sculptures. ⊠ *Av. La Paz 646 tienda 4, Miraflores* ☎ *01/241–5461.*

CLOTHING

All Alpaca. One of several shops in Miraflores specializing in alpaca clothing, All Alpaca sells sophisticated sweaters, ponchos, coats, and more. There's a second shop at Avenida José Larco 1005. ⊠ *Av. Schell 377, Miraflores* ☎ *01/446–0565.*

Alpaca 859. This colorful store in the heart of Miraflores's shopping district has some lovely clothing, as well as a small selection of hand-woven tapestries. ⊠ *Av. José Larco 859, Miraflores* ☎ *01/447–7163.*

Kuna. Lots of stores stock clothing made of alpaca, but Kuna is one of the few to also offer a few articles made from vicuña, a cousin of the llama that produces the world's finest and most expensive wool. They offer an excellent selection of scarves, sweaters, shawls, and coats in an array of colors and styles. Kuna has a second shop in the Larcomar shopping center in Miraflores. ⊠ *Av. Larco 671, Miraflores* ☎ *01/447–1623* ⊕ *www.kuna.com.pe.*

Sol Alpaca. Conveniently located on busy Avenida José Larco, this popular shop offers a colorful mix of alpaca clothing with lovely designs. The selection includes sweaters, shawls, coats, hats, and scarves. They also have shops in the Larcomar shopping center and in the JW Marriott Hotel ⊠ *Av. José Larco 847, Miraflores* ☎ *01/651–7453* ⊕ *www.solalpaca.com.*

HANDICRAFTS

Agua y Tierra. Ceramics, hand-painted or embroidered fabrics, and other handicrafts of the country's Amazonian tribes decorate the windows of this small shop two blocks east of Parque Miraflores, but it also has some Andean handicrafts. ⊠ *Diez Canseco 298, at Alcanfores, Miraflores* ☎ *01/444–6980.*

Andean Treasures. Two blocks north of Larcomar on Avenida José Larco is this modern shop with a selection of quality alpaca clothing and handicrafts that include jewelry, mini *retablos* from Ayacucho and *toritos de pucará* (ceramic bulls from the Puno region). ⊠ *Av. José Larco 1219, Miraflores* ☎ *01/243–2627.*

Fodor's Choice ★ **La Floristeria.** The tiny but charming La Floristeria, in the front the Pasaje El Suche complex, is packed with quality handicrafts from a select group of artisans: hand-painted trays, *retablos ayacuchanas* packed with ceramic figures, jewelry, weavings, candles, and other colorful collectables. ⊠ *Av. La Paz 644, Miraflores* ☎ *01/444–2288.*

JEWELRY

H. Stern. It's unlikely you'll find gold jewelry elsewhere as distinctive as the pieces at H. Stern. The well-regarded South American chain specializes in designs influenced by pre-Columbian art. There are also branches in the Larco Herrera Museum, the Miraflores Park Hotel, and the airport. ⊠ *JW Marriott Hotel Lima, Malecón de la Reserva at Av. José Larco, ground fl., Miraflores* ☎ *01/242–3610* ⊕ *www.hstern.net.*

MALLS

Larcomar. Right in the heart of things is Larcomar, a surprisingly appealing open-air shopping center in Miraflores. It's built into the cliff at the end of Avenida José Larco, so it's almost invisible from the street. The dozens of shops, bars, and restaurants are terraced, and some of them have impressive views of the coast and ocean below. ⊠ *Malecón de la Reserva and Av. José Larco, Miraflores* ☎ *01/625–4343* ⊕ *www.larcomar.com.*

MARKETS

On the northern edge of Miraflores, Avenida Petit Thouars has half a dozen markets crammed with vendors, who will expect you to bargain.

La Portada del Sol. Excellent quality goods can be found at La Portada del Sol. In this miniature mall the vendors show off their wares in glass cases lighted with halogen lamps. Some accept credit cards. ⊠ *Av. Petit Thouars 5411, at Ricardo Palma, Miraflores.*

Mercado Indios. Ask a local about the best place for handicrafts and you'll probably be told to go to Mercado Indios. The selection ranges from mass-produced souvenirs to one-of-a-kind pieces, and since most vendors will bargain, you can often get a very good deal. ⊠ *Av. Petit Thouars 5245, Miraflores.*

BARRANCO

HANDICRAFTS

Fodor's Choice ★ **Dédalo.** Housed in a restored mansion on Barranco's stately Avenida Sáenz Peña, Dédalo specializes in contemporary work, as opposed to the traditional handicrafts sold by most shops. It is packed with the colorful creations of dozens of independent artists and artisans, including an impressive selection of jewelry. The little café in the back garden is a pleasant spot to take a break from exploring Barranco. ⊠ *Av. Sáenz Peña 295, Barranco* ☎ *01/652–5400.*

Las Pallas. On a quiet street one block east of busy Avenida Grau, this shop is in the home of Mari Solari, who has been selling handcrafted goods and folk art for decades. She works with some of the best artisans in the Andes and Amazon Basin. Ring the doorbell and someone will let you in. ⊠ *Cajamarca 212, Barranco* ☎ *01/477–4629.*

ELSEWHERE AROUND LIMA

MALLS

Jockey Plaza. With more than 200 shops, Jockey Plaza is by far the city's largest mall. ⊠ *Av. Javier Prado 4200, Surco* ☎ *01/716–2000* ⊕ *jockeyplaza.com.pe.*

SPORTS AND THE OUTDOORS

BEACHES

Lima's beaches can be nice to walk along in the winter (June to September), when it is too cold to swim. In the summer (December to May), they are mobbed with locals whose picnics often end up in litter along the beach and sea. In general the sand is dark gray and the sea is rough, and there are rip currents. The water is better suited to surfing than swimming.

BARRANCO

Playa Barranquito. A short walk north of the pedestrian bridge at the bottom of Barranco's Bajada de Baños, this narrow beach is one of Lima's most popular. The sand is dark gray, and when the sea is rough it is unsafe for swimming. That doesn't keep Playa Barranquito from getting packed from December to April, when vendors stroll through the crowd selling snacks (which could result in littering on the beach). It's a quiet spot the rest of the year except for the cries of seagulls and the rumble of cars passing on the Circuito de Playas. **Amenities:** food and drink, parking (fee); toilets. **Best for:** sunset; walking. ⊠ *Circuito de Playas, ½ km (¼ mile) north of Bajada de los Baños, Barranco.*

CHORRILLOS

Playa Agua Dulce. The nicest of Lima's public beaches, Playa Agua Dulce is a wide swath of gray sand that slopes into calm water. It gets packed from December to April, when vendors wander through the crowd and families enjoy picnic lunches. **Amenities:** parking, toilets. **Best for:** sunset; walking. ⊠ *Circuito de Playas, 1 km (½ mile) south of Bajada los Baños, Chorrillos.*

ELSEWHERE AROUND LIMA

FAMILY **Punta Hermosa.** Getting here might not be most scenic drive, but it is worth the trip. When the waves are big, surfers ride the break on the beach's northern end. The northern end of the beach gets packed on summer weekends, when it's worthwhile to walk to the southern end. There is a small selection of restaurants at the northern end that offer fresh seafood with an ocean view. ⚠ **The rip currents can be dangerous, especially when the waves are bigger. Amenities:** food and drink. **Best for:** surfing; swimming; walking. ⊠ *Km 40, Panamericana Sur, Punta Hermosa.*

NAZCA AND THE SOUTHERN COAST

WELCOME TO NAZCA AND THE SOUTHERN COAST

TOP REASONS TO GO

★ **Mysteries in the Desert:** Marvel over the mysterious Nazca Lines, giant shapes and figures etched into the desert floor by an enigmatic ancient civilization and best seen from the sky.

★ **Island Life:** Boats cruise around the Islas Ballestas for viewing sea lions, condors, flamingos, and millions of guano-producing seabirds in the Paracas National Reserve.

★ **Wine and Pisco Tasting:** Go wine tasting in the grape-growing valleys near Lunahuaná, Chincha, and Ica and sample Peru's most famous drink, pisco, in the best *bodegas* (traditional wineries).

★ **Seaside Luxury:** Sprawling luxury coastal resorts have sprung up in Paracas. Kick back at the spa or infinity pool and enjoy these posh palaces as bases for exploring area attractions.

★ **Sandboarding:** Test your nerve and skill by sandboarding down the giant dunes at the oasis town of Huacachina, then nurse your injuries in the lagoon's magical healing waters.

1 North of Pisco. Escape from the noise and chaos in Lima by heading to the gorgeous Lunahuaná River valley, or by exploring the Inca burial site at Tambo Colorado. You'll find whitewater rafting on Class IV rapids, and more relaxing opportunities, too—like chilling out with a plate of *langostinos* (shrimp) while sipping pisco from a rustic distillery.

Pucusana · TO LIMA, PUNTA HERMOSA & PUNTA ROCAS
Puerto Viejo · Mala
Asia
Quilmaná · Lunahuaná Valley
Punta Corriene · Lunahuaná
Cerro Azul · 24
San Vicente de Cañete · Imperial
Cinco Cruces
Chincha
ISLAS DE CHINCHA · Bahía Paracas · San Clemente
ISLAS BALLESTAS · Pisco · Hum
Puerto San Martín · Paracas
ISLAS SAGAYÁI · Pozo Sante
Paracas Península
Paracas National Reserve ♦
Laguna Grande
Punta Carreta
Bahía Independencia · Carhua
ISLA INDEPENDENCIA
Punta Grande
Punta de Asma
Faro del Infie
TABLASA DE
PACIFIC OC

2 Pisco and the Paracas Peninsula. Rugged beaches and tiny rocky islands swarm with amazing wildlife on this part of the Peruvian coast, where a new wave of modern resorts has reenergized the shoreline. A recent tourism development has been the cruise ships that dock at Puerto San Martín and spend a day or two in the area.

3 Ica and Nazca. Lush wine-producing valleys, peaceful desert oases, and the enigmatic signs of some of the world's most fascinating ancient cultures hide amid the arid coastal desert in this fascinating corner of Peru. Taste increasingly good wines and potent piscos in Ica, test your skills on a sandboard in Huacachina, and tackle the mysteries of the Nazca Lines in Nazca.

GETTING ORIENTED

3

Southern Peru is connected to Lima by the Panamericana (Pan-American Highway), which runs down the coast to Pisco and the Paracas Peninsula before cutting inland to Ica and Nazca. Between Lima and Pisco are a variety of small coastal towns, all just off the Panamericana. Towns are laid out in the usual Spanish-colonial fashion around a central Plaza de Armas. This is usually a good place to look for services such as banks, lodgings, and transportation.

Updated
by Michael
Gasparovic

From vineyards to rolling sand dunes, surf beaches to rocky islands teeming with wildlife, the area south of Lima is wild and fascinating. This region was home to the Nazca, a pre-Columbian civilization that created the enigmatic Nazca Lines. Hundreds of giant diagrams depicting animals, humans, and perfectly drawn geometric shapes are etched into the desert floor over areas so vast that they can be seen properly only from the air.

The mystery of how, why, and for whom the Nazca Lines were created is unexplained, although theories range from irrigation systems to launch pads for alien spacecraft.

This is also where the Paracas culture arrived as early as 1300 BC and over the next thousand years established a line of fishing villages that still exist today. The Paracas people are long gone, and the Inca Empire conquered the region in the 16th century, yet the Paracas left behind some of Peru's most advanced weavings, ceramics, stone carvings, metal jewelry, and thousands of eerie cemeteries in the desert.

Yet it's not all ancient civilizations, pottery, and mysterious drawings. With a sunny climate, great wines, and charming fishing villages, this region has been a favorite vacation destination for generations of *limeños* eager to escape the big city. It's also been a commercial hub. For years during the mid-19th century, the region was the center of Peru's riches, which took the rather odorous form of guano—bird droppings (found in vast quantities on the islands off the coast of Paracas) that are a rich source of natural fertilizer. Shipped to North America and Europe from the deepwater port of Pisco, the trade proved so lucrative that there was even a war over it—the Guano War of 1864–66, in which Spain battled Peru for possession of the nearby Chincha Islands.

Today the region capitalizes on its natural beauty, abundant wildlife, and enigmatic archaeological sites to draw tourists from all parts of the world.

PLANNING

WHEN TO GO

Although the weather in southern Peru is fairly even and arid throughout the year, the best time to visit is in summer and autumn, November through April, when the rivers are ripe for rafting and kayaking and harvest festivals spice up the small towns. Around Christmas, Carnaval, the grape harvest, Easter, the mid-June religious festivals, and Peru's independence day in July, hotels are often booked to capacity.

FESTIVALS

Ica is a good place to experience local culture in celebratory mood, with several festivals during the year, including Carnaval in February, Ica Week in mid-June, and the Ica Tourist Festival in late September. The Fiesta de la Vendimia (Harvest Festival), at the start of the grape-pressing season, is a highlight.

El Señor de Luren. On the third Monday in October and again at Easter, Ica's streets are lined with carpets of flowers for an overnight pilgrimage, in which thousands of the faithful go in procession with a highly illuminated image of "El Señor" (Christ), said to have come ashore here after a shipwreck in the mid-16th century. ⊠ *Ica.*

Fiesta de la Vendimia. In early March, the grape harvest heralds this week-long celebration of the local wine industry, with winery visits, grape-stomping contests, an agricultural fair, entertainment, a beauty pageant, a parade, and fireworks. ⊠ *Ica* ⊕ *www.facebook.com/vendimiadeica.pe.*

Fiesta de Verano Negro. Afro-Peruvian culture is the focus of this celebration in Chincha in late February and early March, with music, dance, food, and other events. Look for El Alcatraz dance, in which a male dancer tries to set his partner's cloth tail on fire with a candle. ⊠ *Chincha.*

GETTING HERE AND AROUND

With the Panamericana following the coastline all the way to Chile, southern Peru is prime territory to explore by road. Bus travel is easy and inexpensive. Larger companies such as Cruz del Sur, Peru Bus, and Oltursa serve all major towns. Minivans, called *combis,* and share taxis shuttle between smaller towns and usually depart from the Plaza de Armas.

AIR TRAVEL

Although there has been talk of building an international airport near Pisco for years, right now there are only landing strips in Nazca and Paracas that do not accept commercial traffic. The nearest airport to this region is in Lima, where ground transportation can be arranged via bus or tour operator.

BUS TRAVEL

Numerous companies work the route from Lima to Arequipa. Always take the best service you can afford: aside from the comfort issue, cheaper carriers have less stringent safety standards, and the section of highway between Nazca and Cusco is notorious for robbery, especially on overnight services. Cruz del Sur, Oltursa, Peru Bus, and Ormeño provide the most reliable service and have the most departures from Ica, whereas the quality of vehicles and onboard service is notoriously patchy with other operators.

CAR TRAVEL

The Pan-American Highway runs the length of southern Peru, some of it along the coast, some through desert, and some over plateaus and mountains. It's paved and in good condition, but be sure to have fully equipped first-aid and repair kits. Besides breakdowns, hazards include potholes, rock slides, sandstorms, and heat. You'll find many service stations along this route, most of which have clean bathrooms and convenience stores. Off the highway, conditions are less predictable. Roads may be poor in the eastern highlands and around the Paracas Reserve. Four-wheel-drive vehicles are recommended for all driving except on the main highway and within major cities.

Your only real options to rent a car are in Lima or Arequipa.

HEALTH AND SAFETY

The main health advice for the rest of Peru also applies to this region: don't drink the water (or use ice), and don't eat raw or undercooked food.

Theft can be a problem in crowded tourist areas, such as beaches or on economy-class transportation. Police are helpful to most foreign travelers, but procedures can be slow, so take care with your valuables. If you lose something important, like your passport, report it to the police and to your embassy.

RESTAURANTS

Casual dress is the order of the day. Reservations are seldom necessary. If you're on a budget, look for the excellent-value set menus at lunchtime, where a three-course meal can be as little as S/10. Throughout the south seafood is king, and you will never be far from a plate of *cebiche* or *camarones* (shrimp). In Chincha and rural villages closer to Lima, there's Afro-Peruvian fare like *tacu tacu*, a mass of seasoned, pan-fried rice and beans. In Ica, try *tejas*, candies made of *manjar blanco*, a sweet, pudding-like milk spread. A treat available only during harvest festivals is *cachina*, a partially fermented wine.

HOTELS

Accommodations in southern Peru range from luxury resorts to spartan *hostals* that run less than S/30 per night. Top-rated hotels usually have more than standard amenities, which might include such on-site extras as a spa, sports facilities, and business and travel services, and such room amenities as minibars, safes, faxes, or data ports. Midrange hotels might have only some of the extras. There are also basic accommodations, which may have shared baths or be outside the central tourist area. If you're arriving without a reservation, most towns have accommodations around the Plaza de Armas or bus and train stations. *Hotel reviews have been shortened. For full information, visit Fodors.com.*

WHAT IT COSTS IN NUEVO SOLES				
	$	$$	$$$	$$$$
Restaurants	under S/35	S/35–S/50	S/51–S/65	over S/65
Hotels	under S/250	S/250–S/500	S/501–S/800	over S/800

Restaurant prices are the average cost of a main course at dinner or, if dinner is not served, at lunch. Hotel prices are the lowest cost of a standard double room in high season.

NORTH OF PISCO

Tired of the noise, smog, and traffic chaos of Lima? A couple of hours' drive south is all that's required to leave behind any trace of the big city. Tranquil fishing villages, opportunities for white-water rafting, and even some significant Inca ruins are highlights of this easily accessible section of the Peruvian coast. This area is the favored weekend getaway for many *limeños*, some of whom have grand summer residences that are often in gated communities, separate from the homes of local fishermen and farmers. Follow their lead and head south to enjoy the sun, smog-free air, and overflowing plates of hearty *criollo* cooking.

GETTING HERE AND AROUND

Traveling from town to town is easy in this part of Peru—distances are short and no town is more than an hour or so from the last. ■TIP➜ **Car rental is a convenient way to get around, although you'll have to organize this in Lima, as there are no rental services between Lima and Arequipa.** If you don't have a rental car, hotels and travel agencies in Ica and Paracas offer four-hour tours of Tambo Colorado for around S/80.

Minibuses (called *combis*) shuttle between most towns and are the cheapest, although not the most comfortable, way of getting around. Look on the side of the combi for the painted signs displaying its route. If you choose to travel by taxi, agree on a price before setting off.

From Cerro Azul, combis depart to Cañete from the Plaza de Armas for S/3. To get to Lunahuaná, take a combi from Cañete to Imperial for S/1, then another combi to Lunahuaná for S/5. Soyuz and Flores both offer a bus service between Cañete and Pisco for S/5.

CERRO AZUL

71 km (45 miles) south of Pucusana; 15 km (9 miles) north of Cañete.

"*Aquí está tranquilo*" say the locals, and tranquil it certainly is in this small fishing town, made famous by the Beach Boys' song "Surfin' Safari," between Cañete and Pucusana. The hustle and bustle of the old days, when the town made its living as a port for the exportation of guano and pisco, is long gone, and now the only industry you'll see is the fishermen repairing their nets down by the waterfront.

Limeños trickle in on the weekends, arriving as much for the town's charmingly off-beat character as for the peace and quiet. On the weekend the local brass band parades through the streets before and after the church services. The local church, instead of ringing its bell, sets off fireworks in the Plaza de Armas as an unconventional call to prayer.

Walk along the waterfront where fish restaurants dish up deliciously fresh cebiche; then, if you're not too full, scramble over the dunes behind the pink-and-green former customs house to find what remains of the ancient Inca sea-fort of Huarco. In the evenings head to the plaza, where several tiny restaurants serve soups and *chifa* (Chinese/Peruvian fusion cuisine) for a little over S/7.

GETTING HERE AND AROUND

Any bus heading south from Lima will pass by Cerro Azul (S/10–S/15 depending on the bus) on the Pan-American Highway, from where you can catch a combi for S/1 or mototaxi for S/6 to the center.

EXPLORING

Huarco. The ruins of this pre-Hispanic fort are minimal, but they conceal a tragic history. The Huarco were a tiny seaside kingdom that resisted the incursions of the Inca Empire in the 15th century. After the Inca surrounded them, they walled themselves up in this fort and threw themselves into the sea rather than surrender. All that remains are crumbling walls overlooking a precipitous cliff. ⊠ *Cerro Azul.*

ASIA

145 km (90 miles) south of Lima; 125 km (78 miles) north of Pisco.

This is Peru's version of the Hamptons. During the summer months, from about Christmas to March, much of middle- and upper-class Lima flees the capital on weekends to a stretch of beach communities that is anchored in Asia. Here, at the Boulevard de Asia, a temporary satellite city is set up, complete with a go-kart track and concert venues. Many of Peru's familiar chains—such as Pardo's, Wong, Ripley, and Illaria—populate a lively commercial zone that mostly shutters when the summer ends. Most visitors here stay in private residential developments that flank the boulevard for about 20 to 30 km (12 to 20 miles) in either direction. In most cases, if you don't know someone in these communities, your only option is accessing public beaches. Traditionally, this area has been targeted primarily at residents of Lima and hasn't seen many tourists, but that's starting to change. A few hotels have sprung up, including lively properties near the boulevard, and resort-style places farther away. You'll find better beaches elsewhere in Peru, but if hanging with the country's elite is what you're after, then this is the place.

GETTING HERE AND AROUND

To reach Asia, take a bus to Km 97.5 on the Pan-American Highway.

WHERE TO STAY

$$
HOTEL

Aquavit Hotel. In the midst of the action on the Asia beach boulevard, this is a clublike party hotel, where rooms surround a central pool area with palm trees and white daybeds that look straight out of South Beach. **Pros:** convenient; in the middle of everything. **Cons:** can get loud; events

CLOSE UP

Surfing

South of Lima you'll find a string of sandy beaches, most of them backed by massive sand dunes. The water is cold and rough, the waves are big, and lifeguards are nonexistent.

Sound appealing? Then pick up your board and head south to see why Peru is becoming one of South America's hottest surfing destinations.

For a sure bet, head to **Punta Hermosa,** a town near Km 44 on the Pan-American Highway (about an hour's drive south of Lima), which, with its numerous reefs and coves, has the highest concentration of high-quality surf spots and breaks all year round.

Fancy yourself a pro? The largest waves in South America, some 7 meters (23 feet) high, roll into nearby **Pico Alto,** with nearly 20 good breaks around the Pico Alto Surf Camp. Paddle out from Punta Hermosa via Playa Norte to reach the reef, although be warned—these waves are for the very experienced and crazy only!

Excellent surfing is also much closer to shore at the town of **Cerro Azul,** at Km 132 of the Panamericana. Long tubular waves break right in front of the town, so be prepared for an audience. A pleasant fishing village, Cerro Azul is a popular weekend and holiday destination, and the beach gets crowded

during peak times. Go midweek if you want the place to yourself.

Peru doesn't have a huge surfing tradition, but to see where a small slice of local history was made, head to **Punta Rocas,** 42 km (26 miles) south of Lima, where in 1965 Peruvian surfer Felipe Pomar converted himself into something of a national hero when he won the World Surfing Championships. The reef break here provides a classic wave for beginners and advanced surfers alike.

There's even some decent surfing in the middle of Lima. Just off the coast of Miraflores, on the **Costa Verde** beach road, you can find four surfable beaches, all within a 15-minute walk of one another. Right near the Rosa Nautica restaurant, Redondo, Makaha, La Pampilla, and Waikiki are breaks for beginners, but their proximity to the city means the water can be more than a little polluted. Think you've just paddled past a jellyfish? It's more likely a plastic bag.

Surfing in Peru is best from March to December, with May probably being ideal. Although the climate is dry year-round, in winter the Pacific Ocean can get very chilly (although it's never particularly warm, and wet suits are advisable year-round), and coastal fog can leave you with little to look at.

3

take over the pool area some weekends; 20-minute walk to the beach. $ *Rooms from: S/250* ⊠ *Km 97.5, Blvd. de Asia (Panamericana Sur)* ☎ *511/530–7801* ⊕ *www.aquavithotel.com* ⌐ *38 rooms* ⦿ *No meals.*

$$$ ⌂ **Estelar Vista Pacifico Resort.** This resort-style condo hotel was the first

RESORT major international property to open on one of Asia's beaches, and thus far, it's the most complete. **Pros:** some rooms have sea views; breakfast is included; 24-hour room service; great pool and beach area. **Cons:** 10 km (6 miles) from Boulevard de Asia; some service issues. $ *Rooms from: S/545* ⊠ *Km 109, Panamerica Sur, Sarapampa* ☎ *01/630–7788* ⊕ *www. hotelesestelar.com/estelar-vista-pacifico/* ⌐ *116 rooms* ⦿ *Breakfast.*

LUNAHUANÁ

14 km (9 miles) east of Cerro Azul; 150 km (93 miles) south of Lima; 85 km (53 miles) north of Pisco.

Flanked by arid mountains, the beautiful valley of the Río Cañete cuts a swath of green inland from Cañete to reach the tiny but charming town of Lunahuaná, nestled against the river—the center for some of Peru's best white-water rafting. The season is from December to March, when the water is at its highest, creating rapids that can reach up to Class IV. Most of the year, however, the river is suitable for beginners. Rafting companies offering trips line Calle Grau in town.

If you're more interested in whetting your palate, Lunahuaná is a great spot to enjoy the products of the region—wines and piscos from the surrounding wineries and distilleries, and freshwater prawns straight from the river. ■ **TIP→ In March you can celebrate the opening of the grape-pressing season at the Fiesta de la Vendimia.** The rest of the year, join the locals and while away the afternoon trying the variety of cocktails from the pisco stands dotted around the flower-filled main plaza—the *maracuya* (passion fruit) sour is a winner. If the cocktails, sun, and lazy atmosphere don't get the better of you, just down the road from Lunahuaná lie the **Incahuasi** ruins—an Inca site said to have been the military headquarters of Túpac Yupanqui. There's not a great deal to see, although Inca enthusiasts may find it interesting.

GETTING HERE AND AROUND

To reach Lunahuaná, take a bus to Km 143 on the Pan-American Highway to the turnoff to San Vicente de Cañete and Imperial. There you can catch a combi for the hour-long ride to Lunahuaná for S/7.50.

WHERE TO STAY

$$ HOTEL 🏨 **Los Palomas de Lunahuaná.** Set on a curve of the Río Cañete, this whitewashed, contemporary hotel is a laid-back, rambling property surrounded by nature. **Pros:** nice pub; great regional food in the restaurant; beautiful pool area. **Cons:** doesn't feel like Lunahuaná. [$] *Rooms from: S/350* ✉ *Km 35, Langla* ☎ *995–674–019* 🌐 *hotellospalomos.com* 🛏 *17 rooms* 🍴 *Breakfast.*

$$$ B&B/INN 🏨 **Refugio Viñak.** In a breathtaking setting high in the Andean foothills, this cozy lodge accesses more than 80 km (50 miles) of hiking trails that offer a glimpse of Andean life that few tourists will ever see. **Pros:** stunning setting; family-size rooms; all-inclusive. **Cons:** extremely remote, 110 km (68 miles) northeast of Lunahuaná. [$] *Rooms from: S/612* ✉ *Lunahuaná* ☎ *51/421–7777* 🌐 *www.refugiovinak.com* 🛏 *11 rooms* 🍴 *All-inclusive.*

$ HOTEL FAMILY 🏨 **Río Alto Hotel.** The sounds of the river create a restful atmosphere at this hacienda-style hotel just outside Lunahuaná, and its family vibe has made it popular with visitors from Lima. **Pros:** riverside location; pool; flower-filled terrace to kick back on; all-inclusive rates. **Cons:** small rooms; out-of-town location; no travel services. [$] *Rooms from: S/177* ✉ *Km 39.5, Cañete–Lunahuana Hwy.* ☎ *01/284–1125* 🌐 *www.rioaltohotel.com* 🛏 *25 rooms* 🍴 *All-inclusive.*

$$ HOTEL 🏨 **Villasol Hotel.** Listen to the sounds of the Río Cañete from your room or enjoy the river views while floating lazily in the swimming pool at this large hotel that makes the most of its spectacular

riverside location. **Pros:** riverside location; spectacular pool area; river views from some rooms. **Cons:** some rooms only have views of the lawn; unimaginative room furnishings; parking on the front lawns. $ *Rooms from: S/316* ✉ *Km 37.5, Cañete–Lunahuana Hwy.* ☎ *51/284–1127* ⊕ *luzdelosandes.com/villa* ⇄ *55 rooms* ✪ *Breakfast.*

SPORTS AND THE OUTDOORS

Hemiriver Adventures. This outfitter offers rafting, rappeling, ATV, and canopy tours around Lunahuaná. ✉ *Jr. Grau 255* ☎ *999–658–635* ⊕ *www.hemiriver.com* ⌫ *From S/40.*

Warko Adventures. Specialists in rafting and kayaking on the Río Cañete, including multiday trips, this outfitter can also arrange mountain-biking and horseback-riding tours. ✉ *Km 33, Lunahuana* ☎ *997–130–206* ⊕ *www.warkoadventures.com* ⌫ *From S/100.*

> ## GRAPE HARVEST
>
> If you happen to be in the San Vicente de Cañete region in March, drop by Cañete, which holds one of Peru's most exciting Fiestas de la Vendimia (grape-harvest festivals) on the first weekend of that month. The event stems from the town's proximity to the **Valle Cañete**, best known for its fertile vineyards that produce some of Peru's greatest wines. During the rest of the year there's little in Cañete to hold your interest, and most people head straight to the far nicer towns of Cerro Azul, 30 minutes to the north, or Lunahuaná, 45 minutes to the east.

TAMBO COLORADO

132 km (82 miles) southeast of Lunahuaná; 45 km (28 miles) east of Pisco.

The ruins of this administrative center and burial site make up one of the best-preserved Inca sites on the Southern Coast. Although the ruins are somewhat off the beaten track down poor roads, this archaeological complex rarely fails to impress.

GETTING HERE AND AROUND

There is no public transportation to Tambo Colorado. Many hotels and travel agencies in Ica and Paracas offer four-hour tours of the archaeological site for around S/80.

EXPLORING

Fodor's Choice ★ **Tambo Colorado.** The great Inca Pachacutec himself probably stayed at this, one of Peru's most underrated archaeological sites. That's because the labyrinthine alleyways and trapezoidal plaza of this huge adobe settlement were devised as an outpost for soldiers and visiting dignitaries of the far-flung Andean empire, making it the most important Inca site on the Peruvian coast. Today, Tambo Colorado is incredibly well preserved, owing to its bone-dry setting. When you go, you'll feel some of the same grandeur found in the stones of the Sacred Valley around Cuzco.

Tambo Colorado, or Pucahuasi ("red resting place") in Quechua, derives its name from the bright bands of imperial red, yellow, and white with which it was once blazoned. The site comprises several sections laid out around a large central plaza, and you can see the quarters where the great Inca received his guests. ■TIP→ Notice that the plaza's distinctive trapezoid shape is reflected throughout the site— look for trapezoid windows and other openings—and thought to have been an earthquake-proofing measure, necessary in this extremely volatile region. Be sure to visit the museum on the premises, which houses many finds by the great archaeologist Julio C. Tello, the site's discoverer. ⊠ *Via Libertadores, 40 km east of Pisco, Pisco* 🖃 *S/5.*

Huaytara. Catch your breath and drive up to this beautifully restored colonial church, built on the foundation of an Inca temple 2,800 meters (9,200 feet) above sea level. ⊠ *Off Libertadores Wari, 69 km (43 miles) east of Tambo Colorado.*

PISCO AND THE PARACAS PENINSULA

With spectacular natural surroundings and diverse wildlife, Pisco and neighboring Paracas have long been featured as stops on Peru's well-beaten tourist trail. At less than half a day's drive from the capital, for many years Pisco was a favorite holiday destination for *limeños* eager to escape the city. Sadly, the earthquake that struck in August 2007 left little of the colonial town standing and both the city and country reeling from the scale of the destruction. Life continues, however, and as Pisco has struggled to rebuild, the town of Paracas is booming, with a handful of major new resorts. The rugged coastline of the Paracas Peninsula and spectacular, rocky Ballestas Islands draw visitors keen to experience the area's wild scenery and to see flamingos, penguins, sea lions, and every imaginable type of guano-producing seabird.

PISCO

30 km (19 miles) south of Chincha.

Lending its name to the clear brandy that is Peru's favorite tipple and a source of fierce national pride, the coastal town of Pisco and its surroundings hold a special place in the national psyche. It's the point where the Argentinean hero General San Martín landed with his troops to fight for Peru's freedom from Spanish rule. It's the city from which *pisco* was first exported. And it's an important seaport that had its heyday during the 1920s, when guano (bird droppings used as fertilizer) from the nearby Islas Ballestas were worth nearly as much as gold.

Modern-day Pisco shows little evidence of its celebrated past. Instead, what you'll find is a city struggling to get back on its feet after the disaster of August 2007, when a magnitude-8 earthquake shook the town for three minutes. Disregard for planning permission, illegal building extensions, and the use of adobe (mud brick) as the main building material had left a vast number of Pisco's buildings unable to withstand the quake, and hundreds of lives were lost as homes, churches, and hospitals collapsed during the tremor. Most travelers now base themselves in Paracas, just a few kilometers down the coast.

GETTING HERE AND AROUND

If you arrive by bus, you may find yourself dropped off at the Pisco turnoff on the Panamericana rather than in the town itself, so ask for a direct service. If you do end up disembarking on the highway, there are taxis waiting that make the run into town for around S/5. Drivers who work this route have a bad reputation for taking travelers only to hotels from which they receive a commission. Always insist on being taken to the destination of your choice, and ignore anyone who tells you that the hotel has closed, moved, or changed its name. Transportation within Pisco is generally not necessary: the central area is easily covered on foot, although those venturing out at night should take a taxi.

Bus Contacts Oltursa. ⊠ *Carretera Paracas, Paracas* ☎ *511/708–5000* ⊕ *www.oltursa.pe.* **Ormeño.** ⊠ *Calle Francisco Bolognesi 259* ☎ *056/532–764* ⊕ *www.grupo-ormeno.com.pe.*

ESSENTIALS

Currency Banco de la Nación. ⊠ *San Fransisco 155* ☎ *056/532–918.* **Interbank.** ⊠ *Av. San Martín 101* ☎ *056/534–167* ⊕ *interbank.pe/ puntos-de-atencion.*

Medical San Juan de Dios (Hospital). ⊠ *Mz B Lt 5 Ex Fundo Alto la Luna* ☎ *056/535–716* ⊕ *www.hsjdpisco.gob.pe.*

Police Comisaría Sectorial. ⊠ *Francisco Bolognesi 159* ☎ *056/532–884* ⊕ *www.pnp.gob.pe.*

WHERE TO EAT AND STAY

The 2007 earthquake destroyed many accommodations in Pisco, and most have closed up shop or moved to nearby Paracas, which has become the base for most travelers here. It's recommended that you stay in Paracas, but if you must stay in Pisco, the Hostal San Isidro is structurally sound and has been repaired since the quake. If you decide to stay elsewhere, stay away from hotels housed in precarious-looking multistory adobe constructions.

$$
SEAFOOD ✕ **As de Oros.** This 40-year-old Pisco institution may host pool parties and dancing on weekends, but it's the seafood specialties like whole fried *chita* (rock fish) and *sudado de choros* (shellfish stew) that keep the crowds coming. Roast goat, grilled meats, and *sopa seca* (noodles

BEST BETS FOR CRUISE SHIP TRAVELERS

■ **Huacachina.** Go sandboarding or ride dune buggies at this desert oasis.

■ **Islas Ballestas.** Take a speedboat tour to observe Humboldt penguins, sea lions, and dolphins.

■ **Paracas National Reserve.** Search for condors or fossilized shark teeth.

■ **Nazca Lines.** Fly over these mysterious ancient etchings.

■ **Adventure Sports.** Go kite- or windsurfing in Paracas Bay.

in basil sauce) round out the extensive menu. **Known for:** fresh seafood; great regional cooking; dancing on weekends. $ *Average main: S/35* ⊠ *Av. San Martín 472* ☎ *056/532–010* ⊕ *www.asdeoros.com.pe* ⊗ *Closed Mon.*

$$

PERUVIAN

✕ **La Viña de Huber.** Locals recommend this restaurant on the outskirts of town as the best around; judging from the lunchtime crowds, they can't be too far wrong. The three brothers who run the kitchen cook up modern regional Peruvian cuisine such as sole fillets rolled with bacon and served with passion-fruit dipping sauce, or fish stuffed with spinach and sautéed in a pisco and pecan broth. **Known for:** huge portions; northern specialties. $ *Average main: S/35* ⊠ *Calle Cerro Azul 601* ☎ *056/536–456* ⊕ *www.lavinadehuber.com* ▭ *No credit cards.*

$

B&B/INN

🏠 **Hostal San Isidro.** A relaxing oasis away from the dust of the Pisco streets, this friendly, family-run guesthouse is a top place to drop your bags and rest your weary bones. **Pros:** very welcoming hosts; great pool; free laundry service. **Cons:** near the cemetery; expensive dorm rooms; high walls somewhat fortresslike. $ *Rooms from: S/80* ⊠ *San Clemente 103* ☎ *056/563–471* ⊕ *sanisidrohostal.com/inicio.html* ⤳ *18 rooms* ❢⊘ *No meals.*

PARACAS

15 km (10 miles) south of Pisco.

After the 2007 quake, Paracas quickly leapfrogged Pisco as the most important tourist hub on the Southern Coast. Several major coastal resorts from big-name chains like Doubletree and Libertador (now part of Starwood) have since opened, and others quickly followed. The small-town feel and cluster of petite inns and restaurants around a central fishing pier are still there, though for the passing tourist the exploring options have quadrupled. Apart from being the launching point for trips in the Paracas National Reserve and Islas Ballestas, this is a good base for pisco-tasting adventures or dune-buggy riding near Ica, and for trips to the Nazca Lines.

CLOSE UP

Pisco Country

El pisco es peruano! And don't try to tell the locals any different. This clear brandy that takes its name from the port town of Pisco is Peru's national drink and a source of unrelenting patriotic pride. It would take a brave and foolish man to raise the suggestion that pisco was invented in Spain, or worse still, in neighboring Chile. Yes, when in Peru, the only thing you need to know is that *el pisco es 100% peruano.*

Fiery and potent, pisco is hands-down the most popular liquor in Peru, and is drunk on just about every social occasion. Invited to someone's house for dinner? Chances are you'll be welcomed with a pisco sour, a tart cocktail made from pisco, lime juice, egg white, sugar, and bitters. Heading to a party? You're sure to see at least a couple of people drinking Peru libres—a Peruvian take on the classic Cuba libre, using pisco instead of rum and mixing it with Coca-Cola. Of course, the real way to drink pisco is *a lo macho*—strong and straight up. It will certainly put hair on your chest.

Pisco is derived from grapes, like wine, but is technically an *aguardiente*, or brandy. Through a special distillation process involving a serpentine copper pipe, the fermented grapes are vaporized and then chilled to produce a clear liquor. In Peru there are multiple variations of pisco: the single-grape *pisco puro*; a blend of grapes, such as quebranta mixed with torontel and muscatel, called *pisco acholado; pisco aromatico*, made from straight aromatic grapes; and *pisco mosto verde*, in which the green musts are distilled during the fermentation process.

Legend has it that pisco got its name from sailors who tired of asking for "aguardiente de Pisco" and shortened the term to pisco. (The name meant "place of many birds" in the language of the indigenous people, and it still refers to the port city as well as a nearby river.)

Today Peru produces more than 7.5 million liters annually, 40% of which is exported to the United States. In 1988 the liquor was designated a national patrimony, and each year Peruvians celebrate the Pisco Festival in March as well as the National Day of the Pisco Sour on the first Saturday of every February.

Bottoms up!

GETTING HERE AND AROUND

A taxi from Pisco to Paracas runs about S/15, or you can take a half-hour Chaco–Paracas–Museo *combi* to El Chaco for S/3. From Paracas, you can catch a fast motorboat to the reserve and islands.

To visit the Islas Ballestas, you must be on a registered tour, which usually means an hour or two cruising around the islands among sea lions and birds. Motorboat tours usually leave from the El Chaco jetty at 8 and 10 am. For the calmest seas, take the early tour. ■ TIP➜ You'll be in the open wind, sun, and waves during boat trips, so dress appropriately, and prepare your camera for the mists in July and August. It takes about an hour to reach the park from the jetty; you're close when you can see the Candelabra etched in the coastal hills. A two-hour tour costs around S/40. Some tours continue on to visit the Paracas Peninsula during the afternoon for around S/40 extra.

Take a boat trip out to Isla Ballestas to observe the marine birds and sea lions.

TOURS

Guided tours of Paracas National Reserve and the Ballestas Islands are offered by Zarcillo Connections in Paracas. Ballestas Travel represents several agencies that sell park packages. Just about every hotel in Pisco and Paracas will assist in booking tours, and most include transportation to and from the dock at Paracas. Make sure your boat has life jackets.

Ballestas Travel. Half-day boat tours the Islas Ballestas and/or the Paracas National Reserve are the primary tours from this agency. ⊠ *Pisco* ☎ *955–924–285* ⊕ *monica09014.wixsite.com/ballestastravelpisco* ⧉ *From S/40.*

Peru Kite. This company offers kitesurfing and windsurfing in Paracas Bay, including lessons and equipment rentals. ⊠ *Santo Domingo L-36* ☎ *994–567–802* ⊕ *www.perukite.com* ⧉ *From S/200 for 1-hr tuition.*

Venturia. Luxury tours are operated out of the Libertador Paracas hotel, including exclusive lunches in vineyards or at desert tent camps, as well as straightforward boat tours of the Islas Ballestas. ⊠ *Av. Paracas 173* ☎ *01/712–7000* ⊕ *www.tikariy.com.pe* ⧉ *From S/100.*

Zarcillo Connections. Based out of the Zarcillo Paradise hotel in Paracas, this is one of the largest tour operators in the region, with a full range of options from boat tours of the Islas Ballestas to visits to pre-Inca sites such as Tambo Colorado. ⊠ *Av. Principal de ingreso al Chaco 101* ☎ *056/536–636* ⊕ *www.zarcilloconnections.com* ⧉ *From S/40.*

EXPLORING

Fodor's Choice
★
Islas Ballestas. Spectacular rocks pummeled by waves and wind into *ballestas* (arched bows) along the cliffs mark this haven of jagged outcrops and rugged beaches that shelter thousands of marine birds and sea lions. You're not allowed to walk onshore, but you wouldn't want to—the land is calf-deep in *guano* (bird droppings). ■ TIP→ **Bring a hat, as tourists are moving targets for multitudes of guano-dropping seabirds. Also, be prepared for the smell—between the sea lions and the birds, the odor can drop you to your knees.** A boat provides the best views of the abundant wildlife: sea lions laze on the rocks, surrounded by Humboldt penguins, pelicans, seals, boobies, cormorants, and even condors, which make celebrity appearances for the appreciative crowds in February and March. On route to the islands is Punta Pejerrey, the northernmost point of the isthmus and the best spot for viewing the enormous, cactus-shape **Candelabra** carved in the cliffs. It's variously said to represent a symbol of the power of the northern Chavín culture, a Masonic symbol placed on the hillside by General José San Martín, leader of the liberation movement, or a staff of the pre-Inca religious figure Viracocha. ⊠ *Paracas.*

Fodor's Choice
★
Reserva Nacional de Paracas. If a two-hour jaunt around the Islas Ballestas doesn't satisfy your thirst for guano, sea lions, and seabirds, then a land trip to this 280,000-hectare (700,000-plus-acre) park just might. The stunning coastal reserve, on a peninsula south of Pisco, teems with wildlife. Pelicans, condors, and red-and-white flamingos congregate and breed here; the latter are said to have inspired the red-and-white independence flag General San Martín designed when he liberated Peru. Onshore you can't miss the sound (or the smell) of the hundreds of sea lions, while on the water you might spot penguins, sea turtles, dolphins, manta rays, and even hammerhead sharks.

Named for the blustering *paracas* (sandstorms) that buffet the west coast each winter, the Reserva Nacional de Paracas (Paracas National Reserve) is Peru's first park for marine conservation. Organized tours take you along the thin dirt tracks that crisscross the peninsula, passing by sheltered lagoons, rugged cliffs full of caves, and small fishing villages. This is prime walking territory, where you can stroll from the bay to the **Julio Tello Museum,** and on to the fishing village of **Lagunilla** 5 km (3 miles) farther across the neck of the peninsula. Adjacent to the museum are colonies of flamingos, best seen June through July (and absent January through March, when they fly to the sierra). Hike another 6 km (4 miles) to reach **Mirador de Lobos** (Sea-Lion Lookout) at Punta El Arquillo. Carved into the highest point in the cliffs above Paracas Bay, 14 km (9 miles) from the museum, is the **Candelabra.** Note that you must hire a guide to explore the land trails. Minibus tours of the entire park can be arranged through local hotels and travel agencies for about S/40 for four hours. ⊠ *Paracas* ⊕ *www.sernanp.gob.pe/de-paracas* ⊡ *S/5.*

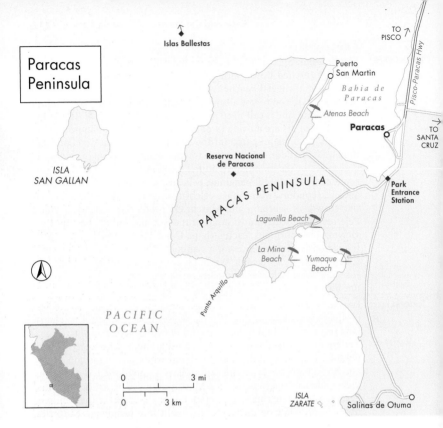

WHERE TO EAT

$ ✕ **El Arizal.** In a waterfront lined with identical-seeming seafood joints,
SEAFOOD this *cebichería* (cebiche restaurant) stands out for its ample menu, *arroz
con mariscos* (seafood with rice), and attentive service. There's also
breakfast while you wait for your boat out to the islands, and the views
of the bay are unbeatable. **Known for:** fresh seafood; bay views; good
service. $ *Average main: S/30* ✉ *Malecon El Chaco s/n* ☎ *056/791–144*
⊕ *elarizal.es.tl.*

WHERE TO STAY

Sleepy Paracas really comes alive only during the Peruvian summer
(December to March), when city dwellers arrive to set up residence
in their shorefront vacation homes. If you're visiting out of season, be
warned—many hotels close during the low season or scale back their
service and concentrate on repairs.

$$$ ⌂ **Aranwa Paracas.** Part of the growing Peruvian Aranwa chain, this
RESORT sprawling upscale resort has a lot going on, making it good for families,
FAMILY active types, spa-seekers, and conference delegates alike. **Pros:** lots of
space; beautiful pools. **Cons:** somewhat overpriced. $ *Rooms from:
S/800* ✉ *El Chaco, La Puntilla Lote C* ☎ *056/580–600* ⊕ *www.aran-
wahotels.com* ⇆ *134 rooms* ⦿ *Breakfast.*

$$$ RESORT FAMILY **Doubletree Hotel Paracas.** The first major resort hotel to hit the Paracas coast, this all-suite, family-friendly retreat opened in 2009 and sits just a few steps down the beach from the more luxurious Libertador. **Pros:** Club de Paco kids' club; variety of dining options; huge pool. **Cons:** pools can become overcrowded on summer weekends; adults without kids might be turned off. [$] *Rooms from: S/645* ✉ *Lote 30–34, Urb. Santo Domingo* ☎ *056/581–919* 🌐 *doubletree3.hilton.com* 🛏 *124 rooms* 🍴 *No meals.*

$$$ RESORT Fodor's Choice ★ **Hotel Paracas Libertador.** The best of the new resorts to have opened in Paracas in recent years, the ultrachic Libertador, now part of Starwood's swanky Luxury Collection, was created from the rubble of the once-famous Hotel Paracas, destroyed in the 2007 earthquake. **Pros:** beachfront location; great prices for basic rooms; one of Peru's most luxurious hotels; private jet for Nazca Lines viewing; all rooms have terraces. **Cons:** wind can pick up at times near the pool. [$] *Rooms from: S/625* ✉ *Av. Paracas 173* ☎ *056/581–333* 🌐 *www.libertador.com.pe* 🛏 *120 rooms* 🍴 *No meals.*

$$$ RESORT FAMILY **La Hacienda Bahia Paracas.** Opened in 2009, this hotel may not be as flashy as the nearby Libertador or Doubletree, but it's nearly as nice, and the daily supervised activities for kids are a hit with families. **Pros:** package deals; amazing pool. **Cons:** slow during the week; only one restaurant; somewhat overpriced. [$] *Rooms from: S/750* ✉ *Santo Domingo Lote 25* ☎ *056/581–370* 🌐 *www.hoteleslahacienda.com* 🛏 *68 rooms* 🍴 *Breakfast.*

$ B&B/INN **Refugio del Pirata.** Friendly and in a terrific location for those heading out to early-morning boat tours, this ramshackle guesthouse is popular with backpackers and tour groups alike. **Pros:** central location in town; lovely terrace with port views; easy to organize tours via the affiliated travel agency on the ground floor. **Cons:** no restaurant; rooms lack style; interior rooms small and dark. [$] *Rooms from: S/170* ✉ *Av. Paracas Lote 6* ☎ *056/545–054* 🌐 *refugiodelpirata.com* 🛏 *14 rooms* 🍴 *No meals.*

$$ RESORT **San Agustín Paracas.** This straightforward Paracas resort, one of the newer additions to the strip, is also one of the more grown-up options, with fewer kids running around and, overall, fewer bells and whistles. **Pros:** nice pool area; quiet and less kids; all rooms have sea views. **Cons:** pricey; fewer amenities than neighboring properties. [$] *Rooms from: S/450* ✉ *Chaco de la Puntilla* ☎ *056/580–420* 🌐 *hotelessanagustin.com.pe/en/* 🛏 *123 rooms* 🍴 *Breakfast.*

SPORTS AND THE OUTDOORS

BEACHES

Most beaches at Paracas are rugged and scenic, top-notch for walking but dangerous for swimming because of riptides and undertow. Beware in the shallows, too—there are often stingrays and giant jellyfish. Calmer stretches include La Catedral, La Mina, and Mendieta, as well as Atenas, a prime windsurfing section. Dirt roads lead farther to Playa Mendieta and Playa Carhaus. Small, open restaurant shacks line the more popular beaches.

ICA AND NAZCA

South of Pisco, the thin black highway cuts through desert vast and pale as cracked parchment, and there's nothing but sand and sky as far as the eye can see. As you gaze out the bus window at mile upon endless mile of arid coastal desert, you'd be forgiven for thinking that there's little to hold your attention in this part of Peru.

You couldn't be more wrong, though. With good wines, year-round sunshine, spectacular desert landscapes, and giant desert drawings left by one of the world's most enigmatic ancient cultures, there's definitely more to this region than meets the eye.

Head to Nazca to puzzle over the mystery of the world-famous Nazca Lines—giant drawings of animals, geometric shapes, and perfectly straight lines that stretch for miles across the desert floor. Who created them and why? Theories range from ancient irrigation systems to alien-spaceship landing sites. Hop on a light aircraft for a dizzying overflight and try to cook up your own theory.

Or try tackling the easier problem of discerning which of Ica's numerous bodegas produces the best pisco, and if you're around in March, have a go at stamping the grapes during the pressing season.

Adrenaline seekers will find their mecca in Huacachina, where the dazzling dunes can be explored in a hair-raising dune-buggy ride or sliding down on a sandboard. The oasis town just outside Ica also draws the health conscious, who come to enjoy the lagoon's reputedly magical healing qualities.

ICA

72 km (45 miles) southeast of Paracas.

A bustling commercial city with chaotic traffic and horn-happy drivers, Ica challenges you to find its attractive side. Step outside the city center, however, and you'll see why this town was the Nazca capital between AD 300 and 800, and why the Nazca people couldn't have picked a better place to center their desert civilization. Set in a patch of verdant fields and abutted by snow-covered mountains, Ica is serene, relaxing, and cheerful, with helpful residents—likely due as much to the nearly never-ending sunshine as to the vast selection of high-quality wines and piscos produced by dozens of local bodegas and distilleries. This is a town of laughter and festivals, most notably the Fiesta de Vendimia, the wine-harvest celebration that takes place each year in early March. Ica is also famous for its pecans and its high-stepping horses, called *caballos de paso.*

The city center's colonial look comes from its European heritage. Ica was founded by the Spanish in 1563, making it one of the oldest towns in southern Peru. The city suffered badly in the 2007 earthquake, however, and sadly many of the colonial-era buildings, including most of the famous churches, were damaged.

Today Peru's richest wine-growing region is a source of national pride, and its fine bodegas are a major attraction. Most are open year-round, but the best time to visit is February to April, during the grape harvest.

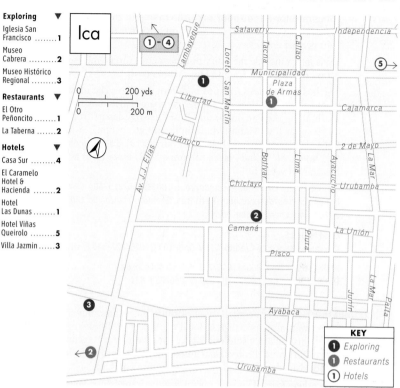

KEY

❶ Exploring

① Restaurants

① Hotels

The Tacama and Ocucaje bodegas are generally considered to have some of the best-quality wines, and the Quebranta and Italia grape varietals are well regarded for pisco. ■TIP→ The Peruvian autumn is the season for Ica's Fiesta de la Vendimia, where you can enjoy parades, sports competitions, local music, and dancing, and even catch beauty queens stamping grapes. It's also a great time to be introduced to the vast selection of local wines and piscos, as well as an opportunity to try homemade concoctions not yet on the market.

The city's excitement also heightens for such festivals as February's Carnaval, Semana Santa in March or April, and the all-night pilgrimages of El Señor de Luren in March and October. Other fun times to visit are during Ica Week, around June 17, which celebrates the city's founding, and the annual Ica Tourist Festival in late September.

GETTING HERE AND AROUND

Surrounded as Ica is by vineyards, tourism here is all about wineries. Most are close to the city and easily accessed by road. ■TIP→ If you don't have your own car (or you don't want to be the designated driver on a winery trip), pick the wineries you'd like to see and ask a taxi driver to give you a price. For some bodegas, there are collectivos (shared taxis) that depart from near the main square for S/2. You can also hop on one of the prearranged tours offered by most hotels. The going rate for a four-hour taxi ride taking in three wineries close to the city is around S/50; if you go on a formal tour, you'll pay up to S/40 per person.

Taxis in Ica include the noisy but distinctive three-wheeled mototaxis. A taxi ride between Ica and Huacachina costs S/8.

The bus companies Ormeños and Peru Bus have the most departures from Ica, though dozens of other companies also make trips north or south along the Panamericana. Buses usually depart from the station on Avenida José Matias Manzanilla and go to Lima (5 hours, S/30), Pisco (1 hour, S/10), and Nazca (3 hours, S/15). Taxi *colectivos* to Lima (3½ hours, S/40) and Nazca (2 hours, S/25) leave from in front of the bus station when full.

Bus Contacts Ormeño. ⊠ *Lambayeque 180* ☎ *056/215–600* ⊕ *www.grupo-ormeno.com.pe/destinos.html.* **Peru Bus.** ⊠ *Matias Manzanilla 130* ☎ *01/205–2370* ⊕ *www.perubus.com.pe/.*

ESSENTIALS

Currency Banco de Crédito. ⊠ *Av. Grau 105* ☎ *056/222–845* ⊕ *www.viabcp.com.*

Mail DHL. ⊠ *Lima 468* ☎ *056/211–592* ⊕ *dhl.com.pe.*
Post Office. ⊠ *Av. San Martín 521* ☎ *056/233–881.*

TOURS

Most hotels can arrange tours of the Nazca Lines, but several travel companies also specialize in local explorations. Book ahead, because the flights are often sold out. Make sure the guide or agency is licensed and experienced. Professional guides must be approved by the Ministry of Tourism, so ask for identification before you hire.

Huacachina Tours. This tour operator will arrange dune buggy and sandboarding around the Huacachina oasis and throughout the Ica desert. They also offer flights over the Nazca Lines. ⊠ *Av. Perotti s/n, Balneario de Huacachina* ☎ *975–612–550* ⊕ *www.huacachina.com* 🖃 *From S/500.*

Ica Desert Trip Peru (Roberto Penny Cabrera). One fellow you can't miss in Ica is Roberto Penny Cabrera, a direct descendent of Ica's founding family, with a home right on the Plaza de Armas . After a long career in mining, Roberto started this company and began offering tours of the nearby desert in his fully equipped four-wheel-drive Jeep. He's fascinated with the fossils of gigantic sharks and whales he's come across and has a collection of huge incisors. ⊠ *Calle Bolivar 178* ☎ *056/237–373* ⊕ *www.icadeserttrip.com* 🖃 *From S/420 per day.*

EXPLORING

Iglesia San Francisco. Soaring ceilings, ornate stained-glass windows, and the fact that it's the only one of Ica's colonial-era churches left standing after the 2007 earthquake make this the city's grandest religious building. Yet even this colossal monument didn't escape the quake unscathed. ■**TIP→** If you look on the floor toward the front of the church you can see the gouges left in the marble blocks by falling pieces of the church altar. It's said that the statues of the saints stood serenely throughout the quake and didn't move an inch. ⊠ *At Avs. Municipalidad y San Martín* 🖃 *Free.*

Museo Cabrera. Curious to find the *real* meaning of the Nazca Lines? Head to this small building on the *Plaza de Armas*, which contains a collection of more than 11,000 intricately carved stones and boulders depicting varied pre-Colombian themes, ranging from ancient surgical techniques to dinosaurs. The charismatic and eccentric founder, Dr. Javier Cabrera, studied the stones for many years, and the staffers are more than happy to explain to you how they prove the existence of an advanced pre-Colombian society who created the Nazca Lines as a magnetic landing strip for their spacecraft (they even have the diagram to prove it!). It's a good idea to make a reservation before you go, as hours are irregular. ✉ *Bolívar 170* ☎ *056/227–676* ⊕ *www.museode-piedrasgrabadasdeica.com.pe* 🖵 *S/35 with guided tour.*

Museo Histórico Regional. It may be a little out of the way, but don't let that stop you from visiting this compact museum with a vast and well-preserved collection on regional history—particularly from the Inca, Nazca, and Paracas cultures. Note the *quipus ,* mysterious knotted, colored threads thought to have been used by the Incas to count commodities and quantities of food. ■**TIP**➔ **Fans of the macabre will love the mummy display, where you can see everything from human mummies to a mummified bird.** The squeamish can head out back to view a scale model of the Nazca Lines from an observation tower. You can also buy maps (S/1) and paintings of Nazca motifs (S/5). The museum is about 1½ km (1 mile) from the main square. It's not advisable to walk, so take the opportunity to jump into one of the distinctive three-wheeled *mototaxis* that will make the trip for around S/5. ✉ *Ayabaca 895* ☎ *056/234–383* ⊕ *museos.cultura.pe/museos/museo-regional-de-ica-adolfo-bermúdez-jenkins* 🖵 *S/7.*

WINERIES

If you can't imagine anything better than sampling different varieties of wine and pisco at nine in the morning, then these winery tours are most definitely for you. Most wineries in the Ica region make their living from tourism and, as a way of boosting sales, devote a good portion of the winery tour to the tasting room. Tours are free, although the guides do appreciate tips.

■**TIP**➔ **Peruvians like their wines sweet and their pisco strong.** If you're unused to drinking spirits straight up, follow this tried-and-true Peruvian technique for a smoother drop: after swirling the pisco around the glass, inhale the vapors. Before exhaling, take the pisco into your mouth and taste the flavor for four seconds. As you swallow, exhale!

Bodega El Catador. A favorite stop on the tour circuit, this family-run winery produces wines and some of the region's finest pisco. Tour guides are happy to show you a 300-year-old section of the distillery that's still in operation. If you're here in March, try to catch the annual Fiesta de Uva when the year's festival queen tours the vineyard and gets her feet wet in the opening of the grape-pressing season. The excellent Taberna restaurant and bar is open for lunch after a hard morning's wine tasting. If you don't want to drive, take a collectivo taxi from near the Plaza de Armas (S/2). ✉ *Km 294, Pan-American Hwy. S, Fondo Tres Equinas 104* ☎ *056/403–516* ⊕ *www.elviejocatador.com/.*

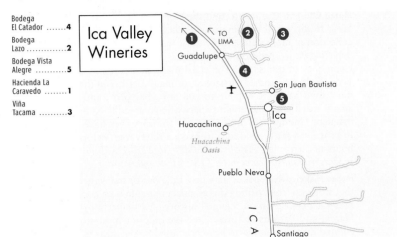

Bodega Lazo. One of the more fun alcohol-making operations to visit is owned by Elar Bolivar, who claims to be a direct descendent of the Libertador Simón Bolívar himself (some locals shrug their shoulders at this). Regardless, Elar's small artisanal operation includes a creepy collection of shrunken heads (Dutch tourists, he says, who didn't pay their drink tab), ancient cash registers, fencing equipment, and copies of some of the paintings in Ica's regional museum. The question is, who really has the originals—Elar or the museum? As part of your visit, you can taste the bodega's recently made pisco, straight from the clay vessel. The pisco is so-so, but the atmosphere is priceless. Some organized tours include this bodega as part of a tour. It's not a safe walk from town, so take a cab if you come on your own. ⊠ *Camino de Reyes s/n, San Juan Bautista* ☎ *959–072–245* ⊕ *www.facebook.com/pg/bodegalazo1809/about/?ref=page_internal.*

Bodega Vista Alegre. A sunny brick archway welcomes you to this large, pleasant winery, which has been producing fine wines, pisco, and sangria since it was founded by the Picasso brothers in 1857. The largest winery in the valley, this former monastery is a popular tour-bus stop, so come early to avoid the groups. Tours in English or Spanish take you through the vast pisco- and wine-making facilities at this industrial winery before depositing you in the tasting room. ⚠ It's not safe to walk here from downtown Ica, so if you don't have your own vehicle, take a taxi. ⊠ *Km 2.5, Camina a la Tinguiña* ☎ *056/232–919* ⊕ *www.vistaalegre.com.pe.*

Hacienda La Caravedo. Dating to 1684, this is one of the oldest working distilleries in the Americas. For the past few years the historic hacienda has been continually upgraded, now that it is the home of internationally famous brand Pisco Portón. Master distiller and pisco celebrity Johnny Schuler designed the new distillery so that it would also move liquid only through the natural forces of gravity, which allows for the same small-batch distillation and control over every bottle. On the guided tours you'll see the traditional pisco-making methods on the estate, from the large wooden press to the gravity-fed channels. Then you'll see the modern additions, such as the roof garden that was planted to offset the carbon dioxide emissions created during fermentation, and a water-treatment system to recycle water from distillation into irrigation water for the vineyards. Tours end with, of course, a tasting. With prior notice, they can set up lunch in the vineyard or Peruvian Paso horseback rides. Reservations are essential. ✉ *Km 291, Panamericana Sur* ☎ *511/711–7800* 🌐 *www.piscoporton.com.*

Viña Tacama. After suffering earthquake damage in 2007, this 16th-century farm hacienda took the opportunity to overhaul its now very modern operation. Internationally renowned, it produces some of Peru's best labels, particularly the Blanco de Blancos and Don Manuel Tannat wines and the Demonio de los Andes line of piscos. Stroll through the rolling vineyards—still watered by the Achirana irrigation canal built by the Incas—before sampling the end result. The estate is about 11 km (7 miles) north from town. ✉ *Camina a la Tinguiña s/n* ☎ *056/581–030* 🌐 *www.tacama.com.*

WHERE TO EAT

$ PERUVIAN 🍴 **El Otro Peñoncito.** Don't be surprised if chef Hary Hernandez comes over to chat during your meal at this half-century-old Ica institution: "Sir Hary"'s passion for food and hospitality is legendary. Among the dishes he might offer are *pollo a la iqueña* (chicken in pecan-and-pisco sauce) or fried trout. **Known for:** traditional coastal cooking; warm hospitality. [$] *Average main: S/30* ✉ *Calle Bolívar 255* ☎ *034/233–921* 💳 *No credit cards.*

$$ PERUVIAN 🍴 **La Taberna.** After a hard morning's wine tasting, stop in this cheerful open-air restaurant in Bodega El Catador to soak up the pisco. Like an outdoor rural dining room, this pleasant spot specializes in local *criollo* dishes such as *carapulcra con sopa seca* ,a stew of dried potatoes and spaghetti in basil sauce, washed down with one of El Catador's wines. **Known for:** traditional coastal cooking; extensive bar with wines and piscos. [$] *Average main: S/45* ✉ *Km 296, José Carrasco González* ☎ *056/403–516* 🌐 *www.elviejocatador.com/* 🕒 *No dinner.*

WHERE TO STAY

$ HOTEL 🏨 **Casa Sur.** This is one of Ica's hidden gems—the two-level former Hotel Austria, in two side-by-side buildings, has been renovated and provides amenities you'd expect to find only in a much larger hotel. **Pros:** quiet; superb attention to detail; good food and great value. **Cons:** high walls make it seem cut off from the city. [$] *Rooms from: S/210* ✉ *Av. La Angostura 367* ☎ *056/256–106* 🌐 *www.casasur.pe* 🛏 *16 rooms* 🍽 *No meals.*

$ 🖼 **El Carmelo Hotel & Hacienda.** Hotel or bodega-related theme park—it's
HOTEL   hard to tell at this oddball spot on the road between Ica and Huacachina,
FAMILY   where rooms are built around a central courtyard complete with ancient
grape press and working pisco distillery. **Pros:** wicker-filled open-air sitting
room; chance to see the pisco-making process up close; zoo and playground
to entertain the kids. **Cons:** out-of-town location; rooms are on the small
side. $ *Rooms from: S/165* ⊠ *Km 301.2, Pan-American Hwy.* ☎ *056/232–
191* ⊕ *www.elcarmelohotelhacienda.com* 🛏 *58 rooms* ⊚| *Breakfast.*

$$ 🖼 **Hotel Las Dunas.** For a taste of the good life, Peruvian style, head to
RESORT   this top-end resort between Ica and Huacachina, a favorite getaway
FAMILY   for Peruvian families. **Pros:** beautiful grounds; activities for children;
decent restaurant. **Cons:** out of town; resort aesthetic. $ *Rooms from:
S/350* ⊠ *Av. La Angostura 400* ☎ *056/256–224* ⊕ *www.lasdunashotel.
com* 🛏 *133 rooms* ⊚| *No meals.*

$$$ 🖼 **Hotel Viñas Queirolo.** There's no better property in the country for expe-
HOTEL   riencing Peru's wine and pisco industry than this charming bodega-based
Fodor's Choice hacienda surrounded by 400 hectares of Santiago Queirolo's verdant
★   vineyards. **Pros:** atmospheric and authentic; unique in the region. **Cons:**
a bit out of the way, making local public transportation impractical.
$ *Rooms from: S/800* ⊠ *Carretera a San José de los Molinos* ☎ *056/254–
119* ⊕ *www.hotelvinasqueirolo.com* 🛏 *20 rooms* ⊚| *Breakfast.*

$$ 🖼 **Villa Jazmin.** This intimate inn garners rave reviews, and the charm-
HOTEL   ing dune setting and small but inviting pool make this a good place to
chill out for a few days while exploring the area. **Pros:** relatively new;
eco-friendly; less crowded than other Ica resorts. **Cons:** rooms can be
dark; the pool is more for lounging than swimming. $ *Rooms from:
S/250* ⊠ *Los Girasoles MZ C-1, Lote 7, La Angostura* ☎ *056/258–179*
⊕ *www.villajazmin.net* 🛏 *20 rooms* ⊚| *No meals.*

SHOPPING

Ica is an excellent place to pick up Peruvian handicrafts with regional
styles and motifs. Tapestries and textiles woven in naturally colored
llama and alpaca wool often have images of the Nazca Lines and histori-
cal figures. In particular, look for *alfombras* (rugs), *colchas* (blankets),
and *tapices* (hangings).

HUACACHINA

5 km (3 miles) southwest of Ica.

Drive 10 minutes through the pale, mountainous sand dunes southwest of
Ica and you'll suddenly see a gathering of attractive, pastel-color buildings
surrounding a patch of green. It's not an oasis on the horizon, but rather
the lakeside resort of Laguna de Huacachina, a palm-fringed lagoon of
jade-color waters whose sulfurous properties are reputed to have healing
powers. The view is breathtaking: a collection of attractive, colonial-style
hotels in front of a golden beach and with a backdrop of snow-covered
peaks against the distant sky. In the 1920s Peru's elite traveled here for
the ultimate holiday, and today the spacious resorts still beckon. The
lake is also a pilgrimage site for those with health and skin problems,
sandboarders who want to tackle the 100-meter (325-foot) dunes, and
budget travelers who pitch tents in the sand or sleep under the stars.

GETTING HERE AND AROUND

Huacachina sits on the opposite side of the highway from the center of Ica. Take any bus to Ica and hire a mototaxi to the oasis for about S/5.

WHERE TO EAT

$
CAFÉ
✕ **La Casa de Bamboo.** This pleasant garden café beside Hostería Suiza has a vegetarian-friendly vibe, with lots of quinua and salads on offer. Dishes on the eclectic menu are all handmade from scratch by the British owner, and range from Thai curries to falafel to pastas and crepes. **Known for:** vegetarian dishes; friendly. $ *Average main: S/15* ⊠ *Av. Perotti s/n* ☎ *944–255–871* ⊕ *www.facebook.com/La-Casa-de-Bamboo-123418741040046/.*

WHERE TO STAY

$
B&B/INN
Fodor's Choice
★
🔲 **El Huacachinero.** Hands-down Huacachina's best budget lodging, this is a beautiful bargain in the oasis of Peru—clean, safe, and with its own little bar featuring a mural of Ica's now-disappeared camel herd. **Pros:** fantastic pool area with hammocks; dune-buggy service and sandboard rental; newly remodeled rooms. **Cons:** often full; noisy parrots; three of the rooms don't have en suite bathroom. $ *Rooms from: S/200* ⊠ *Av. Perotti, Balnearia de Huacachina* ☎ *056/217–435* ⊕ *www.elhuacachinero.com* ⇆ *24 rooms* ⦿ *Breakfast.*

$
B&B/INN
🔲 **Hosteria Suiza.** It may not be the most jumping joint in town, but this laid-back guesthouse is a good spot for enjoying the beauty of the desert landscape and lush oasis without having to deal with the constant party that exists in some other hotels. **Pros:** peaceful atmosphere; lovely garden; friendly staff; great pool. **Cons:** restaurant only serves breakfast; furnishings are a little old-fashioned. $ *Rooms from: S/249* ⊠ *Balneario de Huacachina* ☎ *056/238–762* ⊕ *www.hosteriasuiza.com.pe* ⇆ *35 rooms* ⦿ *Breakfast.*

$$
HOTEL
🔲 **Hotel Mossone.** Imagine life as it was in Huacachina's heyday in the original oasis hotel, with a picture-postcard location fronting the lagoon and gorgeous Spanish colonial–style architecture. **Pros:** fantastic lagoonside location; great pool; lounge bar is the best spot in town for watching the sun set over the dunes; bicycles and sandboards available. **Cons:** often full with tour groups. $ *Rooms from: S/380* ⊠ *Balneario de Huacachina s/n* ☎ *056/213–630, 01/261–9605 in Lima* ⊕ *www.dmhoteles.pe* ⇆ *32 rooms* ⦿ *No meals.*

SPORTS AND THE OUTDOORS
SANDBOARDING

Ever fancied having a go at snowboarding but chickened out at the thought of all those painful next-day bruises? Welcome to the new adventure sport of sandboarding, a softer and warmer way to hit the slopes. Surrounded by dunes, Huacachina is the sandboarding capital of the world: every year European sports fans arrive here in droves to practice for the international sandsurfing competitions on Cerro Blanco, the massive dune 14 km (8 miles) north of Nazca.

With no rope tows or chairlifts to get you up the dunes, the easiest way to try sandboarding is to go on a dune-buggy tour (equipment included), offered by just about every hotel in town. In these converted vehicles you'll be driven (quickly) to the top of the dunes, upon which you can board, slide, or slither down to be picked up again at the bottom.

Drivers push their vehicles hard, so be prepared for some heart-stopping moments. Carola del Sur guesthouse (Avenida Perotti s/n) has the biggest fleet of dune buggies and runs two tours daily at 10 am and 4 pm. It's best to go in the morning or late afternoon, when the sand is not as hot and doesn't melt the wax off your board. Be sure to wear a long-sleeved shirt and long pants!

NAZCA

136 km (85 miles) southeast of Ica.

What do a giant hummingbird, a monkey, and an astronaut have in common? Well, apart from the fact that they're all etched into the floor of the desert near Nazca, no one really seems to know. Welcome to one of the world's greatest mysteries—the enigmatic Nazca Lines. A mirage of green in the desert, lined with cotton fields and orchards and bordered by crisp mountain peaks, Nazca was a quiet colonial town unnoticed by the rest of the world until 1901, when Peruvian archaeologist Max Uhle excavated sites around it and discovered the remains of a unique pre-Columbian culture. Set 598 meters (1,961 feet) above sea level, the town has a dry climate—scorching by day, nippy by night—that was instrumental in preserving centuries-old relics from Inca and pre-Columbian tribes. ■TIP➡ The area has more than 100 cemeteries, where the humidity-free climate has helped preserve priceless jewelry, textiles, pottery, and mummies. Overlooking the parched scene is the 2,078-meter (6,815-foot) Cerro Blanco, the highest sand dune in the world.

GETTING HERE AND AROUND

Be prepared: Nazca is all about tours, and it may seem like everyone in town is trying to sell you one at once. The minute you poke your nose outside the bus door, you'll be swamped with offers for flights over the lines, hotels, and trips to the Chauchilla cemetery. Be wise about any offers made to you by touts at the bus station—if it's cheap, there's probably a good reason why. That said, a tour with a reputable agency is a great way to catch all of Nazca's major sites. Recommended agencies include Alegria Tours and Zarcillo Connections in Paracas.

All buses arrive and depart from the *óvalo* (roundabout). To see the lines from ground level, taxis will make the 30-minute run out to the mirador for around S/50, or do it the local way and catch any northbound bus along the Panamericana for just S/3. ■TIP➡ Flights over the lines are best in early morning, before the sun gets too high and winds make flying uncomfortable. Standard flights last around 30 minutes and cost between US$60 and US$140, depending on the season. You'll also have to pay an airport tax of S/30. There are also similar lines at nearby Palpa; some tour operators offer flyovers of both sites. You can buy flight tickets from travel agencies and many hotels in town, or directly from the airline offices near the airport. Buying tickets in advance will save you time. Tickets are available on the spot at the airport, but because planes won't take off until all seats are filled, you may spend most of your morning hanging around the dusty Panamerica Sur watching while others take off and land.

Bus Contacts **Cruz del Sur.** ⊠ *Lima y San Martín* ☎ *056/480–100* ⊕ *www.cruzdelsur.com.pe.*

ESSENTIALS

Currency **Banco de Crédito.** ⊠ *Calle Lima 495* ⊕ *www.viabcp.com.*

Mail **Post Office.** ⊠ *Jr. Fermin del Castillo 379* ☎ *056/522–016* ⊕ *clientes.serpost.com.pe/prj_tracking/redOficinas.aspx.*

Medical **Hospital de Apoyo.** ⊠ *Calle Callao s/n* ☎ *056/522–010* ⊕ *www.hospitalnasca.gob.pe/.*

Police **Comisaría Sectorial.** ⊠ *Av. Los Incas* ☎ *056/522–084* ⊕ *www.mininter.gob.pe/serviciosMAPA-DIRECTORIO-DE-COMISARIAS.*

TOURS

Nazca Airlines and upstarts Aero Nasca, Aero Paracas, and Alas Peruanas all offer services. These latter lines are small operations with varying office hours, so check at the airport for schedules. Most sightseeing flights depart from Nazca, although Aero Paracas also originates in Lima and Pisco. Note that these flights are often overbooked year-round; arrive early to check in for your flight, as many are full and there's a chance you'll get bumped if you're late.

Safety records for many of the airlines are spotty at best. In 2010 seven tourists were killed when their Nazca Airlines flight crashed in the desert. Airlines change owners and names frequently, so it's hard to know exactly who you are flying with.

Aero Nasca. Thirty-minute flights over the Nazca Lines, 60-minute flights over the Nazca and Palpa Lines together, or a full-day tour from Lima include a transfer from your hotel to the airport and a video introduction about the lines. ⊠ *Aeropuerto Maria Reich, Km 447, Panamericana Sur* ☎ *56/522–688* ⊕ *www.aeronasca.com* 🖙 *From S/250.*

Aero Paracas. This airline offers mostly 30-minute flights over the Nazca and Palpa Lines, though in some cases they will fly from Paracas or Lima. ⊠ *Javier Prado Oeste 870, in Lima, Lima* ☎ *01/641–7000* ⊕ *www.aeroparacas.com* 🖙 *From S/250.*

Alas Peruanas. A variety of flights over the Nazca Lines and other area sites are available. Their longer Discovery tours include flights over the Palpa Lines and Cahuachi ruins. They can also arrange transportation from Ica, Paracas, and Pisco. ⊠ *Calle Lima 168* ☎ *056/522–497* ⊕ *www.alasperuanas.com* 🖙 *From S/250.*

Alegría Tours. Lesser known desert and ruin tours are emphasized here, such as four-hour trips to the Cahuachi cemetery and the Cantallo Aqueducts. They can also add a sandboarding excursion on Nazca's Usaka dunes. ⊠ *Hotel Alegría, Calle Lima 168* ☎ *056/522-497* ⊕ *www. alegriatoursperu.com* 🖙 *From S/100.*

EXPLORING

Cahuachi Pyramids. Within a walled, 4,050-square-yard courtyard west of the Nazca Lines is an ancient ceremonial and pilgrimage site. Six adobe pyramids, the highest of which is about 21 meters (69 feet), stand above a network of 40 mounds with rooms and connecting corridors. Grain and water silos are also inside, and several large cemeteries lie outside the walls. Used by the early Nazca culture, the site is estimated to have existed for about two centuries before being abandoned about AD 200. Cahuachi takes its name from the word *qahuachi* (meddlesome). El Estaquería, with its mummification pillars, is nearby. Tours from Nazca, 34 km (21 miles) to the east, visit both sites for around S/40 with a group and take three hours. ⊠ *Nazca.*

Casa-Museo Maria Reiche. To see where a lifelong obsession with the Nazca Lines can lead you, head to the former home of the German anthropologist who devoted her life to studying their mystery. There's little explanatory material among the pottery, textiles, mummies, and skeletons from the Paracas, Nazca, Wari, Chincha, and Inca cultures, so don't expect any of the area's enigmas to be solved here. What you will see is the environment in which Maria Reiche lived and worked. Her vast collection of tools, notes, and sketches is impressive, but if you're not particularly into her life story and the history of the lines, this can probably be skipped. Reiche, who died in 1998, is buried here in a small tomb. A scale model of the lines is behind the house. Take a bus from the Ormeño terminal to the Km 416 marker to reach the museum, which is 1 km (½ mile) from town. ⊠ *Km 416, Pan-American Hwy., San Pablo* ☎ *034/234–383* 🖃 *S/25.*

Cementerio de Chauchilla. In the midst of the pale, scorched desert, 30 km (19 miles) south of Nazca—the last 12 km (7 miles) of the road is unpaved—this ancient cemetery is scattered with sun-bleached skulls and shards of pottery. *Huaqueros* (grave robbers) have ransacked the site over the years, and while up until a couple of years ago the mummies unearthed by their looting erupted from the earth in a jumble of bones and threadbare weavings, they are now housed neatly inside a dozen or so covered tombs. It's nevertheless an eerie sight, as the mummies still have hair attached, as well as mottled, brown-rose skin stretched around empty eye sockets and gaping mouths with missing teeth. Some are wrapped in tattered burial sacks, though the jewelry and ceramics with which they were laid to rest are long gone. Tours from town take about three hours and cost around S/50. Visits to the cemetery are also packaged with Nazca Lines flights. ⊠ *Carretera a Chauchilla* 🖃 *S/8.*

El Estaquería. These wooden pillars, 34 km (21 miles) west of Nazca, carved of *huarango* wood and placed on mud-brick platforms, were once thought to have been an astronomical observatory. More recent theories, however, lean toward their use in mummification rituals, perhaps to dry bodies of deceased tribal members. They are usually visited on a tour of Cahuachi. ⊠ *Nazca* 🖃 *Free.*

Museo Antonini. For an overview of the Nazca culture and the various archaeological sites in the region, this Italian-run museum is the best in town. The displays, made up of materials excavated from the surrounding archaeological digs, are heavy on scientific information and light on entertainment, although the display of Nazcan trophy skulls will appeal to the morbid, and textiles fans will appreciate the display of painted fabrics from the ancient adobe city of Cahuachi. All the signage is in Spanish, so ask for the translation book at the front desk. Don't miss the still-working Nazcan aqueduct in the back garden. ⊠ *Av. de la Cultura 600* ☎ *056/523–444* 🖃 *S/20, S/25 with a camera.*

Continued on page 136

by Ruth Anne Phillips

NAZCA LINES

On the surface of the southern Peruvian coastal desert or "Pampa" between the Nazca and Ingenio River valleys are the Nazca Lines. The Nazca Lines are enormous figures, geometric designs and straight lines etched into the desert's surface called geoglyphs. There are more than 1,000 enormous figures, geometric shapes and straight lines, some arranged as ray centers. While the most famous of the lines appear on the Pampa de San José near Nazca as well as on the hillsides of the valleys of the Río Grande de Nazca, the geoglyphs are throughout a larger area that comprises 400 square miles.

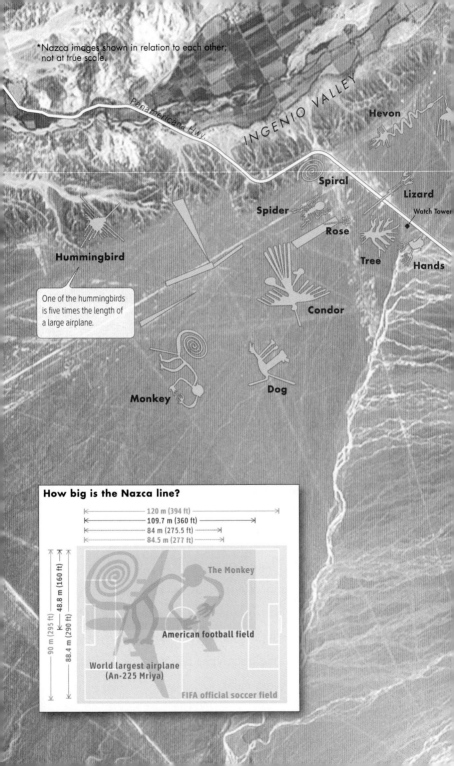

*Nazca images shown in relation to each other; not at true scale.

INGENIO VALLEY

Penamericana Hwy.

Hevon

Spiral

Lizard

Watch Tower

Spider

Rose

Hummingbird

Tree

Hands

One of the hummingbirds is five times the length of a large airplane.

Condor

Monkey

Dog

How big is the Nazca line?

120 m (394 ft)
109.7 m (360 ft)
84 m (275.5 ft)
84.5 m (277 ft)

48.8 m (160 ft)

90 m (295 ft)

88.4 m (290 ft)

The Monkey

American football field

World largest airplane
(An-225 Mriya)

FIFA official soccer field

THINGS TO LOOK FOR

The biomorphic designs include monkeys, birds, a spider, plants, and a number of fantastical combinations and somewhat abstracted humanoid creatures. One of the monkeys is 180 feet long while a hummingbird is five times the length of a large airplane. At least 227 spirals, zigzags, triangles, quadrangles, and trapezoids make up the geometric designs, with one trapezoid measuring over 2,700 feet by 300

A trapezoid.

feet. The straight lines represent the greatest proportion of the geoglyphs: 800 single or parallel lines stretch on for miles, ranging in width from less than two feet to hundreds of feet.

Many of the lines haphazardly overlap each other, which indicates that as a group they were not pre-planned.

CONSTRUCTION
Modern archaeologists have recreated surprisingly simple construction methods for the geoglyphs using basic surveying techniques. Sight poles guided the construction of straight lines and strings tied to posts helped create circular designs. Wooden posts that may have been used as guides or end markers and an abundance of fancy potsherds, possibly used in rituals, have been found along many of the lines.

AGE
The extremely dry climatic conditions of the Pampa have helped preserve the lines; most date from c. 500 AD, during the florescence of the Nazca culture (c. 1–700 AD). A small number, however, may date to after the Nazca period to as late as 1000 AD.

Panamericana Hwy.
(18 miles from Nazca to Ingenio Valley)

TO NAZCA

Astronaut

HISTORY AND MYSTERY

An archaeologist examines the lines.

Though the Nazca Lines are difficult to see from the ground due to their enormous size, some can be seen from nearby hillsides. It's widely believed that the lines were first properly seen from an airplane, but they were "discovered" by archaeologists working near Cahuachi in the mid-1920s. American archaeologist, Alfred L. Kroeber was the first to describe them in 1926, but it was Peruvian archaeologist Toribio Mejía Xesspe who conducted the first extensive studies of the Nazca Lines around the same time.

By the late 1920s, commercial planes began flying over the Pampa and many reported seeing the Nazca Lines from the air. It was not until American geographer and historian, Paul Kosok and his second wife Rose, flew over the Nazca drainage area in 1941, however, that the Nazca Lines became a widely known phenomenon in the United States and Europe.

THE CREATIVE PROCESS

The dry desert plain acts as a giant scratchpad as the darker oxidized surface can be swept away to reveal the lighter, pale pink subsurface. Many of the shapes are made with one continuous line that has piles of dark rocks lining the edges creating a dark border.

Stylistic comparisons between the figural Nazca Lines and images that appear on Nazca ceramics have helped establish their age.

THEORIES ABOUND

The Nazca Lines have incited various scholarly and popular theories for their construction and significance. Kroeber and Xesspe, observing the lines from the ground, believed that they served as sacred pathways. Kosok, seeing the lines from the air, observed the sun setting over the end of one line on the day of the winter solstice and thought they must have marked important astronomical events. German mathematician Maria Reiche, who studied the lines and lived near them for decades, expanded upon Kosok's astronomical theories. Modern scholars, however, have demonstrated that the lines' alignment to celestial events occurred at a frequency no greater than chance. Other theories posit that they were made for earth, mountain, or sky deities. After Cahuachi was determined in the 1980s to have been a large pilgrimage center, the idea that the lines acted as a sacred pathway has gained new momentum. Another plausible theory suggests that the Nazca Lines marked underground water sources.

IT'S THE ALIENS, OF COURSE

Popular theories have promoted the "mystery" of the Nazca Lines. One influential author, Erich von Däniken, suggested in his 1968 best-selling book *Chariots of the Gods* (reprinted several times and made into a film) that these giant geoglyphs were created as landing

Spaceman figure, San Jose Pampa

markers for extraterrestrials. Archaeologists and other scientists have dismissed these theories. The aliens deny them as well.

VISITING THE NAZCA LINES

The best way to view the Nazca Lines is by air in small, low-flying aircraft. Local companies offer flights usually in the early morning, when viewing conditions are best. You can fly over several birds, a few fish, a monkey, a spider, a flower, a condor, and/or several unidentified figures. While seeing the

The "Candelabra of the Andes" or the "Paracas Candelabra" on the Peninsula de Paracas.

amazing Nazca Lines is a great experience, the sometimes questionable-looking airplanes with their strong fumes and pilots who seem to enjoy making nausea-inducing turns and twists can be worrisome. Because of poor safety records, planes are often grounded. Check with your tour operator before booking a trip with any local airline.

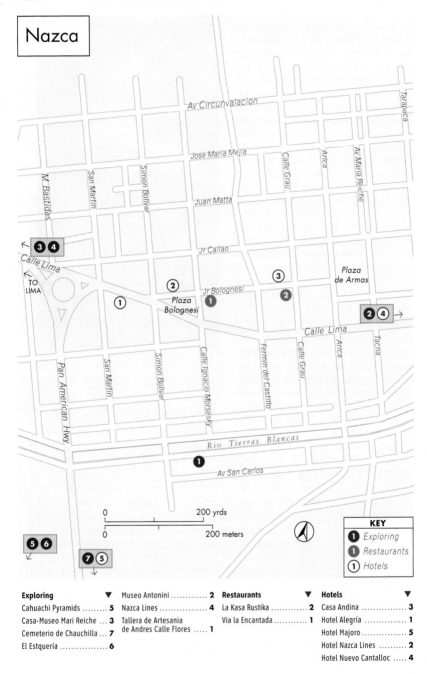

Nazca

KEY
- **1** *Exploring*
- **1** *Restaurants*
- **1** *Hotels*

Fodor's Choice ★ **Nazca Lines.** Even with the knowledge of the Nazca culture obtained from archeological digs, it was not until 1929 that the Nazca Lines were discovered, when American scientist Paul Kosok looked out his plane window as he flew over them. Almost invisible from ground level, the lines were made by removing the surface stones and piling them beside the lighter soil underneath. More than 300 geometrical and biomorphic figures, some measuring up to 300 meters (1,000 feet) across, are etched into the desert floor, including a hummingbird, a monkey, a spider, a pelican, a condor, a whale, and an "astronaut," so named because of his goldfish-bowl-shaped head. Theories abound as to their purpose, and some have devoted their lives to the study of the lines. Probably the most famous person to do so was Kosok's translator, German scientist Dr. Maria Reiche, who studied the lines from 1940 until her death in 1998. ✉ *Pampas de San José* ✣ *20 km (12 miles) northwest of Nazca town.*

Tallera de Artesania de Andres Calle Flores. Everyone comes to town for the Nazca Lines, but it's worth visiting the studio of Tobi Flores, whose father Andres Calle Flores years ago discovered old pottery remnants and started making new pottery based on old designs and forms. He hosts a funny and informative talk in the kiln and workshop, and afterward you can purchase some beautiful pottery for S/30 to S/60. It's a quick walk across the bridge from downtown Nazca; at night, take a cab. ✉ *Pje. Torrico 240, off Av. San Carlos* ☎ *056/522–319* 🎫 *Free.*

WHERE TO EAT

$ PERUVIAN 🍴 **La Kasa Rustika.** All the classics of Peruvian cooking are on offer at this well-loved local hangout. The *corvina a lo macho* (sea bass in shellfish sauce) and the pepper steak are both scrumptious. **Known for:** classic Peruvian cooking; local favorite. [$] *Average main: S/30* ✉ *Bolognesi 372* ☎ *056/324–463* 🌐 *lakasarustika.com.pe/* 🕒 *Closed Sun.*

$ PERUVIAN Fodor's Choice ★ 🍴 **Via La Encantada.** With food that is as modern as the stylish interior, this is the best spot in town to try Peruvian-fusion cuisine. The *pollo a lo oporto,* chicken in a port wine sauce, is a standout, as is the cocktail list, including the tricolor Macchu Pichu pisco cocktail. **Known for:** criollo and international cuisine; friendly atmosphere. [$] *Average main: S/30* ✉ *Calle Bolognesi 282* ☎ *056/522–728* 🌐 *vialaencantada.com.pe.*

WHERE TO STAY

$ HOTEL Fodor's Choice ★ 🏨 **Casa Andina.** Part of a national chain, this hotel offers the best value for the money of any of Nazca's top-end lodgings. **Pros:** welcoming service; good value; Wi-Fi and business center. **Cons:** the pool is on the small side. [$] *Rooms from: S/215* ✉ *Calle Bolognesi 367* ☎ *056/523–563, 01/319–6500 in Lima* 🌐 *www.casa-andina.com/destinos/nasca/standard-nasca/* 🛏 *60 rooms* 🍽 *Breakfast.*

$ HOTEL 🏨 **Hotel Alegría.** Long a favorite with travelers, this classic Nazca hotel is set around a sunny courtyard with swimming pool—a perfect spot to relax after a dusty morning flight over the Nasca Lines. **Pros:** friendly staff; good pool; book exchange. **Cons:** smallish rooms; often full. [$] *Rooms from: S/200* ✉ *Calle Lima 168* ☎ *056/522–702* 🌐 *www.hotelalegria.net* 🛏 *45 rooms* 🍽 *Breakfast.*

$$ ☷ **Hotel Majoro.** Set amid 60 acres of fragrant gardens and surrounded
HOTEL   by cotton fields, this quiet, 80-year-old hacienda and former Augustine
convent, situated 1½ km (1 mile) from the airport, offers a taste of life
on a farm. **Pros:** peaceful atmosphere; lovely gardens and alpacas and
vicuñas on grounds; good travel services. **Cons:** out of town; popular
with tour groups; some airplane noise. $ *Rooms from: S/360* ⊠ *Km
453, Pan-American Hwy. S* ☎ *056/522–481* ⊕ *www.hotelmajoro.com*
⤶ *62 rooms* ⍾⃝⃒ *Breakfast.*

$ ☷ **Hotel Nazca Lines.** Mixing colonial elegance with all the mod-cons,
HOTEL   this historic hacienda is a Nazca landmark, formerly home to Maria
Fodor'sChoice   Reiche (she lived in room 130 for 25 years), and has long drawn inter-
★   national tourists and adventurers seeking to solve the mysteries of the
Lines. **Pros:** magnificent pool; nightly lectures; colonial charm. **Cons:**
busy staff; tour groups; dated. $ *Rooms from: S/190* ⊠ *Av. Bolognesi
147* ☎ *056/522–293, 01/614–3900 in Lima* ⊕ *dmhoteles.pe/eng/hotel/
hotel-in-nasca* ⤶ *78 rooms* ⍾⃝⃒ *Breakfast.*

$$ ☷ **Hotel Nuevo Cantalloc.** At this sprawling hacienda-style resort a
RESORT   10-minute drive from the center of Nasca, the owners have created an
eclectic look that adds modern touches to the farmhouse setting. **Pros:**
two pools; spa. **Cons:** far from town; often empty. $ *Rooms from: S/430*
⊠ *Desvío Puquio Km 3–Km 4, Pan-American Hwy. Sud* ☎ *056/522–
264* ⊕ *www.hotelnuevocantalloc.com* ⤶ *40 rooms* ⍾⃝⃒ *Breakfast.*

THE SOUTHERN ANDES AND LAKE TITICACA

WELCOME TO THE SOUTHERN ANDES AND LAKE TITICACA

TOP REASONS TO GO

★ **Wild Rivers:** Fantastic rapids and gorges make Colca Canyon and Cotahuasi Canyon the region's best-known kayaking, rafting, and hiking spots.

★ **Folk Fiestas:** Whether it's the Virgen de la Candelaria Festival in Puno, Arequipa's annual anniversary, or Semana Santa in Chivay, Peru's culture is celebrated with more than 300 festive folkloric dances featuring brightly colored costumes.

★ **Wildlife:** Llamas, vicuñas, and alpacas roam the Reserva Nacional Salinas y Aguada Blanca, giant Andean condors soar above Colca Canyon, and rare bird species nest at Lake Titicaca and in other highland lakes.

★ **Shopping:** Along with Arequipa's alpaca stores, this region is also a mine of yarn, leather products, guitars, and antiques.

★ **Lake Titicaca:** The birthplace of the sun is a magical sight, as are the floating Uros Islands made of totora reeds.

1 Arequipa. Arequipa is known as La Cuidad Blanca, or The White City, for its dazzling *sillar*—a white volcanic rock from which nearly all the Spanish-colonial buildings are constructed. The most-European-looking city in all of Peru, it's also the most romantic one. It's home to the ice mummy Juanita, the Santa Catalina Monastery, and scores of museums.

2 Canyon Country. Dusty and dry, this is a place of striking geology, wildlife, and history. It's also a playground for adventure-sports lovers. Four hours northeast of Arequipa is Colca Canyon, the second-deepest gorge in the world. It's home to the intense Río Colca, 14 tiny villages, the giant Andean condor, and some of the best hiking in the country. Ten hours away is Colca's less-visited sister gorge, the world's deepest canyon, Cotahuasi Canyon, now a tourist destination in its own right.

GETTING ORIENTED

Arequipa, Colca Canyon, Puno, and Lake Titicaca are often add-ons to a trip to Machu Picchu. They are all part of what is often referred to as the "Southern Circuit," as they are located south of both Lima and Cusco. Rather than just linking the journey between those two cities, however, they make good destinations on their own and offer a different and larger perspective of the country than simply the "Lost City of the Incas."

3 Puno and Lake Titicaca. Puno is known as the folkloric capital of Peru, and its annual festivals shine with elaborate costumes, music, and dancing in the streets. Puno has high-quality hotels and good restaurants, and it's the jumping-off point to Lake Titicaca, the world's highest navigable lake, which encompasses parts of both Peru and Bolivia. Outdoor adventures and unique island cultures are found throughout the lake's islands.

Updated by Maureen Santucci

Though often overshadowed by Cusco and the Sacred Valley, the south of Peru has some of the most dynamic, jaw-dropping geography and exciting cultural attractions anywhere in the country.

Arequipa is Peru's second-largest city, a Spanish-colonial maze, with volcanic white sillar buildings, well-groomed plazas, and wonderful food, museums, and designer alpaca products. Arequipa is close to Colca Canyon, where many head to see the famed gorge for its stunning beauty, depth, and Andean condors. Several hours farther out is the very remote Cotahuasi Canyon, the world's deepest gorge.

A rival in magnificence to Machu Picchu, Lake Titicaca is home to the floating islands. The Uros Islands are around 40 man-made islands—constructed from the lake's totora reeds—and are literally floating. The natives are the Quechua and Aymara peoples, who still speak their respective languages and will introduce you to a way of life that has changed little in centuries.

Puno, an agricultural city on the shores of Titicaca, is the jumping-off point for exploring the lake, and is Peru's folkloric capital. A dusty-brown city most of the time, Puno is a colorful whirlwind during festivals. The region's many fiestas feature elaborate costumes, storytelling dances, music, and lots of merrymaking. Each November and February Puno puts on two spectacular shows for local holidays.

PLANNING

WHEN TO GO
In the mountains and high plains, the blistering sun keeps you warm from May through early November, but nights get cold. Rainy season is from mid-November until April, when it's cooler and cloudy, but rain isn't a guarantee. Use sunscreen, even if it's cloudy.

PLANNING YOUR TIME
Arequipa is a good jumping-off point to the Southern Andes and Lake Titicaca. Acclimatize while taking in the sights, then head to the Colca Canyon. The four-hour drive travels over Patapampa Pass, for views of

the Valley of the Volcanoes, and through the Reserva Nacional Salinas y Aguada Blanca, where herds of wild vicuñas, llamas, and alpacas graze. At the canyon you can go on a multiday hike or relax at a country lodge, but nearly everyone comes to spy condors at Cruz del Condor. Afterward, either continue by car to Puno or head back to Arequipa and on to Puno and Lake Titicaca by bus or plane. There, you can book an overnight island homestay, visit the floating islands, and/or see the Sillustanti ruins. From Puno, some head to Bolivia while others move on to Cusco by bus or plane. Similarly, you can travel to Puno from Cusco and begin your exploration in the opposite direction.

FESTIVALS

Some of Peru's festivals and events provide a good reason to choose a particular time of year to travel, notably Carnaval in February and town anniversary celebrations in June (Chivay) and August (Arequipa). Make your reservations far in advance if you plan to travel at these times.

Corso de Amis. August 15 is the anniversary of the city's founding—in 2015 it was 475 years old—and each year thousands take to the streets all day for the big parade, with music, dancing, traditional costumes, and decorated floats. ⊠ *Arequipa* 🕾 *054/223–265 iPeru tourist office.*

Virgin de la Candelaria. Vast numbers of singers, dancers, and marching bands parade through the streets, accompanying the statue of the Virgin in early February each year in one of Peru's biggest celebrations. You'll also see a huge range of traditional dances, performed in colorful costumes. ⊠ *Puno* ⊕ *www.virgencandelaria.com.*

Virgin del Carmen. In mid-July, each end of the Colca Canyon has two days of celebrations to mark this festival, with singing, dancing, bullfights, food and drink, and parades in Chivay and Cabanaconde. After night falls, impressive fireworks light up the sky. ⊠ *Chivay.*

GETTING HERE AND AROUND

AIR TRAVEL

Flights take between 30 minutes and an hour to fly anywhere in southern Peru, and a one-way ticket costs US$90 to US$190. LATAM (⊕ *www.latam.com*) has daily flights between Lima and Rodríguez Ballón International Airport, 7 km (4½ miles) from Arequipa. Peruvian Airlines (⊕ *www.peruvianairlines.com.pe*), LC Peru (⊕ *www.lcperu.pe*) and Avianca (⊕ *www.avianca.com*) also have daily flights. LATAM and Avianca offer daily flights to Aeropuerto Manco Cápac in Juliaca, the closest airport to Puno and Lake Titicaca. It takes 45 minutes to drive from Juliaca to downtown Puno.

BUS TRAVEL

The road between Arequipa and Puno has been paved, so instead of 20 hours the trip now takes only about six. Service is also good between Puno and Cusco, and so is the road between Puno and Copacabana in Bolivia. Cruz del Sur (⊕ *www.cruzdelsur.com.pe*), CIVA, Inka Express, Flores, and Ormeño (⊕ *www.grupo-ormeno.com.pe/ormeno.php*) have offices in Puno and Arequipa, and each runs daily buses between the two cities. For your comfort and safety, take the best service you can afford; some (but not all) of the nicer ones are also free of the loud music that blares on most buses for the entire journey. There is also the potential for crime on night buses; choosing a reputable company can help avoid this. Several bus companies sell tickets that go direct, so buy one of those or be prepared for a long slog, during which drivers stop for every passerby. Bus stations in Peru are known for crime, mostly theft of your belongings, so always hold on to your bags.

CAR TRAVEL

Car rental services are in Arequipa's center and at the airport. Keep your car travel to daylight hours: night driving poses a number of risks—blockades, crime on tourists, and steep roads. A 4x4 is needed for the canyons. Although the road from Arequipa to Chivay has improved, the last hour of the journey is rough and has steep cliffs. Use even more caution if traveling into Cotahuasi Canyon: only half of the 10-hour drive is paved, and even the paved areas develop potholes that can remain unrepaired.

TAXI TRAVEL

Ask any *arequipeño* and they'll tell you Arequipa has three major concerns: earthquakes, the looming threat of volcanoes, and taxis. The city has the most taxis per capita of any city in Peru. Pint-size yellow cars, namely miniature Daewoo Ticos, clog the streets. Pollution is high, there are accidents aplenty, and rush-hour traffic rivals that of Los Angeles. Taxis are also readily available in Puno although, as a smaller city, the numbers are not as vast as in Arequipa.

TRAIN TRAVEL

Train travel on PeruRail (⊕ *www.perurail.com*) is slow but scenic and more relaxing than a bus blasting reggaeton. A Pullman train ticket means more comfort, not to mention a meal and increased security. The train goes only between Cusco and Puno. It's a popular way to take in the dramatic change of scenery as you ride over La Raya Pass at 4,315 meters (14,157 feet). The trip takes about nine hours and includes a stop at the highest point. The route runs only a few days per week, depending on the season. For a full listing of PeruRail trips, check out the website. It's now possible to book online.

HEALTH AND SAFETY

Visiting mountain towns and Lake Titicaca can bring on *soroche* (altitude sickness). Nonprescription remedies include *mate de coca* (coca tea) and *pastillas de sorojchi* (over-the-counter pills). As these latter contain only caffeine, aspirin, and an aspirin substitute, your own preferred headache remedy is just as good. Drink lots of bottled water and forego alcohol, coffee, and heavy meals at first. Be aware that prescription altitude medication is typically sulfa-based, a substance many people have allergies to. ■TIP→ There is no substitute for proper acclimatization.

Colca Canyon is generally safe, as are Arequipa and Puno. Nevertheless, don't walk alone at night, know where your money is, and educate yourself on the good and bad parts of town. Police presence has increased in Arequipa. Use only recommended taxi companies, or have someone call one for you. But walking around the plaza, even at night, is safe in Arequipa. Hiking El Misti alone is not recommended. Puno is generally safe in the tourist areas, but at night the port and the hills should be avoided.

RESTAURANTS

You can find everything from *cuy* (guinea pig) to wood-fired pizza at the many excellent restaurants in Arequipa and Puno, where dining possibilities range from sophisticated Novo Andino cuisine to traditional fare and international dishes. Food in Arequipa is known for strong, fresh flavors, from herbs and spices to vegetables served with native Andean foods like alpaca meat and *olluco,* a colorful Andean tuber. In the mountains the cool, thin Andean air calls for hearty, savory soups and heaps and heaps of carbs in the form of the potato. Whether they're fried, boiled, baked, with cheese, in soup, or alone, you will be eating potatoes. In Puno fresh trout or kingfish from the lake is served in almost every restaurant. Puno also has a special affection for adobe-oven, wood-fired pizza.

HOTELS

Arequipa and Puno are overloaded with hotels. Although a growing number of resorts and chain hotels are set along the lakeside, most of the properties within the city of Puno are small boutique hotels with local owners pining to get in on the tourist boom in this otherwise agricultural town. As a commercial business center, Arequipa has more high-end hotels that cater to business travelers, and given its fame for being the romance city, it also has lots of small inns. *Hotel reviews have been shortened. For full information, visit Fodors.com.*

WHAT IT COSTS IN NUEVO SOLES			
$	**$$**	**$$$**	**$$$$**
Restaurants under S/35	S/35–S/50	S/51–S/65	over S/65
Hotels under S/250	S/250–S/500	S/501–S/800	over S/800

Restaurant prices are the average cost of a main course at dinner or, if dinner is not served, at lunch. Hotel prices are the lowest cost of a standard double room in high season.

AREQUIPA

150 km (93 miles) south of Colca Canyon; 200 km (124 miles) south of Cotahuasi Canyon.

Cradled by three steep, gargantuan, snow-covered volcanoes, the jaw-dropping white-stoned Arequipa, one of the most visually stunning cities in Peru, shines under the striking sun at 2,350 meters (7,710 feet). This settlement of nearly 1 million residents grew from a collection of Spanish-colonial churches and homes constructed from white sillar (volcanic stone) gathered from the surrounding terrain. The result is nothing less than a work of art—short, gleaming-white buildings contrast with the charcoal-color mountain backdrop of El Misti, a perfectly shaped cone volcano.

The town was a gathering of Aymara Indians and Incas when Garí Manuel de Carbajal and nearly 100 more Spaniards founded the city on August 15, 1540. After the Spanish arrived, the town grew into the region's most profitable center for farming and cattle raising—businesses still important to Arequipa's economy.

The settlement was also on the silver route linking the coast to the Bolivian mines. By the 1800s Arequipa had more Spanish settlers than any town in the south.

Arequipeños call their home La Cuidad Blanca, "The White City," and the "Independent Republic of Arequipa"—they have made several attempts to secede from Peru and even designed the city's own passport and flag. Today the town is abuzz with adventure outfitters leading tours into the surrounding canyons, locals and visitors mingling at bars and cafés in 500-year-old sillar buildings, and shoppers seeking the finest alpaca threads anywhere in the country. ■ TIP→ **On August 15, parades, fireworks, bullfights, and dancing celebrate the city's founding.**

Arequipa enjoys fresh, crisp air, and warm days averaging 23°C (73°F) and comfortable nights at 14°C (57°F). To make up for the lack of rain, the Río Chili waters the surrounding foothills, which were once farmed by the Inca and now stretch into rows of alfalfa and onions.

GETTING HERE AND AROUND

Arequipa's airport is located on the outskirts of the city, and there are plenty of taxis waiting to take you into the center. Many hotels also offer pickup and drop-off. The cost is about S/30.

Walking is the best option around the city center. Most sights, shops, and restaurants are near the Plaza de Armas. For a quick, cheap tour, spend S/5 and catch a Vallecito bus for a 1½-hour circuit around Calles Jerusalén and San Juan de Díos. Taxis are everywhere, and cost about S/4–S/8 to get around the center or to Vallecito.

Arequipa has two bus terminals side by side on Avenida Ibañez and Avenida Andrés Avelino Cáceres. Most people leave out of the older Terminal Terreste, where most bus companies have offices, whereas the newer terminal Terrapuerto sees less traffic.

Rental Cars Avis. ⊠ *Aeropuerto Rodriguez Ballon* ☎ *054/443–887* ⊕ *www.avis.com.pe.* **Hertz.** ⊠ *Aeropuerto Rodriguez Ballón* ☎ *051/445–5716* ⊕ *www.hertz.com.*

Taxi Easy Taxi. ☎ *017/164–600 to report problems* ⊕ *www.easytaxi.com.* **Taxi Turismo Arequipa.** ☎ *054/458–888, 054/459–090* ⊕ *www.taxiturismo.com.pe.*

TIMING

Most sites are open morning and afternoon, but close for a couple of hours at midday. Churches usually open 7 to 9 am and 6 to 8 pm, before and after services.

SAFETY AND PRECAUTIONS

Wear comfortable walking shoes and bring a hat, sunscreen, a Spanish dictionary or phrase book, some small change, and a good map of town. Be street-smart in the Arequipa market area—access your cash discreetly and keep your valuables close. At 2,350 meters (7,510 feet), Arequipa is quite high. If you're coming directly from Lima or from the coast, carve out a day or two for acclimatization.

ESSENTIALS

Currency Banco Continental BBVA. ⊠ *San Francisco 108* ☎ *054/215–060.* **Banco de Crédito BCP.** ⊠ *San Juan de Díos 123* ☎ *054/283–741.* **Caja Municipal Arequipa.** ⊠ *La Merced 106* ☎ *054/380–670.* **Scotiabank.** ⊠ *Mercaderes 410.*

Mail DHL. ⊠ *Santa Catalina 115* ☎ *054/234–288.* **Serpost Arequipa.** ⊠ *Calle Moral 118* ☎ *054/215–247* ⊕ *www.serpost.com.pe.*

Medical Clínica Arequipa SA. ⊠ *Puente Grau y Av. Bolognesi* ☎ *054/599–000* ⊕ *www.clinicarequipa.com.pe.* **Hospital III Regional Honorio Delgado.** ⊠ *Av. Daniel Alcides Carrión 505, La Pampilla* ☎ *054/231–818, 054/219–702,* ⊕ *www.hrhdaqp.gob.pe.* **Hospital Goyeneche.** ⊠ *Av. Goyeneche s/n, Cercado* ☎ *054/231–313* ⊕ *www.hospitalgoyeneche.gob.pe.*

Police Policía de Turismo. ⊠ *Jerusalén 315* ☎ *054/282–613.*

Visitor Information Iperu Oficina de Información Turística. ⊠ *Portal de la Municipalidad 110, Plaza de Armas* ☎ *054/223–265* ⊕ *www.peru.travel/iperu. aspx* ⊠ *Aeropuerto Rodríguez Ballón, Arrivals* ☎ *054/299–191* ⊕ *www.peru. travel/iperu.aspx.*

TOURS

For the standard one- or two-day tours to Colca Canyon most agencies pool their customers, so quality varies little. The following two options offer more personalized service as well and tend to be more attentive to their clients.

Giardino. Since 1995, Giardino Tours has been running tours all over the region, building up a reliable infrastructure and keeping current on any new developments in the area. They have received various awards for providing quality service. ⊠ *Jerusalén 604-A* ☎ *054/200–100* ⊕ *www. giardinotours.com* ⊠ *From S/90.*

Peru Mistika Travel. Although a relative newcomer compared to some of the other long-standing agencies in the Arequipa area, the team has years of experience in tourism in the region and offers a variety of great tours. They bring a fresh outlook and energy to the scene, offering their clients personalized care and service. ⊠ *Calle Santa Marta 304, Of. 208* ☎ *054/636–014* ⊕ *www.perumistikatravel.com* ⊠ *From S/59.*

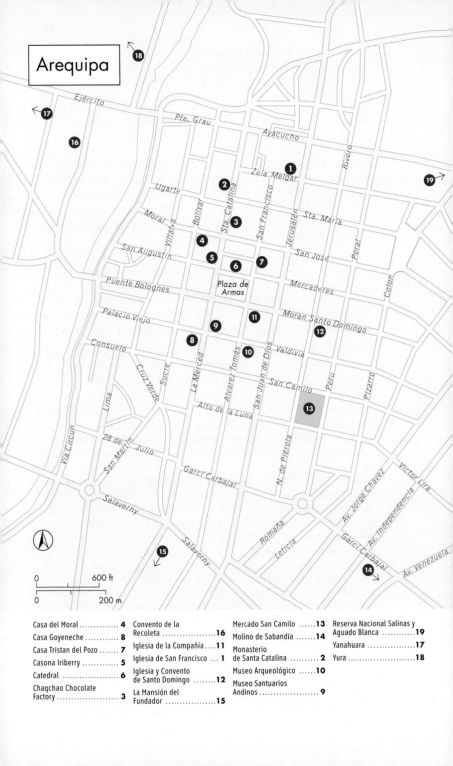

Arequipa

EXPLORING

TOP ATTRACTIONS

Casa del Moral. One of the oldest architectural landmarks from the Arequipa baroque period was named for the ancient *mora* tree (mulberry tree) growing in the center of the main patio. One of the town's most unusual buildings, it now houses the Banco Sur, but it's open to the public. Over the front door, carved into a white sillar portal, is the Spanish coat of arms as well as a baroque-mestizo design that combines puma heads with snakes darting from their mouths—motifs found on Nazca textiles and pottery. The interior of the house is like a small museum with alpaca rugs and soaring ceilings, polished period furniture, and a gallery of colonial period Cusco School paintings. Originally a lovely old colonial home, it was bought in the 1940s by the British consul and renovated to its former elegance in the early 1990s. ⊠ *Moral 318 and Bolívar* ☎ *054/285–371* 🖅 *S/5* ⊙ *Closed Sun.*

Fodor's Choice ★ **Catedral.** You can't miss the imposing twin bell towers of this 1612 cathedral, with a facade guarding the entire eastern flank of the Plaza de Armas. ■ **TIP→ As the sun sets the imperial reflection gives the cathedral an amber hue.** The interior has high-vaulted ceilings above a beautiful Belgian organ. The ornate wooden pulpit, carved by French artist Buisine-Rigot in 1879, was transported here in the early 1900s. In the back, look for the *Virgin of the Sighs* statue in her white wedding dress, and the figure of Beata Sor Ana de Los Ángeles, a nun from the Santa Catalina Monastery who was beatified by Pope John Paul II when he stayed in Arequipa in 1990. A fire in 1844 destroyed much of the cathedral, as did an 1868 earthquake, so parts have a neoclassical look. In 2001 another earthquake damaged one of the bell towers, which was repaired to match its sister tower. ⊠ *Plaza de Armas, between Santa Catalina and San Francisco* ☎ *054/213–149* ⊕ *www.museocatedralarequipa.org.pe* 🖅 *S/10* ⊙ *Closed Sun.*

FAMILY **Chaqchao Chocolate Factory.** Educate your passion for chocolate at this store and workshop where you learn how it gets from bean to bar by making tasty treats from fair-trade Peruvian-sourced cacao. If you don't have time for the workshop, you can shop the store for delicious souvenirs. ⊠ *Calle Santa Catalina 204* ☎ *054/234–572* ✉ *chaqchao@gmail.com* ⊕ *chaqchao.wordpress.com* 🖅 *S/60 for workshop.*

Iglesia de la Compañía. Representative of 17th-century religious architecture, the complex was built by the Jesuits in 1573 and its series of bone-white buildings incorporate many decorative styles and touches—the detail carved into the sillar arcades is spectacular. The side portal, built in 1654, and main facade, built in 1698, show examples of Andean mestizo style, with carved flowers, spirals, birds—and angels with Indian faces—along gently curving archways and spiral pillars. Inside, **Capilla St. Ignatius** (St. Ignatius Chapel) has a polychrome cupola and 66 canvases from the Cusco School, including original 17th-century oil paintings by Bernardo Bitti. Hike up to the steeple at sunset for sweeping views of Arequipa. The former monastery houses some of the most upscale stores in the city and contains two cloisters, which can be entered from General Morán or Palacio Viejo. The main building is on the southeast corner of the Plaza de Armas. ⊠ *General Morán at Álvarez Tomás* ☎ *054/212–141* ⊕ *jesuitasaqp.pe* 🖅 *Chapel S/5.*

4

Fodor's Choice
★
Monasterio de Santa Catalina. A city unto itself, this 5-acre complex of mud-brick, Iberian-style buildings—a working convent and one of Peru's most famed cultural treasures—is surrounded by vibrant fortresslike walls and separated by neat, open plazas and colorful gardens. Founded in 1579 and closed to the public for the first 400 years, Santa Catalina was an exclusive retreat for the daughters of Arequipa's wealthiest colonial patrons. Now visitors can catch a peek at life in this historic monastery. Narrow streets run past the Courtyard of Silence, where teenage nuns lived during their first year, and the Cloister of Oranges, where nuns decorated their rooms with lace sheets, silk curtains, and antique furnishings. Though it once housed about 400 nuns, fewer than 30 call it home today. Admission includes a one-hour guided tour (tip S/15–S/20) in English. Afterward, head to the cafeteria for the nuns' famous *torta de naranja* (orange cake), pastries, and tea. There are night tours on Tuesday and Thursday, but check the times before you go, as they sometimes change. ⊠ *Santa Catalina 301* ☎ *054/221–213* ⊕ *www.santacatalina.org.pe* ⊡ *S/40.*

Fodor's Choice
★
Museo Santuarios Andinos. Referred to as the Juanita Museum, this fascinating little museum at the Universidad Católica Santa Maria holds the frozen bodies of four young girls who were apparently sacrificed more than 500 years ago by the Inca to appease the gods. The "Juanita" mummy, said to be frozen around the age of 13, was the first mummy found in 1995 near the summit of Mt. Ampato by local climber Miguel Zárate and anthropologist Johan Reinhard. When neighboring Volcán Sabancaya erupted, the ice that held Juanita in her sacrificial tomb melted and she rolled partway down the mountain and into a crater. English-speaking guides will show you around the museum, and you can watch a video detailing the expedition. ⊠ *La Merced 110* ☎ *054/215–013* ⊕ *www.ucsm.edu.pe/museo-santuarios-andinos* ⊡ *S/20.*

WORTH NOTING

Casa Goyeneche. This attractive Spanish-colonial home was built in 1888. Ask the guard for a tour, and you'll enter through a pretty courtyard and an ornate set of wooden doors to view rooms furnished with period antiques and Cusco School paintings. ⊠ *La Merced 201 y Palacio Viejo* ⊡ *Free, but if you get a tour a small donation is expected* ⊘ *Closed Sat.–Sun.*

Casa Tristan del Pozo. This small museum and art gallery, sometimes called Casa Ricketts, was built in 1738 and is now the Banco Continental. Look for the elaborate puma heads spouting water. Inside you'll find colonial paintings, ornate Peruvian costumes, and furniture. ⊠ *San Francisco 115* ⊕ *fundacionbbva.pe/casonas/casa-tristan-del-pozo* ⊡ *Free* ⊘ *Closed Sun.*

Casona Iriberry. Unlike the other mansions, Casona Iriberry has religious overtones. Small scriptures are etched into its structure, exemplifying Arequipa's catholic roots. The back of the house is now the Centro Cultural Cháves la Rosa, which houses some of the city's most important contemporary arts venues, including photography exhibits, concerts, and films. The front of the compound is filled with colonial-period furniture and paintings. ⊠ *Plaza de Armas, San Augustin y Santa Catalina* ☎ *054/204–482* ⊡ *Free to look around, charge for certain events* ⊘ *Closed weekends.*

Courtyard in Monasterio de Santa Catalina, Arequipa

Convento de la Recoleta. One of Peru's most extensive and valuable libraries is in this 1648 Franciscan monastery. With several cloisters and
museums, it's a wonderful place to research regional history and culture.
Start in the massive, wood-paneled, wood-floored library, where monks
in brown robes quietly browse 20,000 ancient books and maps, the
most valuable of which were printed before 1500 and are kept in glass
cases. Pre-Columbian artifacts and objects collected by missionaries
to the Amazon are on display, as is a selection of elegant colonial and
religious artwork. Guides are available (remember to tip). To reach the
monastery, cross the Río Chili by Puente Grau. It's a 10- to 15-minute
walk from the Plaza de Armas, but it's best to take a taxi. ⊠ *Recoleta
117* ☎ *054/270–966* ⌧ *S/10.*

Iglesia de San Francisco. This 16th-century church has survived numerous natural disasters, including several earthquakes that cracked its
cupola. Inside, near the polished silver altar, is the little chapel of
the Sorrowful Virgin, where the all-important Virgin Mary statue is
stored. ■TIP➔ **On December 8, during Arequipa's Feast of the Immaculate Conception, the Virgin is paraded around the city all night atop
an ornate carriage and surrounded by images of saints and angels. A
throng of pilgrims carry flowers and candles.** Visit the adjoining convent (S/10) to see Arequipa's largest painting and a museum of 17th-
century religious furniture and paintings. ⊠ *Zela 103* ☎ *054/384–103*
⌧ *Free* ☉ *Convent closed Sun.*

Iglesia y Convento de Santo Domingo. With hints of the Islamic style in its
elegant brick arches and stone domes, this cathedral carries an aura of
elegance. Step inside to view simple furnishings and sunlight streaming

through stained-glass windows as small silver candles flicker along the back wall near the altar. A working Dominican monastery is in back. ✉ *Santo Domingo y Piérola* 📞 *054/213–511* 🎫 *Free.*

La Mansión del Fundador. First owned by the founder of Arequipa, Don Garcí Manuel de Carbajal, La Mansión del Fundador, about 6.5 km (4 miles) outside Arequipa—about a 20-minute journey—is a restored colonial home and church. Alongside the Río Sabandía, the sillar-made home perches over a cliff and is said to have been built for Carbajal's son. It became a Jesuit retreat in the 16th century and in the 1800s was remodeled by Juan Crisostomo de Goyeneche y Aguerrevere. While intimate, the chapel is small and simple, but the home is noted for its vaulted arch ceilings and spacious patio. There's also a cafeteria with a bar on-site. To reach the home, go past Tingo along Avenida Huasacache. ✉ *Av. Paisajesta s/n, Socabaya* 📞 *054/442–460* ⊕ *www. lamansiondelfundador.com* 🎫 *S/13.*

Mercado San Camilo. This jam-packed collection of shops sells everything from snacks and local produce to clothing and household goods. It's an excellent place geared more to locals than tourists so you can spot rare types of potatoes, sample *queso helado* (ice cream), or eat *chicharrones* (deep-fried pork). It's on Calle San Camilo, between Avenidas Peru and Piérola. ✉ *San Camilo 352* 🎫 *Free.*

Molino de Sabandía. There's a colorful story behind the area's first stone *molina* (mill), 7 km (4 miles) southeast of Arequipa. Built in 1621 in the gorgeous Paucarpata countryside, the mill fell into ruin over the next century. Famous architect Luis Felipe Calle was restoring the Arequipa mansion that now houses the Central Reserve Bank in 1966 when he was asked to work on the mill project. By 1973 the restoration of the volcanic-stone structure was complete, and Calle liked the new version so much that he bought it, got it working again, and opened it for visitors to tour. Bring your swimsuit and walking shoes in good weather—there's a pool and trails around the lovely countryside. Adjoining the site is the traditional village of Yumina, which has numerous Inca agricultural terraces. If you're not driving, flag a taxi for S/25–S/30 or take a colectivo from Socabaya in Arequipa to about 2 km (1 mile) past Paucarpata. ✉ *Calle Molino, Sabandia* 📞 *959/839–545* ⊕ *en.elmolinodesabandia.com* 🎫 *S/10.*

Museo Arqueológico. With a solid collection of native pottery and textiles, human-sacrificed bones, along with gold and silver offerings from Inca times, this archaeology museum at the Universidad Nacional de San Agustín provides a background on local archaeology and ruins. ✉ *Calle Alvarez Thomas 200* 📞 *054/288–881* ⊕ *www.unsa.edu.pe/index.php/ arte-y-cultura/museo-arqueologico* 🎫 *S/5* 🕐 *Closed weekends.*

Yanahuara. The eclectic little suburb of Yanahuara, northwest of the city, is perfect for lunch or a late afternoon stroll. The neighborhood is above Arequipa and has amazing views over the city at the lookout constructed of sillar stone arches. On a clear day the volcanos El Misti, Chachani, and Picchu can be seen. Stop in at the 1783, mestizo-style Iglesia Yanahuara. The interior has wrought-iron chandeliers and gilt sanctuaries surrounding the nave. Ask to see the glass coffin that holds a statue of Christ used in parades on holy days. To reach Yanahuara, head across the Avenida Grau bridge, then continue on Avenida Ejército to Avenida Lima, and from here, it's five blocks to the plaza. It's a 15-minute walk or an 8-minute cab ride from the city center. ✉ *Arequipa.*

OFF THE BEATEN PATH

Reserva Nacional Salinas y Aguada Blanca. Herds of beige-and-white vicuñas, llamas, and alpacas graze together on the sparse plant life in the midst of the open fields that encompass this vast nature reserve of desert, grass, and flamingo-filled lakes. Wear good walking shoes for the uneven terrain, and bring binoculars. Also bring a hat, sunscreen, and a warm jacket, as the park sits at a crisp 3,900 meters (12,795 feet). The reserve is 35 km (22 miles) north of Arequipa, just beyond El Misti. If you're headed to Colca Canyon or Puno from Arequipa, you have to pass through the reserve to get there. If you hire private transport, you can visit the cave paintings at Sumbay. The Toccra interpretation center is located 2 hours and 30 minutes from Arequipa and is open to the public from 9 to 4. ✉ *Between Arequipa and Colca Canyon* ☎ *054/257–461.*

OFF THE BEATEN PATH

Yura. About a half-hour drive from Arequipa, this serene little town is settled in the western foothills of the Volcán Chachani. Take the road 27 km (17 miles) farther to reach these rustic thermal baths where you can take a dip in naturally heated water that ranges from 70°F to 82°F. You can soak in any weather and enjoy a picnic along the river in summertime. Admission to the hot springs is S/5, and they're open daily from 8 to 3. From the old Arequipa train station, there's bus service to Yura for S/3 which takes close to an hour. ✉ *Arequipa.*

WHERE TO EAT

Comida Arequipeña (Arequipan cuisine) is a special version of *comida criolla.* Perhaps the most famous dish is *rocoto relleno,* a large, spicy red pepper stuffed with meat, onions, and cheese. Other specialties to try are *cuy chactado* (deep-fried guinea pig), and *adobo* (pork stew), a local cure for hangovers. *Picanterías* are where locals head for good, basic Peruvian meals and cold Arequipeña beer served with *cancha* (fried, salted corn kernels).

The west side of the Plaza de Armas has dozens of restaurants along the balcony above the Portal de San Agustín. The first blocks of Calle San Francisco and Calle Santa Catalina north of the Plaza de Armas are lined with cafés, restaurants, and bars.

$$ INTERNATIONAL

🍴 **Alma de Cocina.** With its placement in the gorgeous Casa Andina Premium hotel, a historic monument, this gourmet restaurant is worth a visit for the setting alone. The menu is quite varied, using local ingredients to create international dishes as well as give a new flair to traditional Peruvian ones. **Known for:** historic setting; nice atmosphere. [$] *Average main: S/48* ✉ *Casa Andina Premium Arequipa, Calle Ugarte 403* ☎ *054/226–907* 🌐 *www.casa-andina.com/en/restaurants.*

$$$ PERUVIAN Fodor's Choice ★

🍴 **Chicha.** With a covered courtyard that evokes images of a traditional yet upscale outdoor picantería, the offerings at celeb-chef Gastón Acurio's stylish bistro provide delicious gourmet twists on typical regional fare. Unlike many restaurants offering fusion menus, the plate sizes here are ample. **Known for:** regionally inspired gourmet dishes; traditional

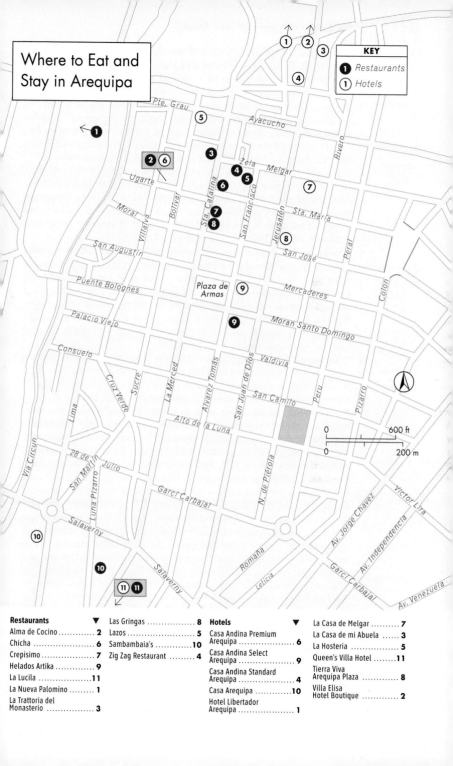

Where to Eat and Stay in Arequipa

KEY

1 Restaurants

① Hotels

yet upscale; decent portion sizes. $ *Average main: S/53* ⊠ *Santa Catalina 210* ☎ *054/287-360* ⊕ *www.chicha.com.pe.*

$ × **Crepisimo.** With an extensive variety of sweet and savory crepes, as
FRENCH well as quality espresso, pisco sours, and craft beers, you could easily spend the day in this artistic, Euro-styled restaurant, little sister to the Zig Zag restaurant on Calle Zela. Check out the terrace for great views of the Monasterio de Santa Catalina and volcanoes. **Known for:** variety of crepes; great service; lively atmosphere. $ *Average main: S/23* ⊠ *Santa Catalina 208* ☎ *054/206-020* ⊕ *www.crepisimo.com.*

$ × **Helados Artika.** The small, retro-style *helados* (ice-cream) café next
CAFÉ to La Compañía is the perfect stop after shopping around town. We recommend the famous arequipeño *queso helado,* translating erroniously to cheese ice cream—it's made with sweet milk, cinnamon, and a dash of coconut. **Known for:** flavor varieties. $ *Average main: S/10* ⊠ *Morán 120* ☎ *054/284-915* ⊟ *No credit cards.*

$ × **La Lucila.** Rivaling La Nueva Palomino for Arequipa's favorite *picante-*
PERUVIAN *ria* (simple, traditional restaurant), La Lucila has been in operation for more than 70 years. Although its beloved namesake owner passed away in 2012, her recipes—iconic regional dishes that have been passed down through generations—live on, as does the simple, rustic atmosphere. **Known for:** traditional regional food; historic location. $ *Average main: S/30* ⊠ *Calle Grau 147, Sachaca* ☎ *054/205-348, 054/232-380* ⊕ *www.picanterialalucila.com* ☾ *No dinner.*

$$ × **La Nueva Palomino.** Chef Mònica Huertas is one of the great promoters
PERUVIAN of Arequipeña cuisine and to many, this is the most authentic restaurant
Fodor'sChoice in town. She uses many of the same classic recipes—some more than a
★ century old—that her mother and grandmother used, and her preparations of regional standards such as rocoto relleno, adobo, *lechón al horno* (oven-roasted pork), chupe de camarones, and queso helado have become the definitive recipes. **Known for:** legendary recipes; authentic local dishes; sprawling grounds and gardens. $ *Average main: S/45* ⊠ *Psje Leoncio Prado 122, Yanahuara* ☎ *054/252-393* ⊕ *www.facebook.com/pg/LaNuevaPalomino* ☾ *Closed Tues. No dinner.*

$$ × **La Trattoria del Monasterio.** This intimate restaurant serves some of
ITALIAN the best Italian food in southern Peru and if you're not sure you want Italian food in Peru, its special location in the Monasterio de Santa Catalina (the entrance is outside the compound, though windows look in) is enough to merit a visit and a meal. A fusion menu featuring homemade pastas, ravioli, gnocchi, risottos, paired with seafood, meats, and creative, savory sauces is offered as well as Novo Andino options, but you can find them elsewhere so stick with the excellent Italian fare here. **Known for:** excellent Italian food; homemade pasta; extensive wine menu. $ *Average main: S/48* ⊠ *Santa Catalina 309* ☎ *054/204-062* ⊕ *www.latrattoriadelmonasterio.com* ☾ *No dinner Sun.*

$ × **Las Gringas.** With interesting and fresh organic ingredients topping
PIZZA their delicious pizzas, this courtyard restaurant is a fun and relaxing place to have dinner or just get a quick bite to eat. Offers gluten-free and vegan options as well as a wide variety of craft beers. **Known for:** great pizza with unusual toppings; vegan and gluten-free options; craft beers. $ *Average main: S/34* ⊠ *Calle Santa Catalina 204* ☎ *054/234-572.*

$$ STEAKHOUSE 🍴 **Lazos.** Although you can get grilled vegetables or fish, this is Arequipa's finest *parrilla*, or steak house, and meat is what you come for—and there is plenty of it, including delicious cuts of beef, alpaca, and sausage. The beautiful, narrow, arched dining room with white sillar walls makes you question whether you should be paying more for the expertly cooked meat. **Known for:** grilled meats; extensive wine list; expensive-feeling setting. [$] *Average main: S/45* ✉ *San Francisco 313* ☎ *054/217–662* 🕓 *No dinner Sun.*

$ PERUVIAN 🍴 **Sambambaia's.** Specializing in both classic Andean meat and fish dishes, as well as international fare, this restaurant is in the quiet residential neighborhood of Vallecito, a 10-minute walk from the Plaza de Armas. Try the chef's favorite, a tender, juicy *lomo al vino tinto* (beef tenderloin in red wine), but if you're craving more something more familiar, wood-oven pizza is another specialty of the house. **Known for:** variety of dishes; lomo al vino tinto; excellent service. [$] *Average main: S/32* ✉ *Luna Pizarro 304, Vallecito* ☎ *054/223–657* 🌐 *www.sambambaias.com.pe.*

$$$ FRENCH Fodor's Choice ★ 🍴 **Zig Zag Restaurant.** Everything here—from its grand iron spiral staircase and sillar stone walls to its Novo Andino cuisine, extensive wine list, and decadent desserts—is done with exquisite detail and attention. The menu, using a fusion of gourmet techniques from the Alps and Andes, is a harmonious mix of fresh local foods. **Known for:** delicious fusion cuisine; elegant architecture; fabulous service. [$] *Average main: S/57* ✉ *Zela 210* ☎ *054/206–020* 🌐 *www.zigzagrestaurant.com.*

WHERE TO STAY

Arequipa has one of the highest-quality collections of inns and hotels anywhere in Peru. Although the larger resorts and chain hotels tend to cater to tour groups and business travelers, there are dozens of charming, small, independently run bed-and-breakfasts within a few blocks of the Plaza de Armas.

$$ HOTEL Fodor's Choice ★ 🏨 **Casa Andina Premium Arequipa.** The city's former coin mint, a national historical monument, became this midsize hotel in 2008, featuring massive colonial-era common rooms with arched stone walls, oil paintings, and period furnishings. **Pros:** historic building; modern comforts; excellent amenities. **Cons:** modern rooms do not have the charm of the colonial ones; not all rooms have views. [$] *Rooms from: S/477* ✉ *Ugarte 403* ☎ *051/213–739* 🌐 *www.casa-andina.com* 🛏 *40 rooms* 🍽 *Breakfast.*

$$ HOTEL 🏨 **Casa Andina Select Arequipa.** You don't get any more central than this midlevel hotel with modern rooms, excellent service, and a superb location right on Plaza de Armas. **Pros:** central location; rooftop pool; great service. **Cons:** somewhat bland decor; interior rooms lack view; central location comes with noise. [$] *Rooms from: S/360* ✉ *Portal de Flores 116, Plaza de Armas* ☎ *054/412–930* 🌐 *www.casa-andina.com* 🛏 *58 rooms* 🍽 *Breakfast.*

$$ HOTEL 🏨 **Casa Andina Standard Arequipa.** As with everywhere else in Peru, the Arequipa version of the Casa Andina chain's classic line of hotels offers comfortable but basic rooms, nicely decorated with Andean

textiles. **Pros:** good location; good breakfast; comfortable but basic rooms. **Cons:** tour-group heavy; no frills. Ⓢ *Rooms from: S/375* ✉ *Calle Jerusalén 603* ☎ *051/213–739* ⊕ *www.casa-andina.com* ↘ *103 rooms* ⊙❘ *Breakfast.*

$$ ▦ **Casa Arequipa.** The individually designed rooms at this neoclassical
B&B/INN boutique hotel are all decked out in luxuriously high-quality motifs
Fodor'sChoice and bedding—every last detail has been considered and applied, and
★ it's all so personalized that it's almost like visiting your best friends.
Pros: impeccable service; comfortable bedding; quiet, upscale residential neighborhood. **Cons:** books up fast; not near any stores; a 10- to 15-minute walk from the center of town (you need a taxi at night). Ⓢ *Rooms from: S/250* ✉ *Av. Lima 409, Vallecito* ☎ *054/284–219* ⊕ *www.arequipacasa.com* ↘ *13 rooms* ⊙❘ *Breakfast.*

$$ ▦ **Hotel Libertador Arequipa.** Amid sprawling gardens outside the town
RESORT center, this 1940 Spanish-colonial villa is an oasis in Old Arequipa, with
sillar arches, wrought-iron window screens, and Peruvian details that give this luxury hotel the intimate feel of an old family home. **Pros:** well maintained; historic charm; Jacuzzi and sauna. **Cons:** older building not for everyone; several blocks from the main plaza. Ⓢ *Rooms from: S/435* ✉ *Plaza Bolívar, Selva Alegre* ☎ *54/215–110, 877/778–2281* ⊕ *www. libertador.com.pe* ↘ *88 rooms* ⊙❘ *Breakfast.*

$ ▦ **La Casa de Melgar.** In a beautiful tiled courtyard surrounded by fra-
B&B/INN grant blossoms and dotted with trees, this 18th-century home is believed
to have been a one-time temporary residence of Mariano Melgar, Peru's most romantic 19th-century poet. **Pros:** high on the charm scale; garden is great for relaxing; close to shops and restaurants. **Cons:** rooms can get cold in rainy season; some rooms are small or have thin walls; front desk staff can be curt. Ⓢ *Rooms from: S/210* ✉ *Melgar 108* ☎ *054/222–459* ⊕ *www.lacasademelgar.com* ↘ *31 rooms* ⊙❘ *Breakfast.*

$ ▦ **La Casa de mi Abuela.** Long a mainstay for budget-minded travelers,
HOTEL La Casa de mi Abuela features about 2,000 square meters of green
FAMILY space, anchored by a lovely pool, and is situated just a five- to seven-
minute walk from the Plaza de Armas. **Pros:** great breakfast buffet; central location; security gate. **Cons:** basic rooms; lots of tour groups. Ⓢ *Rooms from: S/222* ✉ *Calle Jerusalén 606* ☎ *054/241–206* ⊕ *www. lacasademiabuela.com* ↘ *52 rooms* ⊙❘ *Breakfast.*

$$ ▦ **La Hosteria.** For a quiet hotel with old Spanish-colonial charm and
B&B/INN modern amenities, opt for a superior room with a view at this tradi-
tional hacienda. **Pros:** central location; colonial charm; excellent staff. **Cons:** front rooms have street noise. Ⓢ *Rooms from: S/255* ✉ *Bolivar 405* ☎ *054/289–269, 054/281–779* ⊕ *www.lahosteriaqp.com.pe* ↘ *20 rooms* ⊙❘ *Breakfast.*

$$ ▦ **Queen's Villa Hotel.** In the up-and-coming Vallecito neighborhood, a
HOTEL short walk from the center (and removed from its noise), this boutique
hotel has a resort-like pool area, leafy gardens, and a terrace with views over the city to the mountains. **Pros:** quiet neighborhood; great pool; attentive service. **Cons:** uninspiring interior design; away from the plaza. Ⓢ *Rooms from: S/286* ✉ *Luna Pizarro 512, Vallecito* ☎ *054/283–060* ⊕ *www.queensvillahotel.com* ↘ *25 rooms* ⊙❘ *Breakfast.*

4

$ ⌂ **Tierra Viva Arequipa Plaza.** From its inception in 2012, Tierra Viva
HOTEL   has quickly become known as a Peruvian hotel chain offering a great
balance of price and quality, and its Arequipa property is no exception. **Pros:** great quality for reasonable cost; ample buffet breakfast;
central location. **Cons:** rooms are fairly basic. $ *Rooms from: S/210*
⌧ *Calle Jerusalén 202* ☎ *054//234–161* ⊕ *www.tierravivahoteles.com*
⤵ *21 rooms* ⏐◯⏐ *Breakfast.*

$ ⌂ **Villa Elisa Hotel Boutique.** This family-owned boutique hotel is as wel-
B&B/INN   coming as a visit to old friends, with its charming rooms, comfort-
Fodor'sChoice   able beds, pretty gardens, friendly staff, and delicious breakfast. **Pros:**
★   tranquil and welcoming; beautiful grounds; good location. **Cons:** first-
floor room windows are right on garden; not for those who want a
more anonymous hotel experience. $ *Rooms from: S/240* ⌧ *Manuel
Ugarteche 401* ☎ *054/221–891* ⊕ *www.villaelisahb.com* ⤵ *20 rooms*
⏐◯⏐ *Breakfast.*

NIGHTLIFE

Most of the after-dark entertainment revolves around a number of cafés
and bars near the city center along Calle San Francisco, Calle Zela,
and Calle Santa Catalina. Many of these bars and cafés offer creative
cocktails and character; some nights there's live music, typically of the
rock variety. If you're dining around the plaza, there are usually groups
of musicians playing traditional music and hawking their CDs.

BARS

Ad Libitum. Head to this relaxed artistic heaven, popular with thirsty
locals, for cheap cocktails and fun music. There's also a light menu.
⌧ *San Francisco 233* ☎ *054/384–184.*

Fodor'sChoice   **Arequipa Beer Club.** If you are a connoisseur of beers, the sheer number
★   of Peruvian craft beers here may make you a repeat customer. Areq-
uipa shares a courtyard with Las Gringas so you can order one of their
delicious pizzas as you imbibe. ⌧ *Santa Catalina 204* ☎ *054/234–572.*

Café y Vino. For something a bit more relaxed, climb up to the second
floor of the beautiful Claustros de La Compañia complex to this small
wine bar, including some French wine selections, and café serving light
snacks. ⌧ *Morán 118.*

Casona Forum. Enter this large sillar building, open since the late 1980s,
and you'll find a choice of five bars. The bar Retro stages live concerts
and dancing to hits from the '70s to '80s. At Forum you can dine among
tropical furnishings or dance the night away. Terrasse offers great views
while dining and a chance to hone your karaoke skills. At Zero, you
can belly up to the pub-style bar, grab a beer, and shoot some pool, or
you can just hang out at the Chill Out sofa bar. ⌧ *San Francisco 317*
☎ *054/204–294* ⊕ *www.casonaforum.com.*

Istanbul Lounge Bar. This tiny eclectic bar is great for drinks and small
bites. ⌧ *San Francisco 231-A* ☎ *54/214–622.*

GAY AND LESBIAN

Although not as gay-friendly as Lima, there's a small, progressive gay
and lesbian scene.

Imperio. This LGTB club is the place to go for a dance-filled evening, located right in the center of town, making it easy and safe to get to. Straight-friendly as well, the club's cover is lower before midnight, and they offer a variety of themed nights on Saturday. ⊠ *Calle Jerúsalen 201-I* ☎ *972/419–693.*

LIVE MUSIC

Centro Cultural Peruano Norteamericano. It's worth swinging by this venue, not just for announcements of evening concerts of traditional and classical music, but also for art and photography exhibits and other cultural offerings. ⊠ *Melgar 109* ☎ *054/391–020* ⊕ *www.cultural.edu.pe.*

SHOPPING

4

Arequipa has the widest selection of Peruvian crafts in the south. Alpaca and llama wool is woven into brightly patterned sweaters, ponchos, hats, scarves, and gloves, as well as wall hangings, blankets, and carpets. Look for *chullos* (woolen knitted caps with earflaps and ties), transported from the Lake Titicaca region. Ceramic *toros* (bulls), also from the Titicaca area, are a local favorite to hold flowers or money, and you can even see them sitting in the rafters of homes to bring good luck.

At the Plaza San Francisco, the cathedral steps are the site of a daily flea market that has delicate handmade jewelry. Across the street at the Fundo el Fierro, crafts vendors tout bargains on clothing, ceramics, jewelry, and knickknacks in a cobblestone courtyard; deals can be had until about 8 pm. Arequipa is also an excellent place to purchase inexpensive but well-constructed handmade guitars. Avenida Bolognesi has lines of such workshops. Behind the cathedral on the narrow Pasaje Catedral, boutiques sell jewelry and knickknacks made of Arequipa agate, and there are many clothing stores along Santa Catalina where you can find goods made from sheep's wool, alpaca, and vicuña.

In recent years several upscale shopping centers have popped up.

ANTIQUES

Arequipa is a great place to pick up colonial-era antiques, high-quality copies of pre-Columbian ceramics, and even authentic Inca archaeological pieces. As is often the case with these types of stores, open hours can vary so it's best to just have a wander and see what treasures you can discover.

DESIGNER ALPACA CLOTHING

Arequipa is churning out scores of fashionistas who are responsible for creating some of the country's most sophisticated alpaca knits. Since many couturiers make their home in Arequipa, a few have alpaca clothing outlets, such as Jenny Duarte. The Michell Group, the umbrella company of Sol Alpaca, has an ecotourist center called **Mundo Alpaca**, ⊕ *www.mundoalpaca.com.pe*, in Alameda San Lázaro, which houses an upscale boutique as well as a camelid zoo, an art gallery, and a textile museum.

Jenny Duarte. Come here for fine dresses from a French-trained local designer who doesn't shy away from using alpaca and other regional fibers. Her designs are now being sold in Lima, Paris, and Monaco. ⊠ *Cuesta del Ángel 305, Yanahuara* ☎ *054/275–444* ⊕ *www.jennyduarteperu.com/en* ☾ *Closed Sun.*

Kuna. With shops in Lima, Arequipa, Puno, and Cusco, this is one of the go-to destinations in Peru for alpaca scarves, gloves, socks, sweaters, and jackets. ⊠ *Santa Catalina 210* ☎ *054/282–485* ⊕ *www.kuna.com.pe.*

Sol Alpaca. The Michell Group's Sol Alpaca has gone haute couture, constructing fine-quality knits, helping hoist Peru onto the international fashion scene. ⊠ *Santa Catalina 120 A* ☎ *054/221–454* ⊕ *www. solalpaca.com.*

MALLS

Claustros de la Compañia. One of the best things about shopping in colonial cities is you get to do it in beautiful historic buildings. As you wander through the connected courtyards of the Claustros de la Compañia you'll find a variety of small shops with unique wares. Some of these will also have larger outlets located a little outside of the center so be sure to ask if you find pieces that you really like. ⊠ *General Morán 118.*

Patio del Ekeko. If you're looking to scout quality gifts and souvenirs, this is a good shopping complex, with a branch of alpaca store KUNA, Illaria silver, an artisanal foodstuff shop, and more. ⊠ *Mercaderes 141* ☎ *054/215–861* ⊕ *www.elekeko.pe.*

SPORTING GOODS

Andesgear. If you get caught without the right layer of outdoor wear, your hiking boots are falling apart, you need a new backpack, or you just feel the need for a new fleece, this is the place to go. ⊠ *Calle Santa Catalina 210* ☎ *054/418–644.*

CANYON COUNTRY

Colca and Cotahuasi Canyons, the two deepest canyons on earth, are two of Peru's greatest natural wonders. Colca is the far more visited, more accessible of the two, and recently has a seen a boom in five-star resorts and laid-back family inns. Cotahuasi, a little more than 150 meters (nearly 500 feet) deeper than Colca, is much more remote and reached only by the most rugged adventurers, though if you can withstand long, bumpy hours in a car or bus, you'll find an unspoiled terrain rarely visited by outsiders.

COTAHUASI VILLAGE AND VICINITY

379 km (235 miles) north of Arequipa.

Cotahuasi is the largest settlement in canyon country and the first you'll stumble upon. In the hills at 2,680 meters (8,793 feet), whitewashed colonial-style homes line slim, straight lanes before a backdrop of Cerro Hiunao. Most visitors kick off their stay in this Quechua-speaking community of 3,500 residents, where there are a few basic hostels, restaurants, a small grocery store, a 17th-century church with a bell tower, and the Plaza de Armas. Most hiking trails begin or end here. Many families rent burros to tourists to help carry their load, especially kayakers who walk eight hours down to the gorge with their kayaks.

Three hours farther south along a thin track against the canyon wall—which climbs to 400 meters (1,312 feet) above the river—is Chaupo, a

CROSSING INTO CHILE

The border with Chile, about 40 km (25 miles) from Tacna or 440 km (273 miles) from Arequipa, is open daily and very easy to cross. All you need is your passport. From Tacna there are scores of colectivos that will give you a ride to the other side for about S/40, or you can take a bus headed to Arica from Tacna, departing hourly.

Typically, drivers will help with border formalities, even the colectivo drivers. The road journey takes about an hour. Any train aficionado would enjoy the slow, somewhat bumpy but beautiful train ride from Tacna to Arica, which takes more than an hour, leaves twice a day (6 am and 4:30 pm), and costs S/15.

settlement surrounded by groves of fruit trees. You can camp here and hike through Velinga to ruins at Huña before reaching Quechualla, where the ancient farming terraces of Maucullachta, an old Wari city, are visible across the gorge.

In Cotahuasi Village the route forks, leading northeast along the Río Cotahuasi or due north. Either way is possible by 4x4, colectivo, or on foot. Heading northeast, about 10 km (6 miles) out of town, is the village of Tomepampa. After that is the small town of Alca, near the hot springs of Luicho. Even farther east is Puica, at 3,700 meters (12,139 feet). Driving northwest from Cotahuasi Village for two hours will lead you to Pampamarca, a town known for exquisite woven rugs; it's three hours from here to the hot springs of Josla and Uskuni.

GETTING HERE AND AROUND

Cotahuasi Canyon is a travel destination in the making, but outside of expert extreme sports enthusiasts, few people venture here. If you're not taking a bus or coming with a tour operator, driving anything but a 4x4 is asking for trouble. The jagged, rocky dirt roads are full of cliffs and narrow corners. Dry for most of the year, the roads get muddy from December to April (rainy season), a time when you're also likely to encounter random streams flowing across the road.

Hire a guide, regardless of season and not just for safety: because this region is so remote, you're likely to see much more with a guide. All buses travel through the night. Two bus companies go from Arequipa to Cotahuasi daily; each leaves around 4 or 5 pm, arriving in Cotahuasi Village after a 10–12 hour trip, in time for sunrise: Transportes Reyna (☎ *054/430–612*) and Transportes Inmaculada (☎ *054/426–244*).

■TIP→ If you're driving, know that gas stations are few on the long stretch between Corire (near Toro Muerto) and the village of Cotahuasi.

EXPLORING

Cataratas de Sipia. Below the village of Cotahuasi is the valley of Piro, the gateway to the canyon, which is close to this 150-meter (492-foot), three-tiered 10-meter (33-foot) -wide waterfall. ■TIP→ Sipia Falls is the most-visited attraction in the entire canyon.

Cotahuasi Canyon. Colca Canyon may be the region's most famous natural attraction, but at 3,354 meters (11,001 feet), Cotahuasi is the world's deepest gorge, beating Colca Canyon by 163 meters (534 feet). It's nearly twice as deep as the Grand Canyon. The canyon has been carved by the Río Cotahuasi, which becomes the Río Ocuña before connecting to the Pacific. Its deepest point is at Ninochaco, below the quaint administrative capital of Quechualla and accessible only by kayak. Kayak explorations first documented the area in the mid-1990s and measured its depth. Since then, paddling the Cotahuasi River's Class V rapids is to kayakers what scaling Mount Everest is to mountaineers.

The ride from Arequipa to the Cotahuasi Canyon ranks with the great scenic roads of the world. As you pass Corire and Toro Muerto, the road rides the western side of snowcapped Nevado Coropuno (6,424 meters, 21,076 feet), Peru's third-highest mountain, for spectacular views as you descend into the valley of Cotahuasi. ■ TIP→ **Logistically speaking, it's a bumpy 11- to 13-hour bus ride or 10 hours by four-wheel drive from Arequipa.** The pavement ends in Chuquibamba after about five hours of driving, and then resumes for the last hour of the drive, between the Mirador of Cotahuasi as you descend down to the canyon. There is no fee to enter.

SPORTS AND THE OUTDOORS

Many operators in Arequipa and Cusco offer multiday excursions. The most common tours are at least three- to five days although some may last up to 10 days or more. A few local hikers provide custom tours for visitors as well.

HIKING

Cotahuasi Canyon is an awesome place to explore by foot. The backdrop of snowcapped Volcán Coropuna and Solimana is fantastic, the high desert plains offer a rest from the steep upward rocky canyon terrain, and the untouched villages provide a cultural aspect. Hikes can go between 1,830 meters (6,000 feet) and 6,400 meters (21,000 feet) in height, so prepare for the altitude. Temperatures remain about 65°F–70°F during the day, dipping below 45°F on any given night. Ancient Inca paths wind throughout the canyon and its terraces. ■ TIP→ **Beware: Many of these ancient trails are narrow, rocky, and hang over the side of the canyon.** Newer trails parallel some of the ancient ones and are generally safer.

Sipia Falls is a solid three- to four-hour trek from Cotahuasi Village, and it's a hard-on-your-knees hike down that includes two bridge crossings, but the first taste of being in the canyon is a surreal experience. It's also possible to reach the falls by hailing a colectivo or driving your own 4x4 from the Cotahuasi road to the Sipia Bridge, where the road ends. From here it's a 45-minute hike to the falls.

If you're going on a multiday excursion, continue on the trail from Cotahuasi to Sipia to the Chaupo Valley and the citrus-tree village of Velinga, a good place to camp. From Velinga it's on to Quechualla, where you'll pass through the 1,000-year-old Wari ruins, rock forests, and cactus forests. One of the last major points along this route is

CLOSE UP

On The Menu

With its altitude and cool weather, southern Peru is famous for its hearty and savory soups. Quinoa and potatoes typically provide the base, and, with the emergence of Novo Andino cuisine, the addition of meats, vegetables, and spices makes these soups meals in themselves. Cheese, potatoes, cuy, and quinoa make up the diets in traditional villages around Lake Titicaca and the canyons.

SEAFOOD

In coastal towns you'll dine in *cebicherías* and more upscale *marisquerías* (seafood restaurants). The best are along the coast, as well as a few spots in Puno.

Cebiche: Fish or shellfish (marinated in lime juice, cilantro, onions, and chilis), served just after marinating and usually accompanied by *canchas*, toasted corn kernels.

Cebiche mixto is a mix of shellfish and fish and is best along the coast.

Escabeche: With roots from Spain, usually features fish (often chicken) marinated in a vinegar mixture with onions, and other ingredients; found in Arequipa.

MEATS

Cuy chactado: Deep-fried guinea pig.

Filet de cuy: A Novo Andino style of cuy cut in fillets instead of whole; found in Arequipa.

Lomo a la huancaína: Beef strips with egg and a cheese-and-yellow-pepper sauce.

Rocoto relleno: Baked spicy red peppers stuffed with ground beef, olives, and *queso fresco* (creamy white cheese).

SOUPS AND STEWS

Chupe de camarones: Spicy shrimp chowder; found on the coast.

Chupe verde: Potatoes, cheese, eggs, and herbs; found in Arequipa and the canyon country.

Créma de quinua: Creamed soup made of quinoa. Found in mountainous areas near Lake Titicaca and the canyon country.

Hualpa chupe: Chicken, chilis, and spices; found in Arequipa.

Mollejitas: Chicken innards are a specialty in Arequipa.

Sopa a la criolla: Beef, onions, peppers, and potatoes; found in Arequipa.

DESSERTS

Alfajores: Shortbread with a filling of *manjar de leche* (caramel).

Buñuelos: Fried dough sprinkled with sugar.

Cocadas al horno: Macaroons.

Mazamorra morada: Pudding made from purple corn, cinnamon, milk, and sugar—a specialty from small street stands in Arequipa.

Queso helado: The signature ice cream of Arequipa. Creamy coconut ice cream with cinnamon.

REFRESHMENTS

The fizzy red Cola Esococia is the local soda brand in the Arequipa area. Regional beers include Cusqueña and Arequipeña. *Chicha* (a fermented corn drink) is the national beverage for fiestas and celebrations, not to be confused with *chicha morada* (a nonalcoholic drink made from purple corn). *Vino Calliente* is hot-mulled red wine, served across the country but especially in the highlands and in Puno.

4

Huachuy, where you can again camp. Beyond this point things get trickier, as you'll have to cross the Rió Cotahuasi. Many guides use a cable system to reach Yachau Oasis, Chaucalla Valley, and eventually Iquipi Valley.

WHITE-WATER RAFTING

White-water rafters can challenge the rapids anywhere from the upper Cotahuasi, near the village, almost to the Pacific. The river is divided into four sections: the Headwaters, beginning upstream from Cotahuasi Village, Aimaña Gorge, Flatwater Canyon, and the Lower Canyon.

The Lower Canyon is a mix of Class III and V rapids, without much portage. Most rafting tour operators put in at the village of Velinga and use this part of the river for tours.

Cotahuasi rafting trips are run highly infrequently, maybe once or twice a year, and should be booked well in advance. Due to the extreme nature and logistical complications of running this extremely challenging trip, there are only a couple of Peruvian and internationally operators offering it, and they do so between May and June only. You want to book this tour with serious professionals only to avoid cutting corners on safety.

CHIVAY

136 km (85 miles) north of Arequipa.

The largest town in the Colca Canyon region is Chivay, a small, bat-tered-looking village with a population of about 5,000. Most tourist facilities are here, which are not many, but include restaurants, hotels, a medical clinic, and a tourist information center. As you approach Chivay, you'll pass through a stone archway signifying the town entrance, where AUTOCOLCA, the government authority over Colca Canyon, stops cars to ask if they are headed to see the condors. If you're headed to Cruz del Condor or any of the churches in the 14 villages, you must purchase the S/70 Boleto Turistico, which will be asked for again at the entrance of the Mirador and will also get you into specific attractions like the Calera hot springs and church at Cabanaconde. Most agency tours do not include this entry fee in their prices.

Chivay marks the eastern end of the canyon's rim; the other end is Cabanaconde, a developing village where most multiday hikes into the canyon begin and end. As you come into Chivay, the road splits off into two: one, less traveled because of its rocky rutted surface, goes along the canyon's northern edge to the villages of Coporaque, Ichupampa, and Lari; the other follows the southern rim, and although it's a bumpy dirt road, it's better for travel and leads to Cruz del Condor and the small towns of Yanque, Maca, and Cabanaconde.

GETTING HERE AND AROUND

You can explore the area by hiring a private guide, renting a four-wheel-drive vehicle, joining a tour from Arequipa, or going by bus. A standard two-wheel-drive car won't do. Arequipa is the jumping-off point for nearly everyone headed to Colca Canyon, and most will either come on a tour or take a bus that stops at either Chivay, the first town you come to, which takes about five hours to reach from Arequipa, or

Cabanaconde, about another hour farther. Sporadic combi service links each town in the middle.

Chivay is a four-hour drive from Arequipa. The road takes you through the Reserva Nacional Salinas y Aguada Blanca and over the Patapampa Pass, where at 4,825 meters (15,830 feet) you can view nearly the entire Valley of Volcanoes. The road is paved only about half the way; going toward Patapampa Pass is a dirt road, but it has been graded and smoothed out. The last quarter of the ride is rocky. Most who visit Colca Canyon experience altitude sickness along the way, so bring plenty of water. Some of the nicer hotels will have oxygen tanks.

ADVANCE PREP

Cotahuasi is not so traveler savvy yet, so don't expect to just show up in a town, buy a map, hire a guide, and get on your way. You'll want to buy a map of the canyon at the South American Explorers clubhouse in Lima or visit the Colca Trek office in Arequipa. To minimize the amount of hiccups, planning your visit with a tour operator in Arequipa is recommended.

Taxis are a good way to go from town to town if long hikes or mountain biking aren't your thing. Taxis line up around the Plaza de Armas in Chivay. Most rides will cost S/30–S/65.

EXPLORING

Fodor'sChoice
★
Colca Canyon. Flying overhead, you can't miss the green, fertile trough as it cuts through the barren terrain, but it's all an illusion; only scrub brush and cactus cling to the canyon's sheer basalt sides and miles of ancient terraces. ■TIP➔ The canyon is named for the stone warehouses (colcas) used to store grain by an ancient culture that lived along the walls of the gorge.

Carved into the foothills of the snow-covered Andes and sliced by the silvery Río Colca, Colca Canyon is 3,182 meters (10,440 feet) deep. The more adventurous can embark on a hike into the canyon—typically a two-, three-, or five-day excursion. Bird lovers (and anyone with an eye for amazement) can visit the Cruz del Condor. Culture seekers can spend a night with a native family. Light hikers and archaeology aficionados can observe points along the rim, or those seeking pure relaxation can hit one of the all-inclusive lodges with horseback riding and thermal baths.

Fodor'sChoice
★
Cruz del Condor. Cruz del Condor is a haunt for the giant birds, particularly at dawn, when they soar on the thermal currents rising from the deep valley. At 1,200 meters (3,937 feet), the "condor cross" precipice, between the villages Pinchollo and Cabanaconde, is the best place to spot them. ■TIP➔ From June to August you're likely to see close to 20 or more condors during a morning visit. By October and November many of the female birds are nesting, so your chances of eyeing flocks are slim, but you'll likely spot a few birds. It is possible to take a taxi or bus to the Cruz del Condor from Chivay but if you take a tour from there, your guide will likely only speak Spanish. If you want a guided tour in English, you will need to set this up with a tour operator ahead of time in Arequipa or Cusco.

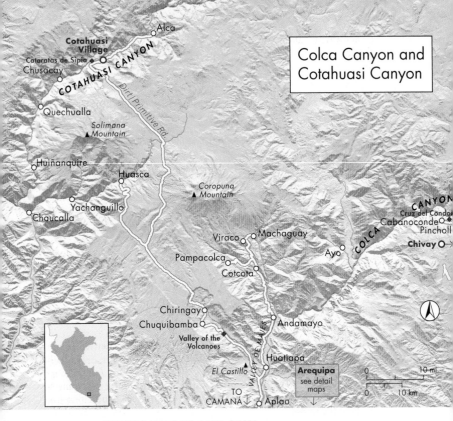

Colca Canyon and Cotahuasi Canyon

WHERE TO EAT AND STAY

Chivay is tiny, but it has plenty of hotels, from budget to moderate, and even a few luxury options. Restaurants are not so plentiful and not varied, especially when it comes to the ubiquitous tourist-oriented buffets. You'll come into town on 22 de Agosto, which leads to the Plaza de Armas, where you'll find long-standing **Inka's Restaurant and Coffee Bar and McElroy's Pub** (a gringo magnet owned by a true Irishman). The best bet though, also on the plaza, is Q'anka Resto Bar, serving delicious meat and fish on volcanic stone, good pizzas, and interesting cocktails and craft beers. There are also a few basic restaurants in Cabanaconde, including the excellent and mostly organic **La Granja del Colca** in a rural area on the highway.

If you're planning on staying one night in Colca Canyon, it makes sense to stay in Chivay. If you'll be in the area for longer, we recommend one of the lodges in the valley, which are more inclusive and offer activities like hiking, biking, and horseback riding, and have a restaurant on-site.

$$$
RESORT
FAMILY
Aranwa Pueblito Encantado del Colca. Although the exterior of this upscale resort and spa along the Colca River feels more condo than boutique, the rooms are modern and airy, the amenities are superb, it houses one of the better restaurants and bars in the area, and it offers a stunning get-away-from-it-all location. **Pros:** full-service spa; secluded

location with stunning views; modern and spacious rooms. **Cons:** inelegant exterior; a taxi ride away from anything else. $\boxed{\$}$ *Rooms from: S/700* ✉ *Cusipampa 1 s/n, Salihua, Coporaque* ☎ *511/207–0440, 1–855/384–6625, 054/383–850* ⊕ *www.aranwahotels.com* ⤵ *41 rooms* ❧ *Breakfast.*

$\$$
B&B/INN
⌂ **Casa Andina Standard Colca.** Part of the national Casa Andina chain, this property is much quainter than their typical urban locations, with stand-alone bungalow-style cabins built of locally quarried rock, thatched roofs, and wood flooring. **Pros:** planetarium (with shows in English) and observatory; good breakfast; cozy lounge and fireplace. **Cons:** disconnected from nature; small bathrooms. $\boxed{\$}$ *Rooms from: S/218* ✉ *Calle Huayna Capac s/n* ☎ *051/213–9739* ⊕ *www.casa-andina. com* ⤵ *51 rooms* ❧ *Breakfast.*

$\$\$\$$
RESORT
FAMILY
⌂ **Colca Lodge.** One of the most complete resorts in Colca, with its own hot springs and solar heating, this hotel is at the same time relaxing and family-friendly. **Pros:** lots of activities; hot springs and full-service spa; solar heating. **Cons:** hot springs closed February and March; minimal decor. $\boxed{\$}$ *Rooms from: S/534* ✉ *Fundo Puye s/n, Caylloma, Yanque* ☎ *054/531–056* ⊕ *www.colca-lodge.com* ⤵ *45 rooms* ❧ *Breakfast.*

$\$\$$
B&B/INN
⌂ **Colca Trek Lodge.** Situated in Pinchollo, a small town just 15 minutes from the Cruz del Condor viewing point, this tranquil lodge is surrounded by gorgeous scenery and in the perfect location for trekking and mountain-climbing excursions. **Pros:** gorgeous location; great food; access to trekking. **Cons:** nothing to do for nonhikers. $\boxed{\$}$ *Rooms from: S/270* ✉ *Calle San Sebastian I–5, Pinchollo* ☎ *054/206–217* ⊕ *www. colcatreklodge.com* ⤵ *12 rooms* ❧ *Breakfast.*

$\$\$$
RESORT
⌂ **El Refugio.** Located about five minutes from Chivay and set in a stunning landscape hugged by mountains and lush greenery alongside a rushing river—the sound will lull you to sleep at night—this peaceful hotel allows you to take refuge from the world without compromising comfort. **Pros:** private natural hot springs; beautiful location ; peaceful escape. **Cons:** remote; many steps to get down to the lodge. $\boxed{\$}$ *Rooms from: S/420* ✉ *Fundo Putuco (carretera rural a Cabanaconde)* ☎ *054/959–603–753, 054/257–901* ⊕ *www.refugiohotelcolca.com* ⤵ *33 rooms* ❧ *Breakfast.*

$\$\$$
B&B/INN
Fodor's Choice
★
⌂ **Killawasi Lodge.** A boutique lodge with rustic-chic decor, Killawasi's location, in the countryside but close to the small town of Yanque, provides the perfect balance of escape to nature and access to local culture. **Pros:** tranquil location; rustic decor; great service. **Cons:** nearby town is tiny; not much else nearby. $\boxed{\$}$ *Rooms from: S/315* ✉ *Calle Caraveli 408, Yanque* ☎ *054/691–072* ⊕ *www.killawasilodge.com* ⤵ *14 rooms* ❧ *Breakfast.*

$\$$
B&B/INN
⌂ **La Casa de Mama Yacchi.** If you're passing through and want to save on your lodging budget, this quiet hotel in the countryside offers great value for basic rooms, many of which have gorgeous views. **Pros:** great value; tranquil location; beautiful views from many rooms. **Cons:** basic rooms; gets cold; taxi needed to get anywhere. $\boxed{\$}$ *Rooms from: S/210* ✉ *Caylloma s/n, Coporaque* ☎ *054/241–206* ⊕ *www.lacasademamayacchi.com* ⊟ *No credit cards* ⤵ *28 rooms* ❧ *Breakfast.*

4

$$$$
RESORT
Fodor's Choice
★

Las Casitas del Colca. The most luxurious property in the Colca area, with service and amenities to match, each thatched bungalow has its own outdoor terrace with private heated pool, heated smooth stone floors, and deep bathtubs beneath skylights for after-dark soaking and stargazing, though you can get an even better view from the outdoor showers. **Pros:** beautiful rooms; gorgeous grounds; private hot springs and full-service spa; top-notch service. **Cons:** pricey; remote location. $ *Rooms from: S/1680* ⊠ *Fundo La Curiña s/n, Yanque* ☎ *996/998–355* ⊕ *www.lascasitasdelcolca.com* ➴ *20 bungalows* ⦿ *Breakfast.*

$$
B&B/INN

Pozo del Cielo. Across the river on top of a hill on the outskirts of Chivay sits one of the most relaxed lodges in the valley, with stunning views over Chivay, the valley, and the volcanoes. **Pros:** lovely views from the outskirts of town; electric blankets and heaters; great service. **Cons:** must walk outside to get to breakfast. $ *Rooms from: S/291* ⊠ *Calle Huáscar B-3 Sacsayhuaman* ☎ *054/346–547* ⊕ *www.pozodelcielo.com.pe* ➴ *38 rooms* ⦿ *Breakfast.*

> ### VALLEY OF THE VOLCANOES
>
> This spectacular, 65-km (40-mile) crevasse north of Colca Canyon includes a line of 80 extinct craters and cinder cones. Looming over the scene is active Volcán Coropuna, the third-highest peak in Peru. Andagua, at the head of the valley, has the best tourist facilities in the area. The valley is about five hours by a rocky, half-paved, half-dirt road from Colca Canyon. There are several multiday hikes from Colca Canyon that must be arranged in Arequipa. If you're going to Cotahuasi or Colca Canyon, you're bound to pass through this high-altitude valley.

SPORTS AND THE OUTDOORS

Most organized adventure-sports activities should be arranged from Arequipa or Cusco, especially rafting and multiday treks into the canyon. Many upper-tier hotels and resorts in the canyon offer packages, have their own tour guides, and have activities like horseback riding and mountain-bike rentals. If you wait to organize a guide until you get to the canyon, you may have trouble finding an English-speaking guide. Therefore, tours are best booked through an agency ahead of time.

HIKING

Bring lots of water (the valley has water, but it's more expensive, as it's "imported" from Arequipa), sunscreen, a hat, good hiking shoes, high-energy snacks, and sugar or coca leaves to alleviate the altitude sickness. And layer your clothes—one minute the wind may be fierce and the next you may be sweltering in the strong sun.

Along the canyon: Along the south side of the canyon, it's possible to do an easy hike from the observation points between Cruz del Condor and Pinchollo. Paths are along the canyon rim most of the way; however, in some places you have to walk along the road. The closer to Cruz del Condor you are, the better the paths and lookouts get.

Another short hike, but more uphill, is on the north rim starting in Coporaque. At the Plaza de Armas, in the corner to the left of the church, you'll see an archway. Go through the archway and take a

Llamas take the high road in Colca Canyon.

right uphill and you'll be on the trail, which goes from wide to narrow but is defined. ■ TIP→ Following it up for about an hour, you'll come to ancient burial tombs (look down) with actual skeletons. The trail climbs up a cliff, which overlooks the valley. It's about a two-hour hike to the top, and in some spots it is very steep and the rocks are crumbly. After the tombs the path becomes confusing and splits in many directions.

Into the canyon: Trails into the canyon are many, and they are rough and unmarked, so venture down with a guide. Several adventure-tour operators provide government-certified hiking guides; local guides are also easily found but may not speak English. Packages range from two- to eight-day treks. The Cabanaconde area is the entry point for most of these.

The most popular multiday hike is the three-day/two-night trek. Starting at Pampa San Miguel, about 20 minutes (on foot) east of Cabanaconde, the trail to San Juan Chuccho (one of the larger villages along the river) begins. The steep slope has loose gravel and takes about four hours. In San Juan Chuccho sleeping options are family-run hostels or a campground. Day two consists of hiking on fairly even terrain through the small villages of Tapay, Cosnirhua, and Malata before crossing the river and into the lush green village of Sangalle, or as locals call it, the oasis, a mini paradise along the Río Colca, with hot springs and waterfalls. On day three, you'll hike four- to five hours uphill to the rim and arrive in Cabanaconde by lunch.

■ TIP→ We do not recommend hiking alone here. So many paths are in this area that it can be overwhelming to even the most experienced trekkers.

Carlos Zárate Aventures. You can hire Carlos Zárate and his hiking and mountain guides for tours to the most difficult and also most common treks in the region. Guides speak Spanish, English, and French. ⊠ *Calle Jerusalén 505A, Arequipa* ☎ *054/294–461* ⊕ *www.colcatrek. com* ⊠ *From S/180.*

Colca Trek. With more than 30 years of experience in adventure tours in the area, Vlado Soto is a pioneer of Colca Canyon trekking. Passionate about outdoor excursions, Vlado is constantly out there himself, checking the routes and investigating new trails. Colca Trek are specialists in longer trekking tours, as well as day trips, city tours, rafting excursions, and mountain biking. You can also get topographical maps of the entire region in their office. ⊠ *Calle Jerusalén 401-B, Arequipa* ☎ *054/206–217* ⊕ *www.colcatrek. com.pe* ⊠ *From S/285.*

WHITE-WATER RAFTING

The Río Colca is finicky. Highly skilled paddlers long to run this Class IV–V river. Depending upon the season, the water level, and the seismic activity of the local volcanoes, the rapids change frequently. In some areas it's more than a Class V, and in other areas it's slow enough that it could be considered a Class II–III. Below Colca Canyon conditions on the Río Majes (the large downstream section of the Río Colca) are reliable, with superb white-water rafting. Skilled rafters start in Huambo by renting mules for S/20–S/30 and for the next eight hours descend to the river. The waters at this point rank in at Class III, but when the Río Mamacocha dumps in, it's Class IV and V rapids.

Paddlers who have tried to run the entire river through the canyon have failed more often than succeeded. There are a few well-known operators to consider, which is important, given the river's intensity.

The following operators specialize in adventure tours in the Colca and Cotahuasi Canyons. For the standard one- or two-day tours of Colca Canyon, see tour operators listed under Arequipa city.

Amazonas Explorer. Based in Cusco and one of the most reputable adventure companies in the country, Amazonas Explorer is one of the few that offer rafting trips in Cotahuasi. Owner Paul Cripps, an inveterate rafter himself, keeps abreast of current conditions and ensures that the best equipment and highest degree of safety practices are employed. ⊠ *Av. Collasuyo 910, Cusco* ☎ *844/380–7378 from U.S., 958/729–904 office in Peru* ⊕ *amazonas-explorer.com* ⊠ *From $3161.*

Bio Bio Expeditions. One of the leaders in kayaking and rafting operators around the world, Bio Bio Expeditions puts on multiday, all-inclusive runs down the Cotahuasi rivers. All guides are trained in first aid and swiftwater rescue. ☎ *800/246–7238* ⊕ *www.bbxrafting. com* ⊠ *From $3300.*

Canyon Life

Quechua farmers once irrigated narrow, stacked terraces of volcanic earth along the canyon rim to make this a productive farming area. These ancient fields are still used for quinoa and *kiwicha* (amaranth) grains, and barley grown here is used to brew Arequipeña beer.

Most of those who live along the rim today are Collagua Indians, whose settlements date back more than 2,000 years. Their traditions persevered through the centuries. In these unspoiled Andean villages you'll still see Collaguas and Cabana people wearing traditional clothing and embroidered hats. Spanish influence is evident in Achoma, Maca, Pinchollo, and Yanque, with their gleaming white sillar (volcanic-stone) churches.

Steeped in colorful folklore tradition, locals like a good fiesta. Some of the larger festivals include La Virgen de la Candelaria, a two-day fiesta in Chivay on February 2 and 3; later in the month Carnaval is celebrated throughout the valley. Semana Santa (Holy Week) in April is heavily observed, but for a more colorful party, don't miss Chivay's annual anniversary fiesta on June 21. From July 14 to 17, the Virgen del Carmen, one of the larger celebrations, kicks off with parades on both ends of the canyon: Cabanaconde and Chivay. All Saints' Day is well honored on November 1 and 2, as is La Virgen Imaculada on December 8.

PUNO AND LAKE TITICACA

Lake Titicaca is one of the most breathtaking parts of Peru, though in literal terms that may have something to do with the altitude. The azure-blue waters of the lake paired with an even bluer sky are a sight to behold indeed. The region is one of the most culturally significant places in the entire Andes. Not only are more festivals held here than anywhere else, but Quechua and Aymara people who inhabit isolated islands like Taquile and Amantani have preserved their customs over centuries with little change. The Islas de Uros, made of floating totora islands, are a magical display of color and originality. This is where the Incas were born, and ancient ruins, such as those at Sullustani, are scattered all over the area. For many travelers a visit to Lake Titicaca is the highlight of their trip.

PUNO

975 km (606 miles) southeast of Lima.

Puno doesn't win any beauty pageants—brown unfinished concrete homes, old paved roads, and dusty barren hills have dominated the landscape for years. It's a sharp contrast to Puno's immediate neighbor, Lake Titicaca. Some people arrive in town and scram to find a trip on the lake, but don't let the dreary look of Puno stop you from exploring its shores; it's considered Peru's folklore capital.

Puno retains traits of the Aymara, Quechua, and Spanish cultures that settled on the northwestern shores of the lake. Their influence is in the art, music, dance, and dress of today's inhabitants, who call themselves Children of the Sacred Lake. Much of the city's character comes from the continuation of ancient traditions—at least once a month, a parade or a festival celebrates some recent or historic event.

> **HIGH SUN**
>
> Don't forget sunblock! At high altitudes the rays can be fierce, even with clouds. Often the brisk mountain temperatures trick you into thinking it's too cool for a burn.

A huge contrast to the constant barrage of people trying to sell you things in Cusco's Plaza de Armas, the city and main plaza of Puno exists for the local residents. Although the number of hotels and restaurants that really cater to the tastes of foreign travelers is growing, it is doing so quite slowly. If you are in the city, stick to the Plaza de Armas and the pedestrian-only streets such as Avenida Lima, and take taxis after dark.

GETTING HERE AND AROUND

Although Puno does not have an airport, you can fly into Juliaca's Aeropuerto Manco Capac, about 45 minutes away. The airport is served by LATAM airlines (⊕ *www.latam.com*) for flights between Juliaca, Cusco, and Lima, sometimes with a stop along the way. Avianca (⊕ *www.avianca.com*) also operates between Juliaca and Lima. Most hotels in Puno will pick you up on arrival; otherwise you can take one of the waiting tourist buses (S/5) or organize a private taxi for about S/60–S/80.

The Terrestre bus terminal is at Primero de Mayo 703 and Bolívar, and many companies also have offices here. Puno is a connection point for trips between Arequipa, Cusco, and La Paz, Bolivia, so there are frequent buses throughout the day for each destination.

The train station for PeruRail for trips to and from Cusco, Estación Huanchaq (*084/581414*), is at the end of Avenida Sol on Avenida La Torre just outside the center of town. Service between the towns runs three or four times a week, depending on the season.

Restaurants, shops, Internet services, banks, and drugstores line the four-block pedestrian-only street Jirón Lima, between Pino Park (sometimes called Parque San Juan after the San Juan Bautista Church nearby) and the Plaza de Armas.

Puno has tricycle taxis, which resemble Asian tuk-tuks and are driven by bicycle pedalers with a carriage and cost only S/3–S/4 to go nearly anywhere in the city. But if you're heading to a mirador high up on the hill and you don't want the pedaler to keel over, take an auto taxi, which costs S/3–S/7. There are also moto-taxis, which cost around S/4.

Bus Cruz del Sur. ⊠ *Terminal Terrestre C-10* ☎ *051/368–524* ⊕ *www.cruzdelsur.com.pe.* **Inka Express.** ⊠ *Jr. Tacna 346* ☎ *051/365–654* ⊕ *www.inkaexpress.com.* **Turismo Mer.** ⊠ *Jr. Tacna 336* ☎ *051/367–223 office, 051/365–617 bus station* ⊕ *www.turismomer.com.*

Trains PeruRail. ⊠ *Estacion Puno, La Torre 224* ☎ *084/581–414* ⊕ *www.perurail.com.*

CLOSE UP

Llamas, Vicuñas, and Alpacas

Llamas, vicuñas, guanacos, and alpacas roam the highlands of Peru, but unfortunately not in the great herds of pre-Inca times. Nevertheless, a few are always around, especially the domesticated llama and alpaca. The sly vicuña, like the guanaco, refuses domestication. Here's a primer on how to tell them apart.

The alpaca is the cute and cuddly one, especially while still a baby. It grows a luxurious, long wool coat that comes in as many as 20 colors, and its wool is used for knitting sweaters and weaving rugs and wall hangings. Its finest wool is from the first shearing and is called "baby alpaca." When full grown it's close to 1.5 meters (5 feet) tall and weighs about 48 kg (106 pounds). Its size and the shortness of its neck distinguish it from the llama. There are two types of alpaca: the common huancayo with short thick legs; and the less-predominant suri, which is a bit taller, and also nicknamed the Bob Marley for its shaggy, curly dreadlocks that grow around its face and chest.

The guanaco, a cousin of the delicate vicuña, is a thin-legged, wild, endangered camelid, with a coarse reddish-brown coat and a soft white underbelly. Its hair is challenging to weave on its own, so often it's mixed with other fibers, like alpaca. The guanaco weighs about 90 kg (200 pounds) and can be up to 1.5 meters (5 feet) long and 1–1.2 meters (3–4 feet) high. Eighty percent of guanacos live in Patagonia, but the other 20% are scattered across the *altiplano* (high plains) of southern Peru, Chile, and Bolivia. It's the only camelid that can live both at sea level and in the high-altitude Andes.

The llama is the pack animal with a coarse coat in as many as 50 colors, though one that's unsuitable for fine wearing apparel. It can reach almost 2 meters (6 feet) from its hoofs to the top of its elongated neck and long, curved ears. It can carry 40–60 kilograms (88–132 pounds), depending on the length of the trip. It can also have some nasty habits, like spitting in your eye or kicking you if you get too close to its hind legs.

The vicuña has a more delicate appearance. It will hold still (with help) for shearing, and its wool is the most desirable. Almost rendered extinct by unrestricted hunting, it is now protected by the Peruvian government. It's the smallest of the Andean camelids, at 1.3 meters (4 feet), and weighs about 40 kg (88 pounds) at maturity. It's found mostly at altitudes over 3,600 meters (11,800 feet).

Taxis **Radio Taxi Milenium.** ☏ *051/353–134.*

SAFETY AND PRECAUTIONS

At 3,827 meters (12,556 feet) above sea level, Puno challenges your system, so eat lightly, skip the alcohol (Trust us!), forgo your morning jog, and take it easy your first two or three days.

▪ TIP→ Walking around the port after dark is not smart. When the sun goes down, the port gets desolate, so if you're at the handicrafts market or are getting back from an outing on the lake and suddenly it's dusk, catch a cab.

ESSENTIALS

Almost all the buses leave from the Terminal Terrestre. Reputable companies include Civa, Ormeno, and Tour Peru. Cruz del Sur is probably the best of the bunch and also leaves from the main terminal. Inka Express and Turismo Mer specialize in buses that run between Puno and Cusco, stopping at various tourist sites along the way to break up the trip.

> **BRING CASH!**
>
> There are ATMs in Chivay but nowhere else in the Colca Canyon or valley area. Soles and U.S. dollars (no bills larger than US$20) are accepted.

Currency Banco Continental BBVA. ⊠ *400 Jr. Lima.* Banco de Crédito BCP. ⊠ *Jr. Lima 510* ☎ *051/352–119.* Scotiabank. ⊠ *Plaza de Armas, corner of Duestra and Jr. Lima.*

Mail Serpost Puno. ⊠ *Av. Moquegua 269.*

Medical Manuel Nuñez Butron National Hospital. ⊠ *Jr. Ricardo Palma 120* ☎ *051/367–128, 051/368–862 emergencies* ⊕ *www.hrmnb.gob.pe.* Medicentro Tourist's Health. ⊠ *Jr. Moquegua 193* ☎ *051/365–909, 951/620–937.*

Police Police. ⊠ *Jr. Deustua 530* ☎ *051/366–271, 051/353–988.* Policía de Turismo. ⊠ *Jr. Deustua 538* ☎ *051/354–764.*

Visitor Information iPeru Oficina Información Turística. ⊠ *Plaza de Armas, corner Jr. Deustua and Jr. Lima* ☎ *051/365–088.*

EXPLORING

TOP ATTRACTIONS

Conde de Lemos Balcony. An intricately carved wooden balcony marks the home where Viceroy Conde de Lemos stayed when he arrived in Puno to counter rebellion around 1668. Behind the cathedral, it is today home to the National Culture Institute of the Department of Puno. ⊠ *Corner of Calles Deustua and Conde de Lemos* 🎟 *Free.*

Fodor's Choice ★ **La Casa del Corregidor.** Reconstructed more than five times, this 17th-century colonial building, once a chaplaincy, is now a brightly colored cultural center. It was originally home to Silvestre de Valdés, a Catholic priest who served as a *corregidor* (a Spanish official who acts as governor, judge, and tax collector) and oversaw construction of the nearby Catedral. The house had a long history of changing owners until its present owner, Sra. Ana Maria Piño Jordán, bought it at public auction. Now a vibrant cultural locale, with an arts cooperative, it houses a fair-trade café, a library, and a few upscale handicraft stores. The exhibition hall displays works by local artists and hosts music events. ⊠ *Deustua 576* ☎ *051/351–921* ⊕ *www.casadelcorregidor.pe* ⊗ *Closed Sun.*

WORTH NOTING

Catedral. Etchings of flowers, fruits, and mermaids playing an Andean guitar called the *charango* grace the entrance of the Spanish baroque-style church. Sculpted by Peruvian architect Simon de Asto, the 17th-century stone cathedral has one of the more eclectically carved facades of any church in the area. Plain on the inside, its main decorations are a silver-plated altar and paintings from the Cusco School. ⊠ *Plaza de Armas* 🎟 *Free* ⊗ *Closed Sun.*

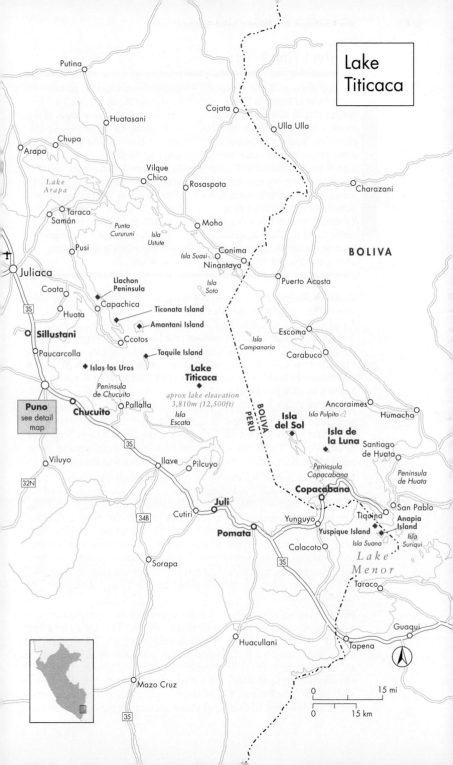

CLOSE UP

Festival Time!

Although any time of year is suitable for traveling to Puno and Lake Titicaca, visiting during a festival of dance, song, and parades is ideal. The streets are flooded with people; the folklore experience is passionate and a lot of fun. Preserving the choreography of more than 140 typical dances, Puno's most memorable celebration is the Festival of the Virgin de la Candelaria, held on February 2 and during Carnaval. A cast of several hundred elaborately costumed Andean singers, dancers, and bands from neighboring communities parades through the streets carrying the rosy-white-complexioned statue of the Virgin. During the rest of the year, the statue rests on the altar of the San Juan Bautista Church. Puno Week, as it's informally known, occurs the first week of November and is equally fun. When Puno isn't having a celebration, it reverts to its true character, that of a small, poor Andean agricultural town. On the lake, Isla Taquile celebrates a vivid festival the last week of July.

Cerrito de Huajsapata. A statue honoring Manco Cápac, the first governor and founder of the Inca Empire, sits on this hill overlooking Puno. Legend has it that there are caves and subterranean paths in the monument, which connect Puno with the Koricancha Temple in Cusco. It's technically a 10-minute walk from town, four blocks southwest of Plaza de Armas, but it's all uphill and a bit off the beaten path. ■TIP→ A few robberies have been reported, so stick with a group or take a taxi. ⊠ Off Calle Choquehanca.

Iglesia San Juan Bautista. This 18th-century church has been entrusted with the care of the Virgin of Candlemas, the focus of Puno's most important yearly celebration in February, the Festival de la Virgen de la Candelaria. The statue rests on the main altar. Worth passing by at night to see the neon exterior lighting. ⊠ Jr. Lima and Parque Pino.

Museo Carlos Dreyer. An exhibit of 501 gold pieces called the "Great Treasure of Sillustani" has classified the intimate museum as one of the most important regional archaeological museums in southern Peru. The museum is named for famed Puno painter and antiques collector Carlos Dreyer Spohr whose oil-on-canvas works you can view here, in addition to exploring exhibits of pre-Hispanic and colonial art, weavings, silver, copper works, delicate Aymara pottery, pre-Inca stone sculptures, and historical Spanish documents on the founding of Puno. Plan to spend about an hour here. ⊠ Conde de Lemos 289 ⊑ S/15 ⊘ Closed Sun.

Museo de la Coca y Costumbres. A hidden gem, this museum pays tribute to the infamous coca leaf and Peruvian folklore. The quaint museum includes a folklore exhibit as well as everything you'd ever want to know about the coca leaf. Presented in English and Spanish, displays are well constructed with educational videos and photographs. The mission is not to promote coca but merely to share the plant's history and culture. The folklore exhibit displays elaborately constructed costumes worn during festivals and shares the history behind the dances.

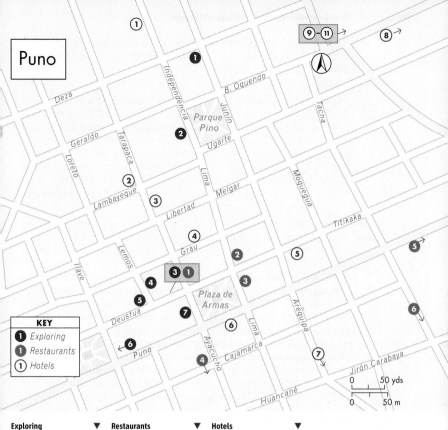

Puno

KEY
- ① Exploring
- ① Restaurants
- ① Hotels

Visit the store and purchase some coca-based products or have your future read in the leaves. ⊠ *Jr. Ilave 581* ☎ *951/927–826* ⊕ *www. museodelacoca.com* 🖃 *S/10.*

WHERE TO EAT

Many small restaurants line Jirón Lima, and include a mix of Novo Andino and classic regional foods. On the menu you'll find fresh fish from the lake and an abundance of quinua dishes, along with typical Peruvian fare like *lechón al horno o cancacho* (highly spiced baked suckling pig); *pesque o queso de quinua* (resembling ground-up barley), prepared with cheese and served with fish fillet in tomato sauce; and *chairo* (lamb and tripe broth cooked with vegetables, and freeze-dried potatoes known as *chuño*). Particularly good are *trucha* (trout) and *pejerrey* (kingfish mackerel) from the lake.

$$
INTERNATIONAL

✕ **Alma Cocina Viva.** Inside the Casa Andina Premium Puno hotel, this contemporary eatery with cozy fireplaces is one of the few upscale options in the city. The lake views alone are worth the visit, and prices are quite similar to the town's lesser alternatives, but it's the menu that's most enticing. **Known for:** views; modern takes on regional ingredients; international food. $ *Average main: S/45* ⊠ *Av. Sesquicentenario 1970–72* ☎ *051/363–992* ⊕ *www.casa-andina.com/private-collection-puno.*

$
CAFÉ
Fodor's Choice
★

✕ **Café Bar.** In La Casa del Corregidor, this laidback café-bar offers some of the best food you can find in Puno, some healthy and some less so, as well as a wide variety of craft beers and great coffee drinks. A collection of teas, cocktails, smoothies, along with more sweet treats like cakes and pies, round out the menu. **Known for:** chill ambiance; snacks; garden seating. $ *Average main: S/24* ⊠ *La Casa del Corregidor, Deustua 576* ☎ *051/351–921* ⊕ *www.cafebar.casadelcorregidor.pe.*

$$
FRENCH

✕ **La Table Del'Inca.** This chic French-Peruvian restaurant, one of the best bets in town for a nice meal out, is set in a beautifully renovated colonial building with walls adorned by paintings from a local surrealist artist. You can order from the à la carte menu but you should opt for the prix-fixe menu (S/80), which will allow you to try more dishes for a a lower price. **Known for:** delicious fusion food; reasonable prix-fixe menu; great atmosphere. $ *Average main: S/40* ⊠ *Jr. Ancash 239* ☎ *994/659–357* ⊗ *Closed Sun.*

$
VEGETARIAN

✕ **Loving Hut Titicaca Vegan.** It's healthy, it's vegan … so what? Puno doesn't have the greatest restaurant selection, and this place is actually decent, and the prices are great. **Known for:** vegan set menu; large portions; reasonable prices. $ *Average main: S/12* ⊠ *Jr. Jose Domingo Choquehuanca 188* ☎ *51/353–523* ⊕ *www.lovinghut.com/pe* ▭ *No credit cards* ⊗ *Closed Sun. and after 7 pm.*

$$
PERUVIAN
Fodor's Choice
★

✕ **Mojsa.** Located in a beautiful colonial building, there are a couple of intimate tables on the balcony overlooking the Plaza de Armas, while the more lively interior rooms make it seem like THE place to eat for both Peruvians and travelers. Mojsa, which means "delicious" in the Aymara language, serves reasonably priced Novo Andino cuisine, fused with fresh traditional and criollo flavors in an elegant space with wood floors and a long bar. **Known for:** beautiful building; reasonable prices; attentive service. $ *Average main: S/37* ⊠ *Lima 635, Plaza de Armas* ☎ *051/363–182* ⊕ *mojsarestaurant.com.*

$ PERUVIAN 🍴 **Restaurant Museo La Casona.** An upscale modern restaurant but with colonial-era artwork and antiques throughout, this two-decades-old local institution is filled with savory aromas of flavorful soups and grilled meats and fish. Try local fare, such as the *lomo de alpaca* (alpaca steak) or their take on quinoa soup, a must-try dish wherever you go in Peru. **Known for:** tasty local fare; ample portions; reasonable prices. [$] *Average main: S/30* ✉ *Av. Lima 423* ☎ *051/351–108* 🌐 *www.lacasona-restaurant.com.*

WHERE TO STAY

Puno can be cold at night, so bring warm clothes. The fanciest hotels have central heating systems, but most others have portable electric heaters in the rooms. Air-conditioning is unheard of here outside of the five-star lodgings but you probably won't want it anyway. Always check heating options when you book, and make sure there are extra blankets on hand when you check in. As Puno has few notable attractions, there is less of a need to stay in town as in other Peruvian cities. On the lakeshore outside town is where the best upscale hotels are located, which allow for lovely views of the lake and a more peaceful setting. Bear in mind, the only convenient restaurants will be those located in the hotels, but as the city still doesn't offer that much in the way of gastronomy, that's not such a detriment.

4

$$ HOTEL 🏨 **Casa Andina Premium Puno.** Out of the two Casa Andina properties in Puno (the other is a less expensive Casa Andina Standard property), this pricier lakeside hotel is the best, offering comfortable rooms with great natural light and all the modern amenities you need. **Pros:** lakeside views; oxygen tank; great service. **Cons:** decor is minimalist; rooms are small. [$] *Rooms from: S/466* ✉ *Av. Sesquicentenario 1970–72, Sector Huaje* ☎ *051/363–992* 🌐 *www.casa-andina.com* 🛏 *45 rooms* 🍽 *Breakfast.*

$ HOTEL 🏨 **Casa Andina Standard Puno.** Basic but comfortable rooms with the typical Casa Andina great service, this standard-level hotel is centrally located, making it easy to head out to tour for the day or have dinner out in the evening. **Pros:** centrally located; clean and comfortable rooms; reliable chain service. **Cons:** lacks atmosphere; basic. [$] *Rooms from: S/248* ✉ *Jr. Independencia 143* ☎ *051/367–803* 🌐 *www.casa-andina.com* 🛏 *50 rooms* 🍽 *Breakfast.*

$$ HOTEL 🏨 **Hotel Hacienda Plaza de Armas.** The most centrally located of all Puno hotels, right in the Plaza de Armas, all rooms are comfortable; some include balconies and Jacuzzis while all have modern bathrooms with bathtubs. **Pros:** central location; colonial features; modern and comfortable rooms. **Cons:** not all rooms have a view; central location brings noise. [$] *Rooms from: S/270* ✉ *Jr. Puno 419, Plaza de Armas* ☎ *051/367–340* 🌐 *www.hhp.com.pe* 🛏 *28 rooms* 🍽 *Breakfast.*

$$ HOTEL 🏨 **Hotel Hacienda Puno.** Panoramic views of Lake Titicaca and its surroundings can be viewed from the endless windows that line the restaurant atop of this Spanish-colonial hotel, and some of the rooms share the view. **Pros:** two blocks from Plaza de Armas; colonial common areas; great views. **Cons:** simple design. [$] *Rooms from: S/270* ✉ *Deustua 297* ☎ *051/365–134* 🌐 *www.hhp.com.pe* 🛏 *64 rooms* 🍽 *Breakfast.*

$ **Intiqa Hotel.** The comfortable rooms here are modern, but the hotel
HOTEL   is also full of local flavor, thanks to plenty of indigenous art and artifacts. **Pros:** modern rooms and bathrooms; historic touches. **Cons:** some
rooms can be noisy. *$ Rooms from: S/203 ⊠ Tarapacá 272 ☎ 051/366–
900 ⊕ www.intiqahotel.com ⤷ 24 rooms ⦿ Breakfast.*

$$$ **Isla Suasi.** An ecological paradise for those who can afford it, this
RESORT   exclusive hotel is on Isla Suasi, on a remote end of Lake Titicaca (a five-
FAMILY   and-a-half hour boat ride from Puno, including a stop at Uruos). **Pros:**
Fodor'sChoice   gorgeous and tranquil setting; lots of activities; private cottage with but-
★   ler. **Cons:** remote. *$ Rooms from: S/645 ⊠ Isla Suasi ☎ 051/351–102
⊕ www.islasuasi.pe ⤷ 23 rooms ⦿ All-inclusive.*

$$ **Libertador Hotel Isla Esteves.** Although it may look a little institutional
RESORT   from the outside, inside this low-rise hotel, which functions more like a
resort, is the most luxurious stay close to the city. **Pros:** lakeside views;
most comfortable rooms in the Puno area; upscale restaurant on-site.
Cons: 10 minutes from town. *$ Rooms from: S/405 ⊠ Isla Esteves
☎ 051/367–780, 877/778–2281 ⊕ www.libertador.com.pe ⤷ 123
rooms ⦿ Breakfast.*

$ **Qelqatani.** On a quiet street about a five-minute walk from Jirón
HOTEL   Lima, this is an affordable, cozy place to lay your head after a day
on the lake, with basic but clean and comfortable rooms. **Pros:** great
value for your money; centrally located; great staff. **Cons:** interior is
dark at night; older building. *$ Rooms from: S/168 ⊠ Tarapacá 355
☎ 051/351–470 ⊕ www.qelqatani.com ⤷ 42 rooms ⦿ Breakfast.*

$$ **Sonesta Posadas del Inca.** Weavings, polished wood, and native art
HOTEL   give character to this thoroughly modern hotel on the shores of Lake
Titicaca, one of Puno's original upscale hotels. **Pros:** on the lake with
outdoor seating; good heating; comfortable beds. **Cons:** five minutes
from town. *$ Rooms from: S/406 ⊠ Sesquicentenario 610, Sector
Huaje ☎ 051/364–111 ⊕ www.sonesta.com/sonestaposadas ⤷ 70
rooms ⦿ Breakfast.*

$ **Tierra Viva Puno Plaza.** Centrally located and modern, this a great base
HOTEL   for your tours, The hotel has comfortable rooms that feature orthopedic
beds, heating, and native weavings that inject color and local flair. **Pros:**
centrally located; comfortable beds; local crafts. **Cons:** fairly simple
design. *$ Rooms from: S/186 ⊠ Calle Grau 270 ☎ 051/368–005 ⊕ tier-
ravivahoteles.com/peru/puno/ ⤷ 30 rooms ⦿ Breakfast.*

$$$$ **Titilaka.** Part of the luxe Relais & Châteaux brand, this is the best
RESORT   hotel on the lake, period—a stylish all-inclusive ecotourism resort with
FAMILY   contemporary flair, in an off-the-beaten-path location. **Pros:** all inclusive
Fodor'sChoice   with gourmet restaurant; luxurious rooms; heated floors; lake views.
★   **Cons:** may be too secluded for some. *$ Rooms from: S/3006 ⊠ Hu-
enccalla, Peninsula Titilaka ☎ 017/005–100, 866/628–1777 ⊕ www.
titilaka.com ⤷ 18 rooms ⦿ All-inclusive.*

NIGHTLIFE

Dozens of small bars and lounges are packed in on Jirón Lima, often one
flight up from the street, although many are dated in style and music.
If you want to enjoy an evening drink, you're best off at your hotel or
enjoying a craft beer at the café bar in the Casa del Corregidor.

SHOPPING

La Casona Parodi. A few small, high-end shops are in this colonial building, selling alpaca sweaters, jewelry, and handicrafts. ⊠ *Jr. Lima 394.*

Mercado Artesanal. Model reed boats, small stone carvings, and alpaca-wool articles are among the local crafts sold near the Port at Puno's Mercado Artesanal. If you find you aren't dressed for Puno's chilly evenings, it's the place to buy inexpensive woolen goods but the cheaper they are, the more likely they are a blend with synthetics, though they will still keep you warm. Open 8–6. Make sure you know where your wallet or purse is while you're snapping a photo of the colorful market. ⊠ *Av. Simon Bolivar and Jr. El Puerto.*

Mercado Central. If you're looking for some fresh produce, Andean cheeses, flowers, or bulk food, stroll through the Mercado Central. Keep a close guard on your belongings. ⊠ *Jr. Tacna between Jr. F. Arbulu and Jr. Oquendo.*

LAKE TITICACA

Forms Puno's eastern shoreline.

Stunning, unpredictable, and enormous, Lake Titicaca is a world of unique flora, fauna, cultures, and geology. Lago Titicaca, which means "lake of the gray (*titi*) puma (*caca*)" in Quechua, borders Peru and Bolivia, with Peru's largest portion to the northwest. Although Peru boasts the largest port in Puno (57% of the lake is in Peru), Bolivia's side has Isla del Sol and Isla de la Luna, two beautiful islands with great views and Inca ruins. The lake itself is larger than Puerto Rico, with an average depth of 7.5 meters (25 feet) and a minimum temperature of 38°F. Lake Titicaca gains 1.5 meters (5 feet) of water in summer (rainy season) and loses it again in winter (dry season).

The Bahía de Puno, separated from the lake proper by the two jutting peninsulas of Capaschica and Chucuito, is home to the descendants of the Uro people, who are now mixed with the Aymara and Quechua. The lakeshores are lush with totora reeds—valuable as building material, cattle fodder, and, in times of famine, food for humans.

Although it's generally cold, the beaming sun keeps you warm and, if you don't slather on sunscreen, burned.

GETTING HERE AND AROUND

A boat is necessary for traveling the lake. Most people go to the islands with a tour, but colectivo boats in Puno Bay will transport you for S/30–S/45. Most boats are super slow and super old, and they won't leave port unless at least 10 people are smooshed aboard. A four-hour trip will take only an hour in one of the newer speedboats that the higher-end tour companies now use.

ESSENTIALS

TOURS OF LAKE TITICACA Excursions to the floating islands of the Uros as well as to any of the islands on Lake Titicaca can be arranged through tour agencies in Puno. Most tours depart between 7:30 and 9 am, as the lake can become choppy in the afternoon. For Amantani and Taquile, you also can take the local boat at the Puno dock for about the same price as a tour, although boats don't usually depart without at least 10 passengers.

All Ways Travel. Aside from standard tours to the floating islands and Sillustani, All Ways Travel makes a concerted effort to discover and run specialty cultural trips to rural communities on islands on the lake, as well as elsewhere in the Puno region. A true socially responsible operator, they invest in ways to help improve the lives of the people in these communities, such as creating libraries. ⊠ *Casa del Corregidor, Jr. Deustua 576, 2nd fl., Puno* ☎ *051/353–979* ⊕ *www.titicacaperu.com* ✉ *From S/90.*

Edgar Adventures. Since 1996, Edgar Adventures has specialized in upscale and adventure trips around the region include standard tours to the Uros, Taquile and Amantani islands, and multiday kayaking trips on Lake Titicaca. ⊠ *Jr. Lima 328, Puno* ☎ *051/353–444* ⊕ *www. edgaradventures.com* ✉ *From S/90.*

Row Peru. Row Peru features a unique way to enjoy the beauty of Lake Titicaca—by paddling outrigger canoes. Rowing allows you to enjoy your surroundings while having a low impact on the environment. You can choose from such options as sunrise paddles, nature paddles, or afternoon visits to the floating islands of Uros. No prior experience is necessary. ⊠ *Hotel Libertador Jetty, Esteves Island, Puno* ☎ *992/755–067* ⊕ *www.rowperu.com* ✉ *From S/117.*

EXPLORING

Fodor's Choice ★ **Amantani Island.** This island has a small set of pre-Inca ruins that are a highlight of a visit here, along with the experience of the traditional life of its mainly agrarian society. Not as pretty as Taquile, Amantani is dusty and brown, though the island is renowned for its homestay programs that bring in boatloads of visitors each day, giving some, albeit touristic, insight into the life of the people here. Facilities and food are basic but cozy. Every tour operator in Puno runs overnight trips here, usually combined with a stop on the Uros Islands and Taquile. Most of the younger generations here speak Spanish and even a smidgen of English, but the older generation speaks only Aymara. Amantani has a population of about 4,500. Sacred fertility rituals are held in its two pre-Inca temples, one of which is dedicated to masculine energy and the other to the feminine. The island is 45 km (28 miles) from Puno and almost three hours away by boat from Taquile.

Anapia and Yuspique Island. In the Winaymarka section of Lake Titicaca, near the Bolivian border, are the Aymara-language islands of Anapia and Yuspique. This off-the-beaten-path two-day trip can be done with a tour operator or on your own but due to logistics, using an operator is probably best. There are 280 families living on the islands, very few of whom speak English or even Spanish.

The trip usually begins in Puno, where you board a bus for two hours to the village of Yunguyo near Punta Hermosa, where you catch a 1½-hour sailboat ride to the flat but fertile Anapia. On arrival hosts will meet visitors and guide them back to their family's home for an overnight stay. The day is then spent farming, tending to the animals, or playing with the children, and also includes a hiking trip to nearby Yuspique Island, where the women cook lunch on the beach. Typically, fresh fish is served with *huatia* (potatoes cooked in a natural clay oven and buried in hot soil with lots of herbs). Yuspique is not very populated, but is home to more than 100 wild vincuñas.

Continued on page 191

THE ISLANDS
of Lake Titicaca

According to legend, under orders from their father, the Sun God, the first Inca—Manco Cápac—and his sister—Mama Ocllo rose from the deep blue waters of Lake Titicaca and founded the Inca empire. Watching the mysterious play of light on the water and the shadows on the mountains, you may become a believer of the Inca myth.

Reed Boat Head, Uros

This is the altiplano—the high plains of Peru, where the earth has been raised so close to the sky that the area takes on a luminous quality. Lake Titicaca's sharp, sparkling blue waters may make you think of some place far from the altiplano, perhaps someplace warm. Then its chill will slap you back to reality and you realize that you're at the world's highest navigable lake, 12,500 feet above sea level. The lake's surface covers 8,562 sq km (3340 sq miles) and drops down 282 meters (925 ft) at its deepest.

Most of Lake Titicaca is a National Reserve dedicated to conserving the region's plant and animal life while promoting sustainable use of its resources. The reserve extends from the Bay of Puno to the peninsula of Capachica. It's divided into two sectors: one surrounds the Bay of Puno and protects the resources of the Uros-Chuluni communities; the other, in the Huancané area, preserves the totora-reed water fields and protects the nesting area of more than 60 bird species, including the Titicaca grebe.

THE FLOATING ISLANDS

Uru woman and totora reeds boat.

ISLAS LOS UROS

Islas Los Uros, known as the Floating Islands, are man-made islands woven together with tótora reeds that grow in the lake shallows. Replenished often with layers because the underbelly reeds rot, these tiny islands resemble floating bails of hay. Walking on them feels like walking on a big waterlogged sponge, but they are sturdy.

VISITING

Trips to the Los Uros typically take 30 minutes. While some travelers marvel at these 62-plus islands, some call them floating souvenir stands. Yes, locals sell trinkets, but visiting the floating islands is a glimpse into one of the region's oldest cultures, the Uros. Now mixed with Aymara culture it's a form of human habitation that evolved over centuries. The closest group of "floating museums" is 7 km (4.35 miles) from Puno.

ISLAND LIFE

The islanders make their living by fishing, trapping birds, and selling visitors well-made miniature reed boats, weavings, and collages depicting island life. You can hire an islander to take you for a ride in a reed boat. Although there's no running water, progress has come to some of the islands in the form of solar-powered energy and telephone stations. Seventh Day Adventists converted the inhabitants of one island and built a church and school.

HOMESTAY TIP

It's tradition for most families not to have visitors help in the kitchen, and on several islands families will not eat with visitors. It's also customary to bring a gift—usually essentials like fruit, dried grains, matches, and candles.

TAQUILE & AMANTANI ISLANDS

Folk dances on Taquile island.

TAQUILE ISLAND

35 km (22 miles) east of Puno in the high altitude sunshine, Taquile's brown dusty landscape contrasts with green terraces, bright flowers, and the surrounding blue waters. Snow-capped Bolivian mountains loom in the distance.

Taquile folk are known for weaving some of Peru's loveliest textiles, and men create textiles as much as the women. Islanders still wear traditional dress and have successfully maintained the cooperative lifestyle of their ancestors. The annual Taquile festival the third week of July is a great time to visit.

Taquile is on a steep hill with curvy long trails, which lead to the main square. There are many ways to reach the top of Taquile where there are Inca and Tiahuanaco ruins—you can climb up the 533 stone steps, or take a longer path.

AMANTANI ISLAND

The island of Amantani is 45 km (28 miles) from Puno and almost three hours away by boat from Taquile. Amantani has pre-Inca ruins, and a larger, mainly agrarian society, whose traditional way of life has been less exposed to the outside world until recently. Not as pretty as Taquile, Amantani is dusty and brown.

Locals were losing population to the mainland before a community-based project helped them dive into the tourist industry and organize homestays. Although the project has been a success, make sure you will be your host's only guests for a more intimate experience.

Most of the younger generations speak Spanish and even a smidgen of English, but the older generation speaks only Aymara. Amantani has a population of about 4,500 Quechua. Sacred fertility rituals are held in its two pre-Inca temples, one of which is dedicated to masculine energy and the other to the feminine.

Amantani woman spinning yarn from wool.

4

IN FOCUS THE ISLANDS OF LAKE TITICACA

ISLA DEL SOL, BOLIVIA

Adventurous travelers, with a couple days to spare, will want to journey on to Bolivia. After crossing the border, and getting to the pleasant lakeside town of Copacabana (visit the striking Moorish-style cathedral), go on by boat to the Isla del Sol, Lake Titicaca's largest island, where there are tremendous views, Inca ruins, and hotels.

Isla del Sol is the best place to visit and to stay on the lake and is the mythological birthplace of the pre-Inca and Inca. The views of the Cordillera Real mountains are amazing, especially at dawn and dusk, and the island has beautiful white sandy beaches and an extraordinary terraced landscape. Ruins include the Inca palace of Pilkokaina and a strange rock formation said to be the birthplace of the sun and moon, and an excellent Inca trail across the island. Alternatively, you can just laze around and soak up the cosmic energy.

En route to Isla del Sol, boats sometimes stop at **Isla de la Luna**, where the ruins of Iñacuy date back to the Inca conquest. You'll find an ancient con-

vent called Ajlla Wasi (House of the Chosen Women). Stone steps lead up to the unrestored ruins of the convent.

The legends that rise out of Lake Titicaca are no more mysterious than discoveries made in its depths. In 2000 an international diving expedition bumped into what is believed to be a 1,000-year-old pre-Inca temple. The stone structure is 660 feet long and 160 feet wide, with a wall 2,699 feet long. The discovery was made between Copacabana and the Sun and Moon islands.

(pictured top and bottom) Isla del Sol, the Island of the Sun, on Lake Titicaca, Bolivia.

After returning to Anapia you'll follow an evening's activities of traditional family life, such as music or dance. All Ways Travel runs tours, with the proceeds going to the families. You can do this trip on your own for about S/300 by following the itinerary and taking a water colectivo from Punta Hermosa to Anapia. Public transportation to the islands only runs on Thursday and Sunday.

Fodor'sChoice
★ **Islas Los Uros.** Known as the floating islands, Islas los Uros are man-made islands woven together with totora reeds that grow in the lake shallows. Replenished often with layers because the underbelly reeds

rot, these tiny islands resemble floating bails of hay and average 3 meters (10 feet) thick. They were originally created so communities could escape from attacks from stronger, more aggressive neighbors. Today they stay in one place. While some travelers marvel at these 40-plus islands, some call them floating souvenir stands. Yes, locals sell trinkets, but visiting the floating islands is a glimpse into one of the region's oldest cultures, the Uros. Now mixed with Aymara culture, it's a form of human habitation that evolved over centuries. The closest group of "floating museums" is 7 km (4.35 miles) from Puno.

The islanders make their living by fishing, hunting, cutting reeds, collecting eggs, trapping birds, and selling visitors well-made miniature reed boats and other handicrafts. Virtually every operator offers a stop to the more touristed of these islands as part of their standard lake tour but you can also find trips (or ask your tour operator specifically) to islands less visited where you can get a more intimate look at the culture.

Llachon Peninsula. One of the peninsulas that form the bay of Puno, Llachon juts out on the lake near Amantani and Taquile. ■TIP➔ **The land is dry and barren with rows of pre-Inca terraces, and original ancient paths and trails, which are great for exploring.** Locals are more than willing to guide visitors on a light trek to Cerro Auki Carus. Here a circular temple remains the sacred place for villagers to honor the Pachamama (Mother Earth). As the highest point on the peninsula, Cerro Auki Carus serves as an excellent viewpoint to admire the splendor of Lake Titicaca. You can venture out yourself from the port in Puno via water colectivo and then arrange a homestay once in Llachon, or for slightly more money, you can have a tour operator arrange the accommodations for you. By land back from Puno it's about two to three hours. Llachon is also a great place to kayak. Cusco-based Explorandes as well as Edgar Adventures offer kayak excursions around here.

Fodor's Choice **Taquile Island.** East of Puno in the high-altitude sunshine, Taquile's
★ brown dusty landscape contrasts with green terraces, bright flowers,
and the surrounding blue waters. Snowcapped Bolivian mountains
loom in the distance.

Taquile folk are known for weaving some of Peru's loveliest textiles,
here created by both men and women. Islanders still wear traditional
dress and have successfully maintained the cooperative lifestyle of their
ancestors. The annual Taquile festival the third week of July is a great
time to visit.

Taquile's steep hill has long, curvy trails leading to the main square,
where islanders often perform local dances for tourists. There are many
ways to reach the top of Taquile, where there are Inca and Tiahuanaco
ruins; the most popular way is to climb up the 533 stone steps, or you
can take a longer path. The island is 35 km (22 miles) from Puno. The
boat trip takes about four hours each way with no transportation on
land once you arrive. Visitors wishing to stay the night are primarily in
the homes of local families. There are a few shops and small restaurants,
as well as an excellent textile store. If you are not prepared for an arduous walk, then you should probably skip Taquile Island, there are tours
that will take you to the other side, avoiding the steps.

SILLUSTANI

30 km (19 miles) northwest of Puno.

Looking out over Lake Umayo, a small body of water just off the main
lake northwest of Puno on the way to Juliaca, these magnificent stone
burial towers are one of the main attractions on Lake Titicaca. The
oldest date back more than 1,100 years, well before the Incas. Restaurants, locals selling textiles and souvenirs, a museum, and bathrooms
are located near the site.

GETTING HERE AND AROUND

There is little to no public transportation to the archaeological site, so
unless you have your own vehicle, opt for a half-day trip here, offered
by every tour operator in Puno for about S/50–S/60.

EXPLORING

Sillustani. High on a hauntingly beautiful peninsula in Lake Umayo is
the necropolis of Sillustani, where 28 stone burial towers represent a
city of the dead that both predated and coincided with the Inca empire.
The proper name for a tower is *ayawasi* (home of the dead), but they're
generally referred to as *chullpas*, which are actually the shrouds used to
cover the mummies inside. This was the land of the Aymara-speaking
Colla people, and the precision of their masonry rivals that of the Inca.
Sillustani's mystique is heightened by the view it provides over Lake
Umayo and its mesa-shaped island, El Sombrero, as well as by the utter
silence that prevails, broken only by the wind over the water and the
cries of lake birds.

Most of the chullpas date from the 14th and 15th centuries, but some
were erected as early as AD 900. The tallest, known as the Lizard
because of a carving on one of its massive stones, has a circumference

of 8.5 meters (28 feet). An unusual architectural aspect of the chullpas is that the circumference is smaller at the bottom than the top. To fully appreciate Sillustani, it's necessary to make the long climb to the top; fortunately, the steps are wide and it's an easy climb. Some schoolchildren will put on dances. If you take photos of mothers and children and pet alpacas, a donation of a few soles will be appreciated.

CHUCUITO

20 km (12 miles) southeast of Puno.

Chucuito (in Aymara: *Choque-Huito*, Mountain of Gold) is the first of several small towns that dot the lake as you travel from Puno into Bolivia. If you aren't interested in architecture and colonial churches, or don't care to see another undeveloped Peruvian town, then chances are you won't enjoy these little towns. Having said that, Chucuito, surrounded by hillsides crisscrossed with agricultural terraces, has one novelty you won't find elsewhere—its Temple of Fertility, or Templo de Inca Uyu.

The temple is the most interesting thing to see in Chucuito. Almost a ghost town, the main plaza has a large stone Inca sundial as its centerpiece. There are two Renaissance-style 16th-century churches, **La Ascunción** alongside the plaza and the **Santo Domingo** on the east side of town. Neither one has been maintained, but both are open for services.

GETTING HERE AND AROUND

You'll need your own vehicle to get here, but once here, your feet are all you'll need. For a more enjoyable way of taking in the sights, there are afternoon horseback riding tours offered by the **Posada de Santa Barbera** 🌐 *hotelposadasantabarbara.com/en/* where you can also spend the night.

Templo de Inca Uyu. Better known as the Temple of Fertility or Temple of the Phallus, this structure doesn't quite meet the dictionary's description of a temple as a stately edifice. Rather, it's an outdoor area surrounded by a pre-Inca and Inca-made stone walls that block the view of a "garden" of anatomically correct phallic stone sculptures. Each meter- (3-foot) -tall penis statue points toward the sky at the Inca sun god, or toward the ground to the Pachamama, the mother earth. From ancient times—and still today—it has been visited by females who sit for hours on the little statues believing it will increase their fertility. Hours are sporadic, so you may need to ask around for the caretaker to get in. ✉ *Chucuito* 🎟 *S/5.*

WHERE TO STAY

$ HOTEL 🏨 **Taypikala Hotel & Spa.** A surprisingly modern hotel given the remote location, rooms are as comfortable and up-to-date as you can find in the city. **Pros:** views of the lake; modern rooms; indoor pool. **Cons:** remote location. [$] *Rooms from: S/231* ✉ *Calle Sandia* ☎ *051/792–252* 🌐 *www.taypikala.com* 🛏 *77 rooms* 🍴 *Breakfast.*

JULI

On Lake Titicaca, 84 km (52 miles) southeast of Puno.

At one time this village may have been an important Aymara religious center, and it has served as a Jesuit training center for missionaries from Paraguay and Bolivia. Juli has been called "Little Roma" because of its disproportionate number of churches. Four interesting churches in various stages of restoration are **San Pedro Mártir, Santa Cruz de Jerusalén, Asunción,** and **San Juan de Letrán.** The latter has 80 paintings from the Cusco School and huge windows worked in stone. Juli has a Saturday-morning bartering market in the main square. It's not a handicrafts market, but a produce and animal market where the barter system is in full effect, and the trade of animals is interesting to watch. It starts at 9 am and is over by noon.

GETTING HERE AND AROUND
You'll need your own vehicle to get here, and the drive from Puno to Juli takes about 1½ hours.

POMATA

108 km (67 miles) southeast of Puno.

This small village on the lake on the way to Copacabana and the Bolivian border is worth a quick stop to visit the spectacular church on the main plaza and enjoy the beautiful views.

GETTING HERE AND AROUND
You will need your own transportation to get here.

EXPLORING
Santiago Apóstol de Nuestra Señora del Rosario. The main attraction in the small lakeside town of Pomata is this church, built of pink granite in the 18th century and containing paintings from the Cusco School and the Flemish School. Its mestizo baroque carvings and translucent alabaster windows are spectacular and the altars are covered in gold leaf. Pomata is also famous for its fine pottery, especially for its Toritos de Pucará (bull figures). ⊠ *Pomata.*

BOLIVIAN SIDE OF LAKE TITICACA

You'll hear much talk about crossing Lake Titicaca from Peru to Bolivia via hydrofoil or catamaran. At this time you cannot go completely across without stopping at the border and walking from Peru into Bolivia or vice versa. ■ TIP➜ You can still use hydrofoils (only through Crillón Tours) and catamarans in your journey to Bolivia's side of the lake from Copacabana on the Bolivian side, then on to the Sun and Moon Islands for an overnight or two on Sun Island.

CROSSING THE BORDER
Bolivia now requires U.S. citizens to obtain a visa to travel in the country. For a price tag of US$160, the visa is good for up to 90 days in a calendar year and lasts 10 years. The application can be done by mail or in person at any Bolivian Consulate or border crossing, but not

A boat sails across Lake Titicaca, on the border between Bolivia and Peru.

online. Additionally, a yellow fever vaccination certificate (approximately US$150 in the United States, valid for 10 years) is necessary for Americans to show upon entry, though proof is not always requested. The vaccine must be taken at least 10 days before exposure.

If you're taking a bus from Puno, three hours into the ride the bus will stop just after Yunguyo for border-crossing procedures. Most higher-end bus services hand you immigration forms on the bus. As you leave Peru, you'll get off to get an exit stamp from Peruvian immigration, and then walk through to the small Bolivian immigration building, where you get an entrance stamp and will have to show your visa. From there you catch up with your bus, which will be waiting for you. Keep all immigration documents, your passport, and visa safe; you may need these when leaving Bolivia. The border closes at 6 pm daily.

Those entering from Peru generally overnight in Copacabana, which provides easy access to the lake and the surrounding countryside. Buses from Puno to Copacabana are available through any operator or by going directly to the Puno Bus Terminal where there are several companies offering this route. Buses cost around S/30 and depart from the Puno Bus Terminal at 7 and 7:30 am, and 2 pm daily. Many buses continue on to La Paz.

GETTING AROUND

The border-crossing tours have packages from US$150 to US$400. Reputable agencies include Crillón Tours and Transturin Ltd.; based in Bolivia, tours go from Puno to La Paz and vice versa. Both include pickup from your hotel in Puno and transfer by first-class bus to the border in Yunguyo (a three-hour drive). After crossing the border, you take a bus to Copacabana, a funky beach town (30 minutes). The most expensive and comfortable way to get to Isla del Sol and Isla de la Luna is by Crillón Tours hydrofoil from the **Inca Utama Hotel,** but cheaper boats leave from Copacabana at 8:30 and 1:30 daily. The journey takes about two hours and costs (Bs)25. Once you are on the island, it's walking all the way, unless a mule has been organized through your hotel ahead of time. The tourist office, on the northern side of Isla del Sol, offers private guides for (Bs)100, or (Bs)10 per person when booking groups of 10 or more.

TOUR OPERATORS

Crillón Tours. The largest and most respected tour operator on the Bolivian side of Lake Titicaca, Crillón Tours offers every sort of trip imaginable between La Paz and Copacabana and can work with most budgets. They operate hydrofoil and boat transfers between the islands and own the best hotel on the Isla del Sol, which you can only stay at through their packages. So if you want to stay on the island, it's a good idea to get a quote from Crillón. ✉ *Av. Camacho 1223, La Paz* ☎ *122/337–533 in Bolivia* 🌐 *www.crillontours.com.*

Transturin. Titicaca catamaran trips, with stops at the Isla del Sol and other attractions, are the main offering of Transturin. ✉ *Achumani Calle 6, No. 100, La Paz* ☎ *122/422–222 in Bolivia, 786/735–5833 from U.S.* 🌐 *www.transturin.com* 🎫 *From (Bs)650.*

WHERE TO STAY

$$$$ HOTEL 🏨 **Inca Utama Hotel & Spa.** Although the location may be too remote for those not traveling on Crillón Tours' hydrofoils, which make their harbor here, the hotel offers a more tranquil place to lodge than many of the properties found right in Copacabana. **Pros:** lakeside location; observatory with powerful telescope; hydrofoil transportation. **Cons:** remote location; rooms can be cold, even with heaters; spa is basic. [$] *Rooms from: (B)871* ✉ *86 Carretera Asfaltada, Huatajata* ✥ *Km 80, off hwy. from La Paz to Copacabana* ☎ *122/337–533* 🌐 *crillontours.com/index.php/en/our-infrastructure-2/inca-utama-hotel-spa* 🛏 *67 rooms* 🍴 *Breakfast.*

COPACABANA, BOLIVIA

79 km (49 miles) from Huatajata.

A pleasant, if touristy, town, Copacabana provides easy access to the lake, the islands, and the surrounding countryside. It is also a major pilgrimage destination for devout Bolivians at Easter, and lost South American hippies all year. A highlight is watching the sunset over the water from the Stations of the Cross, the highest point of Copacabana.

GETTING HERE AND AROUND

Several companies have buses departing from the main terminal in Puno around 7 am and 2 pm for around S/30; the ride takes about 3½ to 4 hours. Buses returning to Puno leave Copacabana around 7:30 am and 1:30 pm, as well as later in the afternoon. It's theoretically possible to drive a rental car from Puno to Copacabana, but passing through Bolivian customs, even if you have all of your paperwork in order, can be a time-consuming hassle. It's easier just to go with public transportation, as a car isn't really needed once you reach Copacabana. In Copacabana's main plaza, the tourist booth is the place to find information about the area.

ESSENTIALS

Virtually everything you need to find in Copacabana, be it a bank, an Internet café, or a restaurant, you will likely find either on the Plaza 2 de Febrero or on the main street that heads down to the pier, Avenida 6 de Agosto. The town is so small and the street numbers so problematic, you'll save time walking around those two areas, rather than trying to wander and find something.

Police Police. ⊠ *Plaza 2 de Febrero, north end* ☎ *02/222–5016, 800/108–687.*

Post Office Copacabana Post Office. ⊠ *Plaza 2 de Febrero.*

Visitor Information Centro de Informacion Turistica. ⊠ *Av. 16 de Julio, esq Av. 6 de Agosto.*

EXPLORING

Cerro Calvario. Marking the highest point of Copacabana are the Stations of the Cross, built in the 1950s for the thousands of pilgrims who summit the hill for prayer and penance on Good Friday. For many tourists, these stone monuments serve as the ideal spot to admire the city and watch the sunset. ⊠ *Trail begins near red chapel at end of Calle Destacamento 211.*

Copacabana Cathedral. The town's breathtaking Moorish-style cathedral, built between 1610 and 1619 and formerly known as the Basilica of Our Lady of Copacabana, is where you'll find the striking sculpture of the Virgin of Copacabana. There was no choice but to build the church, because the statue, carved by Francisco Yupanqui in 1592, was already drawing pilgrims in search of miracles. If you see decorated cars lined up in front of the cathedral, the owners are waiting to have them blessed for safe travel. Walk around to a side door on the left and light a candle for those you wish to remember, then admire the gaudy glitter and wealth of the church interior itself. Throngs of young Paceños do the three-day walk to Copacabana from La Paz to pay homage to the statue with a candlelight procession on Good Friday. You can combine your visit with the semiscramble up past Cerro Calvario (Calvary Hill) on the point above the town. If the climb doesn't knock you out, the view will. ⊠ *Copacabana.*

Horca del Inca. Dating back to the 14th century BC, this structure in the southeast part of the city was originally built by the pre-Inca Chiripa culture as an astronomical observatory. Four of the seven horizontal rock slabs were later destroyed by the Spanish who believed gold was hidden inside. The remains of the ruins show signs of vandalism, yet still warrant a visit for those wanting to blend culture and exercise. The slope is steep and rather challenging, but the view of Lake Titicaca will help alleviate the pain. ⊠ *Off Ruta Nacional 2* 🖼 *(Bs)10.*

WHERE TO EAT

Copacabana has a wide array of hotels, hostels, international cafés, and bars and pizza joints, which reflects its popularity as a weekend destination from La Paz and as the crossing point for travelers from Peru. There's a lot of competition, but most offer the same dishes, none of which are prepared in a particularly memorable—or recommendable—way. The best thing to do for lunch or dinner is wander along Avenida 6 de Agosto and window-shop first. You can find the famous trout dishes everywhere.

$
CAFÉ

✕ **El Condor and The Eagle Café.** If you are dying for a decent cup of organic coffee, this is the place to get your caffeine fix. This cozy spot offers some delicious breakfast options, all of which are vegetarian. **Known for:** great coffee; vegetarian breakfast. $ *Average main: (B)30* ⌂ *Av. 6 de Agosto, inside Residencial Paris* ☎ *No phone* ▭ *No credit cards* ⊘ *Closed after 1:30 pm. Closed weekends.*

$
INTERNATIONAL
Fodor's Choice
★

✕ **La Posta.** On a street where everyone seems to claim the best pizza, La Posta probably does. A variety of other delicious dishes are available from pastas and tacos to local specialties such as the ubiquitous lake trout, at what is the possibly the only restaurant worth making an effort to go to besides that at La Cupula. **Known for:** great pizza; delicious tacos and other fare; craft beers. $ *Average main: (B)60* ⌂ *Av. 6 de Agosto* ⊹ *Block closest to beach* ☎ *591/6818–0949.*

WHERE TO STAY

$$
HOTEL
FAMILY

🏨 **Hostal Las Olas.** This lovely and eclectic boutique property on a hill with a stunning view of Lake Titicaca's azure-blue waters is one of the best options in town. **Pros:** great views; big rooms; eco-friendly. **Cons:** up a hill; the beds could be more comfortable. $ *Rooms from: (B)421* ⌂ *Calle Michel Pérez* ☎ *02/862–2112* ⊕ *hostallasolas.com* ⇨ 8 *rooms* ⦿| *No meals.*

$
B&B/INN
Fodor's Choice
★

🏨 **Hotel La Cupula.** It's worth staying on in Copacabana just to enjoy this alternative-style hotel with gorgeous views looking out over the bay, not least because of the delicious on-site restaurant. **Pros:** excellent value; friendly staff; great vibe. **Cons:** breakfast not included; some rooms lack private bathrooms. $ *Rooms from: (B)194* ⌂ *Calle Michel Pérez 1–3* ☎ *02/862–2029* ⊕ *www.hotelcupula.com* ⇨ 17 *rooms* ⦿| *No meals.*

$$$
HOTEL
Fodor's Choice
★

🏨 **Hotel Rosario Del Lago Titicaca.** One of the nicest accommodations in Copacabana, this colonial-style hotel is a few blocks from the main plaza. **Pros:** great views of the lake; modern rooms; full amenities. **Cons:** suites can fill up fast. $ *Rooms from: (B)684* ⌂ *Calle Rigoberto Paredes and Av. Costanera* ☎ *02/862–2141, 02/245–1341 in La Paz* ⊕ *www.hotelrosario.com/lago* ⇨ 25 *rooms* ⦿| *Breakfast.*

ISLA DEL SOL AND ISLA DE LA LUNA, BOLIVIA

12 km (7½ miles) north of Copacabana.

One of the most popular day trips on Lake Titicaca is to these two mountainous islands a short boat ride from Copacabana. Considered sacred islands, in local mythology this is where the creator god Viracocha emerged from the lake and created the sun and the moon. There are no cars on either island, only steep trails between the ports and villages. Although most visitors come on a day trip, others stick around, taking advantage of the small family-run hostels on Isla del Sol.

GETTING HERE AND AROUND

The most comfortable—and expensive—way to get here is by hydrofoil from the **Inca Utama Hotel** in Huatajata, but cheaper boats leave from Copacabana at 8:30 am and 1:30 pm and return from Isla del Sol's south port at Yumani at 8:30 am, 10:30 am, 1:30 pm, and 4 pm. Some boats may continue on or stop only at the north port, called Challa Pampa, which sees fewer visitors. The journey from Copacabana takes about two hours and costs (Bs)30. Once you are on the island, it's walking all the way, unless a mule has been organized through your hotel ahead of time. The tourist office, on the northern side of Isla del Sol, offers private guides for (Bs)100, or (Bs)10 per person when booking groups of 10 or more.

ESSENTIALS

Tour Operators Andes Amazonia. ⊠ Av. 6 de Agosto, Copacabana ☎ 02/862–2616 ⊕ www.andesamazoniabolivia.com.

Visitor Information Asociacion Turismo Comunitario. ⊠ Av. 6 de Agosto con Av. 16 de Julio, Copacabana ✛ Plaza Sucre ☎ 077/299–088, 7729–9088 ⊕ www.titicacaturismo.com.

Fodor's Choice ★ **Isla del Sol.** The largest of Lake Titicaca's islands, Isla del Sol is the best place to visit and stay on the lake. The views of the Cordillera Real mountains are amazing, especially at dawn and dusk, and the island has beautiful white sandy beaches and an extraordinary terraced landscape. Ruins include the Inca palace of Pilkokaina and a strange rock formation said to be the birthplace of the Sun and Moon, with an excellent Inca trail across the island. Some travelers take a boat to the northern community of Challa Pampa and then hike three- to four hours to the southern community of Yumani where most accommodations (and the main "village") can be found. Although rewarding, the island trail lacks shade and few spots sell water along the way. If your goal is to just laze around and soak up the cosmic energy, then be sure to disembark at the southern boat port of Yumani, unless you are staying at one of the few hotels on the north side. One of the best beaches on Isla del Sol is located on the north end, directly behind the museum. Regardless of your destination, plan on hiking at least 30 minutes uphill from the boat port. Nearly every property is staggered high on the slope, which means that both altitude and fitness should be taken into consideration. If you stay at Crillón Tours' Posada, they will take you to the pier where the walk is a bit longer but avoids the challenging, steep steps up from the Yumani harbor.

Isla de la Luna. En route to Isla del Sol, boats sometimes stop at Isla de la Luna, where the ruins of Iñacuy date back to the Inca conquest. You'll find an ancient convent called Ajlla Wasi (House of the Chosen Women). Stone steps lead up to the unrestored ruins of the convent.

WHERE TO STAY

You will be amply rewarded for your climb up the steps from the port—the higher you go, the cheaper the hostels or *posadas*. They are almost all quite basic so, in most cases, you will be trading a comfy bed for a peaceful retreat with gorgeous views. If you go without a reservation, you'll likely find women or children waiting at Yumani's port to invite you to stay. The north side of the island is more barren but also has attractive options, including a place on the beach itself.

$$$$ B&B/INN **La Estancia Ecolodge.** Staggered on a hillside, each bungalow (named for flora) has an unobstructed view of Lake Titicaca, making it the perfect place to watch the sunrise. **Pros:** excellent views; great showers; dinners integrate local flavors. **Cons:** expensive for location. [$] *Rooms from: (B)1271* ✉ *South end, Isla del Sol* ☎ *22/442–727* 🌐 *www.ecolodge-laketiticaca.com* 🛏 *15 rooms* 🍴 *Some meals.*

$$$$ B&B/INN Fodor's Choice ★ **Posada del Inca Eco Lodge.** Surely the best lodging on the island, your stay at this lovely posada begins with a 30-minute mule ride from the boat dock to the garden-lobby, where fruit trees shade handmade reed couches, and the hillside location offers sweeping views of the lake. **Pros:** high standard of service; good food; most comfortable rooms on the island. **Cons:** must be booked with more expensive hydrofoil tour. [$] *Rooms from: (B)1000* ✉ *South end, Isla del Sol* ☎ *02/233–7533* 🌐 *crillontours.com/index.php/en/our-infrastructure-2/the-posada-del-inca-eco-lodge* 🛏 *20 rooms* 🍴 *Some meals.*

CUSCO AND THE SACRED VALLEY

WELCOME TO CUSCO AND THE SACRED VALLEY

TOP REASONS TO GO

★ **Alpaca Clothing:** Nothing says "Cusco" quite like a sweater, shawl, poncho, or scarf woven from the hair of the alpaca.

★ **Andean Cuisine:** Where else in the world will you find roasted *cuy* (guinea pig) and alpaca steaks rubbing shoulders on fine-dining menus?

★ **Inca Architecture:** Wonder at the ability of the Inca to construct stone walls so precisely, using 15th-century technology, and to position a temple so it would be illuminated best at the exact moment of the solstice.

★ **Layered Religion:** Take a closer look at the walls— every Catholic church was built on the site, and often the foundation, of an Inca *huaca*, or sacred place.

★ **Hotels with History:** Many Cusco hotels are former convents, monasteries, dwellings of sacred women, or palaces of Spanish conquerors.

★ **Sacred Playground:** The Sacred Valley is an adventurer's playground for hiking, biking, rafting, and even stand-up paddleboarding.

1 Cusco. Whether you go before or after your visit to the Sacred Valley and Machu Picchu, you'll be missing out if don't spend some time in Cusco. This city is a mix of new and old: ancient Inca walls holding up baroque colonial buildings, inside of which lie some of the city's most contemporary restaurants and shops. Colonial churches and cultural museums dot the plaza, and funky modern cafés sit side by side with traditional galleries of Cusqueñan art in San Blas. Inca gems are everywhere, even along the traffic-heavy business district of Avenida El Sol, home of Cusco's star attraction, the Qorikancha Sun Temple.

2 Side Trips—The Southeastern Urubamba Valley. What really made the Inca civilization so successful? Their appreciation of a good view! Gorgeous Andean landscapes characterize almost every important Inca site in the area surrounding Cusco. For a bird's-eye perspective on the city, head uphill to the second-most-famous Inca site of them all: Sacsayhuamán.

3 Sacred Valley of the Inca. The Río Urubamba (Urubamba River) meanders through a tranquil valley between the towns of Pisac and Ollantaytambo north of Cusco. The valley towns offer a good selection of hotels and restaurants, stunning views, and a slower pace of life than Cusco. An uncontested hot spot for nature lovers and outdoor enthusiasts, the valley's lower elevation and warmer temperatures are added bonuses, especially for acclimatization.

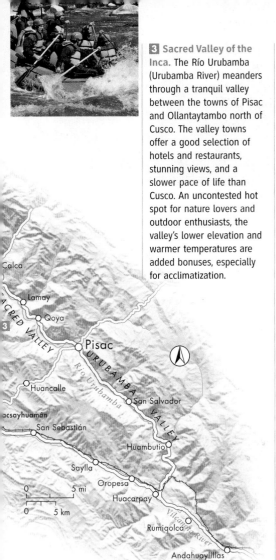

GETTING ORIENTED

At the center of Cusco is the slightly sloped, colonial Plaza de Armas, with streets, most prominently the Avenida El Sol, heading downhill and leading to the more modern sections of the city. Heading uphill takes you to the city's older neighborhoods, notably the artisan quarter of San Blas and its web of pedestrian-only walkways. If you look up and to the left, you'll see that towering over the lot is the archaeological site of Sacsayhuamán, which sits just to the left of the Christo Blanco. This white Christ statue is most clearly seen at night when it's lighted by floodlights.

The Urubamba mountain range on the north side and Cusco and neighborhoods on the south side watch over the river basin known as the Sacred Valley. Transportation to the Sacred Valley is straightforward, with roads fanning out from Urubamba, the valley's small hub city.

5

Updated by
Maureen
Santucci

"Bienvenidos a la ciudad imperial del Cusco," announces the flight attendant when your plane touches down at a lofty 3,300 meters above sea level. "Welcome to the imperial city of Cusco." This greeting hints at what you're in for in Cusco, one of the world's great travel destinations.

The juxtaposition of cultures—Inca and Spanish colonial, but also modern—makes this city fascinating. This is a rare place where, if you take the time to sit and observe, you will see a culture that is going through a transformation in front of your very eyes. Where else can you see a child in traditional dress leading a llama on colonial streets while talking on a smartphone?

The area's rich history springs forth from the Inca tale that describes how Manco Cápac and his sister-consort Mama Ocllo were sent by the Sun and Moon to enlighten the people of Peru. Setting off from Lake Titicaca sometime in the 12th century with the directive to settle only where their golden staff could be plunged fully into the soil, they traveled far across the *altiplano* (high plains) until reaching the fertile soils surrounding present-day Cusco. They envisioned Qosqo (Cusco) in the shape of a puma, the animal representation of the Earth in the indigenous cosmos, which you can still see today on city maps. But not all was Inca in southern Peru. Not far from Cusco sits Pikillacta, a pre-Inca city constructed by the Wari culture that thrived between AD 600 and 1000. It's an indication that this territory, like most of Peru, was the site of sophisticated civilizations long before the Inca appeared.

By the time Francisco Pizarro and the Spanish conquistadors arrived in 1532, the Inca Empire had spread from modern-day Ecuador in the north down through Peru and Bolivia to Chile. Sadly, the city's grandeur could do little to save an empire weakened by internal strife and civil war. Stocked with guns and horses, which the Inca had never seen, and carrying new diseases, against which they had no immunity, the Spanish arrived with the upper hand, despite smaller numbers. In 1532, the Spanish seized Atahualpa, the recently instated Inca ruler, while he was in Cajamarca to subdue rebellious forces. The Inca's crumbling house of cards came tumbling down, though pockets of resistance remained for years in places such as Ollantaytambo.

After sacking the Inca Empire, Spanish colonists instituted new political and religious systems, superimposing their beliefs onto the old society and its structures. They looted gold, silver, and stone and built their own churches, monasteries, convents, and palaces directly onto the foundations of the Inca sites. This is one of the most striking aspects of the city today. The Santo Domingo church was built on top of the Qorikancha, the Temple of the Sun. And it's downright ironic to think of the cloistered convent of Santa Catalina occupying the same site as the equally cloistered Acllawasi, the home of the Inca chosen women, who were selected to serve the Sun in the Qorikancha temple. The cultural combination appears in countless other ways: witness the pumas carved into the cathedral doors. The city also gave its name to the Cusqueña school of art, in which new-world artists combined Andean motifs with European-style painting, usually on religious themes. You'll chance on paintings that could be by Anthony Van Dyck but for the Inca robes on New Testament figures, and Last Supper diners digging into an Andean feast of chinchilla and fermented corn.

The Río Urubamba flows, at its closest, about 30 km (18 miles) north of Cusco and passes through a valley about 300 meters (980 feet) lower in elevation than Cusco. The northwestern part of this river basin, romantically labeled the Sacred Valley of the Inca, contains some of the region's most appealing towns and fascinating pre-Columbian ruins. A growing number of visitors are heading here directly upon arrival in Cusco to acclimatize. The valley's altitude is slightly lower and its temperatures are slightly higher, making for a physically easier introduction to this part of Peru.

PLANNING

WHEN TO GO
Cusco's high season is June through early September (winter in the southern hemisphere) and the days around the Christmas and Easter holidays. Winter means drier weather and easier traveling, but higher lodging prices and larger crowds. Prices and visitor numbers drop dramatically during the November-through-March summer rainy season, except around the holidays.

PLANNING YOUR TIME
The typical tour of the Cusco region combines the city with the Sacred Valley and Machu Picchu in three whirlwind days. We recommend devoting at least five days to get the most out of your visit—including one day to get acclimated to the high altitude.

GETTING HERE AND AROUND
AIR TRAVEL
LATAM (⊕ www.latam.com) connects Cusco with Lima, Arequipa, Juliaca, and Puerto Maldonado. Peruvian Airlines (⊕ www.peruvianairlines.pe) offers direct service between Lima and Cusco, as do LC Peru (⊕ www.lcperu.pe), Avianca (⊕ www.avianca.com), and Star Peru

(⊕ *www.starperu.com*), which can also take you to and from Puerto Maldonado. While LATAM is by far the most expensive for foreign travelers, it is also has the most reliable service by far and the most options in travel times. You can find offices for airlines along the Avenida del Sol but be sure you are dealing with the real thing, as many small agencies post large signs with the airline logos.

BUS TRAVEL

Cusco's main bus terminal is at the Terminal Terrestre in Santiago, not far from the airport. The best company running from Cusco is Cruz del Sur (⊕ *www.cruzdelsur.com.pe*), which has its own terminal on Avenida Industrial in Bancopata. Bus and van travel between Cusco and the Sacred Valley is cheap, frequent . . . and sometimes accident-prone; taxis (shared or private) are by far the better option.

CAR TRAVEL

For exploring the Sacred Valley, a car is nice to be able to get around, but driving anywhere in Peru seems to have its own unwritten rules, so hiring a car and driver or going by taxi is usually the safest option. **Armando Agüero** (☎ 974/213–172 or 953/724–887 ✉ *armandoah@ gmail.com*) is one such driver. He speaks Spanish, English, French, and Portuguese, and can connect with other drivers as needed.

The vehicular tourist route ends at Ollantaytambo. Cusco is the only place to rent a vehicle. Nevertheless, you won't need or want to drive inside the city; heavy traffic, lack of parking, and narrow streets, many of them pedestrian-only, make a car a burden.

TAXI TRAVEL

Cusco's licensed taxis have a small official taxi sticker on the windshield, but these are difficult to see. Choose ones that have the name and number of a company on the top. Fares are S/3–S/5 for any trip within the central city and S/4–S/6 after 10 pm. Have your hotel or restaurant call a taxi for you at night.

Mototaxis—three-wheeled motorized vehicles with room for two passengers—ply the streets of Sacred Valley towns.

Touring the Sacred Valley from Cusco with one of the city's taxis costs about US$60–US$70, but the exact price depends largely on your negotiating skills.

TRAIN TRAVEL

PeruRail is the most established operator in Peru. In 2017, it changed its service between Cusco and Puno, and now offers the route only in sleeper car departing on Tuesdays. Another package has you departing on Thursday morning, visiting Lake Titicaca, and continuing on to Arequipa. Three classes of daily service to Machu Picchu depart from Cusco's Poroy station, about 20 minutes from the Plaza de Armas. Trains depart early in the morning—with the luxury *Hiram Bingham* service departing from Poroy at 9:05 am. Trains depart throughout the day from the Ollantaytambo station. Purchase tickets in advance from the PeruRail sales office in the Plaza de Armas, online (⊕ *www.perurail. com*), or from a travel agency. Inca Rail (⊕ *www.incarail.com*) also has trains from Ollantaytambo to Machu Picchu. *For more information, see Train Travel in Chapter 6, Machu Picchu and the Inca Trail.*

DISCOUNTS AND DEALS

Offering access to 14 of Cusco's best-known tourist attractions, the **Boleto Turístico** (tourist ticket) is the all-in-one answer to your tourism needs. There are four different passes you can purchase. For S/130 you can get a 10-day pass that lets you visit all 14 sites in the city and around the Sacred Valley. Alternatively, you can opt for one of three amended circuits outlined in the Boleto Parcial (partial ticket), each S/70. Although always subject to change, the participating sites have remained the same for some time. Certain big-name attractions (such as the Catedral) have withdrawn from the Boleto Turístico to levy their own fees. Regardless, if you want to see sites such as Sacsayhuamán and Pisac, you have to buy the ticket, which can be purchased at the **Comite de Servicios Integrados Turisticos Culturales del Cusco** (COSITUC) (⊠ *Av. El Sol 103* ☎ *084/261–465* ⊕ *www.cosituc.gob.pe*), open daily 8–6.

HEALTH AND SAFETY

ALTITUDE SICKNESS

You'll likely encounter altitude sickness, known as *soroche,* at Cusco's 3,500-meter (11,500-foot) elevation. Drink lots of fluids, but eliminate or reduce alcohol and caffeine consumption, and eat lightly as much as possible for the first day or two. Many hotels have an oxygen supply for their guests' use that can minimize the effects. The prescription drug acetazolamide can help. Check with your physician about it (allergies to the drug are not uncommon) and about traveling here if you have a heart condition or high blood pressure or are pregnant.

■TIP➔ **Warning: Sorojchi pills are a Bolivian-made altitude-sickness remedy whose advertising pictures a tourist vomiting at Machu Picchu. Its safety has not been documented, and it contains only pain relievers and caffeine, so we don't recommend it.**

SAFETY

Security has improved dramatically in Cusco. A huge police presence is on the streets, especially around tourist centers such as the Plaza de Armas. Nonetheless, petty crime, such as pickpocketing, is not uncommon: use extra vigilance in crowded markets or when getting on and off buses and trains. Robbers have also targeted late-night and early-morning revelers stumbling back to their hotels. Women should not leave drinks unattended at dance clubs; there have been cases in which beverages have been tampered with.

WATER

Tap water is not safe to drink here. Stick with the bottled variety, *con gas* (carbonated) or *sin gas* (plain).

RESTAURANTS

Although many of the restaurants in Cusco and the Sacred Valley have stuck to the same old menus—variations on traditional Peruvian cuisine or often poorly executed standards such as pizza and burritos—this has been gradually changing. The valley is still lagging behind in this area, but Cusco has been adding more and more first-rate fusion as well as international restaurants to its mix. *Prices in the reviews are the average cost of a main course at dinner or, if dinner is not served, at lunch.*

HOTELS

Hotels run the gamut in Cusco and the Sacred Valley. On the low end are backpacker and no-frills spots to hang your hat. On the high end are five-star hotels that can cost more per night than some people's monthly mortgages. Note that what are referred to as *hostals* here are often lovely low-cost bed-and-breakfasts. You can even find these in renovated colonial mansions, allowing you to get the authentic feel without spending a fortune. But for those who like to travel in style, you've got plenty of choices, and virtually all of them in Cusco are in historical buildings, many with Incan foundations. For the lushest options in the valley, check out the offerings in Urubamba. *Hotel reviews have been shortened. For full information, visit Fodors.com.*

WHAT IT COSTS IN NUEVO SOLES				
	$	$$	$$$	$$$$
Restaurants	under S/35	S/35–S/50	S/51–S/65	over S/65
Hotels	under S/250	S/250–S/500	S/501–S/800	over S/800

Restaurant prices are the average cost of a main course at dinner or, if dinner is not served, at lunch. Hotel prices are the lowest cost of a standard double room in high season.

TOURS

One of the most important decisions you'll make when planning your trip is whether or not you want to engage the services of a travel agency. If you speak Spanish and are only doing a quick Lima–Cusco–Machu Picchu trip, it may not be necessary. If not, there are reasons you might consider doing so.

The biggest two concerns most people have when considering using an agency are price and being restricted to a specific itinerary. If you choose a moderately priced Peruvian agency (these are typically ones that will charge about US$750 for a Classic Inca Trail), the percentage that they will mark up a personalized itinerary usually isn't that much beyond what you would pay doing it yourself. As for restrictions, be sure to make it clear to them what your priorities are, and if you want some downtime in places, let them know.

Another question when booking tours is whether to go for a group tour or book a private one. Prices can vary from place to place, but if you are working with an agency, be sure to ask what the difference in price is. For example, a tour to the Sacred Valley with a group is about US$25, not including lunch or admissions. Group size can be up to 30 people and, when it is not high season, you may end up in a bilingual group where more explanation is often given in whichever language the bulk of the group speaks. You can get the same private tour for up to six people for around US$260. Whether it is worth it to you or not will depend on your interests. You'll be able to hear your guide better, explanations can be geared toward your particular obsessions (history, culture, architecture, or plants, for example), you can decide what sites you want to see, and you can stay as long as you like rather than being herded back onto the bus before you're ready. Making your own decisions is key. If you get tired of seeing "rocks," however impressively they have been assembled, you can get your guide to take you to a site that's off the beaten path, on a walk through the country, or to the best *chicheria* (corn beer vendor).

■ TIP➔ **If you need to pay in dollars, as agencies sometimes request, they cannot be even the slightest bit torn. When it comes to soles, many shops do not have change, so it's best to use the larger bills at higher-end shops and restaurants so that you will have small coins and bills for the smaller ones.**

If you want to spend time in Lima, plan to do so at the end of your trip. That way if you run into transportation problems, you will be less likely to miss your flight home.

SELECTING A TOUR OPERATOR

"Holaaaa—trip to Machu Picchu?" With so many touts in Cusco's streets hawking tours to Peru's most famous sight, it's tempting to just buy one to make them stop asking. Anyone who offers an Inca Trail trek departing tomorrow should be taken with more than a grain of salt—Inca Trail hikes need to be booked months in advance. Don't make arrangements or give money to someone claiming to be a travel agent if they approach you on the street or at the airport in Cusco or Lima. It's best to have a recommendation or select one that is listed here or on ⊕ *www.peru.info.Below are several reputable travel agencies.*

TOUR OPERATORS

Amazonas Explorer. For more than 30 years, this company has specialized in top-quality adventure and cultural tours. From gentle half days to two-week adventures, they offer an alternative to rote bus tours and crowds of other tourists. Known for using high-quality equipment and the best guides around, tours include hiking, biking, rafting, and even stand-up paddleboarding. They are the first Peruvian member of 1% for the Planet, which helps fund sustainable tourism and native tree planting. ✉ *Av. Collasuyo 910, Cusco* ☏ *084/252–846, 844/380–7378* ⊕ *amazonas-explorer.com* ✉ *From $110.*

Andina Travel. Specializing in trekking and alternatives to the Inca Trail, Andina Travel also offers standard Sacred Valley and Machu Picchu tours as well as biking and rafting. ✉ *Plazoleta Santa Catalina 219, Cusco* ☏ *084/251–892* ⊕ *www.andinatravel.com* ✉ *From $70.*

Apumayo Expediciones. This operator offers a full gamut of adventure tours and nonconventional treks, rafting and biking and also specializes in trips geared toward people with disabilities. ✉ *Jr. Ricardo Palma N-11, Urb. Santa Monica* ☏ *084/246–018* ⊕ *www.apumayo.com* ✉ *From $70.*

Aspiring Adventures. Started by two longtime professionals in adventure travel, this agency specializes in tours that go off the beaten path. In addition to visiting the must-see sights, you will have the opportunity to engage with Peruvian culture in a more intimate way than with more typical tours. This boutique company excels in personal service, ensuring that the trip you get exceeds even the highest of expectations. ☏ *877/438–1354 U.S. and Canada, 643/489–7474 worldwide* ⊕ *www. aspiringadventures.com* ✉ *From $35.*

Cusco Top Travel & Treks. Run by the wildly talented and witty David Choque, this company specializes in a range of packaged and comfort-class, custom-built tours. ⊠ *Urbanización Cerveceros 3-A, Wanchaq* ☎ *084/234–130, 994/703–027* ⊕ *www.cuscotoptravelperu.com* 🖃 *From $125.*

El Chalan. This operator organizes single-day and multiday horseback-riding tours for all levels (beginner to professional) throughout the Sacred Valley. The ranch uses only the elegant Peruvian Paso horse, a breed known for its smooth, dancing gait that does not bounce the rider up and down like a typical trot. Riders and horses alike are carefully tended to and looked after. ⊠ *Km 75, Autopista Urubamba–Ollantaytambo, Urubamba* ☎ *984/737–897, 084/201–541* ⊕ *www.haciendadelchalan.com* 🖃 *From $95.*

Enigma. Small, customized adventure trips let you enjoy trekking, rafting, mountain climbing, mountain biking, or horseback riding led by professional guides. ⊠ *Calle Fortunato L. Herrera 214, Magisterio* ☎ *084/222–155* ⊕ *www.enigmaperu.com* 🖃 *From $136.*

Explorandes. Established in 1975, this is one of the longest-running tour agencies in Peru. They specialize in adventure tours, including rafting and trekking trips in the area around Cusco, and organizing customized, guided expeditions throughout the Andes in Peru and Ecuador. They also offer special opportunities to visit indigenous communities. ⊠ *Paseo Zarzuela Q-2, Huancaro* ☎ *084/238–380* ⊕ *www.explorandes.com* 🖃 *From $34.*

Gravity Peru. Want to do your touring from the back of a mountain bike? The Gravity Peru people live to ride and are ready and waiting to introduce you to the best trail for your interest and skill level. Full day and multiday rides are available, including a full-suspension MTB bike (value of US$3,000), all equipment, guide, and more. ⊠ *Av. Centenario 707, Cusco* ☎ *984/501–311* ⊕ *www.gravityperu.com* 🖃 *From $150 for a full-day mountain-bike tour.*

Llama Pack Project. This nonprofit organization is dedicated to helping impoverished highland communities regain economic viability in a way that also sustains their culture, by helping to reintroduce pure-bred llamas, which are a more valuable resource than the mixed-breed ones commonly found today. What's this mean for you? The opportunity to go on a half-day, full-day, or multiday trek with these picturesque beasts of burden. You'll have a chance to learn more about the llamas and visit communities or archaeological sites depending on which trek you choose, all while enjoying gorgeous Andean landscapes and contributing to the survival of these villages and their way of life. ⊠ *Km 70.5, Carretera Urubamba-Ollantaytambo s/n, Sector Huincho, Urubamba* ☎ *998/003–114* ⊕ *www.llamapackproject.com.*

Pachamama Explorers. This company has more than 17 years' experience with a specialty in trekking the Inca Trail and alternative routes, as well as in creating customized itineraries. They promoted porter welfare before regulations were set in place. ⊠ *Calle Garcilaso 265, Cusco* ☎ *084/437–547* ⊕ *www.pmexplorers.com* 🖃 *From $140.*

River Explorers. As the name indicates, River Explorers are specialists in one- to six-day rafting and kayaking excursions on the Urubamba and Apurimac Rivers as well as standard trekking tours. ⌧ *Urb. Kennedy A, Brillantes B-36, Cusco* ☎ *084/260–926, 958/320–673* ⊕ *riverexplorers. com* ✉ *From $99.*

SAS Travel. With more than 25 years in business, Cusco-based SAS Travel is one of the longer-running companies in the area and well known especially for its treks. Although the company does offer private treks, they are the ones to call when you prefer hiking with a larger group. ⌧ *Calle Garcilaso 270, Cusco* ☎ *084/249–194* ⊕ *www.sastravelperu. com* ✉ *From $70.*

SUP Cusco. As an alternative to trekking and sightseeing, SUP (Stand-Up Paddleboard) offers leisurely paddleboarding trips on beautiful Piuray Lake in the middle of the Andes, 35 minutes from Cusco en route to the Sacred Valley. Stand-up paddleboarding is suitable for almost everyone; yoga and kayaking are also available from the center. Transportation from Cusco and snacks are included. ⌧ *Piuray Outdoor Center, Pongobamba, Chinchero* ☎ *992/755–067* ⊕ *www. supcusco.com* ✉ *From $70.*

TopTurPeru. This internationally recognized, local company is run by Raul Castelo and family. An archaeoastronomy expert, Raul has been sought out by *National Geographic* and other documentary-filmmaking entities worldwide. That experience stands him and his team in good stead as they design customized travel itineraries and private tours for their clients. ⌧ *Calle Saphi 877 B-6, Cusco* ☎ *084/243–234, 974/215–160* ⊕ *www.topturperu.com* ✉ *From $240.*

Unique Peru Tours. This agency delivers exactly what the name promises: tours that offer something different, such as their signature Salkantay Trek with yoga and massage. Whether you prefer an itinerary oriented toward adventure excursions, cultural tours, or spiritual experiences, or a combination of all three, their highly personalized tours promise to intimately connect you to the history of Peru, past and present, in a trip that matches your specific interests. ⌧ *San Blas* ☎ *982/349–861* ⊕ *www.uniqueperutours.com* ✉ *From $80.*

United Mice. One of the more popular Inca Trail operators, United Mice have been guiding adventurers on multiday hikes since 1987. They also offer a variety of alternative treks throughout the Cusco region. ⌧ *Av. Pachacutec 424 A-5, Cusco* ☎ *084/221–139* ⊕ *www.unitedmice. com* ✉ *From $90.*

Wayki Trek. This unique, indigenously managed operator specializes in Inca Trail and alternative trekking. They are known for great guides and excellent customer service. ⌧ *Calle Quera 249, Cusco* ☎ *084/224–092 coordinations, 012/418–796 booking* ⊕ *www.waykitrek.net.*

5

CUSCO

Cusco is a fascinating blend of old and new. It was once the capital of the Inca Empire, and colonial buildings now top Inca foundations flanked on all sides by the throngs of *mestizos* in colorful dress, visitors headed to Machu Picchu, and locals shopping in the daily markets.

If you arrive in Cusco with the intention of hopping on the train to Machu Picchu the next morning, you'll probably have time only to take a stroll through the Plaza de Armas and visit Qorikancha (the Temple of the Sun) and the Catedral. The city merits exploration, however, at either the start or the end of your trip. We recommend spending at least two days in Cusco, giving you time to acclimate to the altitude and to get to know this city of terra-cotta roofs and cobblestone streets. The churches and some restaurants close for a few hours in the middle of the day. Some of the city's museums close on Sunday, but most are open, sometimes with shorter hours.

Cusco takes its newest role as tourist favorite in stride, and absorbs thousands of travelers with an ample supply of lodgings, restaurants, and services. That a polished infrastructure exists in such a remote, high-elevation locale is a pleasant surprise.

GETTING AROUND

Cusco's Aeropuerto Internacional Teniente Alejandro Velasco Astete (CUZ) is about 15 minutes from the center of town. An army of taxis waits at the exit from baggage claim, and they charge wildly varying rates to take you to the city center. Compare some rates, have your hotel pick you up, or carry your bags out to the street, where the standard price to the center is S/6–S/8.

Cusco's center city is most enjoyably explored on foot. Many of the streets open to vehicular traffic are so narrow that it's simply faster to walk. ■TIP➜ Cusco streets have a habit of changing names every few blocks or even every block. Many streets bear a common Spanish name that everyone uses but have newly designated street signs with an old Quechua name to highlight the city's Inca heritage: the Plaza de Armas is Haukaypata, the Plaza Regocijo is Kusipata, Triunfo is Sunturwasi, Loreto is Intikijlli, Arequipa is Q'aphchijk'ijllu, and intermittent blocks of Avenida El Sol are labeled Mut'uchaka, and so on.

Report any problems with tour companies, hotels, restaurants, and so on to INDECOPI, a tourist-focused government agency.

Cusco has kept steady with the times so that the simplest way to order a taxi is to download the Easy Taxi app on your smartphone, which will find you a taxi close to your location and, with your GPS enabled, help the app to find you as well. If you are not in an area with taxis roaming outside, ask your hotel or restaurant to order you one. If you do pick up a taxi on the street, make sure that it is one that works with a company, recognizable by the name it will typically be touting on the top.

Airport Aeropuerto Internacional Teniente Alejandro Velasco Astete (CUZ).
✉ *Av. Velasco Astete s/n* ☎ *084/222-611.*

Bus Cruz del Sur. ⊠ *Av. Industrial 121, Bancopata* ☎ *084/480–010*
⊕ *www.cruzdelsur.com.pe.* **Ormeño.** ⊠ *Terminal Terrestre de Cusco* ☎ *084/261–704* ⊕ *www.grupo-ormeno.com.pe.*

Rental Car Hertz. ⊠ *Av. El Sol 803* ☎ *084/248–800* ⊕ *www.gygrentacar.com.*
Manu Rent A Car. ⊠ *Av. El Sol 520* ☎ *084/233–382* ⊕ *www.manurentacar.com.*

Train Inca Rail. ⊠ *Portal de Panes 105, Plaza de Armas* ☎ *084/581–860*
⊕ *www.incarail.com.* **PeruRail.** ⊠ *Portal de Carnes 214, Plaza de Armas*
☎ *084/581–414* ⊕ *www.perurail.com.*

ESSENTIALS
Currency Banco de Crédito. ⊠ *Av. El Sol 189* ⊕ *www.viabcp.com.*
Interbank Money Exchange. ⊠ *Portal Comercio 133, Plaza de Armas.*
Scotiabank Money Exchange. ⊠ *Portal de Carnes 244, Plaza de Armas.*
Western Union. ⊠ *Maruri 310* ☎ *084/248–028.*

Mail DHL. ⊠ *Av. El Sol 608.* **SERPOST.** ⊠ *Av. El Sol 800* ⊕ *www.serpost.com.pe.*

Medical Clínica Pardo. ⊠ *Av. de la Cultura 710, Plaza Tupac Amaru*
☎ *084/256–976, 989/431–050 24 hrs* ⊕ *www.clinicapardo-cusco.com.*
Dr. Eduardo Luna. ☎ *984/761–277.* **Hospital Regional.** ⊠ *Av. de la Cultura
s/n, Wanchaq* ☎ *084/231–131* ⊕ *www.hospitalregionalcusco.gob.pe.*

Police INDECOPI. ⊠ *Urb. Constancia Mz A-11-12, Wanchaq* ☎ *084/252–987*
⊕ *www.indecopi.gob.pe.* **Policia Nacional.** ⊠ *Plaza Tupac Amaru* ☎ *084/249–654.* **Tourism Police** (*POLTUR*). ⊠ *Plaza Tupac Amaru* ☎ *084/235–123.*

Visitor Information DIRCETUR (*Dirección Regional de Comercio Exterior
y Turismo*). ⊠ *Plaza Tupac Amaru, Mz. Lote 2, Wanchaq* ☎ *084/223–701*
⊕ *www.dirceturcusco.gob.pe.* **iPerú.** ⊠ *Portal de Harinas 177* ☎ *084/252–974*
⊕ *www.peru.travel/iperu.aspx.*

EXPLORING

PLAZA DE ARMAS
For thousands of years the heart of Cusco, formerly called Haukaypata
and now known as the **Plaza de Armas,** has served as the pulse of the
city. Yet where you once would have found Inca ceremonies and parades
in front of the many palaces that stood here, today you'll find a more
modern procession of postcard sellers, shoe-shiners, and artists angling
for your attention. It's no surprise that they congregate here—with the
stupendous **Catedral** dominating the northeastern side of the plaza, the
ornate **Templo de La Compañía** sitting to the southeast, and gorgeous
Spanish-colonial arcades forming the other two sides, the plaza is one
of the most spectacular areas of Cusco.

TOP ATTRACTIONS
Fodor'sChoice **Catedral.** Dominating the Plaza de Armas, the monumental cathedral is
★ one of Cusco's grandest buildings. Built in 1550 on the site of the palace
of the Inca Wiracocha and using stones looted from the nearby Inca fortress of Sacsayhuamán, the cathedral is a perfect example of the imposi-
tion of the Catholic faith on the indigenous population. The grander
the building, went the theory, the more impressive (and seductive) the

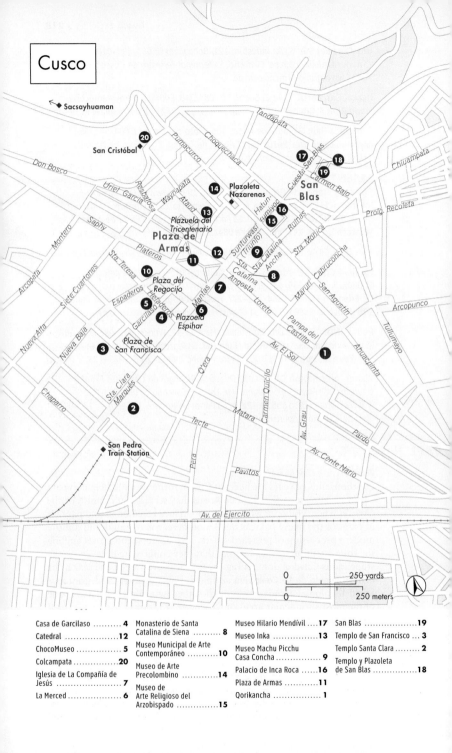

Cusco

Sacsayhuaman

San Cristóbal

Don Bosco

Tandapata

Choquechaca

Pumacurco

Uriel García

Reshalosa

Waynapata

Atauq

Plazoleta
Nazarenas

Plazuela del
Tricentenario

Chihuampata

Carmen Bajo

Cuesta San Blas

San
Blas

Prolg. Recoleta

Saphy

Montero

Arcobata

Nueva Alta

Nueva Baja

Siete Cuartones

Sta. Teresa

Espaderos

Herrajes

Garcilaso

Plaza de
Armas

Plateros

Plaza del
Regocijo

Plazoela
Espihar

Plaza de
San Francisco

Sta. Clara

Marqués

Chaparro

San Pedro
Train Station

Mantas

Qnera

Tecte

Pera

Matara

Carmen Quillo

Pavitos

Av. Grau

Av. del Ejercito

Av. Cente Nario

Pardo

Hatun

Kumiyoc

Ruinas

Sta. Catalina
Ancha

Sta.
Catalina
Angosta

Loreto

Pampa del
Castilla

Sunturwasi
(Triunfo)

Sta. Catalina

Sta. Mónica

Maruri

San Agustín

Cabruconcha

Arcopunco

Tullumayo

Abuacpinta

Av. El Sol

0   250 yards
0   250 meters

ACCLIMATIZING WITH COCA TEA

Take it easy! Cusco is a breathless 3,300 meters (10,825 feet) above sea level—a fact you'll very soon appreciate as you huff and puff your way up its steep cobbled streets. With 30% less oxygen in the atmosphere, the best way to avoid altitude sickness is to take it easy on your first few days. There's no point in dashing off on that Inca hike if you're not acclimatized—altitude sickness is uncomfortable at best and can be very dangerous.

Locals swear by *mate de coca*, an herbal tea brewed from coca leaves that helps with altitude acclimatization. Indigenous peoples have chewed the leaves of the coca plant for centuries to cope with Andean elevations. But the brewing of the leaves in an herbal tea is considered a more refined and completely legal way to ingest the substance, in Andean nations at least. Most restaurants and virtually all hotels have leaves and hot water available constantly.

faith. With soaring ceilings, baroque carvings, enormous oil paintings, and glittering gold-and-silver altars, the cathedral certainly seemed to achieve its aim.

Today Cusco's Catedral is one of the town's star attractions, noted mainly for its amazing collection of colonial art that mixes Christian and non-Christian imagery. Entering the Catedral from the Sagrada Familia chapel, head to your right to the first nave, where you'll find the famous oil painting (reputed to be the oldest in Cusco) depicting the earthquake that rocked the town in 1650. Among the depictions of burning houses and people fleeing, you'll see a procession in the plaza. Legend has it that during the earthquake, the citizens removed a statue of Jesus on the cross from the Catedral and paraded it around the plaza—halting the quake in its tracks. This statue, now known as the Señor de los Temblores, or Lord of the Earthquakes, is Cusco's patron, and you'll find him depicted in many Cusqueñan paintings.

To see the famous statue, head across the Catedral to the other side, where in the nave and to the right of the passage connecting the Catedral to the adjoining Iglesia del Triumfo, you'll find El Señor himself. The dark color of his skin is often claimed to be a representation of the indigenous people of Cusco; actually, it's the effect of years of candle smoke on the native materials used in its fabrication.

Those interested in the crossover between indigenous and Catholic iconography will find lots to look at. Figures of pumas, the Inca representation of the Earth, are carved on the enormous main doors, and in the adjoining Iglesia del Triumfo you'll see an Andean Christ in one of the altars flanking the exit. ■ TIP➜ No one should miss the spectacular painting of the Last Supper, by the indigenous artist Marcos Zapata, where you'll see the diners tucking into a delicious feast of viscacha (wild chinchilla) and chicha (a corn beverage)!

The cathedral's centerpieces are its massive, solid-silver altar, and the enormous 1659 María Angola bell, the largest in South America, which hangs in one of the towers and can be heard from miles away. Behind the main altar is the original wooden *altar primitivo* dedicated

to St. Paul. The 84-seat cedar choir has rows of carved saints, popes, and bishops, all in stunning detail down to their delicately articulated hands. ■TIP→ If you're interested in a more in-depth look, enlist the services of a guide—you'll find them right outside the Catedral. Agree on a price before you start; it will cost a minimum of S/30 per group. Alternatively, there is a free audio guide. ⊠ *Plaza de Armas, Plaza de Armas* ☎ *084/254–285* ⌨ *S/25; combined admission with Templo de San Blas and Museo de Arte Religioso S/30.*

Plaza de Armas (*Haukaypata*). With park benches, green lawns, and

splendid views of the Catedral, Cusco's gorgeous colonial Plaza de Armas invites you to stay awhile. Pull up one of those park benches and the world will come to you—without moving an inch you'll be able to purchase postcards, paintings, and snacks, organize a trip to Machu Picchu, get your photograph taken, and get those dirty boots polished. ■TIP→ What you see today is a direct descendant of imperial Cusco's central square, which the Inca called the Haukaypata (the only name indicated on today's street signs) and which extended as far as the Plaza del Regocijo. According to belief, this was the exact center of the Inca Empire, Tawantinsuyo, the Four Corners of the Earth. Today, continuing the tradition, it's the tourism epicenter. From the plaza you'll see the Catedral and Iglesia de la Compañía de Jesús on two sides, and the graceful archways of the colonial *portales,* or covered arcades, lining the other sides. Soft lighting bathes the plaza each evening and creates one of Cusco's iconic views. Many of the city's frequent parades (and some protests) pass through the Plaza, especially on Sundays. Enjoy the views of colonial Cusco, but note that any attempt to sit on one of those inviting green lawns will prompt furious whistle-blowing from the police. ⊠ *Plaza de Armas.*

WORTH NOTING

Iglesia de La Compañía de Jesús. With its ornately carved facade, this Jesuit church on the Plaza de Armas gives the Catedral a run for its money in the beauty stakes. The Compañía, constructed by the Jesuits in the 17th century, was intended to be the most splendid church in Cusco, which didn't sit too well with the archbishop. The beauty contest between the churches grew so heated that the pope was forced to intervene. He ruled in favor of the Catedral, but by that time the iglesia was nearly finished, complete with baroque facade to rival the Catedral's grandeur. The interior is not nearly so splendid, however, although it's worth seeing the paintings on either side of the entrance depicting the intercultural marriage between a Spanish conquistador and an Inca princess. Tourists are admitted to Masses

under the condition that they participate in them; start wandering around and taking photos and you'll be shown the door. ⊠ *Plaza de Armas* 🖃 *S/10*.

NORTH OF THE PLAZA DE ARMAS

Directly north of the Plaza de Armas, behind the Catedral and to the east and west for about three

blocks, is a section of the city that boasts scores of upscale shops, fine restaurants, and the city's best cultural museum, the Museo de Arte Precolombino. Walk 15 minutes to the northwest to Colcampata, said to be the palace of the first Inca ruler, Manco Cápac. The charming Plazoleta Nazarenas is the perfect place to stroll around and is far quieter than the bustling Plaza de Armas. Many travelers often mistake this section for the artists' neighborhood of San Blas, but San Blas requires a bit more of a hike, about two steep blocks farther, uphill.

TOP ATTRACTIONS

Museo Inka. Everyone comes to "ooh" and "eeww" over this archaeological museum's collection of eight Inca mummies, but the entire facility serves as a comprehensive introduction to pre-Columbian Andean culture. Packed with textiles, ceramics, and dioramas, there's a lot to see here, and displays bear labels in Spanish and English. One room is dedicated to the story of Mamakuka ("Mother Coca"), and documents indigenous people's use of the coca leaf for religious and medicinal purposes. The building was once the palace of Admiral Francisco Aldrete Maldonado, the reason for its common designation as the Palacio del Almirante (Admiral's Palace). ⊠ *Ataúd at Córdoba del Tucumán* 🕾 *084/237–380* ⊕ *museoinka.unsaac.edu.pe* 🖃 *S/10* 🕑 *Closed Sun.*

WORTH NOTING

OFF THE BEATEN PATH

Colcampata. To behold colonial Cusco in all its beauty, take the 15-minute walk up to Colcampata. Following Procuradores from the Plaza de Armas to Waynapata and then Resbalosa, you'll come to a steep cobblestone staircase with a wonderful view of La Compañía. Continuing to climb, you'll find the church of San Cristóbal, which is of little intrinsic interest but affords another magnificent panorama of the city. The church stands atop Colcampata, believed to have been the palace of the first Inca ruler, Manco Cápac. The Inca wall to the right of the church has 11 niches in which soldiers may once have stood guard. Farther up the road, the lane on the left leads to a postconquest Inca gateway beside a magnificent Spanish mansion. ⊠ *Cusco.*

Fodor'sChoice ★

Museo de Arte Precolombino. For a different perspective on pre-Columbian ceramics head to this spectacular museum, known as MAP, where art and pre-Columbian culture merge seamlessly. Twelve rooms in the 1580 Casa Cabrera, which was used as the convent of Santa Clara until the 17th century, showcase an astounding collection of pre-Columbian art from the 13th to 16th centuries, mostly in the form of carvings, ceramics, and jewelry. The art and artifacts were made by the Huari and Nazca, as well as the Inca, cultures. The stylish displays have excellent labels in Spanish and English that place the artifacts in their artistic and historical context. On the walls is commentary from European artists on South American art. Swiss artist Paul Klee wrote: "I wish I was newly born, and totally ignorant of Europe, innocent of facts and fashions, to be almost primitive."

> **WATCHFUL**
>
> To protect historical artifacts from light, guards in Cusco's museums and churches are notoriously watchful about prohibiting all types of photography, flash or not, still or video, within their confines. The exception is the Qorikancha, which allows limited photography, but not of the fragile Cusqueña school paintings on its walls.

Most Cusco museums close at dark but MAP remains open every evening. For a break after a walk around, find your way to the on-site café, one of Cusco's best restaurants (reservations are required for dinner). ⊠ *Plaza de la Nazarenas 231* ☎ *084/233–210* ⊕ *map.museolarco.org* ⛝ *S/20.*

EAST OF THE PLAZA DE ARMAS
TOP ATTRACTIONS

Museo Machu Picchu Casa Concha. Artifacts that Hiram Bingham unearthed during his 1911 "discovery" of Machu Picchu and brought back to Yale University resided with the university for a century. After a hotly contested custody battle, an agreement was reached between Peru and Yale, and the artifacts began to be returned to Peru in 2011. Some can now be seen on display at this small but fascinating museum housed in a colonial mansion built atop the palace of Tupac Yupanqui. While the artifacts are interesting, the real reason to go is for the video, which presents research findings on these pieces. If you have time, visit the museum before your trip to Machu Picchu for a deeper understanding of what is currently known, and still unknown, about this world wonder. ⊠ *Calle Santa Catalina Ancha 320* ☎ *084/255–535* ⛝ *S/20* ☉ *Closed Sun.*

WORTH NOTING

Monasterio de Santa Catalina de Siena. An extensive collection of Cusqueñan religious art is the draw at this still-working Dominican convent, which incorporates a 1610 church with high and low choirs and baroque friezes. Although there's not much to show of it these days, the convent represents another example of the pasting of Catholic religion over indigenous faiths—it was built on the site of the Acllawasi, the house of some 3,000 Inca chosen women dedicated to teaching, weaving Inca ceremonial robes, and worship of Inti, the Inca sun god. The entire complex was given a face-lift in 2010. ⊠ *Santa Catalina Angosta 401* ⛝ *S/8.*

Museo de Arte Religioso del Arzobispado. The building may be on the dark and musty side, but this San Blas museum has a remarkable collection of religious art. Originally the site of the Inca Roca's Hatun Rumiyoq palace, then the juxtaposed Moorish-style palace of the Marqués de Buenavista, the building reverted to the Archdiocese

INTI RAYMI

Inti is the Quechua name for the sun, which the Inca worshipped. Inca rulers were considered to be descended from Inti, thus legitimizing their authority over the people. The most important festival was Inti Raymi, held on June 24, marking the winter solstice and the beginning of the new year. Each June, Cusco is once again home to the Inti Raymi celebration, which begins at the Qorikancha with dances and processions, making its way to Sacsayhuamán, where a variety of ceremonies are performed. There is a cost to the festivities at Sacsayhuamán, but those held in the center of Cusco are free. ■TIP→ If you plan to travel to Peru at this time, reservations should be made well ahead of time because of the influx of visitors.

of Cusco and served as the archbishop's residence. In this primary repository of religious art in the city many of the paintings in the collection are anonymous, but you'll notice some by the renowned indigenous artist Marcos Zapata. A highlight is a series of 17th-century paintings that depict the city's Corpus Christi procession. Free audio guides are available. ⊠ *Hatun Rumiyoq and Herejes, San Blas* ☏ *084/225–211* ⏍ *S/15; S/30 combined admission with Catedral and Templo de San Blas.*

Palacio de Inca Roca. Inca Roca lived in the 13th or 14th century. Halfway along his palace's side wall, nestled amid other stones, is a famous 12-angled stone, an example of masterly Inca masonry. There's nothing sacred about the 12 angles: Inca masons were famous for incorporating stones with many more sides than 12 into their buildings. If you can't spot the famous stone from the crowds taking photos, ask one of the shopkeepers or the elaborately dressed Inca figure hanging out along the street to point it out. Around the corner is a series of stones on the wall that form the shapes of a puma and a serpent. Kids often hang out there and trace the forms for a small tip. ⊠ *Hatun Rumiyoc and Palacio.*

SOUTH OF THE PLAZA DE ARMAS

After the colonial charm of central Cusco and San Blas, head south of the plaza for a timely reminder that you're still in Peru. Traffic, smog, and horn-happy drivers welcome you to the noisy and unattractive Avenida El Sol, where the colonial charm of the city is hidden but for one glaring exception: Cusco's if-you-have-time-for-only-one-thing tourist attraction, the Qorikancha, or Temple of the Sun. Don't miss it. ■TIP→ Plaza Regocijo, although still southwest of the plaza, has re-created itself in the last five years from a once low-level tourist area to a clean, upscale plaza (catering to cusqueños and travelers alike) with gourmet restaurants and high-end shopping.

TOP ATTRACTIONS

Fodor'sChoice ★ **Qorikancha.** If the Spanish came to the new world looking for El Dorado, the lost city of gold, they must have thought they'd found it when they laid eyes on Qorikancha. Built during the reign of the Inca Pachacutec to honor the Sun, the Tawantinsuyos' most important divinity, Qorikancha

CORPUS CHRISTI FESTIVAL

Cusco's Corpus Christi festival in late May or June is a deeply religious affair with Mass in the Plaza de Armas surrounded by 15 statues of saints and representations of the Virgin Mary. The statues are brought from churches in nearby districts and come to Cusco to be blessed. In the early afternoon, the beaded, brocaded, 15-foot statues are hoisted onto the shoulders of teams of men and promenaded around the plaza, with the men genuflecting at various altars and ending at the Catedral. It's a daylong party when the whole city crams into the Plaza de Armas to watch the parade, eat, drink, and make merry. ■TIP➜ Cusco's Plaza de Armas has many second-story restaurants and bars with a view of the action if you want to stay above the fray. Go early for the best views.

translates as "Court of Gold." Conquistadors' jaws must have dropped when they saw the gold-plated walls of the temple glinting in the sunlight. Then their fingers must have started working because all that remains today is the masterful stonework.

If Cusco was constructed to represent a puma, then Qorikancha was positioned as the animal's loins, the center from which all creation emanated; 4,000 priests and attendants are thought to have lived within its confines. Walls and altars were plated with gold, and in the center of the complex sat a giant gold disc, positioned to reflect the sun and bathe the temple in light. At the summer solstice, sunlight reflected into a niche in the wall where only the Inca were permitted to sit. Terraces that face it were once filled with life-size gold-and-silver statues of plants and animals. ■TIP➜ Much of the wealth was removed to pay ransom for the captive Inca ruler Atahualpa during the Spanish conquest, blood money paid in vain since Atahualpa was later murdered. Eventually, Francisco Pizarro awarded the site to his brother Juan. Upon Juan's death, the structure passed to the Dominicans, who began to construct the church of Santo Domingo, using stones from the temple and creating perhaps Cusco's most jarring imperial–colonial architectural juxtaposition.

An ingenious restoration to recover both buildings after the 1953 earthquake lets you see how the church was built on and around the walls and chambers of the temple. In the Inca parts of the structure left exposed, estimated to be about 40% of the original temple, you can admire the mortarless masonry, earthquake-proof trapezoidal doorways, curved retaining wall, and exquisite carvings that exemplify the artistic and engineering skills of the Inca. Bilingual guides are available for a separate fee. A small museum down the hill with an entrance on Avenida El Sol contains a few artifacts from the site but doesn't warrant a huge amount of your time. ■TIP➜ Entrance to the museum is covered in the Boleto Turístico but a separate fee is applied to enter the ruins and the church. For S/15 you can buy a ticket that grants you entrance to the Monasterio de Santa Catalina, and Qorikancha's ruins and church. ✉ *Pampa del Castillo at Plazoleta Santo Domingo* 📠 *S/10 ruins and church; museum entrance via Boleto Turístico.*

WORTH NOTING

La Merced. The church may be overshadowed by the more famous Catedral and Iglesia de la Compañía, but La Merced contains one of the city's most priceless treasures—the Custodia, a solid gold container for Communion wafers more than a meter high and encrusted with thousands of precious stones. Rebuilt in the 17th century, this monastery, with two stories of portals and a colonial fountain, gardens, and benches, has a spectacular series of murals that depict the life of the founder of the Mercedarian order, St. Peter of Nolasco. A small museum is found to the side of the church. ⊠ *Mantas 121* 🕮 *Free for church, S/10 museum* ⊘ *Closed Sun.*

Templo Santa Clara. Austere from the outside, this incredible 1588 church takes the prize for most eccentric interior decoration. Thousands of mirrors cover the interior, competing with the gold-laminated altar for glittery prominence. Legend has it that the mirrors were placed inside in order to tempt locals into church. Built in old Inca style, using stone looted from Inca ruins, this is a great example of the lengths that the Spanish went to in order to attract indigenous converts to the Catholic faith. ⊠ *Santa Clara s/n* 🕮 *Free.*

WEST OF THE PLAZA DE ARMAS

Casa de Garcilaso (*Museum of Regional History*). You'll find a bit of everything in this spot, which may leave you feeling like you've seen it all before. Colonial building? Check. Cusqueña-school paintings? Check. Ancient pottery? Check. Inca mummy? Check. This is the colonial childhood home of Inca Garcilaso de la Vega, the famous chronicler of the Spanish conquest and illegitimate son of one of Pizarro's captains and an Inca princess. Inside the mansion, with its cobblestone courtyard, is the Museo de Historia Regional, with Cusqueña-school paintings and pre-Inca mummies—one from Nazca has a 1½-meter (5-foot) braid—and ceramics, metal objects, and other artifacts. Free guide service is available. ⊠ *Heladeros at Garcilaso* 🕿 *084/223–245* 🕮 *Boleto Turístico.*

FAMILY **ChocoMuseo.** This museum provides a delicious introduction to the history and process of chocolate making, from cacao bean to bar. Workshops allow you to make your own sweets; they are offered three times a day for a minimum of three people at an additional cost of S/75, and advance reservations are required. There is an additional museum location in Ollantaytambo near the archaeological site and in Pisac near the main square. ⊠ *Calle Garcilaso 210, 2nd fl., Plaza Regocijo* 🕿 *084/244–765* ⊕ *www.chocomuseo.com.*

Museo Municipal de Arte Contemporáneo. Take a refreshing turn back toward the present in this city of history. As is typically the case in Cusco, the museum is housed in a colonial mansion. But the art exhibits, which rotate constantly, display some of the best work that contemporary Peruvian artists have to offer. ⊠ *Portal Espinar 270, Plaza Regocijo* 🕿 *084/240–006* 🕮 *Boleto Turístico* ⊘ *Closed Sun.*

Templo de San Francisco. Close to the Plaza de Armas, the Plaza de San Francisco is a local hangout. There's not a lot to see in the plaza itself, but if you've wandered this way, the Templo de San Francisco church is interesting for its macabre sepulchers with arrangements of bones and skulls, some pinned to the wall to spell out morbid sayings. A small museum of religious art with paintings by Cusqueña-school artists Marcos Zapata and Diego Quispe Tito is in the church sacristy. ⊠ *3 blocks south of Plaza de Armas, Plaza de San Francisco* ☎ *084/221–361* ⊕ *www.museocatacumbascusco.com* ✉ *S/10.*

SAN BLAS

Huff and puff your way up the narrow cobbled streets north of the Plaza de Armas about four steep blocks to the trendy artisan district of San Blas. This is *the* spot in Cusco to pick up treasures such as ornate Escuela Cusqueña–style paintings and carved traditional masks. The streets are steep, but you'll have plenty of opportunity to catch your breath admiring the spectacular views along the way.

TOP ATTRACTIONS

Museo Hilario Mendívil. As San Blas's most famous son, the former home of 20th-century Peruvian religious artist Hilario Mendívil (1929–77) makes a good stop if you have an interest in Cusqeñan art and iconography. Legend has it that Mendívil saw llamas parading in the Corpus Christi procession as a child and later infused this image into his religious art, depicting all his figures with long, llama-like necks. ■ TIP→ **In the small gallery are the maguey-wood and rice-plaster sculptures of the Virgin with the elongated necks that were the artist's trademark.** There's also a shop selling Mendívil-style work. ⊠ *Plazoleta San Blas 634, San Blas* ☎ *084/240–527* ✉ *Free.*

San Blas. For spectacular views over Cusco's terra-cotta rooftops, head to San Blas. This is where the Incas brought the choicest artists and artisans, culled from recent conquests, to bolster their own knowledge base. The district has maintained its bohemian roots for centuries and remains one of the city's most picturesque districts with whitewashed adobe homes and bright-blue doors. ■ TIP→ **The area and its surrounds is one of the trendier parts of Cusco, with several of the city's choicest restaurants and cafés opening their doors here.** The Cuesta de San Blas (San Blas Hill), one of the main entrances into the area, is sprinkled with galleries that sell paintings in the Cusqueña-school style of the 16th through 18th centuries. Many of the stone streets are built as stairs or slopes (not for cars) and have religious motifs carved into them. ⊠ *San Blas.*

WORTH NOTING

Templo y Plazoleta de San Blas. The little square in San Blas has a simple adobe church with one of the jewels of colonial art in the Americas—the pulpit of San Blas, an intricately carved 17th-century cedar pulpit, arguably Latin America's most ornate. Tradition holds that the work was hewn from a single tree trunk, but experts now believe it was assembled from 1,200 individually carved pieces. Figures of Martin Luther, John Calvin, and Henry VIII—all opponents of Catholicism—as well as those representing the seven deadly sins are condemned for eternity to hold up the pulpit's base. The work is dominated by the triumphant figure of Christ. At his feet rests a human skull, not carved, but the real thing. It's thought to belong to Juan Tomás Tuyrutupac, the creator of the pulpit. ⊠ *Plazoleta de San Blas, San Blas* ☎ *084/254–057* ✉ *S/15; S/30 combined entrance with Catedral and Museo de Arte Relgioso.*

WHERE TO EAT

Cusco's dining scene is surprisingly vast. Gone are the days when visitors had only touristy restaurants to choose from. You'll encounter everything from Andean grills to Middle Eastern kebab shops. Restaurant employees on Cusco's Plaza de Armas and Plateros and Procuradores streets—any of these could be renamed Restaurant Row—stand in their doorways, touting their establishments, menus in hand, to entice you. Browsing many menus, you will come across the Andean specialties of cuy and alpaca. The former is guinea pig and is usually served roasted (sometimes with peppers stuffed charmingly in its mouth). The latter is the furry llama-like creature you'll see wandering the Cusco streets with its indigenous owner for photo ops. In addition to the wider variety of cuisines, there are also far higher-quality restaurants than there once were. You may not find Cusco to be as cheap a place to eat as before, but what you will pay for a gourmet meal at a place like MAP Café is far less than you would pay at its equivalent in New York or Los Angeles and is just as good.

Lunch is served between 1 and 3. Dinner begins around 7, with prime rush around 8:30, and most restaurants start winding down service about 9:30. Most places stay open throughout the afternoon.

PLAZA DE ARMAS

$$
PERUVIAN
✕ **Ayasqa.** If you're looking for authentic Peruvian food with a show, the dinner buffet at Ayasqa is your best bet as, unlike many buffets, they focus on doing a smaller number of dishes extremely well, giving you the opportunity to taste traditional plates at their finest. If you're more adventurous, go at lunchtime when you can try more exotic options such as tongue, oxtail soup, pig's feet, and beef heart. **Known for:** traditional Peruvian food; creative dishes; locally sourced ingredients. $ *Average main: S/38* ✉ *Portal de Harinas 191, 2nd fl.* ☎ *084/596–973.*

$$
PERUVIAN
✕ **Greens Organic.** Serving delicious food that you can feel good about eating, too, this restaurant's top-quality, locally produced, and organic food makes it the go-to place in town. Whether you are a carnivore or a vegetarian, you'll find options to make your mouth water and ensure you leave satisfied. **Known for:** fresh organic ingredients; healthy options; friendly service. $ *Average main: S/43* ✉ *Santa Catalina Angosta 135, 2nd fl., Plaza de Armas* ☎ *084/243–379* ⊕ *www.cuscorestaurants.com.*

$$
MEDITERRANEAN
✕ **Incanto.** Stylish contemporary design in an Andean setting has made this large upmarket restaurant near the Plaza de Armas a hit with those looking for a classy night out. Dishing up Mediterranean-Andean fusion cuisine, you'll find twists on traditional Italian favorites using Peruvian ingredients and flavors. **Known for:** Italian food with a Peruvian flair; upscale atmosphere. $ *Average main: S/45* ✉ *Catalina Angosta 135, Plaza de Armas* ☎ *084/254–753* ⊕ *www.cuscorestaurants.com.*

$$
PERUVIAN
FAMILY
✕ **Inka Grill.** From fresh quinua-battered shrimp salad to breaded alpaca served with refried beans, rice, banana and fried egg, this popular restaurant located in the Plaza de Armas offers a wide variety of Peruvian and international fare. It's a great place to go when you are with a

group that has varying tastes, as even the pickiest of palates should find something to suit them. **Known for:** variety of options; fine cuts of beef; excellent service. $ *Average main: S/39* ✉ *Portal de Panes 115, Plaza de Armas* ☎ *084/262–992* ⊕ *www.cuscorestaurants.com.*

$$ ✕ **Kion.** There are plenty of *chifa*—Peruvian-Cantonese cuisine—res-
CHINESE FUSION taurants to be found as you wander the side streets of town, but the best by far is Kion, with its modern decor and attentive service. While there are many familiar Chinese offerings on the menu like wontons and fried rice, the Peruvian influences and preparations make it a nice change from your neighborhood wok and indeed from straight-up Peruvian fare. **Known for:** best fusion Chinese; modern Asian decor; Peking duck in three stages. $ *Average main: S/40* ✉ *Calle Triunfo 370, 2nd fl., Triunfo* ☎ *084/431–862* ⊕ *www.cuscorestaurants.com/carta-de-kion.*

$$ ✕ **La Feria.** Traditional Peruvian cuisine, rather than the stuff of gour-
PERUVIAN mands, is a food of the people, served on the street or in family-style restaurants called *picanterías.* At La Feria, you can enjoy good country eating Andean style, with generous portions of such typical fare as slow-cooked pork, beef ribs, *anticuchos* (kebabs), and much more. **Known for:** traditional Peruvian food and atmosphere; varieties of homemade chicha; overlooking the Plaza de Armas. $ *Average main: S/42* ✉ *Portal de Panes 123, 2nd fl., Plaza de Armas* ☎ *084/200–519* ⊕ *www.cuzcodining.com.*

$$ ✕ **Limo.** For an excellent view of the Plaza de Armas with food and
PERUVIAN drinks to match, this is the perfect place to enjoy a drink before dinner
Fodor'sChoice as the sun sets behind the surrounding mountains. Limo is known for
★ its cebiche and fish dishes, not to mention its pisco drinks, but there is plenty more to choose from. **Known for:** great food, especially fish; fabulous pisco drinks; great view of the Plaza de Armas. $ *Average main: S/45* ✉ *Portal de Carnes 236, Plaza de Armas* ☎ *084/240–668* ⊕ *www.cuscorestaurants.com.*

$ ✕ **Papachos.** The brainchild of Gastón Acurio, Peru's most famous
BURGER chef, Papachos is the place to go for a fresh take on the burger. With a sports bar atmosphere, the restaurant has a huge menu with plenty of other choices, but it's the burgers you come here for. **Known for:** great burgers; unique toppings; delicious desserts. $ *Average main: S/33* ✉ *Portal de Belen 115, 2nd fl., Plaza de Armas* ☎ *084/245–359* ⊕ *www.papachos.com.*

NORTH OF PLAZA DE ARMAS

$$ ✕ **Fallen Angel.** Come for the kitschy, fun, over-the-top decor: take your
EUROPEAN pick of seating from a brass daybed, a heart-shaped couch, or leop-
ard- and cheetah-print stools, and dine off bathtubs that double as fish tanks covered with glass tops, watched over all the while by baroque angels, flying pigs, and disco balls in all sizes. The steak-driven menu, just like the decoration, is absolutely fabulous, darling. **Known for:** fun decor; great food, especially steaks; Francisco Pizarro's house. $ *Average main: S/47* ✉ *Plazoleta Nazarenas 221* ☎ *084/258–184* ⊕ *www.fallenangelincusco.com.*

$ ✕ **Justina.** Pizza is the only thing on the menu here so if it's good pizza,
PIZZA along with reasonably priced Chilean wine, you're craving, this is one

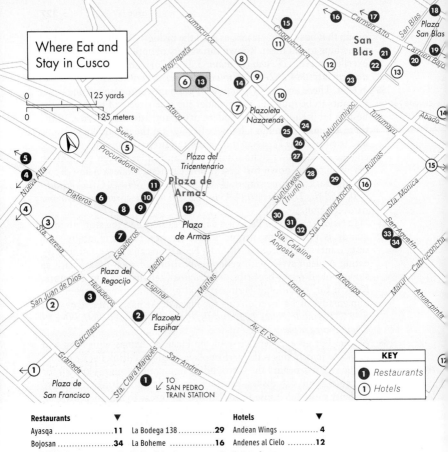

Where Eat and Stay in Cusco

0 — 125 yards
0 — 125 meters

of the best places to get it. The atmosphere is relaxed and cozy, with just a few tables, so get here early. **Known for:** great pizza; reasonably priced wine; just a few tables. $ *Average main: S/32* ⊠ *Calle Palacio 110* ☎ *084/255–475* ⊘ *Closed Sun. No lunch.*

$$$
PERUVIAN

✕ **MAP Café.** Museum eateries don't routinely warrant separate guide listings, but this small, glass-enclosed, elegant café inside the courtyard of the Museo de Arte Precolombino is actually one of the city's top restaurants. It has top prices to boot, but it's still a bargain compared with what this quality meal would cost in New York or Los Angeles. **Known for:** first-class dining and presentation; great service; cool atmosphere in courtyard of museum. $ *Average main: S/65* ⊠ *Plazoleta Nazarenas 231* ☎ *084/242–476* ⊕ *www.cuscorestaurants.com.*

$$
PERUVIAN
Fodor's Choice
★

✕ **Marcelo Batata.** Start with a drink made from one of the many pisco infusions made in-house and then move on to the Peruvian fusion that is Batata's specialty, in particular, mouthwatering alpaca steaks. With a rooftop terrace and a cozy interior dining room, the vibe here is a sweet spot of upscale-but-friendly and romantic. **Known for:** Novo Andino cuisine; pisco infusions; cooking classes. $ *Average main: S/47* ⊠ *Calle Palacio 121, 2nd fl.* ☎ *084/222–424* ⊕ *www.cuzcodining.com/marcelo-batata.htm.*

$$
PERUVIAN

✕ **Uchu.** Although you could easily just feast on the many tasty appetizers at this upscale and minimalist-design spot, you'd be missing out on the real highlight here—cooking an entrée at your table on a heated volcanic stone. Whether you choose beef, alpaca, fish, or shrimp (or any combination), your selection will be the choicest and freshest cut, already seared on the outside, allowing you to complete the cooking to your personal preference. **Known for:** table-side cooking on lava stone; quality meats and fish; ample portions. $ *Average main: S/49* ⊠ *Calle Palacio 135* ☎ *084/246–598* ⊕ *www.cuzcodining.com/uchu.htm.*

EAST OF THE PLAZA DE ARMAS

$
JAPANESE

✕ **Bojosan.** Just as Le Soleil next door makes you feel like you're in Paris, this place, under the same ownership, offers a bit of Japan in the Andes. A 40-year veteran Japanese udon chef was flown in from Paris to help the kitchen get the traditional process—two hours of hands-on work—down pat, and it was a success. **Known for:** authentic udon; Japanese environment; great way to warm up on a cold Cusco night. $ *Average main: S/22* ⊠ *Calle San Agustín 275* ☎ *084/246–502.*

$$
MEDITERRANEAN
Fodor's Choice
★

✕ **Cicciolina.** Everyone seems to know everyone and greet each other with a peck on the cheek at this second-floor eatery, part lively tapas bar, part sit-down, candlelit restaurant. The tapas are delicious and varied while the main dishes offer fabulous Mediterranean cuisine with twists from the Andes. **Known for:** variety of tapas; Mediterranean dishes with Andean twists; best place for romantic dinner. $ *Average main: S/48* ⊠ *Santurwasi 393, 2nd fl., Triunfo* ☎ *084/239–510* ⊕ *www.cicciolinacuzco.com.*

$$
PIZZA

✕ **La Bodega 138.** The wide selection of pizzas, pastas, soups, and salads here, as well as a few great desserts, ensure that you will leave feeling satisfied. In particular, the unique blue cheese, bacon, and *sauco* (elderberry) pizza can't be beat. **Known for:** pizza and pasta dishes; craft beers. $ *Average main: S/35* ⊠ *Herrajes 138* ☎ *084/260–272* ▭ *No credit cards.*

$$$$ ✕ **Le Soleil.** If you're in Peru and
FRENCH missing Paris, you're in luck.
Fodor's Choice Unlike many of the higher-end
★ restaurants in Cusco, this is not
Peruvian fusion—it is French cuisine through and through, right
down to the imported wine and
the fabulous crème brûlée. **Known
for:** authentic French cuisine;
excellent variety of French wines;
fabulous service. $ *Average main:
S/67* ⌧ *Calle San Agustin 275*
☎ *084/240–543* ⊕ *www.restaur-
antelesoleilcusco.com.*

SOUTH OF PLAZA DE ARMAS

$ ✕ **Cafe Dos X 3.** Pouring some of
CAFÉ the best coffee in the city from a
special house blend, this café is a
Cusco icon. Martin Chambi photos help locate the café in Peru, but the
jazz playing and bohemian atmosphere make it feel more cosmopolitan.
Known for: great coffee; cool atmosphere; tasty, low-priced desserts.
$ *Average main: S/6* ⌧ *Calle Marqués 271* ☎ *084/232–661* ▭ *No credit
cards* ⊗ *No dinner. Closed Sun.*

$$ ✕ **Chicha.** Inspired by Gastón Acurio—renowned chef and godfather of
PERUVIAN the Novo Andino culinary craze—hip and hopping Chicha dishes up
regional Cusqueña cuisine with a modern twist. Dishes such as Peking-
style guinea pig (a variation on moo shu) and alpaca curry with quinoa
are great ways to try two of the favorite local delicacies. **Known for:**
new twists on traditional Peruvian dishes; great pisco drinks. $ *Average
main: S/48* ⌧ *Plaza Regocijo 261, 2nd fl., Plaza Regocijo* ☎ *084/240–
520* ⊕ *www.chicha.com.pe.*

$ ✕ **La Bondiet.** This is a great spot to regroup and recaffeinate after a
CAFÉ hard morning's sightseeing. The coffee is quality, there's a huge range
of mouthwatering cakes and slices to dig into, and you can also grab
breakfast and sandwiches, not to mention use the Wi-Fi. **Known for:**
good coffee; ice cream; excellent pastries. $ *Average main: S/16* ⌧ *He-
laderos 118* ☎ *084/246–823* ⊗ *No dinner.*

$ ✕ **Museo del Café.** Café, restaurant, bar, museum, and shop—this place
CAFÉ is somewhat of a one-size-fits-all, housed in the second-oldest colo-
nial mansion in Cusco. The decor is comfortable and welcoming.
Known for: great coffee drinks; tasty food; comfortable, chill atmo-
sphere. $ *Average main: S/24* ⌧ *Calle Espaderos 136, Plaza de Armas*
☎ *084/263–264* ⊕ *www.museodelcafecusco.com.*

$ ✕ **Tacomania.** With a menu that features tacos, enchiladas, burritos,
MEXICAN chimichangas, and fajitas (filled with chicken, tofu, beef, or alpaca),
FAMILY Tacomania is, without a doubt, the closest you will come to South of
the Border in Cusco. Soups and nachos round out the small but deli-
cious menu best washed down with watermelon margaritas. **Known for:**
most authentic Mexican in Cusco; reasonable prices for ample portions;

CORN 1000 WAYS

Corn is a staple of the Peruvian
diet—wander the streets of Cusco
long enough, and you'll soon see
it being popped, steamed, and
roasted into a healthful carbo-
snack. *Chicha*, a corn beer drunk
at room temperature and sold
from rural homes that display a
red flag (and in many restaurants),
is a surprisingly tasty take on the
old corncob, but can have adverse
effects on the foreign tummy. You
may want to stick to the nonalco-
holic chicha *morada*, made from
purple corn.

tasty margaritas. $ *Average main: S/25* ⊠ *Calle Teatro 394* ✛ *Corner of Siete Cuartones* ☎ *084/597–608* ☒ *Closed Sun* ▭ *No credit cards.*

WEST OF THE PLAZA DE ARMAS

$ ✕ **Kintaro.** If you have a hankering for Japanese food, you can get the
JAPANESE real deal at Kintaro where you'll find miso soup, udon, teriyaki dishes, tempura, and authentic sushi; and, of course, hot or cold sake. A lunch menu offers miso soup and an entrée for S/20. **Known for:** authentic Japanese; fresh sushi; salad-plus-main combos. $ *Average main: S/20* ⊠ *Calle Plateros 334, 2nd fl., Plaza de Armas* ☎ *084/260–638* ⊕ *www. cuscokintaro.com* ☒ *Closed Sun.*

$$ ✕ **La Cantina.** More a wine bar than a restaurant, La Cantina's walls are
WINE BAR lined with Italian vintages inviting you to sample them and poured by a
Fodor'sChoice friendly and attentive staff, inviting you to linger. For your meal, there
★ are delicious pizzas with wafer-thin crusts and high-quality ingredients, plus meats and cheeses from the Old Country, and a killer tiramisu for dessert. **Known for:** excellent Italian wines; delicious wafer-thin pizza; imported meats and cheeses. $ *Average main: S/35* ⊠ *Saphy 554, Plaza de Armas* ☎ *084/242–075.*

$$ ✕ **Morena Peruvian Kitchen.** Bright, cheerful, and just off the Plaza de
PERUVIAN Armas, Morena serves their own delicious take on Peruvian standards such as *tacu tacu* (fried beans and rice), here served with *lomo saltado* (an Asian-style beef stir-fry), prawns, calamari, and scallops. Also the menu offers lighter fare like soups, sandwiches, and smoothies, ideal for when you're adjusting to altitude. **Known for:** tacu tacu criollo; pisco drinks; great service. $ *Average main: S/42* ⊠ *Calle Plateros 348-B* ☎ *084/437–832* ⊕ *www.morenaperuviankitchen.com.*

SAN BLAS

$ ✕ **Granja Heidi.** Don't be mistaken: Heidi is not the owner, but rather the
INTERNATIONAL mule who resided on the nearby farm where the owners get much of the produce for this San Blas restaurant. It's all about the farm here, especially the farm-fresh yogurt—something definitely worth trying—as well as lunch and dinner made with fresh ingredients. **Known for:** farm-fresh ingredients; homemade yogurt; delicious desserts. $ *Average main: S/33* ⊠ *Cuesta San Blas 525* ☎ *084/238–383* ⊕ *www.granjaheidicusco.com* ▭ *No credit cards* ☒ *Closed Sun.*

$ ✕ **Green Point – My Vegan Restaurant.** Although there are plenty of veg-
VEGETARIAN etarian options elsewhere, here vegetarians and vegans can order anything on the menu, with a clear, animal-loving conscience. You can even have your coffee with nut milk. **Known for:** extensive vegan menu; inexpensive prix-fixe lunch; vegan products to go. $ *Average main: S/22* ⊠ *Calle Carmen Bajo 235, San Blas* ☎ *084/431–146* ⊕ *www.green-pointveganrestaurant.com* ▭ *No credit cards.*

$ ✕ **Jack's Cafe.** Scrumptious breakfasts can be had all day at this bright
CAFÉ and busy Aussie- and Irish-owned café in San Blas where you can order granola and yogurt, large fluffy pancakes, or a grand "brekkie" with bacon and eggs. Also on the menu are gourmet sandwiches, fresh salads, and a variety of other satisfying dishes. **Known for:** lines; big portions; French toast. $ *Average main: S/20* ⊠ *Choquechaca 509, San Blas* ☎ *084/254–606* ⊕ *jackscafecusco.com* ▭ *No credit cards.*

$ ✕ **Korma Sutra.** Considering that some of the best dishes in England
INDIAN   are curries, it should come as no surprise that the best Indian food
in town is served by a native Brit. You'll find a good assortment of
spiciness here, from mild to mouth-on-fire and, if you're looking to try
alpaca, Korma Sutra offers an interesting take on it. **Known for:** best
Indian food in town; reasonable prices; good portion sizes. Ⓢ *Average main: S/30* ✉ *Tandopata 909, San Blas* ☎ *084/233–023* ⊘ *Closed
Sun. No lunch.*

$ ✕ **La Boheme.** For a quick bite, it's hard to go wrong with real French
FRENCH   crepes; with both savory and sweet to choose from, they're the perfect
meal or pick-me-up any time of day. The prix-fixe lunch is a delicious
deal and there's a great tea selection for an afternoon break. **Known for:**
authentic crepes; prix-fixe lunch; tea selection. Ⓢ *Average main: S/13*
✉ *Carmen Alto 283, San Blas* ☎ *084/235–694* ⊕ *www.labohemecusco.
com* ⊘ *Closed Mon.*

$ ✕ **Le Buffet Francés.** Although not a buffet in the American sense of
FRENCH   all-you-can-eat, this French-owned café tests your restraint with the
Fodor's Choice   best pastries in town, as well as reasonably priced sandwiches on
★   homemade bread, quiches, cheese and meat plates, salads, French
wine, and, every Friday night, a special French dish of the week.
Prix-fixe lunch menus are also available. **Known for:** delicious pas-
tries; fresh homemade food; great coffee. Ⓢ *Average main: S/18* ✉ *San
Blas ✛ Carmen Alto 219* ☎ *960/405–972* ⊕ *www.lebuffetfrances.com*
⊘ *Closed Sun.*

$$ ✕ **Macondo.** Walking through this shop off the busy Cuesta San Blas,
LATIN AMERICAN   part art gallery, part café, and more hip than ever, you may think you
took a wrong turn and ended up in New York City. The menu features
healthy standards such as soups and salads, as well as some splurges
such as bacon-wrapped alpaca. **Known for:** hip and artsy; tasty, albeit
small menu; art shop out front. Ⓢ *Average main: S/35* ✉ *Cuesta San
Blas 571, San Blas* ☎ *084/227–887.*

$$ ✕ **Pacha Papa.** If you've been putting off trying the famous Andean
PERUVIAN   dishes of guinea pig or alpaca, then wait no longer. This fabulous
FAMILY   restaurant, modeled after a typical Peruvian open-air *quinta* with
Fodor's Choice   wooden tables scattered around a large patio, is hands-down the best
★   place in town for Peruvian food. **Known for:** traditional Peruvian
food; great place to try guinea pig; authentic atmosphere. Ⓢ *Average main: S/39* ✉ *Plazoleta San Blas 120* ☎ *084/241–318* ⊕ *www.
cuscorestaurants.com.*

$ ✕ **Quinta Eulalia.** A *quinta* is a *típico* semi-open-air Peruvian restaurant,
PERUVIAN   and Eulalia's is the oldest such place in the city, cooking hearty, filling
portions of down-home food since 1941. Only open for lunch, its specialties include *c hicharrones* (fried pork and cabbage), *trucha al horno*
(oven-baked trout), *lechon* (suckling pig), and *cuy chactado* (deep-fried
guinea pig). **Known for:** real Peruvian food; traditional atmosphere;
generous portions. Ⓢ *Average main: S/28* ✉ *Choquechaca 384, San Blas*
☎ *084/234–495* ☰ *No credit cards* ⊘ *No dinner.*

WHERE TO STAY

No matter what your travel budget, you won't be priced out of the market staying in Cusco: luxury hotels, backpackers' digs, and everything in between await. Most lodgings discount rates during the unofficial off-season of September through May. With a few exceptions, the international hotel chains are absent. In their place are smaller, top-end, independently run lodgings offering impeccable service, even if some lack swimming pools and concierges. Lodgings in all price ranges, whether in a former 17th-century convent or newly built, mimic the old Spanish-colonial style of construction arranged around a central courtyard or patio.

You may have to adjust your internal thermostat in moderate or budget lodgings at this altitude, but all provide extra blankets and may have electric heaters available at an extra charge. High-end establishments have heating. Most places provide hot water around the clock, but if you're wondering, just ask if there's *agua caliente*. Many accommodations keep an oxygen supply on hand for those having trouble adjusting to the thin air.

Lodgings in Cusco keep shockingly early checkout times. (Flights to Cusco arrive early in the morning.) **TIP→ Expect to have to vacate your room by 9 or 10 am, though this is less strictly enforced in the off-season.** All lodgings will hold your luggage if you're not leaving town until later in the day, as well as while you are off on a trek. Breakfast, at least a Continental one (and sometimes something more ample), is included in all lodging rates.

NORTH OF PLAZA DE ARMAS

$$$$ HOTEL Fodor's Choice ★ **Casa Cartagena.** Just a few blocks north of the Plaza de Armas on a quiet cobblestone street lies this elegant boutique hotel where whitewashed walls, exposed wood beams, and Peruvian embroidered pillows temper the trendy lamps and contemporary Italian furniture of this 17th-century restored property. **Pros:** in the historic center of Cusco; elegant mix of old and new; excellent breakfast and service. **Cons:** thin walls; pricey. [$] *Rooms from: S/1575* ✉ *Pumacurco 336* ☎ *084/224–356* 🌐 *www.casacartagena.com* 🛏 *16 rooms* 🍴 *Breakfast.*

$$$ HOTEL **Fallen Angel Guest House.** This luxury boutique hotel features four of the most unusually designed suites you will find anywhere—picture a lofted bedroom with blue-and-brown floral wallpaper, a claw-foot tub with a red canopy curtain, chandeliers, and modern art everywhere. **Pros:** unique style; excellent service; fantastic breakfast included. **Cons:** may be noisy, as it is above the Fallen Angel restaurant, which stays open until 11. [$] *Rooms from: S/600* ✉ *Plazoleta Nazarenas 221, San Blas* ☎ *084/258–184* 🌐 *www.fallenangelincusco.com* 🛏 *4 rooms* 🍴 *Breakfast.*

$$$$ HOTEL **Hotel Monasterio.** One of Cusco's top hotels, this beautifully restored 1592 monastery of San Antonio Abad is a national historic monument. **Pros:** stylish rooms with all the conveniences; stunning public spaces; attentive service. **Cons:** rooms are small for the price tag; *everything* (including Wi-Fi) is charged. [$] *Rooms from: S/1155* ✉ *Palacio 140, Plazoleta Nazarenas* ☎ *084/604–000* 🌐 *www.belmond.com/hotel-monasterio-cusco* 🛏 *122 rooms* 🍴 *Breakfast.*

$$$$
HOTEL
Fodor's Choice
★

La Casona. Colonial with a touch of class, this 11-suite boutique *casa* comes complete with a manicured interior courtyard, stately sitting and dining areas, and rooms with heated floors, antique-looking but modern bathtubs, and marbled showers. **Pros:** serenely situated and spoil-yourself stylish; colonial palace setting; personalized service. **Cons:** books up fast in high season. $ *Rooms from: S/1140* ⊠ *Plaza Nazarenas 113* ☎ *084/245–314, 866/242–2889 reservations from U.S., 855/409–1456 reservations from Canada* ⊕ *www.inkaterra.com* ⬏ *11 suites* ⦿ *Breakfast.*

$$$$
HOTEL
Fodor's Choice
★

Palacio Nazarenas. Following years of careful renovation and rebuilding, Palazio Nazarenas is one of Cusco's most glamorous hotels. **Pros:** excellent and friendly staff; historic setting; central location; top-notch spa. **Cons:** not all rooms have balconies. $ *Rooms from: S/2985* ⊠ *Plaza Nazarenas 144* ☎ *84/582–222* ⊕ *www.belmond.com/palacio-nazarenas-cusco* ⬏ *55 rooms* ⦿ *Breakfast.*

EAST OF THE PLAZA DE ARMAS

$$$
HOTEL

Hotel Libertador Palacio del Inka. Close enough, but still removed from the hubbub of the Plaza de Armas, this hotel has made the most of its gorgeous colonial past while upgrading its room design. **Pros:** lushly appointed and spacious rooms with all the conveniences; some rooms have views to the Sun Temple; close to the action but not in the thick of it. **Cons:** there are other colonial-era hotels with a lower price tag. $ *Rooms from: S/738* ⊠ *Plazoleta Santo Domingo 259* ☎ *084/231–961, 01/518–6500 reservations* ⊕ *www.libertador.com.pe/hotel/palacio-del-inka* ⬏ *203 rooms* ⦿ *Breakfast.*

$
HOTEL

Inkarri Hostal. If all you want is a clean and comfortable place to lay your head, you'll be pleasantly surprised at how much more you get here at this restored colonial mansion with lovely grounds and rooms that, although basic, ensure a peaceful night's sleep. **Pros:** great service; comfy beds; heaters available for an extra fee. **Cons:** basic amenities; can sometimes hear early morning trekkers heading out. $ *Rooms from: S/204* ⊠ *Collacalle 204* ☎ *084/242–692* ⊕ *www.inkarrihostal.com* ⬏ *36 rooms* ⦿ *Breakfast.*

$$$$
HOTEL

JW Marriott Cusco. Step through the enormous original 16th-century doorway and into the plush lobby for a feel of this property, a beautiful and comfortable blend of old and new. **Pros:** large comfortable rooms; close to the historic center; steeped in history. **Cons:** not everyone will appreciate the blending of past and present. $ *Rooms from: S/843* ⊠ *Calle Ruinas 432 and San Agustín* ☎ *084/582–200* ⊕ *www.jwmarriottcusco.com* ⬏ *153 rooms* ⦿ *Breakfast.*

WEST OF THE PLAZA DE ARMAS

$$$
HOTEL

Andean Wings. Housed in a 16th-century colonial mansion, this boutique hotel does an outstanding job of blending the historical backdrop with a modern and artistic design—each room is unique and decorated with original artwork, sometimes with chandeliers, canopy beds, or Jacuzzi tubs. **Pros:** luxurious rooms; attentive service; design is a visual feast. **Cons:** some rooms are smaller with less light; not all designs may be to your taste. $ *Rooms from: S/512* ⊠ *Siete Cuartones 225* ☎ *084/243–166* ⊕ *www.andeanwings.com* ⬏ *17 rooms* ⦿ *Breakfast.*

$$$ ⬚ **Aranwa Cusco Boutique Hotel.** Everywhere you look, there are origi-
HOTEL nal pieces of art juxtaposed with modern furnishings at this luxuri-
ous boutique hotel housed in a 16th-century colonial mansion. **Pros:**
luxury service; historic setting; intimate feel. **Cons:** some rooms have
better views than others. $ *Rooms from: S/510* ✉ *San Juan de Dios 255*
☎ *084/604–444* ⊕ *www.aranwahotels.com* ⬅ *43 rooms* �‖ *Breakfast.*

$$ ⬚ **Costa del Sol Ramada Cusco.** An upscale option at a fraction of the
HOTEL price of some Cusco lodgings, this hotel mixes the best of the new
and old Cusco. **Pros:** excellent value for top-end lodging; mix of
modern and colonial room options. **Cons:** rooms on the modern side
of the hotel are a bit lacking in charm. $ *Rooms from: S/387* ✉ *Calle
Santa Teresa 344* ☎ *084/252–330* ⊕ *www.costadelsolperu.com* ⬅ *90
rooms* �‖ *Breakfast.*

$ ⬚ **Niños Hotel.** If you prefer lodging with a social conscience—and even
HOTEL if you don't—this is a great budget find; proceeds from your stay at
the "Children's Hotel" provide medical and dental care, food, and rec-
reation for disadvantaged cusqueño children who attend day care on
the premises and cheerfully greet you as you pass through the courtyard. **Pros:** wonderfully welcoming staff; charming colonial building;
proceeds benefit a good cause. **Cons:** slightly out of the way; some
rooms are small and very basic; not all rooms have private bathrooms.
$ *Rooms from: S/165* ✉ *Meloq 442* ☎ *084/231–424* ⊕ *www.ninosho-
tel.com* ▭ *No credit cards* ⬅ *20 rooms, 13 with bath* �‖ *No meals.*

$$ ⬚ **Tierra Viva Cusco Plaza.** Part of the Peru-based Tierra Viva hotel chain
HOTEL that can generally be counted on to provide a reliably comfortable
base, this one on Calle Suecia definitely has the most charm of all of
their properties in Cusco. **Pros:** central location; historic building;
some rooms have gorgeous city views. **Cons:** simple decor; lacks the
charm of boutique hotels. $ *Rooms from: S/285* ✉ *Suecia 345, Plaza
de Armas* ☎ *084/245–858* ⊕ *www.tierravivahoteles.com* ⬅ *20 rooms*
�‖ *Breakfast.*

SAN BLAS

$$ ⬚ **Andenes al Cielo.** A boutique hotel housed in a colonial mansion,
HOTEL Andenesis located just a few blocks from the Plaza de Armas but
offers a quiet respite from the crowds there. **Pros:** bargain cost for
a central location; comfortable rooms; lovely setting. **Cons:** not as
luxurious as some of the other Cusco choices; street-facing rooms can
have some noise. $ *Rooms from: S/255* ✉ *Calle Choquechaca 176,
San Blas* ☎ *084/222–237* ⊕ *www.andenesalcielo.com* ⬅ *15 rooms*
�‖ *Breakfast.*

$$ ⬚ **Casa Andina Cusco San Blas Standard.** Part of a national chain, all the
HOTEL Casa Andina hotels exude professionalism and are a great value, but
each hotel differs in style—the San Blas branch, in a colonial house
perched up on the hillside, offers great views over the city's terra-cotta
rooftops. **Pros:** good value for top-end lodgings; excellent location with
spectacular views over Cusco; professional atmosphere and pleasant
service. **Cons:** can be a hard walk uphill to get here; some rooms have
sub-par views over the neighboring houses. $ *Rooms from: S/330*
✉ *Chihuampata 278, San Blas* ☎ *084/263–694, 01/391–6500 Lima
reservations* ⊕ *www.casa-andina.com* ⬅ *37 rooms* �‖ *Breakfast.*

$$ HOTEL FAMILY **Casa San Blas.** This small hotel with a large staff—there's a two-to-one staff-to-guest ratio—prides itself on exceptional service, and the rooms are quite comfortable, with colonial-style furniture and hardwood floors, but with more modern amenities than this restored 250-year-old house would imply. **Pros:** fabulous views; warm welcome from staff; fantastic location. **Cons:** it's a steep uphill walk to get here. [$] *Rooms from: S/444* ✉ *Tocuyeros 566, San Blas* ☎ *084/237–900, 888/223–2806 toll-free in North America* 🌐 *www.casasanblas.com* 🛏 *18 rooms* 🍴 *Breakfast.*

$$ HOTEL **Hotel Rumi Punku.** A massive stone door—that's what *Rumi Punku* means in Quechua—opens onto a rambling complex of balconies, patios, gardens, courtyards, terraces, fireplace, and bits of Inca wall scattered here and there linking a series of pleasantly furnished rooms with hardwood floors and comfy beds covered with plush blankets. **Pros:** great views from the upstairs sauna (US$15 extra); charming rambling layout; great value for the money. **Cons:** located a bit uphill. [$] *Rooms from: S/330* ✉ *Choquechaca 339* ☎ *084/221–102* 🌐 *www.rumipunku.com* 🛏 *40 rooms, 1 suite* 🍴 *Breakfast.*

PERFORMING ARTS

FOLKLORE

If you don't fancy the show at the Qosqo Centro de Arte Nativo, many of the restaurants around the Plaza de Armas (like Ayasqa) offer you a similar package. Starting at around 8 pm you'll be treated to an Andean folkloric show while you're dining, the cost of which is usually included in the meal price. In addition, roving bands of musicians often make their way around the main tourist-oriented restaurants in the center.

Qosqo Centro de Arte Nativo. The cultural center holds folkloric dance performances in its auditorium each night from 6 to 8:30. ✉ *Av. El Sol 872* ☎ *084/227–901* 🌐 *www.centroqosqodeartenativo.com* 🎟 *S/30.*

THEATER

ICPNAC Cusco. Created to promote understanding between Peru and the United States through educational and cultural programs, this center puts on some of the most varied cultural offerings in the city. It also has a small art gallery with new shows every month. ✉ *Av. Tulumayo 125* ☎ *084/224–112* 🌐 *www.icpnacusco.org.*

NIGHTLIFE

Cusco is full of bars and discos with live music and DJs playing everything from U.S. rock to Andean folk. Though dance clubs sometimes levy a cover charge, there's usually someone out front handing out free passes to tourists. Most, if not all, clubs cater to an underthirty crowd. Bars, especially around the Plaza de Armas, frequently position someone in front to entice you in with a coupon for a free drink, but that drink is usually made with the cheapest, rotgut alcohol the bar has available. The drinks may not be great, and the music may not have changed much in the last 5 (or 10) years, but they're good fun if you want to get your dance on. On the brighter side, in recent years as Cusco's culinary scene has moved in, so have more upscale, less clubby lounges.

DID YOU KNOW?

The Inca rebuilt Cusco in the shape of a puma. If you're in Cusco, try to figure out what part of the puma body you're standing in.

PLAZA DE ARMAS

BARS AND PUBS

Limo. For upscale drinks, check out the bar at Limo. While also functioning as a high-end restaurant, the bar here mixes some of the tastiest pisco drinks—in any variation or flavor—around. Not cheap, but if you like pisco sours, don't miss it. ⊠ *Portal de Carnes 236, 2nd fl., Plaza de Armas* ☎ *084/240–668* ⊕ *www.cuscorestaurants.com.*

Norton Rat's Tavern. The second-floor tavern has a great outdoor balcony overlooking the Plaza de Armas, perfect for enjoying a beer (especially if you want an import) and watching the people go by. ⊠ *Santa Catalina Angosta N. 116, Plaza de Armas.*

Paddy Flaherty's. The second-floor, dark-wood Paddy Flaherty's mixes pints of Guinness and old-fashioned Irish pub grub with Philly cheesesteaks, pita sandwiches, and chicken baguettes. ⊠ *Triunfo 124, Plaza de Armas* ☎ *084/247–719* ⊕ *www.paddysirishbarcusco.com.*

DANCE CLUBS

Mythology. Always full, with a mixed crowd of generally young Peruvians and foreigners, the club offers free salsa lessons from about 9 to 11 nightly. After that, you can literally dance the night away to a mix of music from the '80s to today. ⊠ *Portal de Carnes 298.*

Ukukus. Dance the night away at Ukukus, a hugely popular pub and disco that hops with a young crowd, often until 5 am. This is one of the best (and only) places in town to hear live music from local talent, often featuring traditional Peruvian tunes with a modern twist. ⊠ *Plateros 316, 2nd fl.* ☎ *084/254–911.*

NORTH OF PLAZA DE ARMAS

GAY AND LESBIAN

Rainbow flags fly everywhere in Cusco, which might make you think the city is just really gay-friendly. But you're actually seeing the flag of Cusco, based on the banner of Tawantinsuyo, the Inca Empire. The gay scene is actually pretty limited.

Fallen Angel. This bar and restaurant sponsors occasional gay- and lesbian-friendly events, such as cabaret nights, holiday celebrations, and parties. Stop by the restaurant to find out if there's anything going on while you're here. ⊠ *Plazoleta Nazarenas 221* ☎ *084/258–184* ⊕ *www. fallenangelincusco.com.*

EAST OF PLAZA DE ARMAS

BARS AND PUBS

Museo del Pisco. If you only have time for one bar while you're in Cusco, this should be it. Not only do they serve up great pisco drinks, you can also get a pisco tasting on the fly. There's great atmosphere as well as tapas if you want to nosh as you drink. They often have live music as well. ⊠ *Santa Catalina Ancha 398* ☎ *084/262–709* ⊕ *www. museodelpisco.org.*

SHOPPING

Cusco is full of traditional crafts, artwork, and clothing made of alpaca, llama, or sheep wool. Beware of acrylic fakes. For the best-quality products, shop in the higher-end stores. The export of artifacts would require a government permit, so banish any thoughts of waltzing off with the Inca ruler Pachacutec's cape for a song.

Vendors, often children, will approach you relentlessly on the Plaza de Armas. They sell postcards, finger puppets, drawings, and CDs of Andean music. A simple "no, *gracias*" is usually enough to indicate you're not interested; if that doesn't work, just keep walking and say it again. Going to art school is a popular thing for students, so you may find some nice paintings in the mix. Several enclosed crafts markets are good bets for bargains.

PLAZA DE ARMAS

ART AND REPLICAS

Fodor's Choice ★ Ilaria. This is Cusco's finest jewelry store, with an ample selection of replicas of colonial-era pieces. The internationally recognized shop is based in Lima, though there are multiple locations in Cusco, including ones in the Monasterio, Casa Andina Private Collection, and JW Marriott hotels. ⊠ *Portal de Carrizos 258, Plaza de Armas* 🕾 *084/246–253* ⊕ *www.ilariainternational.com.*

CRAFTS AND GIFTS

Arte y Canela. If you're looking for modern twists on folkloric crafts, check out Arte y Canela, which sells a variety of high-end silver jewelry and household goods, all with a regional artistic flair. ⊠ *Portal de Panes 143, Plaza de Armas* 🕾 *084/221–519* ⊕ *www.arteycanela.com.*

SPORTING GOODS

The North Face. There are three locations for this well-known supplier of outdoor wear. In the center, there is one right on the Plaza de Armas and another at Plazoleta Espinar 188. There's a third store in the Real Plaza, Cusco's mall. It's best to buy directly from the company, as there have been problems with inferior knock-off products being sold with the North Face label in Peru. ⊠ *Portal de Comercio 195, Plaza de Armas* 🕾 *084/227–789* ⊕ *www.thenorthface.com.pe/.*

RKF. Forget to pack your winter jacket for the Inca Trail? No problem: check out RKF, where you'll find a variety of quality (mostly imported) outdoor goods from the top brands like Mountain Hard Wear and Columbia. ⊠ *Portal Carrizos 252, Plaza de Armas* 🕾 *084/254–895.*

TEXTILES

Alpaca's Best. With several stores in Cusco, Alpaca's Best sells quality knits but also has a good selection of jewelry. ⊠ *Portal Confituras 221, Plaza de Armas* 🕾 *084/249–406* ⊕ *alpacas-best.com/.*

Ethnic Peru. For fine alpaca coats, sweaters, scarves, and shawls, check out this shop; there are two other central locations at Santa Catalina Ancha and Limacpampa Chico. ⊠ *Portal Mantas 114, Plaza de Armas* 🕾 *084/232–775* ⊕ *www.ethnicperu.com.*

Fodor's Choice ★ **KUNA.** Long-established and ubermodern KUNA has alpaca garments and is one of the only authorized distributors of high-quality vicuña scarves and sweaters. Run by Peruvian design company Alpaca 111, they have shops at the Plaza Regocijo and the Libertador hotel and at the airport. ✉ *Portal de Panes 127, Plaza de Armas* ☎ *084/243–191* ⊕ *www.kuna.com.pe/.*

NORTH OF THE PLAZA DE ARMAS
CERAMICS

Fodor's Choice ★ **Seminario.** This is the Cusco shop of famed ceramics maker Pablo Seminario, now housed in the MAP museum building. Known around the world, it is an ideal place to get a locally made gift that is truly special. Prices are lower at the source, in the Sacred Valley town of Urubamba. ✉ *Plaza Nazarenas 231* ☎ *084/246–093* ⊕ *www.cerami-caseminario.com.*

TEXTILES

La Casa de la Llama. Alpaca gets the camelid's share of attention for use in making fine garments, but this store sells a fine selection of expensive clothing made from the softer hairs sheared from its namesake animal's chest and neck. It's difficult to tell the difference in texture between llama and adult alpaca, at least in this shop. There are some nice gifts for little ones here as well. ✉ *Palacio 121* ☎ *084/240–813.*

EAST OF PLAZA DE ARMAS
TEXTILES

Fodor's Choice ★ **Arte Antropología.** If you're looking for something truly unique, you must make your way here. Part museum, mostly a store, this has been a labor of love for many years as Rosie Barnes and Walter Rodriguez Mamani painstakingly made their way through the legal mire of renovating a colonial manse. The result is simply gorgeous, not least owing to the plethora of one of a kind items that you simply won't find elsewhere, due to locals from all over Peru and Bolvia bringing their heirlooms to sell over the years before the store finally opened. ✉ *Calle Ruinas 105* ☎ *984/623–555.*

SOUTH OF PLAZA DE ARMAS
CRAFTS

Andean Treasures. This reasonably priced crafts shop has many original pieces including tapestries, ceramics, and alpaca clothing. ✉ *Calle Mantas 118* ☎ *084/228–931.*

TEXTILES

Center for Traditional Textiles of Cusco. Sweaters, ponchos, scarves, and wall hangings are sold at fair-trade prices at this nonprofit organization dedicated to the survival of traditional weaving. Weavers from local villages work in the shop, and the on-site museum has informative exhibits about weaving techniques and the customs behind traditional costume. There are additional branches in MAP and Museo Inka. ✉ *Av. El Sol 603* ☎ *084/228–117* ⊕ *www.textilescusco.org.*

Centro Artesanal Cusco. The municipal government operates the Centro Artesanal Cusco, containing 340 stands of artisan vendors. This is often your best bet for buying those souvenirs that you've seen everywhere but not gotten around to purchasing. Prices are typically

CLOSE UP

Alpaca Or Acrylic?

Vendors and hole-in-the-wall shopkeepers will beckon you in to look at their wares: "One of a kind," they proudly proclaim. "Baby alpaca, handwoven by my grandmother on her deathbed. It's yours for S/70."

Price should be the first giveaway. A real baby-alpaca sweater would sell for more than S/200. So maintain your skepticism even if the label boldly says "100% baby alpaca." False labels are common on acrylic-blend clothing throughout the Cusco area. Which brings us to our next clue: a good-quality label should show the maker's or seller's name and address. You're more likely to find high-quality goods at an upscale shop, of which there are several around town. Such a business is just not going to gamble its reputation on inferior products.

Texture is the classic piece of evidence. Baby-alpaca products use hairs, 16–18 microns in diameter, taken from the animal's first clipping. Subsequent shearings from a more mature alpaca yield hairs with a 20-micron diameter, still quite soft, but never matching the legendary tenderness of baby alpaca. (For that reason, women tend toward baby-alpaca products; men navigate toward regular alpaca.) A blend with llama or sheep's wool is slightly rougher to the touch and, for some people, itchier to the skin. And if the garment is too silky, it's likely a synthetic blend. (The occasional 100% polyester product is passed off as alpaca to unsuspecting buyers.)

Although "one of a kind" denotes uniqueness—and again, be aware that much of what is claimed to be handmade here really comes from a factory—the experts say there is nothing wrong with factory-made alpaca products. A garment really woven by someone's grandmother lacks a certain degree of quality control, and you may find later that the dyes run or the seams come undone.

—By Jeffrey Van Fleet

negotiable (and often cheaper than you will find in Pisac), and the more you buy at one stall, the better discount you are likely to get. ⊠ *Tullumayo and El Sol.*

El Palacio de Las Lanas. If you'd rather knit your own sweater than buy one, there are many places where you can buy yarn. Take a walk over toward the San Pedro market, where you will find a number of yarn stores, such as this one, where you can buy packets of the famous baby alpaca yarn. ⊠ *Thupac Amaru 155* ☎ *084/228–741, 974/286–272.*

WEST OF THE PLAZA DE ARMAS
SPORTING GOODS
Speedy Gonzales. Although the shop sells camping equipment, it's also the first place to check if you get to town and want to rent something for your trek. They also do repairs. ⊠ *Procuradores 393, Plaza de Armas* ☎ *992/725–430.*

TEXTILES

Sol Alpaca. Offering fine garments made from alpaca and vicuña fibers, this store is part of the Michell Group, which has more than 75 years of know-how in processing alpaca and is the leading alpaca producer and exporter in the world. There are also stores on Calle Espaderos, Portal de Mantas, Santa Catalina Ancha, and in the Plaza Nazarenas. ⊠ *Santa Teresa 317, Plaza Regocijo* ☎ *084/232–687* ⊕ *www. solalpaca.com.*

SAN BLAS

CERAMICS

Fodor'sChoice **Galería Mérida.** In San Blas, the Galería Mérida sells the much-imitated
★ ceramics of Edilberto Mérida. His characters are so expressive you can practically hear them as you browse through the gallery, which doubles as a museum where you can learn more about this award-winning Peruvian artist and his work. ⊠ *Carmen Alto 133, San Blas* ☎ *084/221–714* ☺ *Closed Sun.*

CRAFTS AND GIFTS

Fodor'sChoice **Galería Mendívil.** Religious art, including elaborately costumed statues
★ of the Virgin Mary, is sold at the shop at the Galería Mendívil. The popular Museo Hilario Mendívil is located across the plaza. ⊠ *Plazoleta San Blas 615–619* ☎ *084/240–527, 084/274–6622.*

Hilo. Like to find fun and unique clothing wherever you travel? This is the store for you. Not remotely Peruvian, Hilo is a boutique shop where you'll find all original pieces unlike anything you've ever seen. Irish-born Eibhlin Cassidy is more artist than mere dressmaker, and if you have the time, she's more than happy to design something especially for you. ⊠ *Carmen Alto 260, San Blas* ☎ *084/254–536* ⊕ *www. hilocusco.com.*

L'atelier by Grid. If you're looking for a different kind of souvenir from Peru, check out the jewelry at this boutique shop in San Blas. The creations of French transplant Ingrid include a variety of one-of-a-kind items, some of which feature Peruvian materials such as antique coins. The rotating display of clothing is also worth a look. ⊠ *Carmen Alto 227 A, San Blas* ☎ *084/246–642.*

SPAS

Healing House. After a day of touring, climbing up and down hundreds of steps, you may be ready for a massage. Healing House is the place to go for a professional treatment with European- and American-trained therapists. This nonprofit also offers yoga classes, a variety of other therapies, as well as seminars, and provides low-cost or free treatments and workshops to locals with limited resources. Limited rooms are available to rent in shared housing for those wanting a more spiritual place to stay. ⊠ *555 Qanchipata, San Blas* ☎ *943/729–368* ⊕ *www. healinghousecusco.com.*

SIDE TRIPS FROM CUSCO

Cusco may be enchantingly beautiful, but with the constant hassle to *buy, buy, buy,* it's not the most relaxing place on Earth. Yet just outside the city lies one of Peru's most spectacular and serene regions, filled with Andean mountains, tiny hamlets, and ancient Inca ruins. In a half-day trip you can visit some of Peru's greatest historical areas and monuments, just beyond Cusco's city limits, such as Sacsayhuamán, perched high on a hill overlooking the city, or the spectacular sights of Qenko, Puka Pukara, and Tambomachay.

The Urubamba Valley, northwest of Cusco and functioning as the gateway to the Sacred Valley of the Inca, which extends farther northwest, attracts the puma's share of visitors going to Machu Picchu, especially those looking to catch their breath—and some R and R—in the region's idyllic setting. Additionally, the Valle del Sur, a stretch of highway running southeast of Cusco to Sicuani, boasts lesser-known, but equally impressive, Inca and pre-Inca sites.

> ## ACCLIMATIZING IN THE SACRED VALLEY
>
> An increasingly popular option for acclimatizing is to touch down in Cusco and head directly to the Sacred Valley. The patchwork of pastures rolls loosely alongside rocky red cliffs, and life sways lazily to the sibilant croon of the Urubamba River; a balmy and breath-catching 2,000 meters (6,562 feet) below the clamoring cobblestone streets of Cusco. Most Sacred Valley hotels will provide transportation to and from the airport in Cusco on request, but be sure to ask about price. It may be cheaper to arrange your own taxi.

GETTING HERE AND AROUND

The sites immediately north of Cusco (Sacsayhuamán, Qenko, Puka Pukara, and Tambomachay) are best and most easily taken in via an organized tour. Although both the Urubamba Valley and Valle del Sur are readily accessible by public transportation, most travelers prefer the convenience of a tour to bouncing between buses—the entire sightseeing circuit is about 170 km (105 miles).

Tours are easily organized from one of the many kiosks in Cusco (US$15–US$30), or if you prefer a more intimate, less tourist-driven trip, you can hire a taxi (US$60–US$70) and a guide (US$80).

SACSAYHUAMÁN

2 km (1 mile) east of Cusco.

This is the second-most important Inca site in the Cusco area after Qorikancha, and a primary reason for going on the standard Cusco City Tour, which also includes Qenqo, Puka Pukara, and Tambomachay.

GETTING HERE AND AROUND

Sacsayhuamán sits a stone's throw from Cusco and is easily visited in a half-day organized tour. A so-called mystical tour typically takes in the Templo de la Luna and other surrounding sites. If your lungs and legs are up to it, the self-guided 30-minute ascent from Cusco to

Ollantaytambo
see detail map

TO MACHU PICCHU

Urubamba
Huaran
Calca
Salineras
Yucay
Huayllabamba
Maras
Moray
Racchi
Huayllabamba
Lamay
Coya
Chinchero
Pisac
Lake Huaypo
Lake Piuray
Ch'uso

Pisac
see detail map

SACRED VALLEY
Taray O
Izcuchaca
Anta
Poroy
RAIL TO
AGUAS CALIENTES
AND MACHU PICCHU
Tambomachay
Puka Pukara
Salapunco
Qenko
Cusco
Sacsayhuamán
Huancalle
San Salvador
San Sebastián
Valle del Sur
Tipón
Saylla
Huambutio
Oropesa
Pikillacta
Huacarpay
Rumicolca
TO URCOS
Andahuaylilla

Río Urubamba
URUBAMBA VALLEY
Vilcanota River

Side Trips from Cusco

0   5 mi
0   5 km

Sacsayhuamán offers an eye-catching introduction to colonial Cusco. The walk starts from the Plaza de Armas and winds uphill along the pedestrian-only Resbalosa Street. Make your way past San Cristóbal Church, hang a left at the outstretched arms of the white statue of Christ, and you're almost there. ⊠ *Km 2, Hwy. to Pisac* ☎ *No phone* 🎫 *S/130 Boleto Turístico*

EXPLORING

Fodor's Choice ★

Sacsayhuamán. Towering high above Cusco, the ruins of Sacsayhuamán are a constant reminder of the city's Inca roots. You may have to stretch your imagination to visualize how it was during Inca times— much of the site was used as a convenient source of building material by the conquering Spanish, but plenty remains to be marveled at. Huge stone blocks beg the question of how they were carved and maneuvered into position, and the masterful masonry is awe-inspiring. If you're not moved by stonework, the spectacular views over the city are just as impressive.

If the Incas designed Cusco in the shape of a puma, then Sacsayhuamán represents its ferocious head. Perhaps the most important Inca monument after Machu Picchu, Sacsayhuamán is thought to have been a religious complex during Inca times. That being said, from its strategic position high above Cusco, it was also excellently placed to defend the city, and its zigzag walls and cross-fire parapets allowed defenders to rain destruction on attackers from two sides.

Construction of the site began in the 1440s, during the reign of the Inca Pachacutec. It's thought that 20,000 workers were needed for Sacsayhuamán's construction, cutting the astonishingly massive limestone, diorite, and andesite blocks—the largest gets varying estimates of anywhere between 125 and 350 tons—rolling them to the site, and assembling them in traditional Inca style to achieve

a perfect fit without mortar. The Inca Manco Cápac II, installed as puppet ruler after the conquest, retook the fortress and led a mutiny against Juan Pizarro and the Spanish in 1536. Fighting raged for 10 months in a valiant but unsuccessful bid by the Inca to reclaim their empire. History records that thousands of corpses from both sides littered the grounds and were devoured by condors at the end of the battle.

Today only the outer walls remain of the original fortress city, which the Spanish tore down after the rebellion and then ransacked for years as a source of construction materials for their new city down the hill, a practice that continued until the mid-20th century. One-fifth of the original complex is left; nonetheless, the site is impressive. Sacsayhuamán's three original towers, used for provisions, no longer stand, though the foundations of two are still visible. The so-called Inca's Throne, the Suchuna, remains, presumably used by the emperor for reviewing troops. Today those parade grounds, the Explanada, are the ending point for the June 24 Inti Raymi Festival of the Sun, commemorating the winter solstice and Cusco's most famous celebration.

These closest Inca ruins to Cusco make a straightforward half-day trip from the city, and provide a great view over Cusco's orange rooftops. If you don't have a car, take a taxi, or if you want to test yourself, the ruins are a steep 30-minute walk up from the Plaza de Armas. ■TIP→ A large map at both entrances shows the layout of Sacsayhuamán, but once you enter, signage and explanations are minimal. You may find guides waiting outside the entrances who can give you a two-hour tour (negotiate the price ahead of time). Most are competent and knowledgeable, but depending on their perspective, you'll get a strictly historic, strictly mystical, strictly architectural, or all-of-the-above type tour, and almost all guides work the standard joke into their spiel that the name of the site is pronounced "sexy woman." It's theoretically possible to sneak into Sacsayhuamán after hours, but lighting is poor, surfaces are uneven, and robberies have occurred at night. ⊠ *2 km (1 mile) north of Cusco, Cusco* ✉ *Boleto Turistico.*

QENKO

4 km (2½ miles) northeast of Cusco.

A stop on the Cusco City Tour, this ceremonial site predicted the season's harvest.

Qenko. It may be a fairly serene location these days, but Qenko, which means "zigzag," was once the site of one of the Incas' most intriguing and potentially macabre rituals. Named after the zigzagging channels carved into the surface, Qenko is a large rock thought to have been the site of an annual pre-planting ritual in which priests standing on the top poured *chicha,* or llama blood, into a ceremonial pipe, allowing it to make its way down the channel. If the blood flowed left, it boded poor fertility for the coming season. If the liquid continued the full length of the pipe, it spelled a bountiful harvest. ■TIP➜ Today you won't see any blood, but the carved channels still exist and you can climb to the top to see how they zigzag their way down. Other symbolic carvings mix it up on the rock face, too—the eagle-eyed might spot a puma, condor, and a llama. ⊠ *Km 4, Hwy. to Pisac, Cusco* 🖃 *Boleto Turístico.*

PUKA PUKARA

10 km (6 miles) northeast of Cusco.

A stop on the Cusco City Tour, this pink-stone Inca site offers great views of the valley below.

Puka Pukara. Little is known of the archaeological ruins of Puka Pukara, a pink-stone site guarding the road to the Sacred Valley. Some archaeologists believe the complex was a fort—its name means "red fort"—but others claim it served as a hunting lodge and storage place used by the Inca nobility. Current theory holds that this center, likely built during the reign of the Inca Pachacutec, served all those functions. Whatever it was, it was put in the right place. Near Tambomachay, this enigmatic spot provides spectacular views over the Sacred Valley. Pull up a rock and ponder the mystery yourself. ⊠ *Km 10, Hwy. to Pisac, Cusco* 🖃 *Boleto Turístico.*

TAMBOMACHAY

11 km (6½ miles) north of Cusco.

Inca-built fountains tap the natural spring at this site on the Cusco City Tour.

Tambomachay. Ancient fountains preside over this tranquil and secluded spot, which is commonly known as "El Baño del Inca," or Inca's Bath. The name actually means "cavern lodge," and the site is a three-tiered *huaca* built of elaborate stonework over a natural spring, which is thought to have been used for ritual showers. Interpretations differ, but the site was likely a place where water, considered a source of life, was worshipped (or perhaps just a nice place to take a bath). The huaca is almost certain to have been the scene of sacred ablutions and purifying ceremonies for Inca rulers and royal women. ⊠ *Km 11, Hwy. to Pisac, Cusco* 🖃 *Boleto Turístico.*

VALLE DEL SUR

The Río Urubamba runs northwest and southeast from Cusco. The northwest sector of the river basin is the romantically named Sacred Valley of the Inca, but along the highway that runs southeast of Cusco to Sicuani, the region that locals call the Valle del Sur is just as interesting. The area abounds with opportunities for off-the-beaten-path exploration. Detour to the tiny town of Oropesa and get to know this self-proclaimed capital of brick-oven bread making, a tradition that has sustained local families for more than 90 years. Or you can side-trip to more pre-Inca and Inca sites. Apart from Andahuayillas, you'll have the ruins almost to yourself. Only admission to Tipón and Pikillacta is included in the Boleto Turístico. A common tour offers an excursion to all three sites.

TIPÓN
26 km (15½ miles) southeast of Cusco.

Tipón. Everyone has heard that the Incas were good engineers, but for a real look at just how good they were at land and water management, head to Tipón. Twenty kilometers (12 miles) or so south of Cusco, Tipón is a series of terraces, hidden from the valley below, crisscrossed by stone aqueducts and carved irrigation channels that edge up a narrow pass in the mountains. A spring fed the site and continually replenished a 900-cubic-meter reservoir that supplied water to crops growing on the terraces. ■TIP→ So superb was the technology that several of the terraces are still in use today and still supplied by the same watering system developed centuries ago. The ruins of a stone temple of undetermined function guard the system, and higher up the mountain are terraces yet to be completely excavated. The rough dirt track that leads to the complex is not in the best of shape and requires some effort to navigate. If you visit without your own car, either walk up (about two hours each way) or take one of the taxis waiting at the turnoff from the main road. ✉ *4 km (2½ miles) north of Km 23, Hwy. to Urcos, Cusco* 🎫 *Boleto Turístico.*

PIKILLACTA
6 km (3½ miles) southeast of Tipón; 7 km (4 miles) southeast of Oropesa.

Pikillacta. For a reminder that civilizations existed in this region before the Incas, head to Pikillacta, a vast city of 700 buildings from the pre-Inca Wari culture, which flourished between AD 600 and 1000. Over a 2-km site you'll see what remains of what was once a vast walled city with enclosing walls reaching up to 7 meters (23 feet) in height and many two-story buildings, which were entered via ladders to doorways on the second floor. Little is known about the Wari culture, whose empire once stretched from near Cajamarca to the border of Tiahuanaco near Lake Titicaca. It's clear, however, that they had a genius for farming in a harsh environment and like the Incas built sophisticated urban centers such as Pikillacta (which means the "place of the flea"). At the thatch-roofed excavation sites, uncovered walls show the city's stones were once covered with plaster and whitewashed. A small museum at the entrance houses a scattering of artifacts collected during site excavation, along with a complete dinosaur skeleton. Across the road lies a beautiful lagoon, Lago de Lucre. ✉ *Km 32, Hwy. to Urcos, Cusco* 🎫 *Boleto Turístico.*

RUMICOLCA

3 km (2 miles) east of San Pedro de Cacha.

Rumicolca. An enormous 12-meter- (39-foot-) high gate dating from the Wari period stands at Rumicolca, sitting a healthy walk uphill from the highway. The Inca enhanced the original construction of their predecessors, fortifying it with andesite stone and using the gate as a border checkpoint and customs post. ⊠ *Km 32, Hwy. to Urcos, Cusco* 🖃 *Free.*

ANDAHUAYLILLAS

40 km (32 miles) southeast of Cusco.

Andahuaylillas. The main attraction of the small town of Andahuaylillas, 8 km (5 miles) southeast of Pikillacta, is a small 17th-century adobe-towered church built by the Jesuits on the central plaza over the remains of an Inca temple. The contrast between the simple exterior and the rich, expressive, colonial baroque art inside is notable: fine examples of the Cusqueña school of art decorate the upper interior walls. ■TIP→ It's the ceiling that is its special claim to fame, for which it is known as the Sistine Chapel of America. ⊠ *Km 40, Hwy. to Urcos, Cusco* 🖃 *S/15.*

SACRED VALLEY OF THE INCA

A pleasant climate, fertile soil, and proximity to Cusco made the Urubamba River valley a favorite with Inca nobles, many of whom are believed to have had private country homes here. Inca remains, ruins, and agricultural terraces lie throughout the length of this so-called Sacred Valley of the Inca. Cusco is hardly the proverbial urban jungle, but in comparison, the Sacred Valley is positively captivating, with its lower elevation, fresher air, warmer temperatures, and rural charm. You may find yourself joining the growing ranks of visitors who base themselves here and make Cusco their day trip, rather than the other way around.

WHEN TO GO

The valley has increasingly taken on a dual personality, depending on the time of day, day of the week, and month of the year. Blame it on Pisac and its famous market. Every Cusco travel agency offers a day tour of the Sacred Valley, with emphasis on Tuesday, Thursday, and Sunday to coincide with the town's larger market days, and they all seem to follow the same schedule: morning shopping in Pisac, buffet lunch in Urubamba, afternoon browsing in Ollantaytambo. You can almost always sign up for one of these tours at the last minute—even early on the morning of the tour—especially if you're here in the September-to-May off-season. Note that the best guides are used for private tours and often get booked up far in advance. On nonmarket days and during the off-season, however, Pisac and the rest of the Sacred Valley are quieter. In any case, the valley deserves more than a rushed day tour if you have the time.

GETTING HERE AND AROUND

Highways are good and traffic is relatively light in the Sacred Valley, but any trip entails a series of twisting, turning roads as you head out of the mountains near Cusco and descend into the valley. Most people get here by way of an organized tour, but you can hire a taxi to take you around. Alternatively, you can take a *collectivo* taxi or van from Cusco (US$2–US$3.50). They depart daily from Pavitos, close to the intersection with Avenida Grau. This is the best place to hire a private taxi to the valley. ■ **TIP→ Watch for the rooftop bulls as you pass through the valley.** The road to Machu Picchu ends in Ollantaytambo; beyond that point it's rail only.

DID YOU KNOW?

Those ceramic bulls often seen on rooftops, especially in the Sacred Valley, are for good luck. The custom began in Pucara (between Cusco and Puno), and the beasts are believed to protect the home and family, bringing good luck, health, and wealth. There is usually a cross between the pair, and there may be other elements as well, such as a condor, sacred in the Andes.

TARAY

23 km (14 miles) northeast of Cusco.

The road from Cusco leads directly to the town of Taray. The Pisac Market beckons a few kilometers down the road, but Taray makes a worthwhile pre-Pisac shopping stop.

FAMILY **Awana Kancha.** Loosely translated as "palace of weaving," Awana Kancha provides an opportunity to see products made from South America's four camelids (alpaca, llama, vicuña, and guanaco) from start to finish: the animal, the shearing, the textile weaving and dyeing, and the finished products, which you can purchase in the showroom. This is a good place to shop for high-quality textiles that you can trust. It makes a great stop for the whole family, as kids can feed the camelids on-site. ⊠ *Km 23, Carretera a Pisac* ⊕ *www.awanakancha. com* ✉ *Free.*

PISAC

9 km (5 miles) northeast of Taray.

The colorful colonial town of Pisac, replete with Quechua-language Masses in a simple stone church, a well-known market, and fortress ruins, comes into view as you wind your way down the highway from Cusco. (You're dropping about 600 meters [1,970 feet] in elevation when you come out here from the big city.) Pisac, home to about 4,000 people, anchors the eastern end of the Sacred Valley and, like much of the region, has experienced a surge of growth in recent years, with new hotels and restaurants popping up in and around town. An orderly grid of streets forms the center of town, most hemmed in by a hodge-podge of colonial and modern stucco or adobe buildings, and just wide enough for one car at a time. (Walking is easier and far more enjoyable.)

Head to the daily Pisac market for local fruits, vegetables, and grains as well as cermics and textiles.

The level of congestion (and fun) increases dramatically each Tuesday, Thursday, and especially Sunday, when one of Peru's most celebrated markets comes into its own, but much more spectacular are the ruins above. Admission to the ruins is included in both the Boleto Turístico and Boleto Parcial.

SIGHTS

Pisac Market. The market is held every day but is even larger on Tuesday, Thursday, and Sunday, when the ever-present ceramics, jewelry, and textiles on the central plaza share the stage with fruits, vegetables, and grains spilling over onto the side streets. Sellers set up shop about 9 am on market days and start packing up at about 5 pm. The market is not so different from many others you'll see around Peru, only larger. Go on Sunday if your schedule permits; you'll have a chance to take in the 11 am Quechua Mass at the Iglesia San Pedro Apóstolo and watch the elaborate costumed procession led by the mayor, who carries his *varayoc*, a ceremonial staff, out of the church afterward. Note that the market is not all it used to be: prices have escalated along with its popularity, and you now typically buy from middle men, not the actual weaver. ⊠ *Plaza de Armas.*

Pisac Ruins. From the market area, drive or take a taxi for S/15–S/20 one-way up the winding road to the Inca ruins of Pisac. Archaeologists originally thought the ruins were a fortress to defend against fierce Antis (jungle peoples), though there's little evidence that battles were fought here. Now it seems that Pisac was a bit of everything: citadel, religious site, observatory, and residence, and may have served as a refuge in times of siege. The complex also has a temple to the

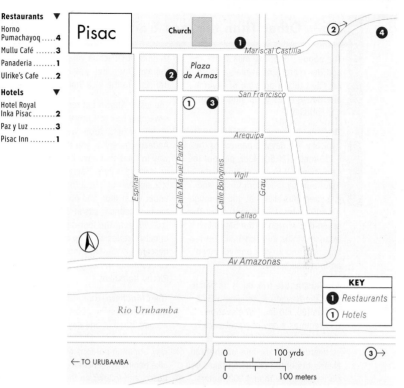

Pisac

Church

Plaza
de Armas

Mariscal Castilla

San Francisco

Arequipa

Vigil

Callao

Espinar

Calle Manuel Pardo

Calle Bolognes

Grau

Av Amazonas

Rio Urubamba

KEY

❶ *Restaurants*

①　*Hotels*

← TO URUBAMBA

0　　　　　100 yrds

0　　　　　100 meters

sun and an astronomical observatory, from which priests calculated
the growing season each year, but this part of the site was closed in
2015 for safety reasons and there is no set date to reopen. Narrow
trails wind tortuously between and through solid rock. You may find
yourself practically alone on the series of paths in the mountains that
lead you among the ruins, through caves, and past the largest known
Inca cemetery (the Inca buried their dead in tombs high on the cliffs).
Just as spectacular as the site are the views from it. ⊠ *Pisac* 🖭 *S/130
Boleto Turístico.*

WHERE TO EAT

$　✕ **Horno Pumachayoq.** The empanadas are fantastic, but that's not the
PERUVIAN　only reason to stop by at this classic empanada place. The real hook is
a "cuy castle," a sort of Barbie mansion for guinea pigs. **Known for:**
traditional oven; guinea pig castle; empanadas. $ *Average main: S/3*
⊠ *Av. Federico Zamballoa s/n* 🕾 *84/203120* ⊘ *No dinner.*

$　✕ **Mullu Café.** Rustic but stylish, Mullu Café has a cosmopolitan flair and
PERUVIAN　specializes in Andean fusion fare. The food and drinks, along with the
upbeat atmosphere, can't be topped. **Known for:** balcony overlooking
Plazade Armas; people watching; Asian dishes. $ *Average main: S/32*
⊠ *Plaza de Armas 352* 🕾 *084/203–073.*

Trails Other Than the Inca Trail

The popularity of the Inca Trail and the scarcity of available spots have led to the opening of several alternative hikes of varying length and difficulty.

The four- to seven-day **Salkantay** trek (typically five days) is named for the 6,270-meter (20,500-foot) peak of the same name. It begins at Mollepata, four hours by road from Cusco, and is a strenuous hike that goes through a 4,800-meter (15,700-foot) pass. The seven-day version of the Salkantay excursion joins the Inca Trail at Huayllabamba, and for this one you need an Inca Trail permit.

The **Ausangate** trek takes its name from the Nevado Ausangate, 6,372 meters (20,900 feet) in elevation, and requires a day of travel each way from Cusco in addition to the standard five to six days on the trail. Nearly the entire excursion takes you on terrain more than 4,000 meters (13,100 feet) high.

Multiday hikes through the **Lares Valley**, north of Urubamba and Ollantaytambo, offer a little bit of everything for anyone who enjoys the outdoors; a series of ancient trails once used by the Inca wind their way through native forests and past lakes fed by runoff from the snowcapped mountains nearby. Excursions also offer a cultural dimension, with stops at several traditional Quechua villages along the way. The Lares trek compares in difficulty to the Inca Trail.

The lesser-known but remarkably rewarding trek to **Choquequirao** (Cradle of Gold) takes in stunning Andean scenery as you make your way to ruins that have been heralded as Machu Picchu's "Sacred Sister." The site, another long-lost Inca city still under excavation and not yet engulfed by mass tourism, sits at 3,100 meters (10,180 feet). The four-day trek entails a series of steep ascents and descents. If you have more time, you can continue trekking on to Machu Picchu from here.

The **Chinchero–Huayllabamba** trek has two selling points: it can be accomplished in one day—about six hours—and is downhill much of the way, although portions get steep. The hike begins in Chinchero, north of Cusco, and follows an Inca trail that offers splendid views as you descend into the Sacred Valley toward the small village of Huayllabamba.

Although the **Rainbow Mountains** near Ausangate have been getting widely sold as a destination, it should be noted that doing this in a single day as it is often marketed is rather long, uncomfortable, and crowded. It's best to do this as a two-day trip from Cusco, including one night of camping.

$ ✕ **Panadería.** The unnamed bakery just off the Plaza Constitución is a
BAKERY   Pisac institution. Empanadas (some vegetarian) and homemade breads are delivered from the clay oven and into your hands. **Known for:** fresh, hot empanadas. $ *Average main: S/3* ✉ *Mariscal Castilla 372* ▭ *No credit cards* ⊘ *No dinner.*

$ ✕ **Ulrike's Café.** German transplant Ulrike Simic and company dish
CAFÉ   up food all day long, making this the perfect refueling stop during a day of market shopping and sightseeing. Breakfast gets under

way before the market does, at 8 am. They've got good à la carte soups and pizzas, too, and yummy brownies, muffins, cheesecake, and chocolate-chip cookies for dessert. **Known for:** familiar comfort food; coffee and desserts. $ *Average main: S/24* ⊠ *Calle Pardo 613* ☎ *084/203–195* ☰ *No credit cards.*

WHERE TO STAY

$
HOTEL
☆ **Hotel Royal Inka Pisac.** Just outside town is a branch of Peru's Royal Inka hotel chain, and the closest lodging to the Pisac ruins. **Pros:** lots of activities; clean and reasonably comfortable. **Cons:** outside town; rooms could use a retouch; extra fee for facilities. $ *Rooms from: S/193* ⊠ *Km 1.5, Carretera a Pisac Ruinas* ☎ *084/203–064, 866/554–6028 in U.S.* ⊕ *www.hotelroyalinka.com* ⤳ *80 rooms* ⦙⊚⦙ *Breakfast.*

$$
HOTEL
FAMILY
☆ **Paz y Luz.** Bright airy rooms, skylighted bathrooms, and mountain views characterize this growing hotel just outside of town. **Pros:** excellent for families and big groups, especially conference cadres. **Cons:** not the most centrally located. $ *Rooms from: S/250* ⊠ *1 km (½ mile) past bridge, on right* ☎ *910/598–781* ⊕ *www.pazyluzperu.com* ⤳ *27 rooms* ⦙⊚⦙ *Breakfast.*

$
HOTEL
FAMILY
☆ **Pisac Inn.** This cozy place is right on the main square, offering a home away from home that can't be beat for location. **Pros:** convenient location; serene space. **Cons:** basic room amenities. $ *Rooms from: S/226* ⊠ *Plaza de Armas* ☎ *084/203–062* ⊕ *www.pisacinn.com* ⤳ *11 rooms* ⦙⊚⦙ *Breakfast.*

HUARAN

On your way from Pisac to Urubamba, and before you get to Huayllabamba, you will pass through Huaran. Even if you're not staying at the absolutely lovely Green House or Green House Villas, it's worth a stop to go to Viva Perú Café for lunch.

WHERE TO EAT

$
CAFÉ
Fodor's Choice
★
✕ **Viva Perú Café.** Enjoy absolutely fabulous sandwiches, salads, homemade ice cream, desserts, craft beer, and much more at this cozy and comfortable café. The outdoor garden area is perfect for enjoying a sunny day under the gaze of the gorgeous Pitusiray mountain. **Known for:** delicious lunch fare; great desserts; comfortable and relaxed atmosphere. $ *Average main: S/22* ⊠ *Km 60.2, Carretera Pisac–Ollantaytambo, Huaran* ☎ *958/301–214* ⊙ *Closed Sun* ☰ *No credit cards.*

WHERE TO STAY

$$ HOTEL Fodor's Choice ★ 🏨 **The Green House.** With just four rooms, this small hotel offers a quiet getaway in a gorgeous rural setting—it's perfect for getting in some nature without having to rough it. **Pros:** quiet and friendly; beautiful grounds. **Cons:** remote location; friendly dogs on-site are not for everyone. [$] *Rooms from: S/345* ✉ *Km 60.2, Carretera Pisac–Ollantaytambo, Huaran* ☎ *941/299–944* 🌐 *www.thegreenhouseperu.com* 🛏 *4 rooms* 🍴 *Breakfast.*

$$$ RENTAL 🏨 **Green House Villas.** For a perfect blend of an independent stay and having your every need catered to, Green House Villas can't be beat. **Pros:** stunning location; beautiful villas and private space; housekeeping and breakfast included. **Cons:** remote location. [$] *Rooms from: S/750* ✉ *Km 60.2, Carretera Pisac–Ollantaytambo, Huaran* ☎ *958/301–214* 🌐 *www.thegreenhousevillas.com* 🛏 *3 villas* 🍴 *No meals.*

HUAYLLABAMBA

On your way from Pisac to Yucay/Urubamba, you will arrive at this small town. There's not much reason to stop unless you happen to be staying at the Aranwa or Inkaterra's Hacienda, but that alone might be reason enough.

WHERE TO STAY

$$ HOTEL 🏨 **Aranwa Sacred Valley Hotel and Wellness.** Set in the beautiful Sacred Valley, the hotel's riverside location is enough to make your stress melt away. **Pros:** excellent service; beautiful property; extensive wellness treatments. **Cons:** located in a remote area. [$] *Rooms from: S/420* ✉ *Antigua Hacienda Yaravilca* ☎ *084/581–900* 🌐 *www.aranwahotels.com* 🛏 *115 rooms* 🍴 *Breakfast.*

YUCAY

46 km (28 miles) northwest of Pisac.

Just a bit outside the much larger Urubamba, Yucay proper is only a few streets wide, with a collection of attractive colonial-era adobe-and-stucco buildings and a pair of good-choice lodgings on opposite sides of a grassy plaza in the center of town.

WHERE TO STAY

$$ HOTEL 🏨 **La Casona de Yucay.** This 1810 home of Manuel de Orihuela, once host to South American liberator Simón Bolívar, features bright, airy, and comfortable rooms arranged in blocks around four courtyards, lush with flowered gardens, all of which received an upgrade in 2017. **Pros:** historic setting; beautiful landscapes; central location for exploring the Sacred Valley. **Cons:** not much else in Yucay itself. [$] *Rooms from: S/405* ✉ *Av. San Martín 104, Plaza Manco II* ☎ *084/201–116* 🌐 *www.hotelcasonayucay.com* 🛏 *54 rooms* 🍴 *Breakfast.*

$$ HOTEL 🏨 **Sonesta Posada del Inca Valle Sagrado.** In the heart of the Sacred Valley, this 300-year-old former monastery offers modern amenities while retaining its charm with details like tile floors, wood ceilings, hand-carved headboards, and balconies that overlook the gardens or the terraced hillsides. **Pros:** good restaurant; historic setting; lovely

surrounding landscape. **Cons:** there's not much else in Yucay. [$] *Rooms from: S/399* ✉ *Plaza Manco II 123* ☎ *084/201–107, 01/712–6060 in Lima, 800/766–3782 in North America* 🌐 *www.sonesta.com/SacredValley* 🛏 *88 rooms* 🍴 *Breakfast.*

URUBAMBA

2 km (1 mile) northwest of Yucay; 29 km (17 miles) northwest of Chinchero.

Spanish naturalist Antonio de León Pinedo rhapsodized that Urubamba must have been the biblical Garden of Eden, but you'll be forgiven if your first glance at the place causes you to doubt that lofty claim: the highway leading into and bypassing the city, the Sacred Valley's administrative, economic, and geographic center, shows you miles of gas stations and convenience stores. But get off the highway and get lost in the countryside, awash in flowers and pisonay trees, and enjoy the spectacular views of the nearby mountains, and you might agree with León Pinedo after all. Urubamba holds little of historic interest, but the gorgeous scenery, a growing selection of top-notch hotels, and easy access to Machu Picchu rail service make the town an appealing place in which to base yourself. Hikers will find that a multitude of small ruins can be visited in a day's outing.

5

ESSENTIALS

Currency Banco de la Nación. ✉ *Av. Señor de Torrechayoc y Jr. Sagrario* ☎ *084/201–291.*

Mail SERPOST. ✉ *Calle Espinar s/n* ☎ *084/201–699* 🌐 *www.serpost.com.pe.*

WHERE TO EAT

$$ PERUVIAN 🍴 **El Huacatay.** The best restaurant in Urubamba, probably in the Valley, El Huacatay was serving Peruvian fusion cuisine before it became trendy, in an intimate atmosphere and with a lovely garden. All that experience has certainly stood them in good stead, and you're likely to need some time to decide between all the enticing possibilities on the menu. **Known for:** gourmet Peruvian fusion cuisine; lovely intimate atmosphere. [$] *Average main: S/42* ✉ *Jr. Arica 620* ☎ *084/201–790* 🌐 *www.elhuacatay.com* ⏲ *Closed Sun.*

$ CAFÉ FAMILY 🍴 **Kaia.** If you're looking for something healthy, with plenty of choices for vegetarians, Kaia is the best bet in the valley for lunch or an early dinner (it closes at 6 pm). With fresh salads, soups, sandwiches, wraps, and all sorts of snacks to choose from, you'll easily satisfy your posthike hunger. **Known for:** healthy choices; vegetarian options; family-friendly. [$] *Average main: S/18* ✉ *Mariscal Castilla 563* ☎ *084/509–754* 🌐 *www.kaiashenai.com/restaurant* 💳 *No credit cards* ⏲ *Closed at 6 pm. Closed Tues.*

$$ ASIAN 🍴 **Kampu.** On a side street behind the Plaza de Armas, Kampu is a delicious surprise, offering spicy curries, pizzas (at night only), some Italian dishes, and a pepper steak that will melt in your mouth. Be sure to check out the special of the day as you walk into this chill but lively locale. **Known for:** curries; pizza in the evening; daily special. [$] *Average main: S/38* ✉ *Jiron Sagrario 342* ☎ *974/955–977* ⏲ *Closed Thurs.*

$ AMERICAN FAMILY 🍴 **Uru Gastropub.** Straightforward delicious fare served in a lovely open setting, the pure beef burgers and other comfort food cooked by this American-Peruvian couple will keep you coming back for more ... and more ... and more. Regular specials mean you never know what treats are in store but, with the obvious care put into it by this friendly pair, you know it's going to be great. **Known for:** great burgers, barbecue, and other American fare; friendly service. [$] *Average main: S/25* ✉ *Jiron Grau 323* ☎ *922/635–333* ⏲ *Closed Mon.* 💳 *No credit cards.*

WHERE TO STAY

$$$$ HOTEL 🏨 **Hotel Libertador Tambo del Inka.** The sprawling complex sits on the edge of Urubamba's curving river—all state-of-the-art, environmentally friendly rooms have hardwood floors, two beds, and great mountain views. **Pros:** secluded with riverfront views; green hotel. **Cons:** huge modern resort; not for those seeking intimate atmosphere. [$] *Rooms from: S/897* ✉ *Av. Ferrocarril s/n* ☎ *511/518–6500, 084/581–777* 🌐 *www.libertador.com.pe* 🛏 *128 rooms* 🍽 *Breakfast.*

$$ HOTEL 🏨 **Hotel San Agustín (Monasterio de la Recoleta).** Offering a unique stay in the beautiful countryside of the Sacred Valley, this scaled-up Recoleta was once a 16th-century Franciscan monastery. **Pros:** unique historic setting; beautiful countryside. **Cons:** slightly outside town. [$] *Rooms from: S/300* ✉ *Jiron Recoleta s/n* ☎ *084/201–666* 🌐 *www.hotelessanagustin.com.pe* 🛏 *32 rooms* 🍽 *Breakfast.*

$$ HOTEL 🏨 **Posada Las Casitas del Arco Iris.** At this incredibly tranquil and cozy retreat in the gorgeous Urubamba countryside, you'll have even more peace of mind knowing that your soles are helping fund health care and education for underprivileged children and adults. **Pros:** gorgeous landscape; private, comfortable rooms; reasonable prices; charitable organization. **Cons:** remote location. [$] *Rooms from: S/450* ✉ *Querocancha* ☎ *084/201–484* 🌐 *www.lascasitasdelarcoiris.com* 🛏 *11 rooms* 🍽 *Breakfast.*

$$$$ HOTEL FAMILY Fodor's Choice ★ 🏨 **Rio Sagrado.** Sprawled across 6 acres of greenery, and situated alongside the Urubamba River, this retreat offers the utmost in tranquility and luxurious comfort, with rooms offering riverfront views and featuring natural materials such as wood and stone to complement the surrounding landscape. **Pros:** gorgeous tranquil location; heated swimming pool; excellent spa. **Cons:** a bit outside town. [$] *Rooms from: S/1155* ✉ *Km 75.8, Carratera Cusco–Urubamba* ☎ *084/201–631* 🌐 *www.belmond.com/hotel-rio-sagrado-sacred-valley* 🛏 *23 rooms* 🍽 *Breakfast.*

$$$$ HOTEL FAMILY Fodor's Choice ★ 🏨 **Sol y Luna Lodge & Spa.** You can't help but relax the minute you set foot on this Relais & Chateaux property featuring private bungalows surrounded by gorgeous flower gardens. **Pros:** tranquil setting; luxurious amenities, including a spa; charitable association attached to hotel. **Cons:** a few miles outside town but easy to get to. [$] *Rooms from: S/1594* ✉ *Fundo Huincho* ✥ *2 km west of Urubamba* ☎ *084/608–930* 🌐 *www.hotelsolyluna.com* 🛏 *43 bungalows* 🍽 *Some meals.*

SHOPPING

Cerámica Seminario. Husband-and-wife team Pablo Seminario and Marilú Behar spent years developing their art into what is now known as the Seminario Style—taking the valley's distinctive red clay and turning it into ceramic works using modern adaptations of ancient indigenous techniques and designs. Their works are world-famous, with pieces seen as far off as the Chicago Field Museum. More than a shop or art gallery, here you have the ability to view the workshop where the magic happens and even speak with the artist directly. The store features decorative and utilitarian pieces, as well as others that are pure art, all of which make fabulous Peruvian gifts for yourself or others. ■ TIP→ Purchases can be shipped to any location. ⊠ *Berriozabal 111* ☎ *084/201–086* ⊕ *www.ceramicaseminario.com.*

CHINCHERO

28 km (17 miles) northwest of Cusco.

Indigenous lore says that Chinchero, one of the valley's major Inca cities, was the birthplace of the rainbow. Frequent sightings during the rainy season might convince you of the legend's truth. Chinchero is one of the few sites in the Sacred Valley that's higher (3,800 meters, or 12,500 feet) than Cusco.

Today tourists and locals frequent the colorful Sunday artisan market on the central plaza, an affair that gets rave reviews as being more authentic and less touristed than the larger market in neighboring Pisac. A corresponding Chinchero produce market for locals takes place at the entrance to town. The market is there on other days, but on Sunday there are artisans who travel from the high mountain villages to sell their wares.

Amble about the collection of winding streets and adobe houses, but be sure to eventually make your way toward one of the weaving cooperatives, where a gaggle of local women will entertain you into understanding the art of making those lovely alpaca sweaters you eyed in the market.

EXPLORING

Centro de Producción Artesanías Andina. This is one of the more organized places to learn about Chinchero's weaving tradition and techniques. Guests are welcomed with a cup of coca tea and then whisked through a series of hands-on explanations of the washing, dyeing, and weaving processes. There is also a good selection of hand-woven sweaters and tapestries for sale from the weavers themselves. ⊠ *Calle Albergue 5.*

Chinchero Market. If you're looking for an authentic market experience, you can see locals come from miles away to sell their produce at the Sunday Chinchero Market. You need to make it there early, though, because it's all over by noon. Open daily, the artisanal markets in Chinchero are some of the best places to find textiles. Within the large market building are smaller owner-operated stands where local weavers sell their own creations. There are also demonstrations of local dyeing and weaving techniques. ⊠ *Road to church.*

Church. A 1607 colonial church in the central plaza above the market was built on top of the limestone remains of an Inca palace, thought to be the country estate of the Inca Tupac Yupanqui, the son of Pachacutec. It's worth a visit if only to see the murals on the walls and ceiling. ⊠ *Chinchero* ⬛ *S/130 Boleto Turístico* ⊗ *Open for Mass on Sun.*

MORAY AND SALINERAS

48 km (29 miles) northwest of Cusco.

Head to Salineras for a look at an ingenious way to harvest salt without mines or the ocean, and to Moray for early, inventive farming and irrigation technology.

GETTING HERE AND AROUND

Moray and Salineras are difficult to reach without a tour and almost impossible during the rainy season. No public transportation serves Moray or Salineras. A taxi can be hired from Maras, the closest village, or from Cusco. Alternatively, it's a two-hour hike from Maras to either site.

Moray and Salineras. Scientists still marvel at the agricultural technology the Inca used at **Moray**. Taking advantage of four natural depressions in the ground and angles of sunlight, indigenous engineers fashioned concentric circular irrigation terraces, 150 meters (500 feet) from top to bottom, and could create a difference of 15°C (60°F) from top to bottom. The result was a series of engineered miniclimates perfect for adapting, experimenting, mixing, matching, and cultivating foods, especially varieties of maize, the staple of the Inca Empire, normally impossible to grow at this altitude. Though the technology is attributed to the Inca, the lower portions of the complex are thought to date from the pre-Inca Wari culture. Entrance to Moray is included in the Boleto Turístico.

The famed terraced Inca salt pans of **Salineras** are still in use and also take advantage of a natural phenomenon: the Inca dug shallow pools into a sloped hillside. The pools filled with water, and upon evaporation, salt crystallized and could be harvested. It costs S/10 per person but is well worth it. ⊠ *Maras* ⬛ *Moray: Boleto Turístico; Salineras: S/10.*

OLLANTAYTAMBO

19 km (11 miles) west of Urubamba.

Fodor'sChoice ★ Poll visitors for their favorite Sacred Valley community, and the answer will likely be Ollantaytambo—endearingly nicknamed Olly or Ollanta—which lies at the valley's northwestern entrance. Ollantaytambo's traditional air has not been stifled by the invasion of tourists. As you walk around, you'll see walls, doors, and water-drainage systems dating from Inca times and still in use today. You can even step into a working Inca-era home, learn about the ancient way of life, and see the guinea pigs, still a delicacy today, running around the kitchen floor. Ask around for the local *mercado,* just off the Plaza de Armas, close to the pickup point for collectivos and taxis. This busy marketplace

Before heading to Machu Picchu, check out the Inca fortress at Ollantaytambo.

quietly evades tourism's grasp and offers a behind-the-scenes peek at life beyond the ruins. The juice stations on the second floor, toward the back, might just be the town's best-kept secret. ■TIP→ Ollantaytambo makes a superb base for exploring the Sacred Valley and has convenient rail connections to Machu Picchu.

Ollantaytambo is also the kickoff point for the Inca Trail. You'll start here at nearby Km 82 if you wish to hike to the Lost City, and lodging here will give you a bit more time to sleep in before hiking. Walk up to discover the **Fortress of Ollantaytambo,** one of the most fantastic ruins in the Sacred Valley.

ESSENTIALS

BCP ATM, on Ventidero 248 inside the entrance to Hostal Sauce, is the most reliable ATM in town. There is also one in the Plaza de Armas if the other one isn't working.

ATMs BCP ATM. ⊠ *Ventiderio 248, inside entrance to Hostal Sauce.*

EXPLORING

Awamaki. If you've made it to the Sacred Valley, you've likely seen your share of woven garments. But it's worth swinging by this fair-trade shop just down the road from the Plaza de Armas on the way to the ruins. All goods are produced as part of the Awamaki weaving project, which supports a cooperative of Quechua women from the Patacancha Valley. The organization also offers a variety of cultural tours, including homestays and weaving courses, all of which you can find out about at the shop. ⊠ *Calle Principal s/n* ☎ *084/214–801* ⊕ *www.awamaki.org.*

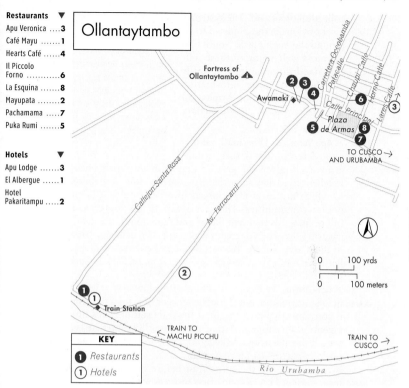

Ollantaytambo

Fortress of
Ollantaytambo ⛰

Awamaki ◆

Plaza
de Armas

TO CUSCO →
AND URUBAMBA

0   100 yrds
0   100 meters

Train Station

TRAIN TO
← MACHU PICCHU

TRAIN TO →
CUSCO

Rio Urubamba

KEY
❶ *Restaurants*
① *Hotels*

Fodor's Choice
★
Fortress of Ollantaytambo. Walk above town to a formidable stone structure where massive terraces climb to the peak of Temple Hill. It was the
valley's main defense against the *Antis* (jungle people) from the neighboring rain forests. Construction began during the reign of Pachacutec
but was never completed. The rose-colored granite used was not mined
in this part of the valley. The elaborate walled complex contained a
temple to the Sun, used for astronomical observation, as well as the
Baños de la Ñusta (ceremonial princess baths), leading archaeologists
to believe that Ollantaytambo existed for more than defensive purposes,
as was typical with Inca constructions. The fortress was the site of the
greatest Inca victory over the Spanish during the wars of conquest. The
Manco Inca fled here in 1537 with a contingent of troops after the disas-
trous loss at Sacsayhuamán and routed Spanish forces under Hernando
Pizarro. The victory was short-lived: Pizarro regrouped and took the
fortress. If you come on your own, take the time to walk up above to
see an Intihuatana ("hitching post of the Sun"). ✉ *Plaza Mañay Raquy*
💰 *S/130 Boleto Turistico.*

Ollantaytambo Heritage Trail. The Old Town's distinctive appearance
can be attributed to Inca organizational skills. They based their
communities on the unit of the *cancha*, a walled city block, each
with one entrance leading to an interior courtyard, surrounded by a

collection of houses. The system is most obvious in the center of town around the main plaza. You'll find the most welcoming of these self-contained communities at Calle del Medio. A tourist information office on the Plaza de Armas can help direct you. ✉ *Ollantaytambo.*

> **WI-FI IN OLLY**
>
> Wi-Fi is nearly everywhere in town. Many hotels offer computer terminals and a place to check your email or look up tour information. There are also some cafés along and near the Plaza de Armas.

WHERE TO EAT

$ PERUVIAN Fodor's Choice ★ 🍴 **Apu Veronica.** This small, family-owned restaurant is sure to outgrow itself, given the passion they pour into their business and the excellent food they serve their customers, using local ingredients many of which are carefully sourced in order to give a helping hand to poorer communities. The specialty here is serving meats on stones full of minerals that add flavor and nutrition to the dishes, as well as ensuring that everyone who walks in gets a little more understanding of the native culture. **Known for:** meats cooked on stone; traditional Peruvian food; great service. [$] *Average main: S/31* ✉ *Calle Ventiderio s/n, 2nd fl.* ☎ *084/214–839, 983/767–932.*

$ CAFÉ 🍴 **Café Mayu.** We recommend hunkering down for at least a day or two in Ollantaytambo, but if you've only got time for a pit stop, Café Mayu is conveniently located right at the train station. This tiny spot serves big-city-style coffee and some quick bites like empanadas. **Known for:** great coffee; delicious baked goods. [$] *Average main: S/8* ✉ *Train Station* ☎ *084/204–014* 💳 *No credit cards.*

$ CAFÉ 🍴 **Hearts Café.** On the corner just before you turn to go down to the train station, Hearts Café offers tasty, down-home soups, sandwiches, baked goods, and fresh juices. This is the place to come if you're craving comfort food like pancakes, French toast, chicken burgers, or birthday cakes made to order. **Known for:** delicious comfort food; tasty desserts; profits support humanitarian programs. [$] *Average main: S/23* ✉ *Ventiderio s/n* ☎ *084/436–726* 🌐 *www.heartscafeperu.com* 💳 *No credit cards.*

$ CAFÉ 🍴 **Il Piccolo Forno.** This little café is the place to go for pizza, lasagna, breads, desserts, and, of course, coffee. There are some vegetarian and gluten-free options, and they also feature a small selection of organic products. **Known for:** pizza; baked goods; great Wi-Fi. [$] *Average main: S/21* ✉ *Chaupi K'ikllu (Calle del Medio) 120* ☎ *940/820–975* 💳 *No credit cards* 🕒 *Closed Mon.*

$ CAFÉ 🍴 **La Esquina.** For a quick bite, healthful or indulgent, this café on the Plaza de Armas is one of the best places in town. Breakfast, sandwiches, soups, and salads will all keep you going as you walk around the ruins, and the baked goods, coffees, and English teas make for great pick-me-ups in the afternoon. **Known for:** great coffee; delicious comfort food; yummy baked goods. [$] *Average main: S/22* ✉ *Plaza de Armas* ☎ *084/204–078* 💳 *No credit cards.*

$ PERUVIAN 🍴 **Mayupata.** Spacious and airy, furnished with large wooden tables and chairs, this restaurant has the unmistakable air of a tourist-friendly Andean establishment. The menu ranges from traditional Peruvian grilled meats and fish to slightly edgier dishes like Andean ravioli (filled with alpaca). **Known for:** Peruvian grilled meats; pizza and other visitor-friendly staples. $ *Average main: S/30* ⊠ *Jr. Concepcíon s/n* ☎ *084/610–258* ▭ *No credit cards.*

$
PIZZA

✕ **Pachamama.** Linen tablecloths, carefully folded napkins, and cruets of olive oil and balsamic vinegar give this pizzeria-restaurant the mark of a sophisticated European eatery. Tables already set with wine glasses invite you to relax and order a bottle. **Known for:** pizza; standard Peruvian fare. $ *Average main: S/30* ⊠ *Plaza de Armas* ☎ *084/204–168* ▭ *No credit cards.*

$
MEXICAN

✕ **Puka Rumi.** Where it lacks the polish and charm of other places in town, Puka Rumi gains ground with its colossal burritos and chicken fajitas—served with a tabletop's worth of sides, including a heaping bowl of homemade guacamole. The menu isn't strictly Mexican, despite what they claim; like the patrons, you'll find an international mix, and the owner is known for only choosing the best-quality meats at the market. **Known for:** burritos and fajitas; high-quality meats. $ *Average main: S/26* ⊠ *Calle Ventiderio s/n* ☎ *084/214–828* ▭ *No credit cards.*

WHERE TO STAY

$
HOTEL
FAMILY

🏠 **Apu Lodge.** Taking its name from the spirit of the mountains, the lodge offers guests clean, bright, and artfully furnished rooms, complete with comfortable beds. **Pros:** gorgeous location; lovely rooms; good place for tour advice. **Cons:** a few blocks from the center of town. $ *Rooms from: S/225* ⊠ *Lari Calle* ☎ *084/436–816* ⊕ *www.apulodge.com* ⟿ *9 rooms* ⦿ *Breakfast.*

$$
HOTEL
FAMILY
Fodor's Choice
★

🏠 **El Albergue.** Right at the train station, the town's first and undoubtedly finest hotel, El Albergue, is absolutely lovely, with spacious rooms featuring dark-wood accents, historic black-and-white photos of the region, and a tranquil garden area. **Pros:** convenient to train; great value for ubercomfort; best restaurant in town on-site. **Cons:** books up fast. $ *Rooms from: S/297* ⊠ *Estación de Ferrocarril* ☎ *084/204–014* ⊕ *www.elalbergue.com* ⟿ *16 rooms* ⦿ *Breakfast.*

$$$
HOTEL

🏠 **Hotel Pakaritampu.** One of Ollantaytambo's better lodgings, with a Quechua name that translates as "house of dawn," has reading rooms with fireplaces and Cusqueña art that invite you to settle in with a good book and a hot cup of coffee on a chilly evening. **Pros:** gorgeous setting and grounds; good restaurant; close to train station. **Cons:** beds are on the hard side; rooms are quite basic. $ *Rooms from: S/572* ⊠ *Av. Ferrocarril s/n* ☎ *084/204–020* ⊕ *www.pakaritampu.com* ⟿ *38 rooms* ⦿ *Breakfast.*

5

MACHU PICCHU AND THE INCA TRAIL

WELCOME TO MACHU PICCHU AND THE INCA TRAIL

TOP REASONS TO GO

★ **Discover Ancient Kingdoms:** Hiram Bingham "discovered" Machu Picchu in 1911. Your first glimpse of the fabled city will be your own discovery, and every bit as exciting.

★ **The Inca Trail:** The four-day hike of the Inca Trail from near Ollantaytambo to Machu Picchu is Peru's best-known outdoor expedition. Spaces fill up quickly, but never fear: tour operators continue to open up new alternative treks.

★ **Amazing Inca Technology:** It was the 15th century, yet the Inca made the stones fit perfectly without mortar. The sun illuminates the windows at the solstice, and the crops grow in an inhospitable climate. And they did it all without bulldozers, tractors, or computers.

★ **Mystery:** Mystics, shamans, spiritualists, astrologers, and UFO spotters, professionals and wannabes, flock to this serene region to contemplate history's secrets.

★ **Majestic Scenery:** The area's stunning mountain landscapes surround you.

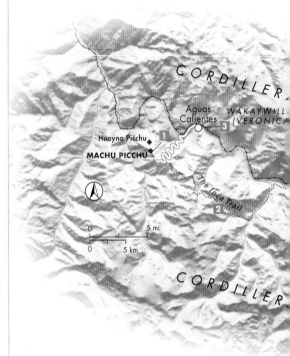

1 Machu Picchu. These two words that are synonymous with Peru evoke images of centuries-old Inca emperors and rituals. Yet no one knows for certain what purpose this mountaintop citadel served or why it was abandoned. Machu Picchu is an easy day trip from Cusco, but an overnight in Aguas Calientes or Ollantaytambo gives you more time to explore and devise your own theories.

2 The Inca Trail. A 43-km (26-mile) sector of the original Inca route between Cusco and Machu Picchu has become one of the world's signature treks. No question: you need to be in good shape, and the four-day excursion can be rough going at times, but it's guaranteed to generate bragging rights and immense satisfaction upon completion.

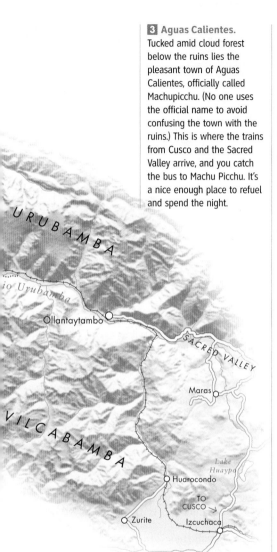

3 **Aguas Calientes.**
Tucked amid cloud forest below the ruins lies the pleasant town of Aguas Calientes, officially called Machupicchu. (No one uses the official name to avoid confusing the town with the ruins.) This is where the trains from Cusco and the Sacred Valley arrive, and you catch the bus to Machu Picchu. It's a nice enough place to refuel and spend the night.

GETTING ORIENTED

The famed ruins of Machu Picchu, accessible only via rail or foot, lie farther down the Río Urubamba, in the cloud forest on the Andean slopes above the jungle. Cusco, the region's largest city, is about 112 km (70 miles) southeast.

6

Ollantaytambo

SACRED VALLEY

Maras

Lake Huaypo

Huarocondo

TO CUSCO →

Zurite

Izcuchaca

URUBAMBA

io Urubamba

VILCABAMBA

Updated by
Maureen
Santucci

More and more people are putting Machu Picchu on their bucket lists each year, and it lives up to its fame as one of the New Seven Wonders of the World. It is indeed a wondrous site to see, so don't let the need to check off a box on your to-do list get in the way of taking the time to really appreciate it.

If you can, go there by trekking the Inca Trail—sleeping in the Andes, walking on paths that the Incas themselves took to get to this sacred site, and entering at dawn through the Sun Gate is absolutely breathtaking. Take some time as well to relax in Aguas Calientes before rushing back to Cusco. It may not have the same charm as that colonial city, but being nestled among green mountains, not to mention getting a hot shower and massage in after hiking around Machu Picchu, is definitely the icing on the cake.

PLANNING

WHEN TO GO

All the high-season/low-season trade-offs are here. Winter (June through August) means drier weather and easier traveling, but it's prime vacation time for those in the northern hemisphere. Don't forget that three major observances—Inti Raymi (June 24), Peru's Independence Day (July 28), and Santa Rosa de Lima (August 30)—fall during this time, and translate into exceptionally heavy concentrations of Peruvian travelers. (Also consider that Sundays are free for *cusqueños*.) The result is higher lodging prices and larger crowds at these times. Prices and visitor numbers drop dramatically during the summer rainy season (October through April). Note that January is the height of rainy season, and the Inca Trail is closed in February. For near-ideal weather and manageable crowds, consider a spring or fall trip.

Entrance to Machu Picchu is now limited to 2,500 visitors a day. In low season this won't present a problem, but if you are traveling during the winter months (North American summer), be sure to purchase your entrance tickets well ahead of time. If your heart is set on hiking Huayna Picchu, the mountain that is in front of Machu Picchu, and which affords great views of the citadel below, you should purchase tickets in advance regardless of the season. If you are not using an agency, you can (in theory) purchase tickets yourself online at ⊕ *www.machupicchu.gob.pe*, although the online purchasing is frequently inoperable.

You often hear rumors that Machu Picchu will be closed to tourism in order to preserve it. Although this is highly unlikely to happen, there are a number of options being discussed in order to help protect it. Among these are requiring all tourists to be accompanied by licensed guides, which may begin as early as July 2017, and restricting the amount of time that you can spend in the citadel. At this point, nothing has been confirmed, but you should check the current status with a tour operator when making your plans.

Although many travelers day trip to Machu Picchu, an overnight in Aguas Calientes (the town below the site) lets you experience the ruins long after the day-trippers have left, and before the first train and tour groups arrive in the morning. ■TIP➜ When booking your return train, it's best not to do that for the same day you are flying out of Cusco, just to be safe.

GETTING HERE AND AROUND

There are two ways to get to Machu Picchu: by foot via a guided trek like the Inca Trail or by train to Aguas Calientes and then an official Consettur tourist bus that takes you to the famed ruins. The 20-minute bus ride offers hair-raising turns and stunning views of the Vilcanota Valley below. Rather than take the bus, you can also walk up to the ruins from Aguas Calientes, but it takes an hour and is uphill the whole way. You cannot drive yourself here. Trains to Aguas Calientes leave from Cusco's Poroy station, which is 20 minutes from the Plaza de Armas, or Ollantaytambo in the Sacred Valley, almost two hours northwest of Cusco.

BUS TRAVEL

If you don't plan on walking up to Machu Picchu (about an hour up the road from Aguas Calientes), you will have to catch a bus, easily identifiable by the Consettur name on the front. Consettur buses depart from the intersection of Imperio de los Incas Avenue and the Aguas Calientes River. Tickets cost US$12 one-way or US$24 round-trip and can be purchased in advance from the small kiosk across the street from the departure point with your passport. Although there are no assigned seats, tickets are issued with your name and ID on them. Buses leave every 10 minutes starting at 5:30 am. The park is open from 6 am to 5:30 pm. During peak season, lines for the first bus can get long, so it's recommended that you arrive by 5 am or earlier. If you're heading back to Cusco, take the bus back down at least an hour before your train departs. Note that the line for the bus back down can get quite long around lunch time, as many people have afternoon trains back to Cusco.

THE SKINNY ON MACHU PICCHU

DAY TRIPPING VS. OVERNIGHT

You can visit Machu Picchu on a day trip, but we recommend staying overnight at a hotel in Aguas Calientes. A day trip allows you about six hours at Machu Picchu, coinciding with the most crowded times. If you stay overnight, you can wander the ruins after most tourists have gone or in the morning before the bulk of them arrive. If you can, opt to spend two nights, one before visiting Machu Picchu so you can be on the first bus up to the ruins in the morning, and one after your visit to allow you time to recuperate especially if you hike Huayna Picchu.

BUYING A TICKET

In theory, Machu Picchu tickets can be purchased online with a Visa card (www.machupicchu.gob.pe) but this option rarely works as there are often technical difficulties with the website; it's advisable to purchase your tickets a month in advance. If you have your heart set on hiking Huayna Picchu, you need to contact a travel agency to purchase the ticket for you, at least 2–3 months in advance. If you arrive without an admission ticket, you must purchase one in Aguas Calientes at the **Centro Cultural Machu Picchu** (⊠ *Av. Pachacutec 103,* ☏ *084/211–196* ✉ *S/152, no credit cards* ⊙ *Daily 5:45 am–8:30 pm*). Purchase must be made with your passport and in person. There is no ticket booth at the ruins' entrance. If you are with a tour, the tickets are most likely taken care of for you. The ticket is valid only for the date it is purchased for so if you arrive in the afternoon and visit the ruins, then stay the night and want to return the next morning, you'll have to buy two tickets. The ruins are open from 6 am to 5:30 pm.

BEING PREPARED

Being high above the valley floor makes you forget that Machu Picchu sits 2,490 meters (8,170 feet) above sea level, a much lower altitude than Cusco. It gets warm, and the ruins have little shade. Sunscreen, a hat, and water are musts. Officially, no food or drinks are permitted, but you can get away with a bottle of water and snacks. Large packs must be left at the entrance. ■TIP➡ **You have to show your passport to enter—if you want it stamped with an image of the ruins, stop by the stand just past the exit.** The office at the entrance has a simple free map of the ruins.

PRACTICALITIES

A snack bar is a few feet from where the buses deposit you at the gate, and the **Belmond Sanctuary Lodge** has a US$40 lunch buffet open to the public. Bathrooms cost S/1, and toilet paper is provided. There are no bathrooms inside the ruins but you may exit and reenter to use them up to two times. After that, you may not reenter.

THE INCA TRAIL, ABRIDGED

Most Cusco tour operators market a two-day, one-night Inca Trail excursion. An Inca Trail permit is required and you must go with a licensed operator; book well in advance. The excursion begins at **Km 104**, a stop on the Cusco/Sacred Valley–Machu Picchu trains. All of the hiking happens on the first day, and you get to enter Machu Picchu through the Sun Gate and spend the night at a hotel in Aguas Calientes. The second day is a visit to the ruins.

TAXI TRAVEL

You can take a collectivo taxi or van from Cusco to Ollantaytambo. They depart daily from Pavitos street near the intersection with Avenida Grau. The trip to Ollantaytambo takes between 1½ to 2 hours and you'll need to arrive 30 minutes before your train departs.

TRAIN TRAVEL

Most Machu Picchu tour packages include rail tickets as well as bus transport between Aguas Calientes and Machu Picchu, admission to the ruins, and lodging if you plan to stay overnight. If you plan to go without a tour, it's an easy train ride from Ollantaytambo in the Sacred Valley to Machu Picchu (the train stops in Aguas Calientes, the town below the ruins). Most visitors board the train in Ollantaytambo, as trains leave more frequently from this station. We recommend taking the train from Ollantaytambo. It is technically possible to take the train from Cusco's Poroy station (which is a 20-minute taxi ride away from the Plaza de Armas) to Machu Picchu, but it is more convenient to take a taxi to Ollantaytambo and board a train there; taxis are quicker than the train and there are more train times available at Ollantaytambo. Two train operators serve Machu Picchu, long-standing PeruRail, which held a near monopoly over train travel from Cusco and Ollantaytambo to Machu Picchu for more than 10 years, and Inca Rail. ■TIP➔ Tourists are not permitted to ride the Tren Local, the less expensive cars intended for local residents only.

PERURAIL **PeruRail** is the longest-standing train operator and offers services from Cusco, Urubamba, Ollantaytambo, and Aguas Calientes. They operate three trains of different classes and offering different services. The least expensive train is the *Expedition*. The cars have comfortable seats and tables, with sky windows for a full peek at the Sacred Valley. The next step up is the *Vistadome*, whose cars have sky domes for great views, snacks and beverages included in the price, and the return trip includes a fashion show and folklore dancing. The luxury *Hiram Bingham* train provides a class of service unto itself (with prices to match). It leaves from Cusco's Poroy station, a 20-minute taxi ride from the Plaza de Armas, and will make a stop in Ollantaytambo if booked from there. The *Vistadome* and the *Expedition* trains depart from both Poroy as well as Ollantaytambo. There is also one *Vistadome* per day traveling to and from Urubamba, which also stops in Ollantaytambo.

Train ticket prices vary by season and time of day. A ticket on the *Expedition* costs between US$109 and US$149 round-trip from Ollantaytambo; a round-trip on the Vistadome from Ollantaytambo costs between US$121 to US$176. A round-trip ticket on the *Hiram Bingham* train costs US$875. One-way-only rates are higher as well.

A full train schedule is available on PeruRail's website, and timetable fliers can be picked up from the office in Cusco's Plaza de Armas.

PeruRail's service is generally punctual. Schedules and rates are always subject to change, and there may be fewer trains per day to choose from during the December to March low season.

In theory, same-day tickets can be purchased, but waiting that late is risky. Procure tickets in advance from PeruRail's sales office in the Plaza de Armas in Cusco; they are open every day, including weekends and holidays, from 7 am to 9:30 pm. You can also purchase tickets online or by phone. Note that trains that include stops in Urubamba tend to fill up quickly.

INCA RAIL **Inca Rail's** new trains allow for more frequent and easier travel from the Sacred Valley, specifically from Ollantaytambo to Aguas Calientes.

There are two types of tickets offered on Inca Rail: Executive Class, which costs between US$108 and US$145 round-trip, and First Class, which costs US$218 to US$242 round-trip and includes a cocktail, lunch and/or dinner, and fresh juices and teas. Coming with a group? Ask about chartering their Presidential Car, which includes welcome champagne, an open bar, a tasting menu, and an observatory lounge.

You can purchase tickets in Cusco at the Inca Rail office in the Plaza de Armas, or by phone. It is also possible to purchase with credit card at *www.incarail.com.*

Train Contacts Inca Rail. ⊠ *Ticket Office, Portal de Panes 105, Plaza de Armas* ☎ *084/581–860 office* ⊕ *www.incarail.com.* **PeruRail.** ⊠ *Ticket Office, Portal de Carnes 214, Plaza de Armas* ☎ *084/581–414 reservations* ⊕ *www.perurail.com.*

HEALTH AND SAFETY

Machu Picchu is a breath-catching 1,000 meters (3,300 feet) *lower* than Cusco. The Inca Trail, however, at its highest point reaches 4,200 meters (13,776 feet). To be on the safe side about altitude effects, locally known as *soroche*, get an ample intake of fluids and eliminate or minimize alcohol and caffeine consumption. (Both can cause dehydration, already a problem at high altitudes.) Smoking aggravates the problem. Some hotels have an oxygen supply for their guests' use, so be sure to ask if you are feeling ill. The prescription drug acetazolamide can help offset the alkalosis caused by low oxygen at high elevations, but bear in mind that you need to start taking it before you get to altitude and that, as a sulfa-based drug, it causes allergic reactions in some.

Tap water is generally not safe to drink. Stick with the bottled variety, *con gas* (carbonated) or *sin gas* (plain). The San Luis and Cielo brands are for sale everywhere.

Aguas Calientes is quite small, with an active police force and is very safe. Mudslides are an occasional problem from October to April, and severe rains in those months can occasionally (though rarely) interfere with train service.

RESTAURANTS

The town of Aguas Calientes near Machu Picchu has numerous restaurants, each offering its own (often not authentic) take on traveler-tested and approved plates like pizza, Mexican, Chinese, as well as typical Andean food. Recently Andean fusion, a gourmet play on traditional Peruvian high-mountain fare, has also found its way to this once gastronomically boring town. Restaurants are busiest between 1 and 3, and then again when dinner begins around 7 and tour groups tend to be gathering. Nevertheless, most places are open all afternoon if you wish to eat in between those times. Things typically start winding down around 9.

HOTELS

There is only one hotel at Machu Picchu itself and that is the Machu Picchu Sanctuary Lodge. It will cost you to stay there no doubt, as it's an exclusive property owned by the Belmond Company, the same people that operate PeruRail, but it's also the only place you can sit in a Jacuzzi and look at the Inca city long after the crowds have left. In Aguas Calientes you'll find many hostels and cheaper hotels lining the railroad tracks—that's not as down-at-the-heels as it first sounds: many rooms have great waterfront views. Aguas Calientes' budget lodgings are utilitarian places to lay your head, with a bed, a table, a bathroom, and little else. A handful of hotels offer surprising luxury for such an isolated location. Their rates can be shockingly luxurious, too.

Not even the top luxury hotels can meet their guests inside the train station anymore. They and all other hotels will meet you just outside the front gate and help you to and from the station with your bags. Lodgings keep surprisingly early checkout times. (Hotels free up the rooms for midmorning Cusco–Ollantaytambo–Machu Picchu trains.) Expect to vacate by 9 am, unless you are in one of the more expensive lodging choices, though this is less strictly enforced in the off-season. All hotels will hold your luggage if you're not leaving town until later in the day.

Many hotels keep the same official rates year-round but unofficially discount rates during the off-season of mid-September through May. It also pays to check the hotel website, if they have one, for current promotions. *Hotel reviews have been shortened. For full information, visit Fodors.com.*

WHAT IT COSTS IN NUEVO SOLES			
$	**$$**	**$$$**	**$$$$**
Restaurants under S/35	S/35–S/50	S/51–S/65	over S/65
Hotels under S/250	S/250–S/500	S/501–S/800	over S/800

Restaurant prices are the average cost of a main course at dinner or, if dinner is not served, at lunch. Hotel prices are the lowest cost of a standard double room in high season.

TOURS

There are no tour operators that are unique to Machu Picchu, and virtually all agencies that operate in Peru sell tours to the site. *For our recommendations, please see Chapter 1, Tour Operators and Chapter 5, Planning section. Note that, as entrance to Machu Picchu requires use of a licensed guide, you are best off organizing this ahead of time so you get the best quality.*

Continued on page 288

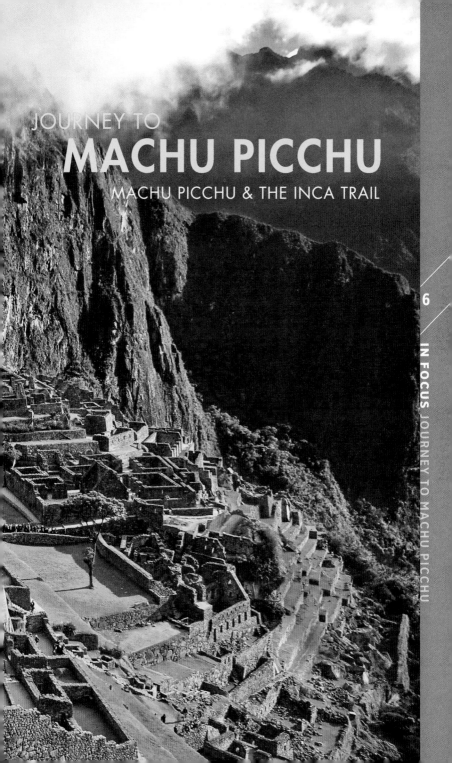

JOURNEY TO
MACHU PICCHU
MACHU PICCHU & THE INCA TRAIL

MACHU PICCHU & THE INCA TRAIL

The exquisite architecture of the massive Inca stone structures, the formidable backdrop of steep sugarloaf hills, and the Urubamba River winding far below have made Machu Picchu the iconic symbol of Peru. It's a mystical city, the most famous archaeological site in South America, and one of the world's must-see destinations.

The world did not become aware of Machu Picchu's existence until 1911 when Yale University historian Hiram Bingham (1875–1956) announced that he had "discovered" the site. "Rediscovery" is a more accurate term; area residents knew of Machu Picchu's existence all along. This "Lost City of the Inca" was missed by the ravaging conquistadors and survived untouched until the beginning of the 20th century.

You'll be acutely aware that the world has since discovered Machu Picchu if you visit during the June–mid-September high season. Machu Picchu absorbs the huge numbers of visitors, though, and even in the highest of the high season, its beauty is so spectacular that it rarely disappoints.

DISCOVERY

American explorer and historian Hiram Bingham, with the aid of local guides, came across the Lost City in 1911. Though the name appeared on maps as early as 1860, previous attempts to find the site failed. Bingham erred in recognizing what he had uncovered. The historian assumed he had stumbled upon

Vilcabamba, the last real stronghold of the Inca. (The actual ruins of Vilcabamba lie deep in the rain forest, and were uncovered in the 1960s.)

Bingham, who later served as governor of and senator from Connecticut, transported—some say stole—many of Machu Picchu's artifacts to Yale in 1912. Although they were intended to be on a short term loan, the artifacts did not begin to make their way back to Peru until 2011. They are now housed in the Museo Machu Picchu Casa Concha in Cusco.

In 1915, Bingham announced his discovery of the Inca Trail. As with Machu Picchu, his "discovery" was a little disingenuous. Locals knew about the trail, and that it had served as a supply route between Cusco and Machu Picchu during Inca times. Parts of it were used during the colonial and early republican eras as well.

Though archaeological adventuring is viewed differently now, Bingham's slog to find Machu Picchu and the Inca Trail was no easy feat. Look up from Aguas Calientes, and you still won't know it's there.

HISTORY

Ever since Bingham came across Machu Picchu, its history has been debated. It was likely a small city of some 200 homes and 1,000 residents, with agricultural terraces to supply the population's needs and a strategic position that overlooked—but could not be seen from—the valley floor.

New theories suggest that the city was a transit station for products, such as coca and hearts of palm that were grown in the lowlands and sent to Cusco. Exactly when Machu Picchu was built is not known, but one theory suggests that it was a country estate of an Inca ruler named Pachacutec,

which means its golden age was in the mid-15th century.

Historians have discredited the romantic theory of Machu Picchu as a refuge of the chosen Inca women after the Spanish conquest; analysis shows a 50/50 split of male and female remains.

The site's belated discovery may indicate that the Inca deserted Machu Picchu before the Spanish conquest. The reason for the city's presumed abandonment is as mysterious as its original function. Some archaeologists suggest that the water supply simply ran out. Some guess that disease ravaged the city. Others surmise it was the death of Pachacutec, after which his estate was no longer needed.

"INDIANA" BINGHAM

Hiram Bingham at Machu Picchu, 1912.

A globe-trotting archaeological explorer, which was an especially romantic figure in early 20th century America, Hiram Bingham was a model for the Indiana Jones character in the film *Raiders of the Lost Ark*.

Storage Houses

Guardhouse

EXPLORING THE RUINS

Everyone must go through the main entrance to have their ticket stamped. You have to show your passport to enter Machu Picchu—if you want it stamped, be sure to stop by the table on the right as you exit the site. From there you work your way up through the agricultural areas and to the urban sectors.

There are almost no signs inside to explain what you're seeing; booklets and maps are for sale at the entrance. As of July 1, 2017, you must purchase your ticket for either the morning shift (6 am–noon) or afternoon (noon–5:30 pm), and you must be accompanied by a licensed guide. You will have just four hours in the site from entrance to exit. If you purchase an entry to hike Huayna Picchu or Machu Picchu Mountain, you may stay in the site until 2 pm.

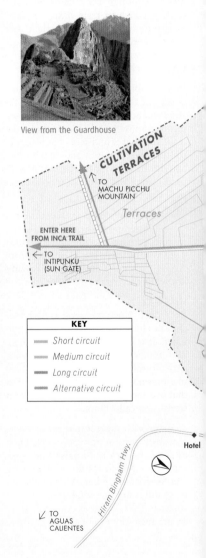

View from the Guardhouse

The English-language names to the structures within the city were assigned by Bingham. Call it inertia, but those labels have stuck, even though the late Yale historian's nomenclature was mostly offbase.

The Storage Houses are the first structures you encounter after coming through the main entrance. The Inca carved terraces into the hillsides to grow produce and minimize erosion. Corn was the likely crop cultivated.

The Guardhouse and Funeral Rock are a 20-minute walk up to the left of the entrance, and provide the quintessential Machu Picchu vista. Nothing beats the view in person, especially with a misty sunrise. Bodies of nobles likely lay in state here, where they would have been eviscerated, dried, and prepared for mummification.

The Temple of the Sun is a marvel of perfect Inca stone assembly. On June 21 (winter solstice in the southern hemisphere; sometimes June 20 or June 22), sunlight shines through a small, trapezoid-shape window and onto the middle of a large, flat granite stone presumed to be an Inca calendar. Looking out the window, astronomers saw the constellation Pleiades, revered as a symbol of crop fertility. Bingham dubbed the small cave below the Royal Tomb, though no human remains were found at the time of his discovery.

CULTIVATION TERRACES

TO MACHU PICCHU MOUNTAIN

Terraces

ENTER HERE FROM INCA TRAIL

TO INTIPUNKU (SUN GATE)

KEY

▬▬	*Short circuit*
▬▬	*Medium circuit*
▬▬	*Long circuit*
▬▬	*Alternative circuit*

Hotel

Hiram Bingham Hwy.

TO AGUAS CALIENTES

Main Gate

Temple of the Sun

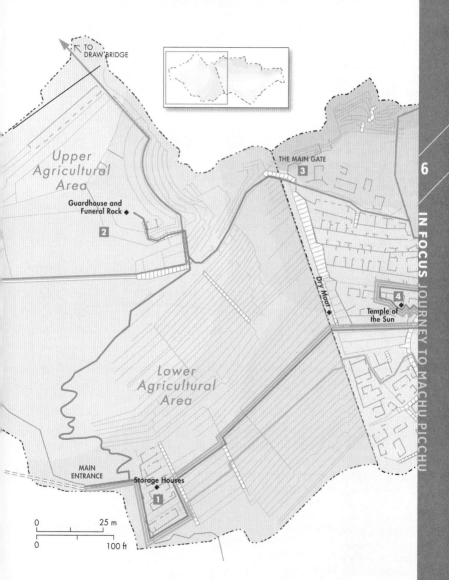

TO
DRAW BRIDGE

Upper
Agricultural
Area

Guardhouse and
Funeral Rock ◆

2

THE MAIN GATE

3

Dry Moat

Temple of
the Sun ◆

4

Lower
Agricultural
Area

MAIN
ENTRANCE

Storage Houses ◆

1

0   25 m

0   100 ft

Principal Temple

Three Windows

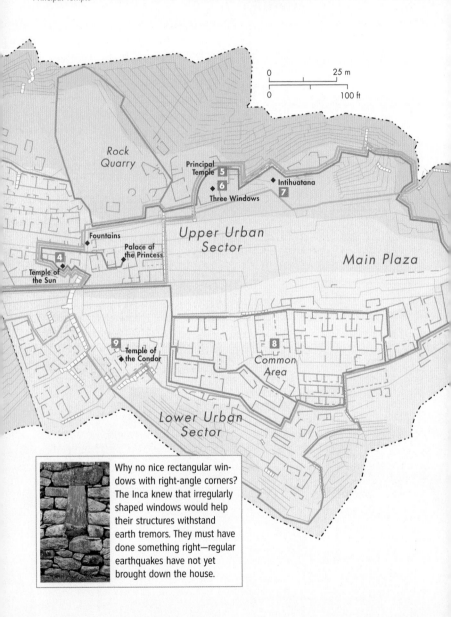

0   25 m
0   100 ft

Rock Quarry

Principal Temple **5**

6
Three Windows

◆ Intihuatana
7

◆ Fountains

Palace of the Princess

4
◆ Temple of the Sun

Upper Urban Sector

Main Plaza

9 ◆ Temple of the Condor

8

Common Area

Lower Urban Sector

Why no nice rectangular windows with right-angle corners? The Inca knew that irregularly shaped windows would help their structures withstand earth tremors. They must have done something right—regular earthquakes have not yet brought down the house.

7 Intihuatana

8 Common Area

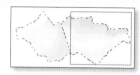

Sacred Rock

URBAN SECTOR

TO
HUAYNA PICCHU →

KEY
▬▬ Short circuit
▬▬ Medium circuit
▬▬ Long circuit
▬▬ Alternative circuit

Temple of the Condor.

9

Fountains. A series of 16 small fountains are linked to the Inca worship of water.

Palace of the Princess, a likely misnomer, is a two-story building that adjoins the temple.

The Principal Temple is so dubbed because its masonry is among Machu Picchu's best. The three-walled structure is a masterpiece of mortarless stone construction. A rock in front of the temple acts as a compass—test it out by placing your smartphone with compass app showing on top of it.

Three Windows. A stone staircase leads to the three-walled structure. The entire east wall is hewn from a single rock with trapezoidal windows cut into it.

Intihuatana. A hillock leads to the "Hitching Post of the Sun." Every important Inca center had one of these vertical stone columns (called *gnomons*). Their function likely had to do with astronomical observation and agricultural planning. The Spanish destroyed most of them, seeing the posts as objects of pagan worship. Machu Picchu's is one of the few to survive—partially at least. Its top was accidentally knocked off in 2001 during the filming of a Cusqueña beer commercial.

The Sacred Rock takes the shape in miniature of the mountain range visible behind it.

The Common Area covers a large grassy plaza with less elaborately constructed buildings and huts.

Temple of the Condor is so named because the positioning of the stones resembles a giant condor, the symbol of heaven in the Inca cosmos. The structure's many small chambers led Bingham to dub it a "prison," a concept that did not likely exist in Inca society.

EXPLORING BEYOND THE LOST CITY

Inca Bridge

Several trails lead from the site to surrounding ruins.

INTIPUNKU (SUN GATE)
You can take a 45-minute walk on a gentle arc leading uphill to the southeast of the main complex. **Intipunku**, the Sun Gate, is a small ruin in a nearby pass. This small ancient checkpoint is where you'll find that classic view that Inca Trail hikers emerge upon. Some minor ancient outbuildings along the path occasionally host grazing llamas. A two- or three-hour hike beyond the Intipunku along the Inca Trail brings you to the ruins of **Huiñay Huayna**, a terrace complex that climbs a steep mountain slope and includes a set of ritual baths.

INCA BRIDGE
Built rock by rock up a hair-raising stone escarpment, The **Inca Bridge** is yet another example of Inca engineering ingenuity. From the cemetery at Machu Picchu, it's a 30-minute walk along a narrow path.

HUAYNA PICCHU
The **Huayna Picchu** trail, which follows an ancient Inca path, leads up the sugarloaf hill in front of Machu Picchu for an exhilarating trek. Limited to 400 visitors daily at two entrance times (7–8 am and 10–11 am), tickets to the trail must be purchased at the same time as your entrance to Machu Picchu. The arduous, vertiginous hike up a steep, narrow set of Inca-carved stairs to the summit and back takes between 2 and 3 hours round trip. Bring insect repellent; the gnats can be ferocious.

MACHU PICCHU MOUNTAIN
Hiking up Machu Picchu mountain is another possibility. Tickets must be purchased at the same time as the entrance to the site itself. Entrance is allowed between 7 am and 10 am.

Huiñay Huayna

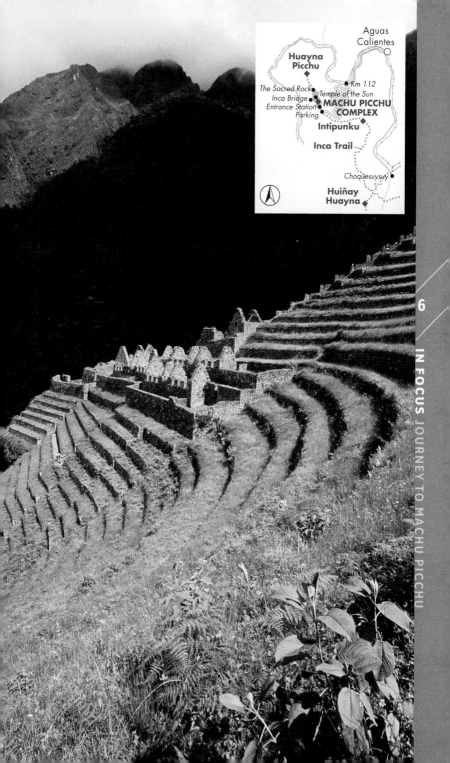

Aguas
Calientes

**Huayna
Picchu**

Km 112

The Sacred Rock
Inca Bridge   Temple of the Sun
Entrance Station   **MACHU PICCHU
Parking   COMPLEX**

Intipunku

Inca Trail

Choquesuysuy

**Huiñay
Huayna**

Walking the Inca trail through the Sacred Valley.

Inca Trail

Patallaqta

INCA TRAIL

One of the world's signature outdoor excursions, the Inca Trail (*Camino Inca* in Spanish) is a 43-km (26-mile) sector of the stone path that once extended from Cusco to Machu Picchu. Nothing matches the sensation of walking over the ridge that leads to the Lost City of the Incas just as the sun casts its first yellow glow over the ancient stone buildings.

Though the journey by train is the easiest way to get to Machu Picchu, most travelers who arrive via the Inca Trail wouldn't have done it any other way. There are limits on the number of trail users, but you'll still see a lot of fellow trekkers along the way. The four-day trek takes you past ruins and through stunning scenery, starting in the thin air of the highlands and ending in cloud forests. The orchids, hummingbirds, and spectacular mountains aren't bad either.

The impressive Puyupatamarca ruins.

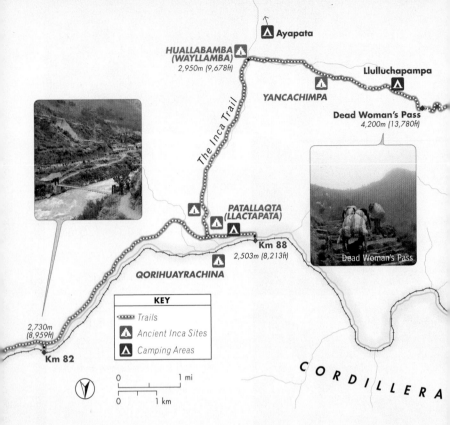

Ayapata

HUALLABAMBA
(WAYLLAMBA)
2,950m (9,678ft)

Llulluchapampa

YANCACHIMPA

Dead Woman's Pass
4,200m (13,780ft)

The Inca Trail

PATALLAQTA
(LLACTAPATA)

Km 88
2,503m (8,213ft)

Dead Woman's Pass

QORIHUAYRACHINA

KEY

••••••• Trails

Ancient Inca Sites

Camping Areas

2,730m
(8,959ft)

Km 82

C O R D I L L E R A

0   1 mi
0   1 km

INCA TRAIL DAY BY DAY

The majority of agencies begin
the traditional Inca Trail trek
at **Km 82** after a two-to-three-
hour bus ride from Cusco.

DAY 1
Compared to what lies ahead,
the first day's hike is a reasonably easy 11 km (6.8 miles).
You'll encounter fantastic ruins
almost immediately. An easy
ascent takes you to the first of
those, **Patallaqta** (also called
Llactapata). The name means
"town on a hillside" in Quechua,
and the ruins are thought to
have been a village in Inca
times. Bingham and company
camped here on their first
excursion to Machu Picchu.

You will see different types of
architecture there, both pre-Inca
and Inca.

At the end of the day, you arrive
at **Huayllabamba** (also called
Wayllamba), the only inhabited
village on the trail and your first
overnight. If the plan is to stay
at Aguas Calientes the third
night, you'll likely press on to
the campsite at Ayapata.

DAY 2
It's another 10-km (6.2 mile) hike,
but with a gain of 1,200 m (3,940
ft) in elevation. The day is most
memorable for the spectacular
views and muscle aches after
ascending **Dead Woman's Pass**

(also known as Warmiwañusca)
at 4,200 m (13,780 ft). The pass
is named for the silhouette created by its mountain ridges—th
resemble a woman's head, nose
chin, and chest.

A tricky descent takes you to
Pacaymayu, the second night
campsite, and you can pat
yourself on the back for completing the hardest section of
the Inca Trail. If cutting out the
third night, you'll likely go on
Chaquicocha.

DAY 3
Downhill! You'll cover the mos
ground today (16 km, 9.9 miles
descending down 1,500 meter

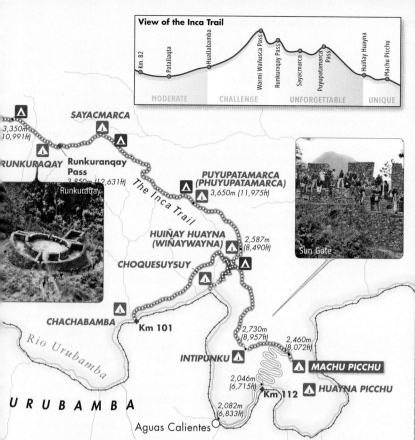

View of the Inca Trail

Km. 82 — Patallaqta — Huallabamba — Warmi Wañusca Pass — Runkuraqay Pass — Sayacmarca — Puyupatamarca Pass — Huiñay Huayna — Machu Picchu

MODERATE — CHALLENGE — UNFORGETTABLE — UNIQUE

SAYACMARCA
3,350m (10,991ft)

RUNKURAQAY
Runkuranqay Pass
3,850m (12,631ft)
Runkuraqay

The Inca Trail

PUYUPATAMARCA
(PHUYUPATAMARCA)
3,650m (11,975ft)

Sun Gate

HUIÑAY HUAYNA
(WIÑAYWAYNA)
2,587m (8,490ft)

CHOQUESUYSUY

CHACHABAMBA
Km 101

Rio Urubamba

INTIPUNKU
2,730m (8,957ft)
2,460m (8,072ft)

MACHU PICCHU
HUAYNA PICCHU

U R U B A M B A
2,046m (6,715ft)
Km 112

2,082m (6,833ft)
Aguas Calientes

to the subtropical cloud forest where the Amazon basin begins. There's some of the most stunning mountain scenery you'll see during the four days. The ruins of **Runkuraqay** were a circular Inca storage depot for products transported between Machu Picchu and Cusco.

You also pass by **Sayacmarca**, possibly a way station for priests traversing the trail.

Most excursions arrive by mid-afternoon at **Huiñay Huayna** (also known as Wiñaywayna), the third night's stopping point, at what may now seem a low and balmy 2,712 m

(8,900 ft). If heading on, you will have lunch here and keep going through the Sun Gate and down to Aguas Calientes to spend the night in a hotel.

There is time to see the ruins of **Puyupatamarca** (also known as Phuyupatamarca) a beautifully restored site with ceremonial baths, and perhaps the best ruins on the hike. At this point you catch your first glimpse of Machu Picchu peak, but from the back side.

DAY 4

This is it. Day 4 means the grand finale, arrival at Machu

Picchu, the reason for the trail in the first place. You'll be roused from your sleeping bag well before dawn to hike your last 6 km (3.7 miles) to arrive at the ruins in time to catch the sunrise. You'll be amazed at the number of fellow travelers who forget about their aching muscles and sprint this last stretch.

The trail takes you past the **Intipunku**, the Sun Gate. Bask in your first sight of the ruins and your accomplishment, but you'll need to circle around and enter Machu Picchu officially through the entrance gate.

PREPPING FOR THE INCA TRAIL

YOU MUST USE A GUIDE

You must use a licensed tour operator, one accredited by SERNANP, the organization that oversees the trail and limits the number of hikers to 500 per day, including guides and porters. (The two-day Inca Trail permits are separate.) There are some 200 such licensed operators in Cusco. *See Chapter 1, Tour Operators section and Chapter 5, Planning section for recommended guides.*

WHEN TO GO

May through September is the best time to make the four-day trek; rain is more likely in April and October and a certainty the rest of the year. The trail fills up during the dry high season. Make reservations months in advance if you want to hike then—weeks in advance the rest of the year. The trek is doable during the rainy season, but can become slippery and muddy by November. The trail closes for maintenance each February.

GETTING READY

Tour operators in Cusco will tell you the Inca Trail is of "moderate" difficulty, but it can be rough going, especially the first couple of days. You must be in decent shape, even if you choose to hire porters to carry your pack, which must be done at time of booking. The trail is often narrow and hair-raising and can be challenging for those with a fear of heights, although most will be fine. Be wary of altitude sickness. Give yourself two or three days in Cusco or the Sacred Valley to acclimatize.

WHILE YOU'RE HIKING

Food: All operators have their own chefs that run ahead of you with the porters, set up camp, and create culinary feasts for breakfast, lunch, and dinner. This will probably be some of the best camp food you'll ever have.

Campsites: There are seven well-spaced, designated campsites along the trail.

Coca Leaves: Coca leaves are a mild stimulant as well as an appetite and pain suppressant. You'll only need about one bag of your own (around S/1) for the trail. Take about 15 of them and pick the stems off. Stack them on top of each other and roll into a tight little bundle. Place the bundle between your gum and cheek on one side, allowing the leaves to soften up for about two minutes. Eventually start chewing to let the juice out. It's quite a bitter taste, but you'll feel better. All tour operators will also serve coca tea during snack breaks.

Bathrooms: Toilets could be a lot worse. You won't be able to sit down, but most flush and there are usually working sinks. You must bring your own toilet paper. Campsites all have toilets, but the trail itself does not. Many tour operators now travel with toilet tents.

Luggage: Pack as lightly as possible in a duffle bag. If you hire porters, current regulations limit the porter's load to 18 kg (39.6 lb) including his own gear. Agencies will typically offer a "half-porter" with a limit of 7 kg (15.4 lb) for your personal gear. Leave the rest of your belongings with your hotel.

PACKING LIST FOR THE INCA TRAIL

You've booked your Inca Trail trek and are ready to pack your duffel bag. But what should you bring? We've compiled a list of essentials here.

DUFFEL BAG PACKING LIST

- Large plastic ziplock bag to keep your things dry

- Waterproof hiking boots with ankle support (broken in)

- Sleeping bag (can be rented), liner, and pad (often provided by agency—ask what type)

- 2 hiking pants (ideally convertible to shorts)

- 2–3 breathable short sleeve and 2–3 long sleeve T-shirts

- 1 medium and 1 thick fleece

- Protective sun hat or baseball cap

- 1 light-weight packable down coat

- 1 set of warm comfortable clothes to change into at campsite or your sleepwear

- 1 set of thermals to sleep in

- 1 pair of warm sleeping socks

- 3–4 pairs of hiking socks

- 3 pairs of hiking liners (prevents blistering)

- Warm gloves and wool hat

- Comfortable sneakers or shoes (to change into at the end of the day—hiking sandals with socks work great as they can back up your shoes as well)

- Flips-flops (to shower on the last day)

- Toiletries, including prescription medicines, pain relievers, face and body wet wipes, feminine products, toothbrush and toothpaste

- 1 set of clothes to change into if you stay in Aguas Calientes after trek (you can get laundry done fast)

GEAR FOR DAY PACK

You will want a small day pack with back support to carry with you as you hike.

- Wear 1 set of layered clothing

- 1–2 water bottles or water bladder

- Hiking poles (can be rented or cheap wooden ones purchased; metal poles must have rubber tips)

- Hat and sunglasses

- Sunscreen and lip balm with sun protection

- Waterproof jacket and pants and backpack cover

- Bug repellent

- Toilet paper, tissues, and hand sanitizer

- Moleskin and Band-Aids for blisters

- Headlamp

- Camera

- Snacks (your operator will also provide snacks)

- Medicine (altitude sickness, antidiarrhea, etc.) and first aid kit

- Small towel

- Cash for tipping porters and staff

—Roxanne Chen

6

AGUAS CALIENTES

But for the grace of Machu Picchu discoverer Hiram Bingham, Aguas Calientes would be just another remote, forgotten crossroads. But Bingham's discovery in 1911, and the tourist boom decades later, forever changed the community. At just 2,050 meters (6,724 feet) above sea level, Aguas Calientes will seem downright balmy if you've just arrived from Cusco. There are but two major streets—Avenida Pachacutec leads uphill from the Plaza de Armas, and Avenida Imperio de los Incas isn't a street at all but the railroad tracks; there's no vehicular traffic on the former except the buses that ferry tourists to the ruins. You'll have little sense of Aguas Calientes if you do the standard day trip from Cusco. But the cloud-forest town pulses to a very lively tourist beat with hotels, restaurants, hot springs, and a surprising amount of activity, even after the last afternoon train has returned to Cusco. It also provides a great opportunity to wander around the high jungle, particularly welcome if you aren't going to make it to the Amazon. Although you won't see wildlife other than several species of hummingbirds, the flora (especially the many varieties of orchids) are worth taking a wander to see. You can find information about the easy and relatively flat walk to Mandor Waterfalls or the more intense hike up Putucusi Mountain at the local iPerú office. ■TIP→ Stay two nights in town if you can so you can be on the first bus to Machu Picchu, take as long as you like touring the ruins, and then relax and enjoy a hot shower after tramping around.

GETTING HERE AND AROUND

Trains to Aguas Calientes depart daily from Cusco's Poroy station, as well as from Ollantaytambo and Urubamba. In spite of its steep side streets, the city is small and easily explored by ambling about on foot. *See Planning above for train travel to Machu Picchu/Aguas Calientes.*

ESSENTIALS

Currency **Banco de Crédito.** ⊠ *Av. Imperio de los Incas s/n.*
Banco de la Nación. ⊠ *Av. Imperio de los Incas 540* ☎ *084/211–323.*

Mail **SERPOST.** ⊠ *Collaraymy L-13.*

Visitor Information **iPeru.** ⊠ *Av. Pachacutec Cuadro 1 s/n* ☎ *084/211–104* ⊕ *www.peru.travel/iperu.aspx.*

EXPLORING

Baños Termales. Aguas Calientes (literally "hot waters") takes its name from these thermal springs that sit above town, however, we don't recommend paying a visit. The baths are not as hot as you might like nor are they up to a high level of cleanliness. Rather than take home a souvenir you'd rather not, consider visiting El MaPi Hotel's spa which is open to nonguests. ⊠ *Top of Av. Pachacutec* ☎ *S/20.*

Mercado Artesanal (*Craft Market*). A warren of vendors' stalls lines the couple of blocks between the train station and the bus stop for shuttle transport up to the ruins. You can find some souvenirs here that you may not see in Cusco. The prices for crafts such as textiles, bags, and

Aguas Calientes

KEY

❶ *Restaurants*

① *Hotels*

magnets may or may not be cheaper (this largely depends on your negotiating skill and patience), but it's a great way to spend time before your train leaves. ✉ *Near train station.*

Museo de Sitio Manuel Chávez Ballón. The museum, dedicated to the history, culture, and rediscovery of Machu Picchu, sits on the way up to the ruins about 2 km (1 mile) from the edge of town at the entrance to the national park. Walking is the best way to get here. Plan on about a 30-minute hike. You'll get a bit more insight at the Casa Concha Museum in Cusco, where the repatriated artifacts returned from Yale University are being exhibited, but there are some interesting pieces on display here, some recovered as recently as 2004. Admission also includes entrance to a small but interesting botanical garden at the same site. ✉ *Puente de Ruinas, 2 km (1 mile) from Aguas Calientes* 🎫 *S/22.*

WHERE TO EAT

Pizza once took Aguas Calientes by storm, and while you can still order up a cheesy pie cooked in the traditional Peruvian wood-burning clay ovens, luxury hotel chefs have raised the bar, creating noteworthy Andean fusion cuisine, or as sometimes it's referred to, Novo Andino fare, a twist on traditionally bland Peruvian food of the high

Andes. The result is creative, gourmet dishes—sometimes influenced by Asian flavors and other times marked by typical California cuisine or European delicacies. You'll often encounter hawkers outside restaurants trying to lure people in, especially at the more generic, run-of-the-mill places where service tends to be on the slow side. Lunchtime is usually the busiest, with dinner being the time to enjoy a more tranquil meal.

INDIGENOUS TERMINOLOGY

Stick to the term "indigenous" (*indígena*) to describe Peru's Inca-descended peoples. Avoid "Indian" (*indio*), which is considered pejorative here, that is, unless you're describing an Indian restaurant. Likewise, among people in Peru, "native" (*nativo*) and "tribe" (*tribú*) conjure up images best left to old Tarzan movies.

$$ FRENCH 🍴 **Bistrot Le P'tit Paris.** Among the best restaurants in Aguas Calientes, this French-owned bistro offers a welcome change from Peruvian cuisine. The dining room and terrace are a bastion of peace and tranquillity, compared to restaurants on the main thoroughfare. **Known for:** raclette; chocolate volcano dessert; oasis of tranquillity. [$] *Average main: S/47* ✉ *Urb. Las Orquideas E-7* ☎ *084/613–693.*

$$$ PERUVIAN Fodor's Choice ★ 🍴 **Chullpi Machupicchu Restaurante.** Located along the tracks heading out of town, the kitchen at this rustic-chic restaurant turns out high-quality gourmet versions of Peruvian classics such as *ají de gallina* with quail eggs and *causa* with salmon tartare. The beautifully presented plates are on the small side, so it's best to order at least two courses, or try the tasting menu of 6, 10, or 15 courses. **Known for:** gourmet food; creative presentation; locally sourced ingredients. [$] *Average main: S/52* ✉ *Av. Imperio de los Incas 140* ☎ *084/211–350.*

$$ ITALIAN 🍴 **Incontri del Pueblo Viejo.** With an owner-chef that hails directly from Italy, you can be sure to find authentic Mediterranean fare here as well as housemade pasta and Peruvian cuisine. The large open space has comfortable seating with a cozy fireplace, and the fair prices, especially on the Italian wines, make this a great value. **Known for:** gourmet Italian food and wine; thin-crust pizza; tiramisu. [$] *Average main: S/42* ✉ *Pachacutec s/n* ☎ *084/211–193.*

$$ FRENCH FAMILY Fodor's Choice ★ 🍴 **Indio Feliz.** An engaging French-Peruvian couple manage one of the best restaurants in Aguas Calientes whose eclectic decor—think maritime kitsch—is worth a visit on its own. Quiche Lorraine, ginger chicken, and spicy *trucha a la macho* (trout in hot pepper and wine sauce) are favorites on the Peruvian-French fusion à la carte menu, but the reasonably priced (S/77) prix-fixe menu is the way to go, offering all the same options plus heavenly homemade bread. **Known for:** quantity meets quality; eclectic atmosphere. [$] *Average main: S/39* ✉ *Lloque Yupanqui s/n* ☎ *084/211–090* 🌐 *www.indiofeliz.com.*

$ CAFÉ 🍴 **La Boulangerie de Paris.** Paris's loss is Aguas Calientes' gain with the authentic French pastries served here, as well as coffee, sandwiches on house artisanal bread, quiche, and more. Eat in or take some of the delicious choices to go—the excellent boxed-lunch options are perfect for enjoying in Machu Picchu, and they open at 5 am so you can pick them up on the way to the bus. **Known for:** oustanding pastries; great coffee; boxed lunch. $ *Average main: S/10* ⊠ *Jr. Sinchi Roca* ☎ *084/211–398* ⊟ *No credit cards* ☉ *No dinner.*

$$ ✕ **Mapacho Craft Beer Restaurant.** Go for the awesome craft beer but stay
PERUVIAN for the delicious food. Faster pub fare to full meals, such as *lomo saltado*
Fodor's Choice (beef stir-fry), grilled chicken, and osso buco are served by friendly,
★ professional staff in a casual setting along the river. **Known for:** great craft beer; friendly, fast service; delicious varied menu. $ *Average main: S/40* ⊠ *Calle Imperio de los Incas 514* ☎ *984/759–634.*

$ ✕ **Palate Bistro.** Although this casual café is part of the Supertramp
AMERICAN backpacker hostel, the food is world-class with burgers, pizzas, and salads that are perfect for satiating an appetite forged by hoofing around Machu Picchu. Unlike many of the places lining the main streets in town, this pizza is worthy of the name, as are the burgers, both with a variety of tasty toppings available such as blue cheese and *jamon serrano* (dry-cured Spanish ham). **Known for:** hamburgers; pizza; rooftop bar. $ *Average main: S/24* ⊠ *Supertramp Eco Hostel, Calle Chaska Tika 203* ☎ *084/435–830* ⊕ *supertramphostel.com/ palate-bistro/.*

$$$ ✕ **Qunuq Restaurant.** A must experience for foodies, the culinary offer-
PERUVIAN ings by Sumaq Hotel's restaurant can easily hold their own against
Fodor's Choice anything the finest restaurants in Lima dish out, along with first-class
★ setting and the utmost in professional yet warm service. The menu features a fusion of flavors giving European dishes like ravioli an Andean slant by stuffing them with *aji de gallina* (creamed chicken) as well as infusing traditional Peruvian fare with international flair. **Known for:** gourmet experience; excellent service; outstanding river trout cebiche. $ *Average main: S/54* ⊠ *Sumaq Hotel, Av. Hermanos Ayar Mz. 1, L-3* ☎ *084/211–059* ⊕ *machupicchuhotels-sumaq.com/.*

$$ ✕ **Toto's House.** This long-standing tourist favorite has long tables
PERUVIAN set up in the center of its cavernous dining room to accommodate
FAMILY tour groups who come for the huge buffet lunch (S/72). Evenings are more sedate with grilled dishes like *trucha andina* (Andean trout), beef, or alpaca set to the entertainment of a folkloric music show. **Known for:** popular buffet lunch; traditional Peruvian dishes; tour groups at lunch. $ *Average main: S/50* ⊠ *Av. Imperio de los Incas 600* ☎ *084/211–020.*

$$ ✕ **Tree House Restaurant.** Perched high above the streets of Aguas Calien-
INTERNATIONAL tes, this small, wood-paneled restaurant serves some of the best international cuisine in town. Fresh, local ingredients are the backbone for such dishes like quinua salad with goat cheese, gnocchi with lamb ragout, and Thai brochettes. **Known for:** romantic setting; fresh local ingredients. $ *Average main: S/45* ⊠ *Calle Huanacaure 180* ☎ *084/435–849* ⊕ *www.thetreehouse-peru.com/indexEN.html.*

WHERE TO STAY

$$$$ 🛏 **Belmond Sanctuary Lodge Machu Picchu.** This upscale hotel at the
HOTEL entrance to Machu Picchu puts you closest to the ruins, a position for which you do pay dearly, but nowhere else can you sit in a hot tub, sip pisco sours or tea, and watch the sunset over the ruins after

One of the pros of spending a night at the Belmond Sanctuary Lodge: you can see Machu Picchu ruins and mountains from the property.

the last of the tourists depart each afternoon. **Pros:** prime location at ruins' entrance with no need to wait on line for bus; personalized service; all-inclusive; views of Machu Picchu. **Cons:** double the price of other luxury options in Aguas Calientes; small rooms and bathrooms. $ *Rooms from: S/4200* ⊠ *Entrance to Machu Picchu* ☎ *084/211–094 hotel, 01/610–8300 in Lima, 800/237–1236 in North America* ⊕ *www.belmond.com/sanctuary-lodge-machu-picchu* ⇄ *31 rooms* ⊚ *All meals.*

$$$
HOTEL
FAMILY

⛲ **Casa Andina Classic Machu Picchu.** Although the feel may be a bit more business than boutique, this is unquestionably the best bet for those wanting a comfortable, modern room and excellent service without a hefty price tag. **Pros:** comfortable modern rooms; friendly and attentive staff; adjoining rooms available. **Cons:** standard rooms near the train tracks; no frills; minimal design. $ *Rooms from: S/657* ⊠ *Prolongacion Imperio de Los Incas E-34* ☎ *511/213–9720* ⊕ *www.casa-andina.com* ⇄ *53 rooms* ⊚ *Breakfast.*

$$$$
HOTEL

⛲ **Casa del Sol Boutique Hotel.** The decor and the setting by the river are what make this hotel special—wood floors, beams, and window frames give rooms an elegant yet warm atmosphere, textile art adorns the walls, and stone-and-marble bathrooms blend perfectly with the natural environment outside. **Pros:** beautiful design and lush comfort; less expensive than other luxury options; suites have balconies with Jacuzzis. **Cons:** train noise from tracks just outside the hotel—ask for a riverside room. $ *Rooms from: S/1320* ⊠ *Av. Imperio de los Incas 608* ☎ *084/211–128* ⊕ *www.hotelescasadelsol.com* ⇄ *28 rooms* ⊚ *Breakfast.*

ALTERNATE ROUTE TO AGUAS CALIENTES

No time to trek or go to the Amazon? If time permits, another option is to take a bus or shared car from Cusco to Santa Maria and from there a taxi to Santa Teresa. (This can also be arranged via private car through an agency). You can overnight here at the EcoQuechua Lodge (*www.ecoquechua.com*), a fantastic opportunity to spend some real quality time in the cloud jungle. This clean and comfortable eco-lodge offers a little bit of paradise, and comes with gourmet dinner included. They can also arrange excursions such as treks, zip line, coffee tours, Machu Picchu, and more. From here a 20-minute taxi ride can take you to the *planta hidroeléctrica* (hydroelectric plant), from which you can hike an easy flat two- to three-hour trail into Aguas Calientes or hop on a PeruRail train (usually US$32 but can vary). Make sure to book your Machu Picchu entrance to include Huayna Picchu and you will get more than enough hiking to get a feel for the trek without the exhaustion. This also makes a nice extension after your Machu Picchu trip and you can take the train from Aguas Calientes to the hydroelectric plant if you have had enough of walking. Note: this excursion is not recommended during rainy season, as the roads to Santa Maria and Santa Teresa have sheer drop-offs and can become dangerous.

6

$$$ HOTEL 🏨 **El MaPi.** Designed to save travelers some dollars and cents without skimping on comfort and class, El MaPi delivers what it promises: simple but stylish rooms, top-tier service, and the same amenities you might expect from one of the more luxurious joints in town. **Pros:** great service; good value; spa with sauna and Jacuzzi open to non-hotel guests. **Cons:** not for those seeking a boutique hotel. [$] *Rooms from: S/704* ✉ *Av. Pachachutec 109* ☎ *084/211–011* 🌐 *www.elmapihotel.com* 🛏 *130 rooms* 🍴 *Some meals.*

$$$ HOTEL 🏨 **Hatun Inti Boutique.** Polished wood floors, white walls, and tasteful furnishings give this hotel an elegantly rustic and homey feel—it's ideal if you want something more upscale that feels like a boutique but don't want five-star prices. **Pros:** prime riverside location; lovely boutique feel; fireplaces; good value for the money. **Cons:** rooms on train side can be noisy; don't confuse this with sister property Hatun Inti Classic when booking online. [$] *Rooms from: S/704* ✉ *Av. Imperio de los Incas 606* ☎ *084/211–365* 🌐 *www.grupointi.com* 🛏 *14 rooms* 🍴 *Breakfast.*

$$$$ RESORT FAMILY Fodor's Choice ★ 🏨 **Inkaterra Machu Picchu Pueblo Hotel.** A five-minute walk from the center of town takes you to this stunning ecolodge, part of the Relais & Châteaux collection of hotels, made up of rustic yet elegant bungalows with exposed beams and cathedral ceilings, set in a minitropical cloud forest. **Pros:** natural setting; many activities, some included in the price; excellent restaurant with breakfast and dinner included; children under 12 stay free. **Cons:** expensive. [$] *Rooms from: S/1594* ✉ *Av. Imperio de los Incas s/n* ☎ *084/211–032, 01/610–0400 in Lima, 800/442–5042 in North America* 🌐 *www.inkaterra.com* 🛏 *83 casitas and villas* 🍴 *Some meals.*

$$$$ HOTEL Fodor'sChoice ★ ⊞ **Sumaq Hotel.** Upscale and comfortable, this five-star hotel sits at the edge of town alongside the Vilcanota River and offers all the amenities plus outstanding service with a smile. **Pros:** great restaurant with breakfast and lunch or dinner included; cooking class and tea time included; fantastic service. **Cons:** luxury costs. $ *Rooms from: S/1265* ✉ *Av. Hermanos Ayar Mz.1 L-3* ☎ *084/211–059, 01/628–1082 in Lima* ⊕ *machupicchuhotels-sumaq.com* ↝ *62 rooms* ⧫ *Some meals.*

$$ HOTEL ⊞ **Tierra Viva Cusco Machu Picchu Hotel.** Tierra Viva has quickly gained a reputation for creating hotels that offer a great balance between quality and price, and this one, standing above the river at the edge of town, is no exception. **Pros:** excellent quality for the price; great location; assisting local artisans. **Cons:** not as high design or comfortable as luxury options; rooms without a river view are not recommended. $ *Rooms from: S/390* ✉ *Av. Hermanos Ayar 401* ☎ ⊕ *www.tierravivahoteles.com* ↝ *42 rooms* ⧫ *Breakfast.*

SPAS

Otto's Spa. In a place where many of the massage therapists have little or no training, Otto and his staff are real gems—professional and talented. A massage is the perfect way to end a day of hiking around Machu Picchu, especially if you climb Huayna Picchu or hike the Inca Trail. At about S/100 for an hour massage plus foot bath and shower, this is truly a bargain. Call for an appointment if the spa is not open; walk-ins are welcome. ✉ *Av. Imperio de los Incas 602* ☎ *984/382–567.*

THE AMAZON BASIN

WELCOME TO THE AMAZON BASIN

TOP REASONS TO GO

★ **The River:** The Amazon River is a natural choice for adventures, but it is best explored on an organized tour.

★ **Wild Things:** Peru's Amazon Basin has more than 50,000 plant, 1,700 bird, 400 mammal, and 300 reptile species. Bring your binoculars.

★ **Sport Fishing:** Anglers can test their skills on dozens of river fish, including the feisty peacock bass.

★ **Nature Lodges:** Staying at a jungle lodge is almost obligatory when visiting the Amazon Basin if you really want to experience the rain forest.

★ **Cruising:** An Amazon River cruise to Pacaya Samiria National Reserve is the most comfortable, though expensive, way to explore this vast wilderness.

1 Madre de Dios. The national parks, reserves, and other undeveloped areas of the southern department of Madre de Dios are among the most biologically diverse in the world. Puerto Maldonado is an ugly frontier town that is mostly used by travelers as a place to fly into, board a boat, and head for a jungle lodge.

2 Iquitos and Nearby. The jungle-locked city of Iquitos has historic architecture, jungle flavors, and a city-on-the-edge attitude with almost 500,000 cooped-up residents. Amazon River cruises and remote nature lodges accessible only by boat offer wildlife observation and rain forest exploration. This region has more people, including indigenous cultures but less wildlife than Madre de Dios.

GETTING ORIENTED

The logistics of travel and isolation make it difficult to visit both the northern and southern Amazon regions— separated by 600 km (370 miles) at their nearest point— during one trip to Peru. The city of Iquitos is the jumping-off point for the northern Amazon; Puerto Maldonado for the southern Amazon tributaries, the Madre de Dios and Tambopata Rivers. Some 1,200 km (740 miles) and connecting flights back in Lima separate the two cities. The Manu Biosphere Reserve, on the upper Madre de Dios River, can be reached by land and river from either Cusco or Puerto Maldonado. Both the north- ern and southern regions are dotted with excellent jungle lodges and can also be experienced on a cruise.

7

Updated by David Dudenhoefer

Peru's least-developed region occupies some two-thirds of the country, an area the size of California. The *selva* (jungle) of the Amazon Basin is drained by the world's second-longest river and its countless tributaries. What eastern Peru lacks in human population it makes up for in sheer plant and animal numbers. There are lodges, cruise boats, and guides for the growing number of people who arrive to see a bit of the region's spectacular wildlife.

The northern Amazon is anchored by the port city of Iquitos—the Amazon Basin's second-biggest city after Manaus, Brazil, and the gateway to the rain forest. From Iquitos you can head out on an Amazon cruise or take a smaller boat to any of a dozen jungle lodges to experience the region's diverse flora and fauna.

Though this area has been inhabited by indigenous groups for more than 5,000 years, it wasn't "civilized" until Jesuit missionaries arrived in the 1500s. The Spanish conquistador Francisco de Orellana was the first white man to see the Amazon. He came upon the great river, which the indigenous people called Tunguragua (King of Waters), on his trip down the Río Napo in search of El Dorado. He dubbed it Amazonas after he was attacked by female warriors along the banks of the river.

Most of the indigenous tribes—many small tribes are found in the region: the Boras, Yaguas, and Orejones being the most numerous—have given up their traditional hunter-gatherer existence and now live in small communities along the backwaters of the great river. You will not see the remote tribes unless you travel far from Iquitos and deep into the jungle, a harrowing and dangerous undertaking. What you will see are people who have adopted Western dress and other amenities, but who still live in relative harmony with nature and preserve traditions that date back thousands of years. A common sight might be a fisherman paddling calmly on an Amazon tributary in his dugout canoe, angling to reel in one of its many edible fish.

The lesser-known southern Amazon region is traversed by one of the big river's tributaries—the Río Madre de Dios. Few travelers spend much time in Puerto Maldonado, the capital of Madre de Dios department, using the city instead as a jumping-off point to the Tambopata National Reserve. The Manu Biosphere Reserve is less accessible but more pristine, located on the upper Madre de Dios River between Cusco and Puerto Malonado. Nonetheless, Tambopata will not disappoint, and much of the jungle outside those protected areas still holds remarkable flora and fauna.

Both Madre de Dios and the Peruvian Amazon are impressive, and while they share much of the same flora and fauna, each region has its own attractions. The Amazon River is notable for its sheer size, and has species that you won't find in Madre de Dios, such as two types of freshwater dolphin and the giant water lily. Because it has fewer inhabitants, Madre de Dios has more wildlife, including rare creatures like the giant river otter, and large flocks of macaws that gather at its *collpas* (clay licks). Whichever region you visit, it will be a true adventure. Be prepared to spend some extra soles to get here. Roads, where they exist, are rough-and-tumble, so the preferred mode of transport is by boat. A dry-season visit is recommended—but, of course, "dry" is a euphemism in the rain forest. You'll most likely jet into Iquitos or Puerto Maldonado, respectively the northern and southern gateways to the Amazon, and climb into a boat to reach one of the region's famed nature lodges.

> ### RIBEREÑOS
>
> Peruvians in the Amazon region are a mix of native and Spanish ancestry. Ribereños (river people) live simple lives close to the land and water, much like their native ancestors. They depend on fish and crops for their survival. Not far from Iquitos are numerous small communities of the Amazon's original peoples. They include the Yagua, Bora, Huitoto, Ticuna, and Cocama, whose people generally speak very little Spanish. If you do visit a native village, be sure to take small bills (soles or dollars) to buy artisanal items.

PLANNING

WHEN TO GO

As you might expect, it rains plenty in the Amazon Basin, though that precipitation is somewhat seasonal. Although there's no true dry season in the Iquitos area, it rains less from June to October, when the river's level drops considerably. For Amazon cruises out of Iquitos, high-water season is best (December–June); tributaries become shallow during the dry months, making it hard to get to oxbow lakes.

The southern Amazon Basin has a pronounced dry season between May and October; and while most lodges are open year-round, some Manu lodges close between December and April. Tambopata sees a well-defined wet season/dry season; Manu's rainfall is more evenly dispersed throughout the year. Plan well in advance for trips in July and August, the peak tourist season, when some jungle lodges often take in large groups and cruise boats can be full. During the dry season, especially July and August, sudden *friajes* (cold fronts) bring rain and cold weather to Madre de Dios, so be prepared for the worst. Temperatures can drop from 32°C (90°F) to 10°C (50°F) overnight. No matter when you travel, bring a rain jacket or poncho.

GETTING HERE AND AROUND

AIR TRAVEL

LATAM flies to Iquitos four times daily from Lima. Peruvian Airlines has three flights daily, and Star Peru flies twice a day. Iquitos's Aeropuerto Internacional Francisco Secada Vignetta is 8 km (5 miles) from the city center. A taxi to the airport should cost around S/15. LATAM has two daily flights from both Lima and Cusco to Aeropuerto Padre Aldamiz, 5 km (3 miles) from the center of Puerto Maldonado. Avianca and Star Peru each have one Lima–Puerto Maldonado flight daily, which stop in Cusco. Star Peru usually has the best deals.

BOAT TRAVEL

Boats are the most common form of transportation in the Amazon Basin and the only way to get to most of the nature lodges, with the exception of those in the cloud forests of Manu. If you stay at any of this region's nature lodges, you will be met at the airport in Puerto Maldonado or Iquitos and transported to a riverbank spot where you board a boat that takes you to your lodge. Once there, most excursions will also be by boat. If you opt for an Amazon cruise, you'll spend most of your time on the water.

BUS TRAVEL

The only areas that can be reached by road are Puerto Maldonado and the buffer zone of Manu National Park. The windy road to Puerto Maldonado from Cusco is a 10-hour bus ride that only a backpacker on a very tight budget would take. Several tour companies offer slower, but incredible, overland trips from Cusco to Manu, including seven hours over rugged terrain via Paucartambo. The road plunges spectacularly from the *páramo* (highlands) into the cloud forest, eventually reaching the Alto Madre de Dios River in Atalaya, where travelers board boats to Manu lodges.

HEALTH AND SAFETY

MALARIA

There is no vaccine for malaria, but prescription drugs help minimize your likelihood of contracting this mosquito-borne illness. Strains of malaria are resistant to the traditional regimen of chloroquine. There are three recommended alternatives: a weekly dose of mefloquine; a daily dose of doxycycline; or a daily dose of Malarone (*atovaquone/proguanil*). Any regimen must start before arrival and continue beyond departure. Talk to your physician well in advance of your trip. Wear long sleeves and pants, and use a mosquito repellent containing DEET whenever you enter the jungle.

YELLOW FEVER

The Peruvian Embassy recommends getting a yellow fever vaccine at least 10 days before visiting the Amazon. Though recent cases of yellow fever have occurred only near Iquitos, southern Amazon lodges in Manu and Tambopata tend to be sticklers about seeing your yellow fever vaccination certificate. Carry it with you.

ZIKA

The Center for Disease Control (CDC) currently recommends that pregnant women should not travel to any area of Peru below 6,500 feet due to Zika virus. The entire Amazon Basin falls within this area. Women who plan to become pregnant should take all necessary precautions (DEET mosquito repellent, long sleeves and long pants, mosquito netting) and speak to their doctors before traveling to this region. Note that Zika is sexually transmitted so partners should also take precautions to avoid Zika. For more information, see ⊕ *wwwnc.cdc.gov/travel/notices/ alert/zika-virus-peru.*

EMERGENCIES

The **Policia Nacional de Turismo** (*0800–22221*), Peru's national police force, handles emergencies. At jungle lodges, minor emergencies are handled by the staff. For serious emergencies, the lodge will contact medical services in Puerto Maldonado, Cusco, or Iquitos.

RESTAURANTS

You can dine out at restaurants only in Iquitos and Puerto Maldonado, the Amazon Basin's two main cities, and even they have limited choices. Your sole dining option is your lodge if you stay in the jungle. The food, usually made of local ingredients, can be quite tasty.

HOTELS

Puerto Maldonado and Iquitos have plenty of small hotels. Iquitos also has a few nicer hotels geared to business travelers. Beyond those urban centers lie the region's jungle lodges, which are reachable only by boat and vary in degree of rusticness and remoteness. They range from tented camps, where rooms consist of a bed inside a screened enclosure under a roof, to upscale eco-lodges with swimming pools and Wi-Fi. Most have limited electricity, however, and only one offers air-conditioning. Showers are often refreshingly cool.

All nature lodges offer fully escorted tours, with packages from one to eight nights including guided wildlife-viewing excursions. They all provide mosquito nets and three meals. Most lodges quote rates per person, based on double occupancy, that include meals and transportation plus most tours, and many take so long to reach that the minimum stay is two nights. *The price ranges given for lodges in this chapter reflect the cost of one night's stay for two people, meals included.* All lodges accept soles and U.S. dollars for drinks and souvenirs. *Hotel reviews have been shortened. For full information, visit Fodors.com.*

WHAT IT COSTS IN NUEVO SOLES			
	$	$$	$$$	$$$$
Restaurants	under S/35	S/35–S/50	S/51–S/65	over S/65
Hotels	under S/250	S/250–S/500	S/501–S/800	over S/800

Restaurant prices are the average cost of a main course at dinner or, if dinner is not served, at lunch. Hotel prices are the lowest cost of a standard double room in high season.

TOURS

Although it's possible to see a bit of the jungle on a day tour from Puerto Maldonado or Iquitos, exploring the Amazon Basin on your own isn't recommended because the areas that you could reach tend to have degraded forest and few animals. If you want to see rain forest wildlife, book a tour with a company that owns one or more lodges located in remote, wild areas.

Amazon Conservation Association. This respected conservation organization protects vast expanses of tropical wilderness and has three biological research stations in pristine, private reserves near the Manu Biosphere Reserve or Tambopata National Reserve that few people visit. In recent years, the organization has built bungalows and begun operating tours that visit one or more research stations on 5- to 10-day trips that begin in either Cusco or Puerto Maldonado. Those tours offer excellent bird-watching and other wildlife encounters, and the profits support conservation. ⊠ *Washington* ☎ *202/871–3777* ⊕ *birding.amazonconservation.org* ✉ *From $625.*

Fodor's Choice ★ **InkaNatura Travel.** InkaNatura Travel runs two- to six-night nature tours to the Manu Biosphere Reserve or the Tambopata National Reserve with overnight stays at any of six nature lodges. These lodges are in some of the most pristine areas that travelers can visit in Peru, so the company's tours offer some of the best exposure to the wildlife of the Amazon Basin available anywhere. They have tours to both Manu and Tambopata out of Puerto Maldonado. ☎ *01/203–5000, 888/870–7378 U.S. and Canada* ⊕ *www.inkanatura.com* ✉ *From $420 per person.*

MADRE DE DIOS

Do the math: 20,000 plant, 1,200 butterfly, 1,000 bird, 200 mammal, and 100 reptile species (and many more yet to be identified). The southern sector of Peru's Amazon Basin, most readily approached via Cusco, is famous among birders, but any traveler will be impressed by the dawn spectacle of macaws and parrots gathered at one of the region's famed *collpas* (clay licks). Ornithologists speculate that the birds ingest clay periodically to neutralize toxins in the seeds and fruit they eat. Madre de Dios also offers a chance to see large mammals, such as capybaras (the world's largest rodent), monkeys, and giant otters. If the zoological gods smile upon you, you may even encounter a tapir or a jaguar. Animal and plant life abounds, but this is the least populated of Peru's departments: a scant 76,000 people reside in an area slightly smaller than South Carolina, and almost two-thirds of them are in Puerto Maldonado.

The southern Amazon saw little incursion at the time of the Spanish conquest. The discovery in the late 19th century of the *shiringa*, known in the English-speaking world as the rubber tree, changed all of that. Madre de Dios saw outside migration for the first time with the arrival of the *caucheros* (rubber men) and their minions staking out claims. The discovery of gold in the 1970s drew new waves of fortune seekers to the region, and you may see the deforestation they've caused from the air on flights between Cusco and Puerto Maldonado.

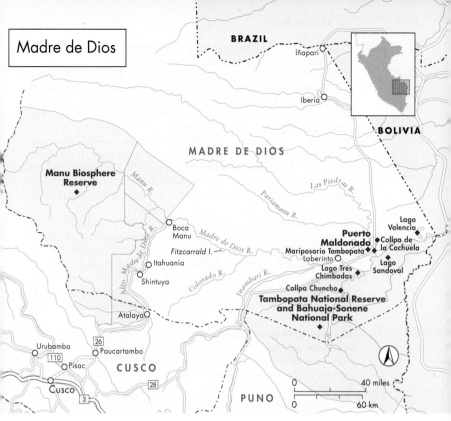

Madre de Dios

Tourism and conservation have triggered the newest generation of
explorers in the species-rich southern Amazon. Two areas of Madre
de Dios are of special interest. One is around the city of Puerto Maldonado, including the Tambopata National Reserve and the adjoining
Bahuaja-Sonene National Park. Easily accessible, they offer lodges amid
primary rain forest and excellent wildlife. Tambopata also serves sustainable agriculture purposes: some 1,500 families in the department
collect Brazil nuts from the reserve and surrounding forest, an economic
incentive to keep the rain forest intact, rather than cut it down. The
Manu Biosphere Reserve, directly north of Cusco, though more difficult
to reach, provides unparalleled opportunity for observing wildlife in
one of the largest virgin rain forests in the New World.

PUERTO MALDONADO

500 km (310 miles) east of Cusco.

The inland port city of Puerto Maldonado lies at the confluence of the
Madre de Dios and Tambopata rivers. The capital of the department
of Madre de Dios, it is a rough-and-tumble town with 60,000 people
and nary a four-wheeled vehicle in sight, but with hundreds of motorized two- and three-wheeled motorbikes jockeying for position on its
few paved streets.

The city is named for two explorers who ventured into the region 300 years apart: Spanish conquistador Juan Álvarez de Maldonado passed through in 1566; Peruvian explorer Faustino Maldonado explored the still-wild area in the 1860s, never completing his expedition (he drowned in the Madeira River). Rubber barons founded this youngster of Peruvian cities in 1912, and its history has been a boom-or-bust roller-coaster ride ever since. The collapse of the rubber industry in the 1930s gave way to decades of dormancy that were ended by the discovery of gold in the 1970s and the opening of an airport 10 years later. High prices for gold and steady improvements to the road there—part of a "highway" connecting Peru with Brazil—have brought an influx of settlers in recent years, which has been a scourge for the region's forests and indigenous peoples.

Nevertheless, Puerto Maldonado bills itself as the "Biodiversity Capital of the World," because it is the jumping-off point for visiting the Tambopata National Reserve and surrounding rain forest. ■TIP→ **Few travelers spend any time in the city, heading from the airport directly to docks, where they board boats to their respective jungle lodges.** Still, Puerto Maldonado has one decent hotel and can be used as a base for day trips. And this is the only place to use an ATM machine or visit a pharmacy.

GETTING HERE AND AROUND
It's fun to get around town in Puerto Maldonado's fleet of mototaxis, semi-open three-wheeled motorized vehicles with room for two passengers in the backseat. They patrol the main streets from dawn to well past dusk.

Airport Aeropuerto Internacional Padre Aldamiz. ⊠ *Ca. Faucett Km 7* ☎ *082/502–029.*

ESSENTIALS
Currency Banco de Crédito. ⊠ *Plaza de Armas, Jr. Daniel A. Carrion 201* ☎ *082/571–193.* **BBVA Banco Continental.** ⊠ *Plaza de Armas, Jr. Arequipa 216* ☎ *082/571–606.*

Mail SERPOST. ⊠ *Av. León Velarde 675* ☎ *082/571–088.*

Medical Hospital Santa Rosa. ⊠ *Jr. Cajamarca 171* ☎ *082/571–046* ⊕ *www.hospitalsantarosa.gob.pe.*

EXPLORING
Collpa de la Cachuela. A 20-minute boat trip up the Madre de Dios River from Puerto Maldonado takes you to this small *collpa* (clay lick) on the riverbank. Each day at dawn, more than 100 parrots, parakeets, and chestnut-fronted macaws gather here from 5:30 am to 8 am to eat the mineral-rich clay. ⊠ *10 km (6 miles) up Madre Dios River from town.*

FAMILY **Mariposario Tambopata.** Tambopata's Butterfly Farm has a large screened-in area full of jungle plants where dozens of colorful butterflies float above the leaves and flowers, and caterpillars hide amidst the foliage. There is information about the biology of those delicate creatures and a chamber full of cocoons, chrysalises, and recently hatched butterflies.

The Mariposario is located close to the airport and has a small restaurant that is a tranquil spot to for a drink or snack. ✉ *Av. Elmer Faucett* ✣ *Km 7, 150 meters before Padre Aldamiz Airport* ☎ *982/353–117* 🌐 *perubutterfly.com* 🎟 *S/18.*

Mirador Turístico (Obelisco). The southern Amazon has a skyscraper! The 35-meter (115-foot) strange tower, shaped like a prison-guard post and surrounded by sculptures, stands at the center of one of Puerto Maldonado's busier intersections. The top offers vistas of corrugated-metal roofs, an odd mix of buildings and, in the distance, the rain forest and river. ✉ *Fitzcarrald and Madre de Dios* 🎟 *S/3.*

Plaza Grau. The best view in Puerto Maldonado is from this grassy plaza one block northeast of the Plaza de Armas. The park is dedicated to Miguel Grau, a Peruvian naval officer in the 19th century. But the attraction isn't the bust of him erected there: rather it's the sweeping view of the Rio Madre de Dios, and the rain forest that lines its banks. ✉ *Jr. Bellinghurst at Jr. Arequipa.*

WHERE TO EAT AND STAY

$ PERUVIAN 🍴 **Burgos's Restaurant.** This funky, thatch-roofed restaurant has one of Puerto Maldonado's best kitchens. Start off with a maracuya sour (a cocktail made with passion fruit and pisco), then sink your teeth into *pollo con salsa de castañas* (chicken in a Brazil-nut sauce), *pescado en hoja* (fish fillet cooked in a leaf with cocona fruit, spices, and peppers), or *lomo* (grilled tenderloin) with *tacacho* (fried plantain balls) and *ensalada de palmito* (heart of palm salad). **Known for:** Amazonian specialties; grilled beef; river views. [$] *Average main: S/30* ✉ *Av. 26 de Diciembre 195* ☎ *082/573–653.*

$ PERUVIAN FAMILY 🍴 **Gustitos del Cura.** Conveniently located on the Plaza de Armas, this popular restaurant is a good spot for a light meal, dessert, or a fresh fruit drink. The menu includes a selection of sandwiches and salads, tamales, and chicken cordon bleu, but most people come for the homemade pastries and ice cream made with *castañas* (Brazil nuts) and local rain-forest fruits such as *aguaje* and *camu camu*. **Known for:** homemade ice cream; light meals; tropical fruit juices. [$] *Average main: S/19* ✉ *Jiron Loreto 258* ☎ *082/572–175* 💳 *No credit cards* 🕒 *Closed Wed.*

$ PERUVIAN 🍴 **Maracuyeah.** It doesn't look like much, but this bamboo-and-wood building on the bank of the Madre de Dios River is a popular spot with locals, especially at sunset. The menu is limited, and people tend to share dishes like *lomo fino* (tenderloin strips sautéed with onions, garlic, and a splash of pisco) served with cassava fries. **Known for:** sunset viewing; typical Peruvian food; loud music. [$] *Average main: S/22* ✉ *Puerto Capitanía, 142 26 de Diciembre* ☎ *993/358–757* 💳 *No credit cards.*

$ HOTEL 🏨 **Hotel Cabaña Quinta.** This hotel (once a tranquil spot with wooden bungalows) has undergone major expansion that has diminished its charm, but it still has Puerto Maldonado's second-best accommodations. **Pros:** central location; quiet; free airport transfers. **Cons:** basic rooms. [$] *Rooms from: S/200* ✉ *Jr. Moquegua 422* ☎ *082/571–045* 🌐 *www.hotelcabanaquinta.com* 🛏 *65 rooms* 🍽 *Breakfast.*

7

$$ HOTEL 🏨 **Wasaí Maldonado Lodge.** Nestled in a patch of rain forest one block from the Plaza de Armas, the Wasaí Maldonado offers the best accommodation in town. **Pros:** river views; jungle setting; good restaurant; free airport transfers. **Cons:** older bungalows can be musty. [$] *Rooms from: S/280* ✉ *Jr. Billinghurst at Jr. Arequipa* ☎ *01/436–8792, 082/572–290* 🌐 *wasai.com* 🛏 *28 rooms* 🍴 *Breakfast.*

TAMBOPATA NATIONAL RESERVE AND BAHUAJA-SONENE NATIONAL PARK

5 km (3 miles) south of Puerto Maldonado.

The lowland rain forests, rivers, oxbow lakes, and palm swamps that surround Puerto Maldonado hold a wealth of colorful creatures—from blue-and-gold macaws to red howler monkeys to iridescent blue morpho butterflies. Much of that wilderness lies within protected areas, indigenous territories, and Brazil-nut concessions, but illegal mining and deforestation by farmers and ranchers destroy vast areas of rain forest here each year. Ecotourism offers an economic alternative to that destruction, and the nature lodges scattered around the Tambopata National Reserve protect significant expanses of rain forest in private reserves, which provide their guests with almost constant exposure to the wonders of tropical nature.

GETTING HERE AND AROUND

Tambopata jungle lodges are possibly the easiest places in the world to experience the Amazon rain forest. They are much more accessible—and affordable—than those in the Manu Biosphere Reserve, Madre de Dios's other ecotourism area. And Tambopata is no poor man's Manu either—its numbers and diversity of wildlife are very impressive. A half-hour flight from Cusco takes you to Puerto Maldonado, the Tambopata jumping-off point. The closest lodges are less than an hour by boat down the Madre de Dios River, but the best lodges for wildlife-watching take anywhere from two to four hours to reach. Some of the lodges offer two-night packages, but a three-night stay is really the least you should spend in this area, and if you really want to see animals, you should book a five-day trip.

ESSENTIALS

TOURS **Amazon Conservation Association.** This respected conservation organization protects vast expanses of wilderness in the Peruvian Amazon and has three biological research stations near the Manu Biosphere Reserve and Tambopata National Reserve. In recent years, the association has built bungalows for tourists, and begun operating bird-watching tours that visit one or more research stations on 5- to 10-day trips. Those tours are opportunities to see all kinds of wildlife, and the profits support conservation. ☎ *202/871–3777 in U.S.* 🌐 *birding.amazonconservation.org* 🎫 *From $650.*

Rainforest Expeditions. The Tambopata experts, Rainforest Expeditions runs three- to seven-day nature tours to lodges near or in the Tambopata National Reserve, with accommodations at one or more of the company's three lodges: the Posada Amazonas, Refugio Amazonas, and Tambopata Research Center. ✉ *Av. Aeropuerto, Km 6, La Joya, Puerto Maldonado* ☎ *01/719–6422, 877/231–9251 in U.S. and Canada* 🌐 *www.perunature.com* 🎫 *From $444.*

Continued on page 313

THE PERUVIAN AMAZON

by Doug Wechsler

Green-winged Macaw (*Ara chloroptera*) foraging high in rain forest canopy.

An observant naturalist living in the Peruvian Amazon can expect to see something new and exciting every day in his or her life. To the casual traveler much of this life remains hidden at first but reveals itself with careful observation.

Western Amazonia may be the most biologically diverse region on earth. The areas around Puerto Maldonado and Iquitos are two of the best locales to observe this riot of life.

In the Tambopata Reserve, for example, 620 species of birds and more than 1,200 species of butterflies have been sighted within a few miles of one eco-lodge. To put that into perspective, only about 700 species of birds and 700 species of butterflies breed in all of North America. Within the huge Manu National Park, which includes part of the eastern slope of the Andes, about 1/10 of the world's bird species can be sighted. A single tree can harbor the same number of ant species as found in the entire British Isles. A single hectare (2.4 acres) of forest might hold nearly 300 species of trees.

This huge diversity owes itself to ideal temperatures and constant moisture for growth of plants and animals and to a mixture of stability and change over the past several million years. The complex structure of the forest leads to many microhabitats for plants and animals. The diversity of plants and animals is overwhelming and the opportunity for new observations is limitless.

STARS OF THE AMAZON

Pink River Dolphin: The long-snouted pink river dolphin enters shallow waters, flooded forest, and even large lakes. Unlike the gray dolphin of river channels, this species rarely jumps out of the water.

Eats: Fish. **Weighs:** 350 lbs. **Myth:** Often blamed for pregnancies when father is unknown.

Red-and-Green Macaw: The loud, raucous shrieks first call attention to red-and-green macaws, the largest members of the parrot family in the Amazon. Clay licks near a number of jungle lodges in Madre de Dios are great places to observe these spectacular birds.

Eats: Seeds of trees and vines. **Weighs:** 3 lbs.
Length: 3 ft. **Odd habit:** Consumes clay from steep banks.

Hoatzin: The clumsy-flying, chicken-sized Hoatzin sports a long frizzled crest and bare blue skin around the eye, suggesting something out of the Jurassic. Its digestive system features a fermentation chamber and is more bovine than avian.

Eats: Leaves, especially arum. **Weighs:** 1.8 lbs.
Unusual feature: Nestlings can climb with claws on their wings. **Favorite Hangout:** Trees and shrubs in swampy vegetation near lakes.

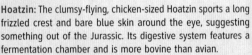

Squirrel Monkey: The small, active squirrel monkeys live in groups of 20 to 100 or more. These common monkeys can be distinguished by a black muzzle and white mask.

Eats: Large insects and fruit. **Weighs:** 2 lbs.
Favorite Hangout: Lower and mid-levels of vine-tangled forest especially near rivers and lakes. **Associates:** Brown capuchin monkeys often hang out with the troop.

Red Howler Monkey: A loud, long, deep, roaring chorus from these large, sedentary, red-haired monkeys announces the coming of dawn, an airplane, or a rainstorm. The swollen throat houses an incredible vocal apparatus.

Eats: Leaves and fruits. **Weighs:** 8 to 23 lbs.
Favorite Hangout: Tree tops and mid-levels of forest.
Unfortunate trait: They will urinate and defecate on you if you walk beneath them.

Three-toed Sloth: This slow-moving, upside down ball of fur is easiest to spot in tree crowns with open growth like cecropias. The dark mask and three large claws on the hands distinguish it from the larger two-toed sloth.

Eats: Leaves. **Weighs:** 5 to 11 lbs. **Favorite Hangout:** Tree tops and mid-levels of forest. **Unusual habit:** Sloths climb to the ground once a week to move their bowels.

Cecropia Tree: The huge, multi-lobed leaves, open growth form, and thin light-colored trunks make cecropias among the most distinctive Amazonian trees. Cecropias are the first trees to shoot up when a forest is cut or a new river island is formed. Their long finger-like fruits are irresistible to birds.

Height: Up to 50 ft. or more. **Bark:** Has bamboo-like rings. **Attracts:** Toucans, tanagers, bats, monkeys, sloths. **Relationships:** The hollow stems house stinging ants that protect the tree—beware.

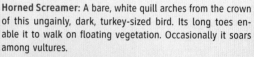

Horned Screamer: A bare, white quill arches from the crown of this ungainly, dark, turkey-sized bird. Its long toes enable it to walk on floating vegetation. Occasionally it soars among vultures.

Eats: Water plants. **Weighs:** up to 7 lbs. **Favorite Hangout:** Shores of lagoons and lakes. **Relatives:** Screamers are related to ducks and geese—who would have guessed?

Russet-backed Oropendola: What the yellow tailed, crow-sized, oropendola lacks in beauty, it makes up for in its liquid voice. The remarkable three-foot long woven nests dangle in groups from an isolated tree—protection from monkeys.

Eats: Insects and fruit. **Favorite Hangout:** Forest near clearings and rivers. **Look for:** Flocks of hundreds going to and from roosting islands in the river at dusk and dawn.

Giant Amazon Water Lily: This water lily has leaves up to 7 ft. across and 6–12 inch white or pink flowers that bloom at night. The edges of the leaves bend upward. Leaf stems grow with the rising flood.

Length: Stems up to 20 ft. **Eaten by:** Fish eat the seeds. **Favorite Hangout:** River backwaters, oxbow lakes. **Sex changes:** Female parts flower the first night, then the flower turns pink and the male parts open.

TIPS:

Don't expect all those species to come out and say hello! The Amazon's great biodiversity is made possible by the jungle's sheltering, almost secretive nature. Here are tips to help train your eye to see through nature's camouflage.

1. Listen for movement. Crashing branches are the first clue of monkeys, and rustling leaves betray secretive lizards and snakes.

2. Going upstream on the river means your boat will stay steady close to shore—where all the wildlife is.

3. Look for birds in large mixed-species flocks; stay with the flock while the many birds slowly reveal themselves.

4. Concentrate your observation in the early morning and late afternoon, and take a midday siesta to save energy for night-time exploration.

5. Wear clothes that blend in with the environment. Exception: hummingbird lovers should wear shirts with bright red floral prints.

6. Train your eye to pick out anomalies—what might, at first, seem like an out-of-place ball of debris in the tree could be a sloth.

7. At night, use a bright headlamp or hold a flashlight next to your head to spot eye-shine from mammals, nocturnal birds, frogs, boas, moths, and spiders.

8. Crush leaves and use your nose when getting to know tropical plants.

Reserva Amazonica canopy walkway.

Wasaí Lodges and Expeditions. With an eco-lodge and a camp on the Tambopata River and a hotel in Puerto Maldonado, Wasaí is able to offer tours that visit this area's two most spectacular spots: the Copa Chuncho and Lago Sandoval. ⊠ *Jr. Billinghurst s/n, Puerto Maldonado* 🕾 *01/436–8792* ⊕ *wasai.com* ✆ *From $384.*

EXPLORING

Fodor'sChoice **Tambopata National Reserve and Bahuaja-Sonene National Park.** A vast
★ expanse of protected wilderness stretches eastward from Puerto Maldonado to Bolivia and southward all the way into the Andean foothills. Its forests, rivers, palm swamps, and oxbow lakes are home to hundreds of bird and butterfly species, monkeys, tarantulas, turtles, and countless other jungle critters. This amazing natural diversity can be experienced from any of a dozen nature lodges scattered along the Madre de Dios River, the Tambopata River,which flows into the Madre de Dios at Puerto Maldonado, or the more distant Heath River.

Together, the contiguous Tambopata National Reserve and Bahuaja-Sonene National Park protect 3.8 million acres: an area the size of Connecticut. Several indigenous Ese'eja communites border the park; "Bahuaja" and "Sonene" are the Ese'Eja names for the Tambopata and Heath rivers, respectively. The Río Heath forms Peru's southeastern boundary with neighboring Bolivia, and the former Pampas de Río Heath Reserve, along the border, is now incorporated into Bahuaja-Sonene. It includes a looks-out-of-place "pampas" ecosystem that resembles an African savannah more than the lush Amazon forest that borders it.

Peru collaborates on conservation with Bolivia, whose adjoining Madidi National Park forms a vast, cross-border protected area that covers 7.2 million acres. Only environmentally friendly activities are permitted in Tambopata. In addition to participating in tourism, local communities collect *castañas,* or Brazil nuts, from the forest floor, and *aguaje* palm fruit in the swampland.

Elevations here range from 500 meters (1,640 feet) to a lofty 3,000 meters (9,840 feet), providing fertile habitat for an astounding diversity of animals and plants. The area holds a world record in the number of butterfly species (1,234). ■TIP➜ These protected areas contains Peru's largest collpas, or clay licks, which are visited by more than a dozen parrot, parakeet, and macaw species each morning. They congregate at dawn to eat the mineral-rich clay in the steep riverbank. ⊠ *Puerto Maldonado* 🕾 *082/573–278.*

Collpa Chuncho. The largest *collpa ,*or clay lick, in this region is located in Bahuaja-Sonene National Park, behind an island on the Tambopata River. On any given morning, hundreds of parrots, parakeets, and macaws congregate here to eat the clay. The action starts at the break of dawn, when flocks of parakeets begin to arrive. They are followed by several parrot species and five macaw species, which first gather in the treetops and wait for a moment when it seems safe to descend to the clay lick. When they do, it is an amazing sight. Collpa Chuncho can only be visited on excursions from various lodges on the Tambopata River. You'll also see other wildlife along the river on the trip here. ⊠ *Tambopata River, 122 km (76 miles) southwest of town, Puerto Maldonado.*

7

DID YOU KNOW?

Walking above the Madre de Dios Preserve, you are walking above one of the world's most diverse bird habitats. More species live here than in all of North America.

Fodor's Choice ★ **Lago Sandoval.** Changes in the course of Amazon tributaries have created countless oxbow lakes, which are formed when the riverbed shifts and the abandoned bend fills with water. Lago Sandoval, created by the Madre de Dios River, lies just inside the Tambopata National Reserve, a short trip form Puerto Maldonado. It is a lovely sight, hemmed with lush jungle and a wall of *aguaje* palms on one end. It is also an ideal spot for wildlife-watching. Herons, egrets, kingfishers, and other waterfowl hunt along its edges; several species of monkeys forage in the lakeside foliage; and chestnut-fronted macaws fly squawking overhead. A family of elusive giant otters lives in Lake Sandoval, making it one of the few places you can hope to see that endangered species. The lake is a 30-minute boat ride east from Puerto Maldonado. Once you disembark, there's a flat-but-muddy 3-km (1.8-mi) hike to a dock in the *aguaje* palm swamp from where you'll be rowed to the actual lake. Unfortunately, Sandoval is very popular, so you'll see plenty of tourists on the trail and lake. ■ **TIP→ Fewer people visit the lake in the afternoon, but it is best experienced by spending a night or two at the Sandoval Lake Lodge.** ✉ *14 km (9 miles) east of Puerto Maldonado, Puerto Maldonado.*

Lago Tres Chimbadas. This oxbow lake, a short hike from the Tambopata River, is a great place to see wildlife, including the endangered giant river otter. It is also home to side-necked turtles, hoatzins, sun grebes, jacanas, and dozens of other bird species. Its dark waters hold black caimans (reptiles that resemble small alligators) and a plethora of piranhas, so try to resist any urge you have to go for a swim. Most people visit Tres Chimbadas on an early morning excursion from the nearby Posada Amazonas. ✉ *42 km (26 miles) southeast of town, Puerto Maldonado.*

7

WHERE TO STAY

Eco-lodges in this area are reached by a combination of bus and boat and range from the jungle luxury of Inkaterra's Reserva Amazónica to the rustic Tambopata Research Center, deep inside the Tambopata National Reserve. Rates for all lodges include transportation, bilingual nature guides, three meals per day, and varied excursions. The Corto Maltes, Hacienda Concepción, and Reserva Amazónica are the region's most accessible lodges. They lie less than an hour down the Madre de Dios River from Puerto Maldonado, whereas the Sandoval Lake Lodge requires an additional 90-minute hike. The next closest is Posada Amazonas, which is two hours from Puerto Maldonado, up the Tambopata River. The rest require boat trips ranging from three to five hours. Whichever lodge you choose, you will be met at the Puerto Maldonado Airport and transported to and from the lodge by bus and boat.

$$$$ RESORT FAMILY 🏨 **Corto Maltes Amazonia.** A short boat ride down the Madre de Dios River from Puerto Maldonado, this lodge provides an affordable introduction to the rain forest and easy access to beautiful Lago Sandoval. **Pros:** good value; spacious, private bungalows; pool; easy to reach. **Cons:** less of a jungle experience than the remote lodges. [$] *Rooms from: S/945* ✉ *Madre de Dios River, 10 km (6 miles) east of Puerto Maldonado* ☎ *082/573–831* 🌐 *www.cortomaltes-amazonia.com* 🛏 *27 bungalows* 🍴 *All meals.*

CLOSE UP

Jungle Days

The knock at the door comes early. "*¡Buenos días!* Good morning!" It's 5 am and your guide is rousing you for the dawn excursion to the nearby *collpa de guacamayos.* He doesn't want you to miss the riotous, colorful spectacle of hundreds of parrots and macaws descending to the vertical clay lick to ingest mineral-rich earth. Roll over and go back to sleep? Blasphemy! You're in the Amazon.

A stay at any of the remote Iquitos or Madre de Dios lodges is not for the faint of heart. You'll need to gear up for a different type of vacation experience. Relaxing and luxuriating it will not be, although some facilities are quite comfortable. Your days will be packed with activities: bird- and wildlife-watching, boat trips, rain-forest hikes, visits to indigenous communities, kayaking, and so on. You'll be with guides from the minute you're picked up in Iquitos, Puerto Maldonado, or Cusco. Most lodges hire top-notch guides who know their areas well, and you'll be forever amazed at their ability to spot that camouflaged howler monkey from a hundred paces.

The lodge should provide mosquito netting and sheets or blankets, and some type of lantern for your room. (Don't expect electricity.) But check the lodge's website, or with your tour operator, for a list of what to bring and what the lodge provides. Your required inventory will vary proportionally by just how much you have to rough it. Pack sunscreen, sunglasses, insect repellent containing DEET, a hat, hiking boots, sandals, light shoes, a waterproof bag, and a flashlight. Also, a light, loose-fitting, long-sleeve shirt and equally loose-fitting long trousers and socks are musts for the evening when the mosquitoes come out. Carry your yellow fever vaccination certificate and prescription for malaria prevention, plus an extra supply of any medicine you might be taking. Bring along antidiarrheal medication, too. You'll need a small day-pack for the numerous guided hikes. Also bring binoculars and a camera, as well as plastic bags to protect your belongings from the rain and humidity. Everything is usually included in the package price, though soft drinks, beer, wine, and cocktails carry a hefty markup.

Few things are more enjoyable at a jungle lodge than dinner at the end of the day. You'll dine family-style around a common table, discussing the day's sightings, comparing notes well into the evening, knowing full well there will be another 5 am knock in the morning.

—By Jeffrey Van Fleet

$$$$ RESORT 🏨 **Hacienda Concepción.** Owned by Inkaterra, Hacienda Concepción is a good option for travelers who want to experience the rain forest in comfort or are short on time. **Pros:** easy to reach; comfortable, screened rooms; near Lago Sandoval. **Cons:** less wildlife than more remote lodges; can hear neighbors from bungalows. [$] *Rooms from: S/1202* ✉ *20-min boat trip east of Puerto Maldonado, Puerto Maldonado* ☎ *800/442–5042 toll-free in U.S. and Canada, 808/101–2224 toll-free in U.K., 01/610–0400 in Peru* 🌐 *www.inkaterra.com* 🛏 *6 rooms, 19 bungalows* 🍴 *All meals.*

$$$$ RESORT Fodor'sChoice ★ **Heath River Wildlife Center.** The spacious screened bungalows at this InkaNatura-owned lodge are among the most comfortable accommodations in Madre de Dios, and they're in a remote area where guests often see such rare animals as tapirs, or jaguars. **Pros:** lots of wildlife; macaw clay lick nearby; nice bungalows. **Cons:** long boat ride. [$] *Rooms from: S/2112* ✉ *123 km (76 miles), or 5 hrs by boat, east of Puerto Maldonado, Puerto Maldonado* ☎ *888/870–7378 in U.S. and Canada, 01/203–5000 in Peru* 🌐 *www.inkanatura.com* 🛏 *10 bungalows* 🍴 *All meals.*

$$$$ RESORT **Los Amigos Biological Station.** Though farther from the Tambopata National Reserve than the other lodges, this off-the-beaten-path biological station lies within a 1,119-acre private reserve that holds most of the same wildlife, including giant river otters, 13 monkey species, and more than 550 bird species. **Pros:** abundant wildlife; few tourists; profits support conservation. **Cons:** 5-hr boat ride; basic meals; no bar. [$] *Rooms from: S/1400* ✉ *5-hr boat ride west of Puerto Maldonado, Puerto Maldonado* ☎ *202/871–3777 in U.S.* 🌐 *birding.amazonconservation.org* 🛏 *6 bungalows* 🍴 *All meals.*

$$$$ RESORT Fodor'sChoice ★ **Posada Amazonas.** Guest rooms are in long buildings with high, thatched roofs, and wide, screenless windows; mosquito nets protect sleepers and kerosene lanterns provide light at night; whereas the bar/restaurant and superior rooms have electricity. **Pros:** abundant wildlife; great excursions; lodge benefits local community. **Cons:** noise from neighboring guest rooms; no screens to keep mosquitoes out. [$] *Rooms from: S/1443* ✉ *2-hr bus and boat trip on Tambopata River south of Puerto Maldonado, Puerto Maldonado* ☎ *877/231–9251 in U.S., 01/719–6422* 🌐 *www.perunature.com* 🛏 *30 rooms* 🍴 *All meals.*

$$$$ RESORT FAMILY **Refugio Amazonas.** One of three lodges on the Tambopata River run by Rainforest Expeditions, the *refugio* lies within a 200-hectare (500-acre) protected forest that is contiguous with the Tambopata National Reserve, so it has plenty of wildlife. **Pros:** surrounded by wilderness; family-friendly; sustainable tourism. **Cons:** no window screens and some rooms have curtain doors; noise audible from other rooms. [$] *Rooms from: S/1794* ✉ *Tambopata River, 3½ hrs by bus and boat south of Puerto Maldonado, Puerto Maldonado* ☎ *877/231–9251 in U.S., 01/719–6422 in Peru* 🌐 *www.perunature.com* 🛏 *32 rooms, 1 villa* 🍴 *All meals.*

$$$$ RESORT **Reserva Amazónica.** With a massive thatched restaurant and airy bungalows overlooking the Madre de Dios River, Reserva Amazónica is this region's fanciest and most expensive lodge. **Pros:** easy to reach; excellent food, service, and guides; comfortable, tasteful bungalows. **Cons:** bungalows close enough to hear neighbors; less wildlife than other lodges; noise from boat motors; quite expensive. [$] *Rooms from: S/2100* ✉ *30-min boat trip east of Puerto Maldonado, Puerto Maldonado* ☎ *866/242–2889 in U.S., 01/610–0400 in Peru* 🌐 *www.inkaterra.com* 🛏 *35 bungalows* 🍴 *All meals.*

$$$$ RESORT **Sandoval Lake Lodge.** Despite its relative proximity to Puerto Maldonado, this lodge sits deep in the rain forest, overlooking lovely Lago Sandoval, inside the Tambopata National Reserve, so there is plenty of wildlife. **Pros:** gorgeous location; abundant wildlife; decent rooms.

Cons: the boat-2-mile-hike-canoe access isn't for everyone. $ *Rooms from: S/1365* ✉ *14 km (9 miles) east of Puerto Maldonado, Puerto Maldonado* ☎ *888/870–7378 in U.S. and Canada, 01/203–5000 in Peru* ⊕ *www.inkanatura.com* ↩ *25 rooms* ⦿ *All meals.*

$$$$
RESORT
⊡ **Tambopata Ecolodge.** Rooms at this thatched lodge on the Tambopata River, have screened windows, mosquito nets, and porches with hammocks where you can rest after a day of exploring the rain forest. **Pros:** decent rooms; good day trips. **Cons:** less wildlife than other lodges; you can hear neighbors in standard rooms. $ *Rooms from: S/1280* ✉ *Tambopata River, 3-hr boat ride south of Puerto Maldonado, Puerto Maldonado* ☎ *084/245–695, 082/571–397* ⊕ *www.tambopatalodge. com* ↩ *34 rooms* ⦿ *All meals.*

$$$$
RESORT
Fodor's Choice
★
⊡ **Tambopata Research Center.** In the heart of the Tambopata National Reserve, this remote, rustic lodge is one of the best places in Peru to experience the wildlife and diversity of the Amazon rain forest. **Pros:** abundant wildlife; excellent guides; sustainable tourism. **Cons:** long boat rides; no screens; little privacy. $ *Rooms from: S/2020* ✉ *Tambopata River, 7 hrs by bus and boat south of Puerto Maldonado, Puerto Maldonado* ☎ *877/231–9251 in U.S., 01/719–6422 in Peru* ⊕ *www. perunature.com* ↩ *24 rooms with shared bath* ⦿ *All meals.*

$$$$
RESORT
⊡ **Wasaí Tambopata Lodge.** Nestled between the Tambopata River and a 3,000-hectare (7,400-acre) private nature reserve traversed by miles of trails, this eco-friendly lodge offers access to lots of wildlife, especially on overnight excursions to the rustic Tambopata Wildlife Center, and early-morning trips to the nearby Collpa Chuncho clay lick to see hundreds of macaws and parrots. **Pros:** gorgeous forest; comfortable bungalows; great excursions; sustainable tourism. **Cons:** older rooms offer limited privacy. $ *Rooms from: S/1248* ✉ *Tambopata River, 100 km (62 miles) southwest of Puerto Maldonado, Puerto Maldonado* ☎ *01/436–8792* ⊕ *wasai.com* ↩ *12 rooms, 7 bungalows* ⦿ *All meals.*

MANU BIOSPHERE RESERVE

90 km (55 miles) north of Cusco.

Manu is a remote and wild area with spectacular scenery that ranges from lush cloud forest to pristine rain forest dominated by massive tropical trees. It is one of the best places in the Amazon Basin to see wildlife, home to a dozen species of monkeys, and more than 1,000 bird species. But visiting this area is expensive; it entails many hours by road plus many more in a small wooden boat on the Madre de Dios River, and nearly all the accommodations are rustic. A trip to Manu is truly an adventure, and it can involve a little discomfort, but the payoff is the opportunity to explore enchanting, pristine areas that few people have seen and are home to a mind-boggling diversity of plants and animals.

GETTING HERE AND AROUND

A Manu excursion is no quick trip. Overland travel from Cusco, which includes at least one overnight in the cloud forest requires a five-day minimum stay. It is also possible to fly to Puerto Maldonado and travel by land and up the Madre de Dios River to the Manu Wildlife Center, which can be done on a four-day tour. The most spectacular trip is to enter by land and river from Cusco—passing amazing Andean cloud-forest and rain-forest scenery along the way—and depart by river and land, either to Puerto Maldonado, where you catch a flight to Lima, or by driving five hours to Cusco.

ESSENTIALS

TOURS **Manu Expeditions.** These Cusco-based specialists in bird-watching and nature tours offer decades of experience in trips deep into the Manu Biosphere Reserve. Trips last four to seven days and include overnights at several remote nature lodges. ☎ *084/225–990* ⊕ *www.manuexpeditions.com* ✉ *From $1397.*

Pantiacolla. Pantiacolla organizes ecotours to Manu with overnights at one or more of the company's three lodges: the Posada San Pedro, Pantiacolla Lodge, and Sachavaca Campsite. Tours range from two nights in the cloud forest to a nine-day expedition into Manu's reserved zone. Pantiacolla's lodges are more rustic than the competition's, but the guides are excellent and the tours are less expensive. ☎ *084/238–323* ⊕ *pantiacolla.com* ✉ *From $450.*

EXPLORING

Fodor's Choice **Manu Biosphere Reserve.** Scientists consider the Manu Biosphere Reserve ★ to be one of the most biodiverse places on Earth, and much of its vast wilderness has barely been studied, since it is still home to uncontacted indigenous groups. Straddling the boundary of the Madre de Dios and Cusco provinces, the reserve is Peru's second-largest protected area, encompassing more than 4½ million acres of pristine tropical forests. Its extraordinary biological diversity is in part due to its precipitous terrain, which ranges in altitude from 3,450 meters (12,000 feet) down to 300 meters (less than 1,000 feet). This geographical diversity results in varied ecosystems: from high-altitude puna grasslands to luxuriant cloud forest to seemingly endless rain forest, which in turn shelter a stunning range of flora and fauna. To top it off, a near total absence of humans means that the animals here are less skittish and more easily observed.

Whereas Manu's highland cloud forest is home to dozens of humming-bird species, the spectacular cock-of-the-rock, and the andean bear (aka spectacled bear), the reserve's lower parts hold most of its more than 200 mammal species, including 13 species of monkeys, which scrutinize visitors with the same curiosity they elicit. White caimans sun themselves on sandy riverbanks, whereas the larger black caimans lurk in the oxbow lakes. With luck, you may see a tapir, giant river otter, or one of the region's elusive jaguars. You are bound to see a sampling of the avian life that has made Manu world famous. The area counts more than 1,000 bird species; one-ninth of those known to science. They include several species of macaws, toucans, jacamars, cocoi herons, harpy eagles, razor-billed currasows, blue-headed parrots, and horned screamers. ■TIP➔ Manu is also home to hundreds of colorful butterfly species and an array of ants, beetles, and spiders, as well as millions of mosquitoes, so be sure to take an ample supply of insect repellent.

A UNESCO World Heritage site, the Biosphere Reserve is divided into three distinct zones. The smallest, and most accessible, is what's known as the "cultural zone," home to several indigenous groups and the majority of the jungle lodges. Access is permitted to all—even independent travelers, in theory—though it would be extremely difficult to visit it on your own. About three times the size of the cultural zone, Manu's "reserved zone" contains various nature lodges, which can only be visited on a guided tour with one of a dozen agencies authorized to take people into the area. The western 80% of Manu is designated a national park and is closed to all but authorized researchers and the indigenous peoples who reside there.

WHERE TO STAY

Accommodations in Manu are scattered along the area's various life zones: from the cloud forest of the eastern Andes—reached by land from Cusco—to the montane and lowland rain forests that line the Madre de Dios and Manu Rivers, which are reached by a combination of bus and boat travel. Lodges here tend to be more rustic and more expensive than lodges near Puerto Maldonado or Iquitos. This is because of the logistical challenges of transporting guests to, and maintaining facilities in, this remote and rainy region. Keep in mind that lodge rates include all meals, a bilingual, naturalist guide, and days of transportation in buses and wooden boats with outboard motors, which consume barrels of gasoline.

$$$$
RESORT
🎋 **Campsite Sachavaca.** This bare-bones camp operated by the tour company Pantiacolla is near Cocha Salvador, an oxbow lake in Manu's Reserved Zone, which is home to an amazing array of wildlife. **Pros:** deep in the rain forest; abundant wildlife. **Cons:** very rustic. $ *Rooms from: S/1300 ⊠ 70 km (44 miles) northwest of Boca Manu, Cocha Salvador, Manu Biosphere Reserve ☎ 084/238–323 ⊕ www.pantiacolla. com ⇄ 8 rooms ⦿ All meals.*

$$$$
RESORT
🎋 **Cock of the Rock Lodge.** This lodge stands at the edge of the cloud forest in the Manu Cultural Zone, and affords an amazing view of the lush Kosñipata River Valley. **Pros:** great bird-watching; gorgeous setting; pleasant climate. **Cons:** expensive; a seven-hour drive from Cusco. $ *Rooms from: S/2668 ⊠ 163 km (101 miles) northeast of Cusco, Cusco ☎ 888/870–7378 in U.S., 800/234–8659 in U.K., 01/203–5000 in Peru ⊕ www.inkanatura.com ⇄ 12 bungalows ⦿ All meals.*

$$$$
RESORT
🎋 **Manu Park Wildlife Center.** Located deep in the wilderness of the Manu Biosphere Reserve, this InkaNatura Travel property has elevated bungalows with screened walls, each with two single beds, mosquito nets, and a private bathroom with a cold-water shower. **Pros:** amazing wildlife; a true adventure. **Cons:** remote; rustic; expensive. $ *Rooms from: S/3094 ⊠ Manu Reserved Zone, 145 km (90 miles) from northwest of Manu Wildlife Center; 400 km (249 miles) northwest of Puerto Maldonado, Puerto Maldonado ☎ 888/870–7378 in U.S., 01/203–5000 in Peru ⊕ www.inkanatura.com ⇄ 7 rooms ⦿ All meals.*

$$$$
RESORT
Fodor's Choice
★
🎋 **Manu Wildlife Center.** Though outside the Manu Biosphere Reserve, the Manu Wildlife Center is still a great place to see animals, since it is close to macaw and tapir collpas and has 30 miles of rain-forest trails. **Pros:** plenty of wildlife; knowledgeable guides; decent rooms. **Cons:**

remote; expensive. $ *Rooms from: S/3094* ⊠ *255 km (158 miles), or 7 hrs, west of Puerto Maldonado, Puerto Maldonado* ☎ *888/870–7378 in U.S., 01/203–5000 in Peru* ⊕ *www.inkanatura.com* ⌁ *22 bungalows* ¶◯¶ *All meals.*

$$$$ ⛺ **Pantiacolla Lodge.** Named for the mountain range that towers over
RESORT it, the Pantiacolla Lodge sits in a 2,223-acre private nature reserve in the Manu Cultural Zone that boasts 600 bird species and an array of mammals. **Pros:** great bird-watching; lots of mammals; beautiful spot. **Cons:** quite rustic; little privacy in bungalows; fewer mosquitoes. $ *Rooms from: S/1300* ⊠ *290 km (180 miles) northeast of Cusco, Cusco* ☎ *084/238–323* ⊕ *www.pantiacolla.com* ⌁ *11 rooms, 8 without bath* ¶◯¶ *All meals.*

$$$$ ⛺ **Posada San Pedro Lodge.** Nestled in the cloud forest of the Manu
RESORT Biosphere ReserveCultural Zone, midway between Cusco and the Pantiacolla Lodge, this small lodge offers earthy accommodations amid extraordinary scenery and bird life. **Pros:** great bird-watching; gorgeous scenery. **Cons:** rustic; little privacy in rooms; shared bathhouse. $ *Rooms from: S/1300* ⊠ *164 km (102 miles) northeast of Cusco, Cusco* ☎ *084/238–323* ⊕ *www.pantiacolla.com* ⌁ *8 rooms without bath* ¶◯¶ *All meals.*

$$$$ ⛺ **Romero Rainforest Lodge.** Offering comfortable accommodations inside
RESORT the Manu Reserved Zone, several hours by boat up the Manu River, the Romero Rainforest Lodge provides access to impressive natural attractions (including two oxbow lakes) without requiring you to rough it too much. **Pros:** decent rooms; stellar wildlife. **Cons:** remote; expensive. $ *Rooms from: S/3094* ⊠ *Manu Biosphere Reserve, 20 km (12 miles) northwest of Boca Manu, 350 km (217 miles) northwest of Puerto Maldonado, Puerto Maldonado* ☎ *084/225–990* ⊕ *www.manuexpeditions.com* ⌁ *8 bungalows* ¶◯¶ *All meals.*

$$$$ ⛺ **Wayqecha Cloud Forest Birding Lodge.** Perched above the cloud forest
RESORT tree line with a sweeping view of Manu's mountainous area, this ecolodge and biological station provides access to a 1,450-acre reserve adjacent to Manu that protects rare bird and orchid species. **Pros:** gorgeous area; home to rare bird species; profits support conservation. **Cons:** cold at night. $ *Rooms from: S/2500* ⊠ *Carretera a Manu s/n* ✢ *3½ hr drive from Cusco via Paucartambo* ☎ *202/871–3777 in U.S.* ⊕ *birding.amazonconservation.org* ⌁ *6 rooms* ¶◯¶ *All meals.*

IQUITOS AND NEARBY

Founded by Jesuit priests in the 1500s, Iquitos was once called the "Pearl of the Amazon." It isn't quite that lustrous today, but it's still a pleasant, friendly town that provides access to the Amazon River, rain-forest wildlife, and various indigenous cultures. Although most travelers fly here specifically for an excursion into the surrounding rain forest, Iquitos has sites nearby that can be visited in a few hours or a day, and deserves at least a night. The city itself may grow on you as you become accustomed to the humid climate and relaxed, easy ways of its citizens. Its malecón (riverwalk) is a popular place for an evening stroll, and you can enjoy a meal of river fish while floating on the river.

GETTING HERE AND AROUND

Several airlines have daily flights to Iquitos, some of which stop at Pucallpa or Tarapoto, adding an hour to the trip, so try to book a direct flight. The best way to travel around the Iquitos area is by boat: hundreds of vessels come and go each day, from tiny dugout canoes bound for jungle enclaves to seagoing ships that travel all the way through Brazil to the Atlantic Ocean.

Various companies run cruises out of the town of Nauta, a 90-minute drive south of Iquitos, providing comfortable—albeit expensive—access to the province's protected areas and indigenous villages. Nature lodges transport guests in swift launches with outboard engines and canvas tops to protect you from the sun and rain.

BORDER CROSSINGS

Various companies offer speedboat service to the Brazilian and Colombian borders. It's a 9- to 10-hour boat ride to the border town of Santa Rosa, across the river from Leticia (Colombia) and Tabatinga (Brazil). The one-way trip costs only US$80. Each company runs twice a week, so boats depart every day; all the ticket offices are on the 300 block of Calle Raymondi, three blocks north of the Plaza de Armas. Just go there and buy a ticket from the company that departs on the day you want to travel.

American citizens don't need a visa to enter Colombia, but they do need one for Brazil.

IQUITOS

1,150 km (713 miles) northeast of Lima.

A sultry port town on the Río Amazonas, Iquitos is quite probably the world's largest city that cannot be reached by road. The city has nearly 500,000 inhabitants and is the capital of the vast Loreto department. It is a colorful, dilapidated town where motorcycles and three-wheeled mototaxis buzz down narrow streets shaded by massive tropical trees, tiny houses built atop wooden rafts float in the nearby river, and indigenous women hawk their handicrafts in the plazas. A large portion of the people who live in Iquitos are members of Amazonian indigenous tribes, and while most have adopted Western dress, you'll find bushmeat and jungle herbs for sale at the local market, and you can learn about the Amazon's native cultures at the Museo de Culturas Indígenas. You can also watch the locals pass in dugout canoes as you sample an Amazon fish fillet at the floating restaurant of Al Frio y al Fuego. Or savor the tropical surroundings while sipping a cool drink on the malecón and contemplate the rain forest foliage that lines the estuary.

The area around Iquitos was first inhabited by small, independent Amazonian tribes. In the 1500s Jesuit missionaries began adventuring in the area, trying to Christianize the local population, but the city wasn't officially founded until 1757.

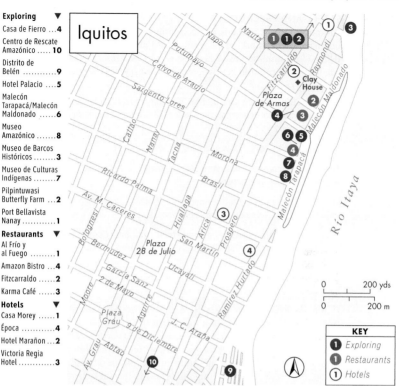

Iquitos saw unprecedented growth and opulence during the rubber boom but became an Amazonian backwater overnight when the boom went bust. The economy slouched along, barely sustaining itself with logging and exotic-animal exports. Then, in the early 1970s, petroleum was discovered. The black gold, along with ecotourism and logging, have since become the backbone of the region's economy, though drug running also provides significant income.

The city's historic center stretches along a lagoon formed by the Río Itaya, near the confluence of the Río Nanay and the Río Amazonas. Most of its historic buildings, hotels, restaurants, and banks are within blocks of the Plaza de Armas, the main square, and the nearby Malecón Maldonado riverwalk.

GETTING HERE AND AROUND

With 10 flights a day, it's easy to get to Iquitos. Some hotels pick guests up at the airport, but there are always taxis available if yours doesn't The most common mode of transportation around town is the moto-taxi, a three-wheeled motorcycle with a canvas top. Service costs S/2, whereas a trip to the outskirts costs around S/10 to S/15. It should cost S/4 to Port Bellavista Nanay, where you can hire a boat to the butterfly farm.

Taxi Taxi Aeropuerto. ☏ *065/241-284.* **Taxi Flores.** ☏ *065/232-014.*

SAFETY AND PRECAUTIONS

Although violent crime is not common in Iquitos, pickpocketing and other petty thefts are—especially in and around the neighborhood of Belén. Use common sense when you're out and about. Malaria and dengue fever are common in town, so use insect repellent containing DEET.

ESSENTIALS

Currency BBVA Banco Continental. ⊠ *Sargento Lores 171* ☎ *01/595–0238* ⊕ *www.bbvabancocontinental.com.* **Banco de Crédito.** ⊠ *Jirón Prospero 200* ☎ *065/234–501.*

Mail Serpost Iquitos. ⊠ *Av. Arica 402* ☎ *065/231–915.*

Medical Clinica Adventista Ana Stahl. ⊠ *Av. de la Marina 285* ☎ *065/252–535* ⊕ *www.clinicaanastahl.org.pe.*

Tour Operators Dawn on the Amazon. ⊠ *Malecón Maldonado 185* ☎ *065/223–730* ⊕ *www.dawnontheamazon.com.*

Visitor Information iPerú. ⊠ *Aeropuerto Internacional Coronel FAP Francisco Secada Vignetta* ☎ *065/260–251.* **Tourist Information Office.** ⊠ *Napo 161* ☎ *065/236–144.*

EXPLORING

TOP ATTRACTIONS

Distrito de Belén (*Belén District*). Iquitos's most fascinating neighborhood lies along, and floats upon, the Itaya River. During high-water season (December–May), tiny houses on balsa-wood rafts float placidly on this Amazon tributary's calm waters. This slummy area has been called the Venice of the Amazon (a diplomatic euphemism), but navigating between its floating homes is really a kick. During the low-water season (June–November), those houses sit in the mud, and the area should simply be avoided. During high-water season, you can visit the floating houses with an Iquitos tour operator. Tours of Belén usually include a visit to the local market, Mercado Belén, where you may see bushmeat, *suris* (palm grubs), love potions, and other goodies for sale. ⚠ Do not visit the Mercado de Belén or the surrounding area alone—muggings are frequent and pickpockets and bag slashers work the market with impunity. Only visit on a tour with a reputable company. ⊠ *East end of, Jr. 9 de Diciembre.*

Malecón Tarapacá (aka Malecón Maldonado). This pleasant waterfront walk between Brasil and Pevas is a good place for an evening stroll. During high-water season, the Itaya River reaches the cement, but during the dry months (May–November), it recedes into the distance. You'll find some lovely rubber-boom-era architecture here, and there are a few bars and restaurants on the malecón's northern end, near the Plaza de Armas. Its southern end gets less traffic, and muggings have been reported there at night, so stick to the three northernmost blocks after 6 pm. ⊠ *Iquitos.*

FAMILY **Museo de Barcos Históricos.** The Ayapua, a 33-meter (108-foot) boat built in Hamburg, Germany, in 1906, navigated the Brazilian Amazon for much of the rubber boom and was brought to Iquitos by the nonprofit Fundamazonia in 2005 to be renovated and turned into a museum. It is now moored next to Plaza Ramón Castilla, on the Itaya River, and contains displays about the rubber boom and historic photos of the region from that era. The bridge has been refurbished, and there is a small bar where you can have a beer or soft drink. ⊠ *Plaza Ramón Castilla* ☎ 065/231–913 ✉ *S/15.*

Fodor's Choice ★ **Museo de Culturas Indígenas.** This small museum housed in a pale blue building on the Malecón Tarapacá has an impressive collection of colorful headdresses made from the feathers of jungle birds and an array of other traditional handiwork by the main Amazonian indigenous tribes. If you're interested in indigenous cultures, you won't want to miss it. The displays include a wealth of information about the lives of the Amazon Basin's native peoples and an array of artifacts collected in Peru, Brazil, Colombia, and the Guianas over the course of decades. They range from the quotidian (clothing, paddles, woven bags) to the ceremonial (musical instruments, headdresses, necklaces with the teeth of jungle animals). Among the more striking items are the jewelry, embroidered cloths and *cushmas* (tunics), painted ceramic wares, blow guns, spears, bows and arrows, and ceremonial headdresses. ⊠ *Malecón Tarapacá 332* ☎ 065/235–809 ✉ *S/15.*

FAMILY **Pilpintuwasi Butterfly Farm.** A 20-minute boat ride and a short walk from the port of Bellavista Nanay will bring you to Pilpintuwasi Butterfly Farm, which raises some 42 butterfly species and serves as home for wild animals that have been confiscated from hunters and wildlife traffickers. It has macaws, a jaguar, a manatee, monkeys (some free roaming), and other animals. During the dry season, you'll need to walk along a forest path for 15 minutes to get there. A private boat to and from Padre Cocha should cost 60 soles, depending on the type of motor. ⚠ Some boat operators may try to take you to a smaller butterfly farm, so insist on Pilpintuwasi; ask for Gudrun. ⊠ *Padre Cocha, Nanay River, 20-min boat trip from Bellavista Nanay* ☎ 965–932–999 ⊕ *www.amazonanimalorphanage.org* ✉ *S/20 without transportation* ⊗ *Closed Mon.*

WORTH NOTING

Casa de Fierro. The most interesting structure on the Plaza de Armas is this "Iron House," which was originally the home of a rubber baron but now houses a pharmacy and a restaurant, on the second floor. The building was forged in Europe and shipped across the Atlantic and up the Amazon River in sections to be assembled at this spot. According to locals, it was designed by Gustave Eiffel (of Eiffel Tower fame), but a Peruvian historian who has studied Eiffel's contribution to South American architecture disputes the claim. ⊠ *Putumayo at Jr. Prospero* ✉ *Free.*

FAMILY **Centro de Rescate Amazónico.** At this animal-rescue center, a short trip south of town, you can get a close look at one of the region's rarest, and most threatened, species: the manatee. Despite being protected by Peruvian law, manatees continue to be hunted for their meat. The center, a collaboration of the Dallas World Aquarium and Zoo and two Peruvian institutions, raises orphaned manatees and nurses injured ones back to health for eventual release in the wild. It also serves as an environmental education center to raise awareness of the gentle creature's plight. ✉ *Km 4.6, Carretera Iquitos-Nauta* ☎ 965–834–685 ⊕ *centroderescateamazonico.com* 💲 *S/20* ⊘ *Closed Mon. mornings.*

Hotel Palacio. Iquitos enjoyed its heyday as a port during the rubber boom a century ago. Some of the wealth of that time can still be detected in the imported *azulejos* (tiles) that cover many of its older buildings. A notable example is the former Hotel Palacio, on the Malecón Tarapacá. The hotel was the city's best when it opened for business in 1908. It has since been converted into a police station and is now looking a little worn, but remains a stately building nonetheless. ✉ *Putumayo and Malecón Tarapacá.*

Museo Amazónico. This "museum" has a few faded paintings and "bronzed" fiberglass statues of local indigenous people. One room holds temporary exhibitions by local artists, sometimes indigenous painters. Although the exhibits are less than enthralling, it's worth popping into this former town hall, constructed in 1863, to admire the ornately carved hardwoods and courtyard garden. ✉ *Malecón Tarapacá 386* ☎ *065/234–031* 💲 *Free* ⊘ *Closed Sun.*

Port Bellavista Nanay. About 3 km (1½ miles) north of downtown Iquitos, at the end of Avenida La Marina, is this muddy beehive of activity with a large open-air market where vendors sell everything from jungle fruits to grilled *suri* (palm grubs). Boats of all shapes and sizes populate the riverbank and seedy bars are perched over the water on wooden posts. You can hire a boat to take you to the Bora and Yagua Indian villages, near San Andrés, or the Pilpintuwasi Butterfly Farm. ✉ *Iquitos.*

WHERE TO EAT

$$$ ✕ **Al Frío y al Fuego.** Step through the unassuming doorway on Avenida
PERUVIAN   La Marina, descend the long stairway to the dock, and a boat will ferry
Fodor's Choice   you to this floating, thatch-roofed restaurant on the Itaya River. The
★   setting is gorgeous, and they prepare excellent versions of traditional dishes such as *patarashca* (a fish fillet topped with herbs and garlic and roasted in a bijao leaf) and *doncella* (Amazon catfish) fillet *à la loretana* (in a mild chili sauce) with *tacacho* (mashed plantain balls with chunks of smoked pork). **Known for:** views of Itaya River traffic; excellent Amazonian dishes. 💲 *Average main: S/52* ✉ *Av. La Marina 134-B* ☎ *965/607–474* ⊘ *No dinner Sun.*

$$ ✕ **Amazon Bistro.** This tastefully restored rubber-boom-era mansion on
BISTRO   the malecón is well worth a visit—if not for a meal, at least for a drink or much-needed espresso. The French-inspired menu features both basic bistro fare (think escargots, fish sautéed in butter, or chicken cordon bleu) and international favorites like hamburgers and pastas. **Known for:** traditional French cuisine; sidewalk-café dining. 💲 *Average main: S/36* ✉ *Malecón Tarapacá 268* ☎ *065/242–918* ⊕ *www. amazonbistro.com.*

$ ✕ **Fitzcarraldo.** Conveniently located on the Malecón Maldonado, this
PERUVIAN   restaurant specializes in traditional regional specialties such as *cecina con tacacho* (a smoked pork steak with fried plantain balls) and *pescado a la loretana* (fish fillet in a mild chili sauce). The restaurant occupies a

historic building and has an air-conditioned room, an airy front dining room with ceiling fans, and sidewalk tables on the malecón. **Known for:** traditional Amazonian dishes; sidewalk tables with river views. [$] *Average main: S/32* ✉ *Malecón Maldonado at Napo* ☎ *065/507–545* 🌐 *www.restaurantefitzcarraldo.com.*

$$ ECLECTIC 🍴 **Karma Café.** This spot serves a tasty mix of international dishes, which together with free Wi-Fi, comfy furnishings (couches and armchairs), and a convenient location between the Plaza de Armas and the malecón, make it a popular traveler hangout. The eclectic food selection includes plenty of vegetarian options, chicken satay, Thai curries, falafel, river fish, and an array of salads and sandwiches. **Known for:** eclectic menu; fruit smoothies; chill-out vibe. [$] *Average main: S/37* ✉ *Calle Napo 138* ☎ *065/222–663* 🌐 *karmacafeiquitos.com* 💳 *No credit cards* ⏲ *Closed Mon.*

WHERE TO STAY

$$ B&B/INN Fodor's Choice ★ 🏨 **Casa Morey.** Built by rubber baron Luis Morey in 1913, this restored mansion offers the most historic setting in Iquitos. **Pros:** lovely building; spacious rooms; some river views; free aiport pickup. **Cons:** street noise, especially weekend nights. [$] *Rooms from: S/310* ✉ *Calle Loreto 200, on Plaza Ramón Castilla* ☎ *065/231–913, 065/223–707* 🌐 *www.casamorey.com* 🛏 *14 rooms* 🍽 *Breakfast.*

$ B&B/INN 🏨 **Época.** Occupying a renovated, turn-of-the-century home at the southern end of the malecón, Época is a comfortable, friendly lodging option with a bit of historic atmosphere. **Pros:** historic atmosphere; peaceful; friendly. **Cons:** guest rooms less charming than common rooms. [$] *Rooms from: S/220* ✉ *Ramirez Hurtado 616* ☎ *065/224–172* 🌐 *www.epoca.com.pe* 🛏 *11 rooms* 🍽 *Breakfast.*

$ HOTEL 🏨 **Hotel Marañon.** It may lack personality, but this small hotel is clean, inexpensive, and centrally located. **Pros:** good value; central location. **Cons:** street noise; very basic rooms; zero personality. [$] *Rooms from: S/160* ✉ *Nauta 289, at Fitzcarrald* ☎ *65/242–673* 🌐 *www.hotelmaranon.com* 🛏 *32 rooms* 🍽 *Breakfast.*

$ HOTEL 🏨 **Victoria Regia Hotel.** Named for the giant lily pads found in the region's lakes, this simple, modern hotel is popular with business travelers. **Pros:** nice rooms; competitive rates; pool; free airport transfers; relatively quiet. **Cons:** rooms are on the small side; those in back are a bit dark. [$] *Rooms from: S/180* ✉ *Ricardo Palma 252* ☎ *065/231–983, 01/421–9195 reservations* 🌐 *www.terraverde.pe* 🛏 *61 rooms* 🍽 *Breakfast.*

NIGHTLIFE AND PERFORMING ARTS

Maybe it's the proximity to the jungle and its innate, inexplicable sensuality. Whatever the reason, Iquitos heats up after dark, and the dancing and bar scene is quite good. You should begin your night with a drink at one of the bars or restaurants along the Malecón Maldonado.

Ajary's. Housed in a large thatched building perched over the water on wooden poles, Ajary's offers the most Amazonian setting for a drink in Iquitos. It is reached via an elevated walkway at the eastern end of Calle Pevas. ✉ *Malecón Maldonado 102, at Calle Pevas* ☎ *065/242–702.*

Arandú Bar. Arandú Bar is the most popular bar on the malecón, with pop and rock music blasting, wild murals covering the walls, and sidewalk tables with river views. ⊠ *Malecón Maldonado 113* ☎ *065/243–434.*

La Noche. With tables on the sidewalk and a second-floor balcony, La Noche is a good spot for a quiet drink on the malecón (riverwalk). ⊠ *Malecón Maldonado 177* ☎ *065/222–373.*

Musmuqui. This two-level, wood-paneled bar, located two blocks north of the Plaza de Armas, lures a young crowd with good music and low prices. It's one of Iquito's most popular watering holes. ⊠ *Raymondi 382* ☎ *065/242–942.*

Noa Disco. The biggest and liveliest dance club in town, Noa Disco is open Thursday–Saturday. DJs play a mix of international and Latin hits from 10 pm till the wee hours, though it doesn't get crowded until about midnight. ⊠ *Fitzcarraldo 298* ☎ *065/222–555* ⊕ *www.noadisco.com.*

Vocé Bar. A large bar fills the center of the room here, providing plenty of spots to pull up a stool, though there are also various tables scattered around and couches lining the wall. On weekends, this place fills up around midnight, and the dance floor stays busy till about 4 am. ⊠ *Jirón Napo at Jirón Condamine* ☎ *065/234–040.*

SHOPPING

Street vendors display their wares on the Malecón Maldonado at night; and around the corner, on the first block of Nauta, by day. Look for pottery, hand-painted cloth from Pucallpa, and jungle items such as preserved piranhas, seed necklaces, fish and animal teeth, blowguns, spears, and balsawood parrots.

Casa del Artesano Amazónico. Handicrafts from several of the province's indigenous cultures can be found in the souvenir stands at the Casa del Artesano Amazónico. ⊠ *Malecón Maldonado 167.*

Centro Artesanal Turístico Anaconda. This collection of handicraft stalls on a wooden platform perched over a seasonal swamp is worth wandering through even if you don't want to buy anything. It's down the stairs from the Malecón Maldonado, at the end of Jirón Napo. ⊠ *Malecón Maldonado s/n, down stairway.*

THE PERUVIAN AMAZON

The Amazon Basin is the world's most diverse ecosystem. The numbers of cataloged plant and animal species are astronomical, and scientists regularly discover new ones. There are more than 25,000 classified species of plants in the Peruvian Amazon (and 80,000 in the entire Amazon Basin), including the 2-meter-wide (6-foot-wide) Victoria Regia water lilies. Scientists have cataloged more than 4,000 species of butterfly and more than 2,000 of fish—a more diverse aquatic life than that of the Atlantic Ocean. Scientists estimate that the world's tropical forests, while comprising only 6% of the Earth's landmass, may hold up to 75% of the planet's plant and animal species. This land is also the largest natural pharmacy in the world: one-fourth of all modern medicines have botanical origins in tropical forests.

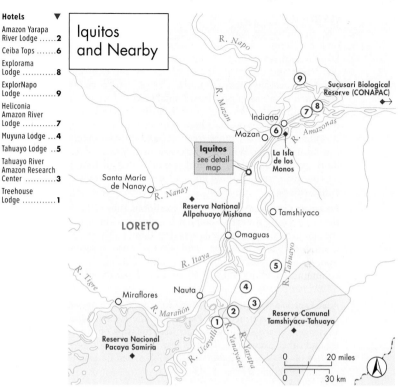

You'll see monkeys, and perhaps a sloth, but most mammals are nocturnal and difficult to spot. ■ **TIP→ You're likely to see an array of birds, butterflies, and monkeys, as well as bufeos (freshwater dolphins) along the Amazon and its tributaries.**

It's interesting and worthwhile to visit a small indigenous village, and take advantage of the opportunity to buy some handicrafts.

The best way to visit the area is on a prearranged tour with one of the many jungle lodges or cruise boats. All have highly trained naturalist guides. Among the activities offered are nature walks, birding tours, nighttime canoe outings, fishing trips, and stops at indigenous villages.

GETTING HERE AND AROUND

With the exception of Reserva Nacional Allpahuayo Mishana, which is a 40-minute drive from town, you'll reach the Amazon's sites by water. You basically have two options: travel to a nature lodge in one of that company's boats or take a cruise. The cruises are more expensive, but quite comfortable, and they allow you to explore different areas on daily excursions in small boats. Otherwise, you can book a stay at a nature lodge, in which case a guide will meet you at the airport, take you to the port, and accompany you to the lodge in a small, fast boat.

ESSENTIALS

TOURS The most popular way to explore the Amazon and its tributaries is on a river cruise, which depart from Iquitos or the port of Nauta, a 90-minute drive south from Iquitos. Those cruises head up the Amazon River and one of its main tributaries, the Ucayali, toward the Reserva Nacional Pacaya Samiria. Cruise boats travel to a different area each day: passengers board smaller vessels to explore tributaries and other sites. An alternative is a tour with a company that has one or more lodges on the Amazon or a tributary. Staying at a lodge, or lodges, allows for more freedom, and more contact with nature (including insects). Whether you cruise or stay at a lodge, you'll enjoy daily excursions led by naturalist guides that include navigating a narrow river, or an oxbow lake, a forest hike, or a visit to an indigenous village.

Fodor's Choice ★ **Amazonia Expeditions.** Amazonia Expeditions runs eight-day trips into the megadiverse Reserva Comunal Tamshiyacu-Tahuayo, with stays at the company's two rustic lodges on the Tahuayo River. The company's naturalist guides are first rate, and part of the profits support conservation, scientific research, and improvement of life in the reserve's remote communities. ☏ *800/262–9669 in U.S.* ⊕ *perujungle.com* ✉ *From $1295 per person.*

Aqua Expeditions. Aqua Expeditions runs high-end nature cruises along the upper Amazon between Nauta and the Pacaya Samiria Reserve. Passengers board small boats each day for trips up Amazon tributaries and other excursions. Cruises last for three, four, or seven nights. ☏ *01/434–5544 in Peru, 866/603–3687 U.S. and Canada* ⊕ *www.aquaexpeditions.com* ✉ *From $2430.*

Delfin. Delfin offers three-, four-, and seven-night Amazon eco-cruises on any of three boats: the luxurious *Delfin I*, which takes eight passengers, and larger *Delfin II*, which sleeps 28, and the more economical *Delfin III*, which sleeps 43. ☏ *844/433–5346 in U.S., 01/719–0999 in Peru* ⊕ *www.delfinamazoncruises.com* ✉ *From $1500.*

Explorama Tours. Explorama Tours runs seven-day trips down the Amazon River that combine stays at its rustic Explorama and ExplorNapo nature lodges and two nights at the more comfortable Ceiba Tops Lodge, with varied outdoor adventures every day. ☏ *065/252–530, 800/707–5275 in U.S. and Canada* ⊕ *www.explorama.com* ✉ *From $1338.*

Green Tracks. Green Tracks is a U.S.-based company that organizes one-week river expeditions up the Amazon to the Pacaya Samiria Reserve and books stays at the area's best nature lodges. ☏ *970/884–6107* ⊕ *www.greentracks.com* ✉ *From $1500 per person.*

EXPLORING

FAMILY **La Isla de los Monos.** A popular spot for explorers of all ages, Isla de los Monos (Monkey Island) is home to more than 40 monkeys of eight species. The 250-hectare (618-acre) island is a private reserve where monkeys that were once held in captivity, or were confiscated from animal traffickers, now live in a natural environment. In addition to the monkeys, there are sloths, parrots, macaws and a small botanical garden. Since most of the animals are former pets, you can get very close to them; maybe even closer than you might want. The easiest way to visit the island is on a tour. ✉ *30 km (18 miles) northeast of Iquitos, Iquitos* ☎ *065/235–887, 965–841–808* ⊕ *laisladelosmonos. org* ☞ *S/20 adults.*

Reserva Comunal Tamshiyacu-Tahuayo. Covering approximately 4,144 square km (1,600 square miles), the Tamshiyacu-Tahuayo Communal Reserve is larger than the state of Rhode Island. It comprises an array of ecosystems that includes seasonally flooded forests, terra firma forests, *aguaje* palm swamps, and oxbow lakes. It holds a wealth of biological diversity, including almost 600 bird species: cocoi herons, wire-tailed manakins, and blue-and-gold macaws among them. It is also home to 15 primate species, including the rare saki and uakari monkeys. The government manages the reserve in coordination with local people (They still hunt and fish here but have reduced their impact on its wildlife.). Local eco-lodges provide employment and support education and healthcare in those communities, which has strengthened their interest in protecting the environment. ✉ *100 km (60 miles) south of Iquitos, Iquitos* ☎ *No phone.*

Reserva Nacional Allpahuayo Mishana. Around Iquitos there are large tracts of protected rain forest, of which Allpahuayo Mishana is the easiest to get to, since it is just 27 km (16 miles) southwest of Iquitos via the road to Nauta. It isn't a great place to see large animals, but it is a good destination for bird-watchers. Scientists have identified 475 bird species in the reserve, including such avian rarities as the pompadour cotinga and Zimmer's antbird. It is also home to several monkey species. ✉ *Km 27, Carretera Iquitos-Nauta.*

Reserva Nacional Pacaya Samiria. This hard-to-reach park comprises a vast expanse of wilderness between the Marañón and Ucayali Rivers, which flow together to form the Amazon. The reserve is Peru's largest, encompassing more than 20,000 square km (7,722 square miles)—which makes it about the size of El Salvador. The landscape is diverse, comprising a patchwork of seasonally flooded forests, oxbow lakes, black-water rivers, *aguaje* palm swamps, and vast expanses of lowland rain forest. So are the animals who inhabit it, including pink river dolphins, black caimans, more than a dozen kinds of monkeys, and more than 500 bird species. As with many South American reserves, there are people living in Pacaya Samiria, around 40,000 according to recent estimates. The park can only be reached by boat, and some cruises visit it's northern sector, which is relatively close to the town of Nauta. ✉ *Confluence of Marañón and Ucayali Rivers* ☞ *S/120.*

Sucusari Biological Reserve (CONAPAC). This smaller, private rain-forest reserve is northeast of Iquitos, near the confluence of the Napo and Amazon Rivers. CONAPAC (the Peruvian Amazon Conservation Organization) manages the 1,000-square-km (386-square-mile) multiuse property, known as the Sucusari Biological Reserve, which can be explored from the ExplorNapo Lodge. ✉ *Near confluence of Napo and Amazon Rivers, 70 km (43 miles) downriver from Iquitos, Iquitos* ☎ *065/252–530* ⊕ *www.explorama.com* ☞ *Free.*

WHERE TO STAY

Rates for the rain-forest lodges near Iquitos are high, but they all include transportation, meals, guide, and two or more excursions per day. Transportation to the lodges is usually in fast boats, and can take 90 minutes to three hours. Three lodges—Ceiba Tops, Explorama Lodge, and ExplorNapo—are owned and operated by Explorama Tours, whereas two—the Tahuayo Lodge and Tahuayo River Amazon Research Center—are owned by Amazonia Expeditions.

$$$$
RESORT

Amazon Yarapa River Lodge. Built from native wood by members of the local community, this lodge is perched at the edge of the Yarapa River, near a seasonal lake, a small "monkey island," and a village. **Pros:** responsible tourism. **Cons:** rustic; limited wildlife; overpriced. *$ Rooms from: S/1733 ⊠ Yarapa River, 150 km (93 miles) southwest of Iquitos, Iquitos ☎ 315/952–6760 in U.S. ⊕ www.yarapa.com ➟ 16 rooms without bath, 8 rooms with bath ⎟◎⎟ All meals.*

$$$$
RESORT
Fodor's Choice
★

Ceiba Tops. With the most comfortable accommodations of any Amazon eco-lodge, complete with a swimming pool and air-conditioned rooms, Ceiba Tops is a good option for people who want to see the Amazon without roughing it. **Pros:** great river view; swimming pool; air-conditioning; easy to reach. **Cons:** less wildlife than some lodges. *$ Rooms from: S/1742 ⊠ Amazon River, 40 km (25 miles) east of Iquitos, Iquitos ☎ 800/707–5275 in U.S., 065/252–533 ⊕ www.explorama. com ➟ 78 rooms ⎟◎⎟ All meals.*

$$$$
RESORT

Explorama Lodge. Built in 1964, this is one of Peru's original nature lodges, and it still provides rustic accommodations and access to the rain forest, but there is much less wildlife here than in the '60s.. **Pros:** in the jungle; good guides. **Cons:** quite rustic; overpriced; not much wildlife; little privacy in rooms. *$ Rooms from: S/1670 ⊠ 80 km (50 miles) east of Iquitos, Iquitos ☎ 065/252–530, 800/707–5275 in U.S. ⊕ www.explorama.com ➟ 40 rooms ⎟◎⎟ All meals.*

$$$$
RESORT

ExplorNapo Lodge. This remote lodge at the edge of a private biological reserve, three hours by boat from Iquitos, has a 1,500-foot-long, 120-foot-high canopy walkway, a medicinal plant garden, and more wildlife than the other Explorama lodges. **Pros:** wildlife; canopy walkway; in the jungle. **Cons:** very rustic; remote; expensive. *$ Rooms from: S/1449 ⊠ On Napo River, 160 km (100 miles) east of Iquitos, Iquitos ☎ 65/252–530, 800/707–5275 in U.S. ⊕ www.explorama.com ➟ 30 rooms without bath ⎟◎⎟ All meals.*

$$$$
RESORT

Heliconia Amazon River Lodge. Perched along the Amazon, a 90-minute boat ride downriver from Iquitos, the Heliconia has comfortable rooms with screened windows and private (hot-water) bathrooms and a blue-tile swimming pool. **Pros:** comfortable rooms; pool; Amazon River views; good value. **Cons:** less wildlife than some lodges. *$ Rooms from: S/1400 ⊠ 104 km (62 miles) east of Iquitos, Yanamono ☎ 01/421–9195, 065/231–983 ⊕ www.amazonriverexpeditions.com ➟ 26 rooms ⎟◎⎟ All meals.*

$$$$
RESORT
Fodor's Choice
★

Muyuna Lodge. Poised at the edge of a seasonally flooded forest on the tranquil Yanayacu River, Muyuna Lodge is surrounded by exuberant tropical forest teaming with wildlife. **Pros:** comfortable bungalows; abundant wildlife; knowledgeable guides; varied excursions;

good value. **Cons:** three-hour boat ride from Iquitos; cold-water showers; kerosene-lit rooms. $ *Rooms from: S/1230* ✉ *San Juan de Yanay-acu, 140 km (87 miles) southwest of Iquitos, Iquitos* ☎ *065/242–858, 995–918–964* ⊕ *www.muyuna.com* ⌁ *17 cabins* ⫮ *All meals.*

$$$$ ⬚ **Tahuayo Lodge.** This rustic eco-lodge owned by Amazonia Expedi-
RESORT   tions is an excellent base for experiencing the rain forest, especially when combined with a stay at the company's Amazon Research Center. **Pros:** plentiful wildlife; personalized tours; responsible tourism; good food; laundry service; solar power. **Cons:** you'll hear your neighbors from your room; cold showers. $ *Rooms from: S/1200* ✉ *Río Tahuayo, 130 km (80 miles) south of Iquitos, Iquitos* ☎ *065/242–792, 800/262–9669 toll-free in U.S.* ⊕ *perujungle.com* ⌁ *15 rooms, 9 with bath* ⫮ *All meals.*

$$$$ ⬚ **Tahuayo River Amazon Research Center.** Staying at this rustic lodge
RESORT   inside the Reserva Comunal Tamshiyacu-Tahuayo means almost constant exposure to tropical nature. **Pros:** deep in the forest; peaceful; abundant wildlife; good food; knowledgeable guides. **Cons:** not much privacy; no bathrooms in room. $ *Rooms from: S/1200* ✉ *Río Tahuayo, 145 km (90 miles) south of Iquitos, Iquitos* ☎ *65/242–792 in Peru, 800/262–9669 toll-free in U.S.* ⊕ *www.perujungle.com* ⌁ *8 rooms with shared bath* ⫮ *All meals.*

$$$$ ⬚ **Treehouse Lodge.** Bungalows at this unique jungle lodge are perched
RESORT   high in the branches of tropical trees, providing an unforgettable bird's-eye view of the rain forest and a 24-hour jungle soundtrack. **Pros:** idyllic treetop setting; good food; friendly staff. **Cons:** mosquitoes in rooms; less wildlife than other lodges; bungalows near river get boat noise; expensive. $ *Rooms from: S/1,880* ✉ *Yarapa River, 152 km (94 miles) southwest of Iquitos, Iquitos* ☎ *801/797–2777 in U.S.* ⊕ *treehouselo-dge.com* ⌁ *10 treehouses* ⫮ *All meals.*

THE CENTRAL
HIGHLANDS

Visit Fodors.com for advice, updates, and bookings

WELCOME TO
THE CENTRAL HIGHLANDS

TOP REASONS
TO GO

★ **Handicrafts:** Ayacucho has *retablos*—three-dimensional scenes of religious and historical events. Quinua has ceramic workshops. The Mantaro Valley has *mates burilados,* silver filigree, and alpaca textiles.

★ **Highland Cuisine:** Enjoy the sublime delights of freshly caught trout, *pachamanca* (herb-roasted meats, potatoes, and vegetables cooked in an earthen oven), and *papa a la huancaína* (potatoes covered in a spicy cheese sauce).

★ **Market Day:** Villagers trek in with their goods ready to hawk and trade. Head to the Mantaro Valley, where there's a market every day.

★ **World's Second-Highest Train:** It's no longer number one, but you can still chug your way from Lima to 4,782 meters (15,685 feet) before dropping down to the valleys surrounding Huancayo.

★ **Jungle Heat:** Head down to Chanchamayo, near Tarma, to escape the dry highland air and enjoy the soothing warmth of the high jungle.

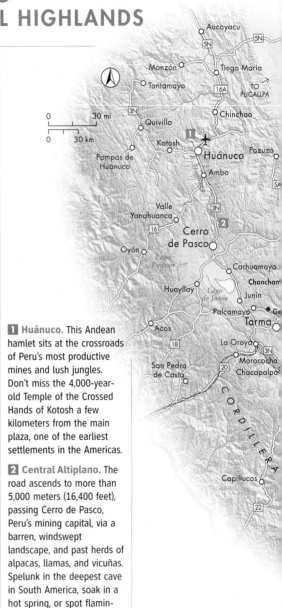

1 Huánuco. This Andean hamlet sits at the crossroads of Peru's most productive mines and lush jungles. Don't miss the 4,000-year-old Temple of the Crossed Hands of Kotosh a few kilometers from the main plaza, one of the earliest settlements in the Americas.

2 Central Altiplano. The road ascends to more than 5,000 meters (16,400 feet), passing Cerro de Pasco, Peru's mining capital, via a barren, windswept landscape, and past herds of alpacas, llamas, and vicuñas. Spelunk in the deepest cave in South America, soak in a hot spring, or spot flamingos on Peru's largest lake after Titicaca.

3 **Central Sierra.** A quintessential Andean town filled with women in traditional garb, crafts capital Huancayo is within a few minutes of vibrant festivals, daily markets, and breathtaking highland scenery. Many come for a weekend on the world's second-highest train, but then stay to study Spanish or explore the small pueblos dotting the surrounding countryside.

4 **Central Valley.** Some of the country's worst roads have kept outside influences away, leaving traditional Andean values intact in places such as Huancavelica. These small villages, perched on the side of countless nameless mountains, can induce more than vertigo; *soroche*, or altitude sickness, will strike the uninitiated, so follow the locals by drinking coca tea and taking it easy while enjoying the breathtaking scenery.

5 **Ayacucho.** Terrorism once cut Ayacucho off from the rest of the country, but with stability, improved roads, and regular flights from Lima, the church-filled town is firmly on the tourist trail. Its centuries-old traditions come to life during the weeklong Semana Santa Easter celebrations, when a passionate and deeply religious fervor blankets the town.

GETTING ORIENTED

A mere hour east of Lima puts you in the foothills of the Andes, a windy, barren landscape where llamas and alpacas graze on vast, puddle-filled fields. Under the blinding highland sun, roads and rails twist around the peaks and pass through ramshackle mountain towns before sliding down through cloud forests and thick jungle en route to Tingo María and Pucallpa. Southeast from Tarma, passing through Huancayo and on to Ayacucho, massive green mountains and the endless *altiplano* (high plains) protect hidden Incan ruins and mesmerizing stone forests.

8

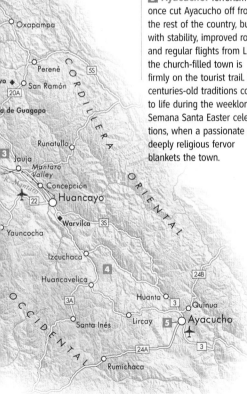

Updated
by Mike
Gasparovic

The Central Highlands are where the massive Andes crash into the impenetrable South American rain forests, and winding, cloud-covered mountain roads dip down into stark desert terrain. Defying the land's complexity, its people continue to eke out a hardscrabble life that time has left unchanged.

Most people in the Andes still depend on the crops they grow and the animals they breed—including guinea pigs and alpaca. Local festivals coincide with the rhythms of the harvest, and traditional recipes and artisanship predate the Inca Empire by hundreds of years. The scenery is stunning, with thundering rivers, blooming potato fields, and hidden waterfalls tucked into the mountainous terrain. Lago de Junín, the country's second-largest lake, sits miles above sea level and crowns the region.

Despite how little daily life seems to have changed over the centuries, the area has served as the backdrop for some of the most explosive events in Peruvian history: fierce wars between the Inca and the Wanka, important battles for independence, and the birth of Peru's most devastating terrorist organization. Sendero Luminoso (the Shining Path) violently shook Peru's political landscape in the Ayacucho region for more than two decades. In the wake of Peru's massive 1969 land reform, Sendero's charismatic leader, Abimaél Guzmán Reynoso, promised an agrarian paradise to Ayacucho's long disenfranchised *campesinos* (peasants). The Central Highlands descended into civil war, and nearly 70,000 people died at the hands of the Shining Path and government-sponsored paramilitaries before Alberto Fujimori's government captured Guzmán in a Lima suburb in 1992 and Oscar Alberto Ramírez Durand, the leader of the Sendero Rojo offshoot, in 1999. The Shining Path is now a small shadow of its former self, controlling narcotrafficking in the *VRAE* (the Apurímac and Ene river Valleys), which abuts the Central Highlands, and occasionally skirmishing with the Peruvian military. Fujimori now resides in the same prison as his foe Guzmán, having been convicted of human-rights abuses committed during the 1992 *auto-golpe* (self-coup) that gave him unlimited power. Now, apart from narcotrafficking and the occasional protest from coca growers and unions, the region is relatively calm.

The Central Sierra is today gaining prominence among tourists, and greater integration with the rest of Peru along with improved security, and transportation options have opened up this remote region to adventurers and cultural travelers alike. To date, it remains one of the most authentic places in the entire country.

No one knows when the first cultures settled on the *puna* (highland plains) or how long they stayed. ■TIP➜ **Archaeologists found what they believe to be the oldest village in Peru at Lauricocha, near Huánuco, and one of the oldest temples in the Americas at Kotosh.** Other nearby archaeological sites at Tantamayo and Garu also show that indigenous cultures thrived here long before the Inca or Spanish conquistadors ever reached the area.

When the Inca arrived in the late 1400s, they incorporated the already stable northern settlement of Huánuco into their empire. It eventually became an important stop along their route between the capital at Cusco and the northern hub of Cajamarca, and today Inca ruins are scattered along the *pampas*. The Spanish built a colonial city at Huánuco in 1539, and the area quickly gained the attention of Spanish explorers, who turned Cerro de Pasco's buried gold, silver, copper, and coal into the center of the mining industry north of the Amazon Basin. They ruled the region—and the country—until 1824, when Simón Bolívar's troops secured Peru's autonomy by defeating the Spanish on the Pampas de Quinua near Ayacucho.

8

PLANNING

WHEN TO GO

This region's best weather falls in the dry season—May through October—when the skies are clear and daytime temperatures are moderate (nights can be frigid). The rainy season is November through April, when many roads are inaccessible.

GETTING HERE AND AROUND
AIR TRAVEL

The airline LC Perú (⊕ *www.lcperu.pe*) flies from Lima to Andahuaylas, Ayacucho, Jauja, Huánuco, and Tingo Maria. Star Perú (⊕ *www. starperu.com*) flies from Lima to Ayacucho and Huánuco. Airlines often cancel flights because of unpredictable weather; always confirm your flight, even outside the rainy season.

BUS TRAVEL

Lima is the country's travel hub. Ormeño, Cruz del Sur, and Expresa Molina, among others, run overnight services (10 hours) from Lima to Ayacucho. Likewise, ETUCSA, Ormeño, Cruz del Sur, and Expresa Molina have many daily buses between Huancayo and Lima (7 hours). You can also reach Huancayo from Ayacucho (12 hours) by overnight service on Turismo Central and Expresa Molina—but prepare for a very rough road. Expresa Molina and Empresa Hidalgo have buses to Huancavelica. GM international has overnight service (7 hours) between Huánuco and Lima. *Colectivos* (shared taxis) travel between the Central Highlands cities, and can be much quicker though slightly more expensive than bus travel. The location of these *paraderos* (taxi stops) changes, so ask your hotel receptionist for directions.

CAR TRAVEL

The Central Highlands have some of the country's most scenic driving routes, and paved roads link Lima and Huánuco to the north and Huancayo to the south. It's five hours from the capital to the crossroads at La Oroya, from which a gorgeous Andean panorama stretches in three directions: north toward Huánuco, east toward Tarma, and south to Huancayo. Most sights around Huancayo in the Valle del Mantaro are accessible by car. You should travel the rugged road from Huancayo to Ayacucho in a four-wheel-drive vehicle, and be sure to bring emergency supplies for the 12-hour trip. Except for the highway, there are mostly dirt roads in this region, so be prepared. There is no place to rent a car in this region.

TRAIN TRAVEL

The train journey from the capital is the most memorable travel option, but service is limited, with bimonthly trips running only from May to November. On the route from Lima to Huancayo, the 12-hour, 335-km (207-mile) railway cuts through the Andes, across mountain slopes, and above deep crevasses where thin waterfalls plunge down into icy streams far below.

HEALTH AND SAFETY

Altitude sickness, or *soroche,* is a common risk in the Andes, though it's not a major concern unless you're hiking or climbing. Hydrate with water and coca tea, avoid alcohol, and move slowly until you have acclimated.

Safety and security have improved dramatically since Shining Path's heyday in the 1980s, and the Central Highlands benefit from a strong military presence. Occasional conflicts do shake the area, though, with illegal coca growers and militant unions often blocking roads, particularly in the area from Huánuco to Pucallpa. This has little effect on tourism, although a regional strike can throw off a tight itinerary.

Petty crime is rarer in the highlands than in Lima. By staying alert and taking standard precautions, you shouldn't have any trouble. Carry your passport and other important identification on you at all times. Call 105 for an ambulance, the fire department, or the police.

RESTAURANTS

Dining out in the Central Highlands is a casual experience. Restaurants are mostly small, family-run eateries serving regional fare. Breakfast is usually bread with jam or butter and juice, but can include anything from eggs to soups. The midday lunch, the day's largest meal, combines soup, salad, and a rice-and-meat dish. You'll find snacks everywhere, from nuts and fruit to ice cream and pastries. Dinner is after 7 pm and tends to be light. Don't worry about dressing up or making reservations. Tipping isn't customary, but waiters appreciate the extra change. All parts of the animal and almost every edible species are considered. Guinea pig husbandry is a centuries-old tradition, so *cuy* served grilled or fried is a menu staple. Highland potatoes, *choclo* (large grained corn), fresh cheese, and rich stews spiced with *aji* (chili pepper) round out the highland culinary experience.

The cuisine of the Central Highlands, which focuses on local ingredients and techniques, reflects its isolation. Huancayo's local specialty is *papa a la huancaína* (potatoes covered in spicy cheese sauce), served cold with a sliced egg and an olive. *Pachamanca* (herb-roasted meats, potatoes, and vegetables) is wrapped in local herbs, then slow-cooked on hot stones in an earthen oven. Huánuco's favorites include *picante de cuy* (guinea pig in hot-pepper sauce), pachamanca, fried trout, *humitas* (a local tamale made of ground corn and stuffed with cheese or raisins), and *caldo de cabeza* (sheep's-head soup). Ayacucho is famous for its filling, flavorful *puca picante* (a nutty pork-and-potato stew), served with rice and topped with parsley. During Semana Santa (Holy Week), the city's favorite drink is the warm *ponche* (flavored with milk, cinnamon, cloves, sesame, peanuts, walnuts, and sugar).

HOTELS

Accommodations in the Central Highlands lean toward the basic. Not all properties have hot water or private baths, and almost none have (or require) air-conditioning. If you don't need pampering, and you don't expect top-quality service, you'll travel easily—and cheaply. The majority of hotels have clean, modest rooms with simple Andean motifs. Bathrooms usually have showers only, and you should confirm that the hot water does function before paying for a room. Most better hotels have a restaurant, or at least a dining room with some type of food service. If you want a homestay experience, ask your hotel or a local travel company, who can often hook you up with hosts in the area.

Rooms are usually available, but if you'll be traveling during the region's popular Semana Santa or Fiestas Patrias (July 28), book tours and hotels early. Also book early around the anniversary of the Battle of Ayacucho in mid-December. *Hotel reviews have been shortened. For full information, visit Fodors.com.*

WHAT IT COSTS IN NUEVO SOLES			
$	**$$**	**$$$**	**$$$$**
Restaurants	under S/35	S/35–S/50	S/51–S/65	Over S/65
Hotels	under S/250	S/250–S/500	S/501–S/800	Over S/800

Restaurant prices are the average cost of a main course at dinner or, if dinner is not served, at lunch. Hotel prices are the lowest cost of a standard double room in high season.

TOURS

A&R Tours. Ayacucho is surrounded by archaeological ruins and natural wonders, all of which can be viewed on a package tour. A&R Tours has city excursions and routes to Huari, Quinua, Valle Huanta, and Vilcashuamán. ✉ *9 de Diciembre 130, Ayacucho* ☎ *066/311–300* ⊕ *www.viajesartours.com* 🖅 *From S/60.*

Dargui Tours. This outfitter offers multiday tours of the region, with a focus on the archaeological ruins around Huancayo. ✉ *Jr. Ancash 367, Plaza Constitución, Huancayo* ☎ *064/233–705* ⊕ *www.darguitours. com* 🖅 *From S/55.*

Incas del Perú. Around Huancayo you can hike, bike, and explore local villages with the amazing Incas del Perú, which also has a Spanish-language school, book exchange, and folk-art collection. They will also arrange volunteering and hiking throughout the Mantaro Valley and high jungle, as well as music, cooking, weaving, and gourd-carving workshops. ✉ *Giráldez 675, Huancayo* ☎ *064/223–303* ⊕ *www.incasdelperu.org* 🖅 *From S/50.*

Max Adventures. For standard day tours around Tarma, including adventure activities like rappelling and mountain biking, call Max Adventures. They also do multiday trips to to the Reserva Nacional de Junín and high jungle around Chanchamayo, including Oxapampa and Villarica. ✉ *2 de Mayo 682, Tarma* ☎ *064/323–908* ⊕ *maxaventuraperu. com* 🖅 *From S/50.*

Perla Tours. Veteran outfitter Perla Tours specializes in day trips around Tarma, with stops like the Gruta de Huagapo cave, as well as longer trips into the central jungle. ✉ *Jr. Moquegua 615, Tarma* ☎ *064/321–796* ⊕ *www.perlatarma.com* 🖅 *From S/45.*

HUÁNUCO

390 km (242 miles) northeast of Lima; 105 km (65 miles) north of Cerro de Pasco.

At first glance, Huánuco looks like any other Spanish settlement: a picturesque collection of colonial buildings and churches surrounded by rocky, forested mountains and cut through by the Huallaga River. History, however, runs far deeper here. Evidence of some of Peru's earliest human settlements, and some of the oldest ruins in the country, were found nearby at Lauricocha and Kotosh. Pre-Inca ruins have turned up throughout these mountains, notably at Tantamayo and Garu. Huánuco was an Inca stronghold and a convenient stopover on their route from Cusco north to Cajamarca. Thousands of Inca relics litter the surrounding *pampas*.

Huánuco's cool, 1,894-meter (6,212-foot) elevation makes for pleasant winter days and crisp nights, but in the rainy summer, a thick mountain fog blankets the town. The Spanish-style architecture reflects the town's 1539 founding, and later buildings tell the story of Huánuco's importance as a cultural hub. Still, the original Peruvian traditions run deep, particularly during the annual Huánuco anniversary celebrations. Mountain hikes, swims in natural pools, and dips in nearby hot springs add to the area's natural appeal.

Exploring ▼

Iglesia La
Merced **1**

Iglesia San
Cristóbal **2**

Iglesia San
Francisco **3**

Kotosh **5**

Pampa de
Huánuco **4**

Tomayquichua ...**6**

Restaurants ▼

Recreo
El Falcon **1**

Hotels ▼

Casa Hacienda
Shismay **3**

Gran Hotel
Cusco **2**

Grand Hotel
Huánuco **1**

KEY

❶ *Exploring*

① *Restaurants*

① *Hotels*

Huánuco

GETTING HERE AND AROUND

Most of Huánuco can be seen on foot or via short, cheap cab rides. A guide is recommended for exploring beyond the city. The area is a major coca-growing region, and farmers are leery about strange characters hanging about. Tours from several agencies on the Plaza de Armas will bring you to the major sites within a few hours of the city for less than S/50. David Figueroa Fernandini Airport (HUU) is 8 km (5 miles) from Huánuco, and has daily flights to Lima.

Airport David Figueroa Fernandini Airport. ✉ *Carretera al Aeropuerto* ☎ *062/513–066.*

Bus León de Huánuco. ✉ *Robles 821* ☎ *062/512–996.* **Transmar.** ✉ *Av. 28 de Julio 1065* ☎ *062/510–414* ⊕ *www.transmar.com.pe.* **Transportes Rey.** ✉ *Av. 28 de Julio 1215* ☎ *062/513–623.* **Turismo Central.** ✉ *Tarapacá 598* ☎ *062/511–806* ⊕ *www.turismocentral.com.pe.*

ESSENTIALS

Currency Banco de Crédito. ✉ *Huánuco 699* ☎ *062/512–213* ⊕ *www.viabcp.com.*

Mail Serpost. ✉ *2 de Mayo 1157* ☎ *062/512–503.*

EXPLORING

TOP ATTRACTIONS

Kotosh. Considered to be one of South America's oldest temples, Kotosh, a 4,000-year-old archaeological site, is famous for the *Templo de las Manos Cruzadas* (Temple of the Crossed Hands). Some of the oldest Peruvian pottery relics were discovered below one of the niches surrounding the main room of the temple, and the partially restored ruins are thought to have been constructed by the Kotosh, one of the country's earliest cultures. Inside the temple you'll see re-created images of the crossed hands. The original mud set is dated 2000 BC and is on display in Lima's Museo Nacional de Antropología, Arqueología, e Historia del Perú. ■ TIP→ The site was named Kotosh, Quechua for "pile," in reference to the piles of rocks found strewn across the fields. Taxi fare is S/20 for the round-trip journey from Huánuco, including a half hour to sightsee. ⊠ *5 km (3 miles) west of Huánuco* 🖼 *S/5.*

WORTH NOTING

Iglesia La Merced. The Romanesque Iglesia La Merced was built in 1566 by Royal Ensign Don Pedro Rodriguez. Colonial treasures include a silver tabernacle, paintings of the Cusco school, and the images of the Virgen Purísima and the Corazón de Jesús that were gifts from King Phillip II. ⊠ *Huánuco and Valdizán* 🖼 *Free.*

Iglesia San Cristóbal. Fronting a landscape of steep, grassy mountain slopes, the Iglesia San Cristóbal, with its three-tiered bell tower, was erected in 1542, the first local church built by Spanish settlers. Inside is a valuable collection of colonial-era paintings and baroque wood sculptures of San Agustín, the Virgen de la Asunción, and the Virgen Dolorosa. ⊠ *San Cristóbal y Beraún* 🖼 *Free.*

Iglesia San Francisco. The 16th-century Iglesia San Francisco, the city's second-oldest church, has Cusco-school paintings and a few colonial-era antiques. Peek inside to see the spectacular gilt wall and arches behind the altar. ⊠ *Huallayco and Beraún* 🖼 *Free.*

Pampa de Huánuco. Also known as Huánuco Viejo, this was formerly the ancient capital city of Chinchaysuyu, the northern portion of the Inca Empire. These highland *pampas* contain Incan ruins and are near the town of La Unión, a S/30 taxi ride from Huánuco. ■ TIP→ During the last week of July, the Fiesta del Sol (Sun Festival) takes place at the ruins. ⊠ *137 km (85 miles) northwest of Huánuco near town of La Unión* 🖼 *Free.*

OFF THE BEATEN PATH

Tomayquichua. This small village was the birthplace of Micaela Villegas, a famous *mestiza* (mixed race) entertainer in the 18th century and the mistress of Viceroy Manuel de Amat y Juniet, a Spanish military hero and prominent colonial official. Also known as La Perricholi, her story was the basis of Prosper Mérimée's comic novella *Le Carrosse du Saint-Sacrement* , and she was an important character along with the viceroy in Thornton Wilder's *The Bridge of San Luis Rey.* A festival in July with parades, music, and dancing celebrates her vitality. Beautiful mountain views are the main attraction of the 2,000-meter-high (6,500-foot- high) area. Sixteenth-century San Miguel Arcángel, one of the first churches built in the Huánuco area, is nearby in the village of Huacar. ⊠ *Huánuco ⊹ 15 km (9 miles) south of Huánuco.*

WHERE TO EAT AND STAY

Restaurants in Huánuco are simple and small, mostly offering local cuisine with a smattering of Chinese and Continental selections. Little eateries cluster around the plaza and markets. **■ TIP→ Most large hotels have a small restaurant.** Hotels are basic, with shared cold-water baths at most budget places. Spend a little more and you'll get lots more comfort, including a private bath, hot water, and a better mattress. But don't expect the Ritz.

$ PERUVIAN 🍴 **Recreo El Falcon.** Perched on the banks of the Huallaga River, this family-style restaurant offers the best of Huánuco cooking, including specialties like *gallina con locro* (chicken soup), pachamanca, and fresh river trout. Come at lunch and lounge on the open-air terrace while you enjoy the view and live music. **Known for:** regional home cooking; generous portions. [$] *Average main: S/22* ✉ *2 de Mayo 190* ☎ *062/516–214* ⏲ *No dinner.*

$ B&B/INN Fodor's Choice ★ 🏨 **Casa Hacienda Shismay.** For lovers of beautiful landscapes and peaceful scenery, Casa Hacienda Shismay, founded in 1851, is a slice of paradise in the highlands of Peru. **Pros:** incredible value; national historic monument; spectacular scenery. **Cons:** 45 minutes from Huánuco; no public transportation; might be too rustic for some. [$] *Rooms from: S/204* ✉ *Shismay* ☎ *062/631–174 in Shismay, 999/036–074 in Lima* 🌐 *www.shismay.com* 🛏 *4 rooms* 🍽 *Breakfast.*

$ HOTEL 🏨 **Gran Hotel Cusco.** This local favorite has a boutiquey feel, with its ample spaces and contemporary photography on the walls. **Pros:** decent price; modern renovations; pool. **Cons:** basic rooms. [$] *Rooms from: S/80* ✉ *Huánuco 616* ☎ *062/517–653* 🌐 *www.hotelcuzcohuanuco.com* 🛏 *60 rooms* 🍽 *Breakfast.*

$$ HOTEL 🏨 **Grand Hotel Huánuco.** The colonial-style building, built in 1943, is chic, swanky, and completely out of place in simple Huánuco, which explains the business travelers wandering its wide halls. **Pros:** on the plaza; first-class service; good restaurant; pool, sauna, and gym. **Cons:** rooms overlooking the plaza are noisy. [$] *Rooms from: S/289* ✉ *Jr. Dámaso Beraún 775* ☎ *062/512–410* 🌐 *grandhotelhuanuco.com* 🛏 *35 rooms* 🍽 *Breakfast.*

CENTRAL ALTIPLANO: HUÁNUCO SOUTH TO TARMA

Heading east, the road from modern, sprawling Lima climbs through the Andes, then splits north–south through the highlands. Working its way through the narrow crevasses and up the rugged hillsides of the Valle Mantaro, the northern road speeds endlessly forward at an elevation of 4,250 meters (13,940 feet) atop the Earth's largest high-altitude plains. This route north connects the mountain towns of La Oroya, Junín, Cerro de Pasco, and Huánuco, where despite battles for independence and intrusions of modern technology, traditional customs remain the way of life. At an elevation of 3,755 meters (12,316 feet), by the confluence of the Río Mantaro and Río Yauli, La Oroya is a town of 33,000 and a main smelting center for the region's mining industry.

8

From here you can head due east to Tarma or continue north by road or rail to the village of Junín. Still farther northwest along the eastern shores of Lago de Junín are Tambo del Sol and Cerro de Pasco.

At an elevation of 4,333 meters (14,212 feet), with more than 70,000 residents, Cerro de Pasco is the world's highest town of its size. It's also the main center for copper, gold, lead, silver, and zinc mining north of the Amazon basin, as the pit mine–turned-lake at the center of town can attest. Coal is excavated from the Goyllarisquisga canyon 42 km (26 miles) north of town, the highest coal mine in the world.

About 80 km (50 miles) east of town, the Valle de Huachón provides gorgeous mountains for hiking and camping, and the trail north toward Huánuco runs along a spectacular road that plunges nearly 2,500 meters (8,200 feet) in the first 30 km (19 miles). Overlooking the land from an elevation of 1,849 meters (6,065 feet), Huánuco is a pleasant stopover between Lima and thick jungles around Pucullpa or before heading south toward Huancayo and into the highlands.

VALLE YANAHUANCA

112 km (70 miles) southwest of Huánuco; 80 km (50 miles) north of Huancayo; 65 km (40 miles) northwest of Cerro de Pasco.

One of the longest-surviving stretches of Inca road, otherwise known as the Qhapaq Nan, passes through the massive rocky outcrops and deep meadows of the Valle Yanahuanca. Forested hills threaded by shallow, pebbled rivers lead 4 km (2½ miles) from the village of Yanahuanca to the village of Huarautambo, where pre-Inca ruins dot the rugged terrain. Continue along the 150-km (93-mile) Inca track and you'll pass La Union, San Marcos, Huari, Llamellin, and San Luis.

TARMA

274 km (170 miles) east of Lima; 65 km (40 miles) southeast of Junín.

The hidden mountain town known as "The Pearl of the Andes" has grown into a city of 55,000 whose traditions and sights illuminate its Peruvian roots. Long before the Spanish arrived, indigenous peoples built homes and temples in the hills that framed the town, the ruins of which local farmers continue to uncover as they turn the rich soil into flower and potato fields, coffee plantations, and orchards. The town's look is Spanish, though, with a small Plaza de Armas and several colonial-style churches and mansions.

At an elevation of 3,050 meters (10,004 feet), Tarma has a cool and breezy climate, with crisp nights all year. ■TIP→ **Get out in these nights, too, as candlelight processions are a major part of the town's many festivals—notably the Fiesta San Sebastián in January, Semana Santa in March or April, Semana de Tarma in July, and Fiesta El Señor de Los Milagros in October.** Tarma is definitely not a tourist town, but a place to visit for true Peruvian traditions and easy access to the jungle to the east.

Tarma's **Oficina de Turismo**, on the Plaza de Armas, can help you find qualified local guides for sights in the region.

Quechua of the Andes

The Quechua are the original mountain highlands dwellers. Their traditions and beliefs have survived Inca domination, Spanish conquests, and the beginning influences of modern technology. Throughout the region, locals speak Quechua before Spanish and wear traditional costumes woven on backstrap looms. Many Quechua make their living by farming maize and coca in the valleys or potatoes and quinua in the higher altitudes, and other families herd llamas and alpacas on the cold, windy *puna.*

QUECHUA ATTIRE

Walk through the narrow, cobbled streets of any village and you'll spot Quechua men by the large, patterned, fringed ponchos draped over their shoulders, their heads topped by matching tasseled cloths beneath big, cone-shape, felt hats. Knee-length pants are held up with a wide, woven belt that often has a local motif—such as the famous mountain train. Despite the cold, men usually wear rubber sandals, often fashioned from old tires.

Quechua women's attire is equally bright, with modern knit sweaters and a flouncing, patterned skirt over several petticoats (added for both warmth and puff). Instead of a poncho, women wear an *aguayo,* a length of sarong-like fabric that can be tied into a sling for carrying a baby or market goods, or wrapped around their shoulders for warmth. Hats for the women differ from village to village; some wear black-felt caps with neon fringe and elaborate patterns of sequins and beads, whereas others wear a plain brown-felt derby. Women also wear rubber sandals for walking and working in the fields but often go barefoot at home.

QUECHUA HOMES

Look for gatherings of stone or adobe-brick homes with thatched roofs as you travel through the mountains. These typical Quechua homes are basic inside and out. Food is cooked either in an adobe oven next to the dwelling or over an open fire inside. Mud platforms with llama wool or sheepskin blankets make do for beds; occasionally a family will have the luxury of a wooden bed frame and grass mattress. All members of the family work in the fields as soon as they are able. Members of the *ayllu* (extended family) are expected to contribute to major projects like harvesting the fields or building a new home.

THE MOROCHUCO QUECHUA

The Morochuco are a unique group of formerly nomadic Quechua who live near Ayacucho on the Pampas de Cangallo. They have light skin and blue eyes, and, unlike other Quechua, many Morochuco men wear beards. The Morochuco are first-rate horse-back riders—women and children included—who use their swiftness and agility to round up bulls on the highland *pampas.* Renowned for their fearlessness and strength, the Morochuco fought for Peru's independence on horseback with Simón Bolívar. Women ride in long skirts and petticoats, whereas men don thick wool tights and dark ponchos. Both men and women wear *chullos,* wool hats with earflaps, beneath a felt hat tied under the chin with a red sash.

8

QUECHUA LESSON

Here's a small sampling of Quechua words. It won't make you fluent, but people appreciate the effort when you learn a few of words of their language.

Words:

House—wasi

Mother—mama

Father—papa, tayta

Son—wawa

Daughter—wawa

Yes—arí

No—mana

Please—allichu

Hello—rimaykullayki, napaykullayki

Phrases:

What is your name?—Imataq sutiyki?

My name is ... —Nuqap ... sutiymi

Good-bye—rikunakusun

Good morning—windía

How are you?—Ima hinalla?

Thank you—añay

Numbers:

Zero—ch'usaq

One—huq, huk

Two—iskay

Three—kinsa, kimsa

Four—tawa

Five—pishqa, pisqa, pichqa

Six—soqta, suqta

Seven—qanchis

Eight—pusaq, pusac

Nine—isqun

Ten—thunka

GETTING HERE AND AROUND

Transportes Chanchamayo, Transportes DASA, and Transportes Junín all offer daily bus service, each two or three times a day, between Tarma and Lima. Transportes Chanchamayo also offers continuing service to Huancayo or La Merced. *Colectivos* to all Central Highlands cities can be found at corners throughout the city; just ask.

ESSENTIALS

Visitor Information Oficina de Turismo. ⊠ *Lima 199* ☎ *064/321–010* ⊕ *turismo.munitarma.gob.pe.*

EXPLORING

Chanchamayo. Tarma sits at more than 3,000 meters (10,000 feet) but is a stone's throw from the *ceja de selva* (high jungle), where many of Peru's citrus plantations lie. For around S/60, you can organize a day trip from Tarma to visit Chanchamayo's magnificent waterfalls, butterfly-filled forests, and local tribal groups. These tours take guests to the major waterfalls in the area, including a refreshing dip in the 30-meter (98-foot) Tirol Falls, a jungle lunch of *cecina* (cured pork) or *doncella* (river fish), a visit to the local Ashaninka tribe at Pampa Michi, and a tasting of local coffees and other artisanal products. For those who won't get to the Amazon during their time in Peru, this is an inexpensive way to experience the pleasures of jungle living. It is also a warm escape from the cool highland air. Peru Latino Tarma offers daily tours. It's also possible to take a bus directly to La Merced, the main town in Chanchamayo. There are simple hotels and restaurants surrounding the small plaza, and you can take tours from there deeper into the central jungle to the fascinating German-Austrian colony of Oxapampa or coffee plantations near Villarica. ✉ *50 km (20 miles) from Tarma, La Merced.*

Gruta de Guagapo. Head northwest of Tarma 28 km (17 miles) to Palcamayo, then continue 4 km (2½ miles) west to explore the Gruta de Guagapo limestone cave system, a National Speleological Area. Guides live in the village near the entrance and can give you a basic short tour, but you'll need full spelunking equipment for deep cavern trips. Numerous tour operators in Tarma offer day trips of the caves and the surrounding villages. It is also possible to arrive at the caves independently by taking a *collectivo* at the corner of Jr. 2 de Mayo and Jr. Puno. ✉ *Palcamayo.*

WHERE TO EAT AND STAY

$ PERUVIAN — 🍴 **Restaurant Chavín de Grima.** This popular travelers' hangout on the plaza has kitschy Andean decor—pictures of snow-covered mountains, patterned wall hangings—and lively lunchtime crowds. They serve tamales and sweet coffee for breakfast, and *comida típica* , including hearty stews, rice dishes, grilled meat, and fish for lunch and dinner. **Known for:** convival atmosphere; hearty fare. [$] *Average main: S/17* ✉ *Lima 270* ☎ *964/647–446.*

$ B&B/INN Fodor's Choice ★ — 🏨 **Hacienda La Florida.** Experience life at a Spanish hacienda at this charming bed-and-breakfast just a 10-minute drive from Tarma. **Pros:** breakfast included; hiking trails lead from property. **Cons:** simple accommodations; car ride from town. [$] *Rooms from: S/245* ✉ *6 km (4 miles) north of Tarma* ☎ *064/341–041 in Tarma, 01/518–8429 in Lima* 🌐 *www.haciendalaflorida.com* 🛏 *5 rooms* 🍽 *Breakfast.*

$$ HOTEL — 🏨 **LP Hotel Tarma.** By far the most luxurious hotel in town, this frequently updated colonial-style mansion surrounded by gardens offers as much warmth as grandeur. **Pros:** historical charm; package deals; lots of amenities. **Cons:** filled during the week with business travelers. [$] *Rooms from: S/279* ✉ *Ramon Castilla 512* ☎ *064/321–411* 🌐 *www.losportaleshoteles.com.pe/hotel/tarma* 🛏 *45 rooms* 🍽 *Breakfast.*

CENTRAL SIERRA: TARMA SOUTH TO HUANCAYO

Traveling onward from Tarma's orchards, you leave the warm cradle of this Andean valley and head back into the crisp air above 3,500 meters (11,482 feet). The road south to Huancayo runs along a high plain buffeted by wind and pocked by herds of highland cattle, and the Río Mantaro leaves a crystalline gash in the otherwise uninterrupted landscape. Draining the massive Lago de Junín, the river has long sustained civilization in the Central Sierra, irrigating corn, artichoke, and potato fields throughout the region.

The hills around Tarma are covered in a pretty patchwork of farmland.

The road is a trip through Peru's complicated history and politics, with Huanca and Inca ruins surrounding Jauja, the former capital of the Peruvian Viceroyalty, and Concepción, home to one of highland Peru's most stunning convents. The trip back in time ends as you approach Huancayo, a modern town enjoying the results of a decade-long mineral boom. Don't be thrown off by its hustle and bustle; Huancayo still pays respects to the traditions of its past, serving up some of the region's best cuisine and finest artisanship, all in the shadows of its colonial churches.

JAUJA

266 km (165 miles) east of Lima; 60 km (37 miles) south of Tarma.

Jauja has the distinction of having been Peru's original capital, as declared by Francisco Pizarro when he swept through the region; he changed his mind in 1535 and transferred the title to Lima. ■TIP→ **Jauja still has many of the ornate 16th-century homes and churches that mark its place in the country's history.** The Wednesday and Sunday markets display Andean traditions at their most colorful, showing the other side of life in this mountain town. Although there are several moderately priced hotels, many travelers come here on a day trip from Huancayo. Those who stay usually visit **Laguna de Paca**, 4 km (2½ miles) from town, which has a few small lakeside restaurants and rowboat rentals.

CONCEPCIÓN

25 km (16 miles) southeast of Jauja; 22 km (14 miles) northwest of Huancayo.

Visitors rarely linger in the small mountain town of Concepción, and neither should you. Aside from being a battle site during the War of the Pacific, where a force of more than 1,000 Peruvian soldiers vastly outmatched 77 Chileans, there is one impressive convent with a historic library.

Convento de Santa Rosa de Ocopa. Originally a Franciscan foundation whose role was to bring Christianity to the Amazon peoples, the 1725 building now has a reconstructed 1905 church and a massive library with more than 25,000 books—some from the 15th century. The natural-history museum displays a selection of regional archaeological finds, including traditional costumes and local crafts picked up by the priests during their travels. A restaurant serves excellent, if simple, Andean food, and several spare but comfortable accommodations are in the former monks' quarters. Take a S/25 taxi ride for a round trip to the convent from Concepción's Plaza de Armas. Admission includes a guided tour. ⊠ *6 km (4 miles) outside Concepción, Concepción* ⌸ *S/5* ⊙ *Closed Tues.*

HUANCAYO

22 km (14 miles) southeast of Concepción; 48 km (30 miles) southeast of Jauja.

It's not hard to see how the modern city of Huancayo, which has close to 260,000 residents, was once the capital of pre-Inca Huanca (Wanka) culture. In the midst of the Andes and straddling the verdant Río Mantaro valley, the city has been a source of artistic inspiration from the days of the earliest settlers and has thrived as the region's center for culture and wheat farming. A major agricultural hub, Huancayo was linked by rail with the capital in 1908, making it an endpoint to what was once the world's highest train line (but is now in second place). Although it's a large town, its little shops, small restaurants, blossoming plazas, and broad colonial buildings give it a comfortable, compact feel.

Huancayo was also a stronghold for the toughest Peruvian indigenous peoples, including the Huanca, who outfought both the Inca and the Spanish. Little wonder that Peru finally gained independence in this region, near Quinua, in 1824. ■ TIP→ Still, the Spanish left their mark with the town's collection of hacienda-style homes and businesses, most with arching windows and fronted by brick courtyards with carefully groomed gardens. For an overview of the city, head northeast 4 km (2½ miles) on Giráldez, 2 km (1 mile) past Cerro de la Libertad Park, to the eroded sandstone towers in the hillsides at Torre-Torre.

8

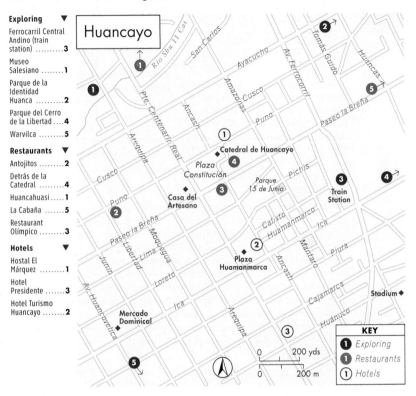

The drive from Lima to Huancayo is breathtaking, with the road rising to more than 4,700 meters (15,416 feet) before sliding down to the valley's 3,272-meter (10,731-foot) elevation. As you enter the city, four-lane Calle Real is jammed with traffic and crammed with storefronts—but look more closely and you'll see the elegant churches and colorful markets tucked into its side streets, hallmarks of local life that make the city so charming. Women with long black braids beneath black-felt hats still dress in multitiered skirts and blouses with *mantas* (bright, square, striped cloths) draped over their shoulders. Note the intricate weavings—particularly the belts with the famous train worked into the pattern.

GETTING HERE AND AROUND

Huancayo's tiny Francisco Carle Airport (JAU) is 45 km (27 miles) north of town near Jauja. LC Perú offers regular flights from Lima. Although Huancayo is big, most of the areas of interest to travelers are within walking distance of the plaza. The exceptions are the crafts villages in the Mantaro Valley. *Combi*vans circle the city streets looking for passengers for the 20- to 40-minute rides to each town, or you can take a comprehensive valley tour from any of the travel agencies in Huancayo for S/50–S/60. Taxis are another option, as they're quite economical.

Bus Cruz del Sur. ✉ *Ferrocarril 151* ☎ *064/223-367* ⊕ *www.cruzdelsur. pe.* **ETUCSA.** ✉ *Puno 220* ☎ *064/226-524.* **Expreso Molina.** ✉ *Angaraes 334* ☎ *064/224-501* ⊕ *www.molinaunion.pe.* **Ormeño.** ✉ *Mariscal Castilla 1379, Tambo* ☎ *964/346-056, 01/472-5679 in Lima* ⊕ *www.grupo-ormeno.com.pe.* **Turismo Central.** ✉ *Ayacucho 274* ☎ *066/223-128* ⊕ *www.turismocentral.com. pe/huancayo.*

ESSENTIALS
Currency Banco de Crédito. ✉ *Real 1075* ⊕ *www.viabcp.com.*

Mail Serpost. ✉ *Centro Cívico Foco 2, Plaza Huamanmarca* ☎ *064/231-101* ⊕ *www.serpost.com.pe.*

Visitor Information Dirección de Comercio Exterior y Turismo de Huancayo. ✉ *Pachitea 201, inside the train station* ☎ *064/222-575* ⊕ *turismo.junin.gob.pe.*

EXPLORING

Fodor'sChoice ★ **Ferrocarril Central Andino.** The Central Highlands' Ferrocarril Central Andino once laid claim to being the world's highest rail route. With the 2006 opening of China's Qinghai–Tibet Railway, the Peru route was knocked down to second place. No matter, though: this is one of the country's most scenic areas, and tracks cut through the mountains and plains all the way from Lima to Huancayo. The line these days is a shadow of what it once was, and trains ply the route only a few times a year; tickets are easy to come by, but you will have to plan around the infrequent departures if you want the journey to be a centerpiece of your visit to Peru. The railway's website lists departure dates, with Lima–Huancayo service operating just a handful of dates between April and November. Trains depart the capital's Desamparados train station for the 12-hour journey to Huancayo. The 335-km (207-mile) route twists through the Andes at an elevation of 4,782 meters (15,685 feet). The engine chugs its way up a slim thread of rails that hugs the slopes, speeding over 59 bridges, around endless hairpin curves, and through 66 tunnels—including the 1,175-meter-long (3,854-foot-long) Galera Tunnel, which, at an altitude of 4,758 meters (15,606 feet) is its highest point. Snacks, lunch, and soft drinks are included in the price. You can request oxygen if you get short of breath over the high passes, and the *mate de coca* is poured freely. The decades-old *Clásico* cars are okay in a pinch, but the newer *Turístico* cars are much more comfortable, with reclining seats and access to the observation and bar car. ✉ *Ticket office, Av. José Gálvez Barrenechea 566, 5th fl., San Isidro* ☎ *01/226-6363* ⊕ *www.ferrocarrilcentral.com.pe* 💲 *S/500 one-way, S/700 round-trip.*

Museo Salesiano. Look for the well-preserved rain-forest creatures and butterflies from the northern jungles among the museum's more than 10,000 objects. Local fossils and archaeological relics are also on display. ✉ *Santa Rosa 299, in Colegio Salesiano* ☎ *064/247-763* 💲 *S/5.*

FAMILY **Parque de la Identidad Huanca** (*Huanka Identity Park*). The focus of the beautiful Parque de la Identidad Huanca is on the pre-Inca Huanca culture, which occupied the area but left few clues to its lifestyle. A 5-km (3-mile) drive from Huancao, the park has pebbled paths and small bridges that meander through blossoming gardens and past a rock castle just right for children to tackle. An enormous sculpture at the park's center honors the local artisans who produce the city's *mates burilados* (carved gourds). ✉ *San Antonio.*

FAMILY **Parque del Cerro de la Libertad.** An all-in-one amusement site 1 km (½ mile) northeast of the city, at the Parque del Cerro de la Libertad you can picnic in the grass, watch the kids at the playground, swim in the public pool, dine at the restaurant, or stroll through the zoo. ■ **TIP→ Folkloric dancers and musicians perform at the Liberty Hill Park amphitheater on weekends.** A 15-minute walk from the park brings you to the site of Torre Torre, a cluster of 10– to 30-meter rock towers formed by wind and rain erosion. ✉ *Giráldez.*

OFF THE BEATEN PATH

Warvilca. This ruined temple was built by the pre-Inca Huanca culture between 800 and 1200 AD. It consists of stone walls enclosing cells where captives were held prior to being sacrificed, as well as underground conduits to bring water to the region—you can still see the sacred spring that flows through the channels, the spring that legend says gave rise to the foreparents of the Huanca people. Several mummies have been discovered at the site. The closest village is Huari, which has a little museum on the main square with ceramic figures, pottery, and a few bones and skulls. ✉ *Huancayo* ✣ *6 km (3½ miles) from Huancayo, near Huari* 🎟 *S/3.*

WHERE TO EAT

The local specialty is *papa a la huancaína,*served cold with an olive and slice of hard-boiled egg. Budget restaurants with set lunch menus are on Arequipa south of Antojitos, as well as along Giráldez. You can pick up a quick morning meal at the Mercado Modelo after 7 am, and juice stands, with fresh fruit brought in daily from the high jungle, are on every street.

$ PERUVIAN

🍴 **Antojitos.** The grilled meats, wood-smoked pizzas, and hearty sandwiches draw a diverse crowd of travelers and locals alike to this dimly lit, wood-paneled restaurant. The daily lunch special is filling and varied, and the locale is an excellent venue for lazy midday people-watching. **Known for:** pizzas; live music. [$] *Average main: S/25* ✉ *Puno 599* ☎ *064/237–950.*

$ PERUVIAN

🍴 **Detrás de la Catedral.** Rustic wood tables and soft candlelight set the mood for a meal of roasted lamb, grilled trout, pasta, and traditional dishes in this cozy restaurant, just steps from the cathedral. Service can be slow, so be prepared to linger or take advantage of the free Wi-Fi. **Known for:** regional Peruvian cooking; intimate atmosphere. [$] *Average main: S/25* ✉ *Ancash 335* ☎ *064/212–969.*

$$ PERUVIAN Fodor's Choice ★

🍴 **Huancahuasi.** A festival-hall atmosphere and mind-blowing updates of Peruvian classic dishes make this Huancayo institution one of the sierra's best restaurants. The versions of papa a la huancaína and *alpaca saltado* (stir-fried alpaca with onions and tomatoes) are like nothing you've had before, and the brightly costumed waiters take joy in introducing the region's cuisine to visitors. **Known for:** exquisite regional cooking; vibrant fiesta-like atmosphere. [$] *Average main: S/35* ✉ *Mariscal Castilla 2222, El Tambo* ☎ *064/244–826* 🌐 *www.huancahuasi.com.*

$ PERUVIAN Fodor's Choice ★ 🍴 **La Cabaña.** Over-the-top decorations and labyrinthine rooms give this restaurant charm, but the food has made it a favorite. Wash down wood-fired pizzas and grilled meats with a pitcher of *calientitos* (hot spiced rum punch). **Known for:** awesome atmosphere; artisanal pizzas. [$] *Average main: S/25* ✉ *Giráldez 675* ☎ *064/223–303* 🕒 *No lunch.*

$$ PERUVIAN 🍴 **Restaurant Olímpico.** This throwback restaurant, open for more than 60 years, still serves a downtown lunch crowd with cheap, hearty Andean specials. It's the kind of place you come to with your grandparents for a lingering Sunday lunch; it's popular and always crowded, but good food is guaranteed. **Known for:** classic Peruvian cooking; social atmosphere. [$] *Average main: S/30* ✉ *Giráldez 199* ☎ *064/219–515* 🌐 *restauranteolimpico.com/huancayo/.*

WHERE TO STAY

$ HOTEL 🏨 **Hostal El Márquez.** Rooms at the El Márquez are relatively modern yet a bit bland; some have flat-screen TVs, heaters, and cathedral views, while others don't, so choose carefully and negotiate hard. **Pros:** centrally located; modern comforts; suites with Jacuzzi tubs. **Cons:** bland; the hot water isn't always hot. [$] *Rooms from: S/190* ✉ *Jr. Puno 294* ☎ *064/219–026* 🌐 *www.elmarquezhuancayo.com* 🛏 *29 rooms* 🍽 *Breakfast.*

$$ HOTEL 🏨 **Hotel Presidente.** The most popular lodging among visiting *limeños* has the comforts of a modern hotel—rooms have contemporary furnishings and Andean fabrics and accents, TVs, Wi-Fi, phones, and private baths with hot water. **Pros:** good amenities; train packages; 24-hour restaurant. **Cons:** mostly business clientele; thin walls; service can be surly. [$] *Rooms from: S/312* ✉ *Real 1138* ☎ *064/231–275* 🌐 *huancayo.hotelpresidente.com.pe* 🛏 *95 rooms* 🍽 *Breakfast.*

$$ HOTEL 🏨 **Hotel Turismo Huancayo.** The hacienda-style exterior of this elegant hotel gives it a worldly charm that sets it above the younger options. **Pros:** excellent service, handy location; sparkling rooms with modern conveniences. **Cons:** street and plaza in front often see protests; quality of rooms varies. [$] *Rooms from: S/312* ✉ *Ancash 729* ☎ *064/231–072* 🌐 *turismo.hotelpresidente.com.pe* 🛏 *95 rooms* 🍽 *Breakfast.*

NIGHTLIFE

Huancayo's nightlife is surprisingly spunky. Many restaurants turn into *peñas* with dancing, live music, and folkloric performances from Friday to Sunday between 7 pm and midnight (though some may start and end earlier). If you arrive around or after the time the show begins, expect to pay a cover of about S/7–S/15. Dance clubs are usually open from about 10 pm to 2 am and have a cover charge of S/10–S/20.

La Cabaña. Listen to rollicking live *folklórico* and pop bands Thursday through Saturday at this cozy bar, which doubles as a pizza restaurant during the week. ✉ *Giráldez 675* ☎ *064/223–303.*

Taj Mahal. Dancing is the main attraction at the Taj Mahal, a rambunctious disco that stays open until 4 am and attracts an upscale clientele of local twenty- and thirtysomethings, along with a few tourists. ✉ *Huancavelica 1052* 🕒 *Closed Sun.–Wed.*

SHOPPING

Huancayo and the towns of the surrounding Valle del Mantaro are major crafts centers. The region is famous for its *mate burilado* (large, intricately carved and painted gourds depicting scenes of local life and historic events), many of which are made 11 km (7 miles) outside town in the villages of Cochas Grande and Cochas Chico. Silver filigree and utensils are the specialties of San Jerónimo de Tunán, and exquisite knitwear, woolen sweaters, scarves, wall hangings, and hats are produced in San Agustín de Cajas and Hualhaus. You will find better prices outside town, especially when buying from the artisans directly.

FOOD

Mercado Mayorista. Stretching around the blocks near the train station is the daily produce market. You'll need several hours to wander through the stalls of local crafts and foodstuffs, where you'll find traditional medicines and spices among such local delicacies as gourds, guinea pigs, fish, and frogs. ⊠ *Ferrocarril.*

HANDICRAFTS

Casa del Artesano. You'll find top-quality, locally made goods near the Plaza Constitución at Casa del Artesano, where independent artists sit shop-by-shop working on their various crafts. ⊠ *Real 475* ⊕ *www. casadelartesano.org.*

Sunday Market. The city's main shopping venue is the Sunday *mercado ,* which is spread down one of the city's main thoroughfares and its side streets for about a kilometer. It is one of the largest weekly markets in the country, yet it still sees few tourists. In particular, look for *mates burilados*, *mantas*, straw baskets, and *retablos* (miniature scenes framed in painted wooden boxes). ⊠ *Av. Huancavelica.*

CENTRAL VALLEY: HUANCAYO TO AYACUCHO

The road from Huancayo to Huancavelica and on to Ayacucho shoots over high green plains before spilling into the folds of the Andes and tracing the cascading Mantaro River along a winding two-lane highway. In the rainy season, landslides or *huaycos* often block the road, making this trip a difficult one. Breathtaking scenery and vertigo-inducing climbs reward travelers who push onward.

Despite its seeming proximity on a map, Ayacucho lies at least 10 hours from Huancayo, as the road swerves south toward Lima, alternately cutting through high-altitude plains and winding in coils alongside steep crevasses. The thin air can be biting in the shade and scorching in the midafternoon sun, which beats down on the dry, barren landscape between the peaks. ■TIP➔ Look for spots of black, brown, and white—wild vicuñas and alpacas that roam this cold, rocky range. Near Pucapampa the road rises to 4,500 meters (14,760 feet), often causing *soroche* in travelers while the resident (and rare) gray alpaca remains quite comfortable.

The road continues to rise higher, passing tiny Santa Inés and Abra de Apacheta, the latter at 4,750 meters (15,580 feet). The ever-changing scenery continues to be even more spectacular, with oxides painting the rocks and creeks a wash of vibrant colors. One of the highest roads in the world is 14 km (9 miles) farther, the 5,059-meter (16,594-foot) pass 3 km (2 miles) north of Huachocolpa. From here the journey is downhill into the wide, windy Valle Huanta, a landscape of lakes and hot springs, caverns, and ruins.

HUANCAVELICA

147 km (91 miles) south of Huancayo.

Spread out high in the Andes, colonial Huancavelica was founded by Spanish conquistadors in the 16th century, and they promptly discovered rich veins of silver and mercury threaded through the rocky hillsides. The abundant mercury was vital in the extraction of silver from mines in Peru and Bolivia, including Potosí. Although mining was difficult at 3,680 meters (12,979 feet), the Spanish succeeded in making the city an important profit center that today has grown to a population of around 40,000.

The Río Huancavelica slices through the city, dividing the commercial district in the south from the residential area in the north. The road between Huancayo and Huancavelica has been completely revamped in recent years, though it still winds through Central Highlands villages and vast pastures, and can be closed during the rainy season because of landslides. ■ TIP➔ If you have a good map (or a good grasp of Spanish) and your own equipment, excellent hiking opportunities exist in the surrounding mountains.

With improved transportation links, Huancavelica's traditional culture and relaxed atmosphere are now more accessible to the adventurous traveler. You'll still see traditional costumes worn by women in the markets and shops, and the narrow, cobbled streets are still lined with elegant, colonial-style mansions and 16th-century churches. Residents from all over the region crowd the sprawling Sunday market as well as the daily food market at the corner of Muñoz and Barranca.

Most crafts and clothing are made in the villages on the outskirts of Huancavelica, and you're welcome to visit the artisans' shops. Other neighboring explorations include the viewpoints from Potaqchiz, a short stroll up the hill from San Cristóbal. Thermal baths can be found on the hillside across from town.

GETTING HERE AND AROUND

Few roads lead to Huancavelica; the town is famously difficult to access, and many mountain villages can be reached only on foot. Buses are tiny, routes are unpredictable, and departure points for collectivos from Huancayo and Ayacucho change constantly, so inquire on-site. The town is quite compact, and a few short streets in the center contain nearly everything of interest. A good, albeit steep, path starts from behind the rail station and has pleasant views of the city and surrounding mountains. The altitude is a common problem for visitors here, so take it slow and drink plenty of bottled water.

ESSENTIALS

Currency Banco de Crédito. ⊠ *Toledo 383* ☎ *067/452–830* ⊕ *www.viabcp.com.*

Mail Serpost. ⊠ *Pasaje Ferrua 105.*

Visitor Information Instituto Nacional de Cultura. ⊠ *Antonio Raimondi 193* ☎ *067/453–420.* **Oficina de Información Turistíca Municipal.** ⊠ *Manchego Munoz 299* ☎ *067/452–870* ⊕ *turismo.munihuancavelica.gob.pe.*

EXPLORING

Feria Dominical. The Sunday *feria dominical* market attracts artists and shoppers from all the nearby mountain towns. It's a good place to browse for local crafts—although you'll get better quality (and sometimes better prices) in the villages. ⊠ *Garma y Barranca.*

Iglesia de San Francisco. Begun in 1673, the Iglesia de San Francisco took nearly a century to complete. The dual white towers and red stone doorway—carved with regional motifs—make the church one of the most attractive buildings in town. ⊠ *Plaza Bolognesi, Godos y Tagle* ☑ *Free.*

Plaza de Armas. Huancavelica's Plaza de Armas is the main gathering place and a wonderful example of colonial architecture. Across from the plaza is the restored 17th-century cathedral, which contains a silver-plated altar. ⊠ *Plaza de Armas* ☑ *Free.*

OFF THE BEATEN PATH

Baños Termales de San Cristóbal. Locals believe that these hot-spring mineral baths, found in the tree-covered slopes north of town, have healing powers. Hundreds of pilgrims come from the surrounding villages during holy days. ⊠ *Av. 28 de abril, San Cristobal* ☎ *067/753–222* ☑ *S/5 private room, S/2 public area.*

WHERE TO EAT AND STAY

Restaurants line Barranca, Toledo, and the streets around the Plaza de Armas. All are casual and have a mix of Andean and Continental cuisine. Most restaurants have an à la carte menu useful for sampling several dishes. Hotels usually have restaurants or at least a small café or dining room.

$

HOTEL

Gran Hostal la Portada. This standard guesthouse provides travelers with a clean bed, hot shower, and friendly service at a bargain price. **Pros:** great location; piping-hot water; rooms on the top floor have nice views of the surrounding mountains; inexpensive, even by local standards. **Cons:** building lacks charm. $ *Rooms from: S/50* ⊠ *Toledo 252* ☎ *067/451–050* ⊕ *www.facebook.com/hostallaportada.huancavelica* ▤ *No credit cards* ⤳ *20 rooms* ⦿ *No meals.*

$$

HOTEL

Hotel Presidente Huancavelica. On the plaza, the town's top hotel is in an attractive, Spanish-colonial building with bland but sizable rooms that have phones, Wi-Fi, and hot showers. **Pros:** historical building; prime plaza setting; comfortable, spacious rooms. **Cons:** mixed amenities; pretty basic for the best hotel in town; expensive. $ *Rooms from: S/490* ⊠ *Plaza de Armas s/n* ☎ *067/452–760* ⊕ *huancavelica.hotelpresidente.com.pe* ⤳ *45 rooms* ⦿ *Breakfast.*

QUINUA

37 km (23 miles) northeast of Ayachuco.

The Battle of Ayacucho, the decisive battle against Spain in the Peruvian War of Independence, took place on the Pampas de Quinua grasslands 37 km (23 miles) northeast of the city, near the village of Quinua, on December 9, 1824. Today a white obelisk rises 44 meters (144 feet) above the pampas to commemorate Peru's independence from Spain and celebrate the role of locals in bringing it about.

■ **TIP→** Quinua is one of the crafts centers of Peru. It's best known for its ceramics, and you'll find various examples on the windowsills and rooftops of the adobe houses. Miniature churches, delicately painted with ears of corn or flowers, are frequently seen symbols of good luck. The ubiquitous ceramic bulls are figures once used in festivities associated with cattle-branding ceremonies. Tours from Ayacucho bring you into the workshops of the many artisans in the village. Among the better-quality workshops are Cerámica Artística Sánchez, Rumi Wasi, and Galería Artesanal Límaco; all are on Jr. Sucre off the main plaza. Tours of Huari, Vilcashuaman, and Vischongo often include Quinua, but you can also get here by bus from Ayacucho.

Museo de Quinua. You can immerse yourself deeper in Latin American revolutionary history through exhibits in the compact Museo de Quinua, which has on display relics from the Battle of Ayacucho. Next door, be sure to visit the room where the Spanish signed the final peace accords recognizing Latin America's independence. Come the first week in December to celebrate the town's role in Peru's democracy, when you'll see extravagant local performances, parties, parades, and crafts fairs. There's a little local market on Sunday. ⊠ *Plaza de Armas* ⊑ *S/2.*

AYACUCHO

114 km (71 miles) south of Huancavelica; 364 km (226 miles) northeast of Pisco.

Tucked into the folds of the Andes, 2,760 meters (9,055 feet) up on the slopes, Ayacucho is a colorful, colonial-style town. Though its looks are Spanish—all glowing white-alabaster mansions with elegant columns and arches—it's primarily an indigenous town inhabited by people who still speak Quechua as a first language and don traditional costume for their daily routine. Locals greet visitors with warmth and amazement, and the city's 170,000 people revere artists with an energy matched only during religious celebrations like Carnaval and Semana Santa. Religion is a serious pursuit, too, in this city of churches, where more than 50 sanctuaries beckon worshippers at all hours.

Civilization in Peru began in the valleys around Ayacucho about 20,000 years ago. Dating back this far are the oldest human remains in the country—and perhaps in the Americas—found in a cave network at Piquimachay, 24 km (15 miles) west of the city. Over the centuries, the region was home to many pre-Hispanic cultures, including the Huari

8

(Wari), who set up their capital of Huari 22 km (14 miles) from Ayacucho some 1,300 years ago. When the Inca arrived in the 15th century, they ruled the lands from their provincial capital at Vilcashuamán.

The Spanish came and conquered the reigning Inca, and Francisco Pizarro founded Ayacucho in 1540. First named Huamanga for the local *huamanga* (alabaster) used in handicrafts, Ayacucho grew from a small village into a broad city known for its many colonial-style churches. Nearly 300 years later it was the center of Peru's rebellion for independence from the Spanish, when the Peruvian army led by Antonio José de Sucre defeated the last peninsular forces at nearby Quinua on December 9, 1824. Iglesia Santo Domingo in Ayacucho sounded the first bells of Peru's independence, punctuating the city's role in achieving the country's freedom.

It took a century more before the city built its first road links west to the coast, and the road to Lima went unpaved through the 1960s. Ayacucho might have opened to tourism then but for the influence of Abimael Guzmán, a philosophy teacher at the University of Huamanga. His charismatic preaching encouraged a Maoist-style revolution as a panacea to the age-old problems of rural poverty among the country's indigenous peoples. He founded Sendero Luminoso (Shining Path) in the late 1960s, and spurred it to militant action in March of 1982, when bombs and gunfire first shook the cobbled streets. The fighting between the Shining Path and the government killed thousands of *ayacuchanos,* and by the mid-1980s the city was cut off from the rest of Peru. Alberto Fujimori's government arrested Guzmán in a posh Lima suburb in 1992, and the Shining Path fell apart thereafter. Although the city is now peaceful, tourism has been slow to establish itself outside of Semana Santa, and the city receives only about a thousand visitors a month. Those who do come consequently enjoy the benefits of hassle-free strolls down the city's well-built pedestrian promenades.

Ayacucho's resulting isolation from the modern world means that to visit is to step back into colonial days. Elegant white huamanga buildings glow in the sunlight, with bright flowers spilling out of boxes lining high, narrow wooden balconies. Beyond the slim, straight roads and terra-cotta roofs, cultivated fields climb the Andes foothills up to the snow. Electricity, running water, and phones are occasionally unreliable, but infrastructure is generally modern, and deep poverty in the region has diminished significantly. Banks and businesses are housed in 16th-century *casonas* (colonial mansions). Women in traditional Quechua shawls draped over white blouses, their black hair braided neatly, stroll through markets packed with small fruit, vegetable, and crafts stalls.

GETTING HERE AND AROUND

Most of the city can be explored on foot, as most tourist amenities, hotels, restaurants, and the bulk of the churches and colonial buildings are within a few blocks of the Plaza de Armas. Getting to out-of-the-way workshops in Santa Ana and La Libertad requires a quick cab ride. Basic city tours (S/25) offered at every agency depart daily and will save you much of the hassle.

Sendero Luminoso (Shining Path)

Fighting what it considered a Marxist revolutionary war, Sendero Luminoso (Shining Path) first formed in the late 1960s under the guidance of philosophy professor Abimael Guzmán and his "Gonzalo Thought." After Peru's military coup in 1968 and its ambitious land reform in 1969, Peru's political left grew and fractured, with Sendero eventually forsaking politics and launching its "revolutionary war" in 1980 after 12 years of military rule. By burning ballot boxes in a town outside of Ayacucho, Sendero launched the opening salvo of its revolution.

Sendero promoted an exotic and violent philosophy of extreme Maoism. Guzmán and his disciples envisioned Peru as an agrarian utopia, and saw in Ayacucho's deep poverty and discontent the preconditions needed to destroy the country's existing political structure and replace it with a peasant revolutionary regime. Sendero's charismatic leadership built a core group of operatives who assassinated political figures and bombed police posts. To spread fear throughout the country, they hung dead dogs from lampposts. Their techniques ever more macabre, Sendero began committing atrocities against the very communities they claimed to be helping. Throughout the Highlands, they used "people's trials" to purge those connected with the capitalist economy, including trade unionists, civic leaders, and the managers of farming collectives. What was once a "shining" path quickly became a bloody road to war.

Sendero's emergence was violent, but the government's response turned the conflict into a civil war. Peru's leaders sent in the military to quell what they viewed as a localized uprising, and the military in turn exacerbated the unrest by violating human rights and committing indiscriminate massacres of peasant populations. The anger of centuries of discrimination and disenfranchisement welled up and unleashed a torrent of senseless violence. The Truth and Reconciliation Commission released a 2003 report estimating that nearly 70,000 people died or disappeared during the conflict. The commission attributes half of these victims to Sendero, and at least one-third to government security forces.

The Dancer Upstairs, a film directed by John Malkovich, is a fascinating look at the search for, and capture of, Sendero leader Guzmán in 1992. With his arrest, Sendero began a rapid decline, although it remains active to this day, driven more by narcotrafficking riches than radical ideology. In 2012 Sendero kidnapped 36 employees of a major gas company near the VRAE (Apruímac and Ene River valley), the country's main coca-growing region. The military freed the employees, but in the process lost three of their own. Profits from the drug trade will likely sustain low-level Sendero activities into the near future.

Meanwhile, although Peru's economy has grown over the last decade, rural Central Highlands peasants still live in desperate poverty, a potent source of conflict in one of South America's most unequal countries.

Joining Guzmán in jail is former President Alberto Fujimori, who spearheaded the fight against Sendero. The former president is serving a 25-year prison sentence for human rights violations.

—By Michael Goodwin

Ayacucho's Alfredo Mendívil Duarte Airport (AYP) is 4 km (2½ miles) from the city. You can take a taxi (about S/6), or catch a bus or *colectivo* from the Plaza de Armas, which will deliver you about a half block from the airport.

Airport Alfredo Mendívil Duarte Airport. ⊠ *Ejército 950* ☏ *066/312–418.*

Bus Cruz del Sur. ⊠ *Av. Mariscal Cáceres 1264* ☏ *0801/11111* ⊕ *www.cruzdel-sur.com.pe.* **Expreso Molina.** ⊠ *9 de Diciembre 469* ☏ *066/319–689* ⊕ *www.molinaunion.pe/inicio.html.* **Internacional Palomino.** ⊠ *Av. Manco Capac 216* ☏ *066/313–899* ⊕ *www.grupopalomino.com.pe/agencia.* **Ormeño.** ⊠ *Jr. Libertad 257* ☏ *064/812–495.*

ESSENTIALS

Currency Banco de Crédito. ⊠ *Plaza de Armas* ⊕ *www.viabcp.com.*

Internet Internet El Hueco - Multiservicios Shaddai. ⊠ *Portal Constitución 9, Plaza de Armas* ☏ *066/315–528.*

Mail Serpost. ⊠ *Jr. Asamblea 293* ☏ *066/312–224.*

Visitor Information iPerú. ⊠ *Cuzco 108, Plaza de Armas* ☏ *066/318–305* ⊕ *www.peru.travel* ⊠ *Alfredo Mendívil Duarte Airport* ☏ *944/492–235* ⊕ *www.peru.travel.* **La Dirección General de Comercio Exterior y Turismo.** ⊠ *Jr. Asamblea 481* ☏ *066/313–162* ⊕ *www.dirceturayacucho.gob.pe.*

EXPLORING

TOP ATTRACTIONS

Casa Ruiz de Ochoa. Across from the Iglesia Merced, one block from the Plaza de Armas, you'll see the colonial-style Casa Ruiz de Ochoa. The intricate 18th-century doorway mixes European and indigenous techniques in a style known as *mestizo*. Climb up to the second floor for a bird's-eye view of the cobbled patio. ⊠ *Dos de Mayo 210* ☏ *066/314–612* 🖾 *Free.*

Catedral. The twin bell towers of Ayacucho's catedral, built in 1612 by Bishop Don Cristóbal de Castilla y Zamora, crown the Plaza de Armas. Step inside to view the cathedral's carved altars with gold-leaf designs, a silver tabernacle, and an ornate wooden pulpit, all built in a style mixing baroque and Renaissance elements. Look for the plaque inside the entrance that quotes from Pope John Paul II's speech during his visit in 1985. ⊠ *Plaza de Armas* ☏ *066/312–590* 🖾 *Free.*

OFF THE BEATEN PATH

Ruinas Huari. Recent excavations at this massive archaeological site have uncovered multilevel underground galleries, burial chambers, circular plazas, arched portals, and other architectural magnificences. Together they make this capital city of the Huari culture one of the most impressive non-Inca ruins in the Peruvian sierra. The Huari flourished from around 700 to 1200 AD, and wandering the quiet alleys of this 5,000-acre complex gives you a sense of how its 60,000 residents lived, worshipped, and died. Especially noteworthy are the temples and communal tombs. There's a small museum on-site with mummies and ceramics, as well as a lounge to rest in after roaming the cactus-covered grounds. The best way to visit is to take a tour from a travel agency in town for S/30, as taxis andcollectivos to the site are sporadic and hard to figure out. ⊠ *Quinua Hwy.* ✛ *22 km (14 miles) northeast of Ayacucho* ☏ *066/312–056* 🖾 *S/3.*

Iglesia Santo Domingo. The 1548 Iglesia Santo Domingo is now a national monument. The first bells ringing out Peru's independence from the Spanish after the Battle of Ayacucho were sounded from here. The church's facade features Churrigueresque architectural elements, a style of baroque Spanish architecture popular in the 16th century, while the interior is coated in *pan de oro* (gold leaf). ⊠ *9 de Diciembre y Bellido* 🎫 *Free.*

La Compañía de Jesús. You can't miss the striking red trim on the baroque-style exterior of this 17th-century Jesuit church. The towers were added a century after the main building, which has religious art and a gilt altar. ⊠ *28 de Julio* 🎫 *Free.*

Museo Cáceres. Located in the Casona Vivanco, a 17th-century mansion, the Museo Cáceres was once the home of Andrés Cáceres, an Ayacucho resident and former Peruvian president best known for his successful guerrilla leadership during the 1879–83 War of the Pacific against Chile. This is one of the city's best-preserved historic buildings, which today houses a mix of military memorabilia and ancient local artifacts, including stone carvings and ceramics. Note the gallery of colonial-style paintings. The **Museo de Arte Religioso Colonial** can also be found within these storied walls, and exhibits antique objects from the city's early days. ⊠ *Casona Vivanco, 28 de Julio 508* 🕾 *066/836–166* 🎫 *S/2* 🕓 *Closed Sun.*

Museo de Arqueología y Antropología Hipólito Unánue. Regional finds from the Moche, Nazca, Ica, Inca, Canka, Chavín, Chimu, and Huari cultures are on display here, at the Centro Cultural Simón Bolívar. Highlights of the archaeology and anthropology museum include ceremonial costumes, textiles, everyday implements, and even artwork from some of the area's earliest inhabitants. The museum is locally referred to as Museo INC. ⊠ *Centro Cultural Simón Bolívar, Independencia 502* 🕾 *066/312–056* 🎫 *S/4.*

Palacio del Marqués de Mozobamba. Built in 1550 and now part of the cultural center for San Cristobal Huamanga University, the Palacio del Marqués de Mozobamba is one of the oldest mansions in Peru. The colonial-era, baroque-style architecture includes *portales* (stone arches) in front and a monkey-shaped stone fountain in the courtyard. ∎TIP➔ **On the left side as you enter, you'll see the remains of Inca stone walls discovered during restorations in 2003.** ⊠ *Portal Unión 37, Plaza de Armas* 🕾🎫 *Free.*

Prefectura. Also known as the Boza and Solís House, the Prefectura is tucked into a 1748 two-story *casona historica* (historic mansion). Local independence-era heroine María Prado de Bellido was held prisoner in the Prefecture's patio room until her execution by firing squad in 1822. The balcony opens out onto a lovely view of the Plaza de Armas. ⊠ *Portal Constitución 15* 🎫 *Free* 🕓 *Closed Sun.*

OFF THE BEATEN PATH **Vilcashuamán and Intihuatana.** Four long hours south of Ayacucho on winding, unpaved roads is the former Inca provincial capital of Vilcashuamán, set where the north–south Inca highway crossed the east–west trade road from Cusco to the Pacific. You can still see the Templo del Sol y de la Luna and a five-tiered platform, known as the Ushnu, crowned

by an Inca throne and surrounded by stepped fields once farmed by Inca peasants. An hour's walk from Vilcashuamán (or a half-hour's walk south past the main road from Ayacucho) is the Intihuatana, where Inca ruins include a palace and tower beside a lagoon. Former Inca baths, a sun temple, and a sacrificial altar are also on the grounds. Check out the unusual 13-angled boulder, one of the odd building rocks that are an Inca hallmark. Ayacucho travel agencies can organize tours of both sites (S/65), or you can catch a bus or colectivo for S/15–S/20. **■TIP→ Ask around to confirm where these public transport options are leaving from, as pickup points change frequently.** ✉ *Km 118, Vilcashuamán Hwy.* 🎟 *S/5.*

WHERE TO EAT

Outside of a few international restaurants catering to visiting tourists, Ayacucho stands by its Andean specialties. The city is famous for its filling, flavorful *puca picante* (a peanut-pork-and-potato stew), served with rice and topped with a parsley sprig. **■TIP→ The city's favorite drink is the hot, creamy, pisco-spiked ponche (flavored with milk, cinnamon, cloves, sesame, peanuts, walnuts, and sugar).** The best time to sample this popular concoction is during Semana Santa. In the first week of November, ayacuchanos are busy baking sweet breads shaped like horses (*caballos*) and babies (*guaguas*) to place in baskets for the spirits at the family gravesites. You'll find inexpensive restaurants where you can grab a cheap *almuerzo* (lunch) along Jirón San Martin. Many restaurants are closed Sunday morning.

$ PERUVIAN
🍴 **Carbon y Vino.** Grilled meats and local fare like puca picante are the stars at this popular lunchtime spot, housed in a pretty old mansion with both front and back patios. During the week, the three-course fixed-price lunch is a steal at S/10. **Known for:** grilled entrées; great fixed-price lunches. [$] *Average main: S/20* ✉ *Bellido 593* ☎ *999/443–318* 🕓 *No dinner* 💳 *No credit cards.*

$$ STEAKHOUSE Fodor's Choice ★
🍴 **Casa Grill.** Dining in this charmingly refitted family home is like dining at Grandpa's house—if Grandpa were an internationally trained grill expert who served only the most exquisite cuts of meat. That's because the steaks, fire-cooked pork, and whole salmon at the sumptuous *parrilla* are the best in Ayacucho, with delicious sauces to boot. **Known for:** best grilled meat in the Central Sierra; warm hospitality. [$] *Average main: S/35* ✉ *Tres Mascaras 390* ☎ *966/137–090* 🕓 *Closed Mon.–Wed.* 💳 *No credit cards.*

$ PERUVIAN
🍴 **La Casona.** Dining in this Spanish-style home is like attending an intimate party in a fine hacienda. The sun bathes the leafy courtyard during lunch, while the clientele tucks into the best of ayacuchano cooking, including heaping plates of puca picante and fried trout. **Known for:** bargain lunch special; hearty local stews. [$] *Average main: S/20* ✉ *Bellido 463* ☎ *066/312–733.*

$ CAFÉ
🍴 **Lalo's Café.** This modern, Parisian-style café attracts the city's well-to-do and NGO workers in the mornings and evenings. It has coffees, teas, pastries, and light meals. **Known for:** decadent cakes; cheap menu lunches. [$] *Average main: S/15* ✉ *Jr. 28 de Julio 178* ☎ *066/311–331.*

$ ✕ **Via Via Cafe.** Perched above the Plaza de Armas, this wood-paneled
PERUVIAN restaurant offers an ample menu that includes both Highlands specialties and backpacker favorites. Enjoy a relaxed breakfast in the
morning or an artisanal ice cream in the afternoon while taking in
the view of the cathedral from the expansive terrace. **Known for:**
great views; dessert; international flair. $ *Average main: S/25* ✉ *Por-*
tal Constitución 4, Plaza de Armas ☎ *066/312–834* ⊕ *www.viavia.*
world/ayacucho.

WHERE TO STAY

$$ ⊞ **Hotel La Crillonesa.** With a lovely rooftop terrace offering panoramic
B&B/INN views of the city and clean, comfy rooms, this budget inn is one of the
best values in the Peruvian sierra. **Pros:** spectacular views from the
terrace; great value; wonderful staff. **Cons:** adjoining street is noisy;
some rooms are rather small. $ *Rooms from: S/40* ✉ *Nazareno 165*
☎ *066/312–350* ⊕ *hotelcrillonesa.com* ⬎ *36 rooms* ⦿ *No meals.*

$$ ⊞ **Hotel Plaza Ayacucho.** The city's most expensive hotel, in a gracious
HOTEL colonial building partly overlooking the Plaza de Armas, has spacious
gardens and opulent sitting areas that belie the modest rooms with
worn carpet and nicked modern furnishings. **Pros:** some rooms overlook Plaza de Armas; the place to stay for Semana Santa. **Cons:** stuffy
atmosphere; some rooms need a makeover. $ *Rooms from: S/300* ✉ *Jr.*
9 de Diciembre 184 ☎ *066/312–202, 066/312–314* ⊕ *www.dmhoteles.*
pe ⬎ *69 rooms* ⦿ *Breakfast.*

$ ⊞ **Hotel San Francisco de Paula.** At this rambling Spanish mansion, folk
HOTEL art, textiles, and local crafts lend charm to a building that dates back
centuries. **Pros:** nice views of city and hills; regional art everywhere;
rooftop restaurant. **Cons:** plain rooms; poor lighting. $ *Rooms from:*
S/130 ✉ *Callao 290* ☎ *066/312–353* ⊕ *www.hotelsanfranciscodepaula.*
com ⬎ *41 rooms* ⦿ *Breakfast.*

$ ⊞ **Hotel Santa María.** Just three blocks from the Plaza de Armas, Hotel
HOTEL Santa María is a quiet, tastefully appointed hotel with brightly colored textiles and minimalist furnishings. **Pros:** colorful decor; helpful
staff. **Cons:** rooms are a bit gloomy. $ *Rooms from: S/160* ✉ *Jr. Areq-*
uipa 320 ☎ *066/314–988* ⊕ *www.jianhoteles.com.pe* ⬎ *22 rooms*
⦿ *Breakfast.*

$ ⊞ **Hotel Santa Rosa.** A block from the Plaza de Armas, the rooms in
HOTEL this pleasant little hotel have a mix of antiques, handmade fabrics, and
contemporary furnishings, plus modern amenities like TV and Wi-Fi.
Pros: beautiful courtyard; good restaurant; local charm with a modern feel. **Cons:** room sizes vary. $ *Rooms from: S/135* ✉ *Jr. Lima 166*
☎ *066/312–083, 066/315–830* ⊕ *www.hotelsantarosa.com.pe* ⬎ *40*
rooms ⦿ *Breakfast.*

$ ⊞ **Via Via Hotel.** This hotel and its eponymous café sit in a restored
HOTEL colonial building on the plaza and offer some of the city's best, most
eclectic lodging. **Pros:** excellent location; views of the plaza; free Wi-Fi.
Cons: some rooms are noisy. $ *Rooms from: S/165* ✉ *Portal Consti-*
tución 4, Plaza de Armas ☎ *066/312–834* ⊕ *viavia.world* ⬎ *20 rooms*
⦿ *Breakfast.*

8

NIGHTLIFE

Maxxo. The best disco in town, Maxxo gets going late and keeps going until the wee hours with a mix of local and international music, and a crowd to match it. ⊠ *Mariscal Caceres 1035.*

Taberna Magía Negra. Admire the local art on the walls and dozens of upside-down black umbrellas on the ceiling while grabbing a drink or pizza at the "black magic" pub. ⊠ *Portal Independencia 65, Plaza Mayor* ☎ *066/328–289.*

SHOPPING

Ayacucho is home to many of Peru's best artists, whom you can often visit at work in their neighborhood shops or galleries. Look for *retablos*, the multitiered, three-dimensional displays of plaster characters in scenes of the city's famed religious processions and historic battles. The busy Mercado Domingo (Sunday Market) in Huanta, an hour north, is fun to visit.

FOOD

Mercado Andrés Vivanco. Ayacucho's produce and meat market is found behind the Arco del Triunfo in a one-story building; shops continue for several streets behind. ⊠ *Jr. 28 de Julio.*

HANDICRAFTS

Mercado Artesanal Shosaku Nagase. The widest selection of handicrafts in Ayacucho, from retablos to sweaters, can be found at Mercado Artesanal Shosaku Nagase, about a kilometer north of the city center near the city jail. ⊠ *Plazoleta El Arco, Av. Maravillas 101.*

Santa Ana neighborhood. The Santa Ana neighborhood is dotted with some of Peru's finest workshops. These local artists and their galleries are clustered around the Plazoleta Santa Ana, and most are happy to share their knowledge and even their life stories with visitors. In particular, look for complex *tejidos* (textiles), which have elaborate, and often pre-Hispanic, motifs that can take more than half a year to design and weave. Many artists painstakingly research their designs, pulling abstract elements from Huari ceremonial ponchos. These creations, made of natural fibers and dyes, can cost US$400 or more for high-quality work. Standouts include the textile workshops of Alejandro Gallardo (Plaza Santa Ana 105) and Edwin Sulca Lagos (Plaza Santa Ana 82), who also makes carpets. And don't miss the beautiful alabaster (*huamanga*) carvings of José Gálvez. ⊠ *Plaza Santa Ana.*

THE NORTH COAST AND NORTHERN HIGHLANDS

WELCOME TO THE NORTH COAST AND NORTHERN HIGHLANDS

TOP REASONS TO GO

★ **The Ancient World:** Along the coast, Chavín, Moche, and Chimú ruins date as far back as 3000 BC. In the highlands are Wari sites, and Kuélap, a stunning complex built by the Chachapoyans a thousand years before Machu Picchu.

★ **Superb Eating:** The North Coast undeniably has one of Peru's most exciting regional cuisines. Abundant shellfish and extensive pre-Columbian influences make for some of Peru's favorite dishes.

★ **Outdoor Adventure:** The Northern Highlands provide plenty of trekking, climbing, and rafting, especially around Huaraz, home of the highest mountains outside of the Himalayas.

★ **Colonial Architecture:** Trujillo, on the coast, and Cajamarca in the highlands are two of the best places for colonial architecture.

★ **Beaches:** The far northern coast offers year-round sun, white-sand beaches, and a relaxed, tropical atmosphere.

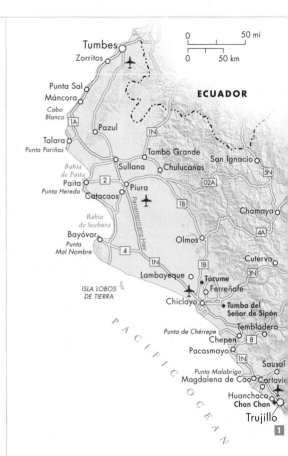

1 The North Coast.
Explore almost unlimited archaeological sites, well-preserved colonial architecture, mangrove forests, and relaxed beach towns with year-round sun and surf. Fresh seafood is abundant, the climate is warmer, and life is more relaxed.

2 Huaraz and the Cordillera Blanca. Stunning snowcapped peaks, natural hot springs, and a lively bar and restaurant scene make this one of the north's most popular areas. With more than 40 peaks above 6,000 meters (19,500 feet) and the fourth-highest peak in all the Americas, this region provides spectacular views and outdoor activities.

3 The Northern Highlands. See a landscape almost untouched by the modern world, with farm pastures, mountains, and herds of cows, goats, and sheep in Cajamarca. Head to Chachapoyas, where the Andes begin their descent to the Amazon, for extraordinary greenery and the astonishing ruins at Kuélap, often compared to Machu Picchu but built more than a thousand years before. This is the Peru that is dying to be discovered.

GETTING ORIENTED

Traveling from one geographic region to another in northern Peru is quite challenging and recommended only for those without time constraints. Instead, choose a region and explore accordingly: for the North Coast, travel from archaeological ruins to the beach in a south–north direction; for Huaraz and the Cordillera Blanca, use the town of Huaraz as your junping-off point for glaciers, snowcapped peaks, and natural hot springs; for the Northern Highlands, fly to Cajamarca or take a bus to Chachapoyas to begin discovering the gateway to the Amazon.

9

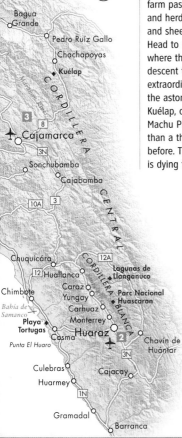

Updated by Mike Gasparovic

Glaciers swathed in mist, virgin tracts of forest, endless stretches of lunar desert: Peru's North Coast and Northern Highlands are as geographically diverse as they are stunning. Once passed over by travelers rushing to get to Cusco, these enchanted regions are increasingly attracting attention from adventurers eager to explore their endless opportunities for hiking, trekking, and surfing—as well as the mysterious ancient cultures that once flourished here.

Nature takes pride of place in northern Peru. Here you'll find soaring, 6,000-meter (19,700-foot) peaks streaked with snow in the Cordillera Blanca, as well as shifting sands guarding hidden tombs along the coast. To the east, ancient cloud forests back up onto the darkest jungles of the Amazon, while in the valleys of the northern sierra, emerald hills stand luminous in the blue haze.

All this means northern Peru is a prime place for outdoor activities. Whether you're on muleback, edging along the turquoise lakes of the Callejón de Huaylas, or a surf god riding the swells at Máncora, you'll find yourself fumbling for superlatives as you pit yourself against Peru's northern land- and seascapes. What's more, in recent years an extensive tourist infrastructure has grown up around these pastimes. Renting gear, finding a mountain lodge, or hunkering down at a luxurious coastal resort is a snap in what Peruvians call *el norte*. And when it's time to refuel, you can do so with rich northern *secos* (stews) and *cebiches*, dishes that Peruvians of every stripe count among the country's culinary glories.

Northern Peru exercises your imagination no less than your body. The region was home to a bewildering number of ancient peoples, as one of the few places on Earth that was a cradle of human civilization. These included the Chavín, who originated a terrifying cult of a fanged jaguar-deity in the underground passages at Huántar, as well as the Moche, a race of brilliant artists who drained the blood of conquered peoples in a gory ritual of human sacrifice. When you add in the greatest tomb discovery since Tutankhamun and the stunning, little-known cloud-city of the Chachapoyas people at Kuélap, you have an archaeologist's paradise that brings out the Indiana Jones in even the most modern of travelers.

PLANNING

WHEN TO GO

The weather along the North Coast is usually pleasant, although a strong sun causes temperatures to climb from November to May. The Northern Highlands weather is more capricious—rainy season is November to early May, and it's drier from mid-May to mid-September. September and October have fairly good weather, but occasional storms can frighten off would-be mountaineers.

PLANNING YOUR TIME

EXPLORING ANCIENT CIVILIZATIONS

If seeing the important archaeological sites, ruins, and museums is your main priority, start your journey in Trujillo with the important Moche pyramids of the Huaca de la Luna and Huaca del Sol, as well as Chan Chan, built by the Chimú people (but be sure to take at least a day to walk around and enjoy the spectacular colonial architecture). From here, head north to Chiclayo and peer into the Tomb of Sipán, see the pyramids at Túcume, and explore world-class historical museums. If you can extend your trip past a week, preferably for another four to five days, take the bus from Chiclayo to Chachapoyas and visit Kuélap, a rival in magnificence to Machu Picchu and built more than a thousand years before.

EXPLORING THE OUTDOORS

If you want to see the spectacular mountains of the Northern Highlands, head up (and up and up) to the mountain town of Huaraz. Drink lots of water and take a day or so to acclimatize to the altitude, taking in the local sights and hot springs. Take a three-day trek around the Cordillera Blanca. Discuss the numerous options with your guide. If you can extend your trip past a week, head to Trujillo to enjoy the architecture and ruins. Note: You can fly to Huaraz, but flights from Lima are very irregular (and expensive), so do your homework beforehand.

REST AND RELAXATION

If you want to take a week to relax, fly from Lima to Piura, walk around the city, eat in one of the excellent restaurants, and sleep in one of the first-rate hotels. After a leisurely breakfast at your hotel (almost always included in the price of your room), head to Máncora or Punta Sal for the next few days. Regardless of where you stay, you'll be able to lie back on the beach or poolside, and—if you're inspired to get out of your beach chair—go on a fishing trip, learn to surf, or try the even more adventurous kitesurfing.

9

GETTING HERE AND AROUND

AIR TRAVEL

The easiest way to get around is by plane. You'll definitely want to fly to destinations like Piura, Tumbes, and Cajamarca. LATAM (⊕ *www.lan.com*), Avianca (⊕ *www.avianca.com*), and Peruvian Airlines (⊕ *www.peruvian.pe*) fly to several cities in the region.

BUS TRAVEL

Bus service throughout the region is generally quite good. Oltursa (☎ *01/708–5000* ⊕ *www.oltursa.pe*) runs all the way up the coast. Other reputable companies for the coastal communities include Cruz del Sur (☎ *01/311–5050 in Lima* ⊕ *www.cruzdelsur.com.pe*), CIVA (☎ *044/251–402 in Trujillo* ⊕ *www.civa.com.pe*), and Transportes Chiclayo (☎ *074/503–548 in Chiclayo* ⊕ *www.transporteschiclayo.com*). For the highlands, Móvil (⊕ *www.moviltours.com.pe*) is a good choice. Whenever possible, pay for a *bus-cama* or *semi-cama,* which gets you an enormous seat that fully reclines, and attendant service that includes at least one meal and a movie. Some buses, such as CIVA's Excluciva buses, have Wi-Fi.

CAR TRAVEL

Driving can be a challenge—locals rarely obey rules of the road—but a car is one of the best ways to explore the region. The Pan-American Highway serves the coast. From there take Highway 109 to Huaraz and Highway 8 to Cajamarca. Small, reputable rental-car agencies can be found in Trujillo, Chiclayo, Piura, and Huaraz. Think twice before driving to archaeological sites; some are hard to find, and it's easy to get lost on the unmarked roads. Consider hiring a driver or taking a tour. Roads in the Northern Highlands are always in some degree of disrepair.

TAXI TRAVEL

Taxi rides in town centers should cost around S/3 to S/8; rates go up at night. A longer ride to the suburbs or town environs costs S/5 to S/20. Negotiate the price before you head off. Taxis hire out their services for specific places, ranging from S/15 and up, depending on the distance, or around S/300 for the entire day.

HEALTH AND SAFETY

Use purified water for drinking and brushing your teeth. If you're out trekking, bring an extra bottle with you. Also, eat foods that have been thoroughly cooked or boiled. If vegetables or fruit are raw, be sure they're peeled. In the highlands, especially Huaraz, relax and take the time to acclimatize for a few days, drinking lots of water to avoid dehydration and altitude sickness.

In the big cities on the coast, be on your guard and take simple precautions, such as asking the concierge at the hotel to get you a taxi and carrying only the cash you need. In small coastal towns or in the highlands, things are more secure, but be aware of your belongings at all times.

RESTAURANTS

The North Coast has excellent seafood, whereas simpler, but equally delicious, meat-and-rice dishes are more common in the highlands. Some of the fancier restaurants in Trujillo and Chiclayo expect you to dress up for dinner, but most spots along the coast are quite casual.

Depending on the restaurant, the bill may include a 10% service charge; if not, a 10% tip is appropriate. Throughout the region, *almuerzo* (lunch) is the most important meal of the day, eaten around 2 pm. *Cena* (dinner) is normally a lighter meal, but always check with restaurants before going out at night: many only serve lunch.

HOTELS

Cities along the North Coast, especially Trujillo and Chiclayo, have a wide range of lodgings, including large business hotels and converted colonial mansions. The latter, usually called *casonas,* offer personalized service not found in the larger hotels. In smaller towns, such as Yungay and Caraz, there are no luxury lodgings, but you'll have no problem finding a clean and comfortable room. The highlands have excellent lodges with horse stables and hot springs; you can also find family-run inns with basic rooms. Assume that hotels do not have air-conditioning unless otherwise indicated.

Finding a hotel room throughout the coastal and highlands areas ought to be painless throughout the year, although coastal resorts like Máncora and Punta Sal are often jammed in summer and during holiday weeks. Sports enthusiasts head to Huaraz and Cajamarca in summer, so make reservations early. Plan at least two months in advance if you want to travel during Easter week, *fiestas patrias* (Peruvian Independence Day, the week of July 28), or Christmas, when Peruvians take their holidays. *Hotel reviews have been shortened. For full information, visit Fodors.com.*

	$	$$	$$$	$$$$
WHAT IT COSTS IN NUEVO SOLES				
Restaurants	under S/35	S/35–S/50	S/51–S/65	over S/65
Hotels	under S/250	S/250–S/500	S/501–S/800	over S/800

Restaurant prices are the average cost of a main course at dinner or, if dinner is not served, at lunch. Hotel prices are the lowest cost of a standard double room in high season.

TOURS

Condor Travel and Mayte Tours both organize tours to the ruins around Trujillo. Clara Bravo and Michael White are great guides for Trujillo, and also lead trips farther afield. Moche Tours is one of Chiclayo's best tour companies for trips to the tomb of El Señor de Sipán.

There are many tour companies in Huaraz; locally owned Eco Ice Tours is among the best, arranging customized trekking and mountain-climbing expeditions. Clarín Tours is said to be one of Cajamarca's best.

In Chachapoyas, contact Vilaya Tours. The company arranges tours to Kuélap, as well as to the remote ruins of Gran Vilaya, which requires a 31-km (19-mile) hike, and to the Pueblo de Los Muertos, which requires a 23-km (14-mile) hike.

Canechi Tours. Aside from beach trips to Mancora and Punta Sal, Canechi arranges day trips around Piura and private transportation around the region. ✉ *Luis Montero 490, Piura* ☎ *073/344–602* ⊕ *www.canechi-tours.com* ✉ *From S/50.*

Clara Bravo and Michael White. Peruvian-born Clara and British-born Michael are two of Trujillo's most reputable guides. They lead tours to all of the region's major archaeological attractions and take tourists on extended circuits. Highly recommended. ⊠ *Cahuide 495, Trujillo* ☎ *044/243–347* ⊕ *trujilloperu.xanga.com* ✉ *From S/20.*

Clarín Tours. With offices in Lima and Cajamarca, Clarín Tours specializes in multiday package deals that include transportation, hotels, and tours in northern Peru, particularly in Cajamarca. ⊠ *Del Batán 165, Cajamarca* ☎ *076/366–829* ⊕ *www.clarintours.com* ✉ *From S/180.*

Eco Ice Tours. This excellent Peruvian-owned company has a full range of adventure and ecotours of the Central Sierra. Choose from day hikes, trekking, or mountaineering—or design your own. ⊠ *Amadeo Figueroa 1185, Huaraz* ☎ *958/032–249* ⊕ *www.ecoice-peru.com.*

Go2Andes. This hiking and trekking operator runs well-prepared trips into the Cordillera Huayhuash and Cordillera Blanca, including technical climbs to Alpamayo and other peaks. ⊠ *Psje. Pacífico 204, Nueva Florida, Huaraz* ☎ *043/428–941* ⊕ *go2andes.com* ✉ *From S/70.*

Mayte Tours. Specializing in organized tours to difficult-to-reach destinations, such as Cerros de Amotape and Santuario Los Manglares, Mayte will also set up secure transportation to Guayaquil and other parts of Ecuador. ⊠ *Jr. San Martín 131, Tumbes* ☎ *972/892–506* ⊕ *maytetours. com* ✉ *From S/80.*

Moche Tours. This is Chiclayo's largest operator, with trips to most archaeological and cultural attractions in the region, including standard day trips and excursions to less-visited destinations like Ferreñafe for the Museo Nacional de Sicán and the Chaparrí bear reserve. ⊠ *7 de Enero 638, Chiclayo* ☎ *074/224–637* ⊕ *www.mochetourschiclayo. com.pe* ✉ *From S/65.*

North Shore Expeditions. Whale-watching (from June to October) and deep-sea sport-fishing trips off the Pacific coast are available here. ⊠ *Km 1,186, Panamericana Norte, Tumbes* ☎ *961/770–728* ⊕ *www.north-shore.pe* ✉ *From S/200.*

Vilaya Tours. With 20 years' experience, Chachapoyas's most reputable operator runs private and customized tours to Kuélap, the sarcophagi of Karajia, the Gocta waterfall, and the Mummy Museum of Leymebamba. ⊠ *Jr. Amazonas 261, Chachapoyas* ☎ *041/477–506* ⊕ *www. vilayatours.com* ✉ *From S/50.*

THE NORTH COAST

Desert, desert, and more desert: so appears Peru's northern coast to the uninitiated. Venture into those miles of sandy barrenness, however, and you'll discover a region that's incredibly fertile in culture, from 2,000-year-old pyramids to ultramodern beach resorts, all fed by a culinary tradition many consider to be the best in the country.

If you're at all archaeologically minded, northern Peru will have you mesmerized upon arrival. That's because it's one of only six places on the planet where civilization arose, and its deserts are littered with ruins to prove it. The complex cultures that developed here—the Moche, Chimú, and Huari, among others—were not only superb artists. They also practiced terrifying rituals of human sacrifice and shamanism that are abundantly on display at the pyramids and tombs in Trujillo and Chiclayo. Meanwhile, the so-called *norte chico* region north of Lima is the site of the oldest cities in the Americas.

Peru's North Coast is more than just history. After your Tomb Raider–style adventures, relax and cool off on the region's stunning beaches, where blazing white sands, first-class resorts, and rides in reed-woven canoes are all standard. As you watch the sun sink over the Pacific, enjoy some of the world's best seafood, in a regional cuisine that extends back to pre-Hispanic times.

GETTING HERE AND AROUND

Once in a city, it's extremely easy to get around via taxis or tour buses; however, getting from city to city requires more planning. There are flights to Tumbes, Piura, Chiclayo, or Trujillo from Lima, but not from city to city; the best option is to start by flying into a city and from there either renting a car or taking one of the many frequent, but long, bus rides to other towns.

BARRANCA

200 km (124 miles) northwest of Lima on the Pan-American Hwy.

A nondescript town with little to visit except a large Chimú temple nearby and one iconic restaurant, this is a stop for those who are either determined to see every archaeological site in Peru or do not have the time to go to Trujillo or Chiclayo but would like to see some northern ruins.

GETTING HERE AND AROUND

To get to Barranca, head north from Lima on the Panamericana (Pan-American Highway) through the bleak, empty coastal desert and past several dusty villages.

EXPLORING

Paramonga. With its seven defensive walls, the gigantic pyramid at Paramonga is worth a look. Nicknamed "the fortress" for its citadel-like walls, it may have only been a ritual center for the Chimú people back in the 13th century. In any case, it was already in ruins when the Spanish arrived in Peru in 1532. A small museum has interesting displays on Chimú culture. The archaeological site sits just off the Pan-American Highway, about 3 km (2 miles) north of the turnoff for Huaraz. For a few soles you can take a taxi to the ruins from the nearby town of Barranca. ⊠ *Pan-American Hwy.* ⓢ *S/5.*

WHERE TO EAT AND STAY

$ ✗ **Don Goyo.** One of the better options in Barranca, Don Goyo offers
PIZZA a large selection of pizza, pasta, and grilled-meat dishes. On the menu is the requisite *pollo a la brasa* (rotisserie chicken). **Known for:** laid-back atmosphere; decent pizzas. ⓢ *Average main: S/15* ⊠ *Jr. Gálvez 506* ☎ *01/235–5484* ▭ *No credit cards.*

$ ✕ **Tato's.** Overlooking the beach, Tato's is something of a cult restau-
SEAFOOD   rant—a rustic eatery known for seafood, from cebiches to fried calamari. The most famous dish on the menu is the *tacu tacu relleno de
mariscos* (refried rice and beans stuffed with shellfish). **Known for:**
hearty portions; fresh seafood. $ *Average main: S/25* ⊠ *Av. Chorrillos
383* ☎ *511/235-2562* ⊘ *No dinner.*

$ ☷ **Hotel Chavín.** A full-service hotel at bargain prices, this is the best
HOTEL   deal in Barranca. **Pros:** extensive facilities for a low price; poolside
FAMILY   bar. **Cons:** on a busy main road; outdated. $ *Rooms from: S/135*
⊠ *Jr. Gálvez 222* ☎ *01/235-2253* ⊕ *www.hotelchavin.com.pe* ⤺ *72
rooms* ⍟ *No meals.*

CASMA

182 km (113 miles) north of Barranca.

Once known as the "City of Eternal Sun," Casma, like Lima, is now
subject to cloudy winters and sunny summers. With its leafy Plaza de
Armas and a number of pleasant parks, however, it makes the best base
for visiting the nearby ruins. If you're not into the archaeology thing,
you might not want to include Casma in your itinerary.

GETTING HERE AND AROUND

Casma lies about six hours north of Lima and just over two hours from
Barranca. Cruz del Sur buses stop here on their Lima–Trujillo routes.
Once in town, mototaxis are the best way to get around.

EXPLORING

Pañamarca. Several ruins can be found near the town of Casma, but
the heavily weathered Mochica city of Pañamarca is the one to see
after Sechín (below). Located 10 km (6 miles) from the Pan-American
Highway on the road leading to Nepeña, Pañamarca has some interesting murals. If they're not visible right away, ask a guard to show
you, as they are often closed off. The site was later occupied by the
Incas. ■ TIP➔ A taxi will take you to the ruins for about S/20 an hour;
negotiate the price before you leave. ⊠ *Casma* ▱ *S/6, includes admission to Sechín.*

Sechín. The origins of Sechín, one of the country's oldest archaeological
sites dating from around 1600 BC, remain a mystery. It's not clear
what culture built this coastal temple, but the bas-relief carvings ringing the main sanctuary, some up to 4 meters (13 feet) high, graphi-
cally depict triumphant warriors and their conquered, often beheaded
enemies. Some researchers have even speculated that this was a center
for anatomical study, due to the sheer number of detached body parts
engraved on the rocks. The site was first excavated in 1937 by the
archaeologist J.C. Tello. It has since suffered from looters and natural
disasters. Archaeologists are still excavating here, so access to the
central plaza is not permitted. ■ TIP➔ A trail leading up a neighboring
hill provides good views of the temple complex and the surrounding
valley. A small museum has a good collection of Chavín ceramics
and a mummy that was found near Trujillo. To get to the ruins, head
southeast from Casma along the Pan-American Highway for about 3

NORTH COAST MENU

The coast is characterized by heaps of fresh seafood, which, when served cold, is a refreshing meal on a hot day. The highlander diet consists of root vegetables, like yucca and potato, and a variety of meats, with all parts of the animal being eaten. Both regions have spicy and nonspicy meals, so ask before you order.

Arroz con pato: Tender duck is paired with rice that's colored green with cilantro in this iconic dish that originated in Chiclayo.

Cabrito con tacu-tacu: This dish of goat kid with refried rice and beans tastes like Peruvian comfort food. It's rich in flavor, but has little spice.

Cangrejo reventado: This is a fresh, spicy dish of boiled crab, eggs, and onions usually served in the shell with a side of yucca.

Cebiche de conchas negras: *Cebiche* (raw seafood with lemon or lime juice and chili peppers) made of black conch, believed to be an aphrodisiac, is an iconic dish in the region, though it's not for everyone. The taste of the conch is quite strong, and seasonal bans should be respected to help with conservation.

Cuy: Guinea pig is one of the more popular dishes in Peru. It's tasty and similar to rabbit, but usually served whole, so you need to decide whether you can deal with seeing a head-on critter on your plate before ordering it.

Parrilladas: At restaurants serving *parrilladas* (barbecues) you can choose from every imaginable cut of beef, including *anticucho* (beef heart) and *ubre* (cow udder).

Shámbar: Particular to Trujillo, this wheat-and-bean stew is a nice, semispicy meat alternative that is served only on Monday.

km (2 miles), turning east onto a paved road leading to Huaraz. The ruins sit about 2 km (1¼ miles) past the turnoff. ✉ *Casma* 🎫 *S/6, includes admission to Pañamarca.*

9

WHERE TO EAT AND STAY

$ SEAFOOD 🍴 **El Tío Sam.** The best restaurant in Casma, this local favorite serves just about every type of seafood imaginable. The *arroz chaufa con mariscos* (shellfish with Chinese-style fried rice) is especially good, but if you're not in the mood for seafood, try the *cebiche de pato.* This isn't traditional cebiche, but cooked duck, served with rice, yucca, and beans. **Known for:** home-style seafood dishes; cebiche with duck. [$] *Average main: S/25* ✉ *Av. Huarmey 138* ☎ *043/580–659* ⏲ *Closed weekends.*

$ HOTEL 🏨 **El Farol.** You'll find a respite from the dusty streets at this pleasant hotel surrounded by gardens. **Pros:** calm and natural beauty transport you away from the city; restaurant overlooking gardens. **Cons:** service requires patience. [$] *Rooms from: S/120* ✉ *Av. Túpac Amarú 450* ☎ *043/411–064* 🌐 *www.elfarolinn.com* 🛏 *28 rooms* 🍽 *No meals.*

PLAYA TORTUGAS

20 km (12 miles) north of Casma.

Between the towns of Casma and Chimbote, this idyllic, perfectly round bay is the area's best beach escape. Facilities are quite simple and are limited to just a few small hotels and restaurants.

GETTING HERE AND AROUND

Playa Tortugas is most easily reached by taxi from Casma. Expect to pay S/20 for the 15-minute drive.

EXPLORING

Playa Tortugas. An easy drive from the Sechín area, this small beach is a low-key base for exploring the nearby ruins. A ghost town in winter, it is much more pleasant, in terms of both weather and people, in summertime. The stony beach, in a perfectly round cove surrounded by brown hills, offers limited hotel and restaurant options, but with its fleet of fishing boats and pleasant lapping waves, it's a relaxing destination. **Facilities:** food and drink; toilets. **Best for:** sunset; swimming. ⊠ *Malecón Grau, Playa Tortuga.*

TRUJILLO

174 km (108 miles) north of Playa Tortugas; 561 km (350 miles) northwest of Lima on the Pan-American Hwy.

Well-preserved colonial architecture, rich local cuisine, and spectacular archaeological sites make Trujillo a must-see tourist destination. Inhabited for centuries by the Moche and Chimú peoples, who practiced human sacrifice and left some of the greatest structures and artworks in pre-Columbian Peru, the town later was conquered by the Spanish and filled with graceful colonial architecture. Today, Trujillo is renowned for its spicy northern cuisine and warm hospitality, which are abundantly on display in its excellent hotels and restaurants. You'll see why this City of Eternal Spring, officially founded in 1534, competes with Arequipa for the title of Peru's "Second City." The only problem is trying to find time to visit all the sights—literally, since many places close from 1 to 4 for lunch.

GETTING HERE AND AROUND

Both LATAM Perú and Avianca fly from Lima to Trujillo's Aeropuerto Carlos Martínez de Pinillos (TRU), 5 km (3 miles) north of the city on the road to Huanchaco.

Almost everything is within walking distance in the center of the city, and for everything else there are reasonably priced taxis. If you don't have a car, ask your hotel to arrange for a taxi for the day or to tour a specific place. For the archaeological sights, another option is to join a day tour from a travel agency.

ESSENTIALS

Currency Scotiabank. ⊠ *Jr. Pizarro 314* ☎ *044/256-600* ⊕ *www.scotiabank. com.pe.*

Mail DHL. ⊠ *Jr. Diego Almagro 579* ☎ *044/593-427* ⊕ *www.dhl.com.pe.*
Post Office. ⊠ *Jr. Independencia 286* ☎ *044/245-941.*

CLOSE UP

Which Culture Was That Again?

It's a common question after a few days of exploring the extensive archaeological sites in the north. So many different civilizations were emerging, overlapping, and converging, that it can be difficult to keep track of them all.

Chavín: One of the earliest major cultures in northern Peru was the cat-worshipping Chavín. The Chavín Empire stretched through much of Peru's Northern Highlands and along the northern and central coasts. Artifacts dating back to 850 BC tell us that the Chavín people were excellent artisans, and their pottery, with its florid, compact style, can be seen in the museums of Trujillo and Lima.

Moche: About 500 years later, a highly advanced civilization called the Moche emerged. It was their carefully planned irrigation systems, still in use today, that turned the desert into productive agricultural land. Their fine ceramics and large pyramids, still standing near present-day Trujillo and Chiclayo, give us insight into their

architectural advances and daily lives. A consistent theme of their art is the ritual combat between captives, followed by elaborate bloodletting ceremonies. Despite voracious *huaqueros,* or looters, the tomb of the Lord of Sipán, discovered in 1987, was intact and untouched, revealing more about their complex culture.

Chimú to Inca: The Chimú came on the scene around AD 850. That civilization continued to conquer and expand until around 1470, when it, like most others in the area, was assimilated by the huge Inca Empire. The awe-inspiring city of Chan Chan, built by the Chimú, sits near present-day Trujillo. Although the Inca center of power lay farther south in the Cusco–Machu Picchu area, its cultural influence stretched far beyond the northern borders of Peru, and it was near present-day Tumbes that Francisco Pizarro, the Spanish pig farmer-turned-conquistador, first caught sight of the glory of the Inca Empire.

9

Medical Hospital Belén. ✉ *Bolívar 350* ☎ *044/480–200* ⊕ *www.hbt.gob.pe.*

Pharmacy Boticas Fasa. ✉ *Jr. Pizarro 512* ☎ *044/899–028.*

Visitor Information iPerú. ✉ *Jr. Independencia 467* ☎ *044/294–561* ⊕ *peru.info.*

ARCHAEOLOGICAL SITES

Chan Chan's Museo del Sitio. Begin your archaeological exploration at this small but thorough museum, which has displays of ceramics and textiles from the Chimú Empire. The entrance fee to the museum includes Chan Chan, Huaca Arco Iris, and Huaca Esmeralda, so hold on to your ticket (you may also go directly to the ruins and purchase the same ticket there, for the same price). From Trujillo, take a taxi or join a tour from an agency. Each location is a significant distance from the next. Guides are available at the entrance of each site for S/10 or more (S/25 Chan Chan) and are strongly recommended, both for the information they can provide and also for safety reasons (a few robberies have occurred in the more remote sectors of the archaeological sites). At the museum,

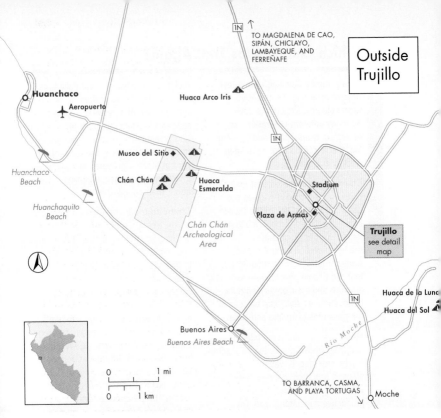

TO MAGDALENA DE CAO,
SIPÁN, CHICLAYO,
LAMBAYEQUE, AND
FERREÑAFE

Huanchaco

Aeropuerto

Huaca Arco Iris

Museo del Sitio ◆

Huanchaco
Beach

Chán Chán

Huaca
Esmeralda

Stadium

Huanchaquito
Beach

Plaza de Armas

Trujillo
see detail
map

Chán Chán
Archeological
Area

Huaca de la Luna

Huaca del Sol

0   1 mi

0   1 km

Buenos Aires
Buenos Aires Beach

Río Moche

TO BARRANCA, CASMA,
AND PLAYA TORTUGAS

Moche

and all sites, there are clean restrooms and a cluster of souvenir stalls and a snack shops, but no place to buy a full meal. ⊠ Ctra. Huanchaco, 5 km (3 miles) northwest of Trujillo ☎ 044/206–304 ⊠ S/20, includes admission to Chan Chan, Huaca Arco Iris, and Huaca Esmeralda; ticket valid for 48 hrs.

Fodor's Choice ★ Chan Chan. With its strange, honeycomb-like walls and labyrinth of wavelike parapets, this sprawling ancient capital is the largest adobe city in the world. Its surreal geometry once held boulevards, aqueducts, gardens, palaces, and some 10,000 dwellings. Within its precincts were nine royal compounds, one of which, the royal palace of Tschudi, has been partially restored and opened to the public. Although the city began with the Moche civilization, the Chimú people took control of the region 300 years later and expanded the city to its current size. Although less known than the Incas, who conquered them in 1470, the Chimú were the second-largest empire in South America. Their territory stretched along 1,000 km (620 miles) of the Pacific, from Lima to Tumbes.

Before entering this UNESCO World Heritage site, check out the extensive photographic display of the ruins at the time of discovery and postrestoration. Then, begin at the Tschudi complex, the Plaza Principal, a monstrous square where ceremonies and festivals were held. The throne of the king is thought to have been in front where the ramp is found. The reconstructed walls have depictions of sea otters at their base. From here, head deep into the ruins toward the royal palace and tomb of Señor Chimú. The main corridor is marked by fishnet representations, marking the importance of the sea to these ancient people. ■TIP→ You will also find renderings of pelicans, which served as ancient road signs, their beaks pointing to important sections of the city. Just before you arrive at the Recinto Funerario, the funeral chamber of Señor Chimú, you pass a small natural reservoir called a *huachaque*. Forty-four secondary chambers surround the funeral chamber where the king, Señor Chimú, was buried. In his day it was understood that when you pass to the netherworld you can bring all your worldly necessities with you, and the king was buried with several live concubines and officials and a slew of personal effects, most of which have been looted. Although wind and rain have damaged the city, its size—20 square km (8 square miles)—still impresses. ⊠ *Ctra. Huanchaco, 5 km (3 miles) northwest of Trujillo* ☎ *044/206–304* ⊕ *chanchan.gob. pe* ✉ *S/20, includes admission to Huaca Arco Iris, Huaca Esmeralda, and Museo del Sitio; ticket valid for 48 hrs.*

Huaca Arco Iris. Filled with intriguing symbolic carvings, and with an urban backdrop, is the restored Huaca Arco Iris, or Rainbow Pyramid. Named for the unusual rainbow carving (the area rarely sees rain), it's also known as the Huaca El Dragón, or Pyramid of the Dragon, because of the central role dragons play in the friezes. This structure, built by the early Chimú, also has a repeating figure of a mythical creature that looks like a giant serpent. On the walls, mostly reconstructions, you will see what many archaeologists believe are priests wielding the knives used in human sacrifices. Half-moon shapes at the bottom of most of the friezes indicate that the Chimú probably worshipped the moon at this temple. You can climb the ramps up to the top of the platform and see the storage bins within. ⊠ *La Esperanza* ✉ *S/20, includes admission to Chan Chan, Huaca Esmeralda, and Museo del Sitio; ticket valid for 48 hrs.*

Fodor's Choice **Huaca de la Luna and Huaca del Sol.** Stark and strange beneath the ash-
★ gray hill that towers over them, these astonishing Moche pyramids were the scenes of bloody human sacrifices. Their exteriors may have eroded, but inside archaeologists have uncovered sinister octopus-shaped reliefs of the great Moche god Ai-Apaec, as well as evidence of a cataclysmic El Niño sequence that effectively destroyed Moche civilization.

The Huacas of the Sun and Moon are located some 10 km (6 miles) outside Trujillo, near the Río Moche. The former is the bigger of the two, but it's not open to the public due to its decayed state. (Built up of 130 million adobe bricks in eight continually expanding stages, its treasures were literally cleaned out of it in 1610, when the Spanish diverted the Río Moche to wash the imperial gold and silver from its innards.) The Huaca of the Moon is awesome in its own right, with numerous exterior and interior walls blazoned with bizarre mythological reliefs. These include spider-like creatures, warriors, and the scowling face of Ai-Apaec, the ferocious god to whom captives were sacrificed at the pyramid's base. These sacrifices probably occurred to propitiate the gods of the weather, but alas, it didn't work. A series of violent El Niño events around the year 600 brought drought and sandstorms, eventually ending the Moche civilization.

The Chan Chan ruins, outside of Trujillo, are the largest adobe city in the world.

When you visit the Huaca de la Luna, you'll start from the top, near the sacrificial altars, and work your way down through the inner galleries to the murals at the base. This was where archaeologists discovered bones of the Moches' victims in recent decades. ■TIP➔ Be sure to allot time for the excellent museum, which includes exhibits of Moche artwork and informative discussions of the culture's history and religion. ✉ *Av. Santa Rosa, off Panamericana Norte* ☎ *044/221–269* ⊕ *huacas-demoche.pe* 🎫 *S/10; S/5 for museum.*

Huaca Esmeralda. Much like the other Chimú pyramids, the most interesting aspects of the ruins are the carved friezes, unrestored and in their original state. The images include fish, seabirds, waves, and fishing nets, all central to the life of the Chimú. Like other Chimú pyramids on the northern coast, the ancient temple mound of Huaca Esmeralda, or the Emerald Pyramid, is believed to have served as a religious ceremonial center. ⚠ The pyramid is in an area that's dangerous for unaccompanied tourists, so go with a guide. ✉ *Huanchaco Hwy., 2 km (1¼ miles) west of Trujillo* 🎫 *S/20, includes admission to Chan Chan, Huaca Arco Iris, and Museo del Sitio; ticket valid for 48 hrs.*

EXPLORING

More than any other city in Peru, Trujillo maintains much of its colonial charm, especially inside Avenida España, which encircles the heart of the city. This thoroughfare replaced a wall 9 meters (30 feet) high erected in 1687 to deter pirates. Two pieces of the wall stand at the corner of Estete and España.

TOP ATTRACTIONS

Casa Urquiaga. The enormous, elaborately carved wooden door is a stunning entrance to this beautifully restored neoclassical mansion from the early 19th century. ■TIP→ **The house is owned by Peru's Central Bank; simply inform the guard that you'd like to go inside and look around.** Don't miss the lovely rococo furniture and the fine collection of pre-Columbian ceramics. ✉ *Pizarro 446* 🕿 ✉ *Free.*

Palacio Iturregui. One look at the elaborate courtyard with its two levels of white columns, enormous tiles, and three-tiered chandeliers and you'll know why this is called a palace rather than a house. From the intricate white-painted metalwork to the gorgeous Italian marble furnishings, every detail has been carefully restored and maintained. Originally built in 1842, it's now the home of the private Club Central de Trujillo. Unfortunately, the club only allows visitors limited access, and permission to enter seems to depend principally on the guard's mood for the day. But if you do go, prepare to be impressed. The grand salon alone is worth it. ✉ *Pizarro 688* 🕿 *044/234–212.*

NEED A BREAK

✕ **Casona Deza Café (***Casona de los Leones***). This beautiful café sits inside the Casa Ganoza Chopitea, which was constructed around 1735 and is one of the best-preserved colonial mansions in Trujillo. The interior has original woodwork and frescoes, and the exterior features a balcony and a unique polychrome facade featuring a male and a female lion (which is why it is sometimes referred to as Casona de los Leones). Known for: colonial atmosphere; cheap snacks.** ✉ *Independencia 630* 🕿 *044/474–756.*

WORTH NOTING

Casa de la Emancipación. This branch of Banco Continental is unlike any bank you've ever been in. Go through the central courtyard and up to the small art gallery on the right. Enjoy the current exhibition—anything from modern to traditional works of art—and see a scale model of Trujillo when it was a walled city. ■TIP→ **Continue to the back, taking in the chandeliers, the large gold mirrors, and the small fountain, and imagine the day that, in this house, the city declared its independence from Spain on December 29, 1820.** It later became the country's first capitol building and meeting place for its first legislature. ✉ *Pizarro 610* 🕿 *044/246–061* ✉ *Free* ☾ *Closed Sun.*

Casa del Mayorazgo de Facala. The open courtyard, from 1709, is surrounded by beautiful cedar columns, greenery … and bankers: as with many colonial mansions in Peru, this one is now owned by a bank. Scotiabank, however, welcomes tourists and clients into the house to see its wonderfully preserved beauty. Notice the classic brown stucco-covered thick adobe walls and Moorish-style carved-wood ceiling. The security guards are happy to answer questions about the house. The entrance is on the corner of Bolognesi and Pizarro. ✉ *Pizarro 314* 🕿 *044/249–994* ✉ *Free* ☾ *Closed weekends.*

Monasterio El Carmen. Still used as a nunnery, this handsome edifice, built in 1725, is regarded as the city's finest example of colonial art. It has five elaborate altars and some fine floral frescos. Next door is a museum, the Pinacoteca Carmelita, with religious works from the

17th and 18th centuries and an interesting exhibition on restoration techniques. Be warned: visiting hours are sporadic. ⊠ *Av. Colón at Av. Bolívar* ☎ *044/233–091* 🖙 *S/5.*

Museo de Arqueología. Originally built in the 17th century, this museum displays pottery and other artifacts recovered from the archaeological sites surrounding Trujillo. There are excellent reproductions of the colorful murals found at the Huaca de la Luna, the pyramids southeast of the city, as well as a lovely courtyard. ⊠ *Jr. Junín 682 at Jr. Ayacucho* ☎ *044/249–322* 🖙 *S/6* ⏾ *Closed Sun.*

FAMILY **Museo del Juguete.** Puppets, puzzles, toys, games—what could be more fun than a toy museum? This private museum houses a large collection of toys from all over the world and shows the transformation of toys through the centuries. ■ TIP→ The toys from pre-Colombian Peru are especially interesting, giving a seldom-seen view into the daily lives of ancient people. You can't play with the toys, so it may not be appropriate for very young children. ⊠ *Jr. Independencia 705* ☎ *044/208–181* 🖙 *S/5.*

NEED A BREAK

Museo Café Bar. Feel like you're part of the colonial history while enjoying a delicious cocktail at this swanky bar and lounge beside the Museo del Juguete. With its wood floors, dark-wood bar, floor-to-ceiling glass cabinets, and cushioned leather seats, it's a relaxed café in the afternoon

and a hopping bar with live jazz in the early evening. ✉ *Jr. Independencia 701* ☎ *044/208-181.*

Plaza de Armas. Brightly colored, well-maintained buildings and green grass with walkways and benches make this one of the most charming central plazas in Peru. Fronted by the 17th-century cathedral and surrounded by the colonial-era mansions that are Trujillo's architectural glory, this is not, despite claims by locals, Peru's largest main plaza, but it is one of the nicest. ✉ *Trujillo.*

FESTIVALS

Considered the cultural capital of Peru, Trujillo is known for its festivities, including an international ballet festival, a contemporary art biennial, and a horse show. Consider coming to town for the Festival Internacional de la Primavera (International Spring Festival), held every year in late September or early October (check local listings for the exact dates). Trujillo is also busy during the last week of January, when it holds a spectacular dance competition called the National Fiesta de La Marinera, which showcases the country's virtuosic, flirtatious national dance.

WHERE TO EAT

Trujillo serves up delicious fresh seafood and a variety of excellent meat dishes. Try the cebiche made with fish or shellfish, *causa,* a casserole made of mashed potatoes and layers of fillings, tasty *cabrito al horno* (roast kid) or *seco de cabrito* (stewed kid), or *shámbar,* a bean stew tinged with mint.

$
ITALIAN
🍴 **Al Dente.** With this simple but classy Italian hideaway, artisanal pizza comes to Trujillo. The pies are indeed tempting—with thin and flaky crust and generous toppings—but don't let them dissuade you from the excellent pastas, which are homemade and inventive. **Known for:** top-notch artisanal pizza; house-made pasta. [$] *Average main: S/25* ✉ *Fatima 693* ☎ *044/372-379.*

$
PERUVIAN
🍴 **El Mochica.** Join the many other enthusiastic diners at this local spot. It's crowded and busy, but a fun place to eat that specializes in regional cuisine—and does it well. **Known for:** fresh takes on seafood classics; elegant setting close to the plaza. [$] *Average main: S/30* ✉ *Bolívar 462* ☎ *044/221-626* 🌐 *elmochica.com/trujillo/.*

$$
PERUVIAN
Fodor's Choice ★
🍴 **Fiesta Gourmet.** Born in Chiclayo decades ago, the Fiesta group is widely considered the preeminent dining choice for those looking for modern interpretations of Peru's northern coastal cuisine such as *arroz con pato* (duck with rice) or suckling goat. This location, a sleek multilevel modern bistro in Vista Alegre, has become the city's top choice for fine dining. **Known for:** dishes that set the benchmark for northern cooking; polished, attentive service. [$] *Average main: S/50* ✉ *Av. Larco 954* ☎ *044/421-572* 🌐 *www.restaurantfiestagourmet.com.*

$$
PERUVIAN
🍴 **Las Bóvedas.** This elegant restaurant in the Hotel Libertador offers diners a beautiful space and delicious food. An impressive *bóveda,* or vaulted brick ceiling, arches over the dining room, and plants fill the niches. **Known for:** northern food; local delicacy, shámbar, on Monday. [$] *Average main: S/45* ✉ *Hotel Libertador, Independencia 485, Plaza de Armas* ☎ *044/232-741* 🌐 *www.libertador.com.pe.*

$
PERUVIAN

✕ **Restaurante Doña Peta.** *Seco de cabrito* (spicy goat stew, a northern delicacy) is the star of the menu at this wildly popular institution among Trujillo locals, and no wonder: the version here is among the best you'll find. Colorfully woven decorations and *marinera* music add to the atmosphere. **Known for:** stick-to-your-ribs goat stews; festive atmosphere. $ *Average main: S/30* ✉ *Alcides Carrion 354* ☎ *949/328–282* ⊘ *No dinner.*

$
ECLECTIC

✕ **Romano.** Although this Trujillo establishment looks like it's seen better days in its five-plus decades, Romano still offers diners good food and friendly service. For dinner, enjoy seafood and pasta dishes, followed by excellent homemade desserts. **Known for:** criollo cooking; excellent desserts. $ *Average main: S/20* ✉ *Pizarro 747* ☎ *044/252–251.*

WHERE TO STAY

$
RESORT
FAMILY

🏨 **Costa del Sol Wyndham Trujillo.** If you want to stay outside the city, this modern hotel is the best place to stay. **Pros:** quiet, attractive setting; good for kids; two pools. **Cons:** can be isolating without a car. $ *Rooms from: S/225* ✉ *Los Cocoteros 500* ☎ *044/484–150* ⊕ *www. costadelsolperu.com/trujillo/* ⇥ *120 rooms* ⦿ *Breakfast.*

$$
HOTEL

🏨 **El Gran Marqués.** This upscale, full-service hotel and spa is minutes from the city center and has solid, comfortable rooms overlooking a pool surrounded by lush gardens. **Pros:** very efficient service; two pools. **Cons:** caters to business travelers and can be impersonal. $ *Rooms from: S/270* ✉ *Díaz de Cienfuegos 145, Urb. La Merced* ☎ *044/481–710* ⊕ *www.elgranmarques.com* ⇥ *50 rooms* ⦿ *Breakfast.*

$
HOTEL

🏨 **Gran Bolívar.** A modern hotel hides behind the historic facade of this centrally located lodging. **Pros:** colonial architecture; beautiful central courtyard; central location; good staff. **Cons:** some rooms have lots of light, but others have very little; tacky decorations. $ *Rooms from: S/155* ✉ *Jr. Bolívar 957* ☎ *044/262–200* ⊕ *www.granbolivarhotel.com* ⇥ *35 rooms* ⦿ *Breakfast.*

$$
HOTEL
Fodor's Choice
★

🏨 **Hotel Libertador.** On the Plaza de Armas, this elegant, upscale hotel is the best choice in Trujillo, with beautiful colonial architecture. **Pros:** central location; beautiful architecture. **Cons:** some rooms are better than others. $ *Rooms from: S/305* ✉ *Independencia 485* ☎ *044/231–741* ⊕ *www.libertador.com.pe/hotel/libertador-trujillo/* ⇥ *79 rooms* ⦿ *Breakfast.*

$
HOTEL

🏨 **Los Conquistadores.** Near the Plaza de Armas, this no-frills business hotel has large rooms with separate sitting areas and common areas away from the noisy street. **Pros:** excellent location; large rooms. **Cons:** bland furnishings; little natural light. $ *Rooms from: S/140* ✉ *Diego de Almagro 586* ☎ *044/481–650* ⊕ *www.losconquistadoreshotel.com* ⇥ *50 rooms* ⦿ *Breakfast.*

NIGHTLIFE

Runa's Martini Lounge. Conveniently set in a lovely colonial building not far from the plaza, this sleek bar and lounge attracts an upscale, 20- to 40-year-old clientele who are content with skipping the club scene. Happy hours and frequent drink promotions keep the cocktail prices down. ✉ *Jr. Independencia 610* ☎ *937/506–594* ⊘ *Closed Sun.*

Tributo. In a converted mansion with a friendly vibe, Tributo has live music, mainly cover or "tribute" (hence the name) bands on weekends. ⊠ *Pizarro 391* ⊘ *Closed Sun.–Wed.*

SHOPPING

Along Avenida España, especially where it intersects with Junín, stalls display locally made leather goods, particularly shoes, bags, and coats. Be wary of pickpockets during the day, and avoid it altogether after sunset.

> **TRUJILLO TIME**
>
> Many of the museums are closed at lunchtime from about 1 to 4 or 4:30. It can be quite hot around midday, so it's best to plan on indoor activities. It's easy to hail a taxi in Trujillo, and the in-town fare of about S/4 is quite reasonable. As always when traveling, be on your guard if you visit the market area—access your cash discreetly and keep your valuables close.

HUANCHACO

12 km (7 miles) northwest of Trujillo.

Less than half an hour away from the city, Huanchaco is a little beach community where surfers, tourists, affluent *trujillanos*, families, and couples easily mix. With excellent restaurants, comfortable hotels, and never-ending sunshine, this is a nice place to unwind for a couple of days or to live it up at one of the many annual fiestas. The Festival del Mar is held every other year during May, the Fiesta de San Pedro every June 29, and multiple surfing and dance competitions happen throughout the year.

■ TIP→ **Head to the beach in the late afternoon to watch fishermen return for the day, gliding along in their caballitos de totora, traditional fishing boats that have been used for thousands of years.** These small boats, made from totora reeds, can be seen in Moche ceramics and other pre-Columbian handiwork. The boat's name, *caballitos*, means "little horse"; fishermen appear to be on horseback as they straddle the boats. Offer them a few soles, and they'll be glad to give you a ride.

GETTING HERE AND AROUND

Huanchaco sits well enough within the Trujillo orbit that taxiing it is the best way to get out here. The drive takes about 15 minutes and the fare runs about S/12. Buses also run between the two points from all parts of the city for about S/3.

ESSENTIALS

ATMs are plentiful here, including a GlobalNet ATM beside the Municipalidad. You can exchange cash at any bank back in Trujillo.

EXPLORING

El Santuario de Huanchaco. Although people come to Huanchaco for the beach, one of Peru's oldest churches, El Santuario de Huanchaco, on a hill overlooking the village, is a nice side trip. The sanctuary was built on a Chimú ruin around 1540. In the second half of the 16th century, a small box containing the image of *Nuestra Señora del Socorro* (Our Lady of Mercy) floated in on the tide and was discovered by locals. The image, which is kept in the sanctuary, has been an object of local veneration ever since. ⊠ *Andrés Rázuri and Unión* ⊟ *Free.*

WHERE TO EAT AND STAY

$$ | ✕ **Big Ben.** Skip the first floor and head upstairs to the terrace for great
SEAFOOD | views of the beach at Huanchaco's largest and most popular restaurant. Enjoy Huanchaquero specialties, including *cangrejo reventado* (baked crab stuffed with egg) and *cebiche de mococho* (algae cebiche). **Known for:** unusual seafood dishes; sweeping beach views. $ *Average main: S/35* ✉ *Av. Victor Larco 1184* ☎ *044/461–378* ⊕ *www.bigbenhuanchaco.com* ☉ *No dinner.*

$ | ✕ **Chocolate Café.** This cute coffeehouse serves as a nice break from
CAFÉ | seafood if you find yourself spending too much time indulging in Huanchaco's cebicherias. The Dutch-and-Peruvian-owned café sources their coffee and other organic ingredients from local and regional producers. **Known for:** gourmet desserts; European atmosphere. $ *Average main: S/15* ✉ *Av. la Rivera 752* ☎ *044/626–973* ☉ *No dinner.*

$ | ✕ **Club Colonial.** This classic Huanchaco eatery, in the hotel of the
SEAFOOD | same name, is on the beachfront and has a sidewalk-facing patio.
Fodor'sChoice | It combines recipes from the old world with ingredients from the
★ | new world, coming up with wonderful combinations of fresh seafood, pasta, greens, meats, and more. **Known for:** European flair with unusual dishes; beachside people-watching. $ *Average main: S/30* ✉ *Av. La Rivera 514* ☎ *044/461–015* ⊕ *www.facebook.com/clubcolonialhuanchaco/.*

$ | 🏨 **Hotel Bracamonte.** This pleasant hotel, across the boulevard from
HOTEL | Playa Huanchaco, is popular with Peruvian families, especially in sum-
FAMILY | mer, giving it a good "neighborhood" feel. **Pros:** if you have kids, this is the place to be; pool in beautiful landscaping; low-season rates. **Cons:** if you don't have kids, this is not the place for you. $ *Rooms from: S/160* ✉ *Jr. Los Olivos 503* ☎ *044/461–162* ⊕ *www.hotelbracamonte.com.pe* 🛏 *33 rooms* ⦿ *No meals.*

$ | 🏨 **Las Palmeras.** Across from the tranquil Playa Los Tumbos, a beach on
HOTEL | the northern end of the waterfront, Las Palmeras is a welcoming hotel (once you get past the gated entrance) with ocean views. **Pros:** pristine and comfortable rooms with terraces and views; very quiet and relaxing; gated hotel feels private. **Cons:** prices vary based on which floor the room is on. $ *Rooms from: S/130* ✉ *Av. Victor Larco 1624* ☎ *044/461–199* ⊕ *www.palmerashuanchaco.com* 🛏 *21 rooms* ⦿ *Breakfast.*

NIGHTLIFE

Huanchakero. A hot spot mainly filled with foreign travelers, this trendy restaurant and pub has an extensive menu with a range of Peruvian and Nikkei food, from sushi to cebiche. Their cocktails, many utilizing pisco that has been macerated in local fruits or herbs, are the most innovative on the strip, and there's loud music for the after-dinner crowd. Service can be hit or miss, and the food is not always consistent, so be warned. ✉ *Av. La Rivera 612* ☎ *044/461–184.*

Sabes? Worth checking out, especially on the weekend, this laid-back spot at the northern end of the main drag has good music and drinks, as well as decent pizza. ✉ *Av. Victor Larco 1220* ☎ *044/461–555.*

SPORTS AND THE OUTDOORS

The beaches around Huanchaco are popular, though the water can be rather cold.

Playa Huankarote. This wide, rocky beach south of the pier is less popular for swimming, but there's good surfing. **Amenities:** none. **Best for:** surfing, solitude. ⊠ *South of municipal pier.*

Playa Malecón. North of the pier, this is the town's most popular beach, and it is filled with restaurant after restaurant. Local craftspeople sell their goods along the waterfront walk, and fishermen line up their *caballitos de totora*, the reed fishing rafts that are used more as a photo op or to rent to tourists than for actual fishing. **Amenities:** food and drink. **Best for:** sunset; surfing; swimming; walking. ⊠ *North of municipal pier.*

MAGDALENA DE CAO

47 km (29 miles) northwest of Huanchaco.

Chances are if you are coming to this small, remote village in the Chicama Valley, it's to see the El Brujo archaeological complex, which is quickly growing in popularity.

GETTING HERE AND AROUND

As the site is about 1½ hours from Trujillo by road and public transportation is sporadic, you'll either want to rent a car or join a tour from Trujillo.

EXPLORING

El Brujo. About 6 km (4 miles) from town lie the three *huacas* of El Brujo: La Huaca Prieta, Huaca Vieja, and Huaca Rajada. The Huaca Vieja in particular has drawn considerable interest due to the 2006 discovery of the well-preserved 1,600-year-old mummy, the Lady of Cao. The discovery of the tattooed Mochica ruler has been compared to the discovery of King Tut's tomb in Egypt, as it completely turned notions of power in pre-Colombian Peru upside down. Her tattoos even suggest that she had the ability to predict supernatural events. You can see her remains, as well as other artifacts found during the ongoing excavations, in the small site museum. The other two *huacas* are still not fully excavated, but the entrance fee covers all three, and they are a short walk from each other. Guides can be hired at the entrance for a small fee. ⊠ *Magdalena de Cao* 🖅 *S/11.*

SIPÁN

165 km (102 miles) north of Magdalena de Cao; 35 km (21 miles) east of Chiclayo.

This tiny village, with a population of about 1,700, doesn't offer much, but nearby is one of the country's major archaeological sites. Arrange for a taxi or tour to take you to the tomb of the Lord of Sipán.

EXPLORING

Tumba del Señor de Sipán (*Tomb of the Lord of Sipán*). The road to the archaeological site, discovered by renowned archaeologist Walter Alva in 1987, is not far from the town of Sipán, and winds past sugar plantations and through a fertile valley. You'll soon reach a fissured hill—all that remains of a temple called the Huaca Rajada. ■ TIP→ **The three major tombs found here date from about AD 290 and earlier, and together they form one of the most complete archaeological finds in the western hemisphere.** The tombs have been attributed to the Moche culture, known for its ornamental pottery and fine metalwork. The most extravagant funerary objects were found in the tomb, now filled with replicas placed exactly where the original objects were discovered. The originals are now on permanent display in the Museo Tumbas Reales de Sipán in Lambayeque. The Lord of Sipán did not make the journey to the next world alone—he was buried with at least eight people: a warrior (whose feet were amputated to ensure that he didn't run away), three young women, two assistants, a servant, and a child. The tomb also contained a dog and two llamas. Hundreds of ceramic pots contained snacks for the long trip. Archaeological work here is ongoing, as other tombs are still being excavated. ⊠ *Sipán* 🏷 *S/10, S/20 for a guide (strongly recommended).*

CHICLAYO

204 km (127 miles) north of Trujillo.

A lively commercial center, Chiclayo is prosperous and easygoing. Although it doesn't have much colonial architecture or special outward beauty, it's surrounded by numerous pre-Columbian sites. ■ TIP→ **The Moche and Chimú people had major cities in the area, as did the Lambayeque, who flourished here from about 700 to 1370.** Archaeology buffs flocked to the area after the 1987 discovery nearby of the unlooted tomb of the Lord of Sipán. Chiclayo is a comfortable base from which to visit that tomb as well as other archaeological sites.

GETTING HERE AND AROUND

LATAM Perú, LC Perú, and Avianca connect Lima with Chiclayo's Aeropuerto José Quiñones González (CIX) just outside the city.

For the most part, you'll need to take a taxi around Chiclayo. Within the city limits, each ride should cost about S/4; ask for help at your hotel to negotiate anything beyond the city. Look at the map before hailing a taxi, though, because some things are within walking distance.

ESSENTIALS

Currency Banco de Crédito. ⊠ *Av. Balta 630* ⊕ *www.viabcp.com.*

Mail Post Office. ⊠ *Elías Aguirre 140* ☎ *074/237–031.*

Medical Clínica del Pacífico. ⊠ *Av. José Leonardo Ortiz 420* ☎ *074/232–141* ⊕ *www.clinicadelpacifico.com.pe.*

Pharmacy Max Salud. ⊠ *Av. 7 de Enero 185* ☎ *074/226–201.*

Visitor Information iPerú. ⊠ *San Jose 823* ☎ *074/205–703* ⊕ *www.peru.travel/iperu.aspx.*

EXPLORING

Cathedral. The enormous Chiclayo cathedral, dating back to 1869, is worth a look for its neoclassical facade on the Plaza de Armas, and its well-maintained central altar. ⊠ *Plaza de Armas* 🏷 *Free.*

Paseo Las Musas. For some fresh air and great people-watching, head to this pedestrian walking path. The path borders a stream and has classical statues depicting scenes from mythology. ✉ *La Florida and Falques.*

OFF THE BEATEN PATH

Túcume. Head 35 km (22 miles) north of Chiclayo to can see an immense pyramid complex, including Huaca Larga, one of the largest adobe pyramids in South America, as well as dozens of smaller ones spread across a dry desert. Most are badly deteriorated. Go first to the small museum, **Museo de Sitio,** and take a tour with an English-speaking guide to learn about the history of the nearby ruins. Then follow your guide and walk 10 minutes to see the 26 giant pyramids, surrounded by the smaller ones, and the areas in between, which have yet to be excavated.

The rugged desert landscape, sprinkled with hardy little *algarrobo* (mesquite) trees, is probably very similar to what it looked like when—so the legend goes—a lord called Naymlap arrived in the Lambayeque Valley, and with his dozen sons founded the Lambayeque dynasty and built the pyramids we see today. **TIP→ Keep an eye out for burrowing owls as you make your way from the entrance toward the pyramids.**

Adjacent to the archaeological site is a lovely hotel designed from adobe and algarrobo wood, **Los Horcones de Tucume** (*951/831–705, www.loshorconesdetucume.com*), whose architect/owner seamlessly incorporated pre-Colombian designs into the walled complex. There are 12 airy guest rooms with private terraces and a small pool at the hotel. They can arrange various horse-riding trips through algarrobo forests and meetings with local *curanderos*, or shamans. ✉ *Chiclayo* ☎ *076/422–027* 🎟 *S/10.*

WHERE TO EAT

Much like Trujillo, Chiclayo and Lambayeque offer *cabrito, causa,* and *tortilla de raya* (skate omelet). The area is more famous for King Kong, a large, crispy pastry that was invented around the time that the original movie premiered. It's filled with *manjar blanco,* a sweet filling made of sugar, condensed milk, and cinnamon boiled down until it's thick and chewy.

$$ | PERUVIAN | Fodor's Choice ★

🍴 **Fiesta Gourmet.** In 1983, the Solis family began serving modern interpretations of *comida norteña* (northern Peruvian cuisine) out of their home. The business exploded, leading to a chain of top-shelf restaurants all over Peru. **Known for:** northern Peruvian cooking raised to an art form; classic surroundings. [$] *Average main: S/50* ✉ *Salaverry 1820* ☎ *074/201–970* 🌐 *www.restaurantfiestagourmet.com* 🕒 *No dinner Sun.*

$ | PERUVIAN | FAMILY

🍴 **Hebrón.** A friendly staff serves a wide range of Peruvian and international specialties from 7 am to midnight daily at this centrally located eatery. *Pollo a la brasa*, sandwiches, grilled meats, *arroz con pato*: it's all there. There's also an excellent breakfast menu, free Wi-Fi, big corner windows for people-watching, and a playground, Hebrónlandia, in the back. **Known for:** kid-friendly environment; grilled chicken; breakfast. [$] *Average main: S/20* ✉ *Av. Balta 605* ☎ *074/222–709.*

$ | PERUVIAN

🍴 **La Parra.** Despite the bland decor, this restaurant serves delicious grilled meats, and specializes in parrilladas, with an extensive menu that includes every imaginable part of the cow. The *anticuchos* (beef heart) and *ubre* (cow udder) are well-prepared house specials. **Known for:** sizzling mixed grills; relaxed, casual vibe. $ *Average main: S/25* ✉ *Manuel María Izaga 752* 🕾 *074/225–198* ☺ *No lunch*.

$$ ✕**Paprika.** With its fusion-tinged menu and contemporary, relaxed

PERUVIAN vibe, this eatery developed by the Costa del Sol hotel chain adds an elegant twist to Chiclayo's food scene. The menu includes not just Peruvian classics, but also inventive takes on local specialties like *espesado chiclayano*, stewed duck served over a base of rice, beans, and *shámbar*. **Known for:** Peruvian classics; imaginative fusion food. $ *Average main: S/35* ✉ *Costa del Sol Wyndham Chiclayo, Balta 399* 🕾 *074/227–272* ⊕ *www.paprika.pe*.

$ ✕**Pizzeria Venecia.** This hugely popular Italian restaurant serves fantastic

PIZZA pizza on a wooden block fresh from the oven. The list of toppings is extensive, and there are some pasta choices as well. **Known for:** great pizza; raucous, hearty vibe. $ *Average main: S/20* ✉ *Av. Balta 413* 🕾 *074/506–418* ☺ *Closed Sun. No lunch*.

WHERE TO STAY

$ 🏨 **Costa del Sol Wyndham Chiclayo.** This modern tower just a few blocks

HOTEL from Chiclayo's main plaza attracts business travelers and tourists on a budget who come for the many amenities. **Pros:** central location; great service; pool and gym. **Cons:** can be noisy outside. $ *Rooms from: S/195* ✉ *Av. Balta 399* 🕾 *074/227–272* ⊕ *www.costadelsolperu.com* 🛏 *82 rooms* ⦿| *Breakfast*.

$ 🏨 **Gran Hotel Chiclayo.** Managed by the Casa Andina chain, this well-

HOTEL known lodging has well-trained staff, spacious rooms, and a good range of amenities, including a pool, casino, restaurant, gym, and spa. **Pros:** central location; first-rate accommodations and amenities. **Cons:** occasionally large business groups overtake the hotel. $ *Rooms from: S/245* ✉ *Av. Federico Villareal 115* 🕾 *074/234–911* ⊕ *www.casa-andina.com* 🛏 *145 rooms* ⦿| *Breakfast*.

$ 🏨 **Intiotel.** With refurbished rooms and noise-proof glass for street-side

HOTEL rooms, this hotel is one of the best deals in Chiclayo. **Pros:** good rooms at a low price; well-equipped gym. **Cons:** dimly lighted hallways; mediocre hotel restaurant. $ *Rooms from: S/130* ✉ *Av. Luis Gonzales 622* 🕾 *074/235–931* ⊕ *www.intiotel.com* 🛏 *65 rooms* ⦿| *Breakfast*.

$ 🏨 **Winmeier Hotel & Casino.** This full-scale casino resort features a whole

HOTEL host of amenities including a poolside bar and outdoor fireplace for cool nights, two restaurants and a karaoke bar, efficient staff, and excellent accommodations. **Pros:** first-rate service and accommodations; central location. **Cons:** run-of-the-mill interior design. $ *Rooms from: S/231* ✉ *Bolognesi 756* 🕾 *074/228–172* ⊕ *www.winmeier.pe* 🛏 *94 rooms* ⦿| *Breakfast*.

NIGHTLIFE

Fodor's Choice **Cafe 900.** This bi-level restaurant and bar opens at 8 am for breakfast
★ and doesn't close until late. Decorated with old guitars and various knickknacks and furnished with leather couches, it's one of the few options in Chiclayo with charm. Tapas and sandwiches dominate the long menu, and there are twenty or so different desserts. The superb cocktail list features new looks at Peruvian favorites, like the *chilcano*

de hierba luisa (made with lemongrass, pisco, lime, bitters, and ginger ale). There's occasionally live jazz and folk music. ☒ *Calle Izaga 900* ☎ *074/209–268* ⊕ *www.cafe900.com* ☉ *Closed Sun.*

Magno. This multistory disco is Chiclayo's place to see and be seen—and to get down to house, Latin pop, reggaeton, and salsa. The grooves are pumpin', and the crowd is mixed and friendly. ☒ *Av. Jose Leonardo Ortiz 490* ☎ *074/236–226.*

SPORTS AND THE OUTDOORS

Pimentel. The closest beach to Chiclayo is this small port town, 14 km (8½ miles) west of the city. Access via taxi should cost about S/25 each way, or bus fare is just a few soles. Although the beach isn't very attractive and the century-old curved pier is now closed to the public, there are many other enjoyable sights along the beach, including a small fleet of *caballitos de totora* and a lively boardwalk lined with restaurants. Walk along and observe the old colonial beach houses, the naval officers in white outside the maritime station, and an excessive number of young Peruvian couples walking hand in hand. **Amenities:** food and drink. **Best for:** swimming, surfing, sunset. ☒ *Malecón Seoane, Pimentel.*

SHOPPING

Mercado Central. Chiclayo's indoor market on Avenida Balta is no longer the city's main market. Once famed for its ceramics, weavings, and charms made by local *curanderos* (folk healers), now there's mainly fresh food for sale, and a nice little "food court" in the back. ☒ *Av. Balta and Vicente de la Vega.*

Mercado Modelo. Beginning at the intersection of Avenida Balta and Avenida Arica, this vast and popular market has fresh meat, vegetables, and fruit from local farms, as well as clothing, DVDs and CDs, handbags, and more. You can also ask at any of the stalls to point you to the southwest corner, where there is an extensive *mercado de brujos* (witchdoctor's market), where dozens of herbalists, *curanderos* , and shamans offer their folk remedies, many of them made of dried animals like armadillos and llama fetuses. Wander around and enjoy, but don't lose your companions in the crowd and keep a close guard on your belongings. ☒ *Av. Balta and Av. Arica.*

LAMBAYEQUE

12 km (7 miles) north of Chiclayo.

This small town has some well-preserved colonial-era buildings, but the reason to come is for the outstanding museums. The museums' exhibits provide details about the Moche civilization, and original artifacts from the tomb in Sipán.

GETTING HERE AND AROUND

The town is small enough to walk around from place to place, or you can take an inexpensive taxi (S/3 within town) to the different museums. To get here from Chiclayo, you can easily hire a taxi or rent a car.

EXPLORING

Museo Arqueológico Nacional Brüning. While not nearly as exciting as the Sipán museum next door, this archaeological museum helps reveal how the different pre-Inca civilizations lived their daily lives. Excellent interpretive displays show how the Moche, Lambayeque, and other pre-Inca cultures such as the Cupisnique, Chavín, Chimú, and Sicán fished, harvested, and kept their homes. There's also a wonderful photography exhibit detailing the archaeologist Hans Heinrich Brüning and his experiences in Peru beginning in the late 1800s. Descriptions are in Spanish, so an English-speaking guide is recommended. ⊠ *Huamachuco and Atahualpa* ☎ *074/282–110* 💰 *S/10, S/20 for a guide.*

Fodor's Choice ★ **Museo Nacional Tumbas Reales de Sipán.** This striking pyramidal complex, which ranks among the country's best museums, displays the real artifacts from the tomb of the Lord of Sipán, one of the greatest archaeological finds of the 20th century. The find showed the world how advanced the Moche and other pre-Inca civilizations in Peru once were, and these stunning exhibits detail what and where every piece of jewelry, item of clothing, or ceramic vase was found. As you descend through the different floors, you'll see spectacular turquoise-and-gold earrings, bizarre hairless dogs buried with the Señor, and life-size mockups of Sipán warriors. This museum is very highly recommended. ■TIP➔ **English-speaking guides are available to help with the Spanish-only descriptions and confusing order of exhibits.** ⊠ *Av. Juan Pablo Vizcardo and Guzmán* ☎ *074/283–977* 💰 *S/10, S/30 for a guide* ⊗ *Closed Mon.*

WHERE TO STAY

$
HOTEL
Fodor's Choice ★ 🏨 **Hosteria San Roque.** The most atmospheric place to base yourself while exploring the Chiclayo area's archaeological attractions is not in the city itself but rather in this 18th-century *casona* in Lambayeque. **Pros:** authentic colonial-era style; romantic manor house; pleasant pool. **Cons:** nothing nearby to do in the evenings. 💲 *Rooms from: S/200* ⊠ *2 de Mayo 437* ☎ *074/282–860* ⊕ *www.hosteriasanroque.com* 🛏 *20 rooms* ⃝ *Breakfast.*

FERREÑAFE

18 km (11 miles) northeast of Chiclayo.

It's produced more winners of the Miss Peru contest than any other town, but Ferreñafe has other charms as well. The Iglesia Santa Lucia, begun in 1552, is a good example of baroque architecture. Nevertheless, most visitors come for its excellent Sicán museum.

GETTING HERE AND AROUND

Minibuses ply the streets of Chiclayo and Lambayeque for the short ride to Ferreñafe, and many tours will stop here on the way to Túcume. Taxis can also be hired. The Sicán museum is on the northern end of town.

EXPLORING

Museo Nacional Sicán. Offering insight into the culture of the Sicán people, this interesting museum also has unique exhibits on such topics as the *El Niño* effect and where the pre-Inca civilizations fit into world history. Visual timelines hammer home just how far back Peruvian history goes. See the exhibits introducing the Sicán (also known as the Lambayeque), including everything from common eating utensils to ceremonial burial urns, models of what their homes might have looked like, and a central room full of treasures from this coastal culture renowned for its amazing headdresses and masks. The replicas of the tombs are especially cool. ⊠ *Av. Batán Grande* ☎ *074/286–469* ⊕ *www.muniferrenafe.gob.pe* ⊠ *S/8* ⊘ *Closed Mon.*

OFF THE
BEATEN
PATH

Chaparrí Reserve. Getting to the Chaparri Reserve on your own can be difficult—it's 75 km (47 miles) northeast of Chiclayo, a little more than an hour's journey—but if you can get a group together or join a tour to this community-owned dry-forest nature preserve, it might just be one of your most memorable experiences in Peru. The 34,412-hectare (85,000-acre) reserve was created to help safeguard rare native species such as the white-winged guan, the Andean Condor, and the guanaco (a type of camelid similar in appearance to a llama). Perhaps their most important work is protecting the spectacled bear, for which they have a rescue center that works to reintroduce rehabilitated animals into this last refuge for populations of the species.

While you can visit the reserve anytime from 7 am to 5 pm, you'll up your chances of seeing wildlife if you stay overnight in the 12-room **Chaparri Ecolodge** (*084/255–718, www.chaparrilodge.com*) in the heart of the reserve. Stays include three daily meals and a guide to the reserve. ■TIP➜ Advance booking for day visits and overnight stays is highly recommended, as space is limited and all visitors must be accompanied by a guide. ⊠ *Chaparrí* ☎ *084/255–718* ⊕ *www.chaparri.org* ⊠ *S/30.*

PIURA

216 km (134 miles) north of Chiclayo.

The sunny climate, friendly people, and good food make Piura a delightful stop on your way north. Since most of the major flight and bus routes to the North Coast beaches travel through Piura, stopping here is not just easy, it's often required.

As a central commercial hub and the country's fifth-largest city (population 380,000), it's hard to believe how relaxed and friendly Piura is to tourists. Historically, however, it's a community used to transition. Founded in 1532 by Francisco Pizarro before he headed inland to conquer the Inca, the community changed locations three times before settling on the modern-day location along the banks of the Río Piura.

GETTING HERE AND AROUND

LATAM Perú, Peruvian Airlines, and Avianca fly between Lima and the Aeropuerto de Piura (PIU), 2 km (1 mile) east of the city. The best way to get around Piura is on foot, as most amenities and attractions are within a short walk of the plaza. Inexpensive and safe taxis are available from the street if you have heavy bags or are ready for a siesta.

ESSENTIALS

Currency Banco de Crédito. ⊠ *Av. Grau 133* ☎ *073/286–190* ⊕ *www.viabcp.com.*

Medical Hospital Cayetano Heredia. ✉ *Av. Independencia s/n, Urb. Miraflores* ☎ *073/287–970.*

Visitor Information iPerú. ✉ *Av. Ayacucho 377* ☎ *073/320–249* 🌐 *www.peru.travel.*

EXPLORING

Catedral de Piura. On the city's main square, the cathedral, built in 1588, is one of the country's oldest churches and is worth a visit. Inside you'll find an altarpiece dedicated to the Virgen de Fátima dating back more than 350 years. ✉ *Plaza de Armas* 🎟 *Free.*

Museo Vicus. This archaeological museum, sometimes called the Museo Municipal, was extensively renovated during the first decade of this century. It houses the city's collection of pre-Columbian ceramics and gold artifacts, primarily from the Vicus culture, as well as changing art exhibits. ✉ *Av. Sullana and Av. Huánuco* ☎ *073/322–307* 🌐 *museos.cultura.pe* 🎟 *S/5* ⏲ *Closed Mon.*

WHERE TO EAT AND STAY

$ PERUVIAN 🍴 **Capuccino.** This attractive restaurant has an extensive international menu offering traditional rice and meat dishes, as well European-inspired salads, sandwiches, and entrées mixing local and imported ingredients. Whether you choose the Thai salad or *lomo saltado* (stir-fried beef and potatoes), expect to savor your meal. **Known for:** alternatives to Peruvian fare; cheery atmosphere. [$] *Average main: S/25* ✉ *Tacna 786* ☎ *074/301–111* 🌐 *www.capuccinogourmet.com.*

$ PERUVIAN Fodor's Choice ★ 🍴 **Picanteria La Santitos.** Ask anyone in Piura the best place in town to go for typical dishes, and they'll tell you to come here. Two dining rooms with cracked white walls—one air-conditioned, one not—and waitresses in flowing peasant dresses make the setting for regional dishes like *tamales verdes* (green tamales) and *seco de chavelo* (fried green bananas and pork) memorable. **Known for:** offbeat regional food; countrified atmosphere. [$] *Average main: S/25* ✉ *La Libertad 1001* ☎ *074/309–475* 🌐 *www.lasantitos.com* ⏲ *No dinner.*

$ HOTEL 🏨 **Costa Del Sol Wyndham Piura.** This excellent hotel, part of the Costa del Sol chain, has modern rooms and facilities and a high-end bar, along with excellent service. **Pros:** catering to business travelers means better all-around service; nice pool area; soundproofed windows. **Cons:** the modern architecture lacks charm; some rooms have little natural light. [$] *Rooms from: S/150* ✉ *Av. Loreto 649* ☎ *073/302–864* 🌐 *www.costadelsolperu.com/piura/* 🛏 *95 rooms* 🍽 *Breakfast.*

$ HOTEL 🏨 **LP Hotel Piura.** A venerable hotel on the tree-shaded Plaza de Armas, the LP (Los Portales) has charming colonial architecture paired with plenty of modern amenities. **Pros:** beautiful colonial architecture; up-to-date technology, including LCD TV and Wi-Fi; valet parking. **Cons:** some rooms are better than others. [$] *Rooms from: S/220* ✉ *Libertad 875* ☎ *074/328–887* 🌐 *www.losportaleshoteles.com.pe/hotel/piura/* 🛏 *87 rooms* 🍽 *Breakfast.*

SHOPPING

Catacaos. The tiny pueblo of Catacaos, 12 km (7 miles) southwest of Piura, is famous for its textiles, gold and silver figurines and jewelry, and excellent pottery. The small market, filled with street stalls and shops, is open daily until 6 pm. Look around as much as you like, but to get the best price, only closely examine what you really want to buy. The town also has excellent *picanterías* to sample northern cuisine. To get to Catacaos, take the Pan-American Highway. A taxi should cost around S/30 round-trip.

MÁNCORA

181 km (113 miles) north of Piura.

This laid-back beach destination, famous for its sunshine and white-sand beaches, has excellent waves for surfing and great opportunities for fishing and adventure sports. Although the relaxed but dusty town has tourist offices, restaurants, and small shops, the real attraction is the line of hotels about 2 km (1 mile) south along **Las Pocitas**, a lovely string of beaches with rocky outcrops that hold tiny pools of seawater at low tide.

GETTING HERE AND AROUND

Comfortable Excluciva and Cruz del Sur buses ply the long 14-hour route between Lima and Máncora. If you wish to fly, LATAM Perú connects Lima with the Aeropuerto de Tumbes (TCP), about 1½ hours away, and LATAM Perú, Peruvian Airlines, and Avianca fly to Piura, about 2½ hours away. Taxis at the airport charge about S/160 for the trip between Máncora and Tumbes, or S/250 between Máncora and Piura. Once you arrive at Máncora, mototaxis are the best way to get around.

WHERE TO EAT

$$
PERUVIAN
Fodor's Choice
★

✕ **La Sirena D'Juan.** Chef Juan Seminario rides his motorcycle to local markets every day to find the fish and produce that make this narrow restaurant the rival of many top eateries in Lima. This means Mediterranean and Asian elements find their way into dishes such as a Nikkei-style *tiradito* (sashimi-style fish with a spicy sauce) and house-made pastas. **Known for:** Asian fusion cuisine; top-notch food. $ *Average main: S/40* ⊠ *Av. Piura 316* ☎ *073/258–173.*

WHERE TO STAY

$
HOTEL
FAMILY

▥ **Hotelier Arte y Cocina.** Sandwiched between the fishing pier and the start of Las Pocitas beach, just south of Máncora, this small hotel is owned by the son of famed Peruvian TV chef Teresa Ocampo, whose recipes are used in the excellent beachfront restaurant, Donde Teresa. **Pros:** quiet and remote yet close to town; great restaurant; large rooms with good amenities. **Cons:** restaurant has sporadic hours. $ *Rooms from: S/240* ⊠ *Acceso Máncora, off Panamericana Norte, Las Pocitas* ☎ *073/258–702* ⊕ *www.hotelier.pe* ⇤ *8 rooms* ⦿ *Breakfast.*

$$$$
RESORT
🛏 **KiChic.** This tiny, Zen-like property on Las Pocitas beach, near other top boutique hotels, is perhaps the first to really do the New Age concept right in Máncora. **Pros:** unique emphasis on wellness; well planned; great rooms and facilities. **Cons:** concept not for everyone; accepts adult couples only; quite expensive. $ *Rooms from: S/860 ⊠ Acceso Máncora, off Panamericana Norte, Las Pocitas* ☎ *073/411–518* ⊕ *www.kichic. com* 🛏 *9 rooms* ⦿| *Breakfast.*

$$
HOTEL
🛏 **Los Corales.** Directly on the beach south of the town, with very reasonable rates, this little lodging is one of the best deals in Máncora. **Pros:** same beachside location and service as other hotels for less; on-site restaurant and pool. **Cons:** one of the oldest properties in town. $ *Rooms from: S/349 ⊠ Acceso Máncora, off Panamericano Norte* ☎ *073/258–309* ⊕ *www.loscorales-mancora.com* 🛏 *15 rooms* ⦿| *Breakfast.*

$$
HOTEL
🛏 **Mancora Marina Hotel.** Better known as MMH, this dramatic white hotel just south of town was designed by Jordi Puig, who designed the MV Aqua luxury riverboats in the Amazon. **Pros:** close to town; beautiful pool; decent restaurant and bar. **Cons:** the beach in front can get dirty. $ *Rooms from: S/284 ⊠ Acceso Máncora, off Panamericano Norte* ☎ *073/258–614* ⊕ *www.mancoramarina.com* 🛏 *12 rooms* ⦿| *Breakfast.*

> **HOLD ON!**
>
> As a general rule, taxis are abundant, cheap, and mechanically safe throughout Peru. Enter the mototaxi, a three-wheeled motorcycle, attached to a double seat, covered by an awning. No metal, no glass, nothing between you, the road, and the other vehicles. The good news? Mototaxis often are slower and go only short distances. Whenever possible, take a regular taxi in a car. Nevertheless, for those places—especially Máncora and Punta Sal—in which mototaxis are the main source of travel, hold on and enjoy the ride!

SPORTS AND THE OUTDOORS

Escuela de Buceos Spondylus. This PADI-licensed dive school runs immersion courses for beginners, and you can get your license for open-water diving, rescue diving, and underwater photography. Dive trips go to Los Organos, Punta Sal, and Cabo Blanco. ⊠ *Av. Piura 216* ☎ *073/496–932* ⊕ *www.buceaenperu.com* 🍴 *From S/300.*

PUNTA SAL

25 km (15 miles) north of Máncora; 85 km (53 miles) southwest of Tumbes.

Sit on the beach, go for a swim, relax in the afternoon sun—what more could you want from a beach resort? That's probably why Punta Sal has become a popular vacation spot in recent years. A few kilometers north of the Pan-American Highway, hotels and resorts abound in this area, while tourists and vacationing *limeños* flock here for the blond-sand beach, comfortable ocean breezes, and sunny climate. It's quieter here than in Máncora, with fewer facilities, so plan on spending most of your time at or near your hotel.

Surfers take to the waves at Máncora, the north's hot spot beach destination.

WHERE TO STAY

$$$
RESORT
FAMILY

Punta Sal Suites & Bungalows Resort. Offering a variety of bungalows, rooms, and beach areas, this upscale, all-inclusive resort is the place to go for luxury and relaxation. **Pros:** top-quality hotel; wide range of activities and sports. **Cons:** regular rooms are nothing special; rates vary by season. $ *Rooms from: S/580* ⊠ *Km 173, Sullana–Tumbes Hwy.* ☎ *072/596–700* ⊕ *www.puntasal.com.pe* ⤳ *27 rooms* ⦿ *All-inclusive.*

TUMBES

183 km (114 miles) north of Piura; 70 km (43 miles) north of Punta Sal.

About an hour's drive north of the beach resorts of Máncora and Punta Sal is Tumbes, the last city on the Peruvian side of the Peru-Ecuador border. Tumbes played a major role in Peruvian history: it was here that Pizarro first glimpsed the riches of the vast Inca Empire in 1528, which he would return to conquer in 1532. In the past, tensions with neighboring Ecuador were high—it wasn't until 1941 that Tumbes became part of Peru after a military skirmish—but things are now *tranquilo*, as Peruvians say. Still, hot, muggy Tumbes is unlike anywhere else in the country. The coastal desert that follows the Pan-American Highway all the way to Chile is no more; in its place is a landscape that is decidedly more tropical, with mangrove forests and banana plantations. For most visitors, Tumbes is just a transit point to or from Ecuador, or a quick stop before an early flight. The city has few attractions or attractive places to spend the night. But for those with the urge to explore, there are several excellent national parks, as well as plenty of inexpensive shellfish—plus an atmosphere you won't find anywhere else in Peru.

If you find yourself crossing the border at Aguas Verdes, be extra aware of your personal belongings. Like many border towns, it has its fair share of counterfeit money, illegal goods, and scams to get money from foreigners.

GETTING HERE AND AROUND

Tumbes is the stopping point for most bus lines that travel the Pan-American Highway for the 18- to 19-hour trip to Lima, including Cruz del Sur. To get to Ecuador there are direct buses with CIFA (*www.cifainternacional.com*) to Guayaquil and Machala, where you can transfer to Cuenca. For most, the airport will be their point of entry. LATAM offers several flights per week from Lima to the Aeropuerto de Tumbes (TCP), which is just a few kilometers north of the city.

WHERE TO STAY

$$ RESORT 🏨 **Casa Andina Select Tumbes.** National chain Casa Andina's first foray into the beach-resort game has proven to be a smart one—this resort in Zorritos, south of Tumbes, is one of the north's most convenient beach getaways. **Pros:** only 40 minutes from Tumbes airport; great pool. **Cons:** isolated. [$] *Rooms from: S/314* ✉ *Panamericana Norte, km 1232, Bocapán, Zorritos* ☎ *072/596–800* 🌐 *www.casa-andina.com* 🛏 *57 rooms* 🍴 *Breakfast.*

$ HOTEL 🏨 **Costa del Sol Tumbes.** In the heart of downtown, this hotel makes for a comfortable option in Tumbes, which has a dearth of nice places to stay. **Pros:** large, inviting pool area; the best hotel in town; sport and fitness amenities. **Cons:** Wi-Fi can be spotty. [$] *Rooms from: S/238* ✉ *Jr. San Martín 275* ☎ *072/523–991* 🌐 *www.costadelsolperu.com* 🛏 *54 rooms* 🍴 *Breakfast.*

HUARAZ AND THE CORDILLERA BLANCA

The Cordillera Blanca is one of the world's greatest mountain ranges. The soaring, glaciated peaks strut more than 6,000 meters (19,700 feet) above sea level—only Asia's mountain ranges are higher. Glaciers carve their lonely way into the green of the Río Santa valley, forming streams, giant gorges, and glorious gray-green alpine lagoons. On the western side of the valley is the Cordillera Negra. Less impressive than the Cordillera Blanca, its steep mountains have no permanent glaciers and are verdant and brooding. A drive along the paved stretch of road through the valley offers spectacular views of both mountain ranges. You'll find an abundance of flora and fauna in the valley and in the narrow gorges that come snaking down from the high mountains. Deer, *vizcacha* (rodents resembling rabbits, without the long ears), vicuñas, pumas, bears, and condors are among the area's inhabitants. You'll also find the 10-meter-tall (32-foot) *puya raimondii* (the world's largest bromeliad), whose giant spiked flower recalls that of a century plant.

Continued on page 409

THE CORDILLERA BLANCA

by Oliver Wigmore

The lofty ice-clad peaks of Cordillera Blanca soar above 6,000 meters (20,000 feet) and stretch for over 100 kilometers (62 miles) north to south across the Andes. These mountains, worshipped by Andean peoples for thousands of years, are now the idols of global adventure tourism.

Explore ancient ruins, ascend icy summits at the crack of dawn, hike isolated alpine valleys, be absorbed by the endless azure blue of glacial lakes, or put your feet up at a mountain lodge.

The formation of the present Andean mountain chain began as the Nazca plate collided with and was forced beneath the South American plate, driving the ocean floor up to produce the world's longest exposed mountain range. This resulted in the formation of the Pacific coastal desert, the highland puna, and the verdant Amazon basin. Since then the Andes have been the bridging point between these diverse environmental and ecological zones. The Cordilleras Blanca, Negra and Huayhuash, and the Callejón de Huaylas Valley were formed 4 to 8 million years ago, producing spectacular peaks and many distinct ecological niches.

The May to September dry season brings the most stable weather—and the big crowds. Increasingly people are battling the rain and snow for the isolation that comes with the off-season.

Peruvians cross a log bridge in the Jancapampa Valley, as the Cordillera Blanca looms before them.

DID YOU KNOW?

Inca legend tells of Huas-carán, a wife who castrated her adulterous husband and fled with her favorite child on her back and the rest in tow. Coming to rest, the Cordillera Blanca was formed by their bodies. Their tears created the Santa and Marañón rivers.

CORDILLERA BLANCA

Taulliraju Mount, Cordillera Blanca, Huascarán National Park, Peru.

The Cordillera Blanca encompasses the mighty Huascarán, Peru's highest peak at 6,767 m (22,204 ft), and Alpamayo 5,947 m (19,511 ft), once proclaimed the most beautiful mountain in the world by UNESCO. Most of the Cordillera Blanca is within the Huascarán National Park, for which an entry ticket is required. Valid for one day or one month, these can be purchased at the entry gates or from the park headquarters in Huaraz.

Thanks to the newly paved road, the glacial lakes are now a popular day trip from Huaraz. Their beauty is still worth the trip.

HIGH POINTS

1. The Santa Cruz Trek: You ascend the Santa Cruz valley, crossing the Punta Union pass at 4,760 m (15,617 ft) beneath the breathtaking peaks, then descend to the spectacular azure blue of the Llanganuco Lakes. One of Peru's most popular alpine treks, it's often overcrowded, with litter and waste becoming a serious problem. For pristine isolation, look elsewhere.

2. Pastoruri Glacier: While you could once ice-climb and ski on this tropical galcier, today a visit allows you to witness the impacts of climate change firsthand. Popular day tours from Huaraz often combine the trip here with a visit to see the impressive Puya raimondii trees.

3. Chavín de Huántar: On the eastern side of the cordillera is Chavín de Huántar, where in around 900 BC the first pan-Andean culture developed. The Chavín culture eventually held sway over much of central Peru. The site can be visited on a long day trip from Huaraz.

4. Olleros to Chavín Trek: A short three-day trek across the Cordillera terminates at Chavín de Huántar. Guiding companies in Huaraz offer this trek with llama hauling your gear.

5. Quilcayhuanca and Cojup Valley Loop: This trek is becoming popular due to its relative isolation and pristine condition. It explores two spectacular high alpine valleys, crosses the 5,000 m (16,404 ft) Pico Choco Pass, passing beautiful glacial lakes, one of which caused the 1941 destruction of Huaraz city in a flood of mud, rocks, and ice.

6. Laguna 69: Spectacular glaciers encircle the lake and give it deep turquoise color. It can be seen on a long day hike from Huaraz. However, spending the night allows you to explore, and you will likely have the lake to yourself once the day trippers leave. This is an ideal acclimation trek.

7. Alpamayo Basecamp: An arduous week-long trek takes you on a northern route through the Cordillera, passing the spectacular north face of Nevado Alpamayo (5947 m/19,511 ft).

8. Huascarán: Peru's highest peak is one of the Cordillera's more challenging summits.

Climbing: Relatively easy three to five day guided summit climbs of Ishinka (5,550 m/18,208 ft), Pisco (5,752 m/18,871 ft) and Vallunaraju (5,684 m/18,648 ft) are arranged at any of the guiding outfitters in Huaraz. Prices and equipment vary—get a list of what's included. Many smaller companies operate purely as booking agencies for the larger companies.

1 The Santa Cruz Trek
Huaicayan
7 Alpamayo 5,947m (19,511ft)
0 3 mi
0 3 km
Cashapampa
Huaripampa
Pirámide
Artesonraju
Caraz
Pisco 5,752m (18,871ft)
Laguna 69 6
Chacraraju
Huandoy
Yanama
Caraz
CORDILLERA BLANCA
(HUASCARAN NATIONAL PARK)
Chopicalqui
Contrahierbas
Huascarán 8 6,768m (22,204ft)
Río Santa
Pueblo Libre
Yungay
Chacas
Utla
Pompey
Musho
Huaypan
Hualcan
Ulta
Mancos
Copa
Shilla
Huaicán
Copa
CORDILLERA NEGRA
Bayoraju
Vicos
Paqcharaju
Copa Chico
Carhuaz
Ranrahirca
Marcará
Akilpo
Kekepatipa
Vicos
Pashpa
Toellaraju
Anta
Joncopampa
Palcaraju
Ishinka 5,550m (18,208ft)
Collón
Taricá
Pucaranra
Jangas
Ranrapaica
Vallunaraju 5,684m (18,648ft)
Pico Choco
COJUP VALLEY
Churup
Monterrey
Wilkawain
Quilcayhuánca and Cojup Valley Loop 5
Pitec
QUILCAYHUANCA VALLEY
Huaraz
Huahulac
Macashca
Río Santa
Chavín de Huántar 3
Pastoruri Glacier 2
4 Olleros
Agocancha

A llama—member of the camelid family and provider of wool for Andean weavers—Chavín, Cordillera Blanca.

GOOD TO KNOW

CLIMBING HISTORY

The first climbers in the region were probably pre-Colombian priests, attempting difficult summits to perform sacred rituals atop icy peaks. This climbing tradition was continued by the Spanish conquistadors who wanted to exploit the rich sulphur deposits atop many of Peru's volcanic cones, and to show their dominance over Mother Nature. Modern climbing in the region took off in 1932 when a German-Austrian expedition completed many of the highest summits, including Huascarán Sur. Since then the peaks of the Cordillera Blanca and Peru have attracted climbers from around the world for rapid-summit sport climbs and solo summits. Extended duration expeditions and large support crews are less common here than in the Himalayas.

SAFETY TIPS

This area is a high alpine environment and weather patterns are unpredictable. Be prepared for all weather possibilities. It's not uncommon to experience snow storms and baking sun over the course of a single day, and at night temperatures plummet. Sunburn, dehydration, exhaustion, and frostbite are all potential problems, but by far the major issue is *soroche* (altitude sickness). It's extremely important to pace yourself and allow enough time for acclimatisation before attempting any long-distance high-altitude treks or climbs.

(above) Cullicocha; (below) Sheperds hut, Huaraz.

ENVIRONMENTAL CHANGE

The warming climate is producing alarming rates of retreat in glacial water reserves of the Cordillera Blanca. The heavily populated Pacific coast relies almost exclusively on seasonal run-off from the eastern Andes for water supplies and hydroelectricity. The feasibility of transporting water across the Andes from the saturated Amazon basin is now being debated.

MAPS

For serious navigation, get the Alpenvereins-karte (German Alpine Club) topographic map sheets, which cover the Cordillera Blanca over two maps (north and south). They are sold by Casa de Guías and the gift store below Café Andino. Many local expedition outfitters sell an "officially illegal" copy with a little persuasion.

The valley between the Cordillera Blanca and the Cordillera Negra is often called the Callejón de Huaylas after the town of Huaylas in the northern part of the valley. ■ TIP➜ This area is possibly the most important climbing and trekking destination in South America. From here, arrange to go white-water rafting, head out on a 10-day trek through the vast wilderness, or stay closer to home—one-day excursions can take you to the 3,000-year-old ruins at Chavín de Huántar, local hot springs, a nearby glacier, and an alpine lagoon. Climbers come during the dry season to test their iron on the more than 40 peaks in the area exceeding 6,000 meters (19,700 feet). The 6,768-meter (22,200-foot) summit of Huascarán is the highest in Peru and is clearly visible from Huaraz on sunny days. To the south of Huaraz, the remote and beautiful Cordillera Huayhuash offers numerous trekking and climbing excursions as well. Some say it's even more impressive than the Cordillera Blanca. The outdoor options are limitless.

The area has been inhabited since pre-Inca times, and Quechua-speaking farmers still toil on the land, planting and harvesting crops much as they did thousands of years ago. The land in the valley is fertile, and corn and oranges are abundant. Up above, potatoes and other hearty crops grow on the steep terrain. The goddess Pachamama has always provided, but she can be iron-willed and even angry at times; every now and then she will shake her mighty limbs and a section of one of the glaciers will crumble. The resulting rock-and-ice fall, called an *aluvión,* destroys everything in its path. In 1970 one such aluvión resulted from a giant earthquake, destroying the town of Yungay and killing almost all of its 18,000 inhabitants. Most of the towns throughout the area have suffered some damage from the numerous earthquakes, so not much colonial architecture survives. What remains are friendly, somewhat rugged-looking towns that serve as excellent jumping-off points for exploration of the area's vast wilderness and mountain ranges, hot springs, and 3,000-year-old ruins.

HUARAZ

400 km (248 miles) north of Lima.

Peru's number-one trekking and adventure-sports destination, Huaraz is an easy starting point for those wishing to explore the vast wilderness of the Cordillera Blanca. Unfortunately, the town has been repeatedly leveled by natural disasters. In the later part of the 20th century, three large earthquakes destroyed much of Huaraz, claiming more than 20,000 lives.

Despite the setbacks and death toll, Huaraz rallied, and today it's a pleasant town filled with good-natured people. Being one of the most popular tourist destinations in northern Peru, Huaraz also has a great international scene, and although the town has few sights, the lively restaurants and hotels are some of the best in the region. ■ TIP➜ Many businesses close between September and May, when the town practically shuts down without its hordes of climbers and trekkers. It can be hard to find an outfitter at this time; call ahead if you plan a rainy-season visit.

GETTING HERE AND AROUND

Most travelers come to Huaraz on an eight-hour bus ride from Lima, though the local airline LC Perú (*www.lcperu.pe*) has several flights per week to the area's small airport in Anta, 32 km (20 miles) north of town. Getting around the city is quite easy, as it is small enough to walk almost anywhere. Or, if you've just arrived and are feeling a little breathless from the altitude, take a taxi for S/5. To enjoy any of the nearby treks and sights, hire a guide, as it's not safe to go alone.

ESSENTIALS

Currency Banco de Crédito. ⊠ *Av. Luzuriaga 691* ☎ *043/421–170*
⊕ *www.viabcp.com.* **Scotiabank.** ⊠ *José de Sucre 760* ☎ *043/721–500*
⊕ *www.scotiabank.com.pe.*

Mail Post Office. ⊠ *Av. Luzuriaga 714* ☎ *043/421–030.*

Medical Hospital Victor Ramos Guardia. ⊠ *Av. Luzuriaga, Cuadra 8*
☎ *043/421–861.*

Visitor Information iPerú. ⊠ *Pasaje Atusparia* ☎ *043/428–812* ⊕ *www.peru.info.*

EXPLORING

Jirón José Olaya. To see Huaraz's colonial remnants, head to Jirón José Olaya, a pedestrian-only street that's one of the few places left untouched by the 1970 earthquake. The handsome white-and-green facades stand east of the town center, on the right-hand side of Raimondi and a block behind Confraternidad Inter Este.The best time to visit is on Sunday, when there's a weekly *feria de comida típica*, a regional street festival with local food and craft stalls. ⊠ *Huaraz.*

Mercado Central. For a down-to-earth look at Andean culture, head to this market, where you'll see fruits and vegetables grown only in the highlands, as well as cuyes, chickens, ducks, and rabbits, all available for purchase alive or freshly slaughtered. ⊠ *Entrance at Jr. de la Cruz Romero and Av. Cayetano Requena.*

Mirador de Rataquenua. The lookout point has an excellent view of Huaraz, the Río Santa, and the surrounding mountains. It's a 45-minute walk up, and the directions are complicated, so it's best to hire a guide or, better yet, take a taxi. ⊠ *Av. Confraternidad Inter Sur and Av. Confraternidad Inter Este.*

Museo Arqueológico de Ancash. What draws visitors to this small museum is the park out back, which houses a delightful assortment of pre-Hispanic statues from the Chavín and Recuay cultures. The musicians, warriors, and gods here will keep you company as you reflect on the mummies and ceramics you've examined in the museum's inner rooms. ■TIP➜ Upstairs numerous skulls bear the scars (or rather holes) from trepanation, the removal of bone from the skull. There are also textiles, metalwork, and a room dedicated to ancient Andean beliefs about the afterlife. ⊠ *Av. Luzuriaga 762* ☎ *043/421–551* ⊡ *S/5* ⊙ *Closed Mon.*

Plaza de Armas. This pretty square is the key spot for people-watching in Huaraz. The cathedral looks splendid when lit up at night, and *tiendas artesanales* (artisanal kiosks) border the central fountain. ⊠ *Luzuriaga and José Sucre.*

Huaraz

Wilcahuaín. Some 8 km (5 miles) north of Huaraz, this small archaeological site contains a Wari temple, dating back to AD 1100, that resembles the larger temple at Chavín de Huántar. Each story of the crumbling three-tiered temple has seven rooms. There's a small museum and basic bathroom facilities and a limited restaurant. Trained and knowledgeable local students will be your guide for a small tip (suggested minimum tip: S/10). ⊠ *Huaraz* ⚓ *Bus service available from corner of 13 de Diciembre and Cajamarca* ⊕ *www. huaraz.es/ruinas-de-wilcahuain.php* 🏷 *S/5* ⊗ *Closed Mon.*

OFF THE BEATEN PATH

Glaciar Pastoruri. A popular day trip from Huaraz is a visit to the Pastoruri Glacier, where you can hike around the 0.9-square-km (0.3-square-mile) glacier. The rapidly shrinking ice field, which could disappear within the next few years, has become a symbol of global climate change. ■**TIP**→ On this trip you'll ascend to well above 4,000 meters (13,000 feet), so make sure you're used to the high altitude. Wear warm clothing, sunscreen, and sunglasses, as the sun is intense. Drink lots of water to avoid altitude sickness. The easiest and safest way to get here is with a tour company from Huaraz. The tour costs about S/30 to S/40 and takes eight hours. You can also hire diminutive horses to take you up to the glacier from the parking lot for about S/15. It's not the most spectacular glacier in the world, but if you've

9

never seen one up close, it's worth the trip. The glacier is 70 km (43 miles) south of Huaraz, off the main highway at the town of Recuay—a journey of about three hours. ✉ *Huaraz* 🎟 *S/5.*

WHERE TO EAT

$ CAFÉ 🍴 **Café Andino.** Equal parts funky and friendly, this café offers light snacks, hot and cold beverages, free Wi-Fi, and a seemingly endless supply of newspapers and books in English. Warm up by the fireplace on a cold night, or sit on the outdoor terrace with your laptop and sip a fresh-pressed cup of tea. **Known for:** good views; cozy; good food. [$] *Average main: S/10* ✉ *Jr. Lucar y Torre 530, 3rd fl.* ☎ *043/421–203* 🌐 *www.cafeandino.com* 💳 *No credit cards.*

$ ECLECTIC 🍴 **Chilli Heaven.** An eclectic mix of Indian curries, Mexican burritos, and Thai favorites makes this cozy dining room a magnet for tourists seeking international edibles. The spicy concoctions are belly warming; a big beer selection helps put out the flames. **Known for:** fajitas; vindaloos; warm hospitality. [$] *Average main: S/25* ✉ *Parque Ginebra* ☎ *043/425–532.*

$$ FRENCH 🍴 **Creperie Patrick.** With a breezy terrace upstairs and a cozy bistro downstairs, this French eatery is an excellent choice. There's couscous and fondue, as well as hard-to-find local dishes such as grilled alpaca. **Known for:** European fare; crepes with fruit and ice cream; great atmosphere. [$] *Average main: S/40* ✉ *Av. Luzuriaga 422* ☎ *043/426–037* 🌐 *creperiepatrick.com* 🕘 *No lunch.*

$ PERUVIAN Fodor's Choice ★ 🍴 **Don Cuy.** To experience the Andean delicacies *huarasinos* eat on special occasions, take a 10-minute taxi ride outside downtown to this excellent *restaurante campestre* (country restaurant beneath a trellised arbor). Here you'll find *pachamanca* (meats and vegetables cooked over coals in a pit), pork cooked in a cylindrical box, and yes, *cuy* or guinea pig (it's actually scrumptious). **Known for:** grilled meats; Andean delicacies; great service. [$] *Average main: S/25* ✉ *Av. Centenario 2621* ☎ *043/232–472* 🕘 *No dinner.*

$ PIZZA 🍴 **El Horno.** "El horno" means "the oven," and this fire-warmed refuge on cold Andean nights makes some of the best pizzas in the Peruvian sierra, with light, flaky crusts and a broad range of toppings. There are also pastas and *parrillas* to line your stomach, as well as salads and even a few Thai curries. **Known for:** wood-fired pizzas; heaping pastas. [$] *Average main: S/25* ✉ *Parque Ginebra* ☎ *043/421–004* 🕘 *No lunch.*

WHERE TO STAY

$ HOTEL FAMILY 🏨 **Hotel El Tumi.** The great location and amenities make this comfy inn a perennial favorite among travelers. **Pros:** great location; comfortable furnishings; good spa and restaurant. **Cons:** some rooms are a bit small. [$] *Rooms from: S/125* ✉ *Jiron San Martín 1121* ☎ *043/421–784* 🌐 *www.hoteleseltumi.com.pe* 🛏 *82 rooms.*

$ HOTEL 🏨 **Hotel San Sebastián.** Perched on the side of a mountain, this hotel has great views of the Cordillera Blanca. **Pros:** reasonable rates; first-rate accommodations. **Cons:** a bit of a hike from Huaraz's city center. [$] *Rooms from: S/230* ✉ *Jr. Italia 1124* ☎ *043/426–960* 🌐 *www.sansebastianhuaraz.com* 🛏 *31 rooms* 🍽 *No meals.*

$$
\begin{array}{l}
\text{\$\$}\\
\text{B\&B/INN}
\end{array}
$$

The Lazy Dog Inn. The Canadian owners who built this eco-friendly adobe lodge are heavily involved with community and environmental activities in Huaraz and the Cordillera Blanca, so if it's a laid-back mountain experience you're after, drop in here rather than stay in town. **Pros:** cabins can sleep four to five people; secluded; close to nature; some rooms have fireplaces. **Cons:** main-floor guest room has shared bathroom; 12 km (7 miles) from town. $ *Rooms from: S/260* ⊠ *Km 3.3, Cachipampa Alto* ☎ *043/978–9330* ⊕ *www.thelazydoginn.com* ⌨ *5 rooms* ♏ *Some meals.*

NIGHTLIFE

To warm yourself up at night, enjoy one of the city's many laid-back bars and dance clubs. Be on the lookout for locally brewed craft beer Sierra Andina.

Cafe Bar 13 Buhos. Homey furnishings and a super-chill vibe make this three-story lounge a cozy nightspot after an all-day trek. The menu includes an in-house brew (called Lucho's) and inexpensive pubgrub like piqueos and burgers. Pool tables and a DJ, add to the relaxed, house-party feel. ⊠ *Parque Ginebra* ☎ *043/429–881.*

Discoteca Xcess. On Friday and Saturday nights this place is packed with locals, who come for cheap drinks and the spacious dance floor. Lots of fun around 2 am, during "*la hora loca.*" ⊠ *Bolivar 571.*

Tambo. The ever-popular Tambo has low ceilings and curvy walls, and there's a large dance floor where you can get down to salsa and Latin pop until the wee hours of the morning. ⊠ *José de la Mar 776* ☎ *043/423–417.*

SPORTS AND THE OUTDOORS
BIKING

If you're an experienced mountain biker, you'll be thrilled at what the area offers along horse trails or gravel roads, passing through the Cordilleras Blanca and Negra.

Mountain Bike Adventures. This shop rents specialized mountain bikes and has experienced guides to take you to the good single-track spots. ⊠ *Jr. Lucar and Torre 530* ☎ *043/424–259* ⊕ *www.chakinaniperu.com* ⌨ *From S/100.*

CLIMBING AND TREKKING

If dreams of bagging a 6,000-meter (19,700-foot) peak or trekking through the wilderness haunt your nights, Huaraz is the place for you. Huaraz sits at a lofty 3,090 meters (10,138 feet), and the surrounding mountains are even higher. Allowing time to acclimatize is a lifesaving necessity. Drinking lots of water and pacing yourself will help avoid high-altitude pulmonary edema (commonly known as altitude sickness, or *soroche* in Peru). ■ **TIP→ The climbing and trekking season runs from May through September—the driest months.** You can trek during the off-season, but trudging every day through thick rain isn't fun. Climbing during the off-season can also be downright dangerous, as crevasses get covered by new snow. Even if you're an experienced hiker, you shouldn't venture into the backcountry without a guide.

9

Guided treks in the region vary by the number of days and the service. You can opt for smaller one-, two-, and three-day hikes, or an expedition of 10 to 20 days. Most guided treks provide donkeys to carry your equipment, plus an emergency horse. So many outfitters are in the area that looking for a qualified company can become overwhelming. Visit a few places, talk with the guides, and make sure you're getting what you really want. Many of the climbs are quite technical and can be dangerous. Deaths do occur on occasion, so it is essential to hire guides with experience.

Casa de Guías. An association of certified freelance guides, Casa de Guías offers excellent advice and personalized trips, including mountaineering and trekking as well as rock- and ice-climbing courses. ⊠ *Parque Ginebra 28/G* ☎ *043/427–545* ⊕ *www.agmp.pe* ⛶ *Prices vary* ☉ *Closed Sun.*

WHITE-WATER RAFTING

There's good rafting on the Río Santa, with Class III and IV rapids. The freezing-cold glacial river water brings heart-pumping rapids. The most-often-run stretch of river is between Jangas and Caraz. The river can be run year-round but is at its best during the wettest months of the rainy season, between December and April. Be prepared with the right equipment; the river is cold enough to cause serious hypothermia.

SHOPPING

Crafts booths on either side of the Plaza de Armas have tables piled high with locally woven textiles.

Montañas Magicas. This outdoors shop stocks many popular brands of gear. ⊠ *Parque Ginebra.*

CHAVÍN DE HUÁNTAR

98 km (61 miles) southeast of Huaraz.

This small, unassuming village thrives on tourists coming to visit the ruins of the same name that are found at one end of town. Few stay overnight—most come here for the day from Huaraz—although those who do will find a few small shops, restaurants, and basic hostels near the Plaza de Armas.

GETTING HERE AND AROUND

If you have a car—and an excellent map and good sense of direction—you can head out and explore the windy, confusing roads. For all others, simply hiring an inexpensive taxi when needed will ensure that you arrive where you need to go. Major trips and treks should be arranged with experienced, certified guides.

Fodor's Choice ★ **Chavín de Huántar.** Indiana Jones would feel right at home in these fascinating ruins, which feature an underground labyrinth of stone corridors and a terrifying idol at their center. The idol, known as the Lanzón, is a 4-meter (13-foot) daggerlike slab with a jaguar's face and serpentine hair, and it was the Holy of Holies for the Chavín people, who were the mother civilization for the Andes. Pilgrims from all over South America would come here to worship, eventually spreading the cult of the so-called Fanged Deity throughout the continent. To make things even crazier, during ceremonies here, Chavín priests and their acolytes would ingest the psychedelic San Pedro cactus, thus facilitating their transformation into the smiling, ferocious god.

Visiting the Chavín archaeological complex, which dates from 1500 BC, is a favorite day trip from Huaraz. The UNESCO World Heritage site sits on the southern edge of the tiny village of the same name, and comprises two separate wings of the main temple, a large U-shaped main plaza, a second plaza surrounded with mysterious carvings, and an on-site museum that houses the grinning stone heads that once looked out from the temple's outer wall. On the drive southeast from the city, you get good views of two Andean peaks, Pucaraju (5,322 meters/17,460 feet) and Yanamarey (5,237 meters/17,180 feet), as well as of the alpine Laguna de Querococha. The eight-hour tour costs about S/50 per person, not including the entrance fee to the ruins. If you'd prefer to get here on your own, regular buses run between Huaraz and Chavín, and you can hire a guide at the entrance to the ruins. ⊠ *Chavín* 🖂 *S/10.*

YUNGAY

59 km (37 miles) north of Huaraz.

On May 31, 1970, an earthquake measuring 7.7 on the Richter scale shook loose some 15 million cubic meters of rock and ice that cascaded down the west wall of Huascarán Norte. In the quiet village of Yungay, some 14 km (8½ miles) away, people were going about their normal activities. Some were waiting for a soccer game to be broadcast on the radio; others were watching the Verolina Circus set up in the stadium. Then the debris slammed into town at a speed of more than 322 km (200 miles) per hour. Almost all of Yungay's 18,000 inhabitants were buried alive. The quake ultimately claimed nearly 70,000 lives throughout Peru.

The government never rebuilt in Yungay, but left it as a memorial to those who had died. It's now a town-size burial ground, and people visit daily. ■TIP➡ Walking through the ruined town, you'll see upturned buses, the few remaining walls of the cathedral, and, oddly, a couple of palm trees that managed to survive the disaster. There's a large white cross at the old cemetery on the hill south of town. It was here that 92 people who were tending the graves of friends and relatives were on high-enough ground to survive. You pay a nominal S/5 to enter the site.

New Yungay was built just beyond the *aluvión* path—behind a protective knoll. It's a modern town with little of interest, though it serves as a starting point for those visiting the spectacular Lagunas de Llanganuco.

GETTING HERE AND AROUND
Buses between Huaraz and Caraz all stop here. Let the driver know you want to get off at Yungay Viejo or Camposanto if you want to go directly to the memorial site.

LAGUNAS DE LLANGANUCO

These two gorgeous mountain lakes, sitting near the base of Mt. Huascarán and within the national park, are the destination of one of the most common day trips from Huaraz. They can be visited year-round.

GETTING HERE AND AROUND

Most visitors arrive here on a day trip from Huaraz or to start a longer trekking excursion, though you can also come by taxi from Yungay. Be prepared to negotiate a wait time, as you won't otherwise find transportation back.

EXPLORING

Fodor's Choice   **Lagunas de Llanganuco.** Make sure your camera memory card is empty
★   when you go to see these spectacular glaciers, gorges, lakes, and mountains. Driving through a giant gorge formed millions of years ago by a retreating glacier, you arrive at Lagunas de Llanganuco. The crystalline waters shine a luminescent turquoise in the sunlight; in the shade they're a forbidding inky black. ■TIP→ Waterfalls of glacial melt snake their way down the gorge's flanks, falling lightly into the lake. There are many *quenual* trees (also known as the paper-bark tree) surrounding the lakes. Up above, you'll see treeless alpine meadows and the hanging glaciers of the surrounding mountains. At the lower lake, called Lago Chinancocha, you can hire a rowboat (S/5 per person) to take you to the center. A few trailside signs teach you about local flora and fauna. The easiest way to get here is with an arranged tour from Huaraz (about S/40 plus entrance fee), though if you are going on the Santa Cruz trek you will probably start here. The tours stop here and at many other spots on the Callejón de Huaylas, finishing in Caraz. ✉ S/5

Fodor's Choice   **Parque Nacional Huascarán (Huascarán National Park).** Laguna Llanganuco
★   is one of the gateways to the Parque Nacional Huascarán, which covers 3,400 square km (1,300 square miles) and was created in 1975 to protect flora and fauna in the Cordillera Blanca. ■TIP→ This incredible mountain range has a total of 663 glaciers and includes some of the highest peaks in the Peruvian Andes. Huascarán, which soars to 6,768 meters (22,200 feet), is the highest in Peru. The smaller Alpamayo, 5,947 meters (19,511 feet), is said by many to be the most beautiful mountain in the world. Its majestic flanks inspire awe and wonder in those lucky enough to get a glimpse. The monstrous Chopicalqui and Chacraraju rise above 6,000 meters (19,700 feet).

Within the park's boundaries you'll find more than 750 plant types. There's a tragic scarcity of wildlife in the park—most have been decimated by hunting and the loss of natural habitats. Among the 12 species of birds and 10 species of mammals in the park, you're most likely to see wild ducks and condors. With a great deal of time and an equal amount of luck you may also see foxes, deer, pumas, and viscachas.

The giant national park attracts campers, hikers, and mountain climbers. Myriad treks weave through the region, varying from fairly easy one-day hikes to 20-day marathons. Within the park, you can head out on the popular **Llanganuco–Santa Cruz Loop,** a three- to five-day trek through mountain valleys, past crystalline lakes, and over a

Cordillera Huayhuash Treks

CLOSE UP

Although much smaller than the Cordillera Blanca, the main chain of the Cordillera Huayhuash is known for its isolation and pristine environment. For years the area remained essentially off-limits to foreign tourism, as it was a major stronghold for the Shining Path movement that wracked much of Peru's Central Highlands with terrorism throughout the 1980s. Today this isolation is what makes the region so special. Treks here are measured in weeks, not days, with road access and tourist infrastructure almost nonexistent. The opportunities to spot rare Andean wildlife are much greater here and the chances of meeting tour groups next to zero.

Cordillera Huayhuash Circuit: The major draw here is the Cordillera Huayhuash circuit. This taxing trek can take up to two weeks, passing some of the region's most spectacular mountain scenery. Access to this trail was traditionally via Chiquián, but the road has been extended to Llamac. Tours and supplies are best organized in Huaraz, although Chiquián does provide some limited facilities, and porters and mules can be arranged here.

Siula Grande (6,344 meters, 20,814 feet): See the mountain made famous by Joe Simpson in his gripping tale of survival in *Touching the Void*.

Yerupaja (6,617 meters, 21,709 feet): The second-highest mountain in Peru.

4,750-meter-high (15,584-foot-high) pass. Other popular hikes include the one-day Lake Churup Trek, the two-day Quilcayhuanca–Cayesh trek, and the two-day Ishinca Trek. Check with guide agencies in Huaraz for maps, trail information, and insider advice before heading out.

Although experienced hikers who know how to survive in harsh mountain conditions may decide to head out on their own, it's much safer to arrange for a guide in Huaraz. You can opt to have donkeys or llamas carry the heavy stuff, leaving you with just a daypack. The most common ailments on these treks are sore feet and altitude sickness. Wear comfortable hiking shoes that have already been broken in, and take the proper precautions to avoid feeling the height (drink lots of water, avoid prolonged exposure to the sun, and allow yourself time to acclimatize before you head out). The best time to go trekking is during the dry season, which runs May through September. July and August are the driest months, though dry season doesn't mean a lack of rain or even snow, so dress appropriately.

Some hikers decide to enter the park at night to avoid paying the hefty S/65 for a multiday pass (from 2 to 30 days), but the money from these fees goes to protect the wonders of the Andes; consider this before you slip in during the dead of night (nighttime safety is a concern, too). You can purchase a pass at the Huaraz office of Parque Nacional Huascarán, at the corner of Rosas and Federico Sal, as well as at Llanganuco. ■TIP➔ **Be sure to carry a copy of your passport with you.** ✉ *Huaraz office of Parque Nacional Huascarán, Rosas 555 and Federico Sal* ☎ *043/422–086* ⊕ *www.sernanp.gob.pe/huascaran* 💲 *S/10 day pass, S/65 multiday pass.*

WHERE TO STAY

$$$ B&B/INN 🏨 **Llanganuco Mountain Lodge.** This quiet, remote lodge, with spectacular views, is right on the edge of the Huascarán National Park, wedged between Llanganuco and Rajururi gorges and adjacent to Keushu lake—a great place to get away from it all. **Pros:** near nature; abundant hiking opportunities; on the lakeshore; all-around pleasant atmosphere. **Cons:** far from everything; no choice at dinner; expensive. [$] *Rooms from: S/750* ✉ *Yungay* ☎ *976/592–524* 🌐 *llanganucomountainlodge.com* 💳 *No credit cards* 🛏 *4 rooms* 🍴 *All-inclusive.*

CARAZ

67 km (42 miles) north of Huaraz.

One of the few towns in the area with a cluster of colonial-era architecture, Caraz is at the northern tip of the valley—only a partly paved road continues north. North of Caraz on the dramatic road to Chimbote is the Cañon del Pato, the true northern terminus of the Callejón de Huaylas. Caraz is an increasingly popular alternative base for trekkers and climbers. While in town be sure to try the ultrasweet *manjar blanco*, Peru's version of dulce de leche.

GETTING HERE AND AROUND

There are frequent buses here from Huaraz, most stopping in Carhuaz and Yungay first. In the other direction your options are fewer.

WHERE STAY

$ B&B/INN 🏨 **Chamanna.** This cluster of *cabañas* (cabins) among beautifully landscaped gardens, with views of mountain streams and towering peaks, is the town's best lodging. **Pros:** location provides peace and quiet; beautiful vistas; good restaurant. **Cons:** hiring taxis and traveling means less time to enjoy the great outdoors; some shared bathrooms. [$] *Rooms from: S/150* ✉ *Av. Nueva Victoria 185* ☎ *044/689–257* 🌐 *www.chamanna.com* 🛏 *10 cabins* 🍴 *No meals.*

THE NORTHERN HIGHLANDS

The green valleys and high mountaintops that make up the Northern Highlands are certainly one of the area's biggest draws, as is the abundance of history in the region. Lamentably, however, few non-Peruvian travelers venture here; it's hard to reach and far from the more popular destinations of Cusco, Puno, and Machu Picchu.

Several major archaeological sites are located around the Northern Highlands. **■ TIP→ The pre-Inca fortress of Kuélap, near Chachapoyas, is one of the region's best-preserved ruins.** Moreover, the region's largest town, Cajamarca, is the center for exploration and was the site of one of history's quickest and wiliest military victories, the capture and defeat of the Inca Atahualpa by the Spanish in 1532, a moment that set the course of Latin American history for the next 500 years. In and around Cajamarca you'll also find a handful of Inca and pre-Inca sites, as well as chances for horseback riding and hiking in the green valleys and hills.

CAJAMARCA

855 km (531 miles) northeast of Lima; 295 km (183 miles) northeast of Trujillo.

Peaceful Cajamarca is one of the most undervisited places in Peru. As the town where the conquistador Pizarro captured and later executed the Inca ruler Atahualpa, it's the crucible of South American history, with abundant ruins testifying to the clash of civilizations that unleashed all of Latin America's subsequent tumult. But even if history isn't your forte, you'll be enchanted by the gently sloping hills, waterfalls, and friendly dairy farms that dot the landscape around this sleeper of an Andean city. That comparatively few foreigners visit only adds to its charm.

For Cajamarca, 1532 was the crucial date. That year, while the Inca was relaxing at the thermal springs just outside town, 168 Spaniards, led by Francisco Pizarro, entered the main square and requested an audience. Thinking to enslave the visiting strangers and steal their horses, Atahualpa agreed, but when he arrived in the plaza with his retinue, he was quickly captured by Pizarro himself and made to witness the slaughter of some 6,000 of his followers. Imprisoned in a stone room, he tried to ransom his life with heaps of gold and silver, but the treacherous Spanish garotted him anyway in 1533.

Visitors to Cajamarca today can see reminders of this tragic history, both in the city's picturesque Plaza de Armas and in the surrounding hills, which feature some choice pre-Hispanic ruins. The town's colonial churches and houses are so well preserved that they were declared a Historic and Cultural Patrimony Site by the Organization of American States in 1986. But for many, the region's chief beauty lies in the lush green sierra outside the city limits. There, cheap day trips allow you to sample the organic dairy products for which the area is famous, as well as shady forests, cataracts, and, at one farm, some of the smartest cows in South America.

GETTING HERE AND AROUND

LATAM Perú and LC Perú fly several times per week between Lima and the Aeropuerto de Cajamarca (CJA), 3 km (2 miles) east of town. Most places are within walking distance, but taxis are abundant if you feel a little breathless from the altitude or want to go somewhere a bit outside the city center. If you like your taxi driver, arrange a pickup for another day. For major exploration outside the city, the best option is to join a day tour; they are quite inexpensive and include transportation. Cajamarca is 2,650 meters (8,694 feet) above sea level. Although not very high by Andean standards, the elevation can still affect some visitors. Take your time, wear sunscreen, and drink plenty of water to avoid altitude sickness.

ESSENTIALS

Currency Banco de Crédito. ✉ *Jr. Apurimac 717* ☎ *44/822–680* ⊕ *www.viabcp.com.* **Scotiabank.** ✉ *Jr. Amazonas 750* ☎ *076/367–101* ⊕ *www.scotiabank.com.pe.*

Mail Post Office. ✉ *Jr. Apurimac 624* ☎ *076/364–065.*

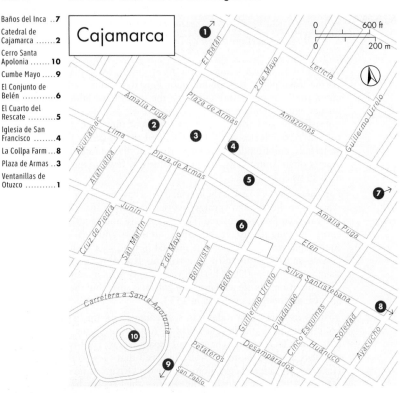

Medical Hospital Regional Docente de Cajamarca. ⊠ *Av. Larry Jhonson* ☎ *076/599–030* ⊕ *www.hrc.gob.pe.*

Visitor Information iPerú. ⊠ *Jr. Cruz de Piedra 601* ☎ *076/365–166* ⊕ *www.peru.info.*

EXPLORING

TOP ATTRACTIONS

Baños del Inca. About 6 km (4 miles) east of Cajamarca are these pleasant hot springs offering several public pools and private baths with varying levels of quality, as well as some spa facilities such as a sauna and massage tables. Each service has a separate price, though everything is quite inexpensive. The central bath, the Pozo del Inca, is where Atahualpa was relaxing when he received news of the conquistadors' arrival in 1532. It's an intact pool with a system of aqueducts built by the Incas and still in use today. Be sure to check out the volcanic pools in the center of the complex, but don't touch! The temperatures there can reach 70°C (160°F). ■TIP→ Don't forget to bring your swimsuit and a towel! ⊠ *Av. Manco Cápac* ☎ *076/348–563* 🎫 *S/6.*

OFF THE
BEATEN
PATH

Ventanillas de Otuzco (*Otuzco Windows*). One of the oldest cemeteries in Peru, the Ventanillas de Otuzco date back more than 3,500 years. The ancient necropolis, 8 km (5 miles) northeast of Cajamarca, comprises several large burial niches carved into a cliff. From afar the niches look like windows: hence the area's name. On closer inspection you see that many of the burial niches have carved decorations. Sadly, the site is slowly being eroded by wind and rain, though measures are being taken to slow the degradation. If you're inspired by this cemetery, you can go about 30 km (18 miles) from Combayo, in the same direction, and visit the better-preserved Ventanillas de Combayo. A three-hour guided tour to Ventanillas de Otuzco costs around S/35. If you prefer to go by yourself, *combis* (small buses) take 30 minutes to arrive from the Plaza de Armas. ✉ *Cajamarca* 🖃 *S/5.*

Cerro Santa Apolonia. At the end of Calle 2 de Mayo steps lead to this hilltop *mirador,* or scenic lookout, where a bird's-eye view of the city awaits. At the top are many carved bricks dating to pre-Columbian times. ■TIP→ One of the rocks has the shape of a throne and has been dubbed the Seat of the Inca. According to local legend, it was here that Inca rulers would sit to review their troops. You'll find pretty gardens and great views of the town. You can either walk or go by taxi (round trip S/6). ✉ *Calle 2 de Mayo* 🖃 *Free.*

El Cuarto del Rescate. This ransom chamber is the only Inca building still standing in Cajamarca. After Pizarro and his men captured Atahualpa, the Inca king offered to fill the chamber once with gold and twice with silver. The ransom was met, up to a marking on the stone wall, but the war-hardened Spaniards killed Atahualpa anyway. Today, visitors aren't allowed in the room itself, but if you look closely, you can still make out the marks the Inca left in an attempt to buy off his captors. ✉ *Jr. Amalia Puga 750* 🖃🖃 *S/5.*

WORTH NOTING

Catedral de Cajamarca. Originally known as the Iglesia de Españoles (Spanish Church, because only Spanish colonialists were allowed to attend services), this cathedral on the Plaza de Armas was built in the 17th and 18th centuries. It has an ornate baroque facade that was sculpted from volcanic rock. Like many of the town's churches, the cathedral has no belfry; the Spanish crown levied taxes on completed churches, so the settlers left the churches unfinished, freeing them from the tight grip of the tax collector. ✉ *Jr. Del Batán and Amalia Puga* 🖃 *Free.*

OFF THE
BEATEN
PATH

Cumbe Mayo. This pre-Inca site, 23 km (14 miles) southwest of Cajamarca, is surrounded by a large rock outcropping, where you'll find various petroglyphs left by the ancient Cajamarcans. There are also petroglyph-adorned caves so a guided tour is highly recommended. This site, discovered in 1937 by the famous Peruvian archaeologist J.C. Tello, also includes some of the most notable aqueducts in the Andes. Constructed around 1000 BC, the aqueduct was designed to direct the ample water from the Andes into the drier area of Cajamarca, where there was a large reservoir. Amazingly, more than 8 km (5 miles) of the ancient aqueduct are intact today. Guided tours cost around S/35 and take about four hours. ✉ *Cajamarca.*

El Conjunto de Belén. Built in the 17th century, this large complex, originally a hospital, now houses the city's most interesting museums and a colonial church. At the **Museo Arqueológico de Cajamarca,** the town's archaeological museum, are exhibits of Cajamarcan ceramics and weavings. The pre-Inca Cajamarcans were especially famous for their excellent patterned textiles, which were often dyed vivid shades of blue. The **Museo Etnográfico** has a few displays of everyday bric-a-brac—there's even an old saddle and a dilapidated coffee grinder—dating back to precolonial times. The **Iglesia de Belén** is a charming church with a polychrome pulpit and cupola. ✉ *Jr. Belén and Jr. Junín* ☎ *076/362–601* ⊕ *museos.cultura.pe* ✍ *S/5* ⊗ *Closed Mon.*

Iglesia de San Francisco. Built in the 17th and 18th centuries, the Church of San Francisco sits proudly on the Plaza de Armas in front of the main cathedral. The church's two bell towers were begun in republican times and finished in 1951. The church was called the Iglesia de Indios (Church of the Indians) as indigenous peoples were not allowed to attend services at the main cathedral; many consider it to be more beautiful than the whites-only cathedral. ■ TIP→ **Inside you'll find catacombs and a small museum of religious art.** To the right of the church, the Capilla de la Virgen de Dolores is one of Cajamarca's most beautiful chapels. A large statue of Cajamarca's patron saint, La Virgen de Dolores, makes this a popular pilgrimage destination for local penitents. ✉ *East side of Plaza de Armas* ✍ *S/4 for museum.*

Plaza de Armas. This main square occupies the same location where Pizarro had his dramatic encounter with Atahualpa, and though all traces of Inca influence are long since gone, it's impressive to stand on the spot where Latin American history began. Today, the fountain, benches, and street vendors make the square a nice place to hang out. ✉ *Cajamarca.*

OFF THE BEATEN PATH

La Collpa Farm. Cajamarca is famous for its dairy products, and you can experience this industry up close at this charming farm 11 km (7 miles) outside town. In addition to sampling the farm's cheeses and sweet *manjar blanco* , you can also visit an artificial lake and check out Peru's biggest all-clay church. The highlight is the "calling of the cows," in which Rosa, Betsy, and Flor answer to their names as they line up to return to their pens. Perfect for kids of all ages. ✉ *Cajamarca* ✍ *S/5.*

WHERE TO EAT

$ ✕ **Cascanuez.** This is the place in Cajamarca for decadent desserts and
BAKERY   delicious coffee. Casanuez translates to "The Nutcracker," and Sugar Plum Fairies would approve of the extensive homemade pastries, tortes, and other tempting treats. **Known for:** artistic local pastries; elegant setting. $ *Average main: S/18* ✉ *Av. Puga 554* ☎ *076/366–089.*

$ ✕ **La Chanita.** In one corner of the Mercado Central, amid stalls selling
PERUVIAN   *charqui* (dehydrated meat) and rainbow-colored displays of quinua, you'll find a lunchtime crowd of people lining up for *cebiche frito* , a locally famous fried version of cebiche where the fish is battered and topped with a spicy mayo and plated with *leche de tigre* and all the other usual cebiche fixings. You'll have to elbow your way to a counter seat; otherwise just take your plate and go. **Known for:** fried cebiche; bustling market setting. $ *Average main: S/7* ✉ *Mercado Central, Jiron Apurimac* ⊗ *No dinner.*

$ SEAFOOD 🍴 **Pez Loco.** Surf and turf, Peruvian style, is the focus at this down-to-earth joint that's half *cebichería*, half *parrilla*. No bells and whistles here, just top-quality steaks, cebiches (try the *mixto*), and seafood classics like *arroz con mariscos*. **Known for:** grilled entrées; seafood. [$] *Average main: S/25* ✉ *San Martín 333.*

$ PERUVIAN 🍴 **Salas.** On the Plaza de Armas, this is the place to get no-frills, typical food from the region. The menu includes authentic regional specialties such as *cuy*, *perico* (a lake fish), and Spanish-style tortillas. **Known for:** cheap daily specials; lively, social atmosphere. [$] *Average main: S/20* ✉ *Av. Puga 637, Plaza de Armas* ☎ *076/362–867.*

WHERE TO STAY

$$ HOTEL 🏨 **Costa del Sol Wyndham Cajamarca.** Set right on Cajamarca's main plaza, this hotel may seem quite modern, but it's actually converted from a historic mansion of a notable local family, and its restaurant has what might be the best view of the city. **Pros:** spa on-site; superb location with good city views; soundproofed windows; good value. **Cons:** the plaza can be quite noisy in the evenings. [$] *Rooms from: S/273* ✉ *Jr. Cruz de Piedra 707* ☎ *076/362–472* 🌐 *www.costadelsolperu.com/cajamarca/* 🛏 *71 rooms* 🍴 *Breakfast.*

$ B&B/INN 🏨 **El Portal del Marqués.** Within Cajamarca's historic district, this lovely *casona* (mansion) surrounds two sunny courtyards, overlooked by rooms furnished in a modern style, with bold color schemes and striking artwork. **Pros:** in the heart of Cajamarca city; attractive rooms with modern conveniences. **Cons:** the city can be noisy. [$] *Rooms from: S/229* ✉ *Jr. del Comercio 644* ☎ *076/368–464* 🌐 *www.portaldelmarques.com* 🛏 *43 rooms* 🍴 *Breakfast.*

$ HOTEL 🏨 **Hotel El Ingenio.** Like many other hotels in the area, this is in a renovated hacienda with extensive grounds, but it is the best bargain in Cajamarca and only a 10-minute walk from the plaza. **Pros:** quality service at a very reasonable price; beautiful, well-tended grounds. **Cons:** some rooms are better than others. [$] *Rooms from: S/168* ✉ *Av. Via de Evitamiento 1611–1709* ☎ *076/367–121* 🌐 *elingenio.com* 🛏 *39 rooms* 🍴 *Breakfast.*

$$ HOTEL FAMILY Fodor's Choice ★ 🏨 **Hotel Laguna Seca.** Come here to pamper yourself—this refurbished hacienda, which has well-manicured garden areas throughout its extensive grounds, offers private and public baths from the nearby thermal hot springs. **Pros:** relaxing; in-room hot-spring water; spa; plenty to amuse children. **Cons:** outside the city limits. [$] *Rooms from: S/290* ✉ *Av. Manco Cápac 1098, Baños del Inca* ☎ *076/584–300* 🌐 *www.lagunaseca.com.pe* 🛏 *42 rooms* 🍴 *Breakfast.*

$$ B&B/INN FAMILY 🏨 **La Posada del Puruay.** In the countryside, this hacienda is far from the noise of Cajamarca and has extensive gardens, a trout hatchery, and green hills for horseback riding and hiking. **Pros:** transported to another time and place; reasonable price. **Cons:** might be too intimate if you don't enjoy socializing with other guests. [$] *Rooms from: S/263* ✉ *Km 4.5, Ctra. Porcón* ☎ *076/367–028* 🌐 *www.posadapuruay.com.pe* 🛏 *13 rooms* 🍴 *Breakfast.*

NIGHTLIFE

Taita. This cavernous disco bar has a near monopoly on Cajamarca's dance scene. The stone walls add to the sonic mayhem. ⊠ *Plazuela Belen, Calle Santisteban.*

Usha Usha. Friendly locals, charming hosts, and sing-alongs with the local musicians that drop in make this watering hole a Cajamarca favorite. The owner, Don Jaime, shares stories and songs to promote local Cajamarca culture. ⊠ *Amalia Puga 142* ☏ *976/461–433.*

SPORTS AND THE OUTDOORS

There are a number of hikes in the area around Cajamarca, from trails along the rivers of the region, to treks leading past Inca and pre-Inca ruins. Most follow the *Capac Ñan,* or Royal Inca Road, that ran from Cusco all the way north to Quito. One of the most popular walks is to the pre-Inca necropolis of **Combayo.** To get to the trailhead, drive 20 km (12 miles) north of the Baños del Inca. The hike takes around four or five hours. The **Ruta del Tambo Inca** takes you to an old Inca *tambo,* or resting point. It's difficult to find this trailhead, and roads sometimes get washed out during the rainy season, so ask in town to confirm the following: Drive 46 km (29 miles) from Cajamarca on the road to Hualgayoc. Near Las Lagunas turn onto a dirt road and follow it to the milk depository at Ingatambo. The trail begins here. The 16-km (10-mile) trip takes about eight hours. The best time to go trekking is during the dry season, May through September.

Clarín Tours. With offices in Lima and Cajamarca, Clarín Tours specializes in multiday package deals that include transportation, hotels, and tours in northern Peru, particularly in Cajamarca. ⊠ *Jr. Del Batán 165* ☏ *076/366–829* ⊕ *www.clarintours.com* ✉ *From S/160.*

SHOPPING

The town of **Llacanora**, 13 km (8 miles) from the city on the road to the Baños del Inca, is a typical Andean farming community, now a cooperative farm, famous for agriculture and making reed bugles. People come to see the traditional village, but there are also several shops around town selling locally produced goods.

CHACHAPOYAS

435 km (271 miles) east of Chiclayo.

Located in the *ceja de la selva* (jungle's eyebrow), Chachapoyas is the capital of Peru's Amazonas region. ■**TIP➔ The town is a good jumping-off point for exploring some of Peru's most fascinating and least-visited pre-Inca ruins.** The giant fortress at Kuélap, the Gocta waterfall, the Karajía sarcophagi, and the ruins of Purunllacta and Gran Vilaya are nearby. Despite the Amazonas moniker, there's nothing junglelike about the area around Chachapoyas. The surrounding green highlands constitute what most people would call a highland cloud forest. Farther east, in the region of Loreto (won by Peru in the 1942 border dispute with Ecuador), you'll find true jungle.

Chachapoyas is a sleepy little town of 20,000. It has a well-preserved colonial center and one small archaeological museum. Difficult to reach because of the poor roads through the mountains, it is most easily accessed from Chiclayo.

GETTING HERE AND AROUND

There are several daily buses between Chachapoyas and Chiclayo, with some originating in Lima. There are also buses from Cajamarca several times per week, as well as from Tarapoto, though they are occasionally canceled because of road conditions. In town everything is close and within walking distance. There are plenty of taxis, but you'll have little chance of needing one. To get to the archaeological sites, you must go with a guide. The most enjoyable and cost-effective way of doing this is with a tour. There's little public transportation, and you cannot hire a guide once at the sites.

> ### DRINKING THE AGUARDIENTES
>
> *Aguardientes* (homemade liqueurs) are common throughout the region. They're made in sundry flavors, including *mora* (blackberry), *maracuyá* (passion fruit), *café* (coffee), and *leche* (milk). Some jungle towns such as Chachapoyas and Pucallpa sell bottles of the stuff and are more than willing to offer tourists a sample of these strong, home-brewed liqueurs.

ESSENTIALS

Currency Banco de Crédito. ✉ *Jr. Ortiz Arrieta 576* ☎ *041/477–430* ⊕ *www.viabcp.com.*

Medical Hospital Regional Virgen de Fatima Chachapoyas. ✉ *Jr. Triunfo, Cuadra 3* ☎ *041/477–092* ⊕ *www.hospitalvirgendefatima.gob.pe.*

Visitor Information iPerú. ✉ *Jr. Ortiz Arrieta 582, Plaza Mayor* ☎ *041/477–292* ⊕ *www.peru.travel.*

EXPLORING

Fodor'sChoice ★ **Gocta Waterfall.** Surprisingly, Gocta, a 771-meter (2,529-foot) waterfall, believed to be the third tallest in the world, wasn't brought to the attention of the Peruvian government until 2006. The falls, about 50 km (31 miles) outside town, are strongest during the rainy season, from November to April, though during the dry season the sun will likely be out and you will be able to swim at their base. Occasionally, on the 2½-hour hike from Cocachimba (you can hire guides there if you are not coming on a tour from Chachapoyas), you may be able to spot toucans or the endemic yellow-tailed woolly monkey. The best way to appreciate the falls is by staying at the charming, 10-room **Gocta Lodge** (*042/526–694, www.goctalodge.com*), especially if you prefer the light of the morning or afternoon. ✉ *Chachapoyas.*

OFF THE BEATEN PATH **Karajía.** Discovered in 1985, the six coffins that make up this uncanny funeral site 48 km (30 miles) northwest of Chachapoyas overlook a ruined village below and are thought to contain the mummies of shamans and great warriors. The Chachapoyas people built them into a sheer cliffside sometime around the year 1460, and today their eerie funeral masks—together with the bones scattered around the site—provide a haunting reminder of the great chieftains that once held sway over the surrounding country. The Karajía sarcophagi, or "ancient wise men" as the locals call them, originally included eight coffins, but two have collapsed due to earthquakes. This has allowed archaeologists to study the contents of the wood-and-clay structures, which were found to house a single individual in the fetal position, along with all the ceramics and other belongings the deceased carried with him into the afterlife. Visitors today can't get close to the sarcophagi due to their remote location, but the view of them watching over the ravine below is awe-inspiring. ⊠ *Chachapoyas.*

Iglesia Santa Ana. The town's oldest church was one of Peru's first "Indian churches," where indigenous people were forced to attend services. It was built in the 17th century and is on a small square of the same name. ⊠ *Av. Santa Ana.*

Pozo de Yanayacu. This small, rocky natural hot spring a few blocks west of the Plaza de Armas isn't much, but is nice to look at. It's said the spring magically appeared during a visit from Saint Toribio de Mogrovejo. ⊠ *Jr. Salamanca.*

OFF THE
BEATEN
PATH

Museo Leymebamba. One of the most fantastic museums in all of Peru, the Museo Leymebamba, which opened in 2000, can be found in this small village 60 km (37 miles) south of Chachapoyas. Inside are more than 200 mummies, some dating back over 500 years, that were discovered high on a limestone cliff above the Laguna de los Condores in 1997, as well as other artifacts from the Chachapoyas culture. If you get a group together, a taxi from Chachapoyas will cost about S/150 round-trip; otherwise you can take a Cajamarca-bound bus (via Celendin) and ask to be let off at Leymebamba. ⊠ *Av. Austria s/n, Leymebamba* ☎ *971/104–909* ⊕ *www.birdsofleymebamba.com/muse-oleymebamba* 💵 *S/12.*

OFF THE
BEATEN
PATH

Purunllacta. About 35 km (22 miles) southeast of Chachapoyas are the ruins of Purunllacta, a good place for hiking. With pre-Inca agricultural terraces, dwellings, ceremonial platforms, and roads extending for more than 420 hectares (1,038 acres), but few tourists, this can be a peaceful spot, but somewhat boring as you have no explanation of what you're seeing. To get here, drive to the town of Cheto. From the town it's a one-hour walk uphill to the site. Few people know about this or go, so ask in Cheto for directions to the trailhead, and don't be alarmed if you have to ask more than one person. ⊠ *Chachapoyas* 💵 *Free.*

WHERE TO EAT

$

CAFÉ

✕ **Café Fusiones.** A great hangout and meeting spot for travelers, this eclectic café with cheery yellow walls and wood-beamed ceilings works with local farming co-ops and has a commitment to organic principles and fair trade. The menu is small, but the quality is good. **Known for:** desserts; sandwiches. 💲 *Average main: S/12* ⊠ *Ayacucho 952, Plaza Mayor* ☎ *41/479–170* ⊕ *cafefusiones.com* ▭ *No credit cards.*

$

PERUVIAN

✕ **El Tejado.** With a pleasant interior courtyard, this is one of the most elegant eateries in Chachapoyas. The *criollo* food is serviceable, and the staff is most attentive when the *dueña* (owner) is around. **Known for:** Peruvian favorites; comfy setting. 💲 *Average main: S/20* ⊠ *Jr. Santo Domingo 424* ☎ *041/477–592* ☾ *No dinner.*

$ STEAKHOUSE 🍴 **La Tushpa.** Probably the best eatery in town, La Tushpa has good grilled steaks served with homemade *chimichurri* (a green sauce made with herbs, garlic, and tomatoes). There are also pizzas and other items from the on-site bakery. **Known for:** grilled meats; very friendly service. [$] *Average main: S/25* ✉ *Jr. Ortiz Arrieta 753* ☎ *041/477–471.*

CERAMIC STOP

About 10 km (6 miles) north of Chachapoyas is the tiny pueblo of **Huancas**, where the citizens are well known for their pottery; this is a good place to buy artisanal goods and locally made ceramics.

WHERE TO STAY

$ B&B/INN 🏨 **Hostal Casa Vieja.** This colorful old house, which dates back to the 1800s, is the finest in Chachapoyas, with a bougainvillea-filled courtyard and pleasant terraces. **Pros:** amazing old house with modern touches; cozy sitting area with fireplace. **Cons:** some rooms are better than others. [$] *Rooms from: S/150* ✉ *Jr. Chincha Alta 569* ☎ *041/477–353, 512/466–7211 in U.S.* 🛏 *14 rooms* 🍽 *Breakfast.*

$ HOTEL 🏨 **Hotel Vilaya.** A pleasant, if slightly antiseptic, hotel in the center of Chachapoyas, the Hotel Vilaya has rooms with simple wooden furnishings and plain walls hung with artwork. **Pros:** central location near Plaza de Armas; good service; Wi-Fi. **Cons:** unattractive building. [$] *Rooms from: S/100* ✉ *Jr. Ayacucho 734* ☎ *041/477–664* 🌐 *www.hotelvilayachachapoyas.com* 🛏 *22 rooms* 🍽 *Breakfast.*

$ HOTEL 🏨 **Puma Urco.** Simple, clean rooms and a friendly staff make this a good budget alternative. **Pros:** good location; inexpensive. **Cons:** very basic rooms; lacks soundproofing. [$] *Rooms from: S/90* ✉ *Jr. Amazonas 833* ☎ *041/477–871* 🌐 *www.hotelpumaurco.com* 🛏 *22 rooms* 🍽 *Breakfast.*

NIGHTLIFE

Licores La Reina. A large selection of *aguardientes* (locally distilled liquors) in flavors that range from *leche* (milk) to *mora* (blackberry) is available at this friendly local bar. Also on tap: mixed drinks typical of the Peruvian jungle and live music on weekends. ✉ *Jr. Ayacucho 544* ☎.

KUÉLAP

72 km (45 miles) south of Chachapoyas.

This phenomenal archaeological site, about two hours from Chachapoyas, is increasingly becoming one of Peru's main attractions. It's much more remote and sees far fewer visitors, which makes it all the more mystical. There are no facilities at the site, so bring everything you need.

GETTING HERE AND AROUND

A visit to Kuélap is an all-day affair, and it's best to visit with a tour group from Chachapoyas. The trip costs around S/95 per person. Vilaya Tours, in the Hotel Vilaya, is highly recommended and has the widest selection of tours in the region. In the past, you used to have to hike (four hours) or take a taxi (two hours) to travel the 4 kilometers (2½ miles) from the village of Tingo to the ruins, but a brand-new cable-car system operated by Peru's government now allows you to cover the same distance in 20 minutes. Remember to bring a hat for protection from the sun. Take frequent rests and drink lots of water to avoid altitude sickness.

EXPLORING

Fodor's Choice ★ **Kuélap.** Consistently compared to Machu Picchu by visitors, this extraordinary citadel high in the cloud forests of Chachapoyas was a walled city sufficient unto itself, housing farmers, shamans, and administrators no less than the "warriors of the cloud" that made up the Chachapoyans' military class. Wandering the circular ruins, with their 12-meter-high (39-foot-high) stone walls and enigmatic carvings of faces and snakes, you catch a haunting glimpse of a fierce people that resisted the Inca Empire to the bitter end.

Kuélap sits at a dizzying 3,100 meters (10,170 feet) above sea level, high above the Río Utcubamba. Consisting of more than 400 small, rounded buildings, it contains lookout towers, huts with grass roofs (now reconstructed), turrets, and rhomboid friezes typical of the region. The most interesting of the rounded buildings has been dubbed *El Tintero* (the Inkpot), and features a large underground chamber with a huge pit. Archaeologists hypothesize that the Chachapoyans kept pumas in this pit, dumping human sacrifices into its depths during religious rituals. The ruins are in surprisingly good condition, considering the antiquity (1,000 or so years) of the site: the Incas appear to have left it alone when they overran the Chachapoyas people in 1472.

For a long time, Kuélap was the least-visited of Peru's major archaeological sites, due to its remoteness. The recent opening of a new *teleférico* (cable car) that whisks visitors up to the hilltop may change all that. But for now, visitors to this magnificent ruin remain pioneers at one of South America's truly exotic destinations. ⊠ *Ctra. Kuélap, Chachapoyas* 🖃 *S/15, cable car S/20.*

UNDERSTANDING PERU

SPANISH VOCABULARY

	ENGLISH	SPANISH	PRONUNCIATION
BASICS			
	Yes/no	Sí/no	see/no
	Please	Por favor	pore fah-**vore**
	May I?	¿Me permite?	may pair-**mee**-tay
	Thank you (very much)	(Muchas) gracias	(**moo**-chas) **grah**-see-as
	You're welcome	De nada	day **nah**-dah
	Excuse me	Con permiso	con pair-**mee**-so
	Pardon me	¿Perdón?	pair-**dohn**
	Could you tell me?	¿Podría decirme?	po-dree-ah deh-**seer**-meh
	I'm sorry	Lo siento	lo see-**en**-toh
	Good morning!	¡Buenos días!	**bway**-nohs **dee**-ahs
	Good afternoon!	¡Buenas tardes!	**bway**-nahs **tar**-dess
	Good evening!	¡Buenas noches!	**bway**-nahs **no**-chess
	Good-bye!	¡Adiós!	ah-dee-**ohss**
		¡Hasta luego!	**ah**-stah **lwe**-go
	Mr./Mrs.	Señor/Señora	sen-**yor**/sen-**yohr**-ah
	Miss	Señorita	sen-yo-**ree**-tah
	Pleased to meet you	Mucho gusto	**moo**-cho **goose**-toh
	How are you?	¿Cómo está usted?	**ko**-mo es-**tah** oo-**sted**
	Very well, thank you	Muy bien, gracias	**moo**-ee bee-**en**, **grah**-see-as
	And you?	¿Y usted?	ee oos-**ted**
	Hello (on the phone)	Diga/Aló	**dee**-gah/ah-**loh**
NUMBERS			
	1	un, uno	oon, **oo**-no
	2	dos	dos
	3	tres	tress
	4	cuatro	**kwah**-tro
	5	cinco	**sink**-oh
	6	seis	saice
	7	siete	see-**et**-eh
	8	ocho	**o**-cho

ENGLISH	SPANISH	PRONUNCIATION
9	nueve	new- **eh**-vey
10	diez	dee- **es**
11	once	**ohn**-seh
12	doce	**doh**-seh
13	trece	**treh**-seh
14	catorce	ka- **tohr**-seh
15	quince	**keen**-seh
16	dieciséis	dee- **es**-ee- **saice**
17	diecisiete	dee- **es**-ee-see- **et**-eh
18	dieciocho	dee- **es**-ee- **o**-cho
19	diecinueve	**dee-es**-ee-new- **ev**-eh
20	veinte	**vain**-teh
21	veinte y uno/ veintiuno	**vain**-te- **oo**-noh
30	treinta	**train**-tah
32	treinta y dos	train-tay- **dohs**
40	cuarenta	kwah- **ren**-tah
43	cuarenta y tres	kwah- **ren**-tay- **tress**
50	cincuenta	seen- **kwen**-tah
54	cincuenta y cuatro	seen- **kwen**-tay **kwah**-tro
60	sesenta	sess- **en**-tah
65	sesenta y cinco	sess- **en**-tay **seen**-ko
70	setenta	set- **en**-tah
76	setenta y seis	set- **en**-tay **saice**
80	ochenta	oh- **chen**-tah
87	ochenta y siete	oh- **chen**-tay see- **yet**-eh
90	noventa	no- **ven**-tah
98	noventa y ocho	no- **ven**-tah- **o**-choh
100	cien	see- **en**
101	ciento uno	see- **en**-toh **oo**-noh
200	doscientos	doh-see- **en**-tohss
500	quinientos	keen- **yen**-tohss

ENGLISH	SPANISH	PRONUNCIATION
700	setecientos	set-eh-see- **en**-tohss
900	novecientos	no-veh-see- **en**-tohss
1,000	mil	meel
2,000	dos mil	dohs meel
1,000,000	un millón	oon meel- **yohn**

COLORS

black	negro	**neh**-groh
blue	azul	ah- **sool**
brown	café	kah- **feh**
green	verde	**ver**-deh
pink	rosa	**ro**-sah
purple	morado	mo- **rah**-doh
orange	naranja	na- **rahn**-hah
red	rojo	**roh**-hoh
white	blanco	**blahn**-koh
yellow	amarillo	ah-mah- **ree**-yoh

DAYS OF THE WEEK

Sunday	domingo	doe- **meen**-goh
Monday	lunes	**loo**-ness
Tuesday	martes	**mahr**-tess
Wednesday	miércoles	me- **air**-koh-less
Thursday	jueves	hoo- **ev**-ess
Friday	viernes	vee- **air**-ness
Saturday	sábado	**sah**-bah-doh

MONTHS

January	enero	eh- **neh**-roh
February	febrero	feh- **breh**-roh
March	marzo	**mahr**-soh
April	abril	ah- **breel**
May	mayo	**my**-oh
June	junio	**hoo**-nee-oh
July	julio	**hoo**-lee-yoh
August	agosto	ah- **ghost**-toh

ENGLISH	SPANISH	PRONUNCIATION
September	septiembre	sep-tee- **em**-breh
October	octubre	oak- **too**-breh
November	noviembre	no-vee- **em**-breh
December	diciembre	dee-see- **em**-breh

USEFUL PHRASES

Do you speak English?	¿Habla usted inglés?	**ah**-blah oos- **ted** in- **glehs**
I don't speak Spanish	No hablo español	no **ah**-bloh es-pahn- **yol**
I don't understand (you)	No entiendo	no en-tee- **en**-doh
I understand (you)	Entiendo	en-tee- **en**-doh
I don't know	No sé	no seh
I am American/British	Soy americano (americana)/inglés(a)	soy ah-meh-ree- **kah**-no (ah-meh-ree- **kah**-nah)/ in- **glehs(ah)**
What's your name?	¿Cómo se llama usted?	koh-mo seh **yah**-mah oos- **ted**
My name is ...	Me llamo ...	may **yah**-moh
What time is it?	¿Qué hora es?	keh **o**-rah es
It is one, two, three ... o'clock.	Es la una/Son las dos, tres ...	es la **oo**-nah/sohn lahs dohs, tress
Yes, please/No, thank you	Sí, por favor/No, gracias	**see** pohr fah- **vor** /no **grah**-see-us
How?	¿Cómo?	**koh**-mo
When?	¿Cuándo?	**kwahn**-doh
This/Next week	Esta semana/la semana que entra	es-teh seh- **mah**-nah/ lah seh- **mah**-nah keh en-trah
This/Next month	Este mes/el próximo mes	es-teh mehs/el **proke**-see-mo mehs
This/Next year	Este año/el año que viene	es-teh **ahn**-yo/el **ahn**-yo keh vee- **yen**-ay
Yesterday/today/ tomorrow	Ayer/hoy/mañana	ah- **yehr** /oy/ mahn- **yah**-nah
This morning/ afternoon	Esta mañana/tarde	es-tah mahn- **yah**-nah/ **tar**-deh

ENGLISH	SPANISH	PRONUNCIATION
Tonight	Esta noche	**es**-tah **no**-cheh
What?	¿Qué?	keh
What is it?	¿Qué es esto?	keh es **es**-toh
Why?	¿Por qué?	pore **keh**
Who?	¿Quién?	kee- **yen**
Where is …?	¿Dónde está …?	**dohn**-deh es- **tah**
the train station?	la estación del tren?	la es-tah-see-on del tren?
the bus stop?	la parada del autobus?	la parada del la pah- **rah**-dah delow-toh- **boos**
the post office?	la oficina de correos?	la oh-fee- **see**-nah deh koh- **rreh**-os
the bank?	el banco?	el **bahn**-koh
the hotel?	el hotel?	el oh- **tel**
the store?	la tienda?	la tee- **en**-da
the cashier?	la caja?	la **kah**-hah
the museum?	el museo?	el moo- **seh**-oh
the hospital?	el hospital?	el ohss-pee- **tal**
the elevator?	el ascensor	el ah- **sen**-sohr
the bathroom?	el baño?	el **bahn**-yoh
Here/there	Aquí/allá	ah- **key** /ah- **yah**
Open/closed	Abierto/cerrado	ah-bee- **er**-toh/ ser- **ah**-doh
Left/right	Izquierda/derecha	iss-key- **er**-dah/ dare- **eh**-chah
Straight ahead	Derecho	dare- **eh**-choh
Is it near/far?	¿Está cerca/lejos?	es- **tah sehr**-kah/ **leh**-hoss
I'd like …	Quisiera …	kee-see-ehr-ah
a room	una habitación	**oo**-nah ah-bee-tah-see- **on**
the key	la llave	lah **yah**-veh
a newspaper	un periódico	oon pehr-ee- **oh**-dee-koh

ENGLISH	SPANISH	PRONUNCIATION
a stamp	un sello de correo	oon **seh**-yo deh koh- **reh**-oh
I'd like to buy ...	Quisiera comprar...	kee-see- **ehr**-ah kohm- **prahr**
cigarettes	cigarrillos	ce-ga- **ree**-yohs
matches	cerillos	ser- **ee**-ohs
a dictionary	un diccionario	oon deek-see-oh- **nah**-ree-oh
soap	jabón	hah- **bohn**
sunglasses	gafas del sol	**ga**-fahs deh sohl
suntan lotion	loción bronceadora	loh-see- **ohn** brohn-seh-ah- **do**-raha
a map	una mapa	oon **mah**-pah
a magazine	una revista	**oon**-ah reh- **vees**-tah
paper	papel	pah- **pel**
envelopes	sobres	**so**-brehs
a postcard	una tarjeta postal	**oon**-ah tar- **het**-ah post- **ahl**
How much is it?	¿Cuánto cuesta?	**kwahn**-toh **kwes**-tah
It's expensive/cheap	Está caro/barato	es- **tah kah**-roh/ bah- **rah**-toh
A little/a lot	Un poquito/mucho	oon poh- **kee**-toh/ **moo**-choh
More/less	Más/menos	mahss/ **men**-ohss
Enough/too much/too little	Suficiente/demasiado/ muy poco	soo-fee-see- **en**-teh/ deh-mah-see- **ah**-doh/ **moo**-ee **poh**-koh
Telephone	Teléfono	tel- **ef**-oh-no
Telegram	Telegrama	teh-leh- **grah**-mah
I am ill	Estoy enfermo(a)	es- **toy** en- **fehr**-moh(mah)
Please call a doctor	Por favor llame a un medico	pohr fah- **vor ya**-meh ah oon **med**-ee-koh

ENGLISH	SPANISH	PRONUNCIATION

ON THE ROAD

Avenue	Avenida	ah-ven-**ee**-dah
Broad, tree-lined boulevard	Bulevar	boo-leh-**var**
Fertile plain	Vega	**veh**-gah
Highway	Carretera	car-reh-**ter**-ah
Mountain pass	Puerto	poo-**ehr**-toh
Street	Calle	**cah**-yeh
Waterfront promenade	Rambla	**rahm**-blah
Wharf	Embarcadero	em-bar-cah-**deh**-ro

IN TOWN

Cathedral	Catedral	cah-teh-**dral**
Church	Templo/Iglesia	**tem**-plo/ ee-**glehs**-see-ah
City hall	Casa de gobierno	kah-sah deh go-bee-**ehr**-no
Door/gate	Puerta/portón	poo-**ehr**-tah/por-**ton**
Entrance/exit	Entrada/salida	en-**trah**-dah/ sah-**lee**-dah
Inn, rustic bar, restaurant	Taberna	tah-**behr**-nahor
Main square	Plaza principal	plah-thah prin-see-**pahl**
Market	Mercado	mer-**kah**-doh
Neighborhood	Barrio	**bahr**-ree-o
Traffic circle	Glorieta	glor-ee-**eh**-tah
Wine cellar, wine	Bodega	boh-**deh**-gahbar, or wine shop

DINING OUT

Can you recommend a good restaurant?	¿Puede recomendarme un buen restaurante?	**pweh**-deh rreh-koh-mehn-**dahr**-me oon bwehn rrehs-tow-**rahn**-teh?
Where is it located?	¿Dónde está situado?	**dohn**-deh ehs-**tah** see-**twah**-doh?

ENGLISH	SPANISH	PRONUNCIATION
Do I need reservations?	¿Se necesita una reservación?	seh neh-seh- **see**-tah **oo**-nah rreh-sehr-bah- **syohn**?
I'd like to reserve a table...	Quisiera reservar una mesa...	kee- **syeh**-rah rreh-sehr- **bahr oo**-nah **meh**-sah ...
for two people	para dos personas	**pah**-rah dohs pehr- **soh**-nahs
for this evening	para esta noche	**pah**-rah **ehs**-tah **noh**-cheh
for 8:00 pm	para las ocho de la noche	**pah**-rah lahs **oh**-choh deh lah **noh**-cheh
A bottle of ...	Una botella	**oo**-nah bo- **teh**-de ... yah deh
A cup of ...	Una taza de ...	**oo**-nah **tah**-thah deh
A glass of ...	Un vaso de ...	oon **vah**-so deh
Ashtray	Un cenicero	oon sen-ee- **seh**-roh
Bill/check	La cuenta	lah **kwen**-tah
Bread	El pan	el pahn
Breakfast	El desayuno	el deh-sah- **yoon**-oh
Butter	La mantequilla	lah man-teh- **key**-yah
Cheers!	¡Salud!	sah- **lood**
Cocktail	Un aperitivo	oon ah-pehr-ee- **tee**-voh
Dinner	La cena	lah **seh**-nah
Dish	Un plato	oon **plah**-toh
Menu of the day	Menú del día	meh- **noo** del **dee**-ah
Enjoy!	¡Buen provecho!	bwehn pro- **veh**-cho
Fixed-price menu	Menú fijo o turistico	meh- **noo fee**-hoh oh too- **ree**-stee-coh
Fork	El tenedor	el ten-eh- **dor**
Is the tip included?	¿Está incluida la propina?	es- **tah** in-cloo- **ee**-dah lah pro- **pee**-nah
Knife	El cuchillo	el koo- **chee**-yo
Large portion of savory snacks	Raciónes	rah-see- **oh**-nehs
Lunch	La comida	lah koh- **mee**-dah

ENGLISH	SPANISH	PRONUNCIATION
Menu	La carta, el menú	lah **cart**-ah, el meh- **noo**
Napkin	La servilleta	lah sehr-vee- **yet**-ah
Pepper	La pimienta	lah pee-me- **en**-tah
Please give me	Por favor déme	pore fah- **vor deh**-meh
Salt	La sal	lah sahl
Savory snacks	Tapas	**tah**-pahs
Spoon	Una cuchara	**oo**-nah koo- **chah**-rah
Sugar	El azúcar	el ah- **thu**-kar
Waiter!/Waitress!	¡Por favor Señor/ Señorita!	pohr fah- **vor** sen- **yor** /sen-yor- **ee**-tah

EMERGENCIES

Emergencies

English	Spanish	Pronunciation
Look!	¡Mire!	**mee**-reh!
Listen!	¡Escuche!	ehs- **koo**-cheh!
Help!	¡Auxilio! ¡Ayuda! ¡Socorro!	owk- **see**-lee-oh/ ah- **yoo**-dah/ soh- **kohr**-roh
Fire!	¡Incendio!	en- **sen**-dee-oo
Caution!/Look out!	¡Cuidado!	kwee- **dah**-doh
Hurry!	¡Dése prisa!	**deh**-seh **pree**-sah!
Stop!	¡Alto!	**ahl**-toh!
I need help quick!	¡Necesito ayuda, pronto!	neh-seh- **see**-toh ah- **yoo**-dah, **prohn**-toh!
Can you help me?	¿Puede ayudarme?	**pweh**-deh ah-yoo- **dahr**-meh?
Police!	¡Policía!	poh-lee- **see**-ah!
I need a policeman!	¡Necesito un policía!	neh-seh- **see**-toh oon poh-lee- **see**-ah!
It's an emergency!	¡Es una emergencia!	ehs **oo**-nah eh-mehr- **hehn**-syah!
Leave me alone!	¡Déjeme en paz!	**deh**-heh-meh ehn pahs!
That man's a thief!	¡Ese hombre es un ladrón!	**eh**-seh **ohm**-breh ehs oon-lah- **drohn**!

ENGLISH	SPANISH	PRONUNCIATION
Stop him!	¡Deténganlo!	deh- **tehn**-gahn-loh!
He's stolen my ...	Me ha robado ...	meh ah rroh- **bah**-doh ...
pocketbook	la cartera	lah kahr- **teh**-rah
wallet	la billetera	lah bee-yeh- **teh**-rah
passport	el pasaporte	ehl pah-sah- **pohr**-teh
watch	el reloj	ehl rreh- **loh**
I've lost my ...	He perdido	eh pehr- **dee**-doh
suitcase	mi maleta	mee mah- **leh**-tah
money	mi dinero	mee dee- **neh**-roh
glasses	los anteojos	lohs ahn-teh- **oh**-hohs
car keys	las llaves de mi automóvil	lahs **yah**-behs deh mee ow-toh- **moh**-beel

TELLING TIME AND EXPRESSIONS OF TIME

What time is it?	¿Qué hora es?	keh **oh**-rah ehs?
At what time?	¿A qué hora?	ah keh **oh**-rah?
It's ...	Es ...	ehs ...
one o'clock	la una	lah **oo**-nah
1:15	la una y cuarto	lah **oo**-nah ee **kwahr**-toh
1:30	la una y media	lah **oo**-nah ee **meh**-dyah
It's 1:45	Son las dos menos cuarto	sohn lahs dohs **meh**-nos **kwahr**-toh
two o'clock	dos	dohs
morning	la mañana	Lah mah- **nyah**-nah
afternoon	la tarde	lah **tahr**-deh
It's midnight	Es medianoche	ehs **meh**-dyah **noh**-cheh
It's noon	Es mediodía	ehs meh-dyoh- **dee** ah
In a half hour	En media hora	ehn **meh**-dyah **oh**-rah
When does it begin?	¿Cuándo empieza?	**kwahn**-doh ehm- **pyeh**-sah?

ENGLISH	SPANISH	PRONUNCIATION

PAYING THE BILL

How much does it cost?	¿Cuánto cuesta?	**kwahn**-toh **kwehs**-tah?
The bill, please	La cuenta, por favor	lah- **kwen**-tah pohr fah- **bohr**
How much do I owe you?	¿Cuánto le debo?	**kwan**-toh leh **deh**-boh?
Is service included?	¿La propina está incluida?	lah proh- **pee**-nah ehs- **tah** een-kloo- **ee**-dah?
This is for you	Esto es para usted	**ehs**-toh ehs pah-rah oos- **tehd**

GETTING AROUND

Do you have a map of the city?	¿Tiene usted un mapa de la ciudad?	**tyeh**-neh oos- **tehd** oon **mah**-pah deh lah syoo- **dahd**?
Could you show me on the map?	¿Puede usted indicármelo en el mapa?	**pweh**-deh oo- **stehd** een-dee- **kahr**-meh-loh ehn ehl **mah**-pah?
Can I get there on foot?	¿Puedo llegar allí a pie?	**pweh**-doh yeh-on foot? a pie? **gahr** ah- **yee** ah pyeh?
How far is it?	¿A qué distancia es?	ah keh dees- **tahn**-syah ehs?
I'm lost	Estoy perdido(-a)	ehs- **toy** pehr- **dee**-doh(-dah)
Where is ...	¿Dónde está ...	**dohn**-deh ehs- **tah**
the Hotel Rex?	el hotel Rex?	ehl oh- **tehl** rreks?
... Street?	la calle...?	lah **kah**-yeh ...?
... Avenue?	la avenida...?	lah ah-beh- **nee**-dah...?
How can I get to ...	¿Cómo puedo ir a...	**koh**-moh **pweh**-doh eer ah ...
the train station?	la estación de ferrocarril?	lah ehs-tah- **syon** deh feh-rroh-cah- **rreel**?
the bus stop?	la parada de autobuses?	lah pah- **rah**-dah deh ow-toh- **boo**-ses?
the ticket office?	la taquilla?	lah tah- **kee**-yah?
the airport?	el aeropuerto?	ehl ah-eh-roh- **pwehr**-toh?

ENGLISH	SPANISH	PRONUNCIATION
straight ahead	derecho	deh- **reh**-chohto
to the right	a la derecha	ah lah deh- **reh**-chahto
to the left	a la izquierda	ah lah ees- **kyehr**-dah
a block away	a una cuadra	ah **oo**-nah **kwah**-drah
on the corner	en la esquina	ehn lah ehs- **kee**-nah
on the square	en la plaza	ehn lah **plah**-sah
facing, opposite	enfrente	ehn- **frehn**-teh
across	al frente	ahl **frehn**-teh
next to	al lado	ahl **lah**-doh
near	cerca	**sehr**-kah
far	lejos	**leh**-hohs

ON THE BUS

I'm looking for the bus stop	Estoy buscando la parada de autobuses	ehs- **toy** boos- **kahn**-doh lah pah- **rah**-dah deh ow-toh- **boo**-sehs
What bus line goes...	¿Qué línea va...	keh **lee**-neh-ah bah...
north?	al norte?	ahl **nohr**-teh?
south?	al sur?	ahl soor?
east?	al este?	ahl **ehs**-teh?
west?	al oeste?	ahl oh- **ehs**-teh?
What bus do I take to go to...	¿Qué autobús tomo para ir a ...	keh ow-toh- **boos toh**-moh **pah**-rah eer ah ...
Can you tell me when to get off?	¿Podría decirme cuándo debo bajarme?	poh- **dree**-ah deh- **seer**-meh **kwan**-doh **deh**-boh bah- **hahr**-meh?
How much is the fare?	¿Cuánto es el billete?	**kwahn**-toh ehs ehl bee- **yeh**-teh?
Should I pay when I get on?	¿Debo pagar al subir?	**deh**-boh pah- **gahr** ahl soo- **beer**?
Where do I take the bus to return?	¿Dónde se toma el autobús para regresar?	**dohn**-deh seh **toh**-mah ehl ow-toh- **boos** pah- rah rreh-greh- **sahr**?
How often do the return buses run?	¿Cada cuánto hay autobuses de regreso?	**kah**-dah **kwahn**-toh ahy ow-toh- **boo**-sehs deh rreh- **greh**-soh?
I would like ...	Quisiera...	kee- **syeh**-rah...

ENGLISH	SPANISH	PRONUNCIATION
a ticket	un billete	oon bee-**yeh**-teh
a receipt	un recibo	oon reh-**see**-boh
a reserved seat	un asiento numerado	oon ah-**syehn**-toh noo-meh-**rah**-doh
first class	primera clase	pree-**meh**-rah **klah**-seh
second class	segunda clase	seh-**goon**-dah **klah**-seh
a direct bus	un autobús directo	oon ow-toh-**boos** dee-**rehk**-toh
an express bus	un autobús expreso	oon ow-toh-**boos** ehks-**preh**-soh
ticketed luggage	equipaje facturado	eh-kee-**pah**-heh fahk-too-**rah**-doh

ACCOMMODATIONS

I have a reservation	Tengo una reservación/una reserva	**tehn**-goh **oo**-nah rreh-sehr-vah-**syohn** / ... **oo**-nah rre-**sehr**-vah
I would like a room for...	Quisiera una habitación por ...	kee-**syeh**-rah **oo**-nah ah-bee-tah-**syohn** pohr ...
one night	una noche	**oo**-nah **noh**-che
two nights	dos noches	dohs **noh**-chehs
a week	una semana	**oo**-nah seh-**mah**-nah
two weeks	dos semanas	dohs seh-**mah**-nahs
How much is it ...	¿Cuánto es ...	**kwahn**-toh ehs ...
for a day?	por día?	pohr **dee**-ah?
for a week?	por una semana?	pohr **oo**-nah seh-**mah**-nah?
Does that include tax?	¿Incluye impuestos?	een-**kloo**-yeh eem-**pwehs**-tohs?
Do you have a room with...	¿Tiene una habitación con ...	**tyeh**-neh **oo**-nah ah-bee-tah-**syohn** kohn ...
a private bath?	baño privado?	**bah**-nyoh pree-**bah**-doh?
a shower?	una ducha?	**oo**-nah **doo**-chah?
air-conditioning?	aire acondiciondo?	**ay**-reh ah-kohn-dee-syoh-**nah**-doh?

ENGLISH	SPANISH	PRONUNCIATION
heat?	calefacción?	kah-leh-fak- **syohn?**
television?	televisor?	teh-leh-bee- **sohr?**
hot water?	agua caliente?	**ah**-gwah kah- **lyehn**-teh?
a balcony?	balcón?	bahl- **kohn?**
a view facing the street?	vista a la calle?	**bees**-tah ah lah **kah**-yeh?
a view facing the ocean?	vista al mar?	**bees**-tah ahl mahr?
Does the hotel have...	¿Tiene el hotel...?	**tyeh**-neh ehl oh- **tehl** ...?
a restaurant?	un restaurante?	oon rrehs-tow- **rahn**-teh?
a bar?	un bar?	oon bahr?
a swimming pool?	una piscina?	**oo**-nah pee- **see**-nah
room service?	servicio de habitación?	sehr- **bee**-syoh deh ah-bee-tah- **syohn?**
a safe-deposit box?	un a caja de valores/ seguridad	**oo**-nah **kah**-hah deh bah- **loh**-rehs/ seh-goo-ree- **dahd?**
laundry service?	servicio de lavandería?	sehr- **bee**-syoh deh lah-vahn-deh- **ree**-ah?
I would like ...	Quisiera...	kee- **sye**-rah ...
meals included	con las comidas incluidas	kohn lvahs koh- **mee**-dahs een- **kluee**-dahs
breakfast only	solamente con desayuno	soh-lah- **men**-teh kohn deh-sah- **yoo**-noh
no meals included	sin comidas	seen koh- **mee**-dahs
an extra bed	una cama más	**oo**-nah **kah**-mah mahs
a baby crib	una cuna	**oo**-nah **koo**-nah
another towel	otra toalla	**oh**-trah **twah**-yah
soap	jabón	hah- **bohn**
clothes hangers	ganchos de ropa	**gahn**-chohs deh **rroh**-pah
another blanket	otra manta	**oh**-trah **mahn**-tah
drinking water	agua para beber	**ah**-gwah **pah**-rah beh- **behr**

ENGLISH	SPANISH	PRONUNCIATION
toilet paper	papel higiénico	pah- **pehl** ee- **hye**-nee-koh
This room is very ...	Esta habitación es muy ...	**ehs**-tah ah-bee-tah- **syohn** ehs muee ...
small	pequeña	peh- **keh**-nyah
cold	fría	**free**-ah
hot	caliente	kah- **lyehn**-teh
dark	oscura	ohs- **koo**-rah
noisy	ruidosa	rruee- **doh**-sah
The ... does not work	No funciona ...	noh foon- **syoh**-nah ...
light	la luz	lah loos
heat	la calefacción	lah kah-leh-fahk- **syohn**
toilet	el baño	ehl **bah**-nyoh
air conditioner	el aire acondicionado	ehl **ay**-reh ah-kohn-dee-syo- **nah**-doh
key	la llave	lah **yah**-beh
lock	la cerradura	lah seh-rah- **doo**-rah
fan	el ventilador	ehl **behn**-tee-lah- **dohr**
outlet	el enchufe	ehl ehn- **choo**-feh
television	el telvisor	ehl teh-leh-bee- **sohr**
May I change to another room?	¿Podría cambiar de habitación?	poh- **dree**-ah kahm-de **byar** deh ah-bee-tah- **syohn**?
Is there...	¿Hay...	ahy...
room service?	servico de habitación?	sehr- **bee**-syoh deh ah-bee-tah- **syohn**?
laundry service?	servico de lavandería?	sehr- **bee**-syoh deh lah-vahn-deh- **ree**-ah?

EMAIL AND THE INTERNET

Where is the computer	¿Dónde está la computadora?	**dohn**-deh eh- **stah** lah kohm-poo-tah- **doh**-rah
I need to send an email	Necesito enviar un correo electrónico	neh-seh- **see**-toh un correo ehn- **byahr** oon koh- **reh**-yoh eh-lehk- **troh**-nee-koh

ENGLISH	SPANISH	PRONUNCIATION
Can I get on the Internet?	¿Puedo conectarme con el internet?	**pweh**-doh koh-nehk- **tahr**-meh ahl **een**-tehr-net?
Do you have a website?	¿Tiene página web?	**tyeh**-neh **pah**-hee-nah web?

BARGAINING

Excuse me	Perdón	pehr- **dohn**
I'm interested in this	Me interesa esto	meh een-teh- **reh**-sah **ehs**-toh
How much is it?	¿Cuánto cuesta?	**kwahn**-toh **kwehs**-tah?
It's very expensive!	¡Es muy caro!	ehs muee **kah**-roh!
It's overpriced (It's not worth so much)	No vale tanto	noh **vah**-leh **tahn**-toh
Do you have a cheaper one?	¿Tiene uno más barato?	**tyeh**-neh **oo**-noh mahs bah- **rah**-toh?
This is damaged—do you have another one?	Está dañado, ¿hay otro?	ehs- **tah** dah- **nyah**-doh, ahy **oh**-troh?
What is the lowest price?	¿Cuál es el precio mínimo?	**kwahl** ehs ehl **preh**-syoh **mee**-nee-moh?
Is that the final price?	¿Es el último precio?	ehs ehl **ool**-tee-moh **preh**-syoh?
Can't you give me a discount?	¿No me da una rebaja?	noh meh dah **oo**-nah rreh- **bah**-hah?
I'll give you ...	Le doy ...	leh doy ...
I won't pay more than ...	No pago más de ...	noh **pah**-goh mahs deh ...
I'll look somewhere else	Voy a ver en otro sitio	voy ah behr ehn **oh**-troh **see**-tyoh
No, thank you	No, gracias	noh, **grah**-syahs

TOILETRIES

toiletries	objetos de baño	ohb- **jeh**-tohs deh **bah**-nyoh
a brush	un cepillo	oon seh- **pee**-yoh
cologne	colonia	koh- **loh**-nyah
a comb	un peine	oon **pay**-neh
deodorant	desodorante	deh-soh-doh- **rahn**-teh

ENGLISH	SPANISH	PRONUNCIATION
disposable	pañales	pah- **nyah**-lehs
diapers	desechables	deh-seh- **chah**-blehs
hairspray	laca	**lah**-kah
a mirror	un espejo	oon ehs- **peh**-hoh
moisturizing lotion	loción humectante	loh- **syohn** oo-mehk- **tahn**-teh
mouthwash	enjuague bucal	ehn- **hwah**-geh boo- **kahl**
nail clippers	cortaúñas	kohr-ta- **oo**-nyahs
nail polish	esmalte de uñas	ehs- **mahl**-teh deh **oo**-nyahs
nail polish remover	quitaesmalte	kee-tah-ehs- **mahl**-teh
perfume	perfume	pehr- **foo**-meh
sanitary napkins	toallas sanitarias	toh- **ah**-yahs sah-nee- **tah**-ryahs
shampoo	champú	chahm- **poo**
shaving cream	crema de afeitar	**kreh**-mah deh ah-fay- **tahr**
soap	jabón	hah- **bohn**
a sponge	una esponja	**oo**-nah ehs- **pohn**-hah
tampons	tampones	tahm- **poh**-nehs
tissues	pañuelos de papel	pah- **nyweh**-lohs deh pah- **pehl**
toilet paper	papel higiénico	pah- **pehl** ee- **hyeh**-ee-koh
a toothbrush	un cepillo de dientes	oon seh- **pee**-yoh deh **dyehn**-tehs
toothpaste	pasta de dientes	**pahs**-tah deh **dyehn**-tehs
tweezers	pinzas	**peen**-sahs

TRAVEL SMART PERU

GETTING HERE AND AROUND

Because of the massive Andes Mountains that ripple through the country, most travelers choose to fly between the major cities of Peru. The good news is that domestic flights can be reasonable, sometimes less than US$100 per segment.

TRAVEL TIMES FROM LIMA		
To	By Air	By Car/Bus
Cusco	1 hour, 20 mins.	21½ hours
Puno	1 hour, 50 mins.	22 hours
Arequipa	1½ hours	15½ hours
Trujillo	1 hour, 15 mins.	9 hours

■ AIR TRAVEL

Almost all international flights into Peru touch down at Aeropuerto Internacional Jorge Chávez, on the northwestern fringe of Lima. Nonstop flying times to Lima are 5 hours, 35 minutes from Miami; 6 hours, 35 minutes from Houston; 7½ hours from New York; and 8 hours, 20 minutes from Los Angeles.

Airlines now include departure taxes on international and domestic flights in the cost of tickets.

The least expensive airfares to Peru are priced for round-trip travel. Airlines generally allow you to change your return date for a fee; most low-fare tickets, however, are nonrefundable.

Airline Security Issues Transportation Security Administration. ⊕ www.tsa.gov.

AIRPORTS

Peru's main international point of entry is Aeropuerto Internacional Jorge Chávez (LIM), 11 km (7 miles) from Lima's historic center and 17 km (10 miles) from Miraflores. It's a completely modern facility with plenty of shops, eateries, and flights that arrive and depart 24 hours a day. ATMs and currency exchange offices are in the arrivals area. ATMs can also be found in the departures area. You will get a better exchange rate from a bank-affiliated ATM or at a currency exchange on the street, so you may want to change or take out a small amount to pay any necessary taxis.

Airport Information Aeropuerto Internacional Jorge Chávez. ⊠ Av. Faucett s/n, Callao ☎ 01/511–6055 flight information ⊕ www.lap.com.pe.

GROUND TRANSPORTATION

If your hotel doesn't offer to pick you up at the airport, you'll have to take a taxi. Arrange a ride with one of the official airport taxis whose companies have counters inside the arrivals area of the terminal. A taxi to most places in the city should cost no more than US$20–US$25. It's a 30-minute drive to El Centro, and a 45-minute drive to Miraflores and San Isidro. During rush hour (8–10 am and 5–9 pm), driving times in Lima can double, so plan accordingly.

FLIGHTS

Dozens of international flights land daily at Lima's Aeropuerto Internacional Jorge Chávez; although most are from other Latin American cities, there are many from the United States as well. Delta flies from Atlanta, American flies from Miami and New York's JFK, United flies from Houston, and Spirit and JetBlue both fly from Fort Lauderdale. South American–based LATAM flies from Los Angeles and Miami; Avianca flies from Miami; and Air Canada flies from Toronto.

If you're arriving from other Latin American cities, you have a wide range of regional carriers at your disposal. LATAM has flights from most major airports in the region, as does Avianca, that now also flies direct between Bogotá, Colombia, and Cusco. Copa (affiliated with United) flies from its hub in Panama

City, Aeroméxico flies from Mexico City, Aerolineas Argentinas flies from Buenos Aires, and Sky Airlines flies from Santiago, Chile.

DOMESTIC

With four mountain ranges and a large swath of the Amazon jungle running through Peru, flying is the best way to travel from Lima to most cities and towns. LATAM, the carrier that operates the majority of flights within the country, departs several times each day for Arequipa, Ayacucho, Cajamarca, Chiclayo, Cusco, Iquitos, Piura, Puerto Maldonado, Pucallpa, Tacna, Tarapoto, Trujillo, and Tumbes. LC Perú flies to Andahuaylas, Arequipa, Ayacucho, Cajamarca, Chiclayo, Cusco, Huancayo, Huánuco, Huaraz, Pucallpa, and Tingo Maria. Peruvian Airlines flies to Arequipa, Cusco, Iquitos, Jauja, Piura, Pucallpa, Tacna, and Tarapoto. Star Perú flies to Cusco, Huánuco, Iquitos, Pucallpa, Puerto Maldonado, and Tarapoto. Avianca flies to Arequipa, Cusco, Iquitos, Juliaca, Piura, Puerto Maldonado, and Trujillo. New in 2017 is Viva Air Peru with flights between Lima and Arequipa, Chiclayo, Cusco, Iquitos, Piura, and Tarapoto.

Airline Contacts Aerolineas Argentinas. ✉ *Dean Valdivia 243, Of. 301, San Isidro* ☎ *800/333-0276 in North America, 800/52-200 in Lima* ⊕ *www.aerolineas. ar.* **Aeroméxico.** ✉ *Av. Alfredo Benavides 1579, Edificio Park II, Of. 405, Lima* ✛ *Miraflores* ☎ *800/237-6639 in North America, 800/53-407 in Lima* ⊕ *www.aeromexico. com.* **Air Canada.** ✉ *Calle Italia 389, Of. 101, Miraflores* ☎ *888/247-2262 in North America, 800/52-073 in Lima* ⊕ *www. aircanada.com.* **American Airlines.** ✉ *José Pardo 392, Miraflores* ☎ *800/433-7300 in North America, 01/211-7000 in Lima* ⊕ *www. aa.com.* **Avianca.** ✉ *José Pardo 811, Miraflores* ☎ *800/284-2622 in U.S., 01/511-8222 in Lima, 800/722-8222 in Canada* ⊕ *www. avianca.com.* **Copa.** ✉ *Los Halcones 105, San Isidro* ✛ *Canaval y Moreyra with República de Panamá* ☎ *800/359-2672 in North America, 01/709-2600 in Lima* ⊕ *www.copaair.com.*

Delta Airlines. ✉ *Víctor Andrés Belaúnde 147, Torre Real 3, Of. 701, San Isidro* ✛ *Via Principal 180* ☎ *800/241-4141 in North America, 01/211-9211 in Lima* ⊕ *www.delta. com.* **JetBlue.** ✉ *Aeropuerto Jorge Chávez, Av. Elmer Faucett s/n, Callao* ☎ *800/538-2583 in U.S., 080/051-061 in Lima* ⊕ *www.jetblue.com.* **LATAM.** ✉ *José Pardo 513, 1st fl., Miraflores* ☎ *866/435-9526 in North America, 01/213-8200 in Lima* ⊕ *www.latam.com.* **Spirit Air.** ✉ *Aeropuerto Internacional Jorge Chávez, Av. Elmer Faucett s/n, Callao* ☎ *801/401-2222 in North America, 01/641-9131 in Lima* ⊕ *www. spiritair.com.* **United Airlines.** ✉ *Av. Victor Andrés Belaunde 147, Edificio Real 5, Of. 101, San Isidro* ☎ *800/864-8331 in North America, 01/712-9230 in Lima* ⊕ *www.united.com.*

Domestic Airlines LC Perú. ✉ *José Pardo 269, Miraflores* ☎ *01/204-1313, 844/209-4603 in North America* ⊕ *www. lcperu.pe.* **Peruvian Airlines.** ✉ *José Pardo 495, Miraflores* ☎ *01/716-6000* ⊕ *www. peruvianairlines.pe.* **Star Perú.** ✉ *José Pardo 485, Miraflores* ☎ *1-757/550-1526 in North America, 01/705-9000 in Lima* ⊕ *www. starperu.com.* **Viva Air Perú.** ☎ *08/005-5786 from Peru, 844/569-7126 from U.S.* ⊕ *www. vivaair.com.*

▌ BUS TRAVEL

The intercity bus system in Peru is extensive, and fares are quite reasonable. Remember, however, that mountain ranges often sit between cities, and trips can be daunting. It's best to use buses for shorter trips, such as between Lima and Ica or between Cusco and Puno. That way you can begin and end your trip during daylight hours. If you stick with one of the recommended companies—such as Cruz del Sur, Ormeño, Inka Express, or CIVA—you can usually expect a comfortable journey.

Second-class buses (*servicio normal*) tend to be cramped and overcrowded, whereas the pricier first-class service (*primera clase*) is more relaxing and much more likely to arrive on schedule.

Bus fares are substantially cheaper in Peru than they are in North America or Europe. Competing companies serve all major and many minor routes, so it can pay to shop around if you're on an extremely tight budget. Always speak to the counter clerk, as competition may mean fares are cheaper than the official price posted on the fare board.

For the 15-plus-hour journey between Lima and Arequipa, Cruz del Sur offers different price tiers, depending on how far the seat reclines, with first-floor seats being more comfortable. Inka Express, which promotes itself to tourists rather than the local market, uses large, comfortable coaches for the popular eight-hour journey between Cusco and Puno. Tickets are US$50, and the trip includes snacks, lunch, and guided visits at points of interest along the way; entrance fees for the sites are not included.

Tickets are sold at bus-company offices and at travel agencies. Be prepared to pay with cash, as credit cards aren't always accepted, although you can typically order and pay by credit card on the Cruz del Sur website. Reservations aren't necessary except for trips to top destinations during high season. Summer weekends and major holidays are the busiest times. You should arrive at bus stations early for travel during peak seasons.

Bus Information CIVA. ⊠ Javier Prado Este 1155, La Victoria ☎ 01/418–1111 ⊕ www. excluciva.pe. **Cruz del Sur.** ⊠ Javier Prado 1109, La Victoria ☎ 01/311–5050 ⊕ www. cruzdelsur.com.pe. **Inka Express.** ⊠ Av. Alameda Pachacutek 499-A, Wanchaq ⊕ Across from Centro Confraternidad ☎ 084/247–887, 984/705–301 ⊕ www. inkaexpress.com. **Ormeño.** ⊠ Javier Prado Oeste 1057, La Victoria ☎ 01/472–5000 ⊕ www.grupo-ormeno.com.pe.

▌ CAR TRAVEL

In general, it's not a great idea to rent a car in Peru. Driving is a heart-stopping experience, as there seem to be unwritten traffic rules that you have to be from here to know. That said, there are a few places in Peru where having a car is a benefit, such as between Lima and points south on the Pan-American Highway. The highway follows the Pacific Ocean coastline before it cuts in through the desert, and stops can be made along the way for a picnic and a swim at the popular beaches around Asia at Kilometer 100. The highway is good, and although there isn't too much to see along the way, it's nice to have the freedom a car affords once you get to your destination.

If you do rent one, keep these tips in mind: outside cities, drive only during daylight hours, fill your gas tank whenever possible, make sure your spare tire is in good repair, and pay extra attention on mountain roads. In some areas, drivers caught using a cell phone receive a hefty fine.

Massive road-building programs have improved highways. Nevertheless, even in some parts of Lima, roads are littered with potholes. Beyond the urban centers, both street signs and lighting can be rare and lanes may be unmarked. Roads are straight along the coast, but in the mountains they snake around enough to make even the steadiest driver a little queasy. Fuel is pricey in Peru, with a gallon costing around of US$3.75.

Then there are the drivers: when they get behind the wheel, Peruvians are very assertive. Expect lots of honking and last-minute lane switching when you're in a city. On highways you'll encounter constant tailgating and passing on blind curves. And remember the ancient car you sold five years ago? Chances are it is now plying Peru's roads. All things considered, it's best to leave the driving to someone else if you can. One option is to hire a car and driver through your hotel; making a deal with a taxi driver for some extended sightseeing is another. Drivers often charge an hourly rate regardless of the distance traveled within Lima; elsewhere, it is typically a set fee according to where you're going. You'll have to pay cash, but you'll likely spend less than you would for a rental car.

The major highways in Peru are the Pan-American Highway (*Panamericana* in Spanish), which runs down the entire coast, the Carretera Central, which runs from Lima to Huancayo, and the Interoceánica, which runs from Lima to Cerro de Pasco and on to Pucallpa before crossing through Brazil to the Atlantic Ocean. Most highways have no names or numbers; they're referred to by destination.

CAR RENTAL

If you plan to rent a car, it's best to shop around online for a good deal and make your booking before you leave home. If you plan to rent during a holiday period, reserve early.

The minimum age for renting a car in Peru is 25, although some agencies offer rentals to younger drivers for an additional fee, and a credit card is required. All major car-rental agencies have branches in downtown Lima as well as at Jorge Chávez International Airport that are open 24 hours. You can also rent vehicles in Arequipa, Chiclayo, Cusco, Piura, Puno, Tacna, and Trujillo.

The cost of rental cars varies widely but is generally between US$30 and US$60 for a compact, US$80 to US$100 for a full-size car or small SUV. A daily US$10 to US$20 collision damage waiver may be added to your bill. Always make sure to check the fine print, as some companies give you unlimited mileage, whereas others give you between 200 and 240 km (124 and 150 miles) free, then charge you a hefty 25 to 60 cents for every kilometer you drive above that. Many rental firms include in your contract a statement saying you may not take the vehicle on unpaved roads, of which there are many in Peru. Many also forbid mountain driving for certain types of vehicles in their fleets.

Always give the rental car a once-over to make sure that the headlights, jack, and tires (including the spare) are in working condition. Note any existing damage to the car and get a signature acknowledging the damage, no matter how slight.

GASOLINE

Gas stations are less plentiful in Peru than in the United States or Europe. In Lima gas stations should be easy to locate, but in Cusco, Arequipa, or smaller cities they may be on the outskirts and are often difficult to find. Make sure to ask your rental company where they're located. Stations along the highways are rare, so don't pass up on the chance to gas up. Many are now open 24 hours.

PARKING

If you have a rental car, make sure your hotel has its own parking lot. If it doesn't, ask about nearby lots. In the cities, guarded parking lots that charge anywhere from US$1 up to US$4 an hour are common. Don't park cars on the street, as theft is common.

ROADSIDE EMERGENCIES

The Touring y Automóvil Club del Perú will provide 24-hour emergency road service for members of the American Automobile Association (AAA) and affiliates upon presentation of their membership cards. (Towing is free within 30 km [18 miles] of several urban areas.) Members of AAA can purchase good maps there at low prices.

Emergency Services Touring y Automóvil Club del Perú. ⊠ *Trinidad Morán 698, Lince* 🕾 *01/611–9999 emergencies, 01/615–9315 information* ⊕ *www.touringperu.com.pe.*

RULES OF THE ROAD

In Peru your own driver's license is acceptable identification, but an international driving permit is good to have. They're available from the American and Canadian automobile associations and, in the United Kingdom, from the Automobile Association and Royal Automobile Club. These international permits, valid only in conjunction with your regular driver's license, are universally recognized; having one may save you headaches with local authorities.

Speed limits are 30 kph–60 kph (18.5 mph–37 mph) in residential areas, 80 kph–100 kph (50 mph–62 mph) on highways. Traffic tickets range from a minimum of US$12 to a maximum of US$120. The police and military routinely check drivers at roadblocks, so make sure your papers are easily accessible. Note that laws, especially outside big cities, can be left to the discretion of the officer, so be polite and respectful at all times. Peruvian law makes it a crime to drive while intoxicated, although many people ignore that prohibition (as everywhere).

▌TRAIN TRAVEL

Trains run along four different routes: between Cusco and Machu Picchu, between Cusco and Lake Titicaca, and, new for 2017, between Lake Titicaca and Arequipa. The second highest train in the world runs between Lima and Huancayo, one or two times a month between May and November; tours last four days. Tickets can be purchased at train stations, through travel agencies, or online. During holidays or high season, it's best to get your tickets in advance.

Two companies offer train service to Machu Picchu. PeruRail, which has served the route since 1999, is operated by Belmond—the same company that runs one of the most luxurious and famous trains in the world, the Venice Simplon Orient Express between London and Venice. It travels to Machu Picchu from Cusco (technically from the nearby town of Poroy, about 20 minutes outside the city) and the Sacred Valley towns of Ollantaytambo and Urubamba. Inca Rail, which began service in 2010 and merged with Andean Railways in 2012, travels between Ollantaytambo and Machu Picchu. Foreigners are prohibited from riding the very inexpensive local trains that cover the route. The Machu

Picchu station is not at the archaeological site itself, but in the nearby town of Aguas Calientes. *See Chapter 6: Machu Picchu and the Inca Trail for more information about these trains.*

In 2017, PeruRail completely revamped their Andean Explorer train service to points south of Cusco. It is now a sleeper train, and the company offers several different options from single-day trips between Cusco and Lake Titicaca, as well as tours that include Arequipa as well. Each departs on a different day of the week, depending on the trip chosen. The newly revamped Andean Explorer from Cusco to the Lake is US$1,300 for two passengers, leaving at 11 in the morning from Cusco, culminating in a sunrise breakfast at Lake Titicaca and including lunch, tour of Raqchi, tea time, predinner drinks, dinner, and, of course, your bed. Note that there are two different train stations in Cusco. Estación Poroy serves the Machu Picchu route, and Estación Wanchaq serves the Lake Titicaca route. Reserve and purchase your ticket as far ahead as possible, especially during holidays or high season. Reservations can be made directly with PeruRail through its website or through a travel agency or tour operator.

Reservations Inca Rail. ⊠ *Portal de Panes 105, Plaza de Armas, Cusco* ☎ *084/581–860 sales and reservations* ⊕ *www.incarail.com.* **PeruRail.** ⊠ *Portal de Carnes 214, Plaza de Armas, Cusco* ☎ *084/581–414 call center* ⊕ *www.perurail.com.*

Train Stations Estación Poroy—PeruRail (Cusco-Machu Picchu Route). ⊠ *Calle Roldan s/n, Poroy, Cusco.* **Estación Wanchaq—PeruRail (Cusco-Lake Titicaca Route).** ⊠ *Pachacutec s/n, Wanchaq, Cusco.*

ESSENTIALS

■ ACCOMMODATIONS

It's always good to take a look at your room before accepting it, especially if you're staying in a budget hotel. If it isn't what you expected, there might be several other rooms from which to choose. Expense is no guarantee of charm or cleanliness, and accommodations can vary dramatically within a single hotel. Many older hotels in some of the small towns in Peru have rooms with lovely balconies or spacious terraces; ask if there's a room *con balcón* or *con terraza* when checking in.

If you ask for a double room, you'll get a room for two people, but you're not guaranteed one large bed. If you'd like to avoid two twins, you'll have to ask for a *cama matrimonial* (literally a marriage bed), but don't worry, no wedding ring is required.

APARTMENT AND HOUSE RENTALS

Apartment rentals are not a viable option in most parts of Peru. They're becoming more common in Lima, however, and several other tourist centers. Aside from the convenience they offer, rentals can be cost-effective—you can often get a roomy two- or three-bedroom apartment for less than you'd pay for a shoe-box-size hotel room. One company that has proven reliable is Inn Peru, which rents apartments in Lima's Miraflores neighborhood; North American–based alternatives include HomeAway and Airbnb.

Contacts Airbnb.com. ☎ *855/424–7262 in North America* ⊕ *www.airbnb.com.* **HomeAway.** ☎ *877/228–3145* ⊕ *www. homeaway.com.* **Inn Peru.** ☎ *01/998–578–350 in Peru* ⊕ *www.innperu.com.*

HOME EXCHANGES

With a direct home exchange you stay in someone else's home while they stay in yours. Some outfits also deal with vacation properties, so you're not actually moving into someone's full-time residence, just their vacant weekend place. Homeexchange.com charges US$150 for a year membership.

Exchange Clubs Home Exchange.com. ☎ *800/877–8723 in North America, 310/798–3864 in North America* ⊕ *www.homeexchange.com.*

HOTELS

Peru's hotels range from bare-bones hostels to luxurious retreats tucked away in forgotten Andean valleys. In general, the highest-quality ones are in major urban centers (Lima, Arequipa, Cusco), but four- and five-star properties can still be found in smaller cities and rural areas that cater to high-end tourism or business. These will generally feature hot water, modern fixtures, and 24-hour concierge service. Midlevel hotels may lack some amenities but still offer a comfortable night's sleep for people who aren't looking for a flat-screen TV. There are many budget hotels that, although they have the word *hostel* in the name, are actually clean, comfortable, no-frills bed-and-breakfasts. At the extreme low end are dormitories aimed at backpackers and budget travelers. Prices tend to reflect the property's age and amenities, but specialty lodges in the jungle or highlands may offer few comforts at any given price point. The name of a hotel does not necessarily have anything to do with its luxuriousness. A *posada*, for example, can be at the high, middle, or low end. *Prices in the reviews are the lowest cost of a standard double room in high season. Our local writers vet every hotel to recommend the best overnights in each price category, from budget to expensive. Unless otherwise specified, you can expect a private bath, phone, and TV in your room. Hotel reviews have been shortened. For full information, visit Fodors.com.*

■ **TIP→ Ask the local tourist board about hotel packages that include tickets to major museum exhibits or other special events.**

■ COMMUNICATIONS

INTERNET

Email has become a favorite way to communicate in Peru. Most large cities have dozens of Internet cafés, and you should be able to find at least one in almost every small town. (Look for a sign with an @ symbol out front.) Even on the shores of Lake Titicaca you can stop in a small shop and get computer access for about US$1 an hour. If you're traveling with your own laptop or wireless device, many of the country's airports, including Lima's Jorge Chávez International Airport and Cusco's Teniente Alejandro Velasco Astete International Airport, offer wireless connections. Hotels increasingly have Wi-Fi as well, if not in their guest rooms then at least in the public areas.

Computer keyboards in South America are not quite the same as those in English-speaking countries. Your biggest frustration will probably be finding the @ symbol to type an email address. On a PC you have to type "Alt+164" with the "Numbers Lock" on or some other combination. If you need to ask, it's called *arroba* in Spanish.

If you're traveling with a laptop that isn't dual voltage (most are these days), bring a converter—otherwise your existing power cord will work just fine. Carrying a laptop could make you a target for thieves. Conceal it in a generic bag, and keep it close to you at all times. In some places, you may need an adapter to convert from your flat prongs to an old-style outlet accepting round ones.

PHONES

The good news is that you can now make a direct-dial telephone call from virtually any point on Earth. The bad news? You can't always do so cheaply. Calling from a hotel is almost always the most expensive option; hotels usually add huge surcharges to all calls, particularly international ones. There are still some call centers but these are disappearing

as most travellers, and Peruvians, have smartphones with Internet access. Calling cards usually keep costs to a minimum, but only if you purchase them locally. And, as expensive as international mobile phone calls can be, they are still usually a much cheaper option than calling from your hotel. Web-based systems, such as Skype and Google Hangouts, are the most inexpensive way to call internationally. The best way to stay connected with your travel agency and tour guides in Peru is to download What's App to your cell phone and use it when you are connected to Wi-Fi; it's widely used in Peru.

To call Peru direct, dial 011 followed by the country code of 51, then the city code, then the number of the party you're calling. (When dialing a number from abroad, drop the initial 0 from the local area code.)

CALLING WITHIN PERU

To get phone numbers for anywhere in Peru, dial 103. For an operator, dial 100, and for an international operator, dial 108. To place a direct call, dial 00 followed by the country and city codes. To call another region within the country, first dial 0 and then the area code.

To reach an AT&T operator, dial 0–800–50288. For Sprint, dial 0–800–50020. For Verizon, dial 0–800–50010.

CALLING OUTSIDE PERU

For international calls, you should dial 00, then the country code. (For example, the country code for the United States and Canada is 1.) To make an operator-assisted international call, dial 108.

Access Codes AT&T Direct. ☎ 800/222–0300 ⊕ www.att.com/esupport/traveler.jsp. **Sprint International Access.** ☎ 866/275–1411 ⊕ support.sprint.com/support/international. **Verizon Wireless.** ☎ 800/711–8300 ⊕ www.verizonwireless.com/solutions-and-services/international/.

LOCAL DO'S AND TABOOS

CUSTOMS OF THE COUNTRY

Peru is one of South America's most hospitable nations. Even in the overburdened metropolis of Lima, people are happy to give directions, chat, and ask a question you'll hear often in Peru, ¿ De dónde eres? (Where are you from?). Peruvians are quite knowledgeable and proud of their country's history. Don't be surprised if your best source of information isn't your tour guide but your taxi driver or hotel desk clerk. That said, always consider what the person offering information might have to gain from directing you to a given hotel or tour agency, and try to ask a few people for information before settling on any one option.

GREETINGS

In the cities, female friends and acquaintances often greet each other with a single kiss on the cheek; males shake hands. Men and women often kiss each other on the cheek, even when being introduced for the first time. Kissing, however, is not a custom among the conservative indigenous population.

SIGHTSEEING

To feel more comfortable, take a cue from what the locals are wearing. Except in beach towns, men typically don't wear shorts and women don't wear short skirts, although these norms are changing in larger cities. Bathing suits are fine on beaches, but cover up before you head back into town. Everyone dresses nicely to enter churches. Peruvian women wearing sleeveless tops often cover their shoulders before entering a place of worship.

OUT ON THE TOWN

Residents of Lima and other large cities dress up for a night on the town, but that doesn't necessarily mean a jacket and tie. Just as in Buenos Aires or Rio de Janiero, you should dress comfortably, but with a bit of style. In smaller towns, things are much more casual, and everyone is used to tourists showing up in hiking gear. The posh clubs in Lima's Miraflores district may not let you enter without proper footwear, so leave the sandals at home.

LANGUAGE

Spanish is Peru's national language, but many indigenous languages also enjoy official status. Many Peruvians claim Quechua, the language of the Inca, as their mother tongue, but most also speak Spanish outside more remote communities. Other indigenous languages include the Tiahuanaco language of Aymara, which is spoken around Lake Titicaca. English is now routinely taught in schools, and many older people have taken classes in English. In Lima and other places with many foreign visitors, locals will often have at least a rudimentary knowledge of the language.

A word on spelling: Because the Inca had no writing system, Quechua developed as an oral language. With European colonization, words and place names were transcribed to conform to Spanish pronunciations. Eventually, the whole language was transcribed, and in many cases words lost their correct pronunciations. During the past 30 years, however, national pride and a new sensitivity to the country's indigenous roots have led Peruvians to try to recover consistent, linguistically correct transcriptions of Quechua words. As you travel, you may come across different spellings and pronunciations of the same name. An example is the city known as Cusco, Cuzco, and sometimes Qosqo. Even the word Inca is frequently rendered as the less-Spanish-looking Inka.

A bit of terminology, too: The word Indio (Indian) is considered pejorative in Peru and Latin America. To avoid offense, stick with indígena (indigenous) to describe Peru's Inca-descended peoples. Likewise, the words nativo (native) and tribú (tribe) rub people here the wrong way.

CALLING CARDS

Public phones use phone cards that can be purchased at newsstands, pharmacies, and other shops. These come in denominations ranging from S/5 to S/50. Your charges will appear on a small monitor on the phone, so you always know how much time you have left. Instructions are usually in Spanish and English. Note that the number of public phones has dwindled greatly with the rise of cell phones.

MOBILE PHONES

Chances are good that you can use your smartphone abroad. Roaming fees can be steep so look into the international plans your provider offers.

If you just want to make local calls, consider buying a new SIM card for a few soles (note that your provider may have to unlock your phone for you to use a different SIM card) and a prepaid service plan in the destination. You'll then have a local number and can make local calls at local rates. If your trip is extensive, you could also simply buy a new cell phone in your destination, as the initial cost will be offset over time. Cell phones in Peru are relatively cheap and often the easiest option.

■TIP➡ If you travel internationally frequently, save one of your old mobile phones or buy a cheap one online; ask your cell-phone company to unlock it for you, and take it with you as a travel phone, buying a new SIM card with pay-as-you-go service in each destination.

Contacts Cellular Abroad. ☏ 800/287–5072 ⊕ www.cellularabroad.com. **Mobal.** ☏ 888/888–9162 ⊕ www.mobal.com. **Planet Fone.** ☏ 888/988–4777 ⊕ www.planetfone.com.

■ CUSTOMS AND DUTIES

You're always allowed to bring goods of a certain value back home without having to pay any duty or import tax. But there's a limit on the amount of tobacco and liquor you can return with duty-free,

and some countries have separate limits for perfumes; for exact figures, check with your customs department. The values of so-called duty-free goods are included in these amounts. When you shop abroad, save all your receipts, as customs inspectors may ask to see them as well as the items you purchased. If the total value of your goods is more than the duty-free limit, you'll have to pay a tax (most often a flat percentage) on the value of everything beyond that limit.

When you check through immigration in Peru, put the white International Embarkation/Disembarkation form you filled out in a safe place when it's returned to you. You will need it when you leave the country. If you lose it, in addition to being delayed, you may have to pay a small fine. You may bring personal and work items; a total of 3 liters of liquor; jewelry or perfume worth less than US$300; and 400 cigarettes or 50 cigars into Peru without paying import taxes. Likewise, travelers can bring one of each type of electronic device (for example, one laptop or one tablet). After that, goods and gifts will be taxed at 20% of their value up to US$1,000; everything thereafter is taxed at a flat rate of 25%. If you happen to be bringing an electronic item to someone as a gift, take it out of the packaging.

U.S. Information U.S. Customs and Border Protection. ⊕ www.cbp.gov.

■ EATING OUT

Most smaller restaurants offer a lunchtime *menú*, a prix-fixe meal (US$3–US$6) that consists of an appetizer, a main dish, dessert, and a beverage. Peru is also full of cafés, many with a selection of delicious pastries. Food at bars is usually limited to snacks and sandwiches. *Prices in the reviews are the average cost of a main course at dinner or, if dinner is not served, at lunch.*

For information on food-related health issues, see Health below.

MEALS AND MEALTIMES

Food in Peru is hearty and wholesome. Thick soups are excellent, particularly *chupes* made of shrimp or fish with potatoes, corn, peas, onions, garlic, tomato sauce, eggs, cream cheese, milk, and whatever else happens to be in the kitchen. *Corvina* (a Pacific sea bass) is superb, as is *paiche* (a fish with a very large mouth that's found in jungle lakes and now being farmed sustainably). Adventurous eaters can try piranha—it's delicious, but full of bones; *cebiche,* raw fish marinated in lime juice then mixed with onions and *aji* (chili peppers), is another option. *Anticuchos* (marinated beef hearts grilled over charcoal) are a favorite street snack, and *pollo a la brasa* (rotisserie chicken) is so popular that the government includes it in its inflation figures. Peru's *choclo* (large-kernel corn) is very good, and it's claimed there are thousands of varieties of potatoes and other tubers, prepared in about as many ways.

Top-notch restaurants serve lunch and dinner, but most Peruvians think of lunch as the main meal, and many restaurants open only at midday. Served between 1 and 3 pm, lunch was once followed by a siesta, though the custom has largely died out. Dinner can be anything from a light snack to another full meal; Peruvians tend to eat dinner between 7 and 10 pm, although in Lima this can extend later to 11.

Unless otherwise noted, the restaurants listed in this guide are open daily for lunch and dinner.

RESERVATIONS AND DRESS

Peruvians dress informally when they dine out. At the most expensive restaurants, a jacket without a tie is sufficient for men. Dress codes have relaxed greatly, particularly in tourist areas. It's common to see shorts and T-shirts in casual restaurants in Lima, and people are used to pretty much everything from tourists in Cusco.

WINES, BEER, AND SPIRITS

Peru's national drink is the pisco sour, made with a type of pale grape brandy called pisco—close to 90 proof—derived from grapes grown in vineyards around Ica, south of Lima. Added to the pisco are lime juice, sugar, bitters, and egg white. It's a refreshing drink and one that nearly every bar in Peru claims to make best. Wines from Ica vineyards include such labels as Santiago Queirolo, Tacama, Taberno and Ocucaje, but a relative newcomer, Intipalka, is probably the country's best. Ica's National Vintage Festival is in March.

Peruvian beer (*cerveza*) is also very good. In Lima try Pilsen Callao or sample the products from craft breweries like Candelaria, Sacred Valley Brewing Company, Nuevo Mundo, Cumbres, and Barbarian. In the south it's Arequipeña from Arequipa, Cusqueña from Cusco, and big bottles of San Juan from Iquitos, where the warm climate makes it taste twice as good. In Iquitos locals make Chuchuhuasi from the reddish-brown bark of the canopy tree that grows to 100 feet high in the Amazon rain forest. The bark is soaked for days in *aguardiente* (a very strong homemade liquor) and is claimed to be a cure-all. In Iquitos, however, it has been bottled and turned into a tasty drink for tourists. *Chicha,* a low-alcohol corn beer, is still made by hand throughout the highlands. An acquired taste, chicha can be found by walking through any doorway where a red flag is flying, though you may want to sample it at a restaurant to be safe.

▌ELECTRICITY

The electrical current in Peru is 220 volts, 50 cycles alternating current (AC). A converter is needed for appliances requiring 110 voltage. U.S.-style flat prongs fit most outlets.

Consider buying a universal adapter, which has several types of plugs in one lightweight, compact unit. Most laptops and mobile-phone chargers are dual voltage (i.e., they operate equally well on 110 and 220 volts), so they require only an adapter. These days the same is sometimes true of small appliances such as hair dryers. Always check labels and manufacturer instructions to be sure. Don't use 110-volt outlets marked "for shavers only" for high-wattage appliances such as hair dryers.

▌EMERGENCIES

The fastest way to connect with the police is to dial 105. For fire, dial 116. For an ambulance, dial 117. The Tourism Police, part of the National Police of Peru, exists for the security and protection of travelers. Officers are usually found around hotels, archaeological centers, museums, and any place that is frequently visited by tourists. They almost always speak English.

Foreign Embassies Australia. ⊠ *La Paz 1049, Piso 10, Miraflores* ☎ *01/630–0500* ⊕ *www.peru.embassy.gov.au/limacastellano/home.html.* **Canada.** ⊠ *Bolognesi 228, Miraflores* ☎ *01/319–3200* ⊕ *www.peru.gc.ca.* **United Kingdom.** ⊠ *Torre Parque Mar, José Larco 1301, 22nd fl., Miraflores* ☎ *01/617–3000* ⊕ *www.gov.uk/government/world/peru.* **United States.** ⊠ *Av. La Encalada, Cuadra 17, Surco* ☎ *01/618–2000* ⊕ *lima.usembassy.gov.*

▌HEALTH

TRAVELER'S DIARRHEA
The most common illness is traveler's diarrhea, caused by viruses, bacteria, or parasites in contaminated food or water. In Lima and much of the center of Cusco, water supplies are chlorinated and should be safe to use for washing fruits and vegetables. Although many *limeños* drink the tap water, travelers should drink bottled, boiled, or purified water and drinks to avoid any issues, even when brushing your teeth. Many higher-quality hotels do purify their water, so inquire with the concierge. In the provinces, water may not be treated. Wash fruits and vegetables before eating, and avoid ice (order drinks *sin hielo*, or "without ice") or make sure the ice cubes are made with purified water. If you buy food from a street vendor, make sure it's cooked in front of you. Avoid uncooked items, ones that have been sitting around at room temperature, and unpasteurized milk or milk products. Fresh fruit juices are generally fine, though it's wise to only purchase them from the cleaner stalls and pay attention to what water they may be adding to your drink. Note that water boils at a lower temperature at high altitudes and may not be hot enough to rid it of the bacteria, so consider using purification tablets. Local brands include Micropur. Mild cases of traveler's diarrhea may respond to Imodium, Pepto-Bismol, or Lomotil, all of which can be purchased in Peru without a prescription. You can also ask your doctor for a prescription for Cipro or other antibiotic commonly used to treat traveler's diarrhea before you travel. Drink plenty of purified water or tea—*manzanilla* (chamomile) is a popular folk remedy as is the *té anís*, which has a licorice taste.

The number of cases of cholera, an intestinal infection caused by ingestion of contaminated water or food, has dropped dramatically in recent years, but you should still take care. Anything raw should be eaten only in the better restaurants.

MOSQUITO-BORNE ILLNESSES
Mosquitoes and sand flies are a problem in tropical areas, especially at dusk; infectious diseases can be passed via mosquitoes. If you are traveling in an area where malaria is prevalent, use a repellent containing DEET and take malaria-prevention medication before, during, and after your trip as directed by your physician. Note: you may have to start antimalarial medication weeks before your trip so ask about it early. You may not get through airport screening with an aerosol can of mosquito repellent, so opt

for a spritz bottle or cream. Local brands of repellent are readily available in pharmacies. If you plan to spend time in the jungle, be sure to wear clothing that covers your arms and legs, sleep under a mosquito net, and spray bug repellent in living and sleeping areas.

⚠ Zika virus is currently being spread by mosquitoes in Peru. The Centers for Disease Control and Prevention (CDC) recommends that pregnant women should not travel to any area of Peru below 6,500 feet. According to the CDC, if your itinerary is limited entirely to areas above 6,500 feet, there is minimal risk of getting Zika from a mosquito. If you are planning to become pregnant, your partner also needs to avoid contacting Zika as it can be spread by sex. See wwwnc.cdc.gov/travel/notices/alert/zika-virus-peru for more information. Speak with your physician and/or check the Centers for Disease Control or World Health Organization websites for health alerts, particularly if you're pregnant, traveling with children, or have a chronic illness.

ALTITUDE SICKNESS

Altitude sickness, known locally as *soroche,* affects the majority of visitors to Cusco, Puno, and other high-altitude locales in the Andes. Headache, dizziness, nausea, and shortness of breath are common. When you visit areas over 10,000 feet above sea level, take it easy for the first few days. Avoiding alcohol will keep you from getting even more dehydrated. To fight soroche, Peruvians swear by *mate de coca,* a tea made from the leaves of the coca plant. (If you are subject to any type of random drug testing through your workplace, know that coca tea can result in a positive test for cocaine afterward.) Some travelers swear by the prescription drug acetazolamide (brand name, Diamox), which should be taken 48 hours before arriving at altitude. Whether that's an appropriate course is for you and your health-care professional to decide.

Spend a few nights at lower elevations before you head higher, especially if you are hiking or climbing in the mountains. If you must fly directly to higher altitudes, plan on doing next to nothing for the first day or two. Drinking plenty of water or coca tea or taking frequent naps may also help. If symptoms persist, return to lower elevations. If you have high blood pressure or a history of heart trouble or are pregnant, check with your doctor before traveling to high elevations.

Chiggers are sometimes a problem in the jungle or where there are animals. Red, itchy spots suddenly appear, most often *under* your clothes. The best advice when venturing out into chigger country is to use insect repellent and wear loose-fitting garments. A hot, soapy bath after being outdoors also prevents them from attaching to your skin.

OVER-THE-COUNTER REMEDIES

Over-the-counter analgesics—available at the airports in Lima and Cusco, as well as most pharmacies in those cities—may curtail soroche symptoms, but consult your doctor before you take these. Always carry your own medications with you, including those you would ordinarily take for a simple headache, as you will usually not find the same brands in the local *farmacia* (pharmacy). If you forgot, however, ask for *aspirina* (aspirin). Try writing down the name of your local medication, because in many cases the pharmacist will have it or something similar.

Medical Insurers International Medical Group. ☎ 800/628-4664 ⊕ www.imgglobal. com. **International SOS.** ☎ 800/523-8662 ⊕ www.internationalsos.com. **Wallach & Company.** ☎ 800/237-6615, 540/687-3166 ⊕ www.wallach.com.

VACCINATIONS AND PREVENTATIVE MEDICINE

No vaccinations are required to enter Peru, however, as of 2017, the Centers for Disease Control and Prevention (CDC) recommends hepatitis A and typhoid inoculations for all travelers to

Peru. Hepatitis B, rabies, yellow fever, and malaria should be discussed with your medical professional, depending on where you will be traveling. It's a good idea to have up-to-date boosters for tetanus, diphtheria, and measles. In those areas where rabies is a concern, many hospitals have antirabies injections, but as these must be taken in a series, prevention is far easier. Children traveling to Peru should have their vaccinations for childhood diseases up-to-date.

According to the CDC, there's a limited risk of Chagas disease. There is some risk of dengue and Zika but these are not preventable by vaccine. If you plan to visit remote regions or stay for more than six weeks, check with the CDC's International Travelers Hot Line.

Health Warnings Centers for Disease Control and Prevention (*CDC*). ☎ 800/232-4636 *international travelers' health line* ⊕ *www.cdc.gov/travel*. **World Health Organization** (*WHO*). ⊕ *www.who.int.*

▌HOLIDAYS

National holidays include New Year's Day (January 1); Easter holiday, which begins midday on Holy Thursday and continues through Easter Monday (March or April); Labor Day (May 1); St. Peter and St. Paul Day (June 29); Independence Day (July 28); St. Rosa of Lima Day (August 30); Battle of Angamos Day, which commemorates a battle with Chile in the War of the Pacific, 1879–81 (October 8); All Saints' Day (November 1); Immaculate Conception (December 8); and Christmas (December 25). There are also regional holidays such as the celebration of the Virgen de Candelaria in Puno (February); Corpus Christi, especially in Cusco (variable dates); and Inti Raymi in Cusco (June 24).

▌MAIL

Letters sent within the country cost S/3.80 for less than 20 grams; letters and cards up to 20 grams sent to the United States and Canada cost S/8.60. Bring packages to the post office unsealed, as you must show the contents to postal workers. Mail service has been improving, and a letter will often reach just about anywhere in a week from any of the main cities. For timely delivery or valuable parcels, use FedEx, DHL, or UPS, although be aware that customs can be very complicated.

DHL, FedEx, and UPS all have offices in Peru. Because of the limited number of international flights, overnight service is usually not available.

▌MONEY

Peru's national currency is the nuevo sol (S/). Bills are issued in denominations of 10, 20, 50, 100, and 200 soles. Coins are 1, 5, 10, 20, and 50 céntimos, and 1, 2, and 5 soles. (The 1- and 5-céntimo coins are rarely seen outside supermarkets in Lima.) At this writing, the exchange rate was S/3.24 to the U.S. dollar. Peru is not one of those "everybody takes dollars" places— many businesses and most individuals are not equipped to handle U.S. currency—so you should try to deal in soles.

You'll want to break larger bills as soon as possible. Souvenir stands, crafts markets, taxi drivers, and other businesses often do not have change. Be aware that U.S. dollars must be in pristine condition, as moneychangers and banks will not accept a bill with even the slightest tear. Likewise, counterfeiting is a big problem in Peru, and you should check all bills (both dollars and soles) immediately to confirm that they are real. The easiest method is to ensure that the color-changing ink does indeed change colors, from purple to black. Do not feel uncomfortable scrutinizing bills; you can be sure that any cashier will scrutinize your bills twice as hard.

Currency Conversion Oanda.com.
⊕ *www.oanda.com.* **XE.com.** ⊕ *www.xe.com.*

■TIP➜ If you're planning to exchange funds before leaving home, don't wait until the last minute. Banks never have every foreign currency on hand, and it may take as long as a week to order. For the best exchange rates, you're better off to wait until you get to Peru to change dollars into local currency.

ATMS AND BANKS

Your own bank will probably charge a fee for using ATMs abroad; the foreign bank you use may also charge a fee, which currently ranges from US$3 to US$6 per transaction. Nevertheless, you may get a better rate of exchange at an ATM than you will at a currency-exchange office and definitely over changing money in a bank. And extracting funds as you need them is a safer option than carrying around a large amount of cash.

■TIP➜ PIN numbers with more than four digits are not recognized at ATMs in many countries. If yours has five or more, remember to change it before you leave.

ATMs (*cajeros automáticos*) are widely available, especially in Lima and most other medium to large cities; you can withdraw cash using a Cirrus- or Plus-linked debit card or a major credit card. Most ATMs accept both Cirrus and Plus cards, but bring at least one of each to be on the safe side. Be sure to inform your bank that you'll be using your cards in Peru, lest they freeze your cards due to suspicious transactions in a foreign country.

ATM Locations MasterCard. ☎ *800/627–8372 in North America, 0800/307–7309 in Peru* ⊕ *www.mastercard.us/en-us/consumers/get-support/locate-an-atm.html.* **Visa Plus.** ⊕ *www.visa.com/atmlocator.*

CREDIT CARDS

It's a good idea to inform your credit-card company before you travel. Otherwise, the credit-card company might put a hold on your card owing to unusual activity—not a good thing halfway through your trip. Record all your credit-card numbers—as well as the phone numbers to call if your cards are lost or stolen—in a safe place, so you're prepared should something go wrong. Both MasterCard and Visa have general numbers you can call (collect if you're abroad) if your card goes missing, but you're better off phoning your issuing bank, since MasterCard and Visa typically just transfer you to the bank anyway.

Although it's usually cheaper (and safer) to use a credit card abroad for large purchases (so you can cancel payments or be reimbursed if there's a problem), note that some credit-card companies *and* the banks that issue them add substantial percentages to all foreign transactions, whether they're in a foreign currency or not. Check on these fees before leaving home, so there won't be any surprises when you get the bill. Some travel-focused credit cards offer zero foreign-transaction fees, which you might want to consider applying for in advance of your trip.

Before you charge something, ask the merchant if any additional fees will be charged on top of the cost. For costly items, try to use your credit card whenever possible—you'll come out ahead, whether the exchange rate at which your purchase is calculated is the one in effect the day the vendor's bank abroad processes the charge or the one prevailing on the day the charge company's service center processes it at home.

Major credit cards, especially MasterCard and Visa, are accepted in most hotels, restaurants, and shops in tourist areas. If you're traveling outside major cities, always check to see whether your hotel accepts credit cards. You may have to bring enough cash to pay the bill.

Before leaving home, make copies of the back and front of your credit cards; keep one set of copies with your luggage, the other at home.

Reporting Lost Cards American Express.
☎ *800/528-4800 in North America,*
800/333-AMEX outside North America
⊕ *www.americanexpress.com.* **Master-
Card.** ☎ *800/627-8372 in North America,*
0800/307-7309 in Peru ⊕ *www.master-
card.com.* **Visa.** ☎ *800/847-2911 in U.S.,*
800/890-0623 in Peru ⊕ *usa.visa.com.*

CURRENCY AND EXCHANGE

You can safely exchange money in a
bank, at your hotel, or at *casas de cam-
bio* (exchange houses). ■TIP➔ Rates are
always better at an ATM or a casa de cam-
bio than a bank.

▮ PACKING

For sightseeing, casual clothing and good
walking shoes are desirable and appropriate; most cities don't require formal
clothes, even for evenings. If you're
doing business in Peru, you'll need the
same attire you would wear in U.S. and
European cities: for men, suits and ties;
for women, suits for day wear, and for
evening, depending on the occasion—ask
your host or hostess—a cocktail dress or
just a nice suit with a dressy blouse.

Travel in rain-forest areas will require
long-sleeve shirts, long pants, socks,
sneakers, a hat, a light waterproof jacket,
a bathing suit (if you want to swim), sunscreen, and insect repellent. You can never
have too many large resealable plastic
bags, which are ideal for protecting official documents from rain and damp and
quarantining stinky socks.

If you're visiting the Andes, bring a jacket
and sweater, or acquire one of the hand-
knit sweaters or ponchos crowding the
marketplaces. Evening temperatures in
Cusco are rarely above 40°F. Layering
is the key, and you may find you are
constantly shedding and adding clothes
throughout the day. For beach vacations,
you'll need lightweight sportswear, a
bathing suit, a sun hat, and lots of sunscreen. Peruvians are fairly conservative, so don't wear bathing suits or other
revealing clothing away from the beach.

Other useful items include a travel
flashlight and extra batteries, a pock-
etknife with a bottle opener (put it in
your checked luggage), a medical kit,
binoculars, and a calculator to help
with currency conversions. A sarong or
light cotton blanket can have many uses:
beach towel, picnic blanket, and cushion
for hard seats. Most important, always
travel with tissues, baby wipes, or a roll
of toilet paper, as restrooms are not
always stocked with these necessities.

*If you're trekking the Inca Trail or other
multiday hike, see the packing list in Chapter 6: Machu Pichu and the Inca Trail.*

Weather Weather.com. ⊕ *www.weather.com.*

▮ PASSPORTS AND VISAS

Visitors from the United States, Canada,
the United Kingdom, Australia, and New
Zealand require only a passport, valid
for six months from date of travel, and
a return ticket to be issued a visa for up
to 183 days at their point of entry into
Peru. Generally, you'll be given a smaller
amount that coincides with your flight
out of the country unless you ask for
more. Even then, it is at the discretion of
the immigration officer.

Make two photocopies of the data page
of your passport, one for someone at
home and another for you, carried
separately from your passport. While
sightseeing in Peru, it's best to carry
the copy of your passport and leave the
original hidden in your hotel room or in
your hotel's safe. When you are going
to travel, such as on the train to Machu
Picchu, take your passport with you. If
you lose your passport, call the nearest embassy or consulate and the local
police. Also, never leave one city in Peru
to go to another city (even for just an
overnight or two) without carrying your
passport with you.

GENERAL REQUIREMENTS FOR PERU	
Passport	Passport required for U.S. residents, valid for 6 months from date of travel
Visa	Not necessary for U.S. residents with a valid passport
Vaccinations	Hepatitis A and typhoid are recommended for all travelers. Hepatitis B, rabies, and yellow fever vaccinations are recommended for travelers visiting certain areas. If you are traveling to another country afterward, confirm that country's requirements; you'll be entering from a country known to have yellow fever, so you may have to have the vaccine.
Driving	Driver's license required
Departure Tax	US$30.74 for international flights; US$10.92 for domestic flights; included in all fares

▮ RESTROOMS

In Lima and other cities, your best bet for finding a restroom while on the go is to walk into a large hotel as if you're a guest and use the facilities there. The next best thing is talking your way into a restaurant bathroom; buying a drink is a nice gesture if you do. Some places will charge a fee of around S/1. Unless you're in a large chain hotel, don't throw toilet paper into the toilet—use the basket provided, as unsanitary as this may seem. Flushing paper can clog the antiquated plumbing. Always carry your own supply of tissues, baby wipes, or toilet paper, just in case.

Public restrooms are usually designated as *servicios higiénicos*, with signs depicting the abbreviation "SS.HH."

▮ SAFETY

Be street-smart in Peru and trouble generally won't find you. Money belts peg you as a tourist, so if you must wear one, hide it under your clothing. If you carry a purse, choose one with a zipper and a thick strap that you can drape across your body; adjust the length so that the purse sits in front of you. Carry only enough money to cover casual spending. Keep camera bags close to your body. Note that backpacks and laptop cases are especially easy to grab or open secretly. Finally, avoid wearing flashy jewelry and watches.

Many streets throughout Peru are not well lighted, so avoid walking at night, and certainly avoid deserted streets, day or night. Always walk as if you know where you're going, even if you don't.

Use only "official" taxis with the company's name emblazoned on the side. Don't get into a car just because there's a taxi sign in the window, as it's probably an unlicensed driver. At night you should call a taxi from your hotel or restaurant. A good bet if you can connect to the Internet from your phone is to download the app for EasyTaxi. You can order a car from your phone; get the make, model, license plate, and name and photo of the driver; and even track his (or her) arrival.

Do not let anyone distract you. Beware of someone "accidentally" spilling food or liquid on you and then offering to help clean it up; the spiller might have an accomplice who will walk off with your purse or your suitcase while you are distracted.

Women, especially blondes, can expect some admiring glances and perhaps a comment or two, but outright come-ons or grabbing are rare. Usually all that is needed is to ignore the perpetrator and keep walking down the street.

▮TIP→ **Distribute your cash, credit cards, IDs, and other valuables between a deep front pocket, an inside jacket or vest pocket, and a hidden money pouch. Don't reach for the money pouch once you're in public.**

Contact Transportation Security Administration (*TSA*). ☎ *866/289-9673* ⊕ *www.tsa. gov.*

▍TAXES

An 18% *impuesto general a las ventas* (general sales tax) is levied on everything except goods bought from open-air markets and street vendors. It's usually included in the advertised price and should be included with food and drink. If a business offers you a discount for paying in cash, it probably means they aren't charging sales tax (and not reporting the transaction to the government).

By law restaurants must publish their prices—including taxes and sometimes a 10% service charge—but they do not always do so. They're also prone to levy a cover charge for anything from live entertainment to serving you a roll with your meal. Hotel bills may also add taxes and a 10% service charge.

Departure taxes at Lima's Aeropuerto Internacional Jorge Chávez are US$30.74 for international flights and US$10.92 for domestic flights—all airlines now include the tax in their ticket prices.

▍TIME

Peru is on eastern standard time (GMT-0500) year-round, with no daylight saving time observed. From November to March the time in Peru is the same as in New York and Miami. The rest of the year, when the United States does observe daylight saving time, Peru is one hour behind the U.S. East Coast.

▍VISITOR INFORMATION

ONLINE TRAVEL TOOLS

Andean Travel Web (an independent site) and the government-run iPerú are two valuable sources of online information. Be wary of seemingly independent information sites that are actually travel agencies. You can still get some good tips from them, but they can be skewed toward their area of expertise or packages they sell.

All About Peru Andean Travel Web.
⊕ *andeantravelweb.com/peru.* **iPerú.**
⊕ *www.peru.travel/.*

INDEX

PHOTO CREDITS

NOTES